THEO-DRAMA
Volume IV

THEO-DRAMA

Volumes of the Complete Work:

HANS URS VON BALTHASAR

THEO-DRAMA

THEOLOGICAL
DRAMATIC THEORY

VOLUME IV
THE ACTION

Translated by Graham Harrison

IGNATIUS PRESS   SAN FRANCISCO

Title of the German original:
Theodramatik: Dritte Band: Die Handlung
© 1980 Johannes Verlag, Einsiedeln
With ecclesiastical approval

Cover by Roxanne Mei Lum

CONTENTS

CONTENTS

CONTENTS

CONTENTS

To the
Catholic University of America
Washington, D.C.
for the conferment
of an honorary doctorate
of humane letters

PREFACE

We have prepared at considerable length for the "action" that is the subject of this volume. First, in the *Prolegomena*, we prepared the way for our use of dramatic categories in the understanding of revelation ("theology"). The next task was to introduce the *dramatis personae* themselves. But here we discovered a tension: on the one hand, the creature is manifestly free before God (volume 2), and, on the other hand, this very freedom is a freedom "in Christ"—and it is only "in Christ" that theological persons can exist at all (volume 3). This tension is so explosive that it was bound to burst into flame in the conflagration of the action; accordingly, we begin this volume "under the sign of the Apocalypse".

The Book of Revelation makes it quite clear that the action set in train by human freedom is not overridden or trivialized by the all-encompassing action of the "Lamb as though it had been slain". What we have here is not the kind of *apokatastasis* that subsumes the Christian's wrestling with God and God's wrestling with him in an overall philosophical perspective (in the manner of Plotinus or Hegel), according to which the world proceeds from the divine and subsequently returns to it. No; for we are faced with a titanic rejection on man's part: he resists being embraced by this very mystery of the Cross. This anti-Christian aversion is something new; it has only existed since the coming of Christ: "If I had not come and spoken to them, they would not have sin." It is only when heaven is wide open that hell too yawns at our feet. So this examination of the action will not unveil what is ultimate; but, where the action is transparent, it will give us an intimation, a shadowy awareness of that ultimate reality. The final drama has not yet taken place.

A special concern of this volume is the precise definition of the concept of "representation", which has suddenly come into prominence after a period of neglect. Unfortunately, Norbert Hoffmann's richly documented essay, "Stellvertretung, Grundgestalt und Mitte des Mysteriums. Ein Versuch trinitätstheologischer Begründung christlicher Sühne" (*Münch. th. Zft.* 30 [1979], 161–91), only appeared after the completion of the present volume, as did Martin Hengel's astonishing contribution, "Der stellvertretende Sühnetod Jesu (*Intern. kath. Zft. Communio* 9 [1980], 1–25, 135–47).[1]

Once again we discern the unity of "glory" and the "dramatic". God's glory, as it appears in the world—supremely in Christ—is not something static that could be observed by a neutral investigator. It manifests itself only through the personal involvement whereby God himself comes forth to do battle and is both victor and vanquished. If this glory is to come within our range at all, an analogous initiative is called for on our part. Revelation is a battlefield. Those who do battle on it can only be believers and theologians, provided they have equipped themselves with the whole armor of God (Eph 6:11).

---

[1] Cf. also Lothar Roos, "Hingegeben für die Vielen. Stellvertretung als Prinzip der Heilsgeschichte" in *Leb. Seelsorge* 30 (1979), 339–53, and several articles by H. J. Lauter in the *Pastoralblatt Köln*.

I. UNDER THE SIGN
OF THE APOCALYPSE

A. THE BOOK OF REVELATION: OUTLINE

1. The Perspective

The Book of Revelation concludes the biblical revelation-event; but it does not do so by continuing the Acts of the Apostles, by prolonging the latter, as it were, into the whole history of the Church and the world. Instead, the seer is lifted up, above the entire sphere of historical revelation in both Old and New Testaments, into a God-given vision that is separate from empirical history (though it integrates it), a vision of all that is taking place between heaven and earth. The vantage point from which the seer is shown these things is neither heaven nor earth but a neutral place between the two; accordingly, what he sees is not a representation of successive historical events—or even of their archetypes—but a sequence of images that, though most closely related to reality, possesses its own intrinsic eidetic truth. It follows that the sequence of images seen in this vision is not built upon historical events of the seer's time, nor is it a symbolic representation of particular epochs of the Church's history. Indeed, the very nature of perceived truth and its expression in the form of speech, as it is presented to us in both Old and New Testaments, should have made it clear that this cannot be so.

> Truth is not presented to us in a developmental form—the only form we know on earth—but in an absolute, fulfilled, accomplished form. It is presented to us as a *fait accompli*, the subject of retrospective contemplation. This applies also to the successions of events and the battles there set forth; they are not segments of concrete historical process but a distillation of things that have long been won and established in the realm of the absolute. . . . This means that all earthly concepts of time are suspended; it is impossible, therefore, to give a temporal interpretation of the visions.[1]

[1] A. von Speyr, *Apokalypse*, 2d ed. (Einsiedeln: Johannes Verlag, 1976), 16. As far as apocalyptic in Daniel is concerned, Gerhard von Rad has already stressed that the prophet surveys world history "like a spectator" (*Theologie des Alten Testaments* I, 2d ed., 335 [cf. the translation by D. M. G. Stalker: *Old Testament Theology* II

The truth of the revealed images is in God; it is guaranteed by the fact that he is their Revealer. Self-contained though they seem, they are closely related to all the Old Testament images associated with visions and revelations. Yet they are original: they cannot artificially have been compiled from them. Thus we must assume that an objective world of images exists in God; excerpts from it are communicated now to this prophet, now to that, until in the Apocalypse of John a kind of *summa* is distilled from it.[2] It is significant that the visions are cast in a language largely woven from Old Testament expressions, although not a single literal quotation has been found.[3] This points to the fact that the seer cannot subsequently have clothed his vision in traditional

---

(SCM Press, 1965), 301–8]). He sees the danger of Gnosticism here, "because there is hardly any mention of the historical and contingent" (4th ed., 320f.). But John, who knew the Lord on earth and doubtless was aware that he and the Lamb were identical, pursues his vision in obedience to the Lord and for the sake of his Church; consequently, there is no danger of Gnosticism here. Moreover, it is not the Apocalypse of John but of Christ (Rev 1:1). Cf. Lohmeyer, *Komm.*, 195, 200. The seer is enabled to observe the actions of the superior powers, not by distancing himself, but by a kind of death (1:17, cf. Dan 8:18; 10:15 ff.); he *must* witness these events and write them down, but this does not dispense him from involvement in them (he weeps, 5:4; he falls down exhausted, 19:10; 22:8). This objectivity is an integral part of subjectivity, not abstracted from it.

[2] Cf. the synopses in the commentaries by H. B. Swete, *The Apocalypse of St. John* (London, 1909), and R. H. Charles, *A Critical and Exegetical Commentary. . . .* (1920).

[3] Even if the visions do not need to have been experienced in a single sequence, nor on the single Sunday on which they began, there is no reason to assume that they were seen in a different sequence from that in which we find them. They do not need to have been the subject of subsequent editorial work. W. Bousset's verdict (*Offenbarung Joh.* [1906], 18) was that "the smaller, more self-contained, more integral the image, the more probably it originates in immediate experience. The larger, more extensive, more complex, more skillfully composed an apocalypse is, the more we have the impression of a purely literary production": such a view may be correct in a case like Enoch, but it is inappropriate where the Book of Revelation is concerned. Parts of the great visions of Ezekiel are complex, but there can be no doubt that they were not "composed" but "seen". For the same reason, we can reject Cerfaux-Cambier's distinction between vision, on the one hand, and "*arrangement littéraire*", on the other (*Apocalypse*, Lect. Div. 17 [1955], 12f., 201ff.). Nor is it necessary to assume, as Rissi does (see note 4 following, 74), that, "in his vision, the seer receives a revelation dealing with material that is familiar to him". George Eldon Ladd: "Apparently he received the visions on Patmos but composed the book at some later time" (*A Commentary on the Revelation of*

and familiar words—as scholars are wont to assume—but that the language is as original as the images to which it belongs. The seer is given not only the substance of his vision but also the proper linguistic medium in which it is to be expressed. Revelation comes from God. As the opening words of the Book of Revelation say, it is given to Jesus Christ, who, by means of his angel, shows it to his servant John and, through him, to his other servants (1:1). Thus there can be no doubt that Jesus Christ, who will designate himself the Alpha and Omega, the First and the Last, stands at the center of events. This does not mean, however, that the "time" referred to begins with his presence on earth.[4] The Old Covenant is present not only in reminiscence or fulfillment (and overfulfillment) but in its own figures and words. For of the twenty-four elders before God's throne, twelve belong surely to the Old and twelve to the New

---

John [Grand Rapids, Mich., 1972], 30). The process whereby Old Testament images attain inner rebirth in the Book of Revelation remains a mysterious one (cf. A. Farrar, *A Rebirth of Images. The Making of St. John's Apocalypse* [London, 1949]). There is no satisfaction in the theory that the prophet took the images he saw and subsequently translated them into symbols and words familiar to him, nor in the view that God employed the imagery familiar to the seer from his knowledge of the Old Testament in order to give him access to the new things that were to be shown him. Our view, rather, is that of L. Cerfaux. On the one hand, Cerfaux assumes an objectively continuous world of images in which the perception of images coincides with their verbal expression ("Il y a comme une grande école de prophétie, avec une tradition voulue par Dieu, les visions que Dieu accorde successivement aux prophètes développent certains grands thèmes fondamentaux", *L'Apocalypse*, Lect. Div. 17 [1955], 69, 28); on the other hand, there is no need to exclude the possibility of a seer having a certain preparedness for his vision on the basis of his familiarity with the Old Testament (185: "Quand l'extase saisissait le prophète, Dieu prenait à son service et élevait jusqu'à lui son intelligence et son imagination", without separating "idées" from "formules imaginatives", 202). But, however true it may be that there is a continuity in the tradition of symbols, we cannot emphasize enough that the content of the symbols is freely and wholly refashioned and redirected with a view to the eschatological reality shaped by Christ. It is only as a result of this sovereign transformation ("maîtrise": 212) that the image-world of antiquity and of prophecy, and of apocalyptic, is sustained and embraced within the ultimate image-world.

[4] At least, this cannot be established beyond contradiction, as Matthias Rissi would like to do in his article "Was ist und was geschehen soll danach", *AThANT* 46 (Zurich: Zwingli, 1965), 45, and previously in "Zeit und Geschichte in der Offenbarung des Johannes" *AThANT* 22 (Zurich: Zwingli, 1952), 40ff.

Covenant; seraphim and cherubim, proclaiming their Trisagion, appear in a form that unites both Covenants. Here we find Temple, altar and the Holy of Holies. But dominant throughout is the sheer juxtaposition (typical of the Old Testament) of pure penal justice and the vision of a reality transfigured. And this in spite of the fact that the Christ-event is always presupposed as something that has taken place, not something still in the future. For example, let us take Ezekiel's vision in which an angel takes burning coals from God's fiery chariot and casts them upon Jerusalem, setting it on fire (Ezek 10:2), and compare it with the scene in Revelation in which an angel takes the censer containing the prayers of the saints, fills it with fire from the heavenly altar and throws it onto the earth, causing thunder and loud noises, lightning and earthquake (8:5); it is clear that the actuality of the first event is wholly preserved in the second. And this in spite of the fact—again—that the work of Christ has been accomplished, in the midst of time, valid for time past and for all future time. We must hold fast to the paradox that goes right through this book: Christ's completed work gives him power to break the seal of world history and unveil it; yet this very opening of the seal brings about a growing sense of fear and foreboding as the end of time approaches. It is not even clear whether the salvific effects of Christ's death become somehow latent in order to allow the aspect of pure judgment to move into center-stage, or whether this salvific efficacy itself summons the opposing powers to the battlefield for a final decisive conflict. Both aspects are present; there can be no doubt that the second aspect predominates from chapter 12 onward. Ultimately the Book of Revelation, coming after all the other books of the New Testament, remains what it is: a window into the ever-greater world of God, which defies all attempts at systematization on our part. Jesus Christ is the Beginning and the End; he has the keys of death and the underworld: people are apt to infer from this that, in the end, no one can be lost. But this is precisely what we are shown, from the case of Babylon to that of the beasts and their adherents. "[John] has to allow both truths to coexist within him, although at no point do they seem to converge."[5]

---

[5] A. von Speyr, *Apokalypse*, 596. Cf. 464: "The Son is present at the same time

So we must also hold fast to this tension: on the one hand, the Lamb is and has always been victorious—the Lord appears to the seer in majesty, with all the emblems of triumph— and yet a struggle is going on (and actually intensifying) in which everything is at stake. The author of the Book of Revelation, however, is not concerned to portray the momentous events of this struggle in their temporal sequence (although, as we shall see, he knows how to heighten tension). He is not a dramatist but someone commissioned to write down objectively the events shown to him. Accordingly, he can alternate between the perspective of the victory that has already been achieved (in the scenes concerning heaven or the Church) and that of the increasingly ferocious hostilities (from the first plagues right up to the final battles). In heaven too, both the Song of Moses and that of the Lamb can be sung simultaneously (15:3).

Thus the Book of Revelation retains its peerless character as a book of vision, opening up perspectives that, once opened, can never be shut. On the other hand, it is only continuing something begun by the entire New Testament (to say nothing of the Old). Not only does it take up the Synoptic apocalypses, often in astonishing detail, to orchestrate them on a mighty scale—and it does the same with the apocalyptic passages in Paul (1 and 2 Th; 1 Cor 15); it also takes up the theme of the tension between the "already" and the "not yet". Ultimate redemption has "already" been achieved: we have only to come to the heavenly Jerusalem (Heb 12:22);[6] but we do "not yet" possess it in fullness since we live by faith, in conflict with the anti-Christian powers (1 Jn) and the more-than-human rulers of darkness (Eph 6). Everywhere, therefore, we find fully developed the dramatic tension that is specific to Christianity. This similarity is more important at the

---

as God's justice is present. . . . Faith means living within the tension between the Old and the New Covenant. There is no easy way of harmonizing them; but the patience that endures all things will allow us to glimpse their underlying unity. However, since all must be fulfilled, there must also be this momentary fulfillment of eternal pain (like a 'still' taken from a film), and of this too the saints must have knowledge" (on Rev 14:12).

[6] On the parallels between the Letter to the Hebrews and the Book of Revelation, cf. C. Spicq, *Hebr.* I, 109, 138.

moment than the difference between them. (The difference is this: in the Book of Revelation, all transitional nuances of the Christian's struggle, in faith, hope, love, conversion and penitence, which are prominent features of the Gospels and Letters, disappear in favor of a stark characterization of the opposing fronts.)

Evidently, this withdrawal from historical truth into visionary truth was the only possible way of presenting a more universal panorama, given that the prospects for the future opened up by the rest of the New Testament were primarily existential in kind —for "it is not for you to know times or seasons that the Father has fixed by his own authority" (Acts 1:7). According to the purely historical analysis of the times—a view that is much too inadequate—this is the period of the cult of Caesar under Domitian, with its resultant persecution of Christians; what is at stake is the position of the Church vis-à-vis the claims of the Roman superpower, which is the *civitas terrena* or *diaboli* and which will assume even more menacing forms in the future. Incidentally, there is not the least hint that the cult of the Emperor's image has been imposed on the communities of Asia Minor to which the seven letters are addressed; in fact, a considerable state persecution had already broken out.[7] However, what is at the center

[7] A. Feuillet, *L'Apocalypse, état de la question* (Paris: DDB, 1963), 79. It may be true that the "letters" (setting aside for the moment their typically apocalyptic preambles and valedictions, from which they cannot be separated) have a different ring to them from the accounts of the visions, but this is no reason to suggest that they are substantially earlier than the main part of the book. The idea that the vision of Christ in 1:9–20 was added later, in order to provide a solemn validation of the letters, lacks all credibility; the two texts are mutually interdependent. Later we shall return to the question of dating, which is connected with the problem of the genuineness of 19:9b–17. At all events, the Book of Revelation is not "a book of consolation written for martyrs by a martyr" (Lohmeyer). There was no persecution of Christians at the beginning of Domitian's reign (Bousset, *Offenbarung*, 134); thus the theme of widespread persecution is prophetic, as in the Gospels.

In his "Die Offenbarung Johannis als metaphysische Grundlage der Politik" in *Die Kraft des Gotteswortes*, ed. O. Karrer (Patmos, 1964), 495–507, Johannes Pinsk suggests that what is new in the Book of Revelation is the growing political tension between the Church and the Empire (a tension that developed only under Nero and Domitian); accordingly, the seer is the first to see Christ as the Lord of history and the world. Though, in my view, this is too narrow a perspective,

here is a more all-embracing law, a law that could be discerned
not only in the relation to Roman state power but, at an earlier stage, in the relation to the "synagogue of Satan" (2:9; 3:9),
the Jews, those who plumb the "deep things of Satan" (2:24),
the Gnostics, the worshipers at "Satan's throne" (2:13) and the
Gentiles. Increasingly, Christ's witnesses could not avoid such
encounters, and so arose the fundamental law of post-Christian
world history: the more Christ's kingdom is manifested as the
light of the world, as a city set on a hill and as leaven, the more
it will meet determined opposition and the more extensive the
satanic counter-strategy will prove. There is nothing new about
this law. It governed much that took place in the Old Testament,
where God stretched out his hands toward a recalcitrant nation
that continually provoked him to anger through its idolatry. Here
love takes the form of vengeance: "I shall not rest until I have
paid them back for their sins" (Is 65:2–7). It informs the New
Covenant: the more the love of Jesus for his people is revealed,
the more it stiffens their resistance, until they resolve to kill him;
so too he weeps for Jerusalem, since it has failed to recognize its
hour and is doomed to be left desolate (Lk 13:34f.). The only
difference between this and the Book of Revelation is that, in
the latter, the law of heightened resistance is vindicated in the
context of the Lamb's established victory. Here, world history
is not a demonstration of progressive integration—Augustine
was right—but is characterized by an increasing polarization;
moreover, it becomes harder and harder to tell the poles apart,
because of the counterfeiting activity of the anti-Trinity and the
anti-Lamb (Rev 13:11). In this way we can grasp something of
the paradox of the Book of Revelation: the Lamb can appear as
the ultimate Victor and as the Lord of all history, while at the
same time he is depicted riding out to do battle and to slaughter
(19:11ff.). On the secular stage, the prior announcement of victory would be regarded as destroying all dramatic tension; on
the apocalyptic stage, however, it is this very victory that causes
the real dramatic action to spark into flame.

Again we find that this corresponds to Jesus' explicit predic-

Pinsk does discern the fundamental law: "The beast is pitiless. . . . But Christ is
pitiless too" (505).

tions of what will happen to his disciples. The mission he gives them is universal in scope; no less universal is the promised help of the Holy Spirit and the promise that the Lord will remain with them all the days, to the end of the world (Mt 28:18–20). But just as categorical and universal are his many predictions of persecution. All men will hate them, and the gospel message will be utterly divisive (Mt 10; Jn 15–16:4; and so forth). Strangely enough, the fate of Christians is predicted to be worse than that of Jesus himself: "If they have called the master of the house Beelzebul, how much more [*pollōi māllōn*] will they malign those of his household" (Mt 10:25).

2. The Place

The acting area in which the apocalyptic drama takes place is the created world, which was structured as "heaven and earth" right from the start—a structure that persists, right from Genesis, throughout Holy Scripture. At the beginning of our study of theo-drama, we described this stage as the locus of all action.[1] We showed that it was erected only for the sake of the action that is to take place on it. God has created heaven and its denizens,[2] just as he has created the earth and all the beings inhabiting the lower cosmos. Within the world, heaven is that created place favored with God's presence; it is more a theological than a cosmological place, as is clear from the fact that the "heaven" that is the counterpart of the earthly world can be "rolled up like a scroll" (6:14) and that, at the Judgment, both heaven and earth flee from before him who judges (20:11). All the same, we cannot simply say that God *is* heaven and that whoever comes to God is automatically in heaven; the visions show only too plainly that the heavenly world is a counterpart to the earthly.

At the center of the heavenly world stands God's throne, and upon it the Lamb "as though it had been slain", yet living, surrounded by the thrones of the twenty-four elders and the "four

---

[1] *Theo-Drama* II, 173–88.

[2] Angels are men's "fellow servants", and thus they refuse to accept any worship offered to them: Rev 19:10; 22:9. On God as the Creator of heaven: 10:6; 14:7. Cf. Ladd, note 3 above, 35.

living creatures" as well as the "seven spirits of God" (1:4; 4:5), which, in the Book of Revelation, represent the Holy Spirit's mode of being. The latter are also the seven eyes of the Lamb, with which it surveys the whole earth (5:6), but at the same time they are the one "Spirit" (2:7) by whom Christ speaks to the communities; in each case, he addresses himself to the Spirit indwelling each community (symbolized by its "angel").[3] But God's presence can also be represented by the heavenly altar (for burnt offerings or incense) or the Temple (when the bowls of God's wrath are being poured out, the Temple is filled with smoke and cannot be entered [15:8]; it is equated with the Tabernacle [15:5]). It is as if the holy things of the Old Testament are also to be found there in their timeless archetypes. In heaven, the twenty-four elders represent the Old and New Covenants; this number remains fixed even if history continues to unroll on earth. In heaven too—"under the altar"—the souls of those who have witnessed with their blood (6:9) are destined for the first resurrection (20:4). But, as for the Lamb who stands on Mount Zion with the one hundred and forty-four thousand who bear his Father's name on their foreheads (14:1−5) and who sing a new song before the throne, the four living things and the elders, it is clear that they must be in heaven, although it does not seem that these, who "have been redeemed from mankind as first fruits for God and the Lamb", have already died. In fact, they are the same one hundred and forty-four thousand who, earlier, when they were being sealed upon their foreheads (7:1−4), were depicted standing on the earth, threatened by the "angels of the winds". And why should not these who have been "sealed" be the same company whom, immediately afterward, the seer observes standing "before the throne and before the

---

[3] "Just as, in a certain sense, he [the Son] allowed himself to be governed by the Spirit during his incarnate life on earth, so he now allows us to glimpse the converse relationship. He speaks in the Spirit's name, and his unity with the Spirit is the same whether the latter is in the mode of self-emptying (in seven spirits) or in the mode of the gathered fellowship in the Lord." A. von Speyr, *Apokalypse*, 131. "The Lord possesses and expropriates the Spirit" (88), and "it is as though the Holy Spirit in him communes with the growing Spirit in man" (111), that is, in the community. Thus he appeals to the Spirit in the community: "The 'angels' embody the Spirit given to the churches; . . . they epitomize the succor that the Spirit gives to the churches" (113).

Lamb, robed in white garments and with palms in their hands"? We would misunderstand the language of the Book of Revelation if we were to object that the one hundred and forty-four thousand (on earth: 7:4) were chosen from the twelve tribes of Israel, whereas the countless host (in heaven: 7:9) come "from every nation and tribe and tongue and people"; for here too Israel is only the living archetype that is fulfilled in the uncountable multitude chosen from all parts of the earth.

All this shows that, in the Book of Revelation, it is quite possible to be both on earth (in the "great tribulation") and in heaven as well; at least people can be *seen* to be in heaven, even if they do not know that they are there. The seer may have seen himself as one of the twenty-four elders without realizing it.[4] So we must reckon with a reality that bridges the gap between heaven and earth without annihilating it; this is the reality of the Holy Church or the Church of the saints, also appearing as the "witnesses" (6:9), the "rest of the offspring [of the Woman], those who keep the commandments of God and bear testimony to Jesus" (12:17), the "called and chosen and faithful" (17:14), who stand by the Logos in his struggle. The Woman who gives birth in anguish, surrounded by stars, also appears as a sign "in heaven", confronting the dragon, who is then "thrown down to the earth" (12:9), whereas the Woman, who surely does not fall from heaven to earth, has a place prepared for her in the "wilderness", where the "earth" protects her from the dragon's lethal flood (12:16). With regard to the Woman, therefore, (that is, the Messianic people), we must say that, despite the aspects of "anguish" and "wilderness", she belongs to both heaven and earth.

However, there is an earth that is in sharp contrast to heaven;

---

[4] "Thus John sees himself—without recognizing himself. Even now, before his death, he plays his part in heaven. The saints who are alive can exert an influence not only on earth but in heaven too. . . . For example, when St. Thérèse says with such certainty that she will spend her heaven doing good on earth, this is because, in some mysterious way, she had already begun her heavenly activity and was actually aware of it to some extent. . . . She says this on the basis of insight into her mission, which is both earthly and heavenly, inseparably one. . . . Her mission comes to her from heaven and has its center of gravity in heaven." A. von Speyr, *Apokalypse*, 226–27.

its characteristics are more theological than cosmological.[5] This is almost always what the Johannine *cosmos* means: the world that is turned away from God, closed in on itself, liable to be led astray by the powers of the abyss. In the black-and-white style of the Book of Revelation, this earth lacks the transforming dimensions of faith and love and is portrayed as impervious to repentance and conversion;[6] even heaven's severest punishments cannot change its course. As we shall show, it is governed from the very outset by the attributes of a fallen world; its borders are constantly threatened by destructive powers (7:1–2; 9:14f.; 16:12).[7] Part of it is the sea, which is seen in a genuine Old Testament sense as a treacherous, ravenous power; beneath it is Hades, the even more frightful abyss that, once unlocked, spews darkness upon the entire world, even obscuring the sun, and emitting demonic spirits to torment mankind (9:2ff.); finally, there is the "lake of fire", in which all that is ultimately opposed to God eternally devours itself. Also from below—from both sea and earth—emerge the first and second beasts, the two embodiments of the dragon; but the beast from the sea is closely associated with the symbol of Babylon, the Great Harlot "with whom the kings of the earth have committed fornication, and with the wine of whose fornication the dwellers on earth have become drunk" (17:2). As for believers, this means that survival on this earth has become doubtful, both physically and spiritually, since "no one can buy or sell unless he has the mark, that is, the name of the beast" (13:17), and since the beast has been granted power "to make war on the saints and to conquer them" (13:7). What is most characteristic, however, is that whatever falls to earth from heaven by way of a blessing is transformed into an instrument of divine punitive justice; or rather, it *is* and *must be* such from the very outset. The images employed here originate in the Old Testament; they come from the judgments upon Babylon and other pagan towns and hostile tribes, and even upon wayward

---

[5] This has rightly been pointed out in connection with the phrase "dwellers on earth" by Paul S. Minear, *I Saw a New Earth: An Introduction to the Visions of the Apocalypse* (Washington/Cleveland: Corpus Books, 1968), 261–69.

[6] Cf. 9:20–21; 16:9. The single exception—if it is such—is 11:13c.

[7] Here the Euphrates is the protective boundary. If it dries up, the powers of evil can invade.

Jerusalem itself; here they are heightened to monstrous proportions. It is as if the Lamb's work of atonement is in the background as a *fait accompli*, but rejected, "blasphemed" (13:6, and so forth), aped and ridiculed (13:3) by the world; thus it necessarily summons "the wrath of the Lamb", "the great day of their anger" (6:16–17: that is, the anger of God and the Lamb).[8] These punishments conceal heaven's love for the guilty earth, but for the present every aspect of love is veiled. Accordingly, the verdict on mankind's cultural "evolution" is negative: merchants and seafarers all worked for the affluence of Babylon, but, now that she has collapsed, nothing is left but a lament for the futility of her glittering luxury, her trade in "men's bodies and souls" (18:13). All that music and the other arts produced in the service of ease and eroticism is lost forever (18:21–24). This has nothing in common with the "works" that "follow" those who have died in the Lord and are pronounced blessed (14:13) or with the "glory" that the kings of the earth shall bring to the heavenly Jerusalem (21:24). When "one like a son of man" reaps the earth with a sharp sickle, and thereupon the earth's vintage is cast into the great wine press of the wrath of God, to be trodden until the excess of blood spurts from it (14:14ff., 19f.), the earth still remains, in this image of judgment, under the heavenly anger.

3. The Time

Time plays an important part in the Book of Revelation. We meet a wealth of time concepts, each with a different nuance: *kairos, chronos, hēmera, hōra, aiōn,* and so forth,[1] as well as time spans that seem to be both precise *and* symbolic ("a time, [two] times, and half a time" = three-and-a-half years = 1260 days = forty-two months). But none of these times can be fitted into the chronol-

---

[8] A. T. Hanson, *The Wrath of the Lamb* (London, 1957), sees this wrath as the historical consequences of rejecting the Cross, but he relativizes the apocalyptic punishments far too much by wrapping them in the whole context of salvation history. Our first task must be to allow the visions their own integrity and special truth.

[1] For an analysis, cf. M. Rissi, 27–37.

ogy of world history. True, the Christ-event dominates this history. It is its center, towering above it. But this is the very point: the Christ-event really is *above* history, rather than *in* it, so that one is reluctant to say that "henceforth" (*ap'arti*, 14:13) means "beginning with Christ's earthly life". In one respect, no doubt, this would agree with the concept of time found, for instance, in Hebrews 11:39, which dates the heavenly salvation from the time of Christ; but, on the other hand, this perspective draws a much sharper distinction between the Old and New Covenants than the Book of Revelation seems to do. It follows from this latter point that we cannot accept the view that the events reported prior to chapter 12 (where the Messiah-child is born) —that is, above all, the first "scaling" of the one hundred and forty-four thousand and the episode with the two prophesying witnesses—refer to the Jewish people, whereas chapter 12 onward portrays situations obtaining in the period of the Church.[2] Against this it must be said that neither part of the book makes any great distinction between the Old and New Testaments, nor is there any reference (most probably not even in chapter 17) to particular historical events, whether contemporary or past; it should all be understood as an eschatological rereading of the great prophecies of the Old Covenant—and this applies also to the portrayal of the heavenly Jerusalem. This means that none of the times mentioned, including the "five months" or the "thousand years", is to be understood quantitatively, but purely qualitatively. This applies most particularly to the "soon" (*tachy*, 3:11; 22:7; *en tachei*, 22:6; *kairos engys*, 1:3): this term expresses an "imminent expectation" that cannot be shaken by intervening delays (for example, the "thousand years"). Lohmeyer, in his commentary (192f.), speaks of "nontemporality" [*Unzeitlichkeit*], the coincidence of past, present and future; but such a manner of speaking is best avoided. It is true, however, that eschatological

---

[2] As does A. Feuillet, *loc. cit.*, 50f., and also in *Rev. Bibl.* (1959), 85: he sees chapters 4–11 as a development of Mark 13, with chapter 11 as a judgment upon Jerusalem's unbelief. In his view, the instance of conversion (an exception) in 11:13 corresponds to the Pauline hope for an eschatological conversion of the Jewish people. Equally unconvincing is the following division by Cerfaux-Cambier (*loc. cit.*): part 1: general (Jewish traditional) eschatology; part 2: (from chapter 12) special Christian eschatology.

time embraces all the events of revelation; thus the portrayal of these events can claim absolute completeness (22:18f.).

As the *eschaton* approaches with increasing urgency, its nearness must not be related exclusively to the constantly new events that irrupt vertically from heaven or exclusively to the purely horizontal, ever-diminishing time span between now and the end. Both aspects are found throughout. At every moment, the quality of the end-time is vertically present, yet as the visions proceed the end does get nearer. Underpinning this paradox will require at least a brief analysis of the succession of visions. Let us say by way of anticipation, however, that, just as we must reject every interpretation of the visions in terms of ecclesiastical and secular history at that period, so we must dismiss the theory that the various sequences of visions "recapitulate" the same events. On the other hand, we cannot deny that certain sequences move inexorably toward the ultimate situation of judgment: this is clearly the case with the sequence of the "seven seals" (where at the sixth the sun is hidden and the stars fall from the sky like unripe fruits, heaven is rolled up and the islands are removed: 6:12–14, cf. the same images in 16:20 and 20:11), at the collapse of the "holy city" (11:13), the twofold harvest scene (14:14–20), the outpouring of the seventh bowl ("it is done!", 16:17), the judgment of Babylon (18:8), the judgment of the beasts after the battle with the Logos (19:20f.) and the judgment of Satan (20:9f.), which leads into the scene of the general judgment of the dead (20:11–15). We could sum this up by saying that each of the individual visions or sequences of visions represents a cross-section between heaven and earth; each cross-section shows both the theodramatic situation between God and the world and a qualitatively different horizontal movement toward the historical end. We discern a certain heightening of the situation with each new vision. On the other hand, the different cross-sections interlock: the opening of the seventh "seal" gives rise to the "seven trumpets", the last three of which are the "three woes" (8:13). Evidently the last of these "woes" (11:14) produces the whole sequence of chapters 12–14, culminating in the "seven bowls of wrath" with which the "wrath of God is ended" (15:1). This is followed by the final judgment scenes, where the beasts, the dragon and all the dead are judged, after which we step over the threshold into the new world and the marriage of the Lamb. Tentatively we might say that the theologico-historical situation becomes more concrete from one cross-section to the next and that the central intervention is the birth of the Messiah, in response to which the dragon and its subject beasts (and Babylon) appear on the scene. And the more concrete the events become, the more everything is concentrated in the ultimately decisive "now": first God "takes his great power" (11:17) and brings about the fulfillment (10:7); then "salvation has now come" (12:10), the "hour of judgment" (14:7) and the "harvest" (14:15); finally "it is done" (16:17) when, God's wrath being at an end and Babylon having fallen, "the Almighty reigns" (19:6) and all his words are proved to be true and fulfilled (21:5).[3] On the one hand, the "now" coincides with the "eternal present" of the "Lamb as though it had been slain"; on the other hand, it signifies the increasingly momentous irruption of the reality of time into that of eternity.

4. The Sequence of Events

If we want to know the meaning of the sequence of events, we must not overlook the impressive introductory vision of Christ as King, Priest and Lord, the First and Last, who has the keys of Death and Hades. The theme of the Alpha and Omega stands at the beginning (1:8, 18) and at the conclusion of the book (22:13); it embraces the entire sequence of visions. While the visions seem to show more and more superhuman and terrible aspects, they never slip from the embrace of the Alpha and Omega. At the beginning, the Pantokrator bends down to his earthly communities (1:8) like a father confessor, testing and purifying them in human form (albeit a sublime one); at the end, he appears as the Guarantor of eternal reward and eternal life, with the promise that he will come soon; faith—perhaps a faith that does not understand—will continue to recognize him,

---

[3] No doubt this idea of the time being "fulfilled" by events (cf. 6:11) is a feature common to all apocalyptic, cf. 4 Esdras 4:35; Wikenhauser, *Offenbarung*, 3d ed. (Regensburg: Pustet, 1959), 63.

even in the unfamiliar forms in which he and his truth appear
in the visions. Initially unfamiliar, the basic figure is the "Lamb
as though it had been slain", known to all who are acquainted
with the Gospel of John.

Following the letters to the churches, the vision-world opens
with the overwhelming sight (4:1–11) of the throne-room of
God, (5:1) who holds in his right hand the sealed scroll containing his decisions concerning the world and its entire history.
No one but the Lamb is worthy to break the seals, for the Lamb
has triumphed "as the Lion of the tribe of Judah, the Root of
David": on the basis of the conclusion and outcome of the whole
drama between heaven and earth, the Lamb can unveil its course
and substance. The hymn of adoration that follows (5:9b–10)
affirms and expounds his function and authority: not only has
the Lamb-as-though-it-had-been-slain proved victorious; by his
blood he has won for God a people of kings and priests out of
all nations, and they will reign over the earth. All creation in
heaven, on earth, in the underworld and in the sea, joins in the
hymn of adoration; it is as though all concur, in advance, with
what the sealed scroll will contain.

It is as though the visions of the seals, like the later series of
sevens (divided into 4 + 3), open up the stage of the entire world
action. Thus the stage is set for a fallen humanity governed by
certain principles, "norms, laws, fundamentals of the world order":[1] life is a struggle that calls for victory (the rider with a
bow); life is a fierce wrestling for superiority (the rider with a
sword); life is controlled by reward and retribution, by justice,
although part of it is out of the reach of these sanctions (the
rider with the scales); and, finally, life is destined for death, an
ultimate death that (as under the Old Covenant) has no prospect
of resurrection (the rider called Death, with Hades in his train).
After these timeless dimensions, the fifth and sixth seals are more
concrete: injustice rules, and the oppressed cry out urgently for
right to be restored: they have to be patient. Finally, history
moves into the phase of judgment, existence showing its essential *Angst* in the face of it. Thus a certain historical movement
(albeit still an abstract one) enters into what seemed to be the

[1] A. von Speyr, *Apokalypse*, 258.

stage's static inauguration: the end is both impatiently and anxiously awaited.

However, the condition of human beings in these various dimensions is not the same. In the first interlude (7:1–17), the proceedings are stopped so that those whom the Lamb has chosen can be sealed with God's sign: they appear on earth as the 12 × 12 × 1000 of the tribes of Israel and in heaven as the countless multitude who come out of tribulation and have washed their robes in the blood of the Lamb, who stand before his throne and God's throne and are led by the Lamb to the streams of the water of life. This vertically ascending vision shows the elect being brought, not to judgment, but, bypassing Death and Hades, to eternal life.[2]

The opening of the seventh seal (8:1) causes a mysterious silence of "about half an hour" in heaven. Is this a silence of recollection? Of adoration? Or of foreboding and apprehension in the face of what will follow the signal to commence the world drama? At all events, it is clear that eternity is not without duration. By way of a prelude, as we have already mentioned, an angel throws to the earth the golden censer of the heavenly liturgy, filled with incense and the prayers of the saints, set alight with fire from the heavenly altar; it occasions terrifying phenomena. Previously the cry of the martyrs called for right judgment; now the prayers of the saints speed its advent,[3] but this acceleration

[2] E. Schick, in his *Die Apokalypse* (Patmos, 1971), sees correctly that, in each case, the "interludes" show the same reality—the Church—in different images: 90, 113f. (where he interprets the episode of the "two witnesses" in an ecclesiological sense) and 153. Cf. Wikenhauser, *Offenbarung*, 67–69.

[3] Various suggestions have been made with regard to 17:9b–17, with its apparently all-too-historical (and in part contradictory) interpretations. Thus the seven heads are both mountains and kings (9b); the harlot who was previously in the wilderness now sits beside waters, which signify nations, etc. (15). People have tried to attribute the passage to a later editor, who wrote at the time of Domitian and backdated his work to the time of Vespasian, the sixth emperor. (The idea that John himself undertook such backdating is even more incredible.) It may be quite correct to date the book to the end of the reign of Domitian (Irenaeus, *Adv. Haer.* 5, 30, 3 = Eusebius, *Hist. Eccl.* 5, 8, 6), but if the cult of the Emperor is strictly enforced in these years (cf. the image of the beast that is to be worshipped: 13:14ff.), the fact is that the seven "letters" reflect no universal persecution of Christians (whereas the prophetic portions strongly emphasize martyrdom). Again, it is quite arbitrary to antedate these letters (n.b., with their

also increases the woes. The seven trumpet blasts that herald the
end (again grouped as 4 + 3) initially have the effect of changing the atmosphere in the world. Corresponding to the censer
that has been thrown down, the first four plagues are primarily
characterized by fire: first, hail mixed with fire and blood; then
a fiery mountain cast into the sea, which changes into blood;
then a star, burning like a torch, falling upon the rivers and
springs and changing them into bitterness; and, finally, there is
the obscuring of all the shining lights of heaven. In each case,
a third of mankind is stricken. Then comes the episode of the
eagle flying through the heavens, uttering a threefold "Woe!"
in anticipation of the remaining three trumpet blasts. And in
fact, the fifth and sixth trumpets introduce a big change in the
atmosphere. First, a (fallen) angel opens the shaft of the abyss;
black smoke emerges and darkens the universe, and out of the
depths come tormenting spirits (half-locust, half-scorpion) who
so sting and torture human beings that they prefer death to life.
Then, terrifying beyond all imagination, the earth is inundated
with demonic horses and riders, their breastplates the color of

---

apocalyptic valedictions!); doing so dismembers a book that has been so carefully
composed as a unity. Some scholars even wanted to take a legend current at the
time (Suetonius, Tacitus), namely, that Nero had not died and would attack Rome
with the help of the Parthians (who did not have ten kings but twelve satraps),
and apply it to 17:10−11. In that case, however, the returning Nero would be
the beast itself; instead of reconquering Rome with the help of the Parthians, he
would hate and destroy it. It is not necessary to suppose that an interpolator has
been at work here, endeavoring to make veiled references to history and using
legends (that cannot be vouched for) for the purpose. Such an assumption would
mean that whole passages would have to be struck out as secondary. Instead, it is
quite possible to interpret 17:9b−17 in the same sense as 17:7−8 (which already
contains the paradox that the beast both "is not" and yet "is to ascend . . .") and
*abandon the attempt to explain the Great Harlot as Rome and the "speaking image" of
13:15 as emperor-worship.* The symbolic language of the "beasts" and "Babylon"
is just as relevant and gripping at every period of the Church's history as at the
time when it was written; to explain this language in terms of historical events of
the period is to distract attention from this here-and-now relevance. The book's
purpose is not to present charades by means of which isolated historical events
can be unravelled (thus 13:18b [the number of the Antichrist] and 17:9b [the
seven "heads" are seven "hills"] should be considered to be real glosses) but to
encourage the gospel attitude of vigilance and readiness in the face of the whole
movement of history; cf. 13:10c; 14:12; 16:15; and the "letters".

fire, with fire and smoke and sulphur issuing from their mouths, grievously wounding both with their mouths and with their tails. They do not have the effect of converting men but only harden them in their abandonment of God and their perverse doings. The new plagues, in the wake of the opening of the abyss and the abolition of life's restraints (the boundary of the Euphrates), give a fantastic portrayal of the demonization of human history ("two hundred million"). Compare Romans 1:28–32. Before the seventh trumpet, heralding the third "woe", there is a new interlude, more dramatic than the first, but also enacted vertically between earth and heaven (11:1–13).

First—an echo of Ezekiel—God's temple and the altar and those who worship there are "measured", but not the outer court, which is given to the "nations", who "will trample over the holy city for forty-two months" (11:2). Over against these "nations" stand God's two "witnesses" (echoing Zechariah 4) with the power of working miracles like Moses and Elijah. They symbolize the chosen people from the first interlude, as well as "those who worship" at the beginning of the second; but now, since God's sacred realm is divided in two, in the presence of God they prosecute the "nations" for their godless activities. Now we have a dramatic heightening of the opposition between the parties and hear of the "beast rising from the abyss" (13:1; 17:8), conquering and killing the witnesses (11:7 = 13:7), whereupon their corpses remain lying "in the street of the great city that is allegorically called Sodom and Egypt, where their Lord was crucified", to the great relief of those who "dwell on the earth", now that they are rid of the troublesome witnesses. After three-and-a-half days, their bodies are instilled with life once more, and they ascend to heaven, to the dismay of those watching them; a tenth of the city collapses as a result of an earthquake. Which city? Not the historical Jerusalem, for here, like temple and altar, it is only a symbol. All the same, there are certain concrete elements: the multitude of the chosen, for instance, is divided into two: a smaller portion ("those who worship"), which is preserved, and the larger portion, which is surrendered to be trampled upon; and, in this "Sodom-Egypt", the Lord was crucified and the prophets were "conquered and killed". In the first interlude, there was a simple juxtaposition of the "servants of God", or the spiritual Israel, on the one hand, and those delivered up to the manner of life of the fallen world, on the other (albeit the former attain salvation through the "great tribulations" of the latter). In the second interlude, this has changed into open hostility; after a sermon in which the offenses are listed, war breaks out.

Following this vision, there is undoubtedly a decisive caesura. The remaining time is short; the end is imminent (10:6). Previously God and Jesus were referred to as "He who is, who was and who is to come" (1:4, 8; 4:8): from now on, the third attribute, "who is to come", is omitted, because "the kingdom of the world has become the kingdom of our Lord and of his Christ" (11:15). Now the Messiah steps forth explicitly. This increased prominence of events corresponds to the seventh trumpet blast and the third "woe", which now follows. The content of this "woe" is the immediate reality of God's mighty power and wrath and his judgment upon the dead (11:17–18); it extends, therefore, up to 20:15.

The visions of chapters 12–13 give further concreteness to the contrast already described. Now the community of the chosen is the Woman, bearing heavenly insignia, who appears in heaven, crying out in her birth-pangs as she gives birth to the Messiah; the dragon threatens to devour the child, but he is "caught up to God". This event is of central significance for the world: its consequence is that the dragon, having been vanquished in heaven, falls to the earth (cf. Lk 10:18), where he is in great rage because the time remaining to him is short. He persecutes the Woman, who is removed to the desert and is protected and nourished there; he makes war on her offspring, "who keep the commandments of God and bear testimony to Jesus" (12:17). The birth of the Child and the resulting fall of the devil mean that a qualitative time threshold has been passed, once and for all. Thus the heightened "woe to the earth" (12:12) and the devil's redoubling of efforts (20:2) in his war against the *civitas Dei* are seen to follow from the fact that he has already been judged. It represents a tremendous step into the open when the devil comes forth in person (as opposed to the mere smoke from the abyss and his demonic offspring in 9:1–21); a further stage is reached when he assumes concrete shape in the two beasts (13:1–18), unmasking himself as the perverse mimic of the divine Trinity. The first beast, rising out of the sea, is the anti-Christian incarnation of evil: thus its wound heals, in contrast to the marks of the Lamb's wounds; in 17:3, it is shown to be one with the Great Harlot, the opposite to the community of Christ. The second beast, which arises out of the earth, is the spiritual and ideological form of the first; it is the lie, which has antipneumatic power to lead men astray, holding them spellbound under totalitarian rule. The appointed span for the beasts' domination is the same as that appointed in 11:2 for the "trampling of the holy city" and in 12:14 for the community's sojourn in the wilderness: it is always a time span ("time") that, because of its intensity, seems to stretch out ("times") but is again shortened ("half a time") by the imminent approach of the end. These three measurements are not to be added together as a series: all three interpenetrate.

Another short interlude (14:1-15) once again shows the Lamb on Mount Zion with the same one hundred and forty-four thousand of the "sealed" in his train. Though many have been "conquered" in the war against the saints (13:7; 11:7), the chosen multitude is unharmed and "virginal" in the face of the godless abominations and spells of the beasts. This preservation is not their own doing; it is because (through the blood of the Lamb) they have been "redeemed from mankind" and are "spotless". At this point we can add 14:13, "Blessed are the dead who die in the Lord": "henceforth" means "in virtue of" the Lamb's redeeming death. "For their deeds follow them": heaven and earth remain bound up with one another, even beyond the judgment: all that has been done and suffered for God's sake will enter into the new world. This "extension" into the new world is possible because of the "endurance of the saints" who "keep the [Old Testament] commandments of God" and the New Testament "faith of Jesus" (14:12). Once again it is stressed that the pre-Christian and post-Christian worlds enjoy equal opportunity, since they are both embraced by the destiny of the Lamb; in this way, the new vision of the elect (14:1ff.) refers back to the earlier vision (7:1ff.).

The cross-section through world history that has shown Satan's beasts as the principles of this history ends in 3 + 2 aspects of judgment. First there are the heralding angels: just as the beast had addressed all nations, so the first angel proclaims to all nations the revealed truth of God, which will now manifest itself in the form of judgment (14:6–7). The second angel proclaims the fall of Babylon, the (female) expression of the first beast; she will be shown in the next vision (14:8). The third angel portrays the fate of those who have been seduced, that is, their eternal torment (14:9–12). This is followed by two images of judgment: the harvest of crops and the vintage (these two are already linked in Joel 4:13). Both are seen in apocalyptic terms as pure wrathful judgment. The first image features the Son of Man; the second, an angel subordinate to "the angel who has power over the fire" (14:14–20).

These pictures of judgment are immediately followed in chapters 15–16 by the series of visions concerning the seven bowls of wrath with which "the wrath of God is ended". Thus they refer to the conclusion of the time of the end and to the final intensification of the struggle between Christian and anti-Christian forces. More than ever, the scene shows the heavenly liturgy (in which those who are predestined and triumphant have a share: 15:2–4) to be simultaneous with the punitive judgment of the earth. After the hymn praising God's judgment, which is righteous and worthy of all adoration, there are solemn descriptions of the seven angels proceeding from the open covenant tabernacle, their liturgical vestments, the giving of the bowls and the filling of the Temple with the incense of the divine anger. This simultaneity of liturgy and judgment is perhaps the most all-pervading leitmotif of the Book of Revelation. It shows how much heaven is involved in earthly destinies but also how little such involvement interrupts the occupations of the heavenly ones. In the constant hymning of the divine attributes of the hidden Father, of the Lamb and of the sevenfold Spirit, there is no neglect of the praise of eternal righteousness, which is just as worthy of worship (15:3–4) as all the other qualities of God's being. The heavenly worship, which includes the prayers of those who have "conquered", is doubtlessly mingled in the bowls of wrath, just as, earlier, the prayers of the saints were mingled in the incense (8:4). (We are not told in 15:2 whether those who have "conquered" have already died or are still living on earth, nor do we know whether they belong to the Old Covenant—

the Song of Moses—or the New—the Song of the Lamb.) Indeed, the praise of God's righteousness is continued even while his wrath is being manifested (16:5–7).

The individual outpourings of wrath show symbolically how the divine anger penetrates the sinner's whole interior and exterior milieu: it is a psycho-physical abscess; it is something that changes the living water into dead water, which the living human being has to drink; it is something that scorches and burns. Nor do these things lead to conversion but—as in the case of the Egyptian plagues, which in many ways serve as a "type" here—to an ever-greater hardening of heart. The plagues are not institutions of mercy: they are judgment; they lay bare the presence, in souls, of the essence of evil. Bowls five to seven deal directly with the beast-principles that lie behind men: the beast's throne is attacked, and his kingdom, the prestige of sin, is thrown into darkness: sin becomes unbearable torment. Then (when the boundary river dries up) a path is opened up for the powers of chaos to enter in and prepare for the final battle against God. Finally, the entire atmosphere linking heaven and earth is affected; all the signs of the end take place (16:18–20), and the last things become actuality: "It is done" (16:17).

However, the new cross-section that follows (chapters 17–18) presents a kind of retrospective "enlargement" of the summary that we have seen (retrospective because Babylon has already fallen: 14:8; 16:9). We must devote special attention to Babylon, the ultimate concrete manifestation of Satan's working through the beast, on which she (Babylon) sits as the Great Harlot (but we need not pay any further attention to the second beast here). From the Old Covenant on, Babylon symbolizes and epitomizes the godless politico-cultural world power, the very opposite of Jerusalem, the *civitas Dei*. It refers neither to the Mesopotamian nor to the new Roman superpower; rather, it is the utterly concrete principle for which and with which "the kings of the earth" (that is, including Rome) "have committed fornication" (17:2) and which "has dominion over the kings of the earth" (17:18). As is often the case in the Old Covenant, fornication is to be understood both figuratively (meaning idolatry) and literally (that is, that which offends against man's incarnational bodily being). Quite consistently, the harlot's cup is filled with the "filth of her fornication" as well as the "blood of the saints" and the "wrath (of God)" (18:3); it is the more concrete expression of the conduct of the beast, which both blasphemes God and wars against the saints.

What follows (17:7–17), that is, the interpretation of the beast and the woman, is the hardest and most disputed passage of the book. In the light of what we have already said, it would seem somewhat perverse suddenly to expect to find a coded portrayal of precise details of contemporary history here or to interpret the ubiquitous symbolic numbers as a key to the succession of Roman emperors, and the Great Harlot as the city of Rome. The (theological) principles and powers of world history have their reality in other dimensions.

The interpretation of the beast is initially mysterious: "The beast . . . was, and is not, and is to ascend from the bottomless pit and go to perdition" (17:8). Thus, as the principle of evil, it is the counterimage to the God "who is and who was and who is to come" (1:8). God is present, here-and-now Being: evil cannot put forward any counterimage to match him. Note that in 17:11 the beast both "was" and "is not" (cf. Gregory of Nyssa, PG 46, 1133A) and that Babylon too is said to have fallen (14:8; 18:2) before ever its presence was beheld or described (17:1ff.; 18:7).

What follows next is even more obscure: the beast's seven heads are said to be seven hills on which the woman sits but also seven kings, "of whom five have fallen, one is, the other has not yet come, and when he comes he must remain only a little while"; as for the beast, "it is an eighth, but it belongs to the seven" (17:10–11). All attempts to interpret this in terms of the sequence of Roman emperors has proved unsatisfactory; we do better to remain at the symbolic level. In the cross-section provided by this vision, most of the high points of the beast's power are past, and the present high point is in transition to a coming short-term one. Then the principle itself will emerge out of its successive embodiments and go to perdition, as the next and final sequence of visions will explicitly show (19:20). Finally, the ten horns of the seven heads (13:1 = 17:3) are interpreted as ten rulers. They do two things: they make war against the Lamb, who vanquishes them (no doubt this anticipates 19:19); then, together

with the beast, they turn against the harlot, "make her desolate
and naked and devour her flesh and burn her up with fire". Details from the history of the period are even less help here. The
"desolation" is described thoroughly in the great lament of 18:1–
24; on the "devouring" and "burning", cf. 19:17ff. and 18:8, 9,
17; 19:3.[4] The essential point is that Babylon's fall is caused by
the beast and the rulers associated with it, that is, evil's final po-

[4] In 20:4, they also participate in the process of judgment in a special way (cf.
1 Cor 6:2). "They are brought to life again in a kind of initial resurrection so that
they may share in Christ's reign. They share in his mission in the world. . . . This
is the first resurrection, namely, holiness." "The two things are equated here: the
holiness of martyrdom and the holiness of bearing witness." A. von Speyr, *Apokalypse*, 656–57. E. Schick's interpretation is in harmony with this (note 2 above),
213; similar, but less accurate, is J. Sickenberger, *Erklärung der Johannesapokalypse*
(Bonn: Hanstein, 1942), 181. This recalls the very widespread view of exegetes
and theologians that Mt 27:52–53 means that the saints who are raised with
Christ will experience a real physical resurrection with a subsequent ascension
into heaven, cf. H. Zeller, "Corpora Sanctorum" in *ZKTh* (1949), particularly
applying to the Apostle John (Cosmas Vestitor, Fulbert of Chartres, Mechthild
of Magdeburg, Giotto's celebrated fresco). H. Bietenhard, *Das tausendjährige Reich*
(Zurich: Zwingli, 1955), adduces parallels to the idea of an "empire of a thousand
years" from late Judaism, in particular the view that the perfection of the world
is preceded by a period of salvation on earth, which can be regarded, in the second and third centuries, as the "Messianic" period (1 Enoch 93 + 91:12–17), *loc.
cit.*, 37–41. Is it really the case, however, that the Book of Revelation is such a
profound fulfillment of Jewish eschatology that the latter should be regarded as
"an integral and integrating component of the Church's eschatology" (153)? Is it
right to say that the conversion of Israel prior to the parousia would introduce
a triumphal phase of the earthly Church (120), "on the one hand, bringing to
fulfillment what the Church now is but also fulfilling here and now, in this aeon,
what the Church will be in the coming aeon . . . whether those who have risen
live in heaven or on earth" (152)? This kind of speculation seems inapt, particularly when, as in Auberlen, *Der Prophet Daniel und die Offenbarung Johannis*, 2d ed.
(1857), 381f., it is linked with the assumption of a kind of spiritist "communication between the heavenly and earthly community, between the upper and the
lower world", a communication that "will have been much more vital and free
than in the period of the Church's history". Contrary to fantasies of this sort, we
must assert that the millennium is one aspect of Christ's "reign" in his Church
(cf. 1:6, 9; 5:10), an aspect affecting the new risen life of the saints (martyrs and
confessors), which does not need to be a merely nonphysical life, as is assumed
by E. W. Hengstenberg, *Offenbarung* II/1 (Berlin, 1850), 380ff. In this context,
we can say with O. Cullmann in his "Königsherrschaft Christi und Kirche im
NT" in *Theol. Stud.* (1941), 14, that a part of Christ's kingdom already reaches
into the new aeon prior to the parousia.

tentiality devours and destroys itself, whereas the beasts opposed
to the Incarnation are conquered by Christ himself (19:19–21),
and the annihilation of the final enemy, the dragon, is reserved
to God alone (20:9).

Babylon's fall is greeted with strongly Old Testament jubilation: this is purely punitive justice (18:1–8). The great lament
of kings, merchants and seafarers, the portrayal of desolation, of
the cessation of all forms of life (18:5–24), is not only a high
point of biblical poetry, it is more: first, it is a judgment on the
essential injustice of all secular economic life; then it looks ahead
to the eschatological cessation of all cultural and social activity:
the Old Testament images applying to the ruin of a city or of
an individual empire are widened here to apply to the whole
of history. This is followed by the sharp contrast of heaven's
thunderous Hallelujah, which looks backward to the sentence
of vengeance that has been carried out (19:2) and forward to
the "marriage of the Lamb" (19:7, 9); as for the present: "God
reigns" (19:6b).

The last series of visions concerning historical events describes
the eschatological battle of the Lamb against the beasts and the
destruction of Satan. This allows us to reflect once more on the
meaning of the cross-sections presented to us in the entire sequence. Each cross-section reveals the total theological situation
of history with regard to the opposition of faith and unbelief,
but it also portrays this situation as it moves toward the end,
judgment. However, since each cross-section shows the whole
situation in a qualitatively unique perspective, we cannot say that
these visions "recapitulate" the same periods or events. Finally,
the cross-sections (each of which embraces the whole) show
opposition becoming more concrete as the end is approached.
This is very clear from chapter 12 onward; the imminent final
battle is now so close to the ultimate total meaning that after
20:11–15 there is no possibility of further vision in intrahistor-
ical categories. Nonetheless, even this final sequence (19:11–
20:15) embraces the whole of salvation history. Here, again, the
center of salvation history is the incarnate and crucified Logos.
(The blood that saturates his robe, 19:13, is surely his own.) But,
given the close resemblance to the sequence in Ezekiel and to
the other Old Testament images, the Old Covenant cannot be

excluded. There are three parts: the Logos rides forth to battle as "King of kings and Lord of lords" to vanquish the beasts, which are thrown into the lake of fire. Then comes the reign of a thousand years while Satan is bound in the abyss. Finally, he is released, and Gog and Magog proceed to make war against the holy city, only to be consumed by fire from heaven; Satan is thrown into the lake of fire along with the beasts. The final picture is the general judgment of the dead, when Death and Hades are also consigned to the lake of fire.

The "times" of these events are coextensive in a way we cannot imagine. The Logos, who in many ways appears as he did at the beginning (1:9–16) and is accompanied by the "heavenly hosts" (who are by no means exclusively angels but also those who are "called, chosen and faithful": 17:14), rides forth once and for all; for there is no time when he does not "judge and make war" with the sword of his mouth. And, since the beast blasphemes and fights against the saints (13:7), it also "makes war with him who sits upon the horse and against his army" (19:19). We are not shown an indecisive struggle between the Logos and the beast: in fighting, the Logos has already judged (19:11); nonetheless he does fight (cf. 1 Cor 15:25), and individual members of his company on earth are actually overwhelmed (11:7; 13:7). The same is not true of the forces coming from heaven.

This should serve to clarify the second picture of the binding of Satan and the thousand-year reign of the saints with Christ. We must not simply equate the thousand years with the period of the Church's history (as Augustine does); but we should take literally what is said about those who lived and died for the testimony of Jesus: "Blessed and holy is he who shares in the first resurrection!" (20:6): the saints and the blessed exercise a bodily presence and influence on the earthly Church that is not shared, to the same degree, by the "rest of the dead" (20:5). The binding of Satan is thus only the necessary counterpart to the saints' exercise of power together with Christ; it can be regarded as a different perspective on his fall from heaven. While this fulfills and transcends the resurrection prophecy of Ezekiel 37, Revelation 20:7–10 (corresponding to Ezekiel 39) interposes the final battle of Satan, in league with Gog and Magog, against "the beloved city", the "camp of the saints". The depiction of the countless deceived ("like the sand of the sea") who come forth from "the four corners of the earth" exhibits a mythical hue: this is the final intensification of the struggle that had always been going on between the two *civitates*. Again there are no episodes; fire descends from God to decide the battle's outcome, and evil's innermost potency is thrown to eternal, self-devouring torment along with the two beasts who are its embodiments. In chapter 12, this potency falls from heaven; in 13 and 17, it emerges from the sea, the earth and the abyss; we are never told where it came from in the first place.

The last judgment is described precisely but, as it were, *sotto voce*. We are not told who sits on the judgment throne. Death's finitude is manifest: the sea and even death and the underworld have to surrender their prey. We are also shown the finitude of the cosmos as a whole: heaven and earth (and the sea: 21:1) flee into oblivion. All that now remain are the dead; they are judged individually according to their works. The lake of fire that swallows death and the underworld is also ready for those whose names are not written in the book of life.

5. The Framework

In the part of the vision that portrayed the drama that takes place between heaven and earth, between God and his world and the dragon and its powers—note that the *civitas Dei* was present in both scenes—the issue was simply that of absolute value or nonvalue, of righteousness or unrighteousness. No attention was paid to the nuances introduced by love, grace and the soul's struggle to attain them. This makes it clear that the visions are not intended to give a glimpse of concrete future world history: their function is to help sustain this concrete struggle in the individual and the community here and now. The seven "letters" introduced by the initial vision, in which Christ holds in his hand the spirits or angels of the communities, form the first half of the framework that serves to situate what is to be seen. In this case, the focus is most precisely on the Christian life and values cultivated in the various communities and in individual groups within them. Thus we read of a love that is perfect and one that has fallen from its erstwhile fullness (2:4); a humility that thinks itself poor yet is rich (2:9); a faith that, in some people, is vulnerable and can turn to unbelief (2:13f.); a kind of progress in Christianity that is insufficiently consistent (2:19f.); a pseudo-vitality that is in fact moribund and needs to be shaken into life (3:1f.); a weakness that yet can hold fast to the Lord in faithfulness (3:8); and, finally, a dangerous lukewarmness that thinks itself rich but in reality is wretchedly poor, blind and naked; it is sharply rebuked, for "those whom I love, I reprove and chasten" (3:17, 19). All these communities are given promises that refer beyond the scenario of the battle visions to the second and concluding part of the framework, namely, that new world created by God where "death shall be no more, neither shall there be mourning nor crying nor pain any more, for the former things have passed away" (21:4). However, the seer beholds "a new heaven and a new earth", that is, it is not simply that the old earth is wound up and absorbed into God's permanent heaven. Most significantly, he sees a downward movement: the New Jerusalem comes down from above[1] and—in an analogy to the Old Covenant—becomes the tabernacle in which God dwells among men (21:2–3). The New Jerusalem is adorned like a bride at her wedding, but this is not a marriage between heaven and earth: she is married to the Lamb who has lived and suffered on earth and now stands on God's heavenly throne. The measurements of the city, radiant with God's glory,

---

[1] We must be cautious about suggesting that this idea of the preexistence, in God, of an eschatological Jerusalem is a feature common to apocalyptic (4 Ezra 7:26 passim; 1 Enoch 90:28ff.; 53:6). M. Rissi is correct here in his *Die Zukunft der Welt* (Basel: Reinhardt, no date), 74. In the first place, it is a trait of the New Testament generally: Galatians 4:26; Hebrews 12:22, whereas in chapter 4ff., what is beheld is by no means the heavenly Jerusalem. The latter comes into view once more in "Behold, I make all things new" (21:5), in a final fulfillment of the promises of Trito-Isaiah (60:1ff.). It is not as if the two aspects can be completely separated. However, the Church's eternal side and eternal origin (for example, the Pauline texts, and Augustine: "de coelo quidem ab initio sui descendit, ex quo per huius saeculi tempus . . . cives eius accrescunt": *Civ. Dei* 20, 17) is one thing; her ultimate shape, once the drama between heaven and earth has been fully acted out, is another. What we have here is not a "vue synthétique de l'Eglise, dans le temps et dans l'éternité", as E.-B. Allo thinks: *L'Apocalypse* (1921), 312ff.

correspond both to (earthly) man and to the (heavenly) angel (21:17), and, although the city comes down from God, it also rests on the foundation of the "apostles of the Lamb"; its gates bear the names of the twelve tribes of Israel, that is, of earthly realities. There is water in the city, but it springs forth from the divine throne; there are trees and leaves and fruit, but they have heavenly powers. Everything else that is described in the city exhibits the same unimaginable union between things that are familiar to earth yet transformed into heavenly realities. It is to this union that the mysterious promises of the "letters" refer. What is already true in the Church, in the hiddenness of faith, that is, that God himself and the Lamb are her temple and her light, is now fulfilled openly and publicly (21:22f.). Similarly, the Church's doors were always open to the world; she was always the light of the world, and the riches of the nations were already hers yet in an invisible manner; now, however, this will be manifest to the eyes of all (21:23–26).

Finally, the beginning and the conclusion fit together as a single framework. Again the Lord speaks: "Behold, I am coming soon" (22:7), to which the Spirit and the Bride reply: "Come" (22:17, 20). As at the beginning, the Lord declares himself to be "the first and the last, the beginning and the end" (22:13): he is the complete framework for that entire drama that embraces world history and the end-time.

B. THE BOOK OF
REVELATION: REFLECTION

The last book of Holy Scripture presupposes the Christ-events of the New Covenant and opens up the vast perspectives they imply. It links up with the magisterial Old Testament prophecy[1] (going beyond the form of intertestamental apocalyptic) and so transcends and integrates it. The Book of Revelation, then, will provide a vantage point from which to survey the form and content of the theodramatic action we intend to portray. Form and content cannot be separated: they presuppose each other. The same applies to the theo-logy in which we must become involved when we come to describe the action of theo-drama: its form is essentially the form of *this* content; its content is essentially the concrete unfolding of *this* form.

1. The Dramatic Form

As we have seen, the center of the Book of Revelation consists of a series of images that show, "in a mirror, dimly" (otherwise it would not be possible at all), the unfolding effects on earth and heaven, time and eternity, of the Christ-event that is set forth in the gospel. But it is not simply that the Book of Revelation is "visionary", whereas the events themselves are "real". On the one hand, through their own inner dynamism, the Synoptic apocalypses and other New Testament apocalyptic passages (like 1 Thessalonians 4–5; 1 Corinthians 15) open out toward the dimensions and scope of the final Book; on the

---

[1] "Ce qui fait l'originalité de l'Apocalypse johannique, c'est que tout en utilisant le style, l'imagerie et les procédés de l'apocalypse juive, elle demeure fidèle à ce qui fait la grandeur de l'ancienne prophétie." Feuillet, *L'Apocalypse, état de la question* (Paris: DDB, 1963), 8, cf. 63. According to E. Fiorenza, in "Gericht und Heil" in *Gestalt u. Anspruch des NT*, ed. Schreiner/Dautzenberg (Echter, 1969), 338, the epistolary framework makes it "clear that the Book of Revelation is not so much an apocalyptic depiction as a prophetical exhortation to the communities." "L'Apocalypse n'est qu'une traduction en clair, dans la lumière du Nouveau Testament, des prophéties de l'Ancien Testament": L. Cerfaux, *Lect. Div.* 17, 89.

other hand, this Book is held together by a beginning and an ending that speak explicitly of the "concrete" love of Christ, of "concrete" Christian life (in the "letters") and "concrete" Christian longing and hope for the heavenly fulfillment. Christ, within this framework, is he "who loves us" (1:5), "who loved you" (3:9), who "reproves and chastens those he loves" (3:19) —which gives evangelical meaning to all Christ's modes of appearance in the world of images.[2] This love both embraces and substantiates the visions. When the Lord makes his appearance as the Alpha and Omega and, taking up the theme of the Prologue of John's Gospel, explicitly refers to himself as the "beginning [JB: 'ultimate source'] of God's creation" (3:14), there is an interpenetration of meaning and image; this disclosure of the beginning and the end makes it possible for there to be such a thing as a theology of history.[3]

Nonetheless, as the preceding analysis has shown, the difference is striking: the images must on no account be resolved in terms of ecclesiastical and world history familiar to us from other sources. The existential history of Christ, of the Church and of the Christian is always held within an overall "bracket"; this bracket or embrace removes the imagery from our manipulation and prevents it from being sucked into the temporal course of history. The images are like a mysterious "dogmatics" that stands, irreducible, over against the actualization of the Church's life. Three things make this especially evident.

---

[2] The specifically Christian quality of the Book of Revelation has often been stressed, for example, by Bousset, 132, and E. Schweizer, *Jesus* (London, 1971), who cites the Book of Revelation to illustrate "the difference between New Testament apocalyptic and Jewish apocalyptic of the period". Cf. also H. Windisch, (*RGG*, 2d ed., 337–38), who simply speaks of the "Apocalypse of the Lamb"; E. Schmitt, "Die christologische Interpretation als das Grundlegende der Apokalypse" in *Th. Q.* (1960), 257–90. In his "Die Christologie der Apokalypse des Johannes" in *Texte und Untersuchungen* 85 (Berlin: Akad. Verlag, 1962), Traugott Holtz focuses on this christocentrism and interprets the many names and predicates of Christ. On p. 61ff., he discusses the explicitly mentioned "love" of Christ that led to the redemption of the elect "through his blood" (5:9; cf. 14:4) and to the Lamb's eternal and visible wound. There is a clear inner continuity here with Paul's and John's doctrine of redemption (*ibid.*, 69).

[3] Cf. A. Halder and H. Vorgrimler, in "Geschichtstheologie", *LThK*, 2d ed., IV, 79.

First of all, there is the process whereby Old Testament images are "reborn" in the Book of Revelation that concludes the New[4] —a process that is hardly accessible to human reason. There is the same analogy and typology between the old and new image as between the Old and New Covenant; a tremendous universalization takes place. Thus, for instance, the smoke that arises "forever . . . day and night" from the ruined Edom (Is 34:10) now becomes the smoke that "goes up for ever and ever" from the self-devouring Great Harlot, Babylon (Rev 19:3), the epitome of all the world's seductive forces. Thus, too, the book that is bound to a stone and thrown into the Euphrates (Jer 51:63f.), indicating the fall of Babylon, becomes that tremendous scene in which the angel casts a great millstone into the sea with the words, "So shall Babylon the great city be thrown down with violence and shall be found no more" (Rev 18:21f.). Many images boldly take up features from farther back than the Old Testament, from (possibly mythical) prehistory; for example, the Proto-evangelion is concluded with the Woman who gives birth in the face of the dragon;[5] Jerusalem has a certain historical continuity with the city of the Jebusites, with "Sodom and Egypt". However, despite this realization, in the gospel, of ancient prophecy, these reborn images remain *images*: they remind believers that the prophetic content of the evangelical words and deeds of Jesus and the Apostles open up dimensions that Christian faith can never change into complacent possession. These dimensions are truly open, for, after all, what we are dealing with is *apo-kalypsis*; yet they remain only significant hieroglyphs that, however legible, conceal their ultimate meaning in the mystery of God. So the Book of Revelation testifies simultaneously to the fact that Old Testament prophecy has been transposed and fulfilled and to the fact

----

[4] Austin Farrar's title "A Rebirth of Images" hits it off splendidly, but the subtitle, "The Making of St. John's Apocalypse" (Westminster: Dacre Press, 1949), leads up a false path; it is not a question of "making", and no known "method of poetic analysis" (20) is of any help. The "rebirth" lies, in fact, in the revelation of the images themselves.

[5] L. Cerfaux, "La Vision de la femme et du dragon de l'Apocalypse en relation avec le Protoévangile" in *Recueil Lucien Cerfaux* III (Gembloux, 1962), 237–51. Cf. F. M. Braun in *Bible et vie chrétienne* 7 (1954), 63–71.

that it continues to exercise a (transformed) actuality and presence.[6]

The second thing that points to a continuous and even intensified *diastasis* is the fact that the acting area, compared to that of the classical Old Covenant, has been expanded. As well as the dimension of "Death and Hades" (6:8), we now have that of the open abyss (9:1f., 11; 20:1; 11:7; 17:8), from which smoke arises to darken the world and from which the beast emerges, and finally the "lake of fire" (19:20; 20:10, 14, 15; 21:8), which blazes and smokes "day and night for ever and ever". Irrespective of the degree to which intertestamental apocalyptic may have prepared the way for this, it remains a fact that, in St. John's Apocalypse, this expansion is a consequence of what the Lamb has done: on the one hand, the Lamb has the key of death and the underworld (1:18), and, on the other hand, the angel who opens the abyss is "given" the key from heaven (9:1). The dragon and his beasts only come out to do battle once the Messiah has appeared (chapter 12f.). The smoke emitted from the abyss corresponds to the heavenly cloud of anger of the divine glory, which comes from above and prevents anyone from entering the heavenly temple (15:7f.). This, again, is prophetic tradition projected into the image-world of the heightened crisis situation in the New Covenant: only since the universal embrace of the Cross does there exist, in a true sense, the demonic world of absolute denial. Accordingly, it is only since the Cross that the concept of "judgment" acquires a seriousness that nothing can relativize.[7] Redemption has come; it is the foundation for everything; yet if a man's name is not written in the book of life, he can be lost.

The third element underlining the *diastasis* is the utterly changed time-reality in the visions as opposed to the apparently linear time of history. In the background, always presupposed, stands the Cross, the real slaying of the Lamb. But, in the vision-images, the struggle that took place there and the victory that was achieved lead to a "war" in heaven (12:7); the battle that

---

[6] Cf. E. Lohmeyer, *Offenbarung*, 2d ed. (1953), 195–96.

[7] D. Mollat, "Jugement", *Suppl. Dict. Bibl.* (1949); J. Blank, *Krisis* (Freiburg: Lambertus, 1964).

breaks out on earth is the result of the dragon's defeat in heaven
(12:13ff.). When the time of reconciliation dawns, it seems to
correspond with a time of intensified struggle and heightened
Old Testament wrath, as if God's victory, once achieved, renews
this wrath and focuses attention on it. The confusing mixture
of tenses is connected with this: a future can suddenly turn into
a preterite "without thereby altering the prophetic meaning";[8]
Babylon's fall is proclaimed before ever it is shown to be a present
reality (14:8), and Babylon is depicted sitting on the beast that
"is not" (17:3, 8). Accordingly, the expressions "soon", "near"
and "a short time" acquire a meaning that cuts obliquely across
earthly time and drops vertically into it. We have already referred
to this in connection with the expression *gegonen*, "it is done".
Yet this apparently confused time matches the time expressions
of the gospel. The gospel is acquainted with a form of "imminent expectation" [*Naherwartung*], which must not be reduced to
a mere "constant expectation" [*Stetserwartung*][9] and nonetheless
cannot be translated in terms of linear, evolutionary time. Nor
(least of all) can it be "privatized by being referred exclusively to
the death-situation of the individual".[10] It is possible to discern
the relatedness of earthly and visionary time in the "letters", and
the former's openness to the latter, but the two cannot be made
to coincide. Earthly time, as depicted in the imagery of the four
horsemen, is one of battle, war, reckoning and a life that leads to
death; but it is also a Christian time characterized by endurance,
hope and a transcendent longing, opening out beyond earthly
time to embrace the eternal kingdom.

Only if we keep in mind this threefold *diastasis*, which cannot
be built into any system, can we say anything meaningful about
the dramatic form of the Book of Revelation. Indeed, if we look

---

[8] J. Sickenberger, *Erklärung der Johannesapokalypse*, 2d ed. (Bonn: Hanstein,
1942), 167.

[9] "The attempt theologically to reinterpret 'imminent expectation' as 'constant
expectation' or 'constant readiness', that is, in short, to understand it as a timeless
existentiale, (remains) a semantic betrayal of Christianity's fundamentally time-
related structure": J. B. Metz, "Hoffnung als Naherwartung oder der Kampf um
die verlorene Zeit" in *Glaube in Geschichte und Gesellschaft* (Mainz: Grünewald,
1977), 152.

[10] *Ibid.*, 153.

solely at the visions, we can subscribe to J. Wellhausen's judgment that "the Apocalypse is not a drama but a picture-book"[11] and that the seer is not involved in what he sees but is "as unmoved as a real-life reporter . . . in the midst of the majestic spectacle".[12] It has often been noticed that the Lamb does not struggle with the hostile powers; he is the Judge who, at most, "makes war" (19:11)[13]—although his victory has already been won. Whenever the decisive final stage is envisaged, its "dramatic" issue is passed over (since it has already taken place in the death of Jesus), and all that is recorded is the collapse of the enemy (19:20ff.; 20:9f.). The theme of the Lamb's victory dominates everything.[14] We should hesitate, therefore, to describe the sequence of images as such, however overwhelming it is, as "dramatic";[15] at most, the word should be reserved for the confrontation of the utterly inimical powers between which men find themselves situated and to which they can succumb (11:7; 13:7). The drama only attains its full shape if we relate the sequence of images to the concrete communities addressed in the "letters" and reflect on their situation as we find it in the

[11] "Analyse der Offenbarung Johannes' " (*Abh. der Kön. Ges. d. Wissenschaften, Göttingen*, phil. hist. Klasse, new series IX, no. 4 [Berlin, 1907]), 3.

[12] *Ibid.*, 10.

[13] C. Brütsch, *Clarté de l'Apocalypse* (Geneva: Labor et Fides, 1955), 9.

[14] Cf. Holtz (note 2 above), 37, and the entire work by Paul S. Minear, *I Saw a New Earth* . . . (Washington/Cleveland: Corpus Books, 1968).

[15] "A drama that proceeds from act to act": H. Bietenhard, *Das tausendjährige Reich* (Zurich: Zwingli, 1955), 95; "the necessity of the eschatological drama": Lohmeyer, *loc. cit.*, 191, 194; "*drame eschatologique*": A. Feuillet, *loc. cit.*, 100; "*un drame élémentaire*", "*le drame eschatologique*", "*. . . certaines analogies avec la tragédie grecque et les oeuvres théatrales*" (etc.): L. Cerfaux, *L'Apocalypse*, 102, 214, 224. Cf. J. W. Bowman's *The Drama of the Book of Revelation* (1953) and his "The Revelation to John: Its Dramatic Structure and Message" in *Interpretation* 9 (1958); R. R. Brewer "The Influence of Greek Drama upon the Apocalypse" in *Anglic. Theol. Rev. Evanston* 18 (1936), 72–92. L. Cerfaux perceptively notes (*loc. cit.*, 224) that, of necessity, the world of images must be related to the historical world of reality if the former is to be regarded as a genuine drama: heaven is "a sort of permanent stage, part real, part fiction, on which allegorical scenes are enacted representing earthly events and the eschatological drama. Moreover, no neat distinction can be made between revelation (the representation of the drama in heaven, or beginning in heaven) and the accomplishment of God's plans. The stage drama enacts and realizes the true and real drama while at the same time showing us the latter's profound significance."

images, magnified and projected onto an eschatological canvas
—in short, if we accept the Book of Revelation as an integral
part of the New Testament. Then the series of "stills" it gives
us will acquire the movement they ultimately signify; then New
Testament existence, biblical existence, will reveal its paramount
dramatic quality.[16] But—it may be objected—does not the New
Testament, in its full form, also testify to the Lamb's unqualified
triumph? In John, surely, the Lamb is the beginning and end of
all things? And in Paul too, does not the Lamb make all his enemies fall down at his feet? In fact, can we not find all the Book
of Revelation's fundamental assertions in the New Testament?
This is true, of course. Even the prophetic glimpses into the
future are analogous to those of the Book of Revelation, as we
have mentioned. With its cross-sections through salvation history in heaven and earth, the Book of Revelation is only writing
in larger characters things that were previously to be found in a
more scattered form "between the lines". In sum, the dramatic
quality of revelation does not lie in any uncertainty as to the
outcome, for God's victory—which does not automatically include the certainty of salvation on the part of any individual—is
already achieved. What is dramatic in revelation is to be found
in its specific uniqueness: namely, that God is at the same time
superior to history and involved in it. This reaches its high point
in the specifically theological law of proportionate polarization:
the more God intervenes, the more he elicits opposition to him.

2. The Dramatic Motif

No one can see God, either in the Old Covenant (Ex 33:20;
19:21; Is 6:5) or in the New (Jn 1:18; 1 Jn 4:12, 20). He "dwells
in unapproachable light" (1 Tim 6:16); so he who sits upon the

---

[16] Thus, taking it with a grain of salt, we can agree with Valentin Tomberg's
verdict: "Nowhere can we find a key to St. John's Apocalypse, for we cannot
interpret it in such a way as to make a philosophico-metaphysical or a historical
system out of it. The key to the Apocalypse is to practice it, that is, to use it as
a book of spiritual exercises calling forth deeper and deeper layers of consciousness." *Meditationen über die grossen Mysterien des Taro* (Meisenheim: A. Hain-Verlag,
1972), 68.

throne remains beyond description (Rev 4:3; 20:11). Even in the heavenly Jerusalem, where all things will be illuminated by the light of the divine glory (21:23), the ultimate source of this light will not be an object of observation. Yet, though the eternal Father is thus removed from us and untouched by the world's events, this is not the same as the philosophical view that proposes a divine principle of unity unconnected with the world at all. For "the Lamb" who sits on the same throne as God, sharing his dignity (5:6, 13; 7:10, 17; 22:1, 3; 3:21), and who, like God, is the "Alpha and Omega" (1:8, 17) and at his first appearance exhibits specifically divine attributes (1:12f.), has received authority over the world from his Father (2:28). Thus, together with the Lamb, the Father has begun to reign over the world (11:15; 14:7). The assumption made by the Book of Revelation is affirmed by the rest of the New Testament: the Son comes forth from the Father; and the Father, out of his love for the world, has given his Son to be slain, "for thou wast slain and by thy blood didst ransom men for God from every tribe and tongue and people and nation" (5:9). The Lamb is God's mode of involvement in, and commitment to, the world; the Lamb is both "worthy" and "able" not only to symbolize God's involvement but to *be* it.

The Invisible One holds nothing back when he hands over his prerogatives to the Lamb; he reserves nothing to himself. Thus, both equally possess "power and wealth and wisdom and might and honor and glory and blessing" (5:12, 13), and the Lamb has the same authority to hand on gifts (*traditio*) to others: "He who conquers, I will grant him to sit with me on my throne, as I myself conquered and sat down with my Father on his throne." (3:21). Just as the Son is the inviolable manifestation of the Father and of his self-giving—thus he is called "faithful", the "witness" and "true" (1:5; 3:14; 19:11), or quite simply "the Word of God" (19:13)—so he gives power to "bear testimony" (12:17; 19:10) to those who are "called, chosen and faithful" (17:14). This motif of *traditio*, "handing on", beginning in God and extending to the creation through him who is "the beginning of God's creation" (3:14), will prove to be a fundamental theme of the theo-drama, constant through all its acts. *Traditio* begins within God (as the doctrine of the Trinity formulates it), and

this prevents God's self-giving to the world from being interpreted mythologically: God is not swallowed up by the world.
It is not through this self-giving to the world that God becomes
a lover—he already *is* a lover. And this same *traditio*, this same
self-giving within the Godhead, also means that God does not
merely hover above the world as the *hen* of philosophy, as the
noēsis noēseōs: rather, the divine self-giving becomes the prototype and archetype of his self-giving to the world and of all the
traditio that flows from it. Only the God of the New Testament
is proof against the twofold threat of being reduced either to an
undramatic philosoph-ism or to a tragic mythology.

If this is so, we can begin to see how the Lamb's already-
having-triumphed can be reconciled with all the—increasing—
challenges to his triumph within the world. The first *traditio*
from Father to Son is beyond all challenge; and, according to
God's free will as Creator, once the Son, the Alpha and Omega,
is constituted as the "beginning and ground of all creation",
the first *traditio* embraces all the endangered and costly *traditiones*
flowing from it. For then God's freedom can set free a creaturely freedom, including the freedom to say No; then he can
"hand over" (*edothē*) "the key of the shaft of the bottomless
pit" (9:1). This "handing-over" is repeated more than twenty
times in the Book of Revelation: the horsemen are given their
insignia and hence their power; the first beast is given the power
to make war against the saints; the second beast is allowed to
give breath to the image of the first beast; the angels too are
given bowls of wrath and the power to hurt the earth, and so
forth. Then the same word is used again and again when the
saints "give" the glory to God at the end of the whole cycle of
traditiones. One is reminded of the great prayer of Jesus, which
has the same leitmotif of handing-over and handing-on: "Thou
hast given [me] power over all flesh, to give eternal life to all
whom thou hast given [me]. . . . The glory which thou hast
given me I have given to them" (Jn 17:2, 22). In the Book of
Revelation, however, we see the reverse side of the *traditio* to the
Son in the express handing-over of power to the hostile forces;
but this very act shows both that these forces are still dependent
on their origin and that a surrender is called for.

This raises once more the pressing question of how the liturgy of adoration can be connected with the theme of slaughter,[1] in other words, the question of the union of the aesthetic and the dramatic. From the vantage point of heavenly worship, the entire maelstrom of world history, with all its punishments, atrocities and sufferings, is a cause of jubilation: here alone in the New Testament, a resounding "Hallelujah" greets the most terrible ruination there portrayed (Rev 19:1, 3, 4, 6). The seven angels with the bowls of God's wrath, in priestly and royal vesture, "celebrate the sacred liturgy of God's righteousness".[2] There was rejoicing in the Old Covenant at God's vengeance against his servants' enemies (Dt 32:43); but here too, at the end of the Bible, we must hold fast to it, albeit in a new and deeper sense. It is of no relevance here that this feature may have been influenced by ancient Christian liturgies[3] nor that there is explicit reference to Old Testament liturgy (Rev 15:3); the really interesting point is that it was possible, even in the Old Testament tradition, to worship God's majesty amid the confusions and collapses of the world as such. Just as, in our *Aesthetics* (in the portrayal of the Old and New Covenants), we found it impossible to proceed without anticipating the present "dramatic theory", so it is here: we are always anticipating the glorious conclusion; the theme of "glory" will accompany us all the way. The worshipper always has the unity of God's "action" in view: the Lamb is worshipped together with God and as God, and *at the same time* is "as though it had been slain": the two states are continuous from *processio* to *missio*, as we showed in the preceding volume. It is not only the *processio* that is adored but equally the *missio*, in which the Lamb, as the "Logos of God", rides forth "in a robe dipped in blood" to "judge and make war", to "rule with a rod of iron; he will tread the wine press of the fury of the wrath of God the Almighty" (19:11–16). "The Spirit", accordingly (2:7, 11,

---

[1] We have already discussed this in *Theo-Drama* II, 33ff.

[2] Cerfaux, *loc. cit*, 138.

[3] J. Peschek, *Geheime Offenbarung und Tempeldienst* (Paderborn, 1929); B. Brinkmann, "De visione liturgiae in Apocalypsi S. Johannis" in *Verb. Dom.* (1931), 331–42; Thomas Forsyth Torrance, "Liturgie et Apocalypse" in *Verb. Caro* 11 (1957), 28–40 (the whole Book of Revelation is "eschatologized liturgy"; "behind the veil of God's wrath, the prayers of the saints determine everything"). Further discussion in A. Feuillet, 61f., 71f., cf. E. Fiorenza, 339.

17, 29; 3:6, 13, 22), is always he who is distributed ("economically") in his gifts and is perpetually at the Son's behest (1:4; 3:1; 4:5; 5:6; 22:6), but ultimately he is the Spirit gathered into one in the Church (22:17). The Book of Revelation is increasingly insistent, almost importunate, in portraying the simultaneity of liturgy and slaughter.

The wrath of God that continues to pour forth right to the end (in the seven bowls of chapter 16) is introduced by a particularly solemn heavenly liturgy (15:5–8), and the total destruction of Babylon (18:21–24) is greeted in heaven with thunderous jubilation (19:1–8). At the end, there is a stark polarization between the lake of fire, into which devil, Death and Hades disappear, and the new world in which there is neither mourning nor crying nor pain any more, "for the former things have passed away" (21:4). Just as the drama originated in the liturgy (at the handing-over, *traditio*, of the sealed scroll to the Lamb), so now it returns to it.

From God's self-involvement, manifest in the slaying and the subsequent reign of the Lamb, light is shed on the inseparable unity of God's wrath and his love. Even if the beasts' blasphemies cannot injure God's "inner" honor, they do affect his "exterior" honor, which he has invested in his world, and so they provoke his anger. No doctrine of atonement may ignore this reality, which is attested a thousand times in Scripture; the Book of Revelation, which concludes the Old and the New Scriptures, once more sets this motif prominently at the center. Wrath is the sign of God's involvement; to that extent, he does "suffer" at the world's hands, as we see from the Lamb who was delivered up (*traditus*) to be slain. God's wrath and the Son's Cross are two sides of a single reality; thus we can understand how the Son "treads the wine press of the fury of the wrath of God the Almighty" (19:15)—and does so "alone", as Isaiah says (63:3). The suffering by which God's wrath accomplishes his work is a divine suffering; vengeance and reconciliation are two sides of the same thing: "For the day of vengeance was in my heart, and my year of redemption has come" (Is 63:4). Thus heaven's sacred fire, when thrown down on the earth, can change into a fire that destroys (Rev 8:5). And it follows that the divine fire spares nothing in the world: in the Book of Revelation, there are really only two categories of people: the "witnesses" who are bound to the slain Lamb (and those who are sealed with God's sign [7:3] and who follow the Lamb everywhere and have been redeemed by the Lamb [14:4]) and those who have submitted to the beasts and are branded with their mark (13:16). As for the first, they too "come out of the great tribulation" (7:14) and have been saved "as through fire" (1 Cor 3:15), and we have no reason to suppose that the two categories are not afflicted and scorched by the same divine fire, for "our God is a consuming fire" (Dt 4:24; Is 33:14; Heb 12:29). The world is full of suffering, burning in God's fire; but there are those who suffer of their own free will, and there are those who suffer unwillingly. God does not adapt himself to the world: the world has to learn how to live in God's element, how to "walk" in the "light" of his "glory" (Rev 21:23f.). The sea of crystal on which the victors stand is "mingled with fire" (15:2), and the Lord's eyes are piercing "like a flame of fire" (1:14; 2:18).

However, this parallelism between the martyrs and the beasts' followers does not say everything there is to be said. We must continually remind ourselves that the increasingly terrible things that are unleashed once the seal of the book of world history has been broken *have already been preceded* by the victory of the Lamb; it is this victory that renders him "worthy" to break the seals (5:5). All the instances of judgment that now become necessary are the result of this victory. Why? Because even the No that echoes through the world is a result of God's Yes. To this apocalyptic rhythm we shall now turn.

3. The Dramatic Rhythm

We have already spoken of this rhythm; it is what constitutes the specifically dramatic element in the theo-drama and is inseparable from the motif. If God, who is "ever-greater", is involved in the drama, we must be prepared, right from the outset, for a continual raising of the stakes. At the same time, it is only through the course of the action that we learn that the greater his involvement is, the greater the resistance it provokes. In the classical Old Covenant, there is no mention of a hell or a devil: the reason for this is that God's heaven is not yet open to man (Heb 11:40). It is only when he who bears the Spirit "not by measure" (Jn 3:34) steps forth that he is confronted with the anti-Spirit, fighting for his power-realm. Only now is it possible for there to be an unforgivable sin against the Holy Spirit (Mt 12:28–32). In spite of Israel's many failures, which led ultimately to its exile, Jesus can say, "If I had not come and spoken to them, they would not have sin; but now they have no excuse for their sin" (Jn 15:22). It is only when Christ is there that antichrists can appear (1 Jn 2:18, 22; 4:3; 2 Jn 7), that the "son of perdition", the "man of lawlessness" (2 Th 2:3, 8) can emerge. It is only when the Woman has given birth in heaven that Satan falls to the earth and his two associates come forth from the depths (Rev 12f.). What was known as the "abomination of desolation" (in the Temple of the holy nation) in Daniel 9:27 will assume worldwide proportions, according to the Book of Revelation. What is at stake is the claim to be equal to God (2 Th 2:4), the blasphemy that is spewed from every mouth (Rev 13:6; 16:9, 11–12). The hostile powers will use stupendous miracles (Rev 13:13ff.) to make people believe that the kingdom of God—which is beyond human definition—can be defined and experienced (Lk 21:8). It is only when God's triune nature has been revealed in the Incarnation of God's Son and the outpouring of the Holy Spirit that it can be countered by a demonic trinity, namely, the primal devil, a pseudo-incarnation and a pseudo-spirit. Similarly, only when the anguished Woman has given birth in heaven can the Great Harlot who seduces the whole world manifest herself.[1] Now that the "Lion of Judah" has triumphed, not only are his followers persecuted; the forces ranged against him have the power to vanquish them (Rev 11:7; 13:7): "they . . . surrounded the camp of the saints and the beloved city" (20:9).

It is no objection against this ever-intensifying rhythm to say that, after all, the Lamb has triumphed right from the start and that his victory will necessarily win through in the final critical moment. It is true that the oppression, persecution and killing of the Lamb's followers actually signify that they have won (in

[1] On the "counterimages" in the Book of Revelation, cf. Günther Bornkamm, "Die Komposition der apokalyptischen Visionen in der Offenbarung Johannis" in *Studien zu Antike und Urchristentum* (1959), 204–22.

martyrdom); they are covictors (cf. 12:11)[2] and hence are pre-destined to reign with the Lamb (1:6; 3:21; 5:10; 22:5); but this, too, is no argument against the "rhythm" of which we are speaking. For it must be said, again, that while heaven's punishments are intended to produce repentance and conversion, they actually have no such effect (with the one exception of 11:13) but rather provoke an even greater hardening of heart among the forces ranged against God (9:20f.; 14:7; 16:9, 11), an even greater blasphemy (16:21). The Old Testament was familiar with the phenomenon of hardening of the heart (Dan 12:10); here it is put forward as a law: "Let the evildoer still do evil, and the filthy still be filthy, and the righteous still do right, and the holy still be holy" (Rev 22:11). Ultimately both poles reach the final extreme: on the one hand, there is the lake of fire, which also consumes all those who are not inscribed in the book of life, burning "for ever and ever" (20:10, 15), and, on the other hand, there is the heavenly Jerusalem, whose inhabitants "shall reign for ever and ever" (22:5).

This last antithesis, it must be said, is the result of the opening of the sealed scroll of world history by the Lamb, who has already triumphed. What this victory sets in motion tends, apparently, to undermine its very success. At all events, the substance—the motif and the rhythm—of the theo-drama transcends all imaginable, intramundane action. The paradoxical result—the apparent contradiction—is that he who encompasses all things, the Alpha and Omega, seems ultimately to be encircled by the final act: this will have to form the central object of faith's pondering on this drama. There must be no question of dismissing straightforward solutions out of hand. All the same, we would do well to note this: it is as the *slain* Lamb that he won his victory; it follows that his disciples' struggle cannot be an armed one, except their armor be the full panoply of faith (1 Th 5:8; Eph 6:14f.), and especially the "endurance and faith of the saints" (Rev 13:10).

---

[2] There are frequent references to victory through battle: Rev 2:7; 2:11; 2:17; 2:26; 3:5; 3:12; 3:21; 5:5; 6:2; 11:7; 12:11; 13:7; 15:2; 17:14; 21:7.

C. THE CONFRONTATION

1. Fire

The Apocalypse, convulsed with lightning, blazing with confla-
grations, provides us only with final, perpendicular excerpts of
the last stages of dramatic action between heaven and earth, God
and his creation. There is no other way of portraying this last act.
This drama, in which God's absoluteness (understood as power
or as love) touches the sphere of the fragile creature, can only be
a fiery event, a history of fire, made up either of devouring or of
healing flames; and everyone who looks back from the vantage
point of the Apocalypse, having heard the account of the entire
action, is bound to sense this, in some fashion at least. Initially,
in the Old Covenant, it is true that this history allows itself to be
written as if it were a piece of secular chronicling; but even here,
the closer the nation's relationship with God becomes, the more
implacably the fire spreads to everything around it. "Our God
is a consuming fire" (Dt 4:24; Heb 12:29): this is clear even as
early as the strange events that surround the covenant with Abraham (Gen 15:7–12, 17–18); then, after Moses' encounter with
the burning bush, the sign of God's holy presence (Ex 3), it is
made plain to all in the concluding of the Sinai covenant, where
the divine Partner makes himself present with peals of thunder,
lightning, thick cloud, smoke and earthquake (Ex 19:16ff.) and
speaks "without form" from the heart of the fire (Dt 4:12, 15,
36). He does so in a voice the people cannot endure: only Moses
can bear it, showing that "God can speak with man and man can
still live" (5:24). Then, however, the invisible word from the
fire must be objectified on the first (5:22) and second (10:1f.)
tables of stone, and not until Elijah is there a realization that
the rock-splitting storm, the earthquake and the fire are only
symbolic forerunners of the "gentle breeze" with which God
touches man at a deeper level (1 Kgs 19:11ff.). Even though the
prophet may be able to call down fire from heaven (2 Kgs 1;
1 Kgs 18:38), and he himself be transported to the divine sphere
of fire (2 Kgs 2:11), henceforth it is the prophet's *word* that will
"burn like fire"—since his mouth has been purified by God's

fire (Is 6:6; Jer 20:9)—and be "a hammer that breaks the rock in pieces" (Jer 23:29), whereas the disobedient people become "wood, and the fire shall devour them" (Jer 5:14). The great Exile and the razing of the Temple are Old Testament eschatology: the devouring inferno is thrown down from above, from the flaming glory of God (Ezek 10:2). One can question whether what happens between the return from the Exile and the manifestation of Jesus can still be regarded as a genuine history of God with his people; the situation is best illuminated by the prayer of the men cast into the fire (Dan 3:24f.): the "remnant of Israel" prays to God from the midst of the pagan gehenna. Not until John the Baptist with his renewed preaching of "fire" are the themes of the great prophets taken up again and brought to their culmination.

There is no chronicling in the New Covenant. Everything is summed up in a single, final Word from God (Heb 1:2). All the same, this Word unfolds dramatically in Jesus' development, work, suffering and Resurrection. It is the acme and the timeless conclusion of dealings between God and man; all subsequent events in the dimension of time, subject to this end-Word and within the embrace of the end-time, can only be "theology of history", that is, a demonstration and exposition of the truth of this Word. Now this fire is dramatic in a heightened sense: God no longer deals with man from without but—by becoming man—from within man and at man's innermost level; Jesus is the man who burns with God's fire. The apocryphal "Whoever comes near me, comes near the fire" is right; "I came to cast fire upon the earth; and would that it were already kindled!" (Lk 12:49). He comes to baptize, no longer with water, but with the Holy Spirit and with fire (Mt 3:11; Lk 3:16); and, when his work is completed, he will send the Spirit upon the Church in the form of fire (Acts 2:3; note the related apocalyptic quotation in 2:19). The mediation of the tables of stone is jettisoned: he himself is the Law and proclaims it in God's name (Mt 5–7); keeping it means personally following him. The stone tables vanish utterly: Jesus, "consumed with zeal for thy house" (Jn 2:17), allows himself to be consumed by the divine fire that burns within him, ultimately becoming flesh and blood that can be consumed by his followers (1 Cor 10:16f.; Jn 6:51–58). This is the stupendous goal of God's dealing with man: man is not consumed by and absorbed into a God who remains sole and alone but is finally given the freedom to perform his true role; he is given an exemplary identity and a mission: "Did not our hearts burn within us while he talked to us on the road, while he opened to us the Scriptures?" (Lk 24:32).

When the divine Word and Spirit enter a man, he is faced with the dramatic challenge to make an appropriate response: "Love one another, as I have loved you", with that unsurpassable love of him "who gives his life for his friends" (Jn 15:12f.). "By this we know love, that he laid down his life for us; and we ought to lay down our lives for the brethren" (1 Jn 3:16). We are only able to perform this deed of our own volition if Jesus is in us and we abide in him: "Apart from me you can do nothing." Thus the fire started by Jesus catches elsewhere, carrying out its other function: he who does not abide in him is cut off, withers and "is thrown into the fire and burned" (Jn 15:6; cf. Mt 7:19; 13:30). No one is spared the fire ("every one will be salted with fire": Mk 9:49); all must face the fire (2 Pet 3:7, 10); on the day when the Son of Man comes to judge, it will not be any different from "the day when Lot went out from Sodom, [when] fire and brimstone rained from heaven" (Lk 17:29). All must go through the testing fire (1 Pet 1:7); then it will be seen whether they and their works survive or, if their works are burned up, they themselves escape "but only as through fire" (1 Cor 3:15), or whether they remain held in the "eternal fire" (Mt 18:8; 25:41; Mk 9:43, and so forth).

We have placed the theme of "fire" at the beginning in this way, like an exclamation mark, in order to set the dramatic atmosphere of biblical revelation and in order to recapitulate everything we have said, by way of introduction, in the three previous volumes. Let us recall the most important elements here. In the world shaped by mythology, there used to be a kind of confused theodramatic dimension; today, however, after having undergone the process of philosophical reflection, it exists only in Christianity (*Theo-Drama* I, 119, 112f.), not even in Islam (*Theo-Drama* II, 43f.), and only in Judaism insofar as it forms a dialectical unity with Christianity (*Theo-Drama* III, 371ff.). But, even in Christianity, it is important that the truth of revelation should not be watered down in a "lyrical" direction— "spirituality"—or dissolved in an "epic" direction—"theology" —(*Theo-Drama* II, 55), as is shown by the tendencies toward the dramatic in modern theological thought, tendencies we twice examined (*Theo-Drama* I, 25–50; *Theo-Drama* II, 62–77). No ("epic") horizon can embrace the totality of free actors in all their mutual confrontations; yet their encounters do not create a multiplicity of independent dramas but are yoked together in a single, total drama that encompasses all the individual interactions (*Theo-Drama* II, 77–89). This is because all encounters between man and God are included in the drama of Christ (*Theo-Drama* III, 33–40). The latter not only supplies the play's content but actually opens up the acting area in the first place (*Theo-Drama* III, 41–56). So it is that the Book of Revelation, with its many distinct episodes, can rightly be called the "Book of the Lamb". As far as the *dramatis personae* are concerned, our lengthy discussion "From Role to Mission" (*Theo-Drama* I, 481–643) led to the realization that man can and must find his identity in his mission. This mission is constitutive of the person, within the mission of Christ (*Theo-Drama* III, 230–59). Christ's mission in turn demonstrates his divine personal being within the divine Trinity (which opens itself up in him and offers itself to man). Even from a philosophical point of view, man's personal mission identifies him simultaneously in his unique personality and his a priori social nature, since he continues to owe his self-being to a human "thou", while owing both himself *and* the "thou" to a divine origin. The man who is receptive to revelation will recognize a manifestation of the divine Trinity in this unity of self-being and being-with (*Theo-Drama* II, 196ff., 205ff., 238ff.). Insofar, however, as God's self-giving in Christ is the purpose of creation, and is thus fundamental to it (*Theo-Drama* III, 250–59; 33–40), when God allows finite freedom to *be*, it follows that full scope is also granted to infinite freedom as the sphere of fulfillment of created freedom. Here the creature, far from experiencing any self-alienation, attains that form of life that is most its own (*Theo-Drama* II, 302ff.) within divine (personal and ontic) grace (*Theo-Drama* II, 312ff.). In its infinity, God's open sphere can accommodate and respond to all the play's eventualities; thus there is no need for God to change as he accompanies the course of the action, even though he gives himself in a new and original way to each actor in each new situation (*Theo-Drama* II, 271–84). God's tri-unity so transcends the play that it is always making itself present in it (*Theo-Drama* III, 505–35).

In all these preliminaries, the actual drama was excluded; we showed nothing more than the acting area (between heaven and earth: *Theo-Drama* II, 173–88) and, more concretely, Christ's inauguration of it (*Theo-Drama* III, 41ff.), the possible relationships of the characters and the possibility that the creature might go astray (*Theo-Drama* II, 37ff.). Furthermore, since there is only one drama, we suggested that the drama of Christ bursts all the dimensions of the purely worldly stage (both tragedy and comedy: *Theo-Drama* II, 83). Hence there must be a struggle: God's struggle for the world and the world's struggle for God (*Theo-Drama* II, 33–36). We indicated certain preliminary sketches of the dramatic struggle (*Theo-Drama* II, 151–69) but kept the central accents of the real play—that is, sin and redemption—for later consideration. The struggle between finite and infinite freedom becomes dramatic only when the creature's opposition to God emerges and goes to the limit; only then do we understand the chasms and tempests of the Apocalypse; only then does the biblical revelation in its entirety become a blazing fire. It is true, of course, that the encounter of the creature with the majesty and glory of God is itself a baffling miracle, to be approached only in adoration and thanksgiving: flashes are continually leaping forth from God's throne of fire, as Ezekiel (1:4) and John (Rev 4:5) saw; this is not the kind of light to which one can become accustomed, but one which illuminates by an ever-new blinding. Revelation can never pass over into "enlightenment". But the depths of this abyss of light are only revealed when the light shines in the darkness that cannot overcome it (Jn 1:5), when the blind see and those who see are made blind (Jn 9:39).

2. The Race

There is another issue to be faced at the beginning of this endeavor, namely, why it is necessary to construct a theological dramatic theory now, if it was not necessary before. If this drama involving God and man has already reached its culmination in Jesus Christ, why has it not been experienced earlier in all the severity of a battle for life and death? Nietzsche is surely right when he says that it is only now that "God is dead"; but it is not Nietzsche but Bloch who is right to say that Jesus Christ has killed him. For, with his "I am" sayings, Jesus has taken religion's "God", who was to be found everywhere in a diffused form—the kind of God whom now, in the post-Christian age, modern transcendental theology would like to reinstate—and relentlessly centered this God on himself: "I am the truth, . . . he who is not with me is against me"; "I am the door; anyone who enters not by the door is a thief and a robber." It took a long time for the diffuse background finally to fade away, leaving behind the great void as an alternative to Jesus. Nietzsche calls it "Dionysos" or "the eternal recurrence", signifying that finite human freedom, with its superhuman aspirations, has been treated as absolute.

The borrowed substance of antiquity lasted a long time, bolstering up man's shrinking "natural piety" behind the figure of Christ or instead of him. These borrowings were entirely natural in the Fathers and in Scholasticism, but eventually—from the Renaissance to the Enlightenment, to Goethe, Hölderlin, Heidegger—they became more and more problematical,[1] particularly since they were increasingly replaced by a metaphysics of spirit and freedom that moved from theism to pantheism to atheism.[2] The vast, all-reconciling, divine horizon, inherited from the Stoics and Neoplatonists and overarching everything—Jewish, Islamic, and Christian thought, right up to Nicolas of Cusa's dialogue between the religions, with its heavenly and ecumenical vision[3]—is rolled up and set to one side. As long as it was

---

[1] Cf. *The Glory of the Lord* V, the chapter "Classical Mediation": 247–450.
[2] *Ibid.*, 451–610.
[3] *Ibid.*, 205–46.

there in the background of consciousness, the biblical world of the Old and New Covenant was almost like an episode, clarifying and symbolizing the deep embrace of infinite and finite freedom. In the same way, as we have already observed, today's transcendental theologians would like to interpret Christ as the "highest, unsurpassable instance" of a self-disclosure to man on God's part that is coterminous with creation as such. However, this attempt comes too late: the stage's background has already been cleared.

In saying this, we are not denying the possibility of a "natural knowledge of God", as defined by the First Vatican Council, nor are we replacing it with the early Barth's interpretation of religion as *hybris*; we are simply saying that, as a result of Jesus Christ's absolute claim, the vague, universally tangible "divinity", "*rerum omnium principium et finem*" (DS 3004), has become profoundly latent; nor has it stopped seeking ever-deeper levels of concealment. Wherever modern technological civilization penetrates areas that are still religious, it also infuses a post-Christian, secular, atheistic consciousness as well. This comes not only through the human beings who make the machines but through the machines themselves; these new fetishes cast a previously unknown spell precisely because they are manipulable. This step into secularity is irreversible; not even the greatest atomic catastrophes would bring people back to the former religious naïveté.

No doubt we shall never know to what degree man's emancipation comes from the biblically fashioned consciousness that he has been redeemed [*er-löst*, "released"] and endowed with personality, and how much is due to the embryonic superiority to nature and the embryonic technology already found in ancient civilizations. The combination of these currents of thought formed a swiftly flowing river, gaining even more impetus through the theory of evolution that put man at the very apex of the world, and in so doing it ushered in an age of anthropocentrism that manifests a prophetic thrust. Whereas yesterday man was nature's child, living and dying in her ample bosom, today he is her master, fashioning her according to his own image: the ideal of "positive humanism". It is superfluous to posit a third party behind this twofold relationship, even if there were such; man is preoccupied with himself and with the world, especially since he can see the evil consequences of his action visibly approaching and has his hands full in trying to avert them.

All this is taking place after God has apparently uttered his last word and made his final move on the chessboard, that is, in the life of Jesus Christ. But was this move intelligible? For, through his Cross and Resurrection, he stepped over the edge of the earthly stage and out into an unimaginable "beyond". And even if, on the other shore, he has won (and who can tell?), is it not true that here, ultimately, he has lost? (After all, we are not expecting a "third kingdom" of the Spirit to follow the age of Christ.) Or is it possible to save the collapsing edifice by incorporating it into the new building? Whereas transcendental theology still thinks in terms of a fundamental religious instinct in man that may already be defunct, liberation theology builds the gospel (in which Cross and Resurrection have become superfluous) into the temple of humanity it is trying to erect. And a soteriology backed up by exegesis shifts the accents in the picture of Jesus to his "solidarity" with the oppressed and marginalized, to such an extent that today the Cross—to which, in former times, the sins of the world were nailed—is nothing more than the logical expression of this solidarity.

True, the mysterious figure of the Nazarene continues to exercise its fascination. But, for the most part, access to this figure is sought outside the official Christianity of the Church, which fails to reflect his features clearly enough and, historically, has compromised him too gravely. However, the modes of access to him that claim to be "immediate", the attempts to be with him "here and now", will continually prove fruitless; all knowledge of Jesus—as the exegetes show us so graphically—always was, and always will be, mediated in and through the Church. Both paths seem blocked: the path through the Church and that which bypasses the Church. Perhaps, after all, the old God's last Messenger has lost the game, and world history proceeds on its way without paying any heed.

Yet, earlier, we saw that the principle of earthly humanity— what Paul calls the "Adam principle"—is always undergirded by the "Christ principle"; for Christ is the world's Alpha even before the "first Adam" (cf. Theo-Drama III, 34). It is therefore a part of Christian faith that this Alpha must also be the Omega, whatever dramatic vicissitudes may intervene. Whatever spectacular, anti-Christian movements world history may produce, it is and remains a fact that the Christ principle is superior to the world: "The second man is from heaven . . . and became a life-giving spirit" (1 Cor 15:47, 45). What is said about the first Adam may be pure speculation, refuted by history. It is an open question whether the fundamental vision of the two principles can be substantiated, whether there are kinds of experiences that speak in favor of Christian faith. Augustine saw his two *civitates*, the divine and the worldly, wrestling together so tightly that it was not always possible to tell which limb belonged to which wrestler; similarly, in our account of theo-drama, we must now describe the apparently mutual embrace of the Adam principle and the Christ principle as they march through history.

There have always been portrayals of various aspects of this struggle. Above (*Theo-Drama* II, 151–69) we have already discussed some of these, expressed in the form of drama. No doubt those authors are right who put the main accent on soteriology, that is, the attempt to understand what happened on Christ's Cross, at a historical hour that yet remains suprahistorical and ever-"now". This will be at the center of our presentation too; but we shall also consider the whole movement of world history that has been set in train by the Cross.

There will be three parts. In the first, Adam, man, unfolds his action, both as an individual and as community. In the second, God acts; first, he prepares the way for Jesus Christ, then he acts in him, and then—most of all—he acts in him on the Cross and in his Resurrection. In the third, God and man encounter one another in history, in what the Book of Revelation has described as the Battle of the Logos.

II. THE PATHOS OF THE WORLD STAGE

A. HORIZONTAL WORLD HISTORY

In what follows we shall take up a single fundamental insight arising from our reflections on the Book of Revelation, namely, that the essential history is that which is enacted in the vertical plane between heaven and earth. For the moment we can leave aside the fact that, largely, this drama excludes considerations of redeeming grace as it concentrates on giving an account of heaven's anger with the world and the world's blasphemy against heaven. This narrowing of the field of vision is bound up with mysterious divine purposes: the New Testament prophet was to be shown only the eschatological crisis toward which history was running, once it had been set in motion by the Lamb's breaking of the seal. All the same, the action taking place between heaven and earth is not one-sided—for example, the mere pouring-out of bowls of wrath from above—for where does the Lamb's supratemporal wound come from, if not from his destiny on earth? And why should his witnesses shed their blood on earth, if not for the sake of heaven? Thus the formal aspect of the vertical, historical relationship always has a material side—though it is not developed as a specific topic.

However, prophetic revelation is necessary if such vertical history is to be unveiled; this is not something earthly man can do. He experiences history anthropocentrically, as something that runs in transitory time, horizontally. In this horizontal time dimension, man's "life in history" must appear as a huge sphinx, "surging back and forth in a thousand complex forms, both free and unfree, in every possible disguise; speaking sometimes through the masses and at other times through individuals; now optimistic, now pessimistic; founding states, religions, civilizations, and then destroying them. At times it is an obscure riddle to itself, led more by dark feelings that arise from the imagination than by reflection; at times it is accompanied by a wealth of reflection; then, again, it is visited by specific intimations of a fulfillment that is to come much later. . . ."[1] Are there any indications that this surging, oscillating reality, rearing itself

[1] J. Burckhardt, *Weltgeschichtliche Betrachtungen* (Kröner, 1969), 9.

up like a tower and then crashing down in pieces, exhibits a law? For some law or principle is essential if we are to grant it a dramatic character. Everything that is produced and enacted on the world's stage by individuals or nations presupposes meaning; it seeks for meaning and posits it. But does the all-encompassing reality that is manifested in all particular action provide a meaning of its own? Or is it not the case, rather, that fragments of meaning flash and sparkle everywhere in the life of the individual and of the community but that these fragments are limited and hence relative, creating contradictory antinomies? Is it not the case that we find a relatively justified thesis being supplanted by an equally relative and justified antithesis, without a satisfying synthesis ever being reached?

Here too, however, in discussing anthropocentric action and its corresponding understanding of history, we must immediately introduce a distinction that we have already considered in some detail (*Theo-Drama* II, 335–426). "Natural" (pre-Christian) man never dreamed of pursuing and understanding horizontal history in the absence of a vertical axis ascending from himself. It did not matter whether he was an animist or a polytheist or a (religious) atheist: the initiative, the irruption of the vertical, with its powers, inspirations and capacity to give meaning, largely predominated over horizontal attempts to find meaning. As a result, these actions and irruptions on the part of the "vertical" always managed to yield a certain totality (even if it was a tragic totality, as in Greek theatre), an attempt to decipher the purely horizontal plot in the categories of drama. In such realms of life as these, even the world view of the "eternal recurrence of all things" could somehow be endured, since the perpendicular epiphany of a total meaning—that which truly brings fulfillment, or at least seems to—could take place time and again.

It is different where the vertical axis (insofar as it is revelation *from* above) is claimed by Christianity as its own, and mankind largely refuses to submit to the claim. Then, ultimately, man's openness *to* the upper realm becomes a purely anthropological fact that belongs henceforth to the immanence of horizontal world history. When this happens, in short, man's "upward" openness, which is the organ of ultimate meaning, is obliged to look for meaning at the horizontal level; hence people's tendency to attribute absolute significance to relative fragments of meaning in history and to commit themselves utterly to such constructions. Thus, in the post-Christian period, we find the development of various philosophies of history—"ideologies" in the strict sense. In this way, certain finite (and hence only partially true) ideas are foisted onto man's spirit, which has an inherent yearning for the absolute; this results in what has been called the "ideological superstructure".

Since man can neither throw off his vertical relationship to the absolute nor entrap the absolute within his own finitude by his own (magical) efforts, he becomes, right from the start, a figure of pathos on the world stage. To the best of his ability, he will attempt to make present, in finite terms, his orientation to the absolute that transcends him; thus arise the temples and kingdoms that are symbols of the absolute. In the post-Christian era, the finite realities that have been thus divinized can be secularized but not the yearning that created them in the first place. For this yearning for the absolute is at the very heart of man; it is the source of his search for meaning as such, including the meaning that he tries to discern in horizontal history. However, none of the passing moments of the world of time can encapsulate that desired absolute meaning—not even that moment, projected into an ever-receding future, when "positive humanism" will have been attained; on the other hand, man rejects that revelation and *incarnation* of absolute meaning that is manifested in terms of finite history. As a result, the pathos of the world stage becomes grotesque, grimacing and demonic. Here, once more, we approach the substance of the imagery of the Book of Revelation.

Let us try to put this in other and more precise words. Instead of starting out from the formal dimensions of the vertical and the horizontal, let us look at the form of the living man who, even though he may have Oedipus' ability to solve the riddle of the Sphinx, finds there nothing but himself—a living Sphinx. He cannot cease puzzling over himself, for he knows what meaning is (even if he can no longer find it) and because meaning lays claim to a certain absoluteness. Yet, in the face of time and death, he can never show this absolute claim to have been fulfilled. This is the pathetic dimension that informs everything that happens on the world stage. We can allow it to have its effect upon us (like the spectators at a Greek tragedy); we can be transported out of our everyday ordinariness into "fear and lamentation" in the face of existence's baffling depths; but this is not enough, as we can see from the fact that the spectators of that time felt they needed a comedy (mostly a grotesque one) to compensate them for the moving effect the tragedy had upon them. Moreover, in the philosophy that replaced the age of high drama, we see a certain inappropriate attitude that preferred to dwell on the pathetic element of tragedy: this pathos is enveloped by an overall view of being in which the pathetic words and cries of lofty heroes, at length brought to their knees, are soothed by an overall vision that is oblivious of history: thus Plato banishes the tragic poets from his social order. People can only cry and scream in a cave haunted by unreal shadows; Socrates did not cry either before or after drinking the cup of hemlock. When a man has turned to look into the light of true wisdom, the spectacle of world history with its blood and tears shrinks to the level of a puppet play. This is the case whether he more or less sets it aside as he ascends to the One (to the *amor intellectualis*, to identity) or tries to include it in a speculative Good Friday that is put forth as a systematic principle or makes it part of a *praxis* oriented to the vanishing point of a positive humanism.

On the one hand, this philosophy wants to do justice to the claim to absoluteness that lies in the pathetic events of the world stage; yet at the same time, on the other hand, it destroys the pathos of the individual fact, since it has no time to take account of it. No philosophy can ever do justice to the groans of a man hidden away in some ancient, medieval or present-day torture chamber. The best philosophy can do, as a human enterprise, is to arrive at the horizon of an abstract absolute *in the presence of which* (whether it is conceived as transcendent or immanent) the historical is enacted. Indeed, it is a secondary matter whether this absolute is thought of in more positive terms, as the *theion* that overarches everything, or in more negative terms, as the "nothing of all that is" (nirvana). Thus philosophy has a twofold role: it imparts a background to the pathos of the finite figures, a background that is implicit in them; and, at the same time, against this very background, it removes this pathos from the historical figures. In doing so, fundamentally, philosophy raises the pathos of historical world being to its second level of potency; just as the dramatic dimension of finitude is reduced in potency by the same instance that confirms and elevates it.

In what follows we must not anticipate the Christian solution of this baneful dilemma; nor must it be rendered—as it were—diffusely omnipresent (by a "transcendental" generalizing tendency and by talking in terms of a "supernatural *existentiale*"), which prevents the dilemma from reaching its full dramatic proportions at all. Rather, our aim must be to show that man's historical situation in this world is in a state of permanent tension: he is constantly on the lookout for a solution, a redemption [*Erlösung*], but can never anticipate or construct it from his own resources; nor does he have even an intimation of it. In retrospect, of course, it is not difficult to create a pseudo-harmony by putting forward Christian philosophies of history that contain the a prioris that emerge from Christian theology, by insinuating articles of Christian revelation into the philosophical *Weltanschauung* (which even the simplest actor in the human tragedy somehow possesses). Such attempts, however, play down the ultimately hopeless situation of finite existence in the face of a transcendence that does not automatically disclose itself, or, put more concretely, in the face of the as yet hidden world plan whereby God becomes man (which implies that God "becomes pathos") and shows himself, through this Incarnation, to be the *triune* God.

We can and must say that the world, as it is in the concrete, in its fallen state, has been conceived and created by God with a view to its redemption by him. But we cannot and must not say that this redemption, which is performed by God in utter freedom, is something of which man has "always been aware", even if only through his own transcendence. True, he can stare spellbound at the point at which the finite, in its decline and demise, must—surely, he thinks—be joined and wedded to the infinite that comes to save it; but, in positing this point where the relative and the absolute conjoin, he is bound to go farther and farther astray, particularly if he is presumptuous enough to try to guess where this point might be or even aim for it. We

shall see clearly why this is so only if we also take human freedom into account—in its autonomy but also in its subjection
to sin. A theodramatic theory must relentlessly insist that, first
of all, the pathos arising from the real world, a pathos full of
obscurity and weakness, should be put fully before us before we
go on to speak of God's free response (*theo-logia* understood as
Theos legōn). If we fail to allow the world time and space to
reveal itself as it is and keep interposing the divine response as
something that was "always there", we risk depriving the world/
God relationship of all dramatic tension. God's merciful *turning
toward* a lost world, in Jesus Christ and, earlier, in the election of
Israel—this fundamentally dramatic act of God in his freedom
—becomes the undramatic, permanent, essential constitution of
a God who, as in Plato and Plotinus, and later in Spinoza and
the Enlightenment, is (and always has been) the eternally radiant
"Sun of Goodness". Accordingly, the picture of man is primarily
determined, not by his frail finitude in which, nonetheless, he
must accomplish things of ultimate value, but by a resignation
with which he commends himself to the unfathomable mystery
of his being (and of all being); this is an attitude to death that
overflows into all his finite acts; it is a Stoicism with Christian
trimmings.

More and more clearly, in the following account, we shall see
that the point at which the "solution"—"redemption"—appears
is not something that can be deduced; it cannot be known. By
way of anticipation, we can say that, in a certain sense, the whole
of world history is present in every individual human life; in each
case, this history begins at the beginning and runs to its end in
death. Yet each individual life is also a minute part of the life
manifested in the whole of history. Who can attempt to do justice to both these aspects at the same time? Not even the belief in a periodic avatar of the divine in an individual human
existence can do this. Moreover, life is inconceivable without
death, which yet appears to be the sudden breaking-off of existence, not its fulfillment; how then can death be included in
the "solution" without forfeiting the very thing it is designed to
achieve, namely, the dissolution of the fundamental limitations
of personal and social existence?

More concretely, let us examine the wounds that existence bears. They are not simply isolated ulcerations; they are connected. And the puzzling thing is that they are not simply negatives either: they are damaged positives, positives that have lost their apexes of meaning. First, there is the dimension of time. At the human level, time corresponds to an end, to death: time, even continuing time, is a gift that is always new, yet bafflingly—"not of its own will" (Rom 8:20)—it is subject to transience and futility. We cannot even imagine time without these aspects. Correspondingly, death is seen as something positive, as a being's ability to come to an end when its *telos* has been reached; but it is negative also, in that this end is always hanging above it like the sword of Damocles. Then there is the entire complex of aspects associated with freedom. Freedom is man's openness to the good as such; it is the power of self-determination, the highest and noblest form of power. But how easily does this freedom become smothered by what the world of nature understands by "power"—the ability to overpower others. Freedom can get lost; it can fail to embrace the good; it can become embroiled in evil in all its countless forms. This evil is a commanding reality in the sphere of human history, permeating the entire life of society and the individual; moreover, it commends itself by assuming the appearance and attractiveness of some good, that is, it is the lie, the disguise. This being so, how is the individual, and history as a whole, to unmask and transform it? Would this not call for a vantage point outside history? And surely no man can take up such a vantage point without surrendering his very existence? (Unless, like Münchhausen, he can extricate himself by climbing up his own pigtail.)

These aspects, that is, death, freedom, power and evil, sharpen the problem of existence to the point of rendering it unbearable. Thus all human life becomes an uninterrupted, chaotic searching and feeling after a totality of meaning. Some are consciously aware that there must be a hidden totality of meaning somewhere; others are unconscious of it. But all must be convinced of it, whether consciously or not, if they are to search for it at all. And yet this totality continues to elude them the more they search for it; it only presents them with fragments of meaning that do not fit together. They cannot be fitted together because

God, in his freedom, has reserved to himself the gift of the synthesis; he will present it to mankind and, in so doing, reveal both who he, God, is and who the authentic man is, the man who exists in the totality of his self.

Even if mankind's intimations and postulates were to converge toward this synthesis, their very claim to have attained it by their own efforts would necessarily cause them to miss it. And yet how hard, how almost impossible it is for man to renounce such a claim! Even if he admits that the individual aspects remain fragmentary, he will try to relate them in a dialectic, with the aim, ultimately, of uniting them in a single whole. Or, taking a single fragment of meaning, he will highlight it—giving it tragic or pathetic status—against the backdrop of the surmised absolute horizon of meaning, claiming that the total meaning can be discerned in and through this (transparent) fragment.

Such false conclusions are inevitable as long as the God-given solution remains hidden. However, this is not only because finitude still claims, ultimately, to possess an absolute meaning but also—and these two things are connected—because freedom, having fallen into sin, gets deeper and deeper into a maze that has no way out. Recognizing that these two aspects cannot be disentangled, we find that the second, tainted with sin as it is, has an effect on the *manner* in which finitude lays its claim to meaning. If we realize this, we shall be even less inclined to accept (on the basis of the belief that this "solution" [*Lösung*] is universally, diffusely, transcendentally present in man) the assumption that the "solutions" [*Lösungen*] proposed by man and projected into the totality are to be read as valid ciphers of redemption [*Er-lösung*]. In the end, such a view proves to be inadequate and false in the face of the shape God has given to redemption in the life and death of Jesus Christ, in the face of the depth of his descent into the whole chaotic labyrinth of worldly existence—a descent that ends in his being forsaken by God, genuinely on our behalf. Here is no stoically resigned, exemplary self-surrender to the mere "mystery" of God. In what follows we shall only speak of the specifically Christian mystery insofar as it is helpful in illuminating man's general situation.

Although all the elements of human existence are, and remain, interwoven in the way we have mentioned, we shall now proceed to introduce them more or less separately. More or less: man exists in two poles that cannot be torn asunder; he is always himself *and* his neighbor. He alone has to give eternity an account of how he has lived, yet the substance of that account is the way he has lived alongside his neighbor. He dies as an individual, but his death occurs in a time dimension he shares with his neighbor. Only as an individual is he free, but his freedom is essentially a freedom together with others who are free. And by "neighbor" here we mean not only those in the individual's private surroundings but the whole that consists of his fellow human beings. Man cannot exist and act on the world stage except in this polarity. The problems arising from his action can be concentrated and reduced to three: (1) Finite existence's claim to meaning and the problematical relationship between development and progress; (2) The multiple values attributable to the time dimension and to death; (3) The relationship between freedom, power and sin.

B. THE CLAIM OF FINITUDE

1. The "Relative Absolute"

The paradoxes associated with a rationality that is embedded in a transitory existence are insoluble. For reason—theoretical and practical—only exists if spiritual-intellectual decisions are made and executed against the background of something that is absolutely valid, absolutely true and good. A judgment arrived at in all conscience ("this is a true fact") does not mean "at the present moment": the judgment is meant to be equally valid tomorrow and in a hundred years' time. And the conscientious and responsible avowal, "I love you", at least at the subjective level, is not intended as a half-truth; it is not meant to hold only for a few weeks. Even if, with regard to his power to love, the lover were not sufficiently sanguine to guarantee his love for ten years, his avowal is still intended to be unconditional; it would reject any attempt to relativize its intention. Naturally, the person who makes a judgment, who pledges himself, who is ready to give an account of his actions here and now, is aware of living in the medium of time (and time is ceaselessly changing everything); he knows that he too, like everything around him, can change and that the perspectives of the "set" that forms the background for his action are continually shifting—unnoticeably, and sometimes quite noticeably too. But, as he moves through this volatile element, through these shifting sands, such knowledge does not stop him from taking his pilgrim's staff and inscribing with it some word that is ultimate.

The great ones of this world endeavor to incise such signs in stone or cast them in bronze, as monuments of absolutist prestige. A pyramid, a colossus, an imperial edict graven in stone, a triumphal arch "immortalizing" a victory—all these things do not actually *create* but only *attest* and *underline* the validity of absolute power and its authority to inscribe supratemporal symbols in the flow of time. But the monuments of those who enjoy the privilege that comes from power, who "make history", only express a desire that is equally that of the insignificant and powerless: all alike want to scratch something true, something

81

valid, into the face of the dwindling day. The poet endowed with the power of words, who *exegit monumentum aere perennius*, may claim thereby to rise higher than Pharaohs and Caesars; his pretention only expresses the fact that he has a little more success in externalizing things than every other man who is at pains to think, judge and act within the dimension of time. In his thinking, judging and acting, every man explicitly and consciously intends certain things he thus expresses to have an ultimate validity—these are the fundamental decisions of his life—whereas a thousand everyday details, of whose fleeting nature he is well aware, share in this ultimate orientation, though he is unconscious of it.

The issue here is not the transitory nature of all the prestige symbols of power or the irreplaceable loss of precious artifacts in all areas of culture or the plundering of Egyptian tombs and Mexican temples or the explosion in the Parthenon or the lost Bach cantatas that were used as packing paper. . . . Nor is it Schiller's complaint, "Even the beautiful must die", and his exquisite lament on the subject (whereas "What is common descends to the Orkus without a sound"); what is important at this point is simply that everyone who exists in history and thus "makes history", either in an extraordinary or in an ordinary way, feels confident to etch something on the stones of time, something that transcends life's fleeting aspect—even if finally, despairing, he comes to view his boldness as a naked illusion.

This is the point at which man lifts himself above the animal, whose head does not rise above the water level of time. Man swims in the river with his head lifted clear, aware of Being's unlimited horizon, its truth and goodness. He finds that Faust's wish, apparently unfulfillable, is already fulfilled: in the "moment" (which naturally passes) he *does* possess "eternity" of a kind. And here we are not thinking of the timelessness of abstract propositions, as in mathematical axioms, that possess an, as it were, secondary "eternity", dependent on the primary; what we have in mind is the presence of Being in the concrete existent. For Being is present in every "situation" (which by definition is limited); each "being-*in-situ*" is not only temporally and spatially within a context of others, similarly "situated": it is also within Being as a whole. It is because of this that we can evaluate "being-*in-situ*" within the world at all.

It is true, of course, that changes in the temporal or spatial situation can obscure or make it harder to discern what was intended, at an earlier stage, as an ultimate utterance or action. Changing "taste" means that we can have no immediate access to the supratemporal ideas the Romanesque, Gothic or Baroque periods wanted to express. But where we fail, wholly or in part, to understand a particular expression, we give it the benefit of the doubt, ready to believe unconditionally *that* its distinctive style was intended to express something more-than-temporal. However many rules of hermeneutics there may be, designed to facilitate our approach to utterances and deeds that are past or otherwise closed to us, they always presuppose a bridge. This bridge is the universal intention of *meaning*, which transcends the changes of time. This would hold good even if Being were thought to communicate itself differently at different epochs. If we are to discern what varies with changing times, there must be some kind of bridge enabling us to step across from one to another.

The fundamental human paradox, namely, the need to write the absolute upon the relative, to put some ultimate mark upon fleeting time, can be expressed in various ways at different periods. There can be civilizations for whom time, with its fleeting nature, is so insignificant that they live perpetually under the sign of the eternal that manifests itself at every moment; such is preeminently the Indian civilization. There can be others who find the impression made on the senses by the epiphany of the eternal in mundane matter to be so overwhelming that the relationship between fleeting moments seems to be of little significance; such are the Greeks. Their historiography is not chronological but a collection of significant aspects and situations. But even nations who attach much more importance to chronology do not need to think in essentially different terms. Thus the Egyptians: the acts and facts of their great ones are in each case—almost more than with the Greeks—permanently valid revelations of Being. This is shown by the care with which they preserved those bodies that were once a manifestation of the Ultimate. This battle against the phenomenon of death is also the heroic battle against finitude's tragic inner contradiction; so conscious are they of being on the side of preponderant, abiding meaning that what is passing can be overlooked as unimportant.

It would be misleading if we were to portray this tragic contradiction as the mark of only one epoch of humanity, the pre-Christian (or rather, the pre- and post-biblical). For, in its own way, the contradiction persists everywhere. It is clearly in evidence in Israel, with its so emphatic belief in the absolute uniqueness and preciousness of existence (since man is in covenant with God). It is also very evident in Christianity, where there is a further deepening of the eternal significance of the temporal moment. However, it is also clearly present (if for the moment we exclude the post-Christian ideologies of "progress") in the consciousness of all those thinkers and writers whose pondering centers on man's fundamental situation. It can be seen as the transparency of the mystery of Being (Heidegger); or as the impossible, that which ought-not-to-be, which instates man in his dignity (Camus); or as that whereby man is accredited as the guardian of the absolute, which prompts him to resist any absolute that would try to assert tutelary rights over him:

> Being here is much, and it seems to us
> that we are needed by what is here, the evanescent
> which, strangely, concerns us. Us, most evanescent of all.
>   *Once* only
> each one, *once* only. *Once* and no more. And we too
> are *once* only. Never again. But to have been this
> *once*, to have been *earthly* if only
> *once*, seems something beyond revoking. . . .
> Let the world extol the angel. . . .
> Show him how blessed a thing can be, how guiltless, how
>   much ours,
> how even suffering's cry purely takes to itself a form. . . .

Thus speaks Rilke: by dint of an enduring love, and by hymning the transitory (and increasingly transitory), he feels he can do something to transpose things into an interior, intramundane space where they will be preserved from passing away. It may be that Heidegger, Camus, Rilke and many others are putting forward soothing, mollifying speculations to cover a phenomenon that, seen in its nakedness, is unbearable: in this context it is immaterial; the point is that they are confronting the facts, and they keep them in view even in the midst of the superstructures they have erected. We cannot get beyond the facts: they are the foundation stone of our existence. Heidegger speaks of "being" [*Sein*] that can only appear, and be stewarded, in this medium of "existence" [*Dasein*]; Camus raises his fist against a heaven in which he does not believe; Rilke addresses himself to the angel who stands above the paradox, yet with a gesture that wards him off, as it were, rather than summons him. None of them do anything to modify the fact: for instance, by pointing out that the individual is of no account vis-à-vis the destiny of the race or that the unique existence is insignificant in the context of the vast multiplicity of reincarnations or that death is swallowed up by the idea of an endless life beyond it.

At this stage, the acknowledgment of the paradox has nothing to do with metaphysics. It is straightforward everyday experience, from which metaphysics will take its starting point as it attempts, from all possible angles, to find solutions. And the more man views and reflects upon existence in the concrete, the more it will be impressed upon him that it contains an inherent anomaly. Man's theoretical and practical spirit cannot be simply the highest form of *bios*; history is something qualitatively different from mere nature. But the way in which super-natural spirit is found to be yoked with mortal nature points to a tragic factor, a disturbance, in the world process. Plato calls this a declension from the "idea"; the Gnostics speak of wisdom falling from its native fullness.

Only now, when the abiding validity of the paradox has been assured, can it be presented without distortion to an epoch in which history is (still) understood primarily in vertical terms. It is possible, with certain qualifications, to call this epoch a predominantly contemplative one insofar as man, in attempting to solve his riddle, looks upward rather than backward or forward. Naturally, the first thing the eye sees is "the starry heaven above me", that inerrant, immortal, regulated order of nature that seems to encompass mortal man on every side; and he finds the echo of this order in the law of the seasons ("Die and become") of which he is a part. Thus one is tempted to say, by way of a short-circuit, that this "contemplative epoch" was only a preparatory one in which man still felt overshadowed by nature and had not yet discovered his own superiority to it, had not yet found his most connatural freedom and historical destiny. There may be some truth in this, but what there is, is only a half-truth. For this cosmological model of the world contains at least two assertions that separate it from mere naturalism. First, there is the consciousness that some dire and baneful fate has divorced the earth (or the entire sublunar world) from heaven. Second, man knows, and cannot shake off the knowledge, that in some way, nonetheless, he belongs to the heavenly world. The myths of "Phaedrus", the "Symposion" and "Phaidon" all circle around this shadowy realization. Even the naturalistic Stoics commend a certain "distance" and are aware of the freedom and the effort necessary if they are to submit themselves to the overarching divine law and assimilate themselves to it. All-embracing nature, in the "contemplative age", is after all only a transparent veil through which the divine is discerned; and of this divinity mortal man bears within him a spark or a reflected radiance.

This is most clearly recognizable if China, India and Hellas are compared with Hebrew religion, which is so totally different. Formally speaking, Judaism, although it points across toward something fundamentally new, exhibits a structure that is comparable to that of the aforementioned world models. Man is "here below", whereas God is "yonder"; man stands forth in all his paradoxes, almost more defenseless and full of riddles than the hero of a Greek tragedy. How, given his absolute mortality, can he have dealings with, and share a covenant with, the God who is absolutely the "living God"? For though he be authorized to regard himself as the "image and likeness of God", he has no right to eternal life but, like Hezekiah, begs for a few more years on earth, since, in any case, there is nothing left in Hades. Classical Israel surely remains the most notable memorial to man's fundamental paradox, because there is no overpainting with metaphysics (as in the case of the neighboring powers of Babylon and, especially, Egypt); we are simply left with the paradox, truth in its most pristine shape. Initially it is not softened by that other great element of Israelite religion, namely, hope in God's promises, which subsequently clarifies to become the expectation of the Messianic kingdom.

2. The Mirage of Progress

In this chapter on the pathos of the world drama, we are proceeding anthropocentrically, observing the way man conducts himself. Thus we are excluding what is distinctively Christian, which, as far as man is concerned, is only a response to God's act and initiative. Israel, however, features prominently in what is to be described here (almost half its entire reality looms up before us, so to speak, in this connection). For in Israel, for the very first time, human history acquires a decidedly horizontal dimension. Salvation is not only from above: it is ahead. While it is true that the vertical axis, that is, the nation's and the individual's relationship with the covenant God, continues to be given its full weight, nonetheless, time now begins to flow into the future. Loving faith in the absolute God is now accompanied by the hope that his salvation will come to earth.

It is significant, however, that this walking forward into the future is understood by Israel as a "waiting"; from time to time it is also interpreted as an active "pressing on" toward the coming salvation, but it is never regarded as a progress that can be measured. The category of "progress" is of an entirely different provenance. Originally it has no religious aspect at all; in fact, it rapidly becomes anti-religious and hence subverts religious energies in order to offer a substitute for religion. The elementally religious potentiality of the Israelite hope was bound, sooner or later, to make a pact with this spurious sister. Together they have become a driving force in world history.

In the face of this hybrid combination, we must first establish in what context "progress" does have an authentic meaning and is in touch with existence, namely, in the life of the individual. It was in the paradox of the "relative absolute" that we first discovered the individual moment of finite existence, or—to put it differently—appreciated its totality as an instant that flickers into life in world history and immediately goes out. But the life of the individual is a finite sequence of moments; later moments incorporate the results of earlier moments and freely adapt them, sometimes positively, by confirming them, and sometimes negatively, by rejecting them, changing the general direction through new decisions. In this way, the quality of absoluteness extends from the perpendicular moment to the horizontal plane of finite temporal succession; only thus can the individual life become a drama, that is, an action of ultimate significance that takes place within a finite framework. It is immaterial that this sequence can be seen in biological terms as the "unfolding" of energies that are already present in germ, in the categories of biological growth, of blossoming, fruiting and decline; in such a context, man is a part of nature: he is undramatic. The important thing is that man is meta-biological; he can imprint a spiritual meaning upon this process, and can do so largely in freedom, notwithstanding all the influences that come from heredity and environment. He can direct this process toward Being—the absolutely true and good—or away from it. We can never catch up with the norm, as the ancients knew; authentic progress,[1] however, consists in a closer and closer orientation to it. Of course, negative progress is also possible: thus we have *The Rake's* (or *The Harlot's*) *Progress* (Hogarth) as well as *The Pilgrim's Progress* (Bunyan). What is dramatic about this progress is not only that a spiritual being, an identity, can learn from his past, enrich himself in his present and plan his future; at each successive "now", he is able, through a free and responsible decision, to stamp the entirety of his finitude with a meaning that reflects, and is guaranteed by, the presence of the absolute (through conversion, for instance). No man can estimate what this meaning is worth in the context of the absolute (since no one can be his own judge); yet the drama enacted on the stage can allow us, as it were, to take a look at the Judge's cards. The drama introduces the spiritual being with his finite progress in all its proportions—albeit "in a mirror, dimly"—to the norm that will judge it.

On the plan of world history, however, progress can only be sought and found where the discoveries of one generation can be taken up and carried farther by the next, that is, in the area of technology. For the ancients, the "technical" was included

---

[1] Plutarch, "Quomodo quis suos in virtute sentiat profectus", 76b, 79b: *Moralia*, ed. F. C. Babbit (1949), I, 408, 420. Cicero, *De finibus* IV, 24.

among the "arts",[2] and there were various views about men being endowed with the arts and the way they developed them. What came first, a Golden Age or (as the Epicureans thought) a life like that of the animals? Did Prometheus steal the fire or discover it by the power of his own *ingenium*? And, most importantly, is the art of politics, for instance, bringing about a better and better society, or has it overreached itself? Is it now heading, driven by inner logic, for its own ruin? This was Plato's view,[3] and it persists as far as Lucretius, who, while he is profoundly impressed by the human mind's ability to plumb the mysteries of nature and perfect the arts and even the political order, sees the entire ascent within the context of a cosmic cycle that will eventually cause everything that has been attained to submerge.[4]

These approaches in the ancient world are subsequently nourished by the empirical science that begins to develop in the Middle Ages. Whereas Albert (like Thomas) still emphasizes progress in philosophical reflection—although the *experimentia*, the knowledge that comes *per experimentum*, is also regarded as important in natural science—Roger Bacon (born c. 1210) puts the accent entirely on the latter, on the invention of instruments and machines: his ideals are airplanes, self-propelling vehicles, submarines and even the prolongation of life.[5] Thus the path is clear: the advances of science can be given pride of place over stagnant philosophy (and theology), preoccupied as it is with abstract problems concerning "being". Francis Bacon (1561–1626) sees the development of experience and experiment as the liberation of human knowledge and enterprise from the crippling tutelage of empty "disputations" and "futile, magical ceremonies"; it is the realization of man's original mandate to rule over the world

---

[2] The idea of technological progress is found everywhere among the ancients, even among the Epicureans; cf. L. Robin, "Sur la conception épicurienne du Progrès" in *La Pensée hellénique* (Paris, 1942), 525ff. In this connection, Thomas (III, d 25, 2, a 2, q 1) refers to Aristotle, *Elench* 33, 183 b 17. Augustine takes this technological progress for granted (*Civ. Dei* XVIII, passim) but never equates it with moral and religious progress.

[3] *Republic* 546a. It would be a mistake, however, to try to trace the law discovered by Plato back to the ancient (cosmological) notions of cyclic recurrence.

[4] *De rerum natura* V, 925–1160, 1440ff., 91–109.

[5] *Opera*, ed. J. S. Brewer, (London, 1859, new ed., 1963), 535f.

of nature. He too envisages airplanes and submarines. In the Age of the Enlightenment, the ideal lies in a "limitless" perfection of mankind; to do what *can be done and devised* becomes part of the canon of man's obligations, with the result that even politics and ethics are seen in this light. As early as 1737, there appeared the *Observations sur le progrès continuel de la raison universelle*, by the Abbé de Saint-Pierre, in which he is pitilessly unconcerned about the death of individuals. In Condorcet's *Esquisse d'un tableau historique des progrès de l'esprit humain* (1793/1794), a science "that not only envisages the progress of the human race but is able to direct and accelerate it" is linked to a law of collective development; according to the latter, the development of a large number of individuals corresponds to that of a single individual, with the result that the idea of progress can now be recklessly applied to society as a whole. Neither Voltaire's scepticism with regard to this notion of progress nor Rousseau's "back to nature" managed to sever the backbone of the pathos of universal progress, nor did the sage distinctions of a Kant, who also thought he could discern nature's hidden plan gradually to bring about a perfect model of the state in which human nature "can fully develop . . . all its endowments".[6] On the one hand, he speaks of this result being wrested from a human being who bears a radical evil within him and is "driven by pride, the lust for power, or greed, to acquire a status among his fellows, whom he cannot bear but cannot do without", so that, in the end, "an agreement to constitute a society, pathologically extracted under compulsion" is eventually transformed "into a moral totality".[7]

> For there are people who are evil-natured and yet are rational, endowed with creativity and even a moral sense. The greater their degree of culture, the more they are aware of the evil they inflict on one another in the pursuit of selfishness; they see no other remedy than—reluctantly—to subject the private aspirations (of individuals) to the common aspirations (of the consensus), that is, to the discipline of civil compulsion. (However, they subject themselves to this discipline only according to laws they have themselves drawn up.) Thus they feel ennobled, telling themselves that

[6] *Idee zu einer allgemeinen Geschichte* . . . (1784): 8th proposition (Weischedel VII) VI, 45.

[7] *Ibid.*, 4th proposition, 38.

they belong to a race that measures up to the definition of man that reason puts forward as an ideal.[8]

On the other hand, Kant is well aware that this kind of social-ethical culture [*Gesittung*] cannot be equated with real moral behavior, which can only come from the individual's free decision.[9] Yet he continues to speak of an "asymptotic" approach,[10] whereby "perfect art" can once again become "nature", which is "the ultimate goal of the human race's ethical constitution."[11]

After all, therefore, the dichotomy envisaged by Kant strongly favors the race or objective "spirit". (According to Hegel, the man who lives in a state that is legally constituted and governed has become truly free.) In Marx' view, history has become nature; Comte sees society divinizing itself at the end of the path of progress. Here, at the latest, we can see that the modern notion of progress, which referred initially only to the technological improvement of the instruments that serve man, eventually—having jettisoned metaphysics—gained control of the political and ethical realm and changed society's entire life into technology. To this technology, the autonomy and dignity of the individual were sacrificed. Integral to the Christian path into the future, in expectation of Christ's final judgment, was the proclamation of this dignity of the person; and it was *on this basis* that Christianity argued for human rights and for justice. Now, however, out from under the Christian message came the Old Testament hope of an earthly future, in the form of the Messianic expectation; it was this that imparted a final religious tincture to the technological notion of progress.

Nonetheless, the element of compulsion that Kant (and Rousseau too) had so emphasized in the process of "ethicizing" the individual, which hardened in Marx into an implacable dialectic, could no longer conceal the fact that it was based on pure power-superiority, both in theory and in practice. And J. Burckhardt was right to diagnose this kind of power in the political (Machiavelli) and the social sphere as "evil" in its divorce

---

[8] *Anthropologie*, ibid., VI, 684f.
[9] Cf. *Mutmasslicher Anfang der Menschengeschichte*, ibid., 92.
[10] A review of Herder's *Ideen*, ibid., 805.
[11] *Mutmasslicher Anfang der Menschengeschichte*, ibid., 95.

from man's religious and moral orientation toward the good. Though it appears in the guise of progress, it has an inherent "tendency toward self-annihilation".[12] The entire modern ideology of progress, even where it wears a religious mask, represents a history of the relationship between earth and heaven that has been tipped up so that heaven is "in the future". Today it has turned into a naked power-struggle between superpowers using naked technological means of annihilation; this is the completely logical conclusion where something intended as an instrument in the service of man has been made into an absolute.

Or should we speak more cautiously? Was not man put on earth to rule the world, to humanize it? Must he not move necessarily away from the predominantly contemplative stance that sees the divine in nature to the different stance of *homo faber*? Yet, once this process has started, who can stop it when "civilization" threatens to turn into pure technocracy and everything natural is turned into a machine? Will it be possible, in the long run, for "nature reserves" to exist *outside* total technological planning, or will they be just another element of it? Are we not faced here with a mechanism that is better described, not as "progress", but as the "unfolding" or "development" of something that is already present in germ?

> Progress demands an idea governing the whole of historical life; it calls for a meaning that will illuminate history. Development unfolds of itself; it can be delayed but not destroyed, for it is a possibility inherent in history. . . . Certainly, we have developed technology, we have invested immense psycho-intellectual resources in this technological development. But who dares to say that we could have stood in its way or held up its infamous triumphal procession? Technology is our fate; it is an integral part of our development, and every development is as merciless and unstoppable as fate. "Progress", by contrast, contains an element of free human decision that is foreign to "development" in this sense.[13]

But if this "development" is only fate and not a free decision— what madness to think that such "fate" would lead to a realm

---

[12] M. Horkheimer/T. W. Adorno, *Dialektik der Aufklärung* (1969), 7.
[13] Hans Jürgen Baden, *Der Sinn der Geschichte* (Hamburg: Wittig, 1948), 80f.

of freedom!—and hence not something to which man has given meaning, what significance can the horizontal history of the human race have, from a purely immanent point of view? (For any transcendent, vertical "judgment" upon the whole of history is outside our present topic.) Perhaps mankind will prove its sublimity by giving itself up and thereby, like a collective Kirillov, demonstrate its own absoluteness? Such an end, in H. Butterfield's calm reflections on world history, would be totally appropriate to the human condition: "It will only put an end to a globe which we always knew was doomed to a bad end in any case. I am not sure that it would not be typical of human history if . . . men should by their own contrivance hasten that end and anticipate the operation of nature or of time—because it is so much in the character of Divine judgement in history that men are made to execute it upon themselves."[14]

This probable end of human history, as envisaged by Butterfield, would bring to a conclusion a destiny of "development" that had been unfolding from its inception; but it would also be the expression of its determination freely to surrender to the pull and current of this destiny, and—in spite of all the warning signs—to regard it as "progress". Finally it would signify a new and unexpected encounter with vertical world history, such as the Book of Revelation depicts in its baffling images. It can be said, in favor of this view, that if collective development is placed under the unequivocal banner of "progress", the goal of such progress remains completely beyond our imagination; this means that, with every (real or apparent) partial success, the goal must be further deferred: it is the "promise that cannot be fulfilled". And—to add a triviality—if *per impossibile* a satisfactory final situation *could* be reached, it would rob all preceding historical present moments of their reality, reducing them to the level of purely instrumental preliminary stages, looking toward a future that cannot presently be envisaged; the individual would be cheated of the reward due to the efforts he had made and the suffering he had undergone. Belief in progress

[14] *Christianity and History* (London: Bell & Sons, 1949), 66. This includes everything that tends toward the self-destruction of mankind in its earthly existence; that is, not only the atom bomb but all the destruction of the ecological foundation for organic life that results from senseless exploitation.

is a flight from time: it flees from everything that, in time, is eternal.

We should also take into account the law that is demonstrated by the whole of history, namely, that genuine spiritual progress, genuine creative achievement of historical stature, never comes about without stubborn wrestling with obstructions. Creative genius is never a matter of the collective but of the individual; the latter is almost always isolated and unrecognized (cf. Walter Muschg's *Tragische Literaturgeschichte*). Only "individuality is the source of the new, of progress. It is a condition of progress that the individual be separated from his community at least for a time, and often with tragic consequences. So history teaches us."[15] This is the law of qualitative progress, as distinct from that of the quantitative amassing of knowledge and know-how that operates almost mechanically. Strange to say, it is the individual, subject to the biological law of blossoming and aging, who is capable of genuine progress because of his freedom; the totality of history, to which this biological law (Spengler, Toynbee) only partially applies, is incapable of qualitative progress. Qualitative progress is seen in the composition of the "Jupiter" Symphony, whereas its mass-production and mass-distribution on disc, tape and radio signify no such progress.

In this way, the dialectic of total progress, now unmasked as a deception, confirms even more what we said in the preceding chapter: it is impossible to unravel the paradox whereby man is forever trying to translate what is absolute into terms that are relative and transitory. Must we wait, perhaps, for the incarnate Logos, who bends down to the earth and writes in the sand with his finger, if we are to discover the meaning of all that is written in the sands of history?

---

[15] Theodor Haecker, *Der Mensch und die Geschichte* (Hegner, 1935), 78f.

C. TIME AND DEATH

1. My Time; Our Time

Everything we shall say here concerning man's time and man's death will only reinforce the paradox of existence, namely, the endeavor to express the absolute through the relative. The individual lives in a finite time. This is not something he takes: it is given him. This, more clearly than anything else, shows him that his very existence is a gift. Within this gift, however, he has freedom to act as seems good to him. Time's givenness is most clearly seen in the fact that man has control neither of its beginning nor of its ending. Its beginning is gentle: a hardly perceptible transition from unconsciousness to consciousness, from life at the purely vital level to an existence that is intellectual, spiritual and responsible. Its end, however and whenever it comes, is abrupt, irrespective of the fact that the exact moment of death occurs at different points depending on the categories used to determine it.

We do not have to decide here whether man has an a priori knowledge of the finitude of his particular time (as Scheler has tried to propose)[1] or acquires this knowledge from his experience of the transience of things and from the death of other people, so being able to envisage his own death. The two aspects are not mutually exclusive. It is possible for the child's experience to be fashioned by the unnoticed fact that its life is "inwardly present to it at every moment as a complete totality" that forms "the background for all particular experiences and vicissitudes",[2] before it becomes aware of the reality that all men die and hence that it must die too. But the higher the constellation of the mind (with its reflex ability) rises within its internal horizon, the more

---

[1] "Tod und Fortleben" in *Schriften aus dem Nachlass* I, *Werke* 10 (1976), 9–64.

[2] *Ibid.*, 23. Later Scheler himself describes the "repression of the idea of death" that is normal in today's achievement-oriented world and which it replaces with a "progress that has neither goal nor meaning", an "ersatz for eternal life" (27, 30). Insofar as modern science's entire way of seeing strives to show us, not an "authentic world", but "only a plan whereby it can be dominated and controlled", "it cannot look at death either" (34).

it chafes against the confines imposed by the inner finitude of biological life. Man cannot say unequivocally that he is locked inside life as in a prison (*sōma-sēma*), for he knows that unique, irrevocable acts and decisions belong to his dignity. Nor can he alter the fact that these acts and decisions are not timeless but occur within a sequence of moments; in other words, time's extension is part of the given as far as he is concerned. Thus he understands "that, in *every* act, the conscious person *transcends* the given insofar as that given represents a 'limit' on the part of the body—which is 'given' him along with the experience";[3] but he also understands that the "space" within which such acts are realized is always his own, restricted time.

Man's spirit may range far and wide, but it is implacably bound to a bodily existence that is to be lived out here and now. This means that, in spite of the multifarious distractions I may find in my particular milieu and among my fellows, I am always thrown back into a fundamental solitude in which my death—my very own death—is unavoidably getting nearer and nearer. This characteristic does not leave man, either in his most spiritual acts or in the two-in-one union of human love, and it suggests that those who say that "authentic" existence lies wholly in the clear *realization* of one's own death and in the resolve to *perform* it have truth on their side after all. Thus not only our "being-with" things but also our "being-with" our fellow men is placed in parentheses; it is part of "one's" mode of existence.[4] For, along with everything

---

[3] *Ibid.*, 42. "The man who knows of death not only from books or from hearsay, and does not merely 'reckon with' death like a life-insurance policy but actually sees it before him, simultaneously sees 'his self'—that is, his spiritual person, his true self—winging its way *beyond* the boundary of life that death represents. Only the man who has risked his own 'self', who has made an interior surrender of it and received it back again as through grace, can be said truly to possess his life henceforth and for all time. . . . This risk-taking and the love that inspires it are the epistemological requirements for beholding the sublimity of existence . . . beyond the body; no observation or deduction can be a substitute for such acts." Scheler, *Der Genius des Krieges* (1915), 123–24.

[4] This objection against Heidegger's interpretation of existence in *Being and Time* is raised by Bernward Plate in his *Die Erfahrung der Zeit und das Mit-Dasein* (Munich: Diss., 1966). Insofar as the "thing" and the "thou" are reckoned as belonging to the same sphere of the non-I, Heidegger's analysis can be called "perhaps even the fulfillment of the transcendental philosophy of the 'I' " (*ibid.*,

else, we shall have to relinquish even the "thou" to whom we now cling when existence eventually comes up against its limit —over which it has no control. Every man dies alone, even if he dies at the same time as another. (There is symbolism in the fact that neither Antony and Cleopatra, Tristan and Isolde, Romeo and Juliet nor Prouèze and Rodrigue die at the same time.)

The time in which I live is primarily "my" (finite) time; the fact that it fits into a neutral, chronological time is only one of its qualities, not to be confused with its essential nature. I may make an objective study of the kind of "time" nature, plants and animals have, but it is not a matter of existential concern to me. My time has enough riddles and paradoxes of its own to keep me occupied. For it is so very much "my" time; it is not like an external medium in which I move; rather, it is given to me as my very own mode of existence. And yet at the same time it is withdrawn from me, since I have no control over my entire past and future, except from the single, here-and-now vantage *point* of my present. My time is so outside my control that I do not know how long it will be, which means that I cannot envisage my existence in an extended duration like a play with several acts. I cannot impart a fully thought-out and constructed "shape" to it, except by imprinting the dramatic "idea" on each present moment. Precisely by doing this, however, it is possible (by means of repentance and a renewed mind and heart) to give a new significance to the past; as for the approaching moments of the future, it is possible to fill them with corresponding significance too.

In his *Confessions* (n.b., his *personal* confessions), Augustine endeavored to portray the paradoxes of his own time, a time that was granted to him *as it was being withdrawn from him*.[5] His time is *distentio*, yet it is held together at every moment and rendered accessible to experience by the power (*vis*) of *memoria*. For the

---

25). It is no surprise, when Husserl makes his return to transcendental philosophy, to find him still saying that "the experience of things is the model for all experience" (83), in spite of his constant attempts to shed light on interpersonality (cf. *Husserliana* XIV–XVI). Heidegger had tried to distance himself from Husserl.

[5] "Sunt enim haec in anima tria quaedam, *et alibi ea non video*: praesens de praeteritis memoria, praesens de praesentibus contuitus, praesens de futuris exspectatio" (*Conf.* XI, 20, 26).

memory can hold fast to what is past and freely reproduce it; it can imagine things never seen; it can sustain the expectation of what is in the future. From this point, we can look ahead to the teachings of Idealism, which see time as the product of a bifurcation of consciousness,[6] and beyond, to Husserl's analysis of "now"-consciousness, in which "retention" and "protention" are inseparable (in the more elementary forms of "memory" and "expectation").[7] But this does not explain how the Augustinian *memoria*, in spite of its "power" to "master" the past and, to some extent, the future, is itself in flux. For the future is continually coming, and the present is continually going; *distentio* is thus not a static, spatial spread but a moving and a stretching forward, a tension, a tendency (*extensio, intensio*) toward something.[8] It is not merely that history *involves* the subject; the subject himself is intrinsically historical.

When Husserl says that "we can no longer speak of the time of the last constitutive consciousness"[9] but only of phases constituting a flux, which, as such, is "absolute subjectivity",[10] it can be shown that this description of time consciousness "in fact assumes a real time 'in' which the phenomenon stands".[11] He assumes a time that is neither produced nor controlled by consciousness: time is *given* to consciousness; consciousness is *admitted* to time. Given, as Augustine shows[12] from a supertemporal or eternal plane; admitted into the biological realm (and hence into the physical realm), whose own form of time can

---

[6] Cf. the excellent analysis of Schelling's and particularly Baader's philosophy of time by F. Kümmel, *Über den Begriff der Zeit* (Tübingen: M. Niemeyer, 1962), 44–121.

[7] "Zur Phänomenologie des inneren Zeitbewusstseins", *Husserliana* X (The Hague, 1961).

[8] "Ecce distentio est vita mea" (*Conf.* XI, 29, 39). Yet, "non distentus, sed extentus . . . secundum intentionem" (*ibid.*). Cf. "Die Vision Augustins" in *Das Ganze im Fragment* (Benziger, 1963), 17–36.

[9] *Loc. cit.,* section 38.

[10] *Loc. cit.,* section 36.

[11] Peter Bieri, *Zeit und Zeiterfahrung* (Suhrkamp, 1972), 199.

[12] This—"the given"—is the context for Heidegger's speculation according to which *being gives time* (*Es gibt Zeit*: "there is time" [lit. "it gives time"]: "time itself remains the gift of an 'it' "): *Zur Sache des Denkens* (Tübingen: Niemeyer, 1969), 18.

only be described in approximate and hypothetical terms.[13] Furthermore, spiritual consciousness participates in this time form in such a way that it becomes an "existence leading to death".

Existence's time can be cut off from outside at any moment, but the biological unfulfillment by no means signifies that the drama of this existence has not been acted out to its end. The Old Testament equating of (biological) "length of days" and (spiritual) "perfection" (Dt 5:16; 30:20; Ps 21:5; 23:6; 91:16; Prov 3:2; Sir 1:12; and so forth) is criticized by the Book of Wisdom, pertinently remarking that perfection is not a matter of a long life; the righteous man who dies "before his time" has come "to perfection in a short while" (Wis 4:7–14)—something that is attested by the many heroes, geniuses (Mozart, Schubert) and saints (Elizabeth of Hungary, Stanislaus, Aloysius, Thérèse, and so forth) who died at an early age. Not only did they "make the most of the time" (Eph 5:16), they used it up in the period of their ascendancy and thus escaped the vicissitudes of an aging process that is not only biological but also spiritual, whereby others find themselves not only old but worn out and empty (Péguy has described this "vieillissement").[14] Better than others, they grasped the moment of opportunity in the time given to them, imprinting so much of the "absolute" on their brief days that, through the *intensio* of their embrace, their entire *oeuvre* seems to have acquired a final and definitive shape.

However, though the individual's particular "time" is his own, this does not mean that people are enclosed in mutually exclusive time dimensions. While these "times" do not mingle and coalesce, they do communicate with one another, for they share an a priori common humanity.[15] In the awakening of the individual self-consciousness, the "thou" is earlier than the "I", for

[13] Cf. the excellent remarks by Karl Rahner: "Theologische Anmerkung zum Zeitbegriff" in *Weisen der Zeitlichkeit. Naturwissenschaft und Theologie*, no. 12 (Freiburg and Munich: Alber, 1970), 215–27. Esp. 225: Rahner understands human time concretely as salvation-historical time. "Extrapolations" from it can be undertaken only "with extreme caution" and yield "limited success"; "the point of departure for understanding any time" must be "the inner time dimension of the individual, not external time, periods of time and time-measurement" (220).

[14] Cf. Albert Béguin, *La Prière de Péguy* (Neuchâtel, 1942), 14–34.

[15] Cf. *Theo-Drama* II, 389f.

the "I" is a response to the preceding call of the "thou"; the "thou" (for example, the mother vis-à-vis the child) produces in the "I" the fundamental ability to go beyond the realm of the "I–thou" and be a responsible part of a "we".[16] Thus both the "I" and the "community of persons"[17] share a "common source". It follows (though it is not easy to hold it in focus) that such a source is common to both the (existential) philosophy that speaks of the lonely "existence leading to death" and the (social) philosophy that assumes a common existence in a physico-spiritual time continuum.

The latter should not be divorced from the "time" of the human subjects who live together, as if it were some neutral "world time". This kind of "world time" where death does not exist is an abstraction compared with the concrete time experienced by persons. But, as a result of contact between one person (with his "death-bound time") and others (with their "death-bound times"), a new "now" comes into being. For one partner, this "now" may be "late", whereas other, younger partners feel it to be "early". The degree of their response to this "now", and involvement in it, will vary depending on the intensity of their shared life; but basically it is this "now" that draws the individual into the totality of human destiny.

This communication shows that all communicating individuals find themselves in the same fundamental situation: all are constrained to inscribe things of absolute validity upon a time continuum that is running out. Moreover, this continuum, which had seemed to be "mine", now appears to be "ours", something for which we have a shared responsibility. In the "I–thou" and "I–we" relationship, the individual's responsibility (for his action and conduct in the face of death) plays a part in the like responsibility of others in the face of death. Thus the individual becomes coresponsible for the common destiny of mankind, not only with regard to the time span in which he lives but also for the generations who will live after him. For instance, he may be directly involved in this destiny by begetting children and bringing them up, and he will be partly responsible for the way

[16] *Ibid.*, 196ff., esp. 208f., 239.
[17] M. Scheler, "Der Formalismus in der Ethik", *Werke* II (1954), 523.

they understand and live out their own responsibilities. Here is a new element of pathos for the individual and for the totality of all individuals: his task of infusing lasting values into the changes and chances of life is no longer limited to his own existence; it extends to that "time" of mankind that is totally beyond his grasp but in which his personal decisions have social consequences he cannot envisage. If a God were ever to require him personally to give an account of his stewardship of his "death-bound time", he would have to appear before the divine judgment seat together with all mankind. He can only work out his own salvation by contributing to the salvation of all. But he does not work out his own salvation by so concentrating on the salvation of all men that he forgets that his own existence is running toward death. He cannot carry out his (authentic) task of self-improvement by being a mere "do-gooder" or world-improver. The two aspects must remain in tension, for "my time" can never be absorbed into "our time". While it is profoundly true that the individual is there for the whole and has been appointed to serve it, he no less has the right to live his (death-bound) time on his own account and in accordance with his own responsibility for the rightness of his decisions and actions. Even from the anthropocentric point of view we are adopting here, in considering the pathos of what takes place on the world stage, the tension between egocentrism and social interaction remains an irreducible one. Even in the ancient world, ethics tried many different ways of finding a balance (largely, it must be said, excluding the problem of slavery) between "autarchy" and the fact that all, including the "wise", were interwoven in the fabric of the *polis*. But for all the most influential thinkers, however different their suggested solutions, the point where personal and social ethics meet is *reason*, which aspires to the sovereign norm of an absolute good. Every individual and all individuals in concert are to inscribe in the flux of time those signs and ciphers that reflect a law that is superior to them both and that orientates each to the other. Both Plato's *Republic* and the Stoics clearly showed that this law does not coincide with what man finds "useful", although it is of great use to man to follow it. For here the individual and the community are subject to the same ethical world law, which is why Plato could construct the state on the analogy of the individual human being's metaphysical organization (by the use of the cardinal virtues). In this perspective, on occasion, the history of mankind was envisaged on the analogy of the development of the individual, mostly, however, along the lines of maturation from childhood to man's estate; death was not taken into account.[18] Not much was to be gained here. It was more important to see concrete time as the time of a mankind consisting of individual mortal human beings, that is, not abstracting it into something indefinite, nonmortal and hence nonhuman. Gregory of Nyssa was surely right to regard mankind's succession of generations, within the stretched span of time, as essentially finite; even in the context of the "macro human being", it is running toward death.[19] Sexual reproduction takes place, according to him, out of the fear of death and as a prophylactic against it.[20] Logically speaking, once the succession of generations has come to an end (with the death of the last man), time too is suspended.[21]

Thus the individual and mankind find themselves equally at a loss when it comes to self-interpretation. This does not mean that, in world history, there may not arise factors of significance not manifested visibly in the life of the individual; but such factors are always emanations of the one human nature that is found in every man (and which in each case is both personal and social) and is thus fundamentally intelligible to him. Such are the

[18] Preeminently Augustine, *De Civ. Dei* X, 14; *En. in Ps.* 118, 16, 6, where he is concerned more with the Church's growth through the ages than with the growth of mankind. Similarly, when the Enlightenment draws the comparison between man and humanity, it will have only this growth in mind. Thus Charles Perrault will say that, compared with the "ancients", we are like adults as against children (*Parallèle des anciens et des modernes*, Paris 1688ff., II, 45-50). In his *Esquisse d'un tableau historique des progrès de l'esprit humain*, to which we have already referred, Condorcet says that mankind learns from the experience of its past, just as the individual does (42-43). Ever since Kant, the parallel has been drawn between the unconscious state of nature and its transition to the state of ethical awareness (through the "Fall") and the individual's emergence out of his first childhood into responsible self-consciousness. But even where civilizations are thought of in terms of a biological cycle, that is, including the phenomenon of dying, people are reluctant to draw the parallel between the individual's "existence unto death" and the corresponding (?) awareness on the part of a nation or a civilization.

[19] *De hom. opif.* 16 (PG 144, 185bc).

[20] *Ibid.*, 188b.

[21] *Ibid.*, 205c.

phenomena of power, triumph and defeat, of the creation and then the destruction of worthy artifacts, and of the good in its beneficence and of evil in its malice. Man (who is both personal and social) is capable of all these things; it will always be futile to try to systematize the ebb and flow of such phenomena as they are realized in history writ large. Just as it is impossible to plot the curve of the individual's existence—since his decisions are free—so it is impossible to plot the curve of history, which is made by countless single decisions. Such calculation could only succeed if the so-called "progress" of amassed technological knowledge had so enslaved mankind that it was no longer capable of making any opposition to it in the form of a free decision. But would such a final phase deserve the name "history"?

Would this not mean that a genuinely human history had sunk back to the level of a biological prehistory, that is, the process whereby life evolved up to the human stage? (For the characteristic of real human history is that it has taken a leap up to an entirely new level.) Even if one were prepared to admit that man is summoned to seize hold of natural evolution and continue it, but now, on the basis of freedom (Teilhard de Chardin, J. S. Huxley), there is no guarantee—no "world spirit" at work behind human freedom—that such evolution, transferred to an entirely different plane, would continue to run according to natural laws. Man, always both personal and social, is alone in a dumb universe, paradoxically obliged to put the imprint of the absolute on what is relative and transitory; in this situation, he will always be faced with sceptical objections, destructive negations. Where the desire for order becomes overwhelming, anarchy and terrorism automatically rear their heads.

2. Gestures of Existence

There has always been a tendency, in Christian thought, to project the Christian reality back into all the dimensions of creation, as if the "mystery hidden for ages in God" (Eph 3:9) were already known to man in a more or less categorial or transcendental manner, in fragments that point forward to the totality; or as if these things are already engraved on man's spirit (which, right from the start, is always the recipient of grace); when confronted with revelation in specific categories, man realizes that, deep down, he was already acquainted with it. However, the "Great Theatre of the World", as it unfolds in reality, does not speak in favor of this kind of "anticipation". Man is not able to anticipate the synthesis of the *Verbum-caro*: it is the only solution and yet could never be arrived at by guesswork. As a result of this inability, man prefers to embrace every other pseudo-solution. This being so, what cannot be guessed becomes what *should not be*; thus the Cross is not a chance occurrence but is strictly necessary. This will become completely clear only when we have discussed the question of evil.

Even now, however, we can foresee the kind of gestures that will be made and the scenes that will be enacted on the world stage. This is true even if, initially, no attempt is made to pre-empt the Christian solution and the light it sheds and particularly where this solution meets with the disappointment of rejection. These gestures are interwoven with the individual and social fabric in a spatio-temporal, finite acting area, which presupposes that this finitude has a reflex consciousness of itself, that is, is illuminated by a spark of the absolute. Such a relationship with the absolute is to be assumed under all circumstances. It arises directly from the insight that man has into the relativity of his own self and of all that resembles him. Because of man's very nature, there is a relationship between him and his "origin and goal", which is outside him and outside the world.[1] Were it not so, even scepticism would be unthinkable.

The point of absoluteness—reason's openness to the totality of being, of the true and the good, and its innate necessity to orientate itself to that totality and be judged by it—can be conceived in manifold ways. Since it is both hidden (the "good beyond all *ousia*") and yet illuminates and permeates all finite reality, it can be thought of as the "nothing" of all that is; or as real Being, compared with which every existent thing is nothing; or as the core of *being* in everything transitory; or as the law of development, reversal or proportion in all passing reality. From the point of view of human reason, it is the highest form

---

[1] Vatican I, c. 2 (DS 3004).

ality or immanent (but in-
y to which all contingent
dom for which all finite,
being presented to us in
whether one or many), a
ction, must first lay aside
into a kind of impersonal
relationship between the
: existent, it is that which
g transitory lacks all sub-
ry must endeavor, in its
t is the absolute law that
nan is meant to discover
: to it. It is the legislating
t look if we are also to
alm of the transitory.
practical possibilities of
alance", between the ab-
enty of scope for tying
down this fluid relationship to a particular religious *Weltanschauung* or letting it petrify into a hostile ideology. Even in the most
diverse forms, however, it will always be a case of manifesting
the absolute in some relative shape, be it in symbols of power
and visible prestige—in divine kingship, imperial laws, temples
and palaces—or in absolute ethical and religious demands—that
is, "leaving everything" and concentrating on the one thing necessary. In this latter way, existence itself is sculpted into a kind
of internal, concave bas-relief representing the absolute; a philosophical, cosmic, mathematical, medical or sociological global
law is distilled out and communicated by the wise man, to the
best of his ability, so that it can be translated into practice in
human society, albeit perhaps in a fragmentary form.

All this is highly abstract. But it would be easy to illustrate
each one of these facets with many examples drawn from world
history and the history of ideas. It can be rendered concrete by
showing that existence's internal finitude does not allow it to realize every valid form of the absolute/relative relationship, since
each of these forms is itself finite and has an equal and opposite
counterform that can claim equal (and equally relative) justifi-

cation. This means that, in the finite world, tensions arise concerning the relationship to the absolute; these harden into ideologies, giving substance to the view that "conflict is the father of all things". Anyone wishing successively to experience these irreconcilable tensions would become a Kierkegaardian dilettante: he would be elevating himself to the level of synthesis and posing as the manipulator of the absolute; in striving for completeness, he would be not only denying his own fragmental nature but—more profoundly—going back on his commitment to the absolute. Nor is this all. As we have shown, existence always has two sides, the individual and the social. They are distinct yet cannot be isolated from one another. Thus, decisions that bring out the individual aspect in its radicality, endeavoring to exhibit its link with the absolute, are bound to fail to recognize the social reality that is inseparable from the individual. For the individual always remains a member of society, a link in the succession of generations. The logic here is implacable: in the end we would be left with pure resignation in the face of the prison of finitude; or, more profoundly, with a despairing scepticism about the task of our existence (that is, to incise some abiding meaning into what is transitory). And it must be said that the latter is an entirely justifiable attitude if such a task is *not* the unshakable foundation of existence.

First, we turn to existence's great historical forces, the potencies and norms that govern its fundamental gestures.

The first fundamental energy is that of *Eros*. Eros rises upon a broad, infrahuman, natural foundation and, in accordance with its aims, is concerned with the maintenance of the species at the natural level. It asserts its claims upon the individual in the name of the species but, for this purpose, presents him with the image of a beloved "thou" as a *fata morgana* of the absolute. Insofar as Eros is a sexual phenomenon, this mirage will dissolve; but insofar as the individual's loving core has been touched, it is able to outlive Eros. Often the will to go on loving persists until it meets the tragic frontier of the death of one of the partners. The discussions on the subject of Eros in Plato's *Symposium* ultimately dissolve it into something "daimonic" that is neither entirely human nor entirely divine: both a movement that infuses and begets the divine in the world of finitude and also, simultaneously, a longing that ascends from the finite world toward the divine. In this way, it provides the theme and the framework for at least half the action that takes place on the world stage—action that is exquisite, comic, tragic, breathing a fragrance of infinity into existence. The more man is aware that, in the long run, the intoxicating moment cannot give what it promises, the greater is his participation in it. If bodily generation is taken seriously, nature goes beyond the aim of union and achieves its goal, namely, the child. In the child we see the unexpected realization and manifestation of an absolute, yet it will soon part from its parents and go to join the stream of successive generations. On the other hand, if the union of the couple is regarded as sufficient in itself, it becomes an *égoisme à deux*, in which two individuals of the species withdraw not only from the purposes of nature but also from the claims of society, whose members they are and remain. For they have to live and work not only for themselves but for the collective. In work, as in love—in a different but equally fragmentary way—they are meant to realize something of the meaning of existence.

At this point we should add something about the ambiguities of *power*. It is a subject to which we shall return. Again we find that power has a broad foundation in nature, where natural selection has taken place through trials of strength. But where power emerges in the region of self-consciousness, it becomes —rightly or wrongly—a means of imprinting something absolute upon what is relative. (For the most part people forget that the absolute has to be thought of in terms of power as well as of goodness, that is, a goodness that is radiant, kind and communicative; the absolute can only represent truth if it is seen in this unity of power and goodness.) As it arises on the foundation of nature, power is primarily self-affirmation, whether it be the affirmation of an individual, a group or a people; and it involves the overpowering and subjugation of others. Thus it causes us to focus on only *one* aspect of the absolute and neglect another, perhaps more fundamental aspect. As a result, power deceives itself and those concerned with it about the true nature of the absolute. Where it prevails by means of oppression, thinking that it alone is right—whether on the basis of the theory that "might is right" or of the ideology that says that a race or class must assert itself with all available means, because it represents some peerless good, some quasi-absolute in the sphere of the relative —it has become demonic, failing to recognize that, beyond everything finite, the absolute is a radiant sun of goodness and righteousness, in the most sublime meaning of the word.

If we ponder the phenomenon of power more deeply, we discover that its emanations can have the same source as goodness. In such a case, the sphere of a power can also be a realm of peace and safety where good things are communicated in justice. Later we shall have to ask why, in the anthropocentric view of life, "the good" is so often half-hidden or totally obscured behind "the powerful".

The little struggles between insignificant individuals and groups are of small interest, providing they do not threaten the general well-being of society, but the great engagements go to make up the main façade of what is regarded and remembered as "world history". It is on this stage that the real heroes step forth—or those whom their contemporaries (or later generations) consider to be such or elevate to that level; not infrequently, bloody weapons are their attribute, whether the blood is spilled by their own hands or those of others. Wherever in the world we find great, powerful symbols of the absolute, they either come from the field of war or are pressing in that direction. So it forms part of children's games; as such it is indulged and overlooked, and people would miss it if it were not there. The radiance of renown, borrowed from the sun of the absolute, transfigures all cruelties. The man who is elevated into the absolute realm of greatness has the power to transfigure himself by gathering around him all the world's beautiful things; indeed he actually calls them into being. All great architecture owes its existence to this power. (Thus David builds his own palace before realizing that Yahweh would be more suitably housed in a temple than in a tent.) We owe most great painting and sculpture, most symphonic music and opera, to the self-glorification of power. (And is there any great museum that does not consist of the booty of war or mammon?)

Art, great art, has a special, reserved place among human endeavors. It is close to that side of the absolute that we call "grace", free gift. Nonetheless it is always the fruit of the highest human effort too. "People imagine that Mozart remained a child all his life; but just consider the will power he showed in his last months."[2] Here the artifact becomes transparent, allowing the absolute to shine through it "in a mirror dimly", revealing permanent, abiding value in something that is unique and of the moment, irrespective of the changes of style and the existence of laws of polarity (classic/romantic, open/closed form, and so forth). Ultimately, however, it is all a writing in the sand, for paintings and architecture decay, and "Mozart and Beethoven can become as unintelligible to mankind in the future as the music of the Greeks is to us, though it was highly praised by contemporaries."[3] Nor can we be certain that the same fate is not in store for the great literature that seems so permanent and lasting to us.

All human drama is concerned with the discovery and appropriation of the point of balance (which is eternally unstable) between two factors: on the one hand, there is what can be realized by the standards of the absolute, and, on the other, there is the fact of transitoriness. Human drama is concerned with what is valid, required and possible here and now. As we have already suggested, this means that we must simultaneously look up to the norm and look down to things of time. It calls for contemplation and action. In trying to realize goals "here below", we are besieged by a mass of secondary norms that can be like clouds obscuring the sun that surpasses them all. Much that is favorable, useful and advantageous is not good when measured against the absolute; or of a dependent goodness that cannot last. Conversely, in looking up to the absolute, we can become so dazzled that we forget that it is our task to transform the transitory realm. "Holiness", outside biblical religion and its environs, and as many people admire it, is mostly a deliberate self-abandonment to the absolute; the dissolution of that human, finite, mortal shape that,

---

[2] J. Burckhardt, "Die historische Grösse" in *Weltgeschichtliche Betrachtungen*, chap. 5 (Kröner, 1969), 221.

[3] *Ibid.*, 226.

in all its pathos as it stands and continues to stand in the face of the absolute, is, *after all, the truer* shape. Those who want to dissolve into the absolute are trying to dodge playing a role on the world stage.

Having reached this stage, we can venture the Christian affirmation that man, the first Adam, was created with a view to the Second. Not only with a view to God; though true, this is an abbreviation that does not do justice to the creature's authentic autonomy. Man was created with a view to the God-man; in him, the equipoise between the absolute and the relative, which man cannot discover, has been established. True, this equipoise comes from God, since it is his Word that becomes man, but not without the earth giving her noblest fruit to cooperate in the Incarnation. So all the attempts to interpret human existence, from whatever angle, circle around the unattainable point of a "balance" that is no longer unstable but permanent. God alone, because of his absolute superiority, can establish such a balance. Tragically, the attempts that come closest to the truth are usually the most dangerous, because they are the most presumptuous (Icarus and his wings): precisely because they are so sure of success, they fail most fundamentally to grasp the humility of the God who humbles himself in taking the form of man. In one way or another, they equate the created image of God with the divine Archetype; either they proclaim some part of man, or some particular man, to be divine, or they actually believe a God to have appeared in human form, yet without being able to accredit himself by undergoing the decisive test of death. Or, where the rhythm of death and reawakening is read from the cycle of nature and projected into human life, only a mythical figure, not a historical one, can correspond to the ideal image. At its core, the dramatic situation on the world stage is one in which man simultaneously aims at, and is bound to fail to attain, the form that brings fulfillment —insofar as this situation is not determined (positively or negatively) by the context of Jesus Christ. It is impossible to approach the latter in a straight line, for the Fulfiller can only be accepted after he has first been rejected (Jn 1:11–12; 3:11, and so forth). First he must be the rejected One who takes away the guilt of this rejection; only through death can he become the accepted One.

Properly speaking, an inventory should be drawn up of the *basic gestures* of which man is capable on his stage. However, such a task would burst the framework we have set ourselves here; all we can do is indicate a few fragments of such an inventory. Basic gestures are those made in the light of Being as a whole, which is also the light of the good, the true and the beautiful; that is, they are made within the experience of the *analogia entis*. This light, however, also illuminates a process that is extended in time, imparting to it a meaning that is regarded as ultimate. This light that comes down from the absolute can only be received by man's free reason, which is open to the whole of Being, through an act of decision without which we cannot speak of drama at all. Without man's free ability to make decisions, the careering of blind fate is undramatic and subhuman. The fundamental element of all dramatic action on the world stage is man's free intelligence, his intelligent freedom that enables him to receive the "instruction" that comes from the absolute light (an "instruction" that is not distinct from the light and does not restrict it), together with the decision that this intelligent and responsible human being makes, embodying it in the form of history. This very act gives a shape to the continuing stream of events (which is actually unforeseeable); it gives drama a beginning, a middle and an end, as Aristotle required.

An initial element in such a decision can be described as the act of *epistrophē*, of *turning-around* or conversion. In this act, the agent (or patient), driven by intramundane, second-order motives, is finally surrounded like a hunted deer: he becomes the focus of an absolute light and, for the first time, becomes aware of it. Even in Plotinus' view of the world, according to which all things flow from the absolute, the One, and return there, there is this moment of conversion, of reflection, of a change of direction: a man sets out from—and to that extent "flees from"—the good and the true (the One); he turns and (as if for the first time) is pierced by its radiance. In the drama of existence, many different things can provoke such a change of direction. A man can be overwhelmingly convinced, in utter solitude, of the perversity and dire consequences of the direction he has taken hitherto. He can encounter someone who compels him to reflect on his life. Often what brings him to this point is the noise of banging on the closed door of death: this calls a halt to the insane, headlong flight of deeds and thoughts, bathing everything that once seemed important in the pale gleam of futility. An act of this kind concentrates existence into a meaning for which man must finally bear responsibility. Either negatively, as in Don Giovanni's descent to hell, where all the dissipation and confusion of his life heretofore are proclaimed as absolute; or positively, as at the end of Schiller's *Maria Stuart*, where everything is refined and concentrated as the heroine prepares to embrace death in purity; or, as at the end of Calderon's *Life's a Dream*, where a selfish life is abandoned in favor of a life of service—of God, of the world—under the light of eternity. Once again, the act of repentance (of which we have already spoken) plays a major part; again, we see that it can only transform the past on the basis of an interplay between a light that is freely bestowed ("grace") and a free decision that is grounded in insight.

There is a second fundamental gesture. This concerns, not the "I" that changes direction, but the *other* person with whom the "I" hitherto shared an (as yet) unresolved drama, an intramundane drama pulled here and there by passions, calculations and power-relationships. All of a sudden, this relationship is seen in the light of an absolute norm: the norm of the true and the good. At this point, there is a demand for a balance between *justice* and *mercy* or forgiveness; not as if the side of truth called for justice and the side of goodness called for forgiveness: in fact, both truth and goodness demand the *unity* of justice *and* forgiveness. It may be that the hero has to go through the "horrendous gate" of "water and fire" if he is to reach mercy. Many a purgatorial fire is lit on earthly stages. The greatest judgment scenes known to the theatre, the conclusion of Aeschylus' *Eumenides* and the fifth act of Shakespeare's *Measure for Measure*, faithfully represent the indivisible unity of absolute truth and goodness. The absolute rejection we find in Marlowe's *Doctor Faustus* ministers not only to a *just* world order but also, most definitely, to one that is good and trustworthy. But a theatre that is true to life knows nothing of "cheap grace", as is shown by Kleist's *Der Prinz von Homburg* and the many forgiveness-scenes in Shakespeare (cf. *Theo-Drama* I, 465–78). In ultimate decisions of this kind, illuminated by an absolute light, it is a question of the all-embracing value of existence; as a result, death—whether imposed from without or accepted from within—is very much a part, a constituent element of existence. The fact that death can be a part of the action shows the profound seriousness of that interpretation of existence that is set forth on the stage. These two events, conversion and judgment (in justice and mercy), reveal the power of the absolute "light" of Being even outside the Christian realm; for, however much the non-Christian world falls short of the christological "balance" between God and the world, Paul is right to put Gentiles side by side with Jews when it comes to judgment, for "Gentiles who have not the law do by nature what the law requires" and so are "a law unto themselves. . . . They show that what the law requires is written on their hearts, while their conscience also bears witness . . ." (Rom 2:14f.). The Roman plays of Shakespeare, Corneille and Racine illustrate the truth of the foregoing and provide a justification for the endeavors of human dramatists to put on stage, "in a mirror, dimly", a representation of the Last Day.

Shall we regard human *love* as a third gesture, or is it too ambivalent? For at times it seems too light-headed and is too lavish with its avowals of eternity in the realm of transitoriness. And at other times, as Eros, it takes itself deadly seriously and (as in *Tristan*) regards itself as the kernel, as the star, of all things. We may well wonder whether it is possible, in the realm external to Christianity—with which we are exclusively concerned at present, a realm in which the divine love has not yet appeared in human form—for Eros to free itself from the intramundane mists so that the light of the absolute norm may shine through. For the Eros of Plato's Diotima has only indirect reference to the intrahuman sphere, unless we recall the incomparable conclusion of the *Symposium*, where Socrates enfolds the beautiful Alcibiades safe and untouched beneath his cloak. But is this still dramatic? And what of Antigone's love for her dead brother? Is

this still Eros? The same question can be applied to all the great
laments for the dead on the Greek stage—most of all, to the
Trojan Women: Is the issue here that of love, or is it not rather
the elegiac quality of all earthly existence in its ruined state?
All the dramatic transformations whereby transitory passion is
changed into a love for our fellow human beings, a love that can
stand in the face of the judgment of eternity, are found within
the Christian realm: Dante's transformation through the love of
Beatrice, which judges him; Rodrigue's purification by Prouèze,
as she withdraws from him and is changed into a "guiding star".
Both plays show the deaths through which Eros must go if it
is to become the agapē that can stand before the judgment of
eternal Light. Eros is too closely bound up with the earthly succession of generations; it cannot throw off this bond, as Soloviev
thought.[4] This shows the questions that are raised when both
Christians and non-Christians speak as though what they expect
to find in the beyond is a kind of unproblematical continuation
of their earthly bonds, friendships and relationships. All that is
"wood, hay, stubble" must be burned (1 Cor 3:12); and what
man can affirm with all confidence that his love is "gold, silver
and precious stones"?

There is one final gesture, though difficult to articulate in an
extra-Christian context. It is the confident awareness that there
is an absolute light, however beclouded by fate and passion. Man
always reaches out for the ultimate, even while he knows he cannot hold it fast. Or—less attractively—it is the idea that he can
ultimately gain control of this light if he adopts the appropriate attitude (*autarchy*). We can call this stance *hope*, although
the word carries little significance in the non-Christian world
(except where the post-Christian milieu has secularized it). Or,
more aptly, we can call it *resignation*, in the best sense of the
word. Man clings to the absolute anchor in the face of all ruination, all hostile gods (as in the *Odyssey*), all implacable opposing forces (as in *Antigone*), even the power of death itself
(as in *Alcestis*). He resists, even in the midst of collapse, where
nothing is possible any more but the nobility of endurance, as

[4] Cf. *The Glory of the Lord* III, 291f.

at the end of the *Nibelungen*. Man retains his nobility even when the struggle for the noble ideal has become—in an earthly perspective—grotesque, as in *Don Quixote*. Then, in the midst of a finitude that can only yield finite things, there springs up the apparently deluded attempt to embrace the Infinite, a hope that takes all energies captive and is prepared to endure all manner of renunciations, as in the pre-Christian *Quest of the Holy Grail*.[5] (The central theme of the Grail can be traced back to the *Epic of Gilgamesh*; at a deeper level, it is continued in so many of the romances of world literature. Of course, the greatest example of such a hope-inspired endeavor, the *Aeneid*, could only be composed from the perspective of the goal attained, the *urbs condita*; thus the open-ended hope could be interpreted as a clearly defined mission, and every apparent breach of faith could be seen as justified by the greater faithfulness to the divine command. On the periphery of this tribe, with its transcendent mission, stand the Titans who (in the name of what higher instance?) rebel against the gods who so restrict them, raising the question of whether the ruling god represents a legitimate form of the highest good or is only an anticipatory form, a projection on man's part, which should rightly be dethroned by him. Aeschylus' *Prometheus* leaves the question open, but, in the lost conclusion of the trilogy, it must have come down in favor of the latter view.

In the foregoing, we have left to one side all those gestures of existence that are based on equipoise, on the balancing-out of purely creaturely states and attitudes. Where there is laughter, there is also weeping; where joy, sorrow; where birth, death; where power, powerlessness and subjection; where shrewdness, folly; where an openness to the absolute, a closed mind. Where *The Great Theatre of the World* is enacted, it can also be interpreted as *The Great Fair of the World* (according to Calderon): it depends on the distance the observer adopts between himself and the actors and their gestures. We are so deeply involved in this world of opposites that the utopia of an existence without antagonisms—all joy and no suffering, all happiness and no pain

---

[5] *La Quête du Graal, mise en langage moderne par Albert Béguin* (Paris, 1945).

or resistance, all friends and no enemies—however desirable it may seem, is (if we are honest) not even imaginable. Or, if we *can* imagine it, we suspect that it might be tedious. The ancients posited the Golden Age in the past; thus they were able to prepare themselves to face an increasingly difficult and spartan existence. In this they were wiser than the modern utopians, who project the Golden Age into the future. True, the evils of the historical world, which seem only to increase the more man himself takes over the helm of world history, will always present us with meaningful possibilities for partial improvement; we shall always have plenty to do, in the constantly changing conditions; we shall always have tasks in hand that can be justified by reference to the absolute good. But this does not affect the fact that we are acting on a finite stage governed by the law of the dyad, of polarity. This *dyad* always shows itself to be dependent on the *monad*; it presupposes it. But it is essentially incapable of dissolving into the latter. This is how it must be according to the principle of analogy, which, in Christian terms, is the principle of our creatureliness before God. The *ana* of the worldly *logos* is an oscillating movement between poles in accordance with a rhythm set from above (*ano*); the spiritual creature knows that, in its *ana*, it must orientate itself by reference to this *ano*.[6] This means that the final gesture of creaturely being is *yearning*. Plotinus describes it as the essence of the *nous*, Augustine gives it a Christian depth by calling it the essence of the creature, and Thomas formulates it as the *desiderium visionis Dei*, though without attributing any specific faculty for it ("supernatural *existentiale*") to the creature. Michelangelo has expressed this yearning perfectly in his depiction of the creation of Adam. However much, in the mind of God, the first Adam is conceived and created explicitly with a view to the Second, we must beware of regarding the former as the anticipatory form (however covert) of the latter. God desires to be perfectly free in giving his answer to man's yearning question and quest; man must never be able to say, "I always knew it deep down." Naturally, God's answer —which ultimately bears the name of Jesus Christ—must be the fulfillment of Adam's yearning. Thus every "theological"

---

[6] E. Przywara, *Analogia entis*, 2d ed., I (Einsiedeln: Johannes Verlag, 1962), 206.

statement is also an "anthropological" one. But every attempt
to preempt the divine Word on the part of man, in his search
for his own fulfillment, will only lead him farther astray. The
shape adopted by the Word of God shows this most clearly: it
is the *Logos tou staurou*, the Word crucified by men. No man
could have hit upon this in his feeling after God. In fact, once
this Word *was* revealed, the majority rejected it as something
undesirable and troublesome, as pure folly.

3. Death

a. The Search for a Starting Point

The pathos that runs through all gestures of existence reaches a
peak in the riddle of death. Death is the ultimate limit of existence; existence gesticulates in the face of death, and death is its
innermost certainty. Man is part of the biological coming-to-be
and passing-away of all cosmic life; to that extent, his dying is
bound to seem the most natural and familiar thing to him, something he cannot imagine *not* to be there. Yet, since man also looks
up to the norm of the absolute, recognizes it and endeavors to
act accordingly, death brings him back more harshly than ever to
the insoluble mystery, the inner contradiction of his existence:
How can a being that is able to recognize truth and has an obligation to do what is good be swallowed up by the law of the
cosmic cycle? From which angle shall we approach this threatening riddle? On the one hand, there is the naked fact of the
paradox that we described at the outset as "the absolute in the
relative": Should we simply accept the paradox? This is what
the Old Testament did in its classical period. So did the Stoic
doctrine of wisdom, however, which took the biological law of
dying and elevated it into a world principle. Stoicism regarded
those men as sages who attained resignation in the face of the
individual's annihilation in the Total Logos. Or is it an authentic feature of the paradox of existence that it must look beyond
its finite time toward a sphere where the unfinished business of
life is resolved? This would involve looking in two directions.
First, toward a theory that would deduce the violence and cru-

elty of specifically human death from some primal trespass, from a primeval Fall that must somehow be recapitulated, transcended and expiated. Second (and in connection with the former), toward a form of survival at least of that aspect of man that distinguishes him from subhuman cosmic life. In this case, we would be facing the multifarious theories of a "fall" that threaten to devalue the dignity and uniqueness of earthly existence, seeing it as something "unreal". We would also be surrounded by the boundlessly fantastic variety of ideas about the world beyond, which are all manufactured out of images and concepts drawn from concrete, temporal existence and projected into dimensions that are imaginary and timeless. Who can distinguish here between what is part of the anthropological deposit (what J. Pieper calls "sacral revelation") and what is only the effusion of an inflamed imagination that is clutching at "immortality"? There is a third alternative, a Christian one: here the problem of the "first Adam" would be approached from the perspective of the "Second Adam". Even if it be true, however, that the Son of Man holds "the keys of Death and Hades" (Rev 1:18), he does so only because these things *are* realities. The fact that they have been eschatologically overcome does not wipe out the immense and baneful effects they have had upon world history. And, as for this "overcoming" itself, the Second Adam's Cross, death and descent into Hades show that death *did* exercise a position of supremacy in the world prior to Christ, a supremacy he acknowledged.

From a methodological point of view, therefore, it would be wrong to start with the substance of the Christian faith and its picture of man. One thinks of Gabriel Marcel's treatment of this subject, which, from a Christian viewpoint, is so convincing: finite existence is burst, exploded by acts of love toward a "thou" who is loved genuinely and not merely erotically;[1] one thinks of F. Wiplinger's passionate heightening of this perspective;[2] one thinks of the many relevant plays—by Claudel,

---

[1] *Gegenwart und Unsterblichkeit* (Frankfurt, 1961); "Tod und Unsterblichkeit" in *Auf der Suche nach Wahrheit und Gerechtigkeit* (Frankfurt, 1964), and also Marcel's plays, cf. *Theo-Drama* I, 379f., 388f., 395.

[2] *Der personal verstandene Tod* (Freiburg/Munich: Alber, 1970).

Bernanos, Wilder, and so forth—mentioned in the *Prolegomena*.[3] In all these cases, a light is shed on the riddle of death; death's absolute veil is lifted a little, in some fashion at least. But it remains linked to the destiny of the Son of Man. If the key position of this destiny is denied, the curtains come down even more impenetrably than before; moreover, even the light shone by mythical imagination upon man's countenance is extinguished. All that remains are the techniques of para-psychology, characteristic of the post-Christian era, which try to penetrate the realm concealed by death. This is a despicable attempt to drag this realm, which is inaccessible to man, down to the level of the here-and-now. A similar technique is the attempt to reactivate earlier existences; this involves a demythologized doctrine of the transmigration of souls. It opposes the Christian idea of the absolute uniqueness of the person and his destiny, seeking to dissolve it back into the pre-Christian understanding of the individual as a mere (personless) subjectivity. The most influential philosophies of modern times, as we shall see, have already retreated to this position.

In our attempts to find a starting point, therefore, we are driven back, after all, beyond the Christian faith and the multifarious pagan fantasies concerning the "other world", to our first position: we must stay with the paradox as it is most impressively embodied by the classical Old Testament. Here death is only the conclusion of man's being alive; mortal man stands before Yahweh, the God of the living, with whom he is covenanted. He does not claim any other prerogative (that is, "eternal life") beyond the salvation promised by this covenant. This, according to the biblical perspective, is evidently the right way to approach the definitive, God-given answer to the paradox of the "first Adam". This answer is the event of the incarnate Word. In a certain sense, it is no misfortune if, after the age of pagan religions, with their proliferating self-projections into the world beyond, man's thought has to be brought back willingly or not to this starting point, distorted in many ways though it may be, since it lacks faith in the living God of the covenant.

Israel found it very difficult to persevere in this attitude; it was hard to renounce additional demands on God and simply to

---

[3] *Theo-Drama* I, 392ff.

accept the gift of the covenant that God offered *now*. So Israel began to cock an eye at other gods who no doubt offered more prospects in the world beyond; it was attracted to the cult of the dead, so strictly proscribed in Israel. Slowly, on the basis of the word of God itself, certain anticipations of the ultimate revelation were unveiled: the prospect of a resurrection of Israel in its entirety at the end of time (Ezek 37); individuals would be raised to "eternal life" and "eternal shame" (Dan 12); and death would be destroyed forever (Is 25:8). This points ahead to something that will be fulfilled in the Resurrection of Jesus (and in his scars) as a promise of universal application: God will keep safe not only the "immortal soul" but also the entire temporal being of living, mortal man. We shall return to this theme at the end of the present section.

However, two things militate against our adopting the starting point of the classical Old Covenant. First of all, there is the problem—becoming more and more explicit as Israel's history unfolds—of the connection between death and (primal) guilt. The second account of creation links the two: death is the punishment for the desire, insinuated by the Tempter, to be equal to God. The Book of Wisdom concurs: "God did not create death" (Wis 1:13); "through envy of the devil death came into the world" (Wis 2:24). Paul continues this line of thought: "Through sin death came into the world" (Rom 5:12); in fact, it entered into the whole cosmos, which, because of man's fall, "was subjected to futility, not of its own will" (Rom 8:20f.). This is a topic of wide implications; it anticipates the following chapter. Thus death stands, inextricably, between nature and un-nature. All theological attempts to separate what is negative and un-natural in death from some positive, natural state that would have been "Adam's", had he not sinned, are highly fantastic. And what a mountain of questions remains! If we are to understand death as a punishment,[4] why are innocent children punished (Ivan Karamazov, Camus)? Why are nature's living things thus punished (assuming that, at a notional level, death can be abstracted from the sphere of living organisms)?

[4] The central thesis in J. Pieper's *Tod und Unsterblichkeit* (Munich: Kösel, 1968), 91ff.

The classical Old Covenant cannot be reconstituted once the myths of the world beyond, and the Christian faith, have been dissolved. For it presupposes the absolute relationship to the living God of the covenant, a relationship that is so strong that, as far as the devout are concerned, it renders the thought of death bearable. In the post-Christian world, the paradox of existence appears without cosmetics, more naked than ever— and the paradox, as we know, posits the existence of (absolute) meaning within the realm of transience. When this happens, something uncanny takes place: either meaning is shifted to the encounter with death itself, or the "absurd" is elevated to the rank of "meaning" (which thus lies in complete freedom from any binding meaning). Or, finally, there is the post-philosophical renunciation of all possibility of discovering any spiritual meaning whatsoever, in the theory of the "natural death".

Since all mythical pictures of the world beyond have faded, and the "postulates" of survival (put forward on the basis of the paradox of existence) cannot, of their essence, be fulfilled, the decisive dialogue is carried on between the Christian and the post-Christian view of death. This dialogue concerning the meaning of existence is conducted on the very edge; one step too many would result in a plunge into pure meaninglessness. It is here, therefore, that the drama that takes place on the world stage attains a peak of intensity.

b. My Death; Our Death

The tension between "my death" and "our death" is only the ultimate consequence of that between "my time" and "our time". We have already described the latter tension, expressly restricting it to the finitude of these two "times". A further aspect emerges here, however: our way of possessing time, and of dying, presupposes the distinctively human connection between organic life and spiritual being. Insofar as we participate in the total organic life of the cosmos, and are ourselves a product of this life, our death has an utterly everyday quality. It is only one "incidence" of death among countless others, occurring every moment. But I can and must adopt a personal attitude to my own dying, to the fact that I shall not be there any more—something of which I am absolutely certain, though the timing of it is uncertain—and to this extent my death is quite different from an "incidence". It is the most lonely encounter with my I-that-is-no-longer, an encounter that sheds a light of absolute seriousness on everything I am still able to experience in the time that remains to me. Kierkegaard: "It is a serious matter really to think of death, to think of it as your destiny, and to realize that in doing so you are doing something that death cannot do, that is, know both that you are and that death is."[5] In this way, death "becomes a reality"—indeed, an inexplicable reality—"in the life of the living".[6] Heidegger develops this by saying that existence's attitude to its own death is a contemplation of its own (possible) impossibility.[7] Insofar as, within its own horizon, it "reveals itself as the *possibility that is one's ownmost, that is nonrelational and that is not to be outstripped [unüberholbare]*",[8] it can never, by its very nature, grasp itself as a totality of being: "Its Being is annihilated when what is still outstanding in its Being has been liquidated."[9] Man's being is bound for death; it is always dying (even if it represses the fact, keeping it at arms' length and treating it as a "case"). This dying is essentially different from the biological "end". That is why, as in Kierkegaard, it is unavoidably permeated by *Angst*. For, within the horizon of what "no longer" is, there is nothing left to be realized; we must simply endure the mere possibility. For Heidegger, this courage in *Angst* is "freedom toward death".[10] But, as he later goes on to show in more detail, it is precisely by thus entering nothingness and standing forth in it that we come to understand the meaning of being as such: a light that comes from the absolute falls on finite existence. Let this be enough for the present. It is not our business, reflecting as we are upon existence in the world, to attempt to see beyond the limits of this paradox.

[5] "An einem Grabe" in *Erbauliche Reden 1844/45* (*Werke*, ed. E. Hirsch [Diederichs, 1952]), 178.

[6] *Ibid.*, 200.

[7] "Death is the possibility of the absolute impossibility of Dasein": *Being and Time*, sec. 50, tr. John Macquarrie and Edward Robinson (Oxford, 1962), 294.

[8] *Ibid.*

[9] *Ibid.*, sec. 46, 280.

[10] *Ibid.*, sec. 53, 311.

This sets us on the way to a penetrating analysis of death's loneliness and its power to dominate the whole of existence. Our steps are directed back to the classical Old Testament: "Happiness enough, to have lived for a time in the sun of the divine covenant!", but also to the many utterances of ancient philosophy, which treat this experience of *being* in finite life as a sufficient justification for existence, for "having been there" [*Da(gewesen)sein*]. As for the individual finite being [*Wesen*] that has actually glimpsed this light of being [*Sein*], it can consider itself blessed when it is reabsorbed into the infinite light, the Logos, the One, Nirvana.

Jaspers too is on this journey into the past. In borderline situations of which death is one, existence [*ek-sistence*] "stands out" beyond all that is of the world, beyond all utility; in a "moment" of existential (not biological) *Angst*, it glimpses being and thus has a foothold beyond temporal dying. True, this is not something that happens once for all; existential *Angst* alternates with biological (which is preoccupied with the fear of extinction); all the same, there are repeated "moments" of *ek-sistence* in which death appears not only as an enemy but also as a friend. Jaspers does not allow us to envisage any other kind of "immortality".[11] Jaspers, a thoroughly modern man, has often (influenced by his wife) dipped into the world of the Old Testament and reflected upon its renunciation of the idea of individual survival beyond death. Great Jewish thinkers of later ages have held fast to this renunciation, including Maimonides,[12] Spinoza and Buber. But we must remember that classical Jewish thought (to which these three do not really belong) is exercised by the *nation*. It is the *nation* that is the subject of such thought; the individual identifies himself with it as far as he is able; the covenant is not concluded with the individual but with the people as a whole. And—if we exclude Plato—we can say something similar of the ancient world: the individual is primarily a product of the *physis* or *archē*; this is its center of gravity and its ground. It looks forward, after its transitory existence,

[11] *Philosophie*, 2d ed. (Springer, 1948), 483–91.
[12] *Mose Ben Maimon, Führer der Unschlüssigen*, ed. A. Weiss (Meiner, 1923), CCLVIII.

to being reabsorbed and reincorporated, and perhaps—where the idea of cosmic recurrence predominates—to being then reborn. Anaximandros' celebrated dictum,[13] though baffling, sees the emergence of the individual from the original ground as a kind of sin, which spreads its effect through finite things and is expiated through death: "The beginning and origin of existent things is the *apeiron* (that which is beyond all limits and cannot be defined). The source from which all existent things come into being is the same source to which they return as they perish through their culpability. For they mete out just punishments to one another on account of their unrighteousness, according to the laws of time." Close to this view is that of Heraclitus, namely, that war is the father of all things, even if the Sage of Ephesus includes growth and disintegration, Eros and Hades, in the one, harmonious revolving of the universe. Parmenides regards the identity of *being* in everything that comes to be as the only reality, with the result that birth and death sink to the level of mere appearance: "How could what *is* pass away or come into existence?"[14] According to Plato, individual souls share in this *being* that is above all coming-to-be, but for the most part he envisages them, after being judged with regard to their past life, entering once again into the cycle of rebirth. He also entertains the idea that man may be brought back into the divine sphere. However, Plato's intuition persists only with difficulty; in his maturity, Aristotle becomes quite indecipherable when he speaks of man being superior to transitoriness; and moderate Stoicism (Panaitios) gives up the notion of individual "immortality" in favor of a return to the eternal universe, urging equanimity in the face of death. Poseidonios endeavors to build Platonic elements into Stoicism, and Cicero, stimulated to engage in philosophy by the death of his daughter, finds consolation in Plato's *Phaedo* but remains in doubt about "immortality". It is the same with Seneca: fundamentally, individuality is suffering, and dissolution into the Whole brings liberation: "We too are first ignited and then extinguished; between these two events we must suffer a little, but beforehand and afterward there is deep

---

[13] Diels I, 89.
[14] Frg. 8; Diels I, 236.

peace."[15] Epicurus puts forward the Sophist doctrine that death does not concern us, for the dying man is still alive, and the dead man no longer feels anything; the fear of death is therefore groundless. Lucretius says that the fear of a judgment in the world beyond is basically nothing but fear of nonbeing. These latter two represent the decline into materialism of the ancient universe-piety, which strove to give absolute precedence to the Whole, the absolute, over everything individual and transitory.[16]

It is impossible, however, for post-Christian man to return to the comfortable security of being part of a chosen people (as in Judaism) or of an all-embracing, divine world of nature (as in paganism). Now the individual experiences himself not only merely as an individual but also as a person. And where personal death is concerned, the philosophies of death no longer present themselves as palliatives, taking the sting out of death by proposing a (Platonic) "immortality" or a (Stoic) home in the universe: on the contrary, they portray death as the most powerful stimulant for utter finitude, enabling it to stand forth, unsupported and unadorned, in nothingness (and hence in *being*). As we saw in Heidegger, this "standing forth" is seen as the true origin of freedom. So it is in Weischedel's sceptical philosophy, which considers that the radical questionability of all philosophical positions calls for a fundamental ethical attitude of "farewell"; this opens up freedom, yet it is a freedom that puts a bar on any radical initiative in life.[17] By contrast, this freedom can be absolutized as the revolt of man's spirit against the absurdity of a death that overtakes us from outside (as Sartre and Camus do in their different ways); or it can be seen (as Adorno does) as a desperate cry for "release" or "redemption" —against all expectation—from the absurd contradiction of existence. These are all modes of what Kierkegaard referred to as "seriousness" in the face of personal, lonely death; a death that, in the wake of Christianity, is experienced much more acutely than before.

[15] Letter to Lucilius, 54, 4f.
[16] On this whole issue: J. Choron, *Der Tod im abendländischen Denken* (Stuttgart, 1967); G. Scherer, *Das Problem des Todes in der Philosophie* (Darmstadt, 1979)— particularly valuable for its conciseness and full documentation.
[17] *Skeptische Ethik* (Frankfurt/Mainz, 1976).

A final remark on this point. Something else has become impossible in the post-Christian situation, something that once linked Jewish and pagan thought, namely, the linking of the mystery of death and the mystery of birth. For birth, although less philosophical attention is devoted to it, is no less a mystery than death. The human being's coming-to-be is due to the race; he comes from a line of descent and can beget and give birth to new members in that line. The biological factor has preeminence among the causes of man's coming-to-be. Nonetheless, the conscious subject has a transcendence that draws him toward the absolute, and this means that he can never attribute himself exclusively to this biological causality. His origins are deeper; he comes from the source of the light that irradiates him. (Paul Häberlin has expressly drawn attention to this mystery of birth.) For the Hebrew mind, there was no contradiction in individual existence feeling safe and secure in the bosom of the nation; as well as the dreary images of Sheol, there is the idea of being "gathered to one's fathers" in the "bosom of Abraham". The pagan mind envisaged this same individual existence returning to the womb of *physis* that had given it birth. But this presupposes a mythical way of thought according to which nature, in its cycle of death and becoming, is essentially divine. Post-Christian man cannot return to this twofold security. The maternal womb that gives birth is a living, fashioning warmth; the grave that receives the corpse is cold and brings disintegration. For us who think in terms of the person, there is no longer any analogy.

Is there an alternative to understanding death in these personal categories?

Yes. There is "our death". There is death as the most everyday occurrence: the dying of old people and sometimes of the young; death in hospitals, death in the newspaper columns, in the statistics of "crime and accidents", and in wars and concentration camps. This is collective death; it is no longer my own, absolutely solitary death; or rather, the solitary nature of it is of no significance here. It is just that "one dies"; this, according to Heidegger, is no longer an existential certainty but an empirical certainty. People tinker with this death, just as they tinker with procreation and birth. It is death seen as a medical problem

("Precisely when does the human being die?" "When should the human being be allowed to die?" "Is passive, or even active, euthanasia permissible?", and so forth). As far as this death is concerned, it is not clear why man, endowed with freedom as he is, should not be allowed to organize and manipulate it. Viewed in this perspective, death has no relation to, or dependence on, any guilt. Nor has it any relation to the metaphysical fact already referred to, namely, that the inscribing of absolute acts and values on a transitory medium is an immense paradox crying out for an interpretation. In the "post-metaphysical age", the only ideal is that of the "natural", "salutary" death (a view put forward as early as Ludwig Feuerbach). This ideal death occurs "at a great age, when a man has had enough of life, as we read in the Old Testament of the Patriarchs and other men who enjoyed God's blessing." A man can be justified in wishing for such a death, provided that "in his wishes and ideas he remains true to human nature".[18]

However, this so-called "natural death", which is accepted wherever a limitedly biological or materialistic view of man is dominant,[19] is "in reality the most artificial death, for it is the fruit of the most refined self-manipulation of man and his environment".[20] It rarely occurs "of its own accord"; medical technology and other forms of life-support are involved to a considerable extent. As G. Scherer rightly perceives, what the idea of the "natural death" has in view is "mastery" of death. This was the case in Stoicism and Epicureanism; now it is promoted

---

[18] *Sämtliche Werke* X, 234f.

[19] A shattering example of this is Walter Schulz, "Wandlungen der Einstellung zum Tod" in J. Schwartländer, *Der Mensch und sein Tod* (Kl. Vandenhoeck-Reihe 1426, 1976), 94ff. "The fact that the human being must ultimately pass away shows human existence to be directionless, lacking in context and lacking any abiding influence" (106). Looking back to Kierkegaard's existential understanding of death: "As far as I am concerned, my death seems the one essential thing, yet I know that my case is only one instance [!] of universal death." "Human death, man's decline and coming-to-an-end, is also an objective process in time" (102). "The biological interpretation of man is a scientifically secure foundation; from its vantage point, death must be regarded as a purely natural process. . . . Metaphysics is an episode; the more it develops, the more it hastens toward its extinction" (99).

[20] J. Schwartländer, 21.

under the banner of technology. However, all such technology can do is to postpone death, which means that man remains a research-object; once further experiments begin to prove unrewarding, he is left to die in a frighteningly inhuman way. In the age of technology, those who are dying or dead are left out of account since they are no longer of any use; heedless, the race pursues its advance and tramples over their graves. Death is publicly suppressed; it is treated as an irrelevance and pushed to the margin of consciousness. The individual follows the public example. The post-Christian philosophy of recent centuries is largely of the opinion that the individual has no right to expect his individuality to be "immortalized"; it should be enough for him to have made some small contribution to the race's destiny, and he should be content to be allowed to give his individuality back to the cosmos—its source. Significantly, this is true of Idealist philosophy, such as that of Fichte or Hegel or Schopenhauer, just as much as of materialist philosophy.

In Fichte, even in his later, religious period, knowing ("spirit") is only an appearance, an image of absolute life. Consequently, it cannot itself claim to be absolute; in fact, if it *does*, it thereby separates itself from life. Even the moves Fichte made in the direction of "dialogism" (the "Realm of the Spirits") fail to overcome this fundamental principle, which—close to Plotinus as it is—calls for all individual *Gestalten* to be swallowed up in infinite life.

The whole pathos of the Hegelian "sublation" tends in the same direction. Certainly, he speaks of the spirit permeating all stages of "I"-consciousness and shared humanity; indeed, Hegel emphasizes that the absolute Idea's self-expropriation—and its adoption of the categories of nature and history—becomes visible in the destiny of one man, Jesus Christ. In the end, however, this is only the visible appearance of a basic spiritual law, namely, that if there is to be a uniting of the "infinite with the finite", the finite must not cling to itself: it must surrender to the infinite. In the realm of religion, too, Jesus' actual Resurrection takes place in the spirit of the community; all religion, seen as a mode of perception, is nothing but an inchoate form of absolute knowledge.

Schopenhauer denies the blind, aimless "will" and its instruments as well as cognitive individuals (who ultimately realize that their desires for happiness cannot be satisfied). Here the individual is bound to tend toward self-dissolution. He "does not demand any personal continuance. He willingly gives up existence as we know it. What, instead of it, he receives and becomes seems nothing in our eyes; that is because, in comparison, our existence is nothing, what Buddhism calls Nirvana, that is, 'that which is extinguished' ".[21]

For Marxists, death is simply the last gesture the individual is able to make. This is particularly the case where such death is undergone for the sake of the social program. This gesture is performed without the strings and claims of Christian martyrdom (E. Bloch),[22] since there is no suggestion of personal reward or personal continuance.

However, where the individual magnanimously surrenders his claim to the unique dignity of his person, he cannot expect society—particularly technocratic society—to respect this dignity. Individuals exist in their hundreds of thousands, and in such a society they can only be its "material"; society will maintain them and control their numbers; it will design factory procedures to annihilate them. That is the age in which we live.

As we have seen, the renunciation of the tension between "my death" and "our death" (which corresponds to that between "my time" and "our time") in favor of a one-sided focusing on "our" death (at the level of the race) only *seems* to diminish the problem of the meaning of death and the connected problem of the meaning of life and existence (in the idea of the "natural death"). In reality, it infinitely intensifies the problem. For the central paradox of existence, called as it is to recognize and implement the absolute in the relative, is regarded as insignificant and simply pushed to one side. On the world stage, this was the real unsolved riddle; now, in a baffling renunciation of thought, it is supinely accepted as a neutral fact that needs no further explanation. The post-Christian age brings about the demise of all mythical and "sacral" revelation concerning man's ultimate

---

[21] *Die Welt als Wille und Vorstellung* in *Werke* 3, ed. Frauenstädt, 583 (the conclusion of the long chapter on death).

[22] *Das Prinzip Hoffnung* (Frankfurt, 1959), 1378. Further discussion in G. Scherer, *Der Tod als Frage an die Freiheit* (Essen, 1971), 32–52.

destiny; at the same time, we discern the unsatisfactory nature of the dualistic philosophy that regarded man as a composite of a mortal part (the body) and an immortal part (the soul), since in reality the human being dies as a body/soul totality. Taken together, these two factors would seem to commend a resigned acceptance of the absurdity of an existence that is both unfulfilled and unfulfillable; either we yield to the increasing dominance of the collective, or we cling, in *Angst*, to an existential "freedom unto death" that is bent back upon itself.

Yet, are we not due an explanation for the stark contrast between the obscurity of man's beginning and ending (at the level of both the individual and the generality) and the clarity with which, at the height of his consciousness, man can distinguish between true and false? And what of the equally stark contrast between the torpor and violence of nature that forms man's infrastructure and his irrefutably luminous awareness that good and evil are irreconcilable? Does not this too call for an explanation? Nor can man himself provide a satisfactory explanation, however he tries; he cannot even come up with an adequate idea of it: his conclusions never add up. This objection applies to his metaphysical reflection on the separation of soul and body (which, after he has died, is left as a lifeless and decomposing "piece of evidence"), for man does not want to be merely a "soul" that survives somewhere or other: he wants to be taken seriously as the flesh-and-blood man he is. It also applies to the theology of the transmigration of souls, according to which man carries over a debit from his earlier existence: man wants to be judged by his unique, free decisions (even if there are many respects in which he has failed in life), and not by the free actions of some unknown "other". Nor is he interested in this temporal, limited existence being prolonged, in time or out of time, after his death—not even if only the agreeable aspects were to be prolonged; for it is in *this* finitude that he came to be and became what he is. He is like a piece of music, which only makes sense in its finite extension; if it were drawn out into infinity it would be unbearable. Nor is it simply a case, when his life has run its course, of having good and bad marks apportioned to him with regard to his achievements, as in a pupil's report at the end of the school year: life is quite different from cramming for an examination. A man's most substantial experiences and decisions have a value that is intrinsic. But what if, after this life, he were to be offered a different, more fulfilling life, freed from the fear of death? This too, a man might say, could devalue his mysterious, here-and-now, mortal existence, through which, as through a blanket of cloud, the light of the true and the good has actually penetrated. Moreover, was it not the times of suffering that opened life's deepest experiences to him?

What, then, in the face of death, becomes of those gestures of existence that we see enacted on the world stage? This raises the question of meaning in a way that cannot be avoided, for "gesture" implies "meaning". We cannot claim that life's full meaning is the sum of gestures in any one life, nor is the cynic right to say that the sum of the fragments of meaning is nil, that is, meaninglessness. In this difficulty we are best advised to use Kant's word: the *postulate*. It is not really man as such who steps forward in the presence of the absolute (whose face he does not know), categorically demanding the solution that is worthy of him. Was he not freely given existence? It is actually his own *given-ness* that calls for clarification, as it would continue to do even if, out of weariness or ennui, man were to renounce every postulate. Existence itself can only stammer its request for clarification, for it has no words of self-justification. There we have it: it requires to be taken seriously in its finitude and justified in the face of the absolute—and there is always much to be judged and condemned. This justification must take place from within, on the basis of its own substance; it must not be "attributed" externally. All the same, this justification is not something it can give itself; indeed, it cannot even envisage it; it must be *given*, as grace and as affirmation. The pathos of the world stage reaches thus far and not a step farther.

At this point we must say a word about Christianity's answer, but only by way of anticipating something that will be set forth in the third, next part of this book, on the subject of "acting from within God's pathos". For there is so much pathos in our transitory life that any answer to it must itself involve pathology or pathos. Such an answer, which cannot be deduced or guessed at in advance, can only come from the absolute; in Christian

terms, it must be given by the living God. And the most im-
probable thing of all is that God does not provide the answer
from outside, from above—like the Spectator-Judge who sits
in state above the Calderonesque world drama—but comes on
stage practically incognito and takes part in the action. He wants
to share not only finitude, with all its happiness and sorrow, but
also the human demise, human collapse and death. This being
the case, existence will not be able to complain that its own
intrinsic significance has been overlooked.

If the impossible happens; if the absolute not only irradiates
finitude but actually *becomes* finite, something unimaginable happens to existence: what is finite, as such, is drawn into what is
ultimate and eternal; what is finite in its temporal extension,
in each one of its moments and their interconnection, and not
merely, for instance, in its final result. The finite, because of its
insight into the true and the good, was always the recipient of
radiance from the absolute; on the other hand, time kept running on, and no moment could hold fast to this radiance and,
as it were, empty it out. Nothing could be exhaustively experienced in its full, eternal dimensions: there always remained a
promise, an unplumbed residue. The "I"—our way of denot-
ing and knowing ourselves—could never say that it filled the
present, that it had made itself fully present. Except in one case,
the case of him who was God's answer: he adopted finitude's
questioning gestures and succeeded in living out our transitory
existence in an ultimate and eternal way. The fact that there *is* this
answering Word of God, who has immersed himself in finitude
and transitoriness (that is, "flesh"), is the heart of the Christian
faith. Moreover, this Word of God also took upon himself our
death, which is an essential part of our existence; he accepted the
inherent tension between "my death", which I anticipate with
fear, and "our death", which is part of our nature as a species. He
fully lived out this death; indeed, since he himself was the absolute Word, he plumbed the abyss of our death far more deeply
than we could ever do. And that is the absolute center of the
heart of the Christian faith. He is the only one who has come
"from above" to provide an answer to the questions of all of
us who are "from below" (Jn 3:13; 8:23), and as such he can
endow the finite with full, eternal significance. And not only

as far as he himself is concerned: for his absolute life and death apply to and affect the entire human race; they are designed to give all a share in this preponderance of eternity, this value in God's sight. His own unique death was the most *lonely* anyone had ever undergone, yet, since he was the absolute answer, he could make it the most *communicable* death: all can share in it. How we are to imagine this will be discussed thoroughly in what follows.

If this is true, we can understand why the prehistory of this event must first of all be purified of all human projections and mythical anticipations of a solution. Thus, in the classical Old Covenant, we have nothing but the naked encounter between mortal man and the absolute God in a covenant that binds them to one another. It did not matter whether man was glad of the light that comes to him from God or, like Job, complained about his finitude; it did not matter whether he confronted God with the unbearable nature of an existence full of suffering, or even, like Qoheleth, wrapped all worldly existence in his tragic scepticism. The question had to be clearly heard in all its pathos.

In addition, it was necessary for man to put forward the postulate that mortality cannot solve all questions. In his death cell, Socrates could talk with his friends about the imperishable nature of existence, and again it did not matter that he was mistaken in many points: unaware that the soul is created, he thought that only that which has-not-come-into-being could be immortal; he did not realize that existence is utterly unique (for its uniqueness is ultimately grasped only in connection with the Word-made-flesh) and so thought in terms of reincarnation. However, he saw very clearly that man, who knows and does both good and evil, must submit his whole existence to judgment; this alone can decide his ultimate destiny. This insight, that is, that there must be a solution that goes beyond existence, a solution that comes down from above, is not only permissible: as we have shown, it is actually immanent in finite existence. This means that the Protestant view, which says that the biblical "resurrection of the dead" precludes philosophical reflection on something allegedly imperishable in man and involves the complete destruction of man, body and soul, in death, contradicts the nature of man as he actually has been created.

At the limit, Jewish apocalyptic, which goes beyond the classical Old Testament position, raises the notion of a resurrection at the end-time; it too postulates and looks forward to an answer that is to come. Everywhere in the broad milieu of the religions, we find this aspiration to immortality and a participation in the life of the absolute; but we must distinguish between the aspiration, the postulate, as such, which cannot be prevented, and the anticipated solutions, which are partly fantastic and partly presumptuous.

What becomes visible in the event of the incarnate Word—"resurrection from the dead"—is not a continuation, in the yonder realm, of earthly existence. This would necessarily have the effect of relativizing earthly existence. "Resurrection from the dead" demonstrates the eternity-content and eternal dignity of an existence that is lived and died in bodily terms and is unique in each case. Nor does it attain this dignity and significance only at the *end* of chronological world time: it has this quality in the very *midst* of world time and *perpendicular* to it. Paradoxically, Jesus' entire existence, once it has been rendered eternal, demonstrates the ultimate quality not only of his deeds and sufferings in time but also, specifically, of his death. But this permanent, definitive nature of his death on the Cross, which will be "proclaimed" until the end of the world (1 Cor 11:26), is permeated by the word of God. For it is the word of God that gives a reply to his question ("My God, why have you forsaken me?"); this same word of God plumbs the very depths of the Son's question, yet in final obedience to the God who sends forth his word. Thus, in the midst of the forsaken Son's questioning, God himself supplies the answer. It is the only possible, the only valid answer. By comparison, every answer proposed by man, after all his brooding and philosophizing, simply falls short. He who is the Word has posed a question—a question that has been raised to absolute significance—in the name of all others who ask it, and this question has pierced the heart of God like an arrow: God's heart opens to reveal the answer.

What is guaranteed by the answer is this: existence in all its gravity can be embraced and kept safe by God's sphere. And it is not merely that its radiant moments are thus lifted into the divine sphere, while the painful moments are sifted out and thrown away. No: the totality is "transfigured", and its meaning is shown in its true light. It is true to say, of course, of this process of re-creation, that "God will wipe away every tear from their eyes, and death shall be no more, neither shall there be mourning nor crying nor pain any more, for the former things have passed away" (Rev 21:4). And it is also true, as Paul says, that "this slight momentary affliction is preparing for us an eternal weight of glory beyond all comparison" (2 Cor 4:17). But nonetheless it is the *tear* that actually elicits the wiping away: it is the "slight momentary affliction" that prepares and *actually brings about* the "weight of glory".

D. FREEDOM, POWER AND EVIL

1. Freedom

The classical gestures surrounding the riddle of death do not fully express the ultimate tensions of the drama of human existence. There is still that horrific and demonic realm that is manifested when pseudo-omnipotent evil unfolds on the world stage—a realm of powers and possibilities that multiply, like the heads of the Hydra, the more they are attacked. These powers and possibilities oppress man's life with torments quite different from the threats posed by death. Everyone knows that the powers of evil are not simply alien and external to him; everyone knows that there is a shaft in him that reaches down to the deepest abysses. Thus he stands in a baffling solidarity with the powers and superior forces of negativity that are ravaging the world around him, while at the same time he is fighting off these same powers as far as he can. They are *powers*: evil is always connected with power, with acquiring power over available natural energies in things and in man's mind, in order to achieve dominance. Consequently, it is often hard to know how far we are threatened and overruled by neutral powers, and how far such threats are put forth by a free intelligence that is manipulating these powers. Man may ask whether, behind the destructive cosmic powers, there is a free intelligence unmistakably bent on evil— the "powers and principalities" of which Paul speaks—but no clear answer is forthcoming.

At least in his own historical area, however, man can detect the interrelationships between freedom, power and evil. He knows from his own experience of himself that evil in the world comes from freedom, a freedom that uses whatever power is available —its own power or someone else's. This power is not intrinsically evil but contains a temptation to evil insofar as it represents a means of domination.

In discussing evil, we need to start with finite freedom. This has been treated in detail in the second volume of *Theo-Drama*, although there we deliberately excluded the evil it occasions, merely noting the points at which evil is wont to emerge. Here it must suffice to recap the earlier discussion as briefly as possible. But where should we begin? With the formal relationship between finite and infinite freedom (that is, in Christian terms, with the problem of creatureliness as such, to which a purely philosophical answer would be sought)? Or should we begin with the relationship between the creature and an infinite freedom that has revealed itself to the creature (that is, in Christian terms, with the fact of a self-revelation freely undertaken by God, which is the subject matter of theology, or rather, of a theologically schooled philosophy)? For the Christian, such a self-revelation on God's part has in fact occurred; indeed, since creation as a whole, and in particular the creation of finite freedom, is always carried out with a view to this self-revelation on God's part, it seems appropriate to start with the second relationship, which has already been shaped by theology. And, if this is the case, if man is the recipient of an essentially super-natural, divine self-revelation (that is, it is not a human postulate), must we not go on to say that God must have anticipated this communication by endowing man, through grace, with a "supernatural *existentiale*" that transcends his creaturely horizon? Otherwise how could man "match up" to this self-disclosure on the part of the Absolute? That being so, how wide would be the scope of created freedom as such? Or how narrow? After all we have said, it is impossible to restrict it to purely internal mundane matters: the paradox of the creature has always included the openness of the totality of being, and hence it has also included truth and goodness as absolute categories. How far do the consequences of such a disclosure extend? At least as far as the ability of finite freedom to decide for or against the norm of an absolute freedom. This applies however veiled or unveiled this norm may be, and however veiled or unveiled we envisage man's response to God's free self-manifestation. Such reflection on the fundamental creaturely form of freedom and its possibilities is all the more necessary since sober examination of world history in the concrete shows us two things. First, by no means the majority of people outside the biblical world, then as now, make an automatic connection between the subjectivity of their finite "I" and an alleged absolute Subject (most forms of Asiatic religion, for instance). Second, post-Christian ideologies (in part arising out of the former situation, for example, China) emphatically reject such a conclusion, regarding it as the ultimate betrayal of human freedom. These two things should make us very careful not to overestimate the influence, in point of fact, of a "supernatural *existentiale*".

Let us briefly summarize our earlier findings. Although we cannot deny that finite freedom has an absolute aspect, it has power over neither its own ground nor its own fulfillment. It does possess itself, yet it is not its own gift to itself: it owes itself to some other origin. Thus it can never catch up with its own ground, nor with its essence;[1] it can only attain fulfillment beyond itself. Moreover, if it is to be itself, it must be continually setting forth for that yonder shore, which initially can be described as the pure manifestation of the totality of being, the manifestation of sheer truth and goodness. All this is infallibly present in the *reflexio completa* once consciousness has awakened. What is consciousness? It is being [*Sein*] that is aware of its indebtedness to a source beyond itself; discerning being [*Sein*] and "letting-be" [*Sein-Lassen*], it affirms everything that is, or may yet be, in being. Insofar as it is bound to affirm its indebtedness, consciousness cannot equate itself with absolute Being; it is only an "image" of this absolute, necessarily related to it since the absolute is its elusive "whence" and "whither". This becomes particularly clear when it reflects on "the good": it possesses itself *as* self-consciousness (and not due to its own efforts, for it is grounded elsewhere), pointing to the fact that its ground is sheer goodness. In the same way, by reflecting on its own essence and looking beyond its existence to an absolute norm of goodness —and thus acquiring a measuring rod for the implementation of goodness under finite conditions—it indicates that its ultimate goal is goodness itself. At the same time, however, consciousness clearly realizes that there is a connection between the good (and the true) and its own self-possession, self-realization.

[1] B. Welte (*Über das Böse*, Quaest. Disp. 6, [1959]), following St. Thomas, has put the paradox of finite freedom very pointedly: he says that man "remains defined by infinity in his irreducible *essence*, and thus, on account of his essence, in a certain sense, he 'is' God . . . , yet, in his *existence*, he can never be such in an undiminished way *in actu perfecto*" (19).

This is bound to suggest the idea that the absolute (of which consciousness is an image) must itself be self-possession, that is, Spirit. Especially since this absolute is good not only *for me* but for *everything* that owes its existence to it and strives toward it. It is only because we experience consciousness in the world as finite that we are repelled by the idea of an infinite consciousness; our experience is that finite consciousness, however objectively open it is, remains imprisoned within its own subjectivity, and this leads us to suppose that the Infinite must be free from this self-involvement and the restrictions it implies. If consciousness takes this fear seriously, it cannot really hold that it is indebted to no one but itself. Here, the fact that consciousness is embroiled in the finitude of *self*-consciousness becomes a tragic destiny that calls for release; the transcendent striving for the absolute turns into the conscious attempt to put an end to consciousness by plunging into an absolute that is not regarded as conscious of itself.

The prior notion is that the gift of (finite) being is also the gift of a "good"; it is a notion that can be twisted, but only on the basis of subsequent reflection upon the dark side of human existence. At the dawn of consciousness, in the child, such a view is impossible. The child cannot imagine that being [*Sein*] is not also goodness [*Gutsein*] and truth [*Wahrsein*]; it cannot conceive that being is an illusion nor that it would be better if the light of being of which it is conscious, irradiating all that authentically *is* and *can be*, were extinguished. The child's act of wonder, along with the indebtedness that it implies, cannot be unmasked and shown to be some kind of evil spell. In this context, when Jesus says that we must be like little children, he means something deeper than that we should abandon the paths of error (all kinds of habit and hardening): he means that we should be receptive to the light that falls on us from the absolute.

He also means, surely, that, given our own subjectivity, which recognizes the true as such and strives to implement the good, we should conclude that the absolute also has the characteristics of a subject, even if (according to Soloviev) this conclusion comes through the mediation of a fellow human being (the child's parent), who summons the child to self-consciousness, in such a way that further reflection is required to distinguish the absolute Subject from the fellow human subject. And precisely because the fellow human subject makes himself known in an open intimacy, the absolute Subject can appear to be openly manifested in a way that, initially, presents no problems. Of course it is possible that, in this area, subsequent reflection has to take some steps backward. For we can "know" a fellow human being, we can know that he exists as an individual, without ever being drawn to him. "Knowing" in this sense is involved in the aforementioned spontaneous "conclusion" from one's own consciousness (and that of others) to the subject-quality of the absolute. Logically speaking, this "conclusion" precedes all supernatural self-disclosure on God's part; it is one of the conditions of its coming about. We must say "conclusion", for there is no direct intuition of the primal, divine Ground, even if the "conclusion" expresses itself psychologically as direct perception.[2] This is an inchoate kind of knowledge, but in it, nonetheless, the divine is grasped as the absolute, the ground—*principium et finis* (DS 3004)—of all that is in the world, "incomprehensible" though it is (DS 3001). As Paul says, God's nature, "his eternal power and deity, have been clearly perceived in the things that have been made" (Rom 1:20).[3] The crucial thing is that this "conclusion" proceeds on the basis of the spirit's self-possession (and the latter must be internally awakened to, and equipped for, such self-possession). Indeed, insofar as the finite spirit is awakened to grasp its own contingence, its ideas of the absolute will largely show those very aspects of which Paul here speaks: the aspect of "eternal power" over against the pseudo-power that exercises itself within the confines of time and the aspect of "eternal deity", which brings out the element of the absolute in contrast to what is relative. The aspect of "goodness" is an intrinsic part of this description, for the whole passage speaks of God's radiance shining through all his works, which is why all should "honor" and "give thanks to him" (Rom 1:21). Accordingly, we can say

---

[2] Cf. E. Przywara, *Religionsbegründung* (Herder, 1923), who takes up the defense of Newman and his illative sense against Scheler and his "perception of essence" [*Wesensschau*].

[3] It does not matter whether an element of gracious revelation is involved here. But Paul is speaking in the tradition of the Wisdom literature, according to which the glory of the Creator is seen in the order and beauty of the creation (Wis 13f.).

that our primary experience of self-possession in freedom is a sense of power—however much our fellow men have a part to play in it—which extends to our environment and the world as a whole. From a philosophical point of view, all freedom is thus seen to be self-possession (*Theo-Drama* II, 220ff.).

Only on this basis can we go farther and allow the second element of the implicit "conclusion" to emerge. The primary experience of free self-possession includes the awareness that the spirit has a unique interior life that may be disclosed to others at will. Surely this must be all the more true in the case of the absolute Spirit? Has he not an interior realm that I cannot approach by my own power, just as my own inner world is inaccessible to others? We recall Paul's apt and celebrated words: "What person knows a man's thoughts except the spirit of the man that is in him? So also no one comprehends the thoughts of God except the Spirit of God" (1 Cor 2:11). Man's own experience teaches him that, if he is to know God inwardly, it can only come about through God's free self-disclosure. At this precise point, we have the final paradox of the human being; Thomas Aquinas perceived and formulated it with the utmost clarity, and Henri de Lubac (*Surnaturel*, 1946) has brought it into the center of attention once more. Put simply: man is dependent on the free self-disclosure of his fellow human beings if he is to be himself —and he cannot force this self-disclosure. In a similar way, since man is created to be receptive to absolute truth and goodness, he is dependent on God's self-disclosure: it is not something he can postulate. This paradox is prior to all talk of the "supernatural *existentiale*", however true it may be that nature is created for the sake of supernature, for the sake of the Incarnation of God, and however true it may be that the paradox of nature has its ultimate explanation in this supernatural order (to which some kind of "supernatural *existentiale*" may belong). The paradox is an integral part of the primal fact of self-consciousness insofar as the latter recognizes itself to be a gift, and hence an "image". De Lubac is right, therefore, to emphasize that there does not need to be a supernatural element of any kind in the natural *desiderium visionis*, in the longing to know God *as he is in himself*. This can —and must—be shown to be quite separate from the fact that

God has always willed to reveal something of his inner life and to empower human beings to receive it. Finally, the logical priority of the natural paradox over any "supernatural *existentiale*", however understood, explains why—contrary to all appearances —all preempting of the fulfillment envisaged by God is hubris, all the more so, the nearer it seems to come to that fulfillment. "Seems to come": no man will ever hit upon the solution God has in store, that is, the Incarnation of the Logos and his atoning death on the Cross on our behalf. Within the perspective of the "supernatural *existentiale*", one could produce a spectrum of apparent approximations and regard them as real approaches to God's plan, insofar as "christological grace" is thought to bring a premonition of God's historical action in Christ. But, in biblical terms, the only locus of such anticipations is the Old Testament, in which the Word of God undergoes a historical period of preparation with a view to becoming incarnate.

Applying this to our present topic, we must ask, is man bound to discern this second element implicit in his "conclusion" regarding the absolute? Is he bound to carry it out? For there are plenty of reasons for not doing it, for allowing this second element to become absorbed into the first. Concretely, the perception of an absolute element within my own free self-consciousness could lead all that is relative and contingent in my spirit to be relegated to the periphery, in favor of concentrating on the naked absolute that is at work in me. In such a case, the "whither" and "whence" of the individual spirit would simply have to be dissolved into what is only real and permanent, the truth and goodness that are at its core, namely, the Atman that is identical with the Brahman. In Christian terms, the creaturely realm is understood as the work of the powerful and kind divine Creator: it is good and owes its existence to God; in this other context, however, compared with the reality of Spirit, which is exclusively real, the creaturely realm appears non-true, non-real and hence illegitimate: it *should not be*. The only thing that counts in me is the absolute point by which I measure everything and by which I steer. It is simultaneously in me and above me. It is *above* me: all that is relative and limited—the locus of my psychological "I"—must be sacrificed to what alone has substance. Yet it is *in* me: that freedom that has first to be won through sacrifice is already hiddenly present in germ in *"my"* being.

In a view such as this, the movement by which man goes beyond himself and touches what is transcendent and absolute is *equated* with the latter's transcendence. The forms of this equation are manifold. They are abundantly evident in the religions of the East. They recur in the Aristotelian tradition (to say nothing of the Pre-Socratics) as represented by Averroes and his school. They attain a position of dominance in German Idealism, at the conclusion of which Schopenhauer turns to the East, whereas Feuerbach and Marx draw the anthropocentric and atheistic consequences of the short-circuit reasoning that lies at the bottom of this Idealism. All the aged Fichte can do is to endeavor to escape his own devastating conclusions by regarding self-consciousness, not as an "image" (of God, in the Christian sense), but as a mere schema of "absolute Life". But where this absolute Life becomes the Marxist life of the total society, there can be just as imperious a demand for the sacrifice of the mere image or schema, that is, of the individual, as in oriental mysticism. Karl Barth's chapter on "Mysticism and Atheism" needs to be seriously taken to heart once again in view of the current state of the world. The former is predominantly prebiblical, the latter predominantly post-Christian, but both ignore the fact of creatureliness and the creature's indebtedness to an extrinsic source.

Within the confines of the world, the *desiderium visionis* cannot be satisfied. Hence, if it does not seek its peace in God, it gives rise to all the familiar forms of fanaticism and anarchism, and the terrorism that destroys all order whatsoever. In the first part of Faust, Goethe's hero is driven to and fro by this *desiderium*, and even if, initially, his victims are from the bourgeois world, it does involve a pact with the devil. The devil—fading all the while, it must be said—accompanies him through part two, as the Faustian longing is elevated and refined; yet, to the very end, it remains embroiled in finitude (including war, violence and murder). Redemption comes partly through grace and partly because "he has striven". But the classical-romantic Faust-figures are followed by the political Fausts of our century: thus, as a result of the clear realization that man, as constituted, can provide no hope of

ultimate satisfaction, we have Nietzsche's Superman. And everywhere, beside Faust, beside Hegel, Marx, Lenin, Stalin, beside
Zarathustra and Hitler, we discern the shadow of a demon, insinuating that all that exists "deserves to be destroyed" [Goethe's
Mephistopheles—TRANS.]; that negativity is the creative, the innermost essence of spirit; and that the "absolute point" in man
is only the cause of his eternal search for power—and as such
implies the destruction of everything that has been.

All these *Weltanschauungen* and practical attitudes have one thing
in common: they all want to resolve the paradox of the human
being, his manifest restlessness and orientation to God, solely
within human nature. The only way to do this is for man to be
centered on his "absolute point", the point at which he touches
Being as such, the true and the good. This in turn leads to a
neglect of man's relativity and time-bound nature; in Christian
terms, it involves a disincarnation, a flight from time and presence. He may flee vertically, into the timeless zone of the Superman, or horizontally, into the future of the classless society. Here
the extremes of Buddhism and Marxism meet in the negation
of the present, for it is only in the present that we can grasp that
which *is*.

This disincarnation, dissolving the concrete human being in
favor of an idea he has of himself, is a sign that he is unwilling to endure the paradox that he is. In fact, the paradox can
only be endured if man's inner, Faustian restlessness is resolved
at its real, destined goal, that is, in the God who has taken the
initiative in revealing, proclaiming, disclosing and giving himself. For man, fashioned by the Logos, is essentially constructed
along dia-logical lines: any mono-logical interpretation is bound
to destroy him.

In his *The Sickness unto Death* (1849),[4] Kierkegaard has given
a peerless description of this state of affairs—though it should
be noted that, as a Protestant, he sees man's relationship with
God governed entirely by God's revelation of himself.[5] Man, he

---

[4] Quoted from the translation by Howard and Edna Hong (Princeton University Press, 1980).

[5] 95, 96; but cf. his critique of the Socratic concept of sin ("'sin is ignorance"),

says, is a synthesis of the infinite and the finite, of the eternal and the temporal, of the possible and the necessary (that is, he is the locus of possible decisions, but he is also constrained by facts and earthly necessities). This objective relationship "re-lates to itself", that is, it is subjective, reflex, and thus it pro-vides a first definition of man as "spirit" or "self".[6] On the basis of this definition, this relation-to-itself is free: "The self is freedom."[7] But the self, in its free self-consciousness, recog-nizes that the entire relationship is not something it has cre-ated: it has been established "by another", in whom alone it can reach "equilibrium and rest".[8] This "other" is "an infinite self",[9] namely, God. And, in the presence of God, the self is given its second definition: it is a "theological self".[10] The only ontological attitude appropriate to the self is this: "In relating itself to itself and in willing to be itself, the self rests transpar-ently in the power that established it."[11] Kierkegaard calls ev-ery other attitude "despair", whether man despairs and refuses to be himself or despairs and resolves to be himself: ultimately these two opposites are interchangeable.[12] He can despair, not wanting to be himself, by allowing what is absolute in him to gain the upper hand in the form of the "fantastic"; thus he loses hold of finitude.[13] Alternatively, he burrows into his own fini-tude and pronounces that he cannot find anything infinite in it.[14] He can also lose himself in the rhythm of absolute-and-relative to such an extent that he forgets his own self-relationship, his true freedom, in "despairing ignorance".[15] Finally, aware of his freedom, he can succumb to "despair in weakness" and be un-willing to *be* this freedom, this self;[16] or, in the same conscious-ness, man can experience the "despair of defiance", in which he

---

which presupposes a hidden knowledge of God even in the case of pagans: 42ff. It is inconsistent, therefore, for Kierkegaard to say that "the pagan did not have his self directly before God. The pagan and the natural man have the merely human self as their criterion" (81).

[6] 13ff.	[7] 29.
[8] 13f.	[9] 68.
[10] 79.	[11] 14, 30, 49.
[12] 20, 49.	[13] 30–32.
[14] 33f.	[15] 42f.
[16] 49f.	

posits his own self as absolute, over against the eternal self of God[17]—even if, in torment, man complains to God about his condition.[18] In the Christian perspective, all these forms of despair constitute a sickness of the spirit, the sickness unto death, in which man endeavors to destroy himself. As such, they are sin.

In what follows, we shall have to discuss man's revolt against his essential structure. Here we were concerned simply with the appropriate attitude to be adopted by created freedom, as ruthlessly set forth by Kierkegaard. He shows that created freedom cannot be brought to a state of "balance" between its opposing elements unless it recognizes its creatureliness, its "transparency", allowing God to shine through. Only thus can it discern and grasp itself; only thus can it be truly free. However, this requires man to acknowledge that he himself is a synthesis that lacks fulfillment, an oscillation that can never come to rest except in God and in the divine self-disclosure. Kierkegaard is entirely right here.

A final point. Wherever the self tries to prescind from its rootedness in God and establish its own autonomy, it is attempting to consolidate its freedom; it is attempting to seize power. And so long as God appears primarily in the form of power —omnipotence—the self can use this as an excuse, as a positive encouragement, to set itself up, likewise, as a "power" over against God. After all, is it not the "image" of God? What is needed, therefore, is the second level of reflection that we have described above. This facilitates the insight that God may disclose and give himself, thus transcending the notion that freedom means power; true freedom is thus seen in self-giving. It will never be possible to say, philosophically or theologically, exactly how far concrete existence can move out of its own (natural) structure and feel its way toward such an insight, and how far it is helped toward the latter by God's prior self-disclosure. In this regard, no further illumination can be brought to the twilight that surrounds Plotinus' characterization of "spirit"— for instance—according to which "spirit" is a yearning eternally circling around the mystery of the One; for an instant,

---

[17] 67.   [18] 74.

when the supernatural glory flashes forth, it participates in the absolute. But a seemingly slight transposition (or is it in reality a *metabasis eis allo genos*?) will bring us from there to man's longing for God, as seen by Christianity in Gregory of Nyssa and Augustine.

2. Power

We have examined the many aspects of power. Now we shall examine it as a link between the discussion of freedom and the discussion of evil. This is because freedom, as we have said, is the most fundamental expression of man's power, and, in this sense, power is eminently part of the goodness of creation. On the other hand, evil is so closely allied to power (as it is both possible and actually practiced in the world) that in one respect it can be described as evil itself. Recalling the Book of Revelation, we must remember that, in each case, the opposing "powers" were "given" power (Rev 9:3; [9:10]; 13:5, 11, 13, 14, 15; 16:9, 10), ultimately "from above" (cf. Jn 19:11). In other words, there is a higher power, superior to the unity that persists between evil and power. But it is not for nothing that Paul sees the "powers", "principalities" and "rulers" that govern the world as being primarily hostile (cf. 1 Cor 2:8; Eph 6:12; 2 Cor 4:4, which sums this up in the phrase "the god of this world", just as John speaks of "the prince of this world": 12:31; 14:30; 16:11). Initially we must avoid saying that power is evil, for freedom —relative or absolute freedom—is a good. On the other hand, the intimate connection between evil and power stares us in the face.

In a special way, power is the cause and the sphere of decisions, particularly ultimate ones, that is, decisions between God and the demonic. To that extent, it is a central topic of theodrama. And theo-drama is concerned with the interplay of finite and infinite freedom. As we shall go on to show, this interplay is impossible without the making of decisions at a fundamental level.

We have already given an exhaustive treatment of the bi-polar nature of finite freedom;[1] it has shown that the two poles, that is, genuine autonomy, on the one hand, and the necessity of an express indebtedness on the other, cannot be reduced to the one or the other. It is in the finite spirit's *reflexio completa* that it understands, possesses and loves itself. But it has not given this self-possession to itself; it is a gift from infinite freedom (which thus becomes normative), and it must transcend itself in the latter's direction if it is to possess itself in accord with its own truth. The truth of the first element prevents its freedom from being heteronomous, for the "nomos" is *genuinely* communicated and given *to it*; yet it comes from the absolute, and as such it is *given* with a view to the absolute.

The Stoics were right to say that the highest power given (note: *given*) to a conscious subject is the power of self-determination, since it cannot be overridden by any external power. But, in freedom's givenness, we see the radiant goodness of absolute freedom, which *gives* the most precious thing it has; and we also see the radiant omnipotence of this same absolute freedom, since it *has* what it gives. Nikolai Berdyaev put forward the absurd idea that human freedom comes, not from God, but from a ("Boehmean") "un-ground" that is both nothingness and absolute freedom.[2] He was attempting to relieve God of responsibility for evil and to preserve man's full autonomy; but this notion practically destroys the second pole of finite freedom (since man is no longer under a divine norm) and robs God of his omnipotence in order to preserve his goodness. Thus Berdyaev is compelled to adopt a gnostic tone and speak of a "tragedy of God". An annihilating abyss of freedom, however, devoid of

[1] 81ff. above and *Theo-Drama* II, 207–42.

[2] "In Boehme, the un-ground, which I call primal freedom, is within God, whereas I posit it outside God. . . . God has no power of any kind. . . . Man is a spiritually independent being and his relationship with God is characterized by his freedom and (in contrast to Schleiermacher) not by dependence": *Essai d'autobiographie spirituelle* (Buchet/Chastel, 1958), 221–23. Quite logically, the God/creature relationship is replaced by divine humanity, the ultimate absolute; the historical Christ is only a *Realsymbol* of this, for example, 223: "God is born in man, man in God. God needs man"; 262: "The Lover (God) cannot exist without his beloved (man)."

being and reason, is just as unacceptable as the ground of all things as Schopenhauer's blind will.

In order to see the true dialectic of power in which created freedom is involved, we need rather to consider the latter's intrinsic relation to its origin, which is the identity of absolute freedom and absolute power. Robert Spaemann has set forth this definition of divinity, taking as his starting point the "complaint, the protest and the accusation against God", which only makes sense if God has the omnipotence of the Creator and is responsible for the goodness of created reality.[3] Now, however, the polar constitution of finite freedom becomes the reason why the self-actualization of this freedom, at its summit, must lead irresistibly to a choice (Blondel's "option"): if it is authentically to lay hold of itself *as* freedom, it cannot see itself as purely autonomous but must also realize that that is a gift, owing its existence to some other source. This highest act of freedom in no way means that freedom should be defined as essentially "freedom to choose" (*liberum arbitrium*) "between good and evil". Man in God can possess a fully realized freedom *and* have this choice behind him; so it is, at least, in the case of the blessed who behold the face of God. But as Henri de Lubac has shown in his *Surnaturel*,[4] it does mean that God cannot create a freedom that is so confirmed in the good that it does not need to choose; such a freedom (and this applies to the pure spirits too!) would have been robbed of its supreme *dignity*. That is why, in *Theo-Drama*, volume 2, 271ff., we spoke of a necessary "latency", according to which God initially keeps his free, inner self hidden: thus he gives the creature the opportunity to lay hold of its own freedom, a freedom that both is its own *and* comes from an external source. "It is not simply a case of doing all the good one wants to do, and of deciding to do it in an act of free good will. The important and hard thing is to do it in the right manner, in a spirit of humility and calm, sensing the presence of another will

---

[3] "Die Frage nach der Bedeutung des Wortes 'Gott'" in *Einsprüche, Christliche Reden* (Einsiedeln: Johannes Verlag, 1977), 13–35, this ref., 23.

[4] Paris: Aubier, 1946, esp. part 2: *Esprit et liberté dans la tradition théologique*, 185–321. Even if, ever since they were created, the angels have an intuitive grasp of their own goodness, their vocation to blessedness remains "supernatural", according to St. Thomas, and as such it is withheld from their intuition (255).

by which one has to take one's bearings."[5] Here, for Blondel, lies the choice between losing and gaining one's freedom; here too, therefore, is the original locus of perversity, of moral evil in the world.[6] Once again, therefore, we find ourselves in the presence of a central aspect of the theological drama. Every philosophical or theological system that attempts to circumvent the supreme act whereby freedom lays hold of itself, robs the God/creation relationship of its intrinsic dramatic tension. This is true whether this is done through the idea that a being could have been created confirmed goodness or through the separation of man's ethical autonomy from the inner reference of his free acts to the divine norm (Kant), or—as we have already described—through the identification of the absolute religious norm with the transcendence of finite consciousness. Dramatic tension cannot be circumvented in a creation of free beings if the dignity of their freedom is to be maintained—a point that applies in all aspects of the theodicy.

It follows that, in laying hold of itself and choosing correctly, finite freedom becomes aware that it has an inviolable power inseparable from the absolute norm of the good. The "good" reveals itself the moment this freedom is bestowed, drawing aside the veil to show that absolute power is identical with absolute self-giving. Thus all ethical conduct is rooted in religion.

At this very point, however, the possibility of separating power and goodness suggests itself, where the one who chooses sets himself up as the standard of the good, thus subordinating goodness to his own exercise of power. This is the primal temptation, autonomy, being "like God, knowing good and evil" (Gen 3:5); this is the original sin against which Jesus has to fight in unmasking Pharisaism. For, even if the Pharisee recognizes that

---

[5] Blondel, *L'Action* (1893), 376.

[6] J. Pieper, in his *Über den Begriff der Sünde* (Munich: Kösel, 1977), seems to overlook this: he describes the assertion that sin is possible because man is free as "unfortunately illusory" because "it does not pertain to the nature of the free will to be able to decide in favor of evil"; "not-being-able-to-sin" must remain "the prerogative of a higher freedom" (100–101). This latter statement is certainly true in the case of fully self-possessed freedom. However, we are considering the act whereby man lays hold of himself in the first place.

the law comes from God, he has cut it loose from its source and taken over the direction of it himself; ultimately the law's commands and prohibitions are in his power. Once this point has been reached in human history, power has become the authority determining what is ethically permitted and forbidden. On the basis of such a historically concrete state of affairs, we can agree with Jakob Burckhardt in his verdict on power. Two things must be borne in mind if we are to understand it correctly. First, we must realize that the *desiderium naturale*, arising from created freedom, is directed toward God and hence *cannot be satisfied* on earth; if it is diverted from its goal and subordinated to the power of individual freedom, it results in a relentless heightening of power on the plane of immanence. We must savor the full effect of Burckhardt's dictum: "Power as such is evil, no matter who wields it. It is not something constant, but a craving; therefore it is unfulfillable, intrinsically unhappy and is bound to make others unhappy."[7] Second, Burckhardt is considering power in the political context, where the state, in its dealings with other states, has to be concerned primarily for its own interests; for the state is not a subject directly indebted to the absolute, like the individual. Hence the realistic conclusion: "It is clear—one thinks of Louis XIV, of Napoleon and of revolutionary popular religion—*that power is evil in itself* (*Schlosser*) and that, without regard to any religion, the egoism that is denied to the individual is attributed to the state as a right. Weaker neighbors are subjugated, annexed or otherwise reduced to the level of vassals, not so that they shall no longer present a hostile threat (that is the least cause of anxiety), but lest someone else take them over. . . . Once this path is pursued, there is no stopping; everything becomes feasible . . . and 'the others do just the same'."[8] Lord Acton's celebrated verdict was, "Power tends to corrupt, and absolute power corrupts absolutely"[9] (note the use of the words *tends* and *absolute*). We can go farther back, however. There is Hobbes' absolutizing of state power, which sovereignly defines what is good and what evil. There is Mon-

[7] *Weltgeschichtliche Betrachtungen*, loc. cit., 97.

[8] *Ibid*., 36. On the reference to F. C. Schlosser, cf. R. Marx' note in the Kröner edition, 340: "He acknowledged only one kind of morality: private morality."

[9] *Life of Mandell Creighton* (1904) I, 372.

tesquieu, who says that experience shows that everyone in a position of power is inclined to misuse it and will proceed until he
comes up against some limit. Only a contrary power can bring
power to a halt.[10] Long ago Augustine had attributed the marks
of the *civitas terrena*, that is, war, slavery and death, to the *libido
dominandi*.[11]

Burckhardt regarded power as one of the three forces dominating world history, along with religion and culture. It is "evil",
in his view, in that it is isolated from the other two. Thus isolated, it is not only evil but also meaningless: it is incapable
of putting meaning into existence; that is why it always has to
link up with ethico-religious and cultural values, or hide behind
them. If "those in power" are to keep their power, they must
appear to be "benevolent", *euergetēs* (Lk 22:25). If the individual
must embellish his claim to absolute freedom by some form of
altruistic ethics, thus imitating the divine identity of power and
goodness that alone can impart meaning to existence, the same
thing applies to the presumptions of political power: "As time
goes by, even the state that is erected exclusively on violence and
calamity is compelled to develop some kind of law and ethical
code."[12]

Thus we have entered the highly opaque field of problems associated with that whole area—so influential on world history
—that Augustine contrasts with the *civitas Dei*. In his view, this
area oscillates between the earthly state, which has a duty to look
after the public good, and the *civitas diaboli*. Neo-Scholasticism
tried to say that the "impure" side of this reality was concerned

[10] *De l'esprit des lois* (1748) XI, 4.

[11] *Civ. Dei* XIII, 14; XV, 4; XVIII, 49.

[12] Burckhardt, 37. But a little earlier he observes that "the subsequent incorpo-
ration of stolen goods does not acquit the robber." On the literary genesis and
interpretation of the *Weltgeschichtlichen Betrachtungen*, cf. W. Kaegi, Jacob Burckhardt VI/1 (Basel and Stuttgart, 1977), 3–116. The state's will to power was a
central topic even in the book's first draft; a marginal note, "justice has to give
way to power" (Kaegi, 33), is of relevance to what is to be discussed in the next
two sections. From this vantage point, we can understand why Burckhardt sees
"the duality of freedom and power" behind the three forces dominating world
history (Kaegi, 74) and accordingly extols the small state.

with "secondary" natural law, that is, the natural law that pre-supposes man's fallenness, in contrast to the "primary", paradisal natural law. Given man's sinfulness and egoism, the element of compulsion on the part of the state is unavoidable; the state is right to bear and wield the sword for the sake of the *bonum commune* (Rom 13:1–6). It is a fact, however, that this power, which is instituted to defend the common good, has to assert itself against other powers, and to do this it must employ the means of power; at best, therefore, all that can be achieved is a "balance of power" between the state and the various indi-vidual interests. Thus, given the actual constitution of human society, the state is a power structure protecting a "justice" that is only a partial aspect of that goodness characterizing the divine self-giving. For that same reason, it can seem to be nothing but collective egoism, a feature that emerges particularly in interna-tional politics. The misuse of power, which is always a possi-bility, has been paralyzed in the course of time through a suc-cession of "inventions":[13] Plato spoke of "restraining power" through laws, because his ideal plan of a state in which power and (philosophical) spirit were identical seemed utopian even to him; he had to acknowledge that legal power was a neces-sary evil in order to limit the abuse of power. Locke spoke of "limiting power" by binding the state to inalienable fundamental rights, giving inferiors the right to use force in resisting injus-tice. Montesquieu spoke of "apportioning power": if the mis-use of power is to be avoided, *"il faut que . . . le pouvoir arrête le pouvoir"*; constitutions provide a range of means to this end. Finally, John Rawls spoke of a "balance of power", where the differences in individual power are just only if they produce ad-vantages for all, particularly for the weakest members of soci-ety. The benefits of all these measures are clear. Equally evident are their limits and their precarious nature, particularly since the profoundly significant emancipation of the modern state from the compact between state and religion, which had existed for a thousand years.[14] This separation is associated with the techno-

---

[13] On this issue, cf. Alois Riklin, "Erfindungen gegen Machtmissbrauch" in *Wandlungen in Wirtschaft und Gesellschaft*, Festschrift für A. Jöhr, ed. E. Küng (Tübingen: Mohr, 1980), 125–46.

[14] B. Welte, basing himself on A. Gehlen, *Urmensch und Spätkultur*, 3d ed. (1975),

logical thrust of modern rationality and is irreversible.[15] People
have often wondered how far Christianity's absorption of the
other religions has contributed to this emancipation; Augustine
even considered the matter, and the transition from Romans 13
to the Book of Revelation is witness to the problems involved.
But since man's religious and ethical initiatives cannot be suppressed, society continues to produce new associations aiming
to ease the world's distress. Such associations cut right across
state structures in their effective pursuit of justice between men
and of selfless goodness. Our age is characterized by the opposition between the state politics that seeks to balance interests and
a disinterested "humanism" that, while it owes its existence in
large measure to Christianity, extends far beyond the Church. It
proves most fruitful where this "humanism" refuses to acquire
power in order to assert itself (this is the problem and the danger of liberation theology). Anyone who reflects realistically on
mankind's situation will see that this tension cannot be resolved.
But once power has stepped out of the context of religion and
ethical justice, it is heading for an eschatological confrontation.
We must examine this in more detail.[16]

The dignity of the person comes out clearly if the person in
question both knows that his personal autonomy is a gift and
allows the image of God to radiate through him. In this way, the
person attains authentic power and attracts those further aspects
of power for which he is personally responsible, that is, acquired
knowledge and ability; the parental authority, which initiates the
child, as a historical being, into social intercourse; and the authority of the teacher and the corporation director, and so forth.

---

discusses this emergence of the state from an all-embracing religious interpretation of the world in his *Die Würde des Menschen und die Religion* (Knecht, 1977).
Welte endeavors to show that the former compact is in accord with man's nature
and can (and should) continue to exert its influence, though now from a subter-
ranean level.

[15] "It is clear that we cannot go back to a stage prior to modern autonomy and
rationality, with all the fruits they have borne." Welte, 50.

[16] The topic of power (and its derivatives) has very many ramifications. We can
deal with only selected aspects here. For a brief survey of the main themes, cf. J.
Schwartländer's article "Macht" in *Handbuch philos. Grundbegriffe* (Kösel, 1973).

Such personal exercise of power is an integral part of social life; it operates best when the two sides of power as exercised by the human being, that is, power and goodness (or love), are found equally, both in the person who gives orders and in the person who obeys. In modern times, however, this socio-personal power structure, which is inherent in man's nature and was never seriously challenged in the older civilizations, is in conflict with the emergence (not only in the political sector but everywhere) of a hegemony of instrumental rationality that aims primarily at manipulating nature. The latter view reduces nature to the level of brute fact; in principle, therefore, it can dispense with the aspect of personal indebtedness and of goodness; it sees itself simply as an instrument of power and operates as such. Heidegger showed that the modern metaphysics—and here its entire development is unmasked—reached its high point in Nietzsche's "will to power"; this plain and unadorned exposition cannot be pushed to one side.[17] Descartes was the first to base an entire metaphysics solely on the self-conscious subject: through self-consciousness, the subject is given to himself *as being* ("I am"); this foundation gives the subject the required certainty so that he can scientifically ("mathematically") master what is presented to him (in "extension").[18] Kant will develop his epistemology with the same aim in view. "All thought, from its very first concepts, is ordered toward a utility that blossoms in technology and science."[19] For Descartes, "there is no need to speak of God except in connection with the need for an absolute guarantee for human knowing, that is, in order to secure man's domination of the world."[20] Despite the similarity between Descartes' conception of truth and that of Augustine, he is doing something profoundly different, for now "man's claims arise, on a truth-basis he himself has discovered and established, from that 'liberation' whereby he bids farewell to his primary indebtedness to the biblical and Christian revelation of truth and to Church

[17] Heidegger, *Nietzsche* I/II (Neske, 1961).

[18] Cf. the title: "Discours de la méthode, pour bien conduire sa raison et chercher la vérité dans les sciences" (1637).

[19] Ulrich Hommes, *Transzendenz und Personalität* (Frankfurt: Klostermann, 1972), 63.

[20] *Ibid.*, 53.

teaching. . . . 'Freedom' now means that man replaces certainty of salvation with that certainty through which and in which he becomes certain that he *is*. Thus he attains self-reliance."[21] From this vantage point, we can understand the history of the modern era and the manifold forms its self-liberation has taken.

> An essential constituent of this freedom, at all points, is that man has attained control over what his own humanity is; such control, essentially and explicitly, implies power. Accordingly, it is only in the modern era that power can become a fundamental reality; indeed, power's "coming to power" *is* the history of modern times. . . . Man's aim is to secure unconditional mastery over the whole earth through the highest possible, unconditional development of all his potential: this is the hidden spur that drives modern man to newer and newer projects.[22]

In "presenting things to himself" ("imagining" them), man puts them at the disposal of the ego; insofar as they are pure extension, they are rendered measurable and so can be employed in "machine technology". Heidegger shows that there is nothing strange in the fact that the apparent primacy of knowledge in Descartes and Kant is transformed into the primacy of the absolute will to power in Nietzsche: not simply because, historically, this transformation is mediated through many factors (for example, through Leibniz' doctrine of energy, according to which there is a unity of *perceptio* and *appetitus*),[23] but "because Descartes' metaphysics, even if it did not know it, always was a metaphysics of the will to power",[24] insofar as its sole aim, as Nietzsche says, "was to render things manipulable".[25] Nietzsche considers this "will to power" to be the absolute and, in so doing, relegates the "highest values" that formerly were established by Being in its self-giving. (In any case, they have become devalued because of profound historical change.) Thus power itself becomes "the principle of a new scale of values".[26] This is the will to power: "resolute commitment to oneself"

[21] Heidegger II, 143.
[22] *Ibid.*, II, 144–45.
[23] *Ibid.*, II, 237f.
[24] *Ibid.*, II, 236.
[25] *Ibid.*, II, 183 (quote).
[26] *Ibid.*, I, 34.

and "being master not only of oneself but also of things beyond oneself"; thus "the will is a potentiality that leads to power."[27] Indeed, it leads to ever greater power; hence the idea of the superman. And this ever-intensifying development must be equated with Being-as-such. As Nietzsche says: "At its height, the will to power wishes to imprint the mark of *being* upon the process of *becoming.*" Logically speaking, this inevitably involves the idea of the eternal recurrence of the same things.[28]

Insofar as Nietzsche thinks along quasi-biological lines (the ego is in reality the "body"), his new scale of values occupies a position beyond good and evil (not far from Lorenz' "evil so-called"). Looking at what were once considered the "highest values", he marvels at the creative power of man, who was able to project all this out of the infinite store of his vitality:

> All the beauty and sublimity we have lent to both real and imaginary things, I claim on man's behalf as his property and manufacture. This is his finest *apologia.* For man is a poet, a thinker, a god, love, power! O the kingly generosity by which he has endowed all things, so that he himself feels *poor* and *wretched*! This was hitherto his greatest self-forgetfulness: he wondered and worshipped, concealing from himself the fact that *he* had created the very object of his wonder.[29]

Here we have an extreme development: the pole of human freedom that owes its existence to the grace imparted by infinite freedom now becomes a function, together with that very grace, of the autonomous self's exercise of ever-increasing power. All grace comes from *itself.* In Christian metaphysics, the *desiderium* could not be satisfied by earthly things but only by God, that is, it was a longing that had its source in God and flowed back to him; in Nietzsche's *Nachtlied*, however, we read: "There is in me something unsatisfied, insatiable. . . . I live in my own light, I drink the very flames that come forth from within me. I do not know the happiness of those who receive. . . ."

---

[27] *Ibid.*, I, 52.

[28] Cf. Heidegger's great treatise "Die ewige Wiederkehr des Gleichen", *loc. cit.*, I, 255–472, and II, 7–29.

[29] *Wille zur Macht* (large octavo edition) XV, 241.

In order to counter this inability to receive, which Heidegger regards as the mark of our age, an age that thinks it can "produce" everything, he developed a philosophy in which "man's essence [*Wesen*] is governed by the inherence [*Wesen*] of the truth of *being* in and through *being* itself",[30] so that, ultimately, man must be nothing but pure receptivity for the wealth and poverty of being.[31] He is ultimately nothing but gratitude for the gift of being, for the fact that "there is" being. Behind a philosophy such as this, there is the best of a natural philosophy of freedom as we find it perfected in Christianity, not denying that man has a commission to rule the earth, but linking this task with thoughts of God. Only on this basis can man fashion the earth in a meaningful and fruitful way.

We can go beyond Heidegger's formulations and assert that all the philosophy of the scope of human power and reason that is based on Descartes lacks the complement and correction of a philosophy of *prayer*. This fundamental act does not emerge as a specific topic again until we come to the thought of Blondel and Ulrich. Since this fundamental act is missing, power grows and distorts until it becomes a tyranny over the earth, exploiting it and heedlessly laying it waste. Yet this technocracy, this manipulation of things and of man (who has himself become a thing) can no longer be recognized as a phenomenon originating in power.

> For it is characteristic of the resultant manipulation that it does not actually apply force, nor does it confront man openly in the form of coercion; he is subject to it without violence and without external conflict. In contrast to all relationships based on power, modern manipulation simply ignores the aspect of free will in man; thus it pursues a quasi-anonymous annihilation of personal existence that is even more radical than that undertaken by force. This is what makes the modern technocracies—not technology itself—much more menacing.[32]

The threat they present is greater since they wrap themselves up in the "destiny of the age"—and no one can do anything

[30] *Loc. cit.*, II, 194.
[31] Cf. *ibid.*, II, 246ff.
[32] J. Schwartländer, 873.

about that. Is it not our duty to tear aside this curtain and expose a negative human decision at the root of this "destiny", a decision in which, as in the case of original sin, all subsequent denizens of the age are entrammeled? Is not the "darkness of God" in which we live (Buber) a clear sign of a hidden culpability, a guilt that burrows deeper into the darkness to escape detection? Thus our reflections on the nature of power form a link between a consideration of freedom, on the one hand, and of guilt and sin, on the other. In concluding our examination of the pathos of human history, we must now turn to the latter pole, that is, guilt and sin.

3. Evil

a. The Power of Evil

Having dealt with freedom and power, we inevitably come to the topic of evil. For only in the context of evil does the dramatic tension of personal and social existence finally explode. It is possible to envisage a dramatic struggle between something good and something better, but, for such a struggle for primacy to be genuine, the "good" would have to be convinced that it was better than the "better"—and this would be impossible without accusing the latter (the "better") of heresy and obscuring our view of the absolute, normative good.

We are attempting to discuss the phenomenon of evil within the horizontal perspective of the "pathos of the world stage". It will not be easy to reach satisfying results in this area. As we shall show, evil necessarily veils and misconstrues itself; accordingly, an absolute authority is needed if the true nature of evil is to be unveiled. Such an authority can be exercised to greater or lesser effect, which means that we must reckon with an analogical scale of unveilings and, hence, of insights into the nature of evil. The final unveiling takes place in the context of the Bible. In the Old Testament, it emerges in the theology of the covenant with God; this is transcended in the New Testament by the theology of the God-man who "takes away" the world's guilt—thus exposing it, in its full malice, as "sin".

If we take this maximum definition of sin, its full unveiling, as final and normative, we can agree with Karl Barth's oft-repeated assertion:

> We only see how *serious* this opposition [between God and man] is, and how utterly unbearable the reality of sin is, when we ponder the fact that it is God *himself* who, in the life of Jesus Christ, undertakes to carry out the wrathful judgment upon sin. If it were simply the case of smoothing out a certain unevenness in the way the world runs, or of ameliorating the relative imperfection of the human situation . . ., God would not have needed to become man, nor would the Son of God have needed to die on the Cross. Proponents of the Neo-Protestant doctrine of sin are right here. . . . All of us seem to have a very modest view of man's culpability and the menace of evil, judging by what we think we should and can do to eradicate it and counteract its effects (for example, in our endeavors in the fields of education, politics and morality). How small our estimate of the damage must be, considering the piecemeal solutions we propose for it! The question posed by Anselm: "*Quanti ponderis est peccatum?*", gets its answer from the Cross of Christ—or else it gets no answer at all. . . . Once we have realized that *this* is what our reconciliation with God cost—in the very person of his Son—we can say goodbye to the comfortable, frivolous attitude that imagines that the evil we do is limited by the good we do; only then can we bid farewell to the notion that, in the face of this "compensation effect", we are excused and have nothing to fear.[1]

On the other hand, we must complement this view by pointing out that, in the Old Covenant, God tolerated something very like cultic "compensations" for guilt; behind these Old Covenant "sin offerings", most pagan religions can show quite analogous attempts on man's part to reconcile himself with God. Does this fact not indicate a universally human insight—obscured, perhaps, but nonetheless present—into a more-than-human dimension of evil, of guilt and of sin? Our next task will be to turn our attention to this awareness.

[1] K. Barth, *Kirchliche Dogmatik* IV/1 (1953), 455–57; cf. *Church Dogmatics* (Edinburgh: T. & T. Clark, 1958).

The possibility of evil arises out of the polarity of human freedom. Human freedom *has been* genuinely handed over and entrusted to itself; but, in addition, it *knows* this. In laying hold of itself, therefore, it must acknowledge its indebtedness and so transcend itself *in a single act of choice*. It is for the sake of this choice that the absolute good communicates itself to us in a hidden, latent manner, whereas the *fact* of the gift, as perceived by finite freedom, is under full illumination.

This is the starting point. It is expressed in the chief elements of the Yahwist paradise legend: man, equipped with freedom, was created "very good" by God. His relation to his origin was unclouded and without alienation; it gave him freedom of operation within the whole "garden", and the prohibition against eating from the tree served to remind him of his dependence on the origin of all these gifts. At this stage, prior to his exercise of choice, man is "good" in a preethical sense; his freedom has not yet taken charge of itself. According to Idealist philosophy's interpretation of the legend, the serpent's temptation obliges him to choose; he sins and thus gains access to free self-consciousness. But it is not man's sin that gives access to self-consciousness: even if he had rejected the temptation, his exercise of choice would have left him in a state that was very different from the "indifferent" primal goodness (which we should not interpret as a state of *Angst*, as Kierkegaard does). It is true that, in this highly symbolic episode, the Yahwist is trying to depict the origin of evil, and masterfully does so;[2] but the proffered temptation— "to be like God"—clearly shows that the negative option was not *necessary*.

The negative option *can* be embraced if the person exercising the power of choice regards his freedom's "autonomy pole" as something absolute, with the result that his indebtedness to God and orientation to him are dissolved and destroyed; not through mere carelessness and neglect, but because of the lure of "being like . . .", that is, of deliberately obliterating the difference

---

[2] For a more detailed interpretation, cf. the exhaustive three-volume work by Eugen Drewermann, *Strukturen des Bösen. Die jahwistische Urgeschichte in exegetischer, psychoanalytischer und philosophischer Sicht* (Schöningh, 1977–1978). For Drewermann, these three perspectives are preliminary; they lead to a paradox that "only becomes meaningful in the context of theology, of God" (vol. 3, LXIII).

between God and the creature. However, insofar as the twin poles of finite freedom inseparably coinhere, autonomy cannot be conceived apart from the dynamism of its "whence" and "whither"; it is this that makes it a real image and likeness of absolute freedom. As a result, when man exclusively opts for his own autonomy, this dynamism is attributed to the latter and, as it were, incorporated into it: he becomes his own origin and goal. But while man's autonomy is genuinely *given to him* in a fundamental and permanent sense, it is impossible to think of the Giver being absent; in fact, he is the One who, in the act of constant presence—both in his omnipotence and in his total goodness—communicates to the finite being something that is fundamentally his own. Thus, in attributing its own gift-quality to itself, finite freedom is alienating something that belongs to the absolute and is inseparable from it and attempting to put it at the disposal of finite freedom.

Three things follow from this. The "dynamism" of which we have spoken is meant to point finite freedom in the direction of infinite freedom, but, when it is attributed solely to the former, it is only the aspect of *power* that is so adopted. This is because the absolute's aspect of *goodness*, insofar as man experiences it as self-giving, cannot be fitted into the categories of autonomy. Autonomous freedom, once it has been set forth as absolute, can only understand *itself* as the norm of the good. In other words, it has the good in its power, which is an internal contradiction, since, in the absolute, the good is identical with power. We have already devoted some attention to the topic of "power"; now too, though at a deeper level, we are moving toward a philosophy of the "will to power", a will that, in superior fashion, itself determines what is good and evil ("you will be like God, knowing good and evil"). This contradiction, which is kept secret from self-absolutizing freedom, not only deprives finite freedom of its harmonious relationship with absolute freedom: it also deprives it of such a relationship with itself. Its undeniable finitude has usurped an element of the infinite; this renders its finitude unintelligible and causes it to reject it. Either it regards its finitude as something of no account and tries to abolish it, or it uses it as an arbitrary plaything to convince itself of its own omnipotence (cf. Sartre). This internal contradiction is necessarily transferred to every interpersonal relationship: what was intended as a relationship of loving solidarity becomes a relationship of mutually antagonistic absolute entities. We see this in the paradise legend itself, where Adam puts the blame on Eve, and Eve puts it on the serpent.

We have already touched on the second point. The contradiction must be kept hidden: what is at stake is the absolute identity of someone who is refusing to acknowledge his indebtedness. Both things are always present and take effect: the act of concealment and its result. The contradiction is hidden, it is no longer visible. These two together show us that evil is *the lie*. If it were possible to stop this act of concealment and just keep the result, the subject would have been presented with a kind of new truth; the latter's acceptance would have brought about a kind of new innocence. But the contradiction adverted to cannot be resolved, for it involves freedom itself; what has been chosen continues to put forth its influence; the choice persists. At the beginning of the Letter to the Romans, Paul explicitly speaks of the pagans "not acknowledging" God's divinity; this failure to ac-know-ledge presupposes a prior (and persisting) "knowing". If evil is the lie, it necessarily implies two things. There must be a primary consciousness of what is fundamentally true, of what should be the case; and there must be a constant attempt to reassure oneself that it is *not* true and is *not* the case. Such self-reassurance is all the easier since, in choosing one's own autonomy as something absolute, one has (by definition) chosen the highest good in the world; this yields a vast number of "goods" of a personal and social nature, dependent on this supposedly highest good and ministering to it; these can be posited and realized. Indeed, it is suggested that liberation from "heteronomy" vis-à-vis some absolute is actually necessary if all intramundane "goods" are to attain their full development. So man reassures and convinces himself. Strangely depicted in the primitive Yahwist narrative, again, we find the fundamental lie inextricably bound up with the production of an intramundane hierarchy of values. The spiritual craving "to be like God" is transferred to the physical craving for the apple (man as spirit and body). Then the sexual relationship is perverted by the overpowering dominance of the man over the woman (man as male and female). Brotherhood is destroyed (in the Cain and Abel episode) and revenge (Lamech) is elevated to the level of law. The Promethean "One World" (in the building of the Tower of Babel) is exploded by the intrinsic lie (the desire to reach up as high as God).

Once again, the third point emerges from what has been said about the other two. The power that has been usurped must conceal itself by the lie; the lie cannot abolish itself. The power is usurped: in fact, it belongs to him who is almighty and utterly good and manifests his presence. In seeking to arrogate this power to itself, finite freedom does two things: it separates power from self-giving goodness, and it sets itself up against the absolute good—thereby incurring the judgment of the latter. Judgment reveals that the usurped power is actually God's power over the usurpers. The one who attempts to seize absolute power is overwhelmed by it; he has no defense against it. Seeking "liberation" through total autonomy, he is so fettered by it (for total autonomy belongs to God) that release can only come from God. We have already seen this in the fact that sin is a lie; the freedom that refused to acknowledge God was bound to maintain this lie, but, by pursuing this course, it actually worked against its own true nature, since part and parcel of this nature is its transcendence backward and forward, that is, pointing to God as its origin and its goal. Thus it is overwhelmed by the very power of self-transcendence with which it has been endowed and becomes "bent in upon itself". Augustine calls this "*incurvatio in se ipsum*".

Something more must be said, however, if we are to understand how finite freedom becomes fettered in this way. We have already stressed that man is created to "behold" and "possess" God and that, consequently, his ultimate goal can only be a supernatural one. While he knows that he himself is not absolute, he can grasp that he is an image of the absolute (in his reason and freedom), an image that is essentially modeled on the Archetype. This, we asserted, is part of the creaturely structure of finite freedom as such. It reveals its origin in God and its constant orientation to him, but that is all. If this orientation to God is to be fully realized, not only is the creature essential: God's free self-disclosure is required. If this divine self-disclosure takes place—and in the biblical view this is the ultimate reason why God created the world from out of himself—something must be added to finite freedom. It must essentially be *summoned* by the divine freedom; it must be called to disclose itself, open itself, to the divine self-disclosure. This challenge must be so radical that it goes farther than a mere "conclusion" from the image to the archetype; it must be unmistakably audible, whether finite freedom opens up or closes itself to it. It must be like some characteristic mark, deeply burned into its structure. Since this mark persists even when man turns away from grace, we can term it a "supernatural *existentiale*", but must not seek to unpack its contents any further. It is more than a natural "orientation": it is an "invitation".

If this element of the divine freedom is built into the concrete structure of finite freedom, we can understand more fully why the sinner, unwilling to transcend himself, and so disregarding this element, thereby excludes himself from it—with dire and inevitable consequences. In such a case, the divine initiative is necessary if he is to be liberated from his turning from God. A child that has misbehaved to its mother can only resolve to ask her forgiveness if it is sure of her abiding, personal love; it is through the power of this love that it can turn over a new leaf. Where God is concerned, the sinner's repentance does not occur as a result of some "natural" reflection upon the idea of a merciful God; it results from living faith (or at least a faith that *was* alive) in a God who graciously communicates himself. Repentance itself is due to the effective power of God's grace.

On the other hand, the sinner's overpowering by the power he has usurped (and which God has only "lent" him) really represents the "power of darkness" (Lk 22:53). This overwhelming power is greater than the power placed at man's own disposal; thus it is not a merely static, superior quantity, dominating man, the inferior: it continually puts forth its power here and now, tending to bind and entangle the sinner even more. Evil creates an undertow leading to further evil. The sinner's self-righteousness vis-à-vis absolute truth (which, by lying, he denies) tends to make him assert that he is absolutely right. Consequently, he uses all the means at his disposal to prove this. The prime means of underpinning the lie is to use sophistical short-circuits in reasoning and distorted aspects of the truth. In this way, the sinner builds a kind of "bulwark" against the real truth; he hides behind its illusion, knowing all the while that the truth he has "wickedly suppressed" (Rom 1:18) will eventually come to lay siege against his citadel. This metaphor comes from Paul, who says that his weapons "are not worldly but have divine power to destroy strongholds. We destroy arguments [*logismoi*: not merely opinions but sophistries too] and every proud obstacle to the knowledge of God, and take every thought [*noēma*: an individual idea, established teaching or world view] captive to obey Christ" (2 Cor 10:4-5). We recall this metaphor of a pitiless battle simply in order to focus on the dramatic situation: God's ever-greater power and goodness are opposed to the more and more entrenched position of evil. This dramatic tension is revealed by the "wrath of God against all ungodliness and wickedness of men" (Rom 1:18); in the Old Testament, it is depicted in countless images.[3] As these biblical references show, evil's power not only to take man captive but to plunge him into more and more evil is manifest in its full proportions only in the face of the divine revelation. Here, initially, the unity of power and goodness in God must show itself in the form of wrath, so that the power of his goodness can be seen as his mercy upon the sinner. Or, putting it in Old Testament terms: "We have all become like one who is unclean, and all our righteous deeds are like a polluted garment . . ., for thou hast hid thy face from us, and hast delivered us into the hand ['into the *power*'] of our iniquities. Yet, O Lord, thou art our Father . . ." (Is 64:6ff.). This idea forms the transition to an assessment of the inner analogy of the sinner's situation vis-à-vis God, according to his distance from or nearness to God's revelation. The question to be asked here is whether this analogy is only a subjective one (extending from the relative ignorance of the pagans to the deeper knowledge of the Jews and to the deepest knowledge found among Christians), or whether it is actually objective, in the sense that the deeper the insight into the God who discloses himself in love, the more it causes sin to increase. This would bring us face to

---

[3] Cf. the wealth of material assembled in vol. 1 of Louis Ligier's *Péché d'Adam et péché du monde* (Paris: Aubier, 1960).

face once more with that law of mutual heightening that runs right through the theological drama and of which we spoke at the end of the first part of this volume. The best illustration of this is Luke 12:47–48, where the two servants receive different beatings for their disobedience: one knows the master's will, whereas the other does not know it.

b. The Analogy of Sin

The only possible basis for such an analogy is the assumption that God's grace and self-disclosure, which are doubtless offered to all men, are not shared by all of them in the same subjective clarity and intensity. Nor does this conflict with the Pauline assertion that all men, Gentiles and Jews alike, are "liars" (Rom 3:4), "under the power of sin" (3:9); "all have sinned, and fall short of the glory of God" (3:23). Paul is nonetheless aware of a considerable difference between the sin of Gentiles and the sin of Jews (to say nothing of the sin of Christians: cf. Heb 6:4ff.; 10:29f.).

Sin arises in the case of *Gentiles* (in biblical terms, those who have not come into contact with God's historical revelation) because, while they are bound to know God—this is a basic law applying to all men—they do not want to acknowledge him (Rom 1:18ff.). What Paul says is rooted in the tradition expressed in the Book of Wisdom, namely, that the Gentiles should have recognized God from the beauty of his handiwork, as Creator; instead, in their "search for God" and in their "desire to find him", they have falsely regarded his works as divine and—what is worse—they have carved idols and worshipped them (Wis 13). The origin of these idols and their cult, which is "the beginning, cause and end of every evil" (Wis 14:27 JB), is explained in terms of psychology and ethnology and thereby, in some manner, excused (a father makes an image of his dead child; the nation needs a statue of its remote king whom it "does not know": Wis 14:18).

According to this tradition, the Gentiles are not the recipients of a historical revelation. Thus Paul can call the Gentiles "*atheoi en tōi kosmōi*" (Eph 2:12),[4] and the Old Testament initially dismisses them as "stupid" (Is 28:9–11; 33:19; Jer 4:22; 5:15, 21; Dt 32:21–29), "foolish" and "lacking discernment" (Is 44:18f.). As a result, they have to rely primarily on their reason if they are to arrive at an awareness of their contingence and hence of the reality of God. This tool, however, is relatively ineffective (even presupposing the inner light of grace) in bringing man into the presence of the living God; that is why, in paganism, religious constructs remain stuck at a twilight stage. We shall return to this aspect later.[5] A rough outline will suffice for the present.

There is an essential ambivalence in pagan religiosity, and hence in pagan sin. This is because, in the absence of a historical revelation, man (who seeks God) cannot avoid making an image (or images) of God. It is part of his very nature. And such images, given man's sinfulness, are bound to obstruct his view of God's truth. Considered in the abstract, the Old Testament prohibition against images might seem to be purely "positive"; its implacable stance might seem exaggerated. But in view of the inevitability of pagan idols and their problematical ambivalence, we begin to see the full force of the prohibition. The idol shows the two things inextricably intertwined: since man is a creature of both spirit and sense, he needs to create "a visible picture" of God if he is to approach him. This is legitimate. Furthermore, in setting up this picture, man is anticipating the divine picture that God himself will eventually provide. One argument for the legitimacy of this procedure is the fact that, when enlightened pagan religion "demythologizes" the images, it usually (though there are exceptions) forfeits the concrete relationship with the absolute mediated by these images: the absolute becomes nonpersonal, pantheistic, even verging on the atheistic. On the other hand, the static image distorts man's living receptivity for the personal word and inspiration that God addresses to him. The knowledge of God infused into man's conscience is replaced by artificial mechanisms by which man tries to find out what is the will of God.

---

[4] Cf. Jer 10:25, Ps 79:6.
[5] See below, III A 3.

A similar twilight atmosphere pervades the pagan cult, particularly the practice of sacrifice. Here the genuine awareness of worship and atonement due to the deity is mixed up with man's attempt to create a proper relationship with God by his own efforts, and particularly to make appropriate compensation for faults and sins he has committed. On the one hand, there is an acknowledgment of God's power, before which man does obeisance; yet, on the other hand, man feels empowered and able to draw God's power over to his side. How can the relationship between these two power-perspectives be clearly defined? Once again we see that the aspect of power in God (and hence in man) is given priority over the aspects of goodness and self-giving. Even if the goodness of the gods is not overlooked (for man is essentially dependent on it), it is subordinated to their power: the deity is perceived as having power to bring about both salvation and disaster; consequently, man must move and persuade him to work salvation. (The predominance of power in the context of the divine is evident in many religions—not only in primitive religions either—in their terrifying and grimacing representations of gods.)

We can insist on the legitimacy of pagan religious institutions because, apart from the element of idol worship, many of these institutions could be adopted by Old Testament divine worship, for example, the Temple, the oracles and the most diverse forms of sacrifice expressing allegiance and atonement. At the same time, this (secondary) adoption, on Israel's part, of religious institutions from pagan nations in no way indicates an origin comparable to that of biblical revelation. In fact, the ambivalent nature of these institutions persists deeply into the Old Testament and has to be overcome there step by step. Only in the New Testament is the institution *as such* fully purified of ambivalence, although it can continue to be misused by sinful man. Many attempts have been made, on the part of scholars of the history of religions and of the philosophy of religion, to say that the religious area provides us with no analogy for anything institutional; against this view we must assert that these institutions do most definitely share in the ambivalent nature of all religious attitudes; they are an objective expression of the divided consciousness of sinful man: on the one hand, he knows of his sinfulness and of the necessity of removing it, and, on the other hand, he thinks he himself knows the ways in which it can be removed. Accordingly, the biblical verdict on the sinfulness of the "nations" will not be unequivocal. On the one hand, God's wrath descends on the nations, who are found guilty no differently from Israel: "God has consigned all men—Jews and Gentiles—to disobedience, that he may have mercy upon all" (Rom 11:32). Nor do the prophets cease announcing God's judgment upon the individual "nations", whether because of their pride or because of their forgetfulness (and hence their sin). In the Book of Revelation, the self-divinization of the King of Tyre (Ezek 26–28) and the utter egoism of Assyria and Babylon ("I am, and there is no one besides me", Zeph 2:15; Is 47:8) become the epitome of sin. All the same, there is a certain ignorance on the part of the nations: they have not encountered the living God; this diminishes their sin or, rather, makes it seem less crass than the sin of Israel, which causes Israel to occupy the bottom place in the judgment, lower than Sodom and Samaria (Ezek 16:53ff.). As Jesus said to the towns that would not believe in him: "It shall be more tolerable on the day of judgment for Tyre and Sidon than for you" (Mt 11:22).

Ultimately this assessment of the sins of the Gentiles is founded on a naïvely anthropocentric view—because they lack a historical revelation—of their relationship to God. They are "God-seekers" (Wis 13:6; Acts 17:27), but, in Paul's speech at Athens, whether God will allow himself to be found is an open question. This anthropocentrism is a fact, despite Paul's emphatic mention of Gentile "piety"; the latter can be largely a product of their fear of the gods. (Primitive religiosity doubtless has a lot to do with man's feeling of powerlessness in the face of a vastly superior cosmos.)[6] Anthropocentrism persists, moreover, despite the sense of the human person's intrinsic value, a sense that, in any case, is less developed here than in the context of biblical religion, where it is undergirded and strengthened by the aspect of

---

[6] Even if it is a mistake to see the "divine" simply as a development of the "powerful" as such, as G. van der Leeuw does in his phenomenology of religion (Mohr, 1933).

the theocentric. Pagan egocentrism can unfold on an individual
plane just as well as on the collective plane (in the notion of the
polis), where it is clothed in the form of the "golden rule"—
which makes it clear that this rule is subject to the same analogy
as that of the concept of sin that we are at present discussing.
The "golden rule", widely instanced in paganism and found in
the Old and New Testaments (Mt 7:12), can form the basis of
an ethics that is entirely egocentric, indeed egoistic, as well as of
one that is selfless. It depends on whether the ego sees itself as
the central reference point of all conduct or as sharing responsibility for the world with all others. There can be no doubt that
this second alternative was clearly envisaged by Plato's Socrates:
indeed, he gave his life in its defense. But there is no ultimate
guarantee for the ethics of selfless love until Yahweh puts forth
his unmerited act of deliverance, conclusively summed up in the
example of Christ.

    In this connection, we can recall the puzzling passage in Ro-
mans 5:13–14: "Sin indeed was in the world before the law was
given, but sin is not counted where there is no law. Yet death
reigned from Adam to Moses, even over those whose sins were
not like the transgression of Adam." Here, no doubt, Paul is
thinking less of the Jews (between Abraham and Moses) than
of pagans. The pagans, equally, have sinned, as is clear from
the way they act contrary to conscience (Rom 2:15); thus death
comes to them also as a punishment for sin. But they have not
infringed a positive law issued by God, like that given to Adam
in paradise and to the people of Israel ever since Moses. For
that reason, the sins of the pagans are not to be weighed in the
same way as those of Adam and the Jews. This is substantiated
by the notion of God's "patience", to which we shall have to
return. Nonetheless Paul speaks of pagans likewise undergoing
a (penal) death, which shows that he takes their sin seriously.
Pagan anthropocentric thought affects man concretely and centrally in his three dimensions: in death (for man tries to remove
the sting of death by saying that the soul is immortal, that is, does
not die when man dies); in the man-woman relationship (which
becomes perverted in homosexuality: Rom 1:24–27); and in his
relationship with his fellow men (which is also damaged in all
its aspects: Rom 1:28–31). Their guilt reaches its peak in the

fact that they not only realize the suicidal nature of such things but "approve those who practice them" (1:32).

When we come to the phenomenon of sin in *Israel*, we can no longer consider it on the purely anthropological, horizontal plane, for here it is God, or someone speaking and acting in his name and commissioned by him, who makes the sinner aware of his sin. "You are the man", says Nathan to David, and David does not accept this revelation, this verdict, purely externally: he acknowledges its truth inwardly. This makes it clear, once again, that there is an ambivalence about conscience in the sinner: while it uncovers some things, it may bury other things even deeper; it accuses but also excuses.[7] On the other hand, Israel's covenant with Yahweh puts the nation under a harsh light that exposes heart and reins, exposes everything to the light of day. This is a divine light before which no man can stand unless he is totally open to it and surrenders himself totally to it; it is a gracious and (for that very reason) a challenging light; it reveals the precise conditions under which man can exist in the covenant. That is why, *in the whole of history, Israel is the place where the nature and the burden of sin is most directly manifested—* albeit this history grows in intensity up to the great prophets— bringing to a climax the dramatic action that is set in train by the covenant between God and man. The resolution of the conflict, raised to an ultimate pitch of intensity, occurs in Jesus Christ, in the "fifth" and last act of the covenant drama, where we witness man's tragic fall into the final No to God—and his *katharsis* in a way that could not have been anticipated. According to Paul's radical theology of the law, the latter comes to unveil sin in all its depth (Gal 3:19–23; Rom 5:20: 7:7ff.) but in order to facilitate what was primarily intended by the covenant (with Abraham), namely, man's surrender to God in faith. This is by no means a forced interpretation of the drama of the Old Covenant but an apt summary of it.

While the covenant with Israel was particular, its range is universal in that it points backward (to Abraham and Noah) and

[7] Romans 2:15 can be understood in this sense: the Gentiles' "conscience" shows them that the law is written on their hearts, for "their conflicting thoughts accuse or perhaps excuse them".

forward (by way of promise). First of all, it focuses on the intensity of the absolute: the covenant with God is pure, free goodness on his part, but behind it is the whole weight of the divine omnipotence. The covenant God designates himself as a "zealous" and "jealous" partner and thus contrasts himself with the pagan image of God: "Jealousy is the divine power that is put in the service of injured love; it indicates that righteousness that is essentially oriented to salvation."[8] The fact that God's love reacts violently to the violence done to it by men[9] is explained by God's total investment of himself and by the utterly astonishing indifference, rejection and hardness of heart on man's part. Thus God's "jealousy" is compared to a "consuming fire" (Dt 4:24; Is 33:14; Zeph 1:18). The "consuming" of sin can signify both judgment and salvation.

It is not only in Abraham but also in Moses that faith's surrender to the God of the covenant has an absolute primacy over the keeping of the individual covenant precepts ("laws", "commandments"). The prophets, and preeminently Isaiah, will continue ceaselessly to lay stress on this insight. The particular, ascertainable transgressions against the commandments—transgressions that have direct social consequences and can thus be identified—are only the results of a fundamental evil, namely, a falling away from the covenant relationship, betrayal, unfaith, disobedience, culpable forgetfulness of God, the sinful failure to "know God". These are central themes of the prophetic tradition.

Evidently, the basic structure of human freedom remains intact: the autonomy pole assumes control of the pole of transcendence, while the covenant relationship has greatly intensified man's awareness of coming from God and being destined for him. Israel has become infatuated with its own beauty (a beauty that comes from God and is for him); Israel has "become sated" and hence forgetful of God. It is precisely this culpable forgetfulness that produces its idolatry; Israel's idols are projections of its lusts, designed to replace the God who makes it feel uncomfortable; its dealings with idols are branded as fornication and

---

[8] B. Renaud, "Je suis un Dieu jaloux" in *Lect. Div.* 36 (Cerf, 1963), 148.

[9] "[Jalousie divine:] la réaction violente de la Sainteté de l'Amour divin, révélé dans le cadre de l'Alliance contre tout ce qui porte atteinte à cette réalisation entre Jahvé et son peuple." *Ibid*.

adultery, that is, a declension from the spousal covenant of love with the true God. The uncovering of this fundamental sin is portrayed with the starkest images: "I will uncover her lewdness in the sight of her lovers, and no one shall rescue her out of my hand" (Hos 2:10).

Sin is unmasked as man's wrenching himself loose from the divine power, which *is* goodness and *calls for* goodness, if man is to exercise his own power in a pure manner. This applies to the politics of the kings of Israel: they attempt to bypass trust in God and, against the warnings of the prophets, endeavor to conclude pacts with the great powers, who ultimately overpower them. It applies to social and economic distress within the country itself, where the party of the powerful—the kings, courtiers, big landowners, but also those who are supposed to be wise, the judges who take bribes—oppress and exploit the poor people. This twofold echo, in the anthropological sphere— in politics and society—of the fundamental sin shows how profoundly the God of the covenant is also the true Creator-God (Deuteronomy, Isaiah) to whom man owes his very nature.

The more God's power over creation, and hence over all nations, is made manifest, the clearer the pagans' culpability becomes. Thus it is seen to be a plain fact that all mankind is guilty before God: "There is none that does good, no, not one" (Ps 53:4). God sees this when he surveys the earth. The same judgment awaits Jerusalem and the Gentiles (Jer 9:24f.; 25:11-32). God cannot find a single edible grape in his vineyard (Micah 7:1); he cannot find "any that act wisely, that seek after God. They have all gone astray, they are all alike corrupt; there is none that does good, no, not one" (Ps 14:2-3). This universality points to all men's inner solidarity in sin[10]—a topic we shall have to examine in more detail—but does not in any way diminish the individual's culpability (cf. Ps 51). The world's sin piles up so high before God that it seems incapable of being forgiven (Is 22:14)—an anticipation of the sin against the Spirit of which the New Testament speaks.

The tension is heightened until it becomes unbearable, and the prophet has a special place in this heightening, at the very core

[10] This topic is dealt with in detail in Ligier, I, 85ff., 92ff.

of the drama. Commissioned by God, he is the one who lays the guilt bare, although, on the other hand, he belongs to the "people of unclean lips" (Is 6:5); he is sent to this people with the certainty that his message will be rejected. Those whose hearts are hardened it will harden even more, and this clash between the people and God will express itself in the prophet's destiny. He is caught between the hammer and the anvil. The hammer can be God himself, using the prophet to make his judgment known to the people; so we have the symbolic penances imposed on men, which are like an incipient Incarnation of the Word of God.[11] But the hammer can be the people, who vent on the prophet the anger of their resistance to God. The "Suffering Servant"— the embodied covenant (Is 42:6)—consigned to the humiliation of atonement both by God and by the people, is already anticipated in Jeremiah and Ezekiel, for example, when the latter has to "bear the punishment of the house of Israel" (Ezek 4:4–6). Hosea's physical, sexual union with the harlot points in the same direction.

Again, the abrupt juxtaposition of prophecies of disaster (including the annihilation of the people and the dissolution of the covenant) and prophecies of salvation (the breathing of new life into the dead bones, the emergence of a new shoot out of the moribund trunk) expresses the inseparably two-sided unity of the divine action. It is the same fire that destroys and purifies. Of course such action from above calls for the response of conversion, of the profession of allegiance, of penance, from below. But there is insistence upon the fact that man's initiative, which God does not force, only comes about because of a preceding intervention on God's part, by which he causes the hardened hearts to melt. The two-sided prophecy points to a single goal, the "Day of Yahweh", which will be both judgment and redemption.

After the Exile, the picture of guilt shifts, adopting a different concrete form with a view to the New Covenant. Israel has given up its idolatry; it endeavors to keep the law and thinks that, by immersing itself in it (and thus in God's purposes for the world), it has attained a God-given wisdom. While this deepen-

---

[11] *The Glory of the Lord* VI (San Francisco: Ignatius Press, 1991), 224–30.

ing of faith and piety on the part of "Yahweh's poor" signifies a genuine return to the covenant, new and more subtly covert dangers emerge elsewhere. In "wisdom", we see the attempt to reach a complacent or rational grasp of the way God rules the world. In the keeping of the Commandments, there is the tendency to regard oneself as guiltless, distinct from the "sinners" and "godless" of whom the later Psalms speak so much. This more covert tendency to autonomy (more covert, that is, than open idolatry) will be taken up by Jesus when he comes to his final unmasking of sin.

It is more difficult to discuss the nature of sin in the *New Testament*. Here sin is portrayed, on the one hand, as a final intensification of the Old Testament No to God's Word (now made flesh). On the other hand, the New Testament takes as its vantage point the post-Easter vanquishing of sin and the reconciliation of the world to God. The images and colors in which this intensification is presented are largely borrowed from the Old Testament—the energy of its speech remains unrivalled—while the images depicting a life forgiven and reconciled to God attain a luminosity and intimacy hitherto unknown. Something else has changed too. On the basis of the Cross, the dividing wall between the Jews, chosen for the covenant, and the pagans, who live "without God in the world", is torn down. Now, as a result of the Incarnation of the Word, mankind as a whole is irradiated by that light from above that "lightens every man" (Jn 1:9). Not only is the same God the Creator and Lord of the covenant as in the Old Testament; the same Jesus Christ is the "beginning of God's creation" (Rev 3:14) and the one who reconciles this creation to God. Thus, in his light, both a true anthropology (including an understanding of sin) and a true theology (that is, God's self-manifestation to men) can attain full development. In this way, justice is done to all that is true in pagan, anthropocentric ethics, and the "golden rule" is given a definitive interpretation in the light of Christ: "As you did it [not] to one of the least of these, you did it [not] to me" (Mt 25:40, 45).

The Old Testament expectation of the Day of Yahweh—ambivalently seen both as an annihilating judgment and as the saving power of God's covenant faithfulness—attains objectivity in the New Testament, where it becomes the way to the Cross, the final judgment (Jn 12:21ff.) and the ultimate overthrowing of all that is hostile to God (Jn 16:33). At the subjective level, however, within the perspective of Jesus' consciousness and his words, the primary result is the promise of ultimate salvation: in him, the kingdom of God is beginning to take hold on earth, and the people who sit in darkness have seen a great light. But at the same time, just as clearly, a warning is addressed—in genuine prophetic style—to all who disregard or reject the approaching salvation. The promise of salvation is magnified beyond anything found in the Old Testament: Jesus not only promises a coming salvation but actually forgives sins, since he *is* salvation, personally present. (This is the deeper meaning of his miracles, cf. Mk 2:5, 9–11.) In his Beatitudes, he promises eschatological salvation to the "poor"; he opens up access to God, the loving Father, for all who accept his message, including those who have gone astray. In his cursing of the towns that did not receive him with faith, on the other hand, he seals the curses of the prophets on the "nations" or on the secessionist North Kingdom. In his "woes" against the Jerusalem that kills the prophets, he ratifies the latters' prediction of the great Exile, which will now prove to be the ultimate destruction, in which Jerusalem is left alone and desolate (Mt 23:34–39). In prophetic language, he can sum up those with whom he is confronted as an "adulterous and sinful generation" (Mk 8:38). He can speak of the coming judgment in quite general terms (just as the Baptist could speak of the "wrath to come" but also of a coming "baptism with the Holy Spirit and with fire": Lk 3:7, 16); but when it comes to concrete mention of the judgment, it is, not God, but the Son of Man who will pronounce it. The verdict will depend on how a man has responded to him, Jesus, God's concrete Word (Mk 8:38). If a man has recognized in him the presence of God's Holy Spirit and has resisted him, his sin is unforgivable; indeed, it is more grievous than those sins that could not be forgiven in the Old Testament, for it cannot be forgiven "in this age or in the age to come" (Mt 12:32). Underlining this intensification, we now find that the "eternal fire" of Gehenna has opened up below Sheol (Mt 5:22, 29f.; 10:28; 18:9; 23:33; 25:41), balancing, as it were, the heaven that is now open to all.

Even though the Gospels speak with less asperity than the prophets, the antithesis of the choice set before man has become a stark one. In the very shadow of the imminent Passion, we have the great sermon in which Jesus lashes the Pharisees and lays their sins bare; his strictures apply to all the leaders in Israel who have tried to usurp God's power for the purpose of their own self-perfection. The prophets too had turned primarily against the nation's leaders: whatever their position or function—kings, priests, judges, court prophets, sages, politicians —they were chiefly responsible for the people's sin. Isaiah and the other prophets reject these leaders' allegedly superior conduct and point back to the true, original, covenant faith. Jesus does the same: "Woe to you, scribes and Pharisees, hypocrites! for you tithe mint and dill and cumin and have neglected the weightier matters of the law, justice and mercy and faith; these you ought to have done, without neglecting the others. You blind guides, straining out a gnat and swallowing a camel!" (Mt 23:23f.). It is by these very leaders, who succeed in changing the people's mind, that Jesus is condemned to the Cross. The "Son" undergoes the fate of the "servants", the prophets, who were sent out on a mission that *was* in vain from the very first, as the New Testament emphasizes (Is 6:9-10; Mt 13:14f.; Mk 4:12, 18; Lk 8:10; Jn 12:40f.).

We have only one thing to say about the Passion of Jesus at this point. The depiction of it, which is above all emotion, which is objective and in fact *liturgical*, is designed as the unveiling of the whole sin of mankind. Thus it starts with the Christian traitor, is continued by the Jews and is brought to a conclusion by the Gentiles. The Christian un-faith of Judas Iscariot regresses to what seems to be the Jewish faith in the Messiah; the latter, however, measured against the response of Abraham, Moses and the prophets, is unmasked as a political trust in power. It is not even un-faith. The words, "We have no king but Caesar", reveal its pagan quality. It is a striking fact that all those guilty of the murder of the Word of God try to slip out of the net in which God has caught them: Judas, by handing back the blood-money; the Jews, by invoking a law that calls for the death of Jesus; Pilate, by washing his hands in token of his innocence. Thus we see that the central sin of world history, in all its patent objectivity, is still designed, at the subjective level, as an excuse, a lie.

Jesus takes upon himself the entire sin of the world. Having been "made sin", he "confesses" it on the Cross in a confession that is—for the first time—total. In return, at Easter, he is given an "absolution" that embraces the whole world.[12] In view of all this, the post-Easter preaching sees even the deepest guilt in the light of the reconciliation that has been achieved: "I know, brethren, that you acted in ignorance, as did also your rulers. . . . Repent therefore, and turn again, that your sins may be blotted out" (Acts 3:17, 19). It took many years of bitter experience before it was eventually realized that the majority of the Jews would not repent but rather would become the most zealous opponents of the new faith. The Book of Revelation will call them the "synagogue of Satan" (2:9).

Paul, the theologian of salvation history, depicts the world's sin in the darkest hue (Rom 3:9; 7:14; Gal 3:22), but this depiction is only one side of a diptych; the other side is always of greater moment: where sin abounds, "grace much more abounds" (Rom 5:15, 17, 20). And in his mature theology, even Paul, in spite of his irritation on account of the Jews (they "killed both the Lord Jesus and the prophets, and drove us out, and displease God and oppose all men by hindering us from speaking to the Gentiles that they may be saved—so as always to fill up the measure of their sins": 1 Th 2:15f.), has a certain understanding for their blindness; he expounds its function in salvation history and opens up a perspective of eschatological salvation for them (Rom 10–11). He sets no limits to Christian hope, for it builds on the fundamental reconciliation between God and all men and on the equally fundamental reconciliation between Jews and Gentiles; thus, according to God's will, it looks forward to the salvation of all (1 Tim 2:4). But, on the one hand, he adopts Jesus' analysis of the way the law has been misused, that is, contrary to the covenant of faith, and sharpens it: now, in his view, the law appears primarily as a cause of sin and as a judgment upon the sinner. On the other hand, Paul does not suggest

[12] Cf. Adrienne von Speyr, *Confession* (San Francisco: Ignatius Press, 1985).

that Satan, the "god of this world" (2 Cor 4:4), and the powers associated with him, have been simply dethroned: Christ's war against these powers continues through world time (1 Cor 15:24). There *is* a region outside the community of salvation, a region subject to Satan (1 Cor 5:5; 2 Cor 2:11; 1 Tim 1:20). Indeed, Satan can act as tempter and persecutor even within this inner realm of salvation (1 Cor 7:5; 2 Cor 11:14; 12:7; 1 Th 2:18). Thus Christians are entangled in a struggle against superhuman powers and cannot survive without "the whole armor of God" (Eph 6:10–18). Paul envisages a final battle that will take place when "the secret power of godlessness", which is "already at work", will no longer be subject to any restraint; "the coming of the lawless one by the activity of Satan will be with all power and with pretended signs and wonders, and with all wicked deception for those who are to perish, because they refused to love the truth and so be saved. Therefore God sends upon them a strong delusion, to make them believe what is false" (2 Th 2:7–11). This power is already concentrating itself in opposition to God, and prior to the Lord's coming, during the period of "rebellion", it will be embodied in the "man of lawlessness", the "son of perdition, who opposes and exalts himself against every so-called god or object of worship, so that he takes his seat in the temple of God, proclaiming himself to be God" (2 Th 2:3–4). Paul's expressions are borrowed from the imagery of the prophetic tradition, Daniel in particular (11:36), as developed by Jewish apocalyptic. The only specifically Christian affirmation is that it is not God (cf. Ps 11:4; Ps 33:6) but the returning Christ who, "with the breath of his mouth", will slay the one who usurps God's place in the Temple (2:8). This strong link with Old Testament eschatology means that there is a clear hiatus between what is described as the "secret power of godlessness" and the Johannine Antichrist.

Not until John does the core of that negative power emerge— in the post-Easter Church—as the open refusal to accept Jesus Christ as the Word of God who has come in the flesh. In the Letters, the whole traditional eschatological imagery disappears; everything is concentrated on man's Yes or No to the Incarnation of the Son of the Father. Therefore the No can be attributed not only to a personalized representative of evil but also to "many antichrists" (1 Jn 2:18); they indicate the approaching end. For John, the denial of Jesus' divine-human nature is crucial, for it rejects the proof that God is love. To "dissolve Jesus" (*ho lyei ton Jēsoun* 4:3) is to dissolve the Christian, trinitarian God and his saving work. John regards a No to Jesus as final and irrevocable. Such a denial scorns the only path to salvation, and the one who has thus fallen away has put himself beyond the community's intercession (1 Jn 5:16)—indeed, beyond that of Jesus himself (Jn 17:9).

This same abyss yawns in Hebrews 6:4ff. before the man who, having received the grace of a living faith in Christ, goes on to despise it. Once God has given his Son, he has nothing more to give; thus the guilty person cannot hope for any further grace of conversion. He has "spurned the Son of God, and profaned the blood of the covenant by which he was sanctified, and outraged the Spirit of grace" (Heb 10:29). The Letter of Jude and 2 Peter are profoundly and awfully aware of this possibility. These sinners, with their mocking attitude and their godless, dissolute behavior, are still within the community itself but are working to destroy it. Since they are "devoid of the Spirit", they "set up divisions" in the Church (Jude 18f.). Believers are urged to "save some, by snatching them out of the fire" (22f.); this implies that the others, who are beyond rescue, are already burning in this fire.

In this way, the idea of a sin that is mortal moves away from the imagery of Jewish eschatology and in the direction of the post-Christian final struggle, which is the central theme of the Book of Revelation.

Of course, the foregoing is not an exhaustive presentation of sin in the New Testament. The criterion for right and wrong conduct is the discipleship of Jesus, walking in his Spirit; Paul, in particular, draws out the implications of this in his *paranesis* and his *Haustafeln*—his catalogues of virtues and sins. In the latter, however, sins are always betrayals of love as it is found incarnate in Christ (hence the special importance that attaches to the body and its holiness, since it is the temple of the Spirit of Jesus, cf. 1 Cor 6:12–20). After what has been said about creation and redemption having the same foundation in Christ, it is no surprise that Paul can actually borrow points from pagan ethics (cf. Phil 4:8); after the Incarnation of the Word of God, in other words, the anthropological dimensions of sin are fully manifested side by side with the theological and christological dimensions.[13] Jesus spoke of the love of one's fellow men as the second commandment, after the love of God, but gave it equal *rank* with the latter (Mt 22:38–39).

c. "Original Sin"

What theology calls *peccatum originale*, the "sin of origin", has deep roots in the theology of the Old and New Testaments, yet it remains one of those "mysteries" of biblical revelation that can never be completely solved.[14] (The German term *Erbsünde*, which came into use with the German mystics, is restricted in scope and misleading.) It casts a further shadow over the pathos of the world stage, which is already dark enough. We need not discuss it in detail here, but only insofar as it heightens the dramatic tension of the situation that exists between God and man.

The fundamental affirmation is this. A decision against God on the part of one individual—not *any* individual, but the one who founded the family of mankind—has plunged this whole family, not into personal sin, but into a lack of grace. This has consequences for nature's entire make-up. This deprivation is not only the source of the countless personal sins of individuals but the cause of all men's inability, on the basis of the powers they still retain, successfully to strive toward their destination in God. There is an initial difficulty in conceiving this kind of socially transmitted deprivation (which must be carefully distinguished from the concept of personal sin or guilt), since sinning (unlike acting in grace and love) isolates man, diminishes or destroys his relationship to the community. Consequently, while it is possible to appreciate that man's estrangement deprives others of a power of love that might otherwise support and benefit them, it

[13] Cf. the introduction to the chapter "Das Wesen der Sünde" and the theological, christological and anthropological interpretation given it by Leo Scheffczyk in his *Wirklichkeit und Ereignis der Sünde* (Augsburg: Winfried, 1970).

[14] M. J. Scheeben, "The Mystery of Sin: Sin in General; Original Sin" in *The Mysteries of Christianity* (1865), 243–310.

is not obvious that it deprives them of something fundamental and radical in their relationship with God.

P. Schoonenberg[15] takes the first aspect, which is clearly evident, as the starting point for his attempt[16] to find a middle position between Scripture's portrayal of man's universal sinfulness—to which history is witness—and the specific dogma of "original sin". He describes it as the individual's "freedom-in-situation", a freedom that exists prior to any particular decision. The individual remains free but lacks the context and the relationships with the community within which to exercise the act of love.[17] Physically he is free, but morally he is unable to develop his freedom. This grace-less situation, according to Schoonenberg, should be conceived not only at an external, social level (as Pelagius did) but in existential terms, insofar as it precedes all the individual's free decisions.[18] He then tries to reduce "official Church teaching" to the positing of this *existentiale*. But, while it is essential to stress the aspect of mankind's historical solidarity,[19] the latter fails to explain the theological assertion, namely, that this solidarity is so total that newborn children (even of Christian parents) carry this defect within them from birth, not merely after reaching the age of reason and becoming acquainted with the power of sin. It may be true that there is a "history of sin" that "gathers momentum like an avalanche" (cf. Gen 6:12) and reaches its climax in the murder of God on Calvary (according to Schoonenberg, it is this that makes "original sin" universal and irrevocable),[20] but the Church's understanding of "original innocence" is quite clearly at a deeper level; the historical mode of transmission is only the vehicle of a meta-historical state of affairs.

If we consult the Scriptures of the Old and New Covenants, we find a convergence of indications to the effect that, behind the incontrovertible universality of sin in mankind (we have

---

[15] *Theologie der Sünde. Ein theologischer Versuch* (Einsiedeln: Benziger, 1966).

[16] His sketch is meant to be "no more than an essay", ending "with a question mark": 213.

[17] *Ibid.*, 92, cf. 121, 129ff.

[18] *Ibid.*, 138. On the differences between Schoonenberg and Pelagius: 166ff.

[19] Schoonenberg thinks it should be emphasized much more strongly: 115.

[20] *Ibid.*, 138, 199.

already presented texts illustrating this), the universality is itself rooted in a mysterious solidarity on the part of all men. At decisive points, this solidarity is traced back through a line of descent. J. Scharbert has demonstrated this—in the teeth of a widespread prejudice—in the case of the Old Testament. He is even able to cite respected exegetes and theologians in his support,[21] yet his demonstration operates at a much deeper level. The texts he adduces from the culture of Israel's neighbors are, in part, astonishing: "No child was ever born of its mother sinless", says a Sumerian text of the seventeenth century B.C., and, in the Hittite "Prayers of Murshilish II" (born 1345), the king entreats the gods to turn away the plague they have justly visited upon the people, saying, "The sin of the father comes upon the son"; he acknowledges solidarity with this sin: "Yes, it is so, we have done this." Egyptian texts are also quoted. A man's sin can threaten all the areas of his life, "particularly his family, his relations, his descendants and his circle of friends; if the king is the guilty one, . . . so is the entire nation: this was held to be self-evident."[22] This is true not only of cultures that see things solely in terms of their clan relationships and hence trace their ancestry back to a progenitor, as is the case with nomads and semi-nomads like the Hebrews. The latter "actually embraced all nations in one vast family tree of mankind (Gen 4f., 10f.); this leads back to a progenitor called simply 'man' (ādām)."[23] In clan societies, all correct behavior is community-related; conversely, wrong conduct is what threatens the peace of the community. Thus the concepts of sin (hatta'âh) and guilt (āwōn) always include their effects on national life.[24] The Yahwist, in his account of man's fall into sin, attributes man's solidarity in sin to the first progenitor of all human beings; ancient oral tradition must have played a part in this.[25] The first community between God and man is already envisaged in the form of a covenant: the grace of paradise is linked to contractual conditions; if they are kept, Adam can enjoy "life", that is, uninterrupted fellowship with God, death at an advanced age, the favor of his fellow men,

---

[21] Prolegomena eines Alttestamentlers zur Erbsündenlehre, Quaest. Disp. 37 (Herder, 1968), 13ff.

[22] Ibid., 28.   [23] Ibid., 37.

[24] Ibid., 54.   [25] Ibid., 64.

and so forth. This life, moreover, is depicted as taking place in a primordial community. The breach of the covenant, inspired by the serpent and carried through by man and woman, has irreparable effects for mankind. "The Yahwist regards it as self-evident that the children and all the descendants of the first human couple are born into a condition radically lacking in peace —as a result of sin—and share in the consequences of transgression." Yet man is not simply banished into the harsh world: God gives him a hope that the power of evil will one day be broken (Gen 3:15).[26] The genealogical schema loses its hold as the national consciousness grows during the period of the Kings, but "the prophets and theologians of history are aware of an original sin on the part of Israel." The prophets trace this original sin back to the national Patriarch (Jacob in Hosea; Ezekiel says that Jerusalem comes of idolatrous parentage) and to the idolatry practiced in the wilderness (Amos, Jeremiah); they are "all adulterers, a company of treacherous men" (Jer 9:2). The Elohist and the Chroniclers, too, "regard it as axiomatic that all generations and members of the people are inextricably entangled in the sins of the fathers".[27] This does not mean that those who come after, and have to bear their fathers' guilt and atone for it, are innocent (cf. the proverb of the "sour grapes" in Isaiah 37:29f.; Ezekiel 18:2f.); they have to admit that they too have transgressed (Lam 5:16). Original sin and personal sin constitute a unity. In addition, the view exists in Israel (perhaps influenced by foreign wisdom traditions) that every man is infallibly bound to sin (1 Kings 8:46), that man is sinful from his mother's womb, as Psalm 51:5 puts it: "Behold, I was brought forth in iniquity, and in sin did my mother conceive me"—an expression meaning "in animal desire". Ligier suggests that this mention of the sinful mother also contains a reference to the adulterous Jerusalem.[28] From the Exile on, however, the documents reveal a growing synthesis of ideas, and the Yahwist's clan-based concepts become part of it. (The Priestly Codex knows, at least, that "all flesh is corrupt": Gen 6:11f.; 7:21; in addition to the many rites of expiation, it is acquainted with the great Day of Atone-

---

[26] *Ibid.*, 70–71.   [27] *Ibid.*, 87.
[28] Ligier I, 99–151.

ment.) The teachers of wisdom take up the theme of original sin as found in the Yahwist account: now, because of a woman's sin, all must die (Sir 25:24): "Through envy of the devil death came into the world, and all who belong to him undergo it" (Wis 2:24).

In the New Testament, the "Second Adam" steps forth to provide a new start for the whole race, but in doing so he does not in any way undermine the old solidarity in, and transmission of, sin. We recall Jesus' words addressed to the "faithless and adulterous generation" that has always killed the prophets and so will kill him too: "Fill up, then, the measure of your fathers" (Mt 23:32). On the other hand, Jesus knows that he is the presence of God's saving will, which embraces the whole human race. As John puts it, God's saving will is not subsequent to, and conditional upon, the occurrence of sin: it was in the beginning ("before Abraham was" . . . "in him"—the life and light of men—"all things were created"). The presupposition, as Paul makes clear, is always the natural human community (with its solidarity) that is the object of God's saving will, created with a view to the latter. It is important to read 1 Corinthians 15:45–50 together with Romans 5:12–21: in Romans 5, the two solidarity principles are "simultaneous" (Adam and Christ) but in such a way that the first (which establishes solidarity in sin) is always overtaken by the second (which causes reconciliation and grace to overwhelm the former). This implies that the first exists with a view to the second and that its very structure is governed by it. In 1 Corinthians 15, by contrast (without any direct mention of guilt), we have the—in some respects—logical priority of the first, earthly Adam over the "last" Adam, who comes from heaven, of the mortal over the immortal; here the first Adam, from the earth (that is, creaturely), has no innate right to the fulfillment brought by the Second, the "life-giving (divine) Pneuma." Nonetheless, the principle of solidarity and community found in the first Adam, which asserts itself in the succession of generations, is the creaturely foundation on which God can build his freely given solidarity-in-grace, in Christ. Clearly, whenever a new member of the human family is born into the world, the creature—with its defects, that is, concretely speaking, with original sin—once more steps forth as the material on which God will work to "clothe the perishable with imperishability" (1 Cor 15:54). The grace that comes from above and that is pledged to us in Christ could not achieve the prototypical solidarity of all (as the "Body of Christ") unless it met with a creaturely solidarity that is ultimately derived from this prototype.

Man is always situated between two principles[29] that, depending on his free choice, govern his perdition or salvation. This already becomes clear in the Old Testament, insofar as man's solidarity in perdition is accompanied by the original promise given to him when he is banished from paradise. This is rendered tangible in Enoch, who "walked with God" (Gen 5:24ff.), and in the covenant with Noah. In Abraham, it becomes a promise of blessing to all nations, a promise that, according to Paul, is fulfilled in Christ (Gal 3:16). The Old Testament concepts that Paul adopts to describe the dire situation applying to everyone: "All have fallen short of the glory of God" (Rom 3:23)—on the basis of a relationship of succession going back to the originating principle—have been subject to so much theological reflection in the Old Testament[30] that they do not need any further "de-

[29] It is possible to say "that 'original sin', as a negative fact, is countered by the positive fact of redemption; thus, from Adam on, man is originally sinful, in a vacuum in which he lacks grace; at the same time, however, Christ draws him into the sphere of grace. This implies that man is objectively oriented to Christ, mankind's gracious and grace-giving Head. From the very outset, Christ draws man to faith and sacramental life." L. Scheffczyk, "Wirklichkeit und Geheimnis der Sünde" (see note 13 above), 270.

[30] The Yahwist traces man's dire situation back to a progenitor of all men. In doing so, he is going beyond narrowly clan-based concepts and also beyond the later idea of Israel's national solidarity, which attributed the threatened situation of an entire nation to a remote guilt (Jerusalem's origins, Jacob's deception). This latter idea was based on the notion of "corporate personality" (J. de Fraine, *Adam und seine Nachkommen* [Cologne, 1962]), a slightly different version of the fundamental idea of the solidarity of all mankind. The various biblical notions circle around a realistic appraisal of this solidarity, seeing it as an *inner* quality of the individual. Trent expressed this as "*propagatione, non imitatione transfusum*" (DS 1513), which by no means anathematizes sexuality as such (its *libido*: Augustine) as the means of transmitting the original guilt but does see sexuality as the real bond linking all individuals and making them an indivisible community. Sexuality as such, even when it is sanctified by the Christian sacrament, belongs to the sphere of the first Adam. Thus even the child of Christian parents comes into the world bearing

mythologizing". However we understand the first principle—
and we have all acted according to its law, whether at a mono-
genist or polygenist level—it destines the entire ensuing race to
a disproportion between nature and the grace originally intended
for it. Thus it results in a disorder that was not envisaged by nature and in a form of death that was not originally designed for
it. Now, death, unless it is undergirded by the grace of Christ's
death, is a dying to God.

In Romans 5:12, the fact that all men die and perish is the primary sign that some original sin has spread through the whole
race, just as "all have sinned" by personally incurring the hand-
icap that brings disaster. Here, however, "hereditary death" is
only a symptom of the "reign of sin, leading to death" that is
explicitly mentioned in 5:21. As far as Paul is concerned, behind the personal sin of all men, the "sin of the world", there
lies some undeniable principle of origin that is responsible for
it.[31] But the "last Adam" did not remain beyond the bane of
death and the sin that causes it. In becoming man, he desired to
take upon himself this very death in order to heal the disastrous
sickness, so that "those who are subject to death because of sin"
(Rom 8:10) have the possibility of putting this death, and all
the suffering associated with it, under the sign of the Second
Adam. In this way, what seems finally to throw the sinner back
upon himself—death—can be understood and experienced as
something that is open to the world's reconciliation with God.

These remarks on "hereditary" or original sin, all too short
as they are, thus bring us to our main topic, that is, the dramatic
dimension of life, by uncovering man's eminently dramatic constitution in the face of the goal of his existence. While inclined,
on the basis of a natural impulse that is not yet affected by sin
("concupiscence"), to affirm his own nature in his own interests,
man is called to pursue a supernatural goal and so to transcend
himself. But since every man is entangled in the consequences of
original sin, his situation becomes more critical: his natural de-

---

"original sin". (Hence the kernel of truth in Augustine's theory.) The exception
is Mary (DS 1516), insofar as she was destined to be the direct associate of the
Second Adam.

[31] Cf. Ligier II, 266ff.: "De la mort au péché".

sire for God (*desiderium naturale*) is weakened by a negative desire to be-for-himself. Thus he finds himself turned away from the principle of redemption; only with the assistance of grace can he win through to the self-conquest that is required of him. Man's very constitution is *agonal* [Gk *agonia*: "contest, struggle, agony" —TRANS.].[32] For the "old Adam" always retains the urge to shut himself within his finitude and mortality and to content himself with goals at the purely natural level; moreover, the grace of the Second Adam—a grace that invites man—has itself adopted an *agonal* form as a result of the world's sin. There is now no other path to self-fulfillment but by dying to oneself (with Christ).

From God's point of view, "original sin" does not cause any interruption of the offer of grace: it only transforms it. No longer is the form of this grace based on the Son's mediatorship in creation (and the creation of man) but on the redemptive grace of the Cross and on the Son's bearing of the world's sin. It is only on mankind's side, at most, that we can speak of an "interruption", since mankind cannot originally have been created in a state of estrangement from God (this is the heart of the doctrine of man's original state), even if grace was required from the very outset if the proper "selfless" choice was to be made. Now, however, because of its sinful determination to "be itself", mankind is turned away from God, and this makes it difficult for it to lay hold of grace (which is the grace of the Cross). To that extent, we can talk only "dialectically" of original sin.[33]

Within this dialectic, instead of lamenting the wound that goes right through human nature, or being indignant at it (as if we had nothing to do with it), we have the right, and even the duty, to be grateful to God for mankind's solidarity in its destiny vis-à-vis God. For our shared nakedness, our common lack of an inner orientation toward God and his grace, has caused him to make

---

[32] Cf. Trent's statement that the concupiscence that remains even in the baptized is not evil as such, "quae cum *ad agonem* relicta sit, nocere non consentientibus et viriliter per Jesu gratiam *pugnantibus* non valet" (DS 1515).

[33] "Dialektisches Verhältnis zweier Existentialien", K. Rahner, article "Erbsünde" in *Sacr. Mundi* I (1967), 1109. "Thus, from the outset, man's situation moves dialectically toward the decision in favor either of faith and love or of personal sin; he is an 'original sinner' from Adam on, and he is redeemed by Christ and destined for him": *ibid.*, 1114.

known to us a deeper and more painful form of his love. Now, for the first time, he has shown us to what depths this love is ready to descend, once it has decided to give a share in absolute love and blessedness to the creatures it has freely (and without any necessity whatsoever) called into existence. For if it is true that God will have to demand more of man once he is subject to original sin—a more rigorous conversion, a more ruthless process of education ("My son, do not despise the Lord's discipline or be weary of his reproof, for the Lord reproves him whom he loves, as a father the son in whom he delights": Proverbs 3:11–12 = Hebrews 12:5f.), he makes it clear that this is a genuine requirement of absolute love: his love has already taken upon itself all the rigorous demands, the extreme chastening, which would aptly apply to us. Seen from the highest angle, our solidarity in sin is the necessary condition if God's last and final initiative for his entire mankind is to be revealed. For he did not take upon himself the sin of chosen individuals, but the sin of all, without selectivity (DS 624, 2005). This is the heart of the theo-drama.[34]

d. Guilt and the World's Suffering

Original sin lies somewhere on the periphery of what we can still grasp; we can reach some understanding of it from the profound solidarity of all human destinies. The worldwide reality of suffering, which extends beyond the human world to the world of animals, has its center of gravity beyond that periphery. Of

[34] This is put splendidly by C. S. Lewis: The archetypal man turned away from God, and this resulted in "the emergence of a new kind of man . . . a new species, never made by God, had sinned itself into existence. . . . God might have arrested this process by miracle: but this . . . would have been to decline the problem which God had set Himself when He created the world, the problem of expressing His goodness through the total drama of a world containing free agents, in spite of, and by means of, their rebellion against Him. The symbol of a drama . . . is here useful to correct a certain absurdity which may arise if we talk too much of God planning and creating the world process for good and of that good being frustrated by the free will of the creatures. . . . In fact, of course, God saw the crucifixion in the act of creating the first nebula . . . ; the resulting conflict is resolved by God's own assumption of the suffering nature which evil produces." *The Problem of Pain* (London, 1940; 29th impression: Collins, 1990), 66–67.

course there is that suffering that culpable human beings inflict on one another—involving so much calculation, so much inventiveness, from personal insults right up to wars, with their ever more terrible weapons. Such suffering can be laid to the account of the human economy of sin. At a human level, we can understand that sin must be expiated, either by the sinner himself or perhaps by some other in his stead, for it is evident that, in intending evil, man not only disturbs the order of being as a whole but actually damages his own good nature. Indeed, he may even ruin it entirely. If, behind the established world order, we see a God who has founded it in love and thus accompanies it, it is not hard to understand that his love can appear in the mode of anger, punishing the disruption of his order by the imposition of suffering. We do not even need to think primarily of great transgressions here. It is enough to think how, in their ordinary, everyday lives, comfortable people who consider themselves decent simply forget God. Compared with those around them, they do nothing startlingly sinful; then, stirred out of their lethargy by some sudden incursion of suffering, they become aware that their existence had no direction. Suffering has an educative function, makes us aware of the seriousness of life and death and of man's final goal. Furthermore, suffering spurs man on to fight against it; this is most definitely part of his task in the world, stimulating him to make countless discoveries. More again: suffering prompts countless people to engage in acts of love of neighbor; the recompense enjoined by the law court always presupposes some suffering that sets the process in motion. People must go hungry so that others may have compassion and selflessly give them bread. People must be sick or in prison so that others may hit upon the idea of visiting them. . . . In the drama between heaven and earth, therefore, human suffering is in many ways an element contributing to the gravity of the action.

If we recall the Book of Job, however, we shall be quick to dismiss this kind of domestication of suffering—which would turn it into an intelligible moral utility—as a shortsighted, petit-bourgeois rationalism. It does not matter whether Job really is as innocent as he avows: the constantly reiterated theme is the disproportion between any transgression he may have committed and the suffering meted out to him. His suffering goes beyond what can be viewed as "just" and humanly bearable; it has become The Unendurable per se. Man, looking at the events taking place on the world stage, has the disconcerting impression that some of the elements in the interaction between heaven and earth are beyond his control. It is as if a searchlight is picking out the center of the stage as the locus of his acting, whereas the outer areas are lost in obscurity. The searchlight's compass is not only that of his own understanding—for example, an ethical law of compensation—but also that of the biblical revelation, which illuminates only enough of the acting area as is necessary for man to have a right relationship with God. The truth of the Bible addresses itself to practical existence. This may (and should) remind man that the God with whom he has to do is "always greater": God has allotted a certain region of the world for man's "dominion", but this by no means extends to all created things; moreover, God reacts to man's behavior in a way that cannot be anticipated from the vantage point of finitude.

The world's suffering exceeds our human powers of comprehension. As such it points in the direction of two things: in the first place, there can be depths, in creation itself, that man has no power to dominate; and, in the second place, God can react to human conduct—that is, sin—in a way that is far more divine than man can imagine. The Book of Revelation clearly points to these two dimensions, speaking in chillingly sober objectivity of such appalling suffering. Here it is as if the pedagogical aspects of the world's suffering, those aspects that are somehow accessible to human intelligence, are deliberately bypassed and left behind. The suffering visited on the sinful earth by a wrathful justice only hardens the guilty and makes them turn away even more decisively. This means, if we now leave the special atmosphere of the Book of Revelation, that even suffering that is "justly" imposed from above is not, and cannot be, recognized and appreciated as such. Nor will it be. For there is always the baffling suffering of—in particular—the relatively innocent, the children (which prompts Ivan Karamazov to refuse to accept the admission ticket to God's heavenly concert). There are always those who are overpowered, suppressed and exploited by the mighty, who cannot defend themselves and have to endure it all; those whose human dignity is abused, perhaps because of their heroism, or who are robbed of their freedom or shot for a piece of land. There are always the "poor", the "hungry", those who "weep" or are "persecuted" (whom Jesus calls "blessed" in Luke 6:20ff.), or who are tortured beyond endurance either by malady or by men. If we assume that, in the eyes of the heaven that decrees or allows it, all this is regarded as just, is it not incumbent on us to foment a rebellion on earth against this heaven with its incomprehensible "justice"? Such a rebellion—the expression of sin's exasperation—must be prepared to stomach a contradiction: it is campaigning against a God whose actions on earth are bound to seem unjust yet who must nonetheless exist as a good God if rebellion is to be possible at all.

Suffering in the world, more than anything else, makes it difficult for people to approach God. He may be just (or even loving!) in himself, but he is unable to act in such a way as to appear credibly so on earth. What is man supposed to do in this darkness? Suffering cries much too loudly: he cannot fail to hear it, nor can he integrate it into an all-embracing system of world harmony—for example, as the "necessary shadow" that must be there for the sake of the beauty of the whole picture. It cries too loudly: it will not let a man dream up some personal escape-route (whether Buddhist or Stoic) out of existence and leave the others behind him, still suffering. (Feeling sorry for them does them no good.) It cries too loudly, yesterday, today and tomorrow, to warrant any consolation in terms of a remote future. Anyway, how can man himself, damaged and torn as he is, overcome suffering by his own efforts? Is there any other path but "the absurd", and hence despair? No answer can be constructed out of words and concepts to give an overall view. "So I tell you: reject every answer, however well-intentioned, so long as it consists only of words. Every answer that originates in thought alone, be it philosophical, theological, dialectical or political thought, is worthless. No answer is to be found in words."[35]

If man is not to fall prey to the internal contradictions of rebellion, he can only wait for God's own answer. And God gives no answer but the folly of the Cross; for the Cross is the only

[35] Bernard Bro, *Le Pouvoir du mal* (Cerf, 1976), 18.

thing to rise above the "folly" of the world's suffering. Men are not brought to acknowledge God by the justice of the heavenly bowls of wrath; even in the Book of Revelation, the Lamb only triumphs "as though it had been slain". It is not God's powerfully presented answer that actually brings an answer to Job's question. Job's "call for an advocate, a redeemer, can only be understood as the unanswerable cry of the pre-Christian world, which is eventually given its answer in Christ. Job is stronger than the old God. The Bringer of Sorrow cannot answer Job, the Sufferer can. Not the Hunter, but the Hunted."[36] The answer is not given by the Suffering Servant either, the representative sufferer, oppressed both by sinners and by God, for it is not God who suffers in him. Only "the Logos of the Cross" will embrace and undergird the world's suffering, a lived, bleeding Word that calls out for meaning and for God and that ends in the cry of death. Only this Word—so faint that, in the maelstrom of questions and accusations, it is hardly audible—will be able to be the answer that comes from God. "The demand made of God was so immense", says Claudel, "that only God's Son could answer it. He gave, not an explanation, but his presence, according to the gospel words: I have not come to bring enlightenment, to banish doubt, but to *fulfill*. . . . The Son of God did not come to do away with suffering but rather to suffer with us; not to abolish the Cross, but to stretch himself upon it. Of all the special privileges of humanity, God wanted to adopt only this one."[37]

However much weight we attach to the consequences of moral evil in mankind, it by no means exhausts the sum of suffering in the world. There remains all the physical suffering to which animal nature is exposed as a result of birth and death; for nature exists by eating and being eaten. In addition, there are all the natural geological catastrophes. And man is involved in all this insofar as he is the apex of organic creation and thus connected with the animal universe. This makes him a kind of centaur, as we have already observed,[38] which complicates his moral exis-

[36] Dorothee Sölle, *Leiden* (Stuttgart/Berlin: Kreuzverlag, 1973), 148.

[37] *Positions et propositions* II (Gallimard, 1943), 245.

[38] *Theo-Drama* II, 337–38.

tence: in part, he is subject to the grace-less laws of the biological cosmos, and, in part, he is superior to them and is obliged, as far as he is able, to submit them to moral control.

When Teilhard de Chardin endeavors to describe the world's development from the primal nebula up to man, he seems to regard it as a fundamental law, applying from the very lowest stages, that "nothing is constructed except at the price of an equivalent destruction."[39] "As a matter of fact, from the real evolutionary standpoint, something is finally burned in the course of every synthesis in order to pay for that synthesis."[40] Coming to the sphere of life, we find that life "passes over a bridge made up of accumulated corpses, and this is a direct effect of multiplication."[41] "Life is more real than lives. . . . This dramatic and perpetual opposition between the one born of the many and the many constantly being born of the one runs right through evolution."[42] But it is only in an "appendix" that Teilhard the phenomenologist deals with the problem of evil in this vast process. "I have not (and this in the interests of clarity and simplicity) considered it necessary to provide the negative of the photograph. . . . Surely [the abysses] were obvious enough. I have assumed that what I have omitted could nevertheless be seen. . . . Evil of disorder and failure . . . —how many failures have there been for one success . . . , how many sins for a solitary saint? . . . This is relentlessly imposed by the play of large numbers." Then the "evil of decomposition": "sickness and corruption", "death is the regular, indispensable condition of the replacement of one individual by another along a phyletic stem. Death—the essential lever in the mechanism and upsurge of life." Moreover, there is the "evil of solitude and anxiety" for the individual (and man in particular) who awakens in a world that is baffling and seems to lack meaning. Finally: "the evil [that is, the pain] of growth" (*mal de croissance*): nothing great is achieved without effort. Thus, under the "veil of security and harmony . . . , evil appears necessarily through the very structure of the system." "A universe that labors, that sins and that suffers." All upsurge must be "rig-

---

[39] *The Phenomenon of Man* (tr. London: Collins, 1959), 56.

[40] *Ibid.*, 56.   [41] *Ibid.*, 123.

[42] *Ibid.*, 123.

orously paid for". "Suffering and failure, tears and blood": these are all "so many by-products (often precious, moreover, and re-utilizable)" on the path toward spirit.[43]

Some people have attempted to render prehuman suffering in the world more plausible by suggesting that, from the start, in both the physical and the biological spheres, there exist "prelim-inary sketches" of human freedom. This human freedom "pre-determines the form of its own development"—the ultimate goal of evolution.[44] This is not convincing, however: it cannot be certain in advance that human freedom will make a negative decision, and the mere element of freedom of *choice* cannot itself be regarded as a source of evil.

Strangely enough, at the conclusion of his treatise, Teilhard himself opens up another perspective, leaving the reader to ver-ify it (since, as a mere phenomenologist, he feels he has no com-petence to do so).

> But is that really all? Is there nothing else to see [beyond this description of evil]? In other words, is it really sure that, for an eye trained and sensitized by light other than that of pure science, the quantity and the malice of evil *hic et nunc,* spread through the world, does not betray a certain *excess,* inexplicable to our reason, if to *the normal effect of evolution* is not added the *extraordinary effect* of some catastrophe or primordial deviation.

The results of science are "always ambiguous beyond a certain point." But how does it come about that, "even in the view of the mere biologist, the human epic resembles nothing so much as a way of the Cross"?[45]

Teilhard is pointing to theology, but not to its center; he is pointing to the periphery to which we referred at the beginning of this section. Here looms the insoluble question of whether the "excess" of suffering ascertained by the phenomenologist has not something to do, even at the level of the subhuman world, with the "principalities and powers" of which Paul speaks. Has it not something to do with the "god of this world", the "prince"

[43] *Ibid.,* 339–41.
[44] Gisbert Greshake, *Der Preis der Liebe. Besinnung über das Leid* (Herder, 1978), 27–48.
[45] Teilhard, 341–42.

and "ruler" of this world, whose original fall from God is responsible for the deep rent that goes from the bottom right up to the top—where it emerges as mankind's tragic history? The stubborn persistence of this topic in Scripture and also in the life of Jesus should cause us to pay greater attention to it, particularly since, compared with similar themes in antiquity and the surrounding Near East, it has quite a different ring about it. What Teilhard feels to be an "excess" is precisely the experience that is manifested in the Gospels, Letters and Book of Revelation.

Man's relationship to this spirit world cannot be pinned down. On the one hand, man, who feels that he is the crown of creation, is humiliated by the existence of this spirit world. It makes him a second-order creation, appearing on a stage on which action has already taken place. This is the origin of the strange idea we find in Augustine and Anselm, and continued into the High Middle Ages, that man was created in order to fill the gaps arising in the ranks of the angels. On the other hand, on the basis of the structure of human freedom, we can exclude totally any suggestion that man has no direct communication with God but can only attain him through the intermediary of a "heavenly hierarchy"; especially since the central dramatic events, as they are revealed to him, actually take place between man's earth and God's heaven, culminating in God's becoming a man (and not an angel). If these principalities and powers continue to exist, however, they are not annihilated by Christ's victory, but, as Paul describes it with some precision, they are "deprived of their power", their "influence" (*katargein*, 1 Cor 15:24), or, in Augustine's metaphor, they are "fettered". At this point, the paradox mentioned by the Book of Revelation acquires concrete relevance: the hostile power that Jesus sees "falling like lightning from heaven" (Lk 10:18) is cast down to the earth and manifests "great wrath, because he knows that his time is short" (Rev 12:12). Thus Jesus' exhortations to watch and pray, Peter's (1 Pet 5:8) and Paul's (Eph 6:11f.) exhortations to fight against the devil with the weapons of God, are not mere mythology. Corresponding to the final, behind-the-scenes stripping away of power from these "powers", there is a temporal, foreground "empowering" of the followers of Jesus: this accords with the whole thrust of the Book of Revelation.

This topic is introduced here not so much for man's sake as in order to throw some light on the fact of physical suffering in the world. C. S. Lewis has made the most concrete attempt to relate physical suffering, in its consequences, to a "redemption" (however conceived) of the subhuman world and of the "futility" (Rom 8:20) that weighs upon it.[46] He is aware that, in doing so, he is moving away from the center and toward the periphery and that all that he surmises remains at the level of "speculation". It is salutary to remember, however, that Scripture itself has already engaged in speculation in this same direction: God's concession in the covenant with Noah, namely, that man (who now fills all animals with "fear" and "dread") may use dead animals for food, is regarded as a secondary stage; the original plan was for both man and animals to eat plants (Gen 1:29–30). Man's ontological connection with the cosmos that upholds him is undeniable; its solidarity with him is also attested in its yearning for salvation.[47] For, in the new heaven and the new earth, the world will not begin again from the beginning; God's old creation will be drawn into his life and so transfigured, and man's works will "follow him" and help to shape his blessedness. If this is the case, creation's suffering must also attain its transfiguration in a way that is beyond our imagining.[48]

At this very point, however, we come up against a final problem that threatens our whole theodramatic approach. Paul says, "I consider that the sufferings of this present time are not worth comparing with the glory that is to be revealed to us" (Rom 8:18). And, "For this slight momentary affliction is preparing for us an eternal weight of glory beyond all comparison" (2 Cor 4:17). Does this not mean that the whole drama is dissolved as it heads toward a completely undramatic destination? Has it not become a mere prelude to something inert, lying beyond the action, described (in 1 John 3:2) as "seeing God as he is"? Jesus

---

[46] "Animal Pain" in *The Problem of Pain*, 103–14.

[47] Romans 8:20 (assuming that *ktisis* really means creation as a whole and not, as some have tried to show, the world of humans).

[48] C. S. Lewis tries to bring out the concrete possibilities of a positive "elevation" of the animal world into the transfigured human world. He does so with a certain humor, which shows that he is well aware of the limits of his speculation.

compares the disciples' sadness to the pangs of a woman about to give birth: she forgets them in the joy of having given birth to a child. Does this not suggest that the only substantial, abiding fruit is the final state, beyond all the turmoil of earthly existence? In other words, can we not "forget" all dramatic tension?

It must be said that, in a certain sense, the drama in which the created world is rescued is, in fact, a prelude to the real action. As such, the real action must be the *being* of the redeemed children of God, in God's world, once they have been brought back to him and to themselves. What the Book of Revelation calls the "marriage of the Lamb" is not the conclusion but the beginning of a *life* that is to characterize the new aeon. This is portrayed only in shadowy images borrowed from the ancient world, but they suffice to evoke the superabundant, ever-flowing, event-quality of this life: myriad nations throng an open city to which all the treasures of the earth are brought; there the rushing waters of life are constantly heard, the trees of life constantly blossom and bear fruit. Now, at last, things that were formerly only in-cipient will really begin: "Behold, God tabernacles among men; they will be his people and he will be their God." And what is meant by: "They will reign for ever and ever"? Surely this implies activity, action that is fulfilling and fulfilled.

Mysteriously, however, even what we call our "drama"—or rather, that part of it that is deemed worthy to last—will be *present*, not *past*. It is true that "every tear will be wiped away, and death will be no more, nor suffering, nor mourning, nor pain". These things ("the former things") have "passed away", for the One who sits upon the throne says, "Behold, I make all things new." Not: Behold, I make a totally new set of things, but: Behold, I refashion and renew all that is. And our faith tells us that this "new" reality was already present in the "old", in our drama, though in a hidden form: "For you have died, and your life is hid with Christ in God. When Christ who is our life appears, then you also will appear with him in glory" (Col 3:3f.). For the present, our real life is hidden in God; it is only manifest to God and in his presence (as the Book of Revelation shows). So what will be manifested in glory is the depth and truth of our present life. And this depth and truth consist, not in our will's opposition to the divine will, but rather in that part of us that is in harmony with it. Our recalcitrance is sin, alienation and the lie; the core of the drama consists, not of such things but, on the contrary, of that interplay, that wealth of dialogic possibilities, that is found in the permanent, reciprocal relationship between finite freedom—once it has been finally liberated—and infinite Freedom. But this prospect points, beyond our present scope, to the subject of the final volume: "the final act".

We have been summarizing all the action (the "pathos") that takes place on the "world stage", revealing deeper and deeper layers. We have endeavored to show what the dramatic action (the play) looks like from the perspective of finite, time-bound man, in his subjection to death, free to commit evil and implicated in the world's suffering. His attempt to manufacture a redeemed existence out of all this—and this is the attempt of all nonbiblical religions that try to break out of the structures that govern earthly existence—is bound to lead, if it is consistently followed through, to man's self-dissolution. It proves impossible, by any means, to remove either guilt or suffering from existence as a whole. Wherever such attempts at deliberate self-redemption are carried out, they lead logically—consciously or unconsciously—to further involvement in guilt. At this point, an entirely different pathos needs to enter the drama, namely, the pathos of God. However, God does not step onto the stage to show contempt for his vanquished opponent. In an action that man could never have anticipated, he steps to his opponent's side and, from within, helps him to reach justice and freedom. Finitude, time and death are not negated: they are given a new value in a way that is beyond our comprehension. Indeed, even what is hostile to God, in all its profound abysses, is not abandoned; God does not turn his back on it: it is taken over and reworked. Who is responsible for this, man or God? These alternatives are superseded once the chief Actor appears on stage. The question *Cur Deus Homo* will be equally vital, equally relevant, as long as the world lasts.

III. ACTING FROM WITHIN GOD'S PATHOS

A. THE LONG PATIENCE OF GOD

(Theo-Drama in History
Prior to the Time of Christ)

1. Fundamental Considerations

From a theodramatic point of view, world history before Christ cannot be divided into acts. The only tangible articulation is the way the destiny of Israel is specially picked out by God, setting the pattern for his action in Christ. Whatever momentous world developments may seem to be going on in prehistorical times (largely inaccessible to us) and historical times (of which we have a certain knowledge), no theodramatically relevant departures can be ascertained. We can see this—within the Old Testament model—in that the primordial accumulation of mankind's guilt up to the Flood, when God regrets having ever created the world (Gen 6:7f.), is something that lies quite definitely behind us: "I will never again curse the ground because of man, for [that is, although] the imagination of man's heart is evil from his youth. . . . And God blessed Noah and his sons, and said to them: . . . 'I establish my covenant with you and your descendants after you, and with every living creature. . ., the waters shall never again become a flood to destroy all flesh'" (Gen 8:21; 9:1f.; 9:9ff.). The bow in the clouds is the cosmic sign that the bond between heaven and earth will never again be severed. This covenant is concluded prior to the separation of Jew from Gentile; it points back to a first promise (Gen 3:15f., a promise that outlasts God's anger with the world) but at the same time constitutes history's true point of departure. Right from the start, therefore, it is clear that the (Old and New Testament) references to God's wrath and judgment on all succeeding history are to be read within the context set by the covenant with Noah.

The drama that takes place between God and mankind proceeds toward its center in the Incarnation of the Word of God in Christ; accordingly, no individual episode of it can be wrenched from this process and evaluated separately. But this applies also to all aspects of God's attitude to the world. However difficult it may be, we must not separate the graciousness of God, which is so often attested in the Old Covenant, from his anger at sin and at breaches of the covenant (which is mentioned about a thousand times in the Old Testament). Nor should we be surprised that the maelstrom of anger that lashes pagans and Jews at the beginning of the Letter to the Romans is succeeded by assertions of the "riches of his kindness and forbearance [*anochē*] and patience", intended to lead the sinner "to repentance" (Rom 2:4; cf. 9:22). Thus we arrive at the strange concept of the "*parēsis*" of sins formerly committed (Rom 3:25), which can only mean "letting them go".[1] This, as the context makes clear, is in view of God's ultimate plan, namely, "the demonstration of his (covenant-) righteousness" in the pillar of atonement, the "propitiation" (*hilastērion*)—Jesus Christ—set up in the midst of history, to be embraced "by faith". Technically, this "letting go" is no different from the word *hyperidōn* used in Paul's Areopagus address: "God overlooked the times of ignorance" and now—in the preaching of the gospel—announces the opportunity of repentance for "all men everywhere" (Acts 17:30). This attitude on God's part is one in which he reserves both grace and judgment; it is a kind of "third time", "the time of God's patience, in which he endures sins in virtue of the coming redemption. It is not chronologically distinct from the time of grace and wrath, but in substance it is distinct from both."[2] It is one way in which God "is there" for the world; if God's "being there" were regarded as outside time and history (because God is eternal and envisages the redemption in Christ), his dealings with the world would hover "transcendentally" above the Incarnation.

On man's side, there is a similar oscillation that corresponds to God's historical "reserve" [*Verhaltenheit*]: man is both sustained and rejected, he is both free and fettered in his relation to God. This oscillation can be very clearly observed in the case of the Jewish law (Paul puts his finger on the dialectic involved here). But it can also be seen in the law inscribed on the hearts of pagans

---

[1] Cf. Bauer, *ThW*, article "*paresis*"; S. Lyonnet, *Exegesis Ep. ad Rom.* I–IV (Rome, 1963), 222–38.

[2] Cf. Lyonnet, 235–36.

—for it is not said that this latter law *cannot* be kept (Rom 2:12ff.). All the same, in God's case, the provisional attitude of reserve is only possible with a view to Christ; accordingly, in man's case, we must say that the twi*light* of the pre-Christian world (insofar as it is a genuine *light*) anticipates and is a reflection of Christ— from whom "faith" (or, according to Ephesians, the Church) is inseparable. Whatever is illuminated by this light in Judaism and paganism is "faith" (going back to "Abraham", Romans 4, and even to "Abel", "Enoch" and "Noah", Hebrews 11), a faith, however, that hovers in uncertainty and cannot "attain fulfill-ment" until Christ appears (Heb 11:40). Just as it would be a mistake to see the forgiveness of sins in the Old Covenant (for example, on the great Day of Atonement) as a mere "postpone-ment" of punishment until the Day of Judgment or as a merely juridical matter (though never attaining the fullness and depth of the forgiveness of sins that comes in Jesus Christ), it would be equally false to assume that human freedom prior to Christ was so fettered that it permitted no kind of free activity vis-à-vis God. To use Israel as an example once more—for in Israel the issues become clear—the fact that the law (cf. 2 Cor 3 and 1 Cor 10) or the Old Testament priesthood and its sacrifices (Heb) are "types" of what was to come does not rob them of all inner "truth". Nor, on the other hand, can we take the type's external "husk" and extract from it some "truth" that would simply equate the pre-Christian truth with the Christian and post-Christian. The first extreme is that adopted by the rigid Protes-tant opposition between law and gospel; the second is the theory developed by certain of the Church Fathers, who assumed that the "initiates" of the Old Covenant had an anticipatory share in the New. Initially, the Mosaic law adopts a highly positive view (making it possible for the covenant partner to draw near to God, cf. Martin Buber); only subsequently (in the gospel and in an extreme formulation in Paul) does it manifest its threaten-ing side that encourages man's hybris. This polar tension must be maintained without allowing it to ossify into a "dialectic".

In other words, God's saving involvement with the world rests on the single point of the Incarnation of his Word in Jesus Christ. Sooner or later everything else converges on it or emerges from it; this can, in a certain sense, produce a crescendo as the central point is approached, but there is no question of any human activity taking off at the same level as the event of Incarnation. It will not do, therefore, to say that the Incarnation is the "unsurpassable high point" in a range of saving initiatives on God's part that stretches back before the Incarnation and continues after it.

This does not stop us from at least asking in what way it is "*conveniens*" that Christ appeared in history just when he did, with the necessary preparations involved. It was a problem for the Church Fathers; on the basis of their straightforward overview of history, they asked: Why did the Redeemer come so late in historical time—just before the end? The answers to this question result in a theology of history that is either optimistic (Irenaeus, Basil, Theodoret and others)[3] or pessimistic (Philaster,[4] Gregory of Nyssa).[5] The former is based on the view that the Logos progressively enters into the history of mankind, the latter on an ever-deteriorating relationship between mankind and God and a continual accumulation of sin.[6] In the first place,

---

[3] Material in H. de Lubac, *Catholicism: Christ and the Common Destiny of Man* (San Francisco: Ignatius Press, 1988), 246ff. The *Letter to Diognetus* lays great stress on the *time of God's patience*: "God, the Lord and Creator of the universe . . . was not only friendly to man but full of *forbearance* too. He is, always was and ever will be such. . . . But when he had conceived the great, ineffable idea [of the Redemption], he shared it with his Son. As long as he kept his wise counsel to himself, as a secret, it seemed as if he were unconcerned about us, as if he were untroubled. But when, in his beloved Son, he unveiled and revealed *what had been his purpose from the first*, he thereby imparted everything to us: he granted us both a share in his favors and the ability to see him and grasp him with the mind. Who would ever have expected this? Having arranged everything between himself and his Son, he allowed us to be led around by disordered desires just as we wished, right up to the present time. . . . Not that he in any way took pleasure in our sins, but because of his *forbearance*. Not that he was pleased with that time of unrighteousness, but because he wanted to *prepare* for the present time of righteousness; so that we, having shown our own inability to enter the kingdom of God on our own account, should be enabled to do so by the power of God. . . . God did not hate us . . . ; instead of remembering the evil, he manifested *forbearance and patience* and, out of pity, took our sins upon himself. . . . O blessed exchange!" (chaps. 8–9).

[4] *Ibid.*, 261.

[5] PG 44, 1180BC; PG 45, 1152B; cf. Cyril Alex., *Adv. Anthrop.*, PG 76, 1121A–25D.

[6] Greek philosophical ideas form the background of both theories. In the former case, it is the basic idea of *paideia* (on which de Lubac lays too little emphasis,

however, the historical phenomena of growth and decline are so tightly and obscurely intertwined in the various cultures—and particularly so as they unfold in history—that we cannot speak of a theologically relevant theory of history. What is clearly seen as progress in one area can be equally clearly seen as the trigger, the beginning, of a decline in another.[7] Furthermore, modern archaeology has so utterly shattered the theologians' earlier chronological scheme of things that it has become irrelevant to ask whether the Incarnation came "early" or "late". The most we could do, from today's perspective, is to point out that, in spite of the millions of years that lie behind the existence of mankind, more human beings have lived since Christ than lived before him.

This could impart a somewhat different hue to the concept of the "end-time". During the period of preparation, from time immemorial, there have indeed been civilizations, advanced and many-sided; but there had never been anything like a single mankind. It is well known that the Fathers speculated on the providential coincidence of Christ's appearance and the *pax Augusta*; we can add to this the spread of *koinē* and what Hegel describes as the element of abstract universality that characterized the Roman Empire. Is this coincidence not—we may wonder—the decisive start of something that, after much hesitation and obscurity, has asserted itself as today's "one-world" consciousness? Here, surely, we have a phenomenon that is new to world history, corresponding at a purely historical level to the univer-

---

cf. Hal Koch, *Pronoia und Paideusis* [Berlin, 1932]), in the second case, it is antiquity's celebrated theory of the descending series of ages of the world, cf. Hesiod's *Work and Days*, 109–201. De Lubac considers that "these two modes of explanation are not contradictory, since they belong to different categories" (263), and he refers to page 231, note 41: "What is truly progress can sometimes appear to be deterioration: the corruption of a particular period or society, for example, may be bound up with a development of civilization and a deepening of moral conceptions that are, in themselves, true progress. *Corruptio optima pessima.* Not that history allows us to establish a law of inversely proportionate progress. . . . But human progress renders the possibilities for evil more and more formidable. Culture can become an obstacle to grace. . . . "*Homines iam expolitos et ipsa urbanitate deceptos*", says Tertullian (*Apolog.* c. 21, n. 30), and within culture, we include 'religious culture' itself."

[7] Cf. the previous note.

sal claim of Christianity; for Christianity has theologically (and not merely sociologically) transcended the national religion of the Jewish people.

If this is true, it follows that the Incarnation's particular point in time—mankind's "axial time", the change of aeons or the "fullness of time"—has a theological relevance even within history itself. It is the moment at which the two universalisms or "catholicisms", that is, that of Christianity and that of mankind, begin to enter into dramatic competition with each other. Initially, of course, this dramatic tension takes the form of the struggle between the young Church and the totalitarian claims of the Roman Empire in its "universal religion"; and such claims, as Augustine's *City of God* shows, doubtless have their predecessors in the great empires of Assyria and Babylon. But, for Augustine, these empires, including that of Rome, are only historically transient concretions of a counterplan that is fundamentally antithetical to that of Christianity. This antithetical model actually develops religious counterpositions; as time goes on, it will put them forward with even greater clarity and impressiveness. Augustine's "two-empires" formula can be interpreted in several directions and can be applied to world history both before and after Christ; yet we can borrow two elements from it in our present context. First, the theology of pre-Christian history is governed by an underlying dramatic antithesis that is partly hidden and partly manifest. Second, this antithesis enters a qualitatively new stage as a result of the appearance of Christ, insofar as the latter's program of the "kingdom of God" is now opposed by counterprograms that are far more sharply defined than hitherto.

How can we shed light on the theodramatic character of historical time prior to Christ? The best way is to hold fast to Israel's religious history, which in one respect has been lifted out from the "nations" and presented as a model. This model both *demonstrates* the relationship between divine and human freedom and *exercises* this relationship through the course of history. This is not to say that Israel's history is nothing else but a manifest model of something that is going on in the same way elsewhere, albeit (more) hiddenly. Such a view would be opposed by that inner continuity, attested by the entire New Testament, between the Old and New Covenants, a continuity that does *not* exist between the other religions and the Church. The Gentiles may have their gods, their cults and even their prophets, but they are still "dogs" compared with the "children" (Mk 7:27), they are still "godless" (Eph 2:12) and "lawless" (1 Cor 9:21). In spite of this distinction, Israel is aware—increasingly—that it is the favorite among all the other children of God (and God is the Lord of all nations, including those who do not genuinely know him). It knows that it is the light to which all nations will be drawn, at least at the time of the end, and in this sense it is the model, in the terms of world history, for all human relationship with God. No less relevant, even if Israel is less aware of it, is the fact that its religious forms come partly from pagan origins and become partially assimilated to alien cults in the course of time. (The categories of covenant, law, priesthood, sacrificial and temple worship and prophecy all have their analogies in the extrabiblical realm.) If such borrowing is thus widespread and possible in the "true religion", it shows that the antecedent forms cannot be dismissed as simply negative.

2. Israel as the Model

Earlier we were concerned primarily with the manifestation of God's glory and only subsequently with man.[1] This time, right from the start, our topic is the interplay of infinite and finite freedom, which had only been broached then in a third step.[2] This topic emerges, not so much at the preliminary stage of the history of the Patriarchs, as in the central theme of the Sinai covenant and its continuing effects. There has been increasing recognition in recent decades of the extent to which the form of the making of the covenant was already there in the surrounding cultures.[3] The form of covenant found among the Hittites and Assyrians, particularly, becomes highly significant when trans-

---

[1] Cf. *The Glory of the Lord* VI, "The Old Covenant", where we first treated God's "glory" (33–86) before going on to discuss man as "image", and in particular as "secularity before God" (87–143).

[2] *Ibid.*, 144–211, 215–98.

[3] *Ibid.*, 150, note 2; 151, note 3.

posed to the covenant between Yahweh and his people. Initially, the "treaty of sovereignty" between a superior king and a vassal rests one-sidedly on the former's grace and favor, and sometimes the preamble of the treaty reminds the vassal of his unworthiness. But nonetheless, the protection guaranteed in the treaty's clauses is dependent on the vassal's precisely defined obedience; this makes the "gracious act" into a genuine treaty. Thus Israel is chosen by God in sovereign freedom, and the commands given to his partner in the context of the theophany have a primarily salvation-oriented thrust. (Ideally, they are the ways in which the nation must live in fellowship with God and subsequently in God's land.) But the conditions attaching to them do not emerge in retrospect; they are there from the outset. Right from the start, failure to keep them attracts God's curse, a curse that is all the more terrible since the grace of election was so unique.

If the Sinai covenant did not have these two sides from the very beginning, it would not have taken human freedom seriously. To some extent we can agree with recent large-scale portrayals of the history of Israel that show that, in an initial period, the idea of the religious "covenant" was stronger than that of the "law" and the keeping of the Commandments and that once the prophets had announced the end of the covenant, the keeping of the law attained a fateful dominance in the post-Exilic period.[4] If it is correct at all to regard the promulgation of the Commandments as an event of salvation (rightly summed up in the "chief commandment" of Deuteronomy), it was obscured as Judaism developed: the law was made absolute.[5] Against that, however, it has been rightly demonstrated that the covenant's two-sided character—precisely because God's grace takes man seriously—must have existed from the start; this is proved by the alternatives of blessing and curse, so clearly attached to the Commandments. As W. Zimmerli asks, "Is the word of Yahweh that is addressed to Israel in his commandment only a word of

[4] M. Noth, *Die Gesetze im Pentateuch* (1940).

[5] G. von Rad, *Old Testament Theology* (London: SCM, 1965). Even more emphatically than before, according to von Rad, the great prophets had investigated the carrying out of the law; they established conclusively that Israel had not fulfilled God's requirements (II, 399). In this sense, they were the harbingers of legalism.

concern, designed to hold on to the people at all costs? Or is it not rather a holy fire that burns up the unholy?"[6]

Israel's history begins and continues in a sequence of breaches of the covenant, each of which is followed by Yahweh's initiative in bringing his people home. But, theologically speaking, this to-and-fro rhythm cannot be the ultimate truth of the covenant; it cannot be God's ultimate purpose, it cannot be the only conclusion. At the time of the prophets, the situation becomes more acute and suggests only one alternative: the arrogant presumption on the part of the people (and often on the part of the priests too) that God will always come to save them (Hos 6:1–3) is met by the prophets' insight that God's patience is at an end and that the covenant, which has been continually broken, is now to be regarded as terminated. A retrospective look at the history of the covenant, right to its beginnings, showed that God's Commandments were never kept and that God had never been really "known" and loved.

Jacob-Israel, wrestling with God for a whole night, had finally wrung a blessing from him. But was there not something altogether ambivalent about man "wrestling" with God? This is Hosea's view: he sees the Patriarch of the nation as a cunning deceiver (12:4) who even allowed himself to become a slave for the sake of a woman (12:12).[7] Will the nation that springs from him have any more integrity? There is something appalling about Joshua's dialogue with the people at Sichem, in which he challenges them to choose whether they will serve Yahweh or not.

> "We will serve the Lord, for he is our God." But Joshua said to the people, "You cannot serve the Lord; for he is a holy God; he is a jealous God; he will not forgive your transgressions or your sins. If you forsake the Lord and serve foreign gods, then he will turn and do you harm, and consume you, after having done you good." And the people said to Joshua, "Nay; but we will serve

[6] W. Zimmerli, *Das Gesetz und die Propheten. Zum Verständnis des Alten Testaments* (Göttingen: Vandenhoeck und Ruprecht, 1963), 83.

[7] Cf. Deutero-Isaiah 43:26–28: "Put me in remembrance, let us argue together; set forth your case, that you may be proved right. Your first father sinned, and your mediators transgressed against me. . . . Therefore I delivered Jacob to utter destruction and Israel to reviling."

the Lord." Then Joshua said to the people, "You are witnesses against yourselves. . . ." And they said, "We are witnesses" (Jos 24:19–22).

He who put into Joshua's mouth the words "You cannot serve the Lord" must have regarded the people's stubborn insistence as sheer blindness. Accordingly, we shall find lengthy confessions of guilt (notably Ps 106; cf. Is 63:7–64:11; Neh 5:1–11; Dan 9, and so forth) that depict even the wilderness wandering, as well as subsequent history, as one long catena of transgressions. At the call of Isaiah, the word of the Lord affirms that his mission will be in vain. "Israel does not know, my people does not understand" (Is 1:3). All classes of the people have made a pact against Jeremiah (1:18–19): the king, the scribes ("The wise men shall be put to shame. . ., they have rejected the word of the Lord": Jer 8:9), the army, the people. Israel is delivered up to exile without hope of rescue. Ezekiel draws out the ultimate consequences: "The menace lying dormant in the law breaks out here with full force."[8] The nation was already adulterous prior to its election in Egypt; in fact, it was adulterous time out of mind (Ezek 23). Time and again during the wilderness wandering, Yahweh had determined to dissolve the covenant; the only thing holding him back was the thought of his own holiness, of his name. This time, however, he will finally scatter the people among the nations (Ezek 20:23). Ezekiel goes to the length of paradoxical assertions (referring to God's demand for the first-born, which served as a pretext for the sacrifice of children to Moloch): "Moreover I gave them statutes that were not good and ordinances by which they could not have life; and I defiled them through their very gifts in making them offer by fire all their first-born" (Ezek 20:25f.). "God's anger and judgment are bound up with each other in God's commandment."[9]

These unpalatable words from the prophet bring us into the area of Paul and his dialectic of law: the law is in itself "holy, righteous and good", but its apodictic character makes it an irritant, and so it "works death" (Rom 7:12f.), it brings a curse, because it cannot be kept in its entirety (Gal 3:10). And it is

[8] W. Zimmerli, 126.
[9] *Ibid.*, 128. Also Zimmerli's commentary on Ezekiel, I (1969), 449–50.

by undergoing this death-under-a-curse that Christ transcends the law that "came in" (Rom 5:20) to keep us "under restraint" (Gal 3:19, 23); thus he takes us with him to share in his death (Gal 2:19f.).

If we survey the history of law in the Old Testament, its tragic dimensions become clear. Initially (up to the Exile), there are gross breaches of the covenant by unfaithfulness ("fornication" with foreign cults); so the prophets urge the people to have a genuine covenant attitude ("If you will not believe [that is, hold to the covenant], surely you shall not be established": Is 7:9) and insist on the power of the commandments. Later there emerges a new, more refined unfaithfulness to the law that thinks that, in this way, it can assure itself of God's favor. It is this new form of "magic" (which was always forbidden in Israel) that causes Jesus to speak of a "perverse and adulterous generation" (Mt 17:17).

Israel lives as one nation among others. Therefore, besides the law, there are other fundamental elements of the Old Covenant that must have been adopted and adapted from the religions and institutions of its neighbors. All these elements are in the same twilight as the law, indefinably situated somewhere half-way between "religion" in the general sense and New Testament faith. But, as far as the phenomenology of forms is concerned, the step from paganism to Judaism is less great than that from Judaism to what heightens and surpasses it, that is, Christianity, with its incarnational and pneumatic dimensions. First of all, we have the whole constellation of "priesthood", "temple worship" and "sacrifice", which the late Priestly Document projects back into the wilderness wandering, whereas Amos attests that at that time there was no such thing (Amos 5:25); and many psalms agree with Jeremiah in stressing that God does not require this odor of sacrifice; he scorns it. A time is coming when sacrifices will have had their day (Hos 9:4). As for the introduction of kingship into Israel, it is even more equivocal, as 1 Kings 8 shows. God half rejects it as treason against his own Kingship and half recognizes it and uses it as a peg on which to hang (Davidic) Messianic prophecy, just as the Aaronic priesthood is acknowledged as having a connection with the ancient "priests according to the order of Melchizedek" (that is, going back beyond

Judaism to a pagan priest of El) and with the "Lamb of God who takes away the sins of the world". Since this kingship is questionable from the outset, it can be withdrawn from Israel on the day of the latter's exposure. "Where is now your king, to save you; where are all your princes, to defend you—those of whom you said, 'Give me a king and princes'? I have given you kings in my anger, and I have taken them away in my wrath" (Hos 13:9-11). The attempts made after the Exile to recreate institutions that had collapsed lead to secularization (the priest-kings) and fall victim to self-criticism (Qumran versus the Temple sacrifices) or annihilation (the final destruction of the Temple). What remains is the dialectic of law: on the one hand, a genuine covenant faith and secret manifestations of divine possession (Merkabah mysticism, the Cabbala) and, on the other, self-justification, reaching its extreme of atheistic self-creation in the modern forms of secularized Judaism.

All this is intended to show only one thing, namely, that Israel, whose ultimate election (Rom 11) cannot be questioned, is a model instance of the "twilight" nature of all pre-Christian religion. (The difference is that, in the pagan religions, this "twilight" feature is not subjected to any critique.) The religion of Israel is a necessary prehistory (a *paidagogia*: Gal 4:2) leading up to the Incarnation of God. The pagan demonisms (1 Cor 10:20), which, at root, are not without a genuine searching after God (Acts 17:27), are somehow "dead" in sin; they only come to life and assume their full proportions when the light of the divine covenant and law falls upon them (Rom 7:8). It is only within this perspective that the two sides of pagan religion can be evaluated: on the one hand, it evinces wonder in the presence of the glory of God in creation, a wonder that goes as far as worshipping the works his wisdom has created; and, on the other hand, it manifests an inability to deduce the Maker from the works and to worship him (Wis 13:1-9). Ultimately, after all, this inability reveals a refusal to attribute to God what it knows to be his work (Rom 1:19-21).

There is one thing, however, that comes into prominence in Israel that remained hidden in the other religions. In a more or less visible way, the latter circle around themselves, growing and declining, experiencing times of illumination and of obscurity. They lack the divine barb that is applied to Israel, compelling it, in the course of a genuine theodramatic history, to utter an ever-clearer Yes or No. In Israel, where the tale of God's covenant with mankind emerges into the bright light of history, there is a kind of ruthless provocation that is designed to elicit a decision. As God steers history toward its climax, this decision is elicited from both sides: man is provoked to an ever more polarized No or Yes, and God's judgment of the "twilight" aspect of law issues in the mysterious contraries of salvation and rejection.

On man's side, there is a law of constant heightening, clearly formulated by Hosea: "The more I called them, the more they went from me" (Hos 11:2). Jeremiah's whole destiny bears witness to it: the more clearly he proclaims God's decrees, the more he is mocked, persecuted and hated. Ezekiel's huge frescoes complete the picture: the daughter of Gentiles (Ezek 16:3), Jerusalem, whom Yahweh has lifted up, nourished, adorned and married, continually estranges herself from him: in the judgment, Jerusalem will be the last to be justified, after Sodom (the city of pagan vice) and the heretical Samaria. This law of heightening does not apply to the "nations": it addresses the Christian future, and that is where it will attain fulfillment.

On God's side, at the very apex of the Old Covenant, the covenant's provisional ambiguity experiences a kind of polarization. The covenant was designed as grace and salvation, yet it contained within it—since the people could not match up to a full response but continued to "wrestle" with God—an element of wrath, something that called for an expiation that the sacrifices of the law could not provide. In Deutero-Isaiah, we find, in an entirely new and pure form, the announcement of salvation to the people, which has done "double penance" (40:2), typically pointing back via Moses and Abraham to the covenant with Noah: "For a brief moment I forsook you, but with great compassion I will gather you. In overflowing wrath for a moment I hid my face from you, but with everlasting love I will have compassion on you, says the Lord, your Redeemer. For this is like the days of Noah to me: as I swore that the waters of Noah should no more go over the earth, so I have sworn

that I will not be angry with you and will not rebuke you"
(Is 54:7–9).

Against this, however, we have the figure of the "Suffering
Servant", who seems to gather into himself, in his mysterious
destiny, all the counterforces that oppose this announcement of
salvation. He embodies the "covenant of the people", and since
—like the earlier prophets, for example, Elijah—he feels he has
"labored in vain" (49:4), Yahweh raises him even higher and
pronounces him to be "a light to the nations" (49:6). He is the
perfect hearer of God's word, and, at the same time, he is despised, abused, spat upon by men (50:5–6); finally, in the great
poem of 52:13–53:12, he is rejected by mankind, though he
bears its sins as its representative: "He was wounded for our
transgressions, he was bruised for our iniquities, . . . he opened
not his mouth, like a lamb that is led to the slaughter, and like a
sheep that before its shearers is dumb. . . . Yet it was the will of
the Lord to bruise him; he has put him to grief; . . . he makes
himself an offering for sin. . . ." The victory that corresponds
to this extreme humiliation is indicated only briefly. Just as the
announcement of salvation had looked back, beyond Moses, to
Noah, so this counterimage points beyond God's burning anger
in the face of the broken covenant: it points to some event that
is as yet undecipherable, which will unequivocally fulfill the
covenant, not only for Israel but for the whole world. This is
the New Covenant of which Jeremiah spoke, in which God will
put his spirit into men's hearts, so enabling them to understand
the commandment of salvation from within and to follow it
(Jer 31:31–34; cf. Ezek 36:24–27).

But should this new grace cost God—as it were—nothing?
Can we say that, when Yahweh allows his Servant to be thus
treated by sinners, it does not affect him? And when he has
to destroy Israel: "My heart recoils within me, my compassion
grows warm and tender. . . . For I am God and not man, I will
not execute my fierce anger" (Hos 11:8), can we say that it does
not cost him anything? "I will betroth you to me for ever; I
will betroth you to me in [that is, for the price of] righteousness and justice, in [that is, for the price of] steadfast love, and
in mercy" (Hos 2:21f.). "At the betrothal, which in the Old Testament is the actual marriage agreement, the man has to pay a

price for his betrothed. Yahweh promises to pay this price himself."[10]

All instances of the forgiveness of sins in the Old Covenant, whether collective or individual, are moving forward toward this promised goal. This is particularly true of the ceremony of the great "Day of Atonement". They are moving toward the goal, but it has not yet been reached, as is shown by the detailed treatment of the Yom-kippur theme in the Letter to the Hebrews. Under the Old Covenant, forgiveness operates within the flux of time and so needs to be renewed annually, whereas the fulfillment that comes with Christ breaks through the limits of time; God's forgiveness gains entrance "once for all" into the eternal sanctuary through the Priest who offers himself.

This brings us back to God's mysterious patience in the pre-Christian ages, where everything—grace and the wrathful judgment—hovers in a kind of indefinite state. The latter cannot be simply identified with what takes place on the Cross; on the other hand, it is not entirely different from it, either—as if Old Testament forgiveness—the "overlooking of sins"—were a mere "postponement" (unless we were to understand this postponement as anticipating Good Friday).[11]

From this position, we can move our focus back to the phenomenon of pre-Christian religion as such, of which Israel can be regarded as an exemplary model. Before proceeding, however, we can briefly raise the question of the expectation of redemption at the end of Old Testament history and—in a remote analogy to it—in contemporaneous antiquity. We have shown elsewhere[12] how the indefinite, transitional period of the centuries after Israel's return from the Exile up to the birth of Christ went beyond the inherited tradition in three ways: first of all there

---

[10] W. Zimmerli, *Das Gesetz und die Propheten*, 113.

[11] "Good Friday comes at the end of antiquity; this eschatological event concludes the period of God's patience [*anochē*]. The period of 'God's wrath' is also the period of God's patience and his waiting. . . . If the former time was a period of 'postponement' and 'restraint' on God's part, it is also true that men's expiatory sacrifices and rites were not able to do what they were intended to do." O. Michel, *Der Brief an die Römer*, 4th ed. (1966), 109f.

[12] In the part entitled "The Long Twilight": *The Glory of the Lord* VI, 301–416.

was the forward thrust, the increasing hope of a Messiah; then there was the upward thrust of "apocalyptic", which embraces the dimensions of heaven and hell; and finally the aspect of "wisdom", which sees the realm of creation as transparent, allowing us to discern the presence of the divine Spirit within it. Once again, however, these three extrusions are seen to be essentially ambivalent. The Messianic hope could articulate itself in terms of Jewish (Maccabean, Zealot) politics *or* in the patent yearning of "Yahweh's poor" for a salvation that only he could bring. Apocalyptic could present itself as a genuine vision of the expected Son of Man (Daniel, parts of Enoch) *or* as a hybrid invasion of the beyond on the part of human curiosity, occasionally coupled with a tragically stubborn resistance to God (4 Esdras). Wisdom could genuinely beat a path toward its incarnation in Christ, *or* it could develop into a hardened human self-reliance; Jeremiah had already broken up this hard surface ("The wise men shall be put to shame", 8:9), and Paul eventually clears it away: "I will destroy the wisdom of the wise . . . , for the foolishness of God is wiser than men" (1 Cor 1:19, 25). In this "long twilight", therefore, the void experienced in three dimensions is either filled out with human materials or kept open, in genuine poverty, in the expectation that God will fill and fulfill it.

There is a remote analogy to this in late antiquity, although here the two sides of the twilight reality are so intertwined that they can hardly be disentangled. We have already portrayed the basic phenomenon as the "bridge never built": from one bank, it is built out on a "philosophical pillar", aiming to reach religion but collapsing in "theurgy". From the other bank, it is built out on the "mythical pillar", but, once it loses the myth's concreteness, it gets lost in philosophico-magical speculation.[13] The ancient world's yearning for redemption is expressed most patently in the work of Virgil,[14] and is seen in Plotinus too, as a fundamental longing of soul and mind.[15] Both authors will become important references in Christian thought and literature. But the

---

[13] *The Glory of the Lord* IV, 216–48.
[14] *Ibid.*, 249–79.
[15] *Ibid.*, 280–313.

clarity remains purely relative; in Stoic and Epicurean philosophies, in the mystery religions, in gnostic and Hermetic theorems, everything is muddied by the hybris of self-redemption.
The only process whereby the pure gold can be extracted from
the vast amalgam is that of the Christian discernment of spirits,
which refines everything in the fiery cauldron of faith.

3. Pre-Christian Religion

Israel's relationship with God is a "twilight" one. This means
that even its most faithful adherents had to endure the long period of God's patience, since "apart from us they should not
be made perfect" (Heb 11:40). The same is true of the other
religions, but even more so, since they are deeper in shadow.
In coming to an assessment of these religions, we must not fall
into the extreme of K. Barth, who regards them as pure human
hybris, resisting the divine revelation. Nor must we embrace
the other extreme, which strips all that is historical away from
God's will for the salvation of all men. According to the latter
view, God's salvific will is timeless (though, of course, it has
its historical climax in Christ) and addresses every man, at least
in the "transcendental" mode, whatever the objective religious
traditions are and whatever paths of salvation are offered to man
in history.

In the previous volume,[1] we have already dealt with the basic
issue with regard to the position of the world religions in the
theo-drama, namely, the relationship of the created *imago Dei*
to the grace that God holds out to him, and the necessary in-
adequacy of all objective systems of religion. What we did not
discuss was the aspect of culpability that always finds expression
in these systems. Tragically, this culpability extends from the
individual sinful subject to the objective system, and from there
—having acquired a quasi-official character—it has an intensified feedback effect on the subject. Here we must devote some
attention to this aspect of culpability. It will provide the necessary, complementary (and theodramatic) element to the op-

[1] *Theo-Drama* III, 410–18.

timistic approach so energetically put forward by K. Rahner, according to which the pre-Christian (and post-Christian) religions are "Christologies searching for a subject",[2] and searching, moreover, "in the Holy Spirit".[3]

Non-Christian religions do two things at the same time. They attempt to say what man is and why he exists, in relation to the world, on the one hand, and to the absolute, on the other. Therefore they also resist the answer that God, in sovereign freedom, provides in the person of Jesus Christ. The term *Vorgriff* ("pregrasp", "anticipatory understanding") expresses both elements: the anticipation of a solution that is the product of man's searching and the resultant blocking of the way to God's solution. The interplay of these positive and negative aspects yields the dramatic tension that "transcendental Christology"—even when it endeavors to take history seriously—cannot really entertain. Why, when Christ appeared, was he not greeted by pagans, Jews and Christians as the Bringer of Salvation who had been found at long last? Surely because all "searching Christologies" *did not want to find* precisely what God the Creator had kept "hidden for ages . . . the unsearchable riches of Christ", in order to manifest it through the Church in the fullness of time (Eph 3).

In setting forth the structure of subjective and objective religion, it is sufficient, as we have shown elsewhere, to start from the *imago Dei* implanted in man,[4] without denying its primary locus in the supernatural relation to the God who reveals himself.[5] The image is, a priori, dependent for its fulfillment on its prototype (which can only lie in the absolute), since, in its three tensions (spirit-body, man-woman, individual-collective),[6] it is essentially incapable of fulfillment. Furthermore, man's forward march seems to offer no prospect of reconciling the empirical forms of the human being with his *Gestalt*, which is drawn to the absolute and which only the latter can fill.

It is inevitable, then, that fragmentary attempts at a solution

---

[2] *Grundkurs des Glaubens* (Herder, 1976), 288ff., 310ff.

[3] *Ibid.*, 308–10ff.

[4] *Theo-Drama* III, 416 note 31.

[5] Cf. the excursus on the "image and likeness of God" in *Theo-Drama* II, 316–34.

[6] *Ibid.*, 346–94.

should be put forward, containing a covert claim to absoluteness. For the paradox whereby Christ is God's final word and final deed in history (true Incarnation, true Cross, true Resurrection) cannot be envisaged by man: moreover, it *must not be allowed* to happen. Man's thought (and "faith") circles around the central light; it is continually attracted by the paradox but must always withdraw from it lest, like the moth, it is burned up by the flame. Thus the partial solutions lead to one aspect of the *imago* being regarded as absolute and the other aspects (which are in fact indispensable and complementary) being denied— a development that involves man in guilt and has a destructive effect on him.

Here we have not space to set forth the whole wealth of relevant material from the history of religions. A glance at the allegedly "advent" character of late antiquity must suffice.

As far as the spirit-body tension is concerned, we have first of all the doctrine adumbrated by Plato, which has come down to us through Hellenistic philosophy. This doctrine speaks of a "whole [that is, sound] cosmos" that, both spiritually and physically, seems to offer the transient human being a dwelling-place in the *cosmos* after the dissolution of the narrower religion of the *polis*. This over-arching "wholeness" is the *divine*, but it deceives the individual human being in that, if he is to enter it, he must lay aside his individuality and be given back, body and soul, to the Whole. The Stoics, Epicurus, Plotinus,[7] are no different here from Indian teaching on salvation. When, later on, thought takes a pessimistic turn, this Whole splits into a nether sphere of disastrous fate and an upper sphere that affords rescue. The inevitable result is that man too is split into a part that is subject to death (be it body or psyche) and a part that is immortal (spirit) and can escape into the "whole" fullness (*pleroma*). In the Hermetic cults, this rescue can be performed by a self-revealing God, but generally this God appeals to the *pneuma* or spark that is already indwelling the "Gnostic", whereas the common "psychic" does not possess it.

If man is torn into two opposite values, it follows that mankind

[7] On the question of Plotinus' "metaphorical language", where he speaks of the individual soul being redeemed by dissolving into the cosmos, cf. C. Andresen, article "Erlösung" in *RAC* 6 (1966), 93.

is also torn into a part that is receptive to salvation—individuals
—and a part that is not—the mass of people. There is no sight
whatsoever of any link between the individual and the community such as that provided by the (Christian) idea of a *person* distinguished by a mission. Even less to be expected in Gnosticism
is any concern about the individual's body being included in salvation. Suggestions of a belief in resurrection, which are found
in Parsism, which may have influenced the latest pre-Christian
Judaism, failed to reach other parts of the ancient world. Occa-
sional references to the dead appearing in bodily form do not
amount to a counterargument. The axis of personal eschatology
remains the soul's immortality, the rescuing of all that is most
valuable in man; here the body can either make a contribution
through ascetic practice or, in libertinism, reveal its insignifi-
cance.

Plato could speak in mythical terms of a "creation". But
nowhere was there an existential relationship such as existed in
Israel between the Creator and a creature who felt it owed its existence to itself alone. At the very point where God is addressed
as Father (Cleanthes, Epictetus), we find the dominant ethical
ideal of the autarchy of the sage: he is self-sufficient and therein
becomes—allegedly at least—"like God". Strictly speaking, in
fact, the situation is the reverse: man thinks he can find his ideal
in complete self-sufficiency and so attributes this ideal to God
as well. In the ancient myths, the gods were largely entangled
in the world process (a view that is given renewed currency
by a post-Christian process theology); only with the advent of
the Platonic, Stoic and Epicurean demythologizing of the divine
were both God and man released from this entanglement. When
Paul proclaims at the Areopagus that the Creator of the world
does not live in temples and cannot be ministered to by human
hands "as though he needed anything" (Acts 17:25), he is not
telling his hearers anything new. "God is truly God; thus he
has no need of anything", Euripides had already said,[8] a dictum
that was often repeated.[9] But this apparent "point of contact"
for Christian preaching is only ambivalent insofar as it could be

[8] *Heracles*, 1345f.
[9] For example, Seneca, Ep. 95, 47, 50.

used (in Stoicism, Epicureanism and in Plotinus) to show that the human *imago* (in the *analogia* of identity) was quasi-divine. By striving to reach up to and penetrate the divine sphere with its own inborn and sinful *desiderium naturale*, the created image loses a sense of the distance between itself and the divine. At the price of its own completeness (and yet for the *sake* of that completeness), it leaves the body behind: "First of all you must tear up the garment you wear, the garment of ignorance, the armor of evil, . . . the living death, the corpse endowed with sense, the grave you carry around with you, the thief who lives in your house, the comrade who hates you by what he loves and envies you in what he hates."[10]

On the other hand, typically creaturely aspects such as the duality of the sexes can be projected into the heavenly world (for example, the *syzygy* and other divine pairings), albeit in a degree of abstractness that ignores the connection between reproduction and death. Often enough, in this connection, the subordination of woman remains a feature. (It is no accident that, for the Gnostic, the material world is the product of a *sophia* that has fallen from original fullness and must be brought home by a male Redeemer.) It may be that the *syzygy* idea forms the remote background to the meditation on Christ and the Church found in Ephesians 5, but the gap between the two remains unbridgeable.

In popular and state religion, the various forms of prayer and sacrifice remain in place, both publicly and in private. Here it is impossible, however, to distinguish the pure from the essentially impure, from the attempt to bind the divine by magical means. If (like Walter F. Otto)[11] we concentrate solely on the positive sides of mythical religion, the latter can seem like an epiphany of the divine, almost on the same level as Christianity. But this would be to gloss over the many negative aspects, such as the attempts to intervene from below in the sphere of divine freedom—for example, the magical prayers found in Babylonian religion and right up to late antiquity in Egypt and the Greek

---

[10] Hermes Trismegistos, Tr. 7, 2 (ed. Nock-Festugière, 1945), 52–54.

[11] *Die Gestalt und das Sein*. Gesammelte Abhandlungen über den Mythos und seine Bedeutung für die Menschheit, 2d ed. (Darmstadt, 1959).

and Roman endeavors to ascertain the will of the gods by means of oracles and the inspection of entrails.

Closest to the Christian mystery come attempts to deal with suffering in the world. Yet most religions take a path diametrically opposed to Christ's. They try to avoid suffering, render it harmless and powerless; religion becomes a technique to that end. The sacrificial cults take a different way: they attempt to pacify an angry deity by the killing of a victim, for example, a scapegoat. Here, as we have shown elsewhere, a death that is freely undertaken for the sake of one's country (Menoikeus), political aims (Iphigeneia), a beloved husband (Alcestis, and so forth)[12] can closely approach the mystery of Christ. Nonetheless, the representative sacrifice is either demanded by the wrathful God, or else it is a self-portrayal of human greatness, and in neither case can it bring about inner and universal atonement such as envisaged by the stupendous concluding image of Old Testament prophecy: the final Suffering Servant poem. If we were to examine ancient Babylonian and Egyptian expiatory rites, we should also find an amalgam of highly significant features anticipating later revelation, together with elements of untenable mythology. And it remains a fact that these expiatory rites are just as tied to the rhythms of the seasons and of growth as were the Jewish atonement rites (which needed constant repetition) and the ideas of resurrection found in most mystery religions (Osiris, Marduk, Esmun, Tammuz, Adonis, Mithras).

The frenzied dance of religious projections moves this way and that, but, however close to the Christian mystery some features of it seem to come, other features show it to be radically remote from Christianity. The totality established by God in Jesus Christ is—at least outside the Old Covenant—unapproachable. The kaleidoscope of forms, each containing an element of apparent "truth"—which is why, later, Christians can adopt and transform these forms so that we can see through them to the Christian mystery—gives no evidence of intrinsic movement toward the extraordinary and unique event of Christ. They may be *logoi spermatikoi*, but this "seed" can only germinate in Christian soil, and only after a "conversion" that involves far more than

---

[12] Cf. *The Glory of the Lord* IV, 141ff.

the mere supplying of a missing element: what is required is the death and new birth that the Bible calls *metanoia*.[13] Only with the greatest reticence, therefore, should we speak of "pre-Christian religions exercising a positive salvific function".[14] It would be better to locate them within the period of God's long patience, in which he "overlooks" all prior perversity. God makes it possible for us to "wrestle" with him, in both a good and a bad sense.

No religion can come up with the "catholicity" that will be the mark of God's revelation in Jesus Christ. No religion can manufacture the totality that characterizes the covenant (inchoate in the Old Covenant and only attaining fullness in the New) between the true God and an unabridged creation. It follows that, outside the biblical realm, it is impossible to find that rhythm, that continual heightening, which—beginning in the Old Covenant —dominates the story of Christ.

Whether we can really speak of a particular expectation of redemption, on the part of the nonbiblical world at the time of Christ, must remain uncertain. Much can be said in favor of it, and apologetics has made much use of such evidence; but the countercurrents—systems of self-redemption, political and mythical redeemer-figures, as well as a certain mundane indifference—blur the outlines of any such expectation. No clear thrust can be detected. It may be that an awareness of the need for redemption is in the air, as it were, but it is not sensed with the same precision as in Israel, which has arrived at a critical point in its salvation history. Israel feels the weight of its sinfulness; it knows that its relationship with its God has become questionable. The "nations" feel the vague, diffuse pressure of a general culpability on the part of all being; they sense that they have fallen prey to fate; and they try to escape by means of ritual and technique.

[13] Cf. *Theo-Drama* III, 418ff.
[14] K. Rahner, *Grundkurs des Glaubens*, 307.

4. Transition to Soteriology

If, on this basis, we look around for an event that should once and for all bring about reconciliation between God and the world, we are bound to take Israel—the model instance—as our starting point. Even so, this will not enable us to deduce the ultimate event in advance. The atonement rites and practices found among the "nations", once they have been purged of all elements of magical influence on the deity, become part of the context of ideas that characterizes the mind and heart of Israel.

In the background, there is the all-embracing image of God's fundamental reconciliation with creation: the covenant with Noah. But, while God's wish to destroy creation lies firmly in the past, a twofold shadow still lies over this "eternal covenant" (Gen 9:16). For God knows that man's heart is evil from his youth (Gen 8:21); this is a kind of natural phenomenon that must be taken into account. Second, there is the warning that, if spilled, the "blood of life"—particularly that of human life, which is created in the image of God—will be required of man. In the very heart of the reconciliation, a strict justice is established among men, inclined to evil as they are.

If, from this perspective, we look beyond the covenant with Abraham to the Sinai covenant and its subsequent history in Israel, we find an increase in tension: once again, when God freely initiates the covenant, we sense that he is doing something final and unconditional. For he takes into account the possibility that man may break the covenant; such an eventuality will not dissolve the covenant but will result in the punishment of the breach (Lev 26:14ff.; Dt 28:15−68). Grace is given freely and unconditionally on God's side; thus, since man's election gives him a theological status and ethical obligations, he must make an appropriate response. We can only speak of a final reconciliation-event, therefore, within this tradition of election and covenant.[1] The Old Testament speaks of God jealously guarding his covenant and wrathfully avenging breaches of it; these are necessary corollaries of his gracious love. Where infinite, absolute Freedom chooses

[1] J. Galot's treatment of this topic is perhaps the most consistent. Cf. his "La Rédemption, mystère d'alliance" (*Mus. Less.*, sec. théol. 59 [DDB, 1965]).

a finite freedom, the qualities of the former *must* characterize the latter. When God makes a covenant with man, even if this choosing on God's part is pure grace, it implies that man has the dignity of a free creature. Accordingly, such a choosing also implies the *demands* of covenant righteousness. "Righteous" (as in Hebrew) means a "di-*rect*-ion" toward the "right", and ultimately this "right" is defined by the divine grace offered to man. This is the source of Anselm's insight, when he says that it is impossible for God alone to bring about reconciliation—however much all initiative lies with him.[2]

At this stage, we can turn our undistracted attention to the manifold aspects of the mystery of atonement, presented to us in the event of Jesus Christ as the solution to the pre-Christian impasse; and we must approach this mystery with the reverence that befits it. For it is impossible to designate this dramatic climax in the relations between God and man with a single, isolated concept. There is God's initiative, yet it cannot do without man's cooperation; there is God's reconciled love, yet the jealous and wrathful side of his love still call for reconciliation. There is sinful man's inability to achieve a more spontaneous reconciliation with God, an inability that must be remedied if the reconciliation is to prove effective; only thus can man—impotent as he is—be drawn into reconciliation from the very outset and not only at the end of the process. These complex questions bring us to the very heart of the theo-drama, for there can only be a dénouement when all the dimensions of the mystery are before us (right from the Trinity, via Christology, to the doctrine of the Church and of mankind and the world in general). In the previous volume, we portrayed the theological persons involved; only on the basis of the doctrine of reconciliation can they really begin to play their parts on the stage.

[2] *Cur Deus Homo* I, 12.

B. SOTERIOLOGY:
A HISTORICAL OUTLINE

1. Scripture

a. The Life of Jesus and the "Hour"

Volume 3 has prepared the way for the following considerations. It has shown us that the entire thrust of the Gospels, Synoptic and Johannine, arises from the tension between the "life of Jesus" and that unknown yet crucial "hour" toward which it is running.[1] We can discern this tension even in the work of the Synoptic authors themselves. There is no doubt that, from early times, the Passion narrative was put together by the primitive Church as an integral whole, perhaps existing in several versions, and that in addition there must have been a supplementary account of the activity of Jesus from his "beginnings" (*archē*: Mk 1:1; Lk 1:2), that is, since his appearance on the public stage, also existing possibly in several versions.[2] It is disputed precisely where the Passion narrative begins; in recent times there have been attempts to trace its beginning back to Mark 8:27ff., that is, the unveiling of the mystery of the suffering Son of Man (in answer to Peter's confession: "You are the

---

[1] *Theo-Drama* III, 109ff. This caesura is overlooked in a certain kind of Protestant Christology (from Schleiermacher to Hofmann and Ritschl) that sees the Cross merely as the ultimate consequence of Jesus' "faithfulness to his vocation". (Cf. Althaus, *Theol. Aufsätze* I [1927], 23f.). The Temptation story, with its particular dramatic quality, which Luke interprets as a kind of prelude to the later temptations connected with the Passion, cannot be used as a serious argument against the caesura to which we are drawing attention here. The Temptations do not exemplify that (supra-active) passivity that concludes all action: rather, they constitute a testing of Jesus in the thick of his Messianic activity. On the dramatic dimensions of the Temptation episode, cf. Duquoc, *Christologie* I (Paris: Cerf, 1972), 52–71 (with refs.).

[2] Cf. H. Schürmann, "Der 'Bericht vom Anfang', ein Rekonstruktionsversuch auf Grund von Lk 4:14–16" (1964), reprinted in *Textgesch. Untersuchungen zu den Evangelien* (Düsseldorf: Patmos, 1968), 69–80.

Christ").[3] Whether or not it actually begins there is not so important for our purposes. More significant is the evident fact that Jesus' question about who he is (and his assertion, in reply to Peter's confession, that "the Son of man must suffer") marks a decisive turning point in the account of the life of Jesus. Even in the Synoptics, the end phase of Jesus' life is clearly distinct from the time of deeds, of teaching and working miracles. In John, this final phase has great emphasis; he calls it "the hour". To be meaningful, the revelation of *what* will happen to Jesus must come after the disciples have somehow realized, on the basis of Jesus' deeds, *who* he is.[4] The coincidence (however provisional and incomplete) of Jesus' self-revelation and the faith of the disciples (crowned in Matthew by the promise made to Peter) clearly indicates the *akmē* and the turning point in the "life of Jesus". Only within this perspective can Jesus himself unfold the necessity of his suffering and being rejected—and of course, as we have already said, we cannot expect that, prior to undergoing the "hour", Jesus would give a detailed presentation of the theology involved in it.[5] In any case, he in no way anticipates the tremendous moment of this hour, preferring to leave the knowledge of it with the Father (Mk 13:32), just as he will leave its interpretation to the Spirit and those whom the Spirit will inspire (Jn 16:13–15). Thus we can leave it an open question whether Jesus himself explained his death in terms of "ransom" (Mk 10:45)[6] or not.[7] In the latter

---

[3] Thus R. Pesch, *Das Markusevangelium* (Herders theol. Komm. z. N. T., 1977), part 2: excursus, "Die vormarkinische Passionsgeschichte". Page 1 lists the passages alleged to belong to it. In this case, the pre-Markan Passion narrative would "encompass a third of the entire Gospel" (*ibid.*, 5). It would date from very early times, probably in the original Jerusalem community of the "Galileans" (*ibid.*, 21).

[4] According to J. Guillet, *Jésus devant sa vie et sa mort* (Paris: Aubier, 1971), 9ff., this identification of Jesus cannot be on the basis of some external teaching regarding his person but must arise from internal insight on the part of the disciples.

[5] *Theo-Drama* III, 115f.

[6] *Theo-Drama* III, 115f., with reference to J. Jeremias, to which should be added M. Hengel (note 15 below).

[7] X. Léon-Dufour: "Jésus n'a jamais fait la théorie sur lui-même." "La Mort rédemptrice du Christ selon le NT" in: X. Léon-Dufour, et al., *Mort pour nos péchés* (Brussels: Fac. Univ. St. Louis, 1976), 37.

case, the eucharistic expression "for many" (an expression that most definitely belongs to the "hour") would call for a specific interpretation.

Life prior to the "hour" is by no means a mere anteroom, even if Jesus' mission—given the conditions of human temporality and human strength—had to be a limited one, limited to the conversion, healing and gathering of Israel; the universality of God's saving will became evident only indirectly, in the opening-up of Israel's mission to all nations. The encounter with believing pagans explicitly brings out this "open" aspect: it is possible to find greater faith outside Israel than within it, a theme that, nonetheless, is still an Old Testament one (cf. Ezek 5:6; 16:44; Jonah). Within the limitations of time, Jesus is the light of the world; his fleeting radiance (Jn 8:12; 12:35) should be taken advantage of, for in the night that is coming (Jn 11:11), the "hour of darkness" (Lk 22:53), one can only stumble about. In this limited span of time, he is the teacher of truth, speaking with divine authority; we are urged to listen with an understanding ear (Mt 11:25, and so forth), because we shall not always have this opportunity to hear him. For a time he is the One who gathers the disciples and the crowds, but the hour is coming when "the shepherd will be smitten and the sheep scattered" (Mt 26:31). The authority with which he speaks and acts during the limited time is itself unlimited: it is founded (not only psychologically but also theologically) on the events of the "hour"—events that are limitless in scope. Moreover, his entire preaching, beginning with the manifesto of the Sermon on the Mount, has that "hour" as its goal, not only ethically but theologically. Thus he urges his hearers to leave everything, not to resist, to love their enemies, to follow him unconditionally, to take up their cross daily, to give away even what is most necessary (the widow's mite), to take the lowest place. Those who want to accompany Jesus are confronted with the overwhelming demands of a supertemporal scale of values; they are urged—bafflingly—to be careful about nothing; this shows that the whole thrust of Jesus' life is toward a timeless "time", is drawn to it, thinks and plans on that basis. In this it is quite different from the atmosphere of the Old Testament, of Judaism, of a wisdom that is ultimately this-worldly. Right from the start—"the time is fulfilled, the kingdom of God is at hand" (Mk 1:15), "at the very gates" (Mk 13:29)—the eschatological movement has begun, even if, in the process, much light can still be shed on the order of creation and related matters.[8] Everything has an impetus toward what is coming; yet what is coming does not lie beyond Jesus' existence (in the way that the prophets could indicate realities lying in the future), although it transcends his present activities. What is coming is what the "hour" will contain.

Jesus refuses to anticipate either the time or the content of the hour, yet he sees them both, time and content, as something that God has immutably appointed (*dei*) and that he, the Son, has unconditionally to go through. So he longs for it with his whole being (Lk 12:50). This is his mission's center of gravity, his ordeal by fire.[9] It is impossible, therefore, for him not to have been aware of its scope, "formally", as it were, right from the start. This is clear from the claims that accompany his words and deeds. In substantiating his claim—to embody God's majestic authority on earth—he makes no explicit reference to the "hour"; this shows his theological naïveté. But let us add that, in not anticipating the hour—as is appropriate to the Son's obedience—he formally embraces the totality of the world that is to be reconciled, whereas the changing details of the Passion render this formal embrace concrete in the most diverse ways. This is like a circling searchlight, picking out now this, now that layer of some immense reality (the world's sin) or of some vast crowd (sinners) so that all can participate in the event; between these periods of illumination, everything slips back into the confined, hopeless darkness of suffering. His mission is multi-dimensional: it has room enough for everyone.

In the Bible, "*hora*" usually refers to a somehow special, definite time, a right or favorable point in time (cf. for example, Lk

---

[8] H. Schürmann, "Das hermeneutische Hauptproblem der Verkündigung Jesu. Eschatologie und Theologie im gegenseitigen Verhältnis" (1959), reprinted in *Trad. gesch. Untersuchungen, loc. cit.*, 13–35.

[9] This presupposes all that we have said in the third volume of *Theo-Drama* concerning "Christ's Person and Mission".

1:10; 14:17; Mt 10:19 par.; Acts 3:1). In the Book of Revelation, it means a time appointed by God (14:7; 14:15; 18:10, and so forth).

In the Synoptic Passion accounts, *hora* is both the time of the Passion as determined by the Father—"he fell on the ground and prayed that, if it were possible, the hour might pass from him" (Mk 14:35)—and the corresponding temporal "hour" in which the disciples should have been watching and praying with Jesus (Mt 26:40). The former, qualitative meaning predominates: "The hour is at hand, and the Son of man is betrayed into the hands of sinners" (Mt 26:45). And finally we have "The hour has come" (Mk 14:41). Thus Jesus, addressing his enemies, calls it "your hour, and the power of darkness" (Lk 22:53). This darkness holds tangible sway from the sixth to the ninth hour (Mt 27:45), and "at the ninth hour", when Jesus utters his cry of dereliction, there is the complete unfolding of that qualitative, timeless dimension in Jesus' life that (even more explicitly in John) constitutes his "hour", something that explodes the chronological concept of time, although it projects into earthly time. This is the expected time, the time that has now come.

The Son's obedience, which John so strongly emphasizes, causes him to wait for the unforeseeable hour just like any ordinary man,[10] and, on the other hand, from his lofty vantage point, he asserts that the hour has *not yet* come, or *has* come. What is special about his relationship with time becomes clear in John 7:6: "My (proper) time (*kairos*) has not yet come, but your time is always here." Ordinary people do not live, as he does, with a view to a particular hour. It is as if he is "saved up" for this hour and hence protected against any premature action: "No one laid hands on him, for his hour had not yet come"—a situation familiar to the Synoptics too (Lk 4:30; cf. also Jn 10:31, 39). It would be hard to find any other interpretation than this of the "hour" in Jesus' answer to his Mother: "My hour has not yet come" (Jn 2:4): the "hour" is the Passion

---

[10] Just as believers have to wait for the "unexpected hour" of the Lord's coming: Matthew 24:44; Luke 12:39 (cf. the simile of the "thief" in Mark 13:33 par.; Revelation 3:3; and of the bridegroom who comes unexpectedly: Matthew 25:10–13; and of the watching servants in Luke 12:35ff.).

that John sees simultaneously as the glorification[11]—even if the subsequent miracle is described as the beginning of Jesus' glory. The hour has really come only when the Passion events begin to take place in close succession. Thus we have the scene in the Temple that, in the Fourth Gospel, replaces the scene in Gethsemane: "The hour has come for the Son of man to be glorified" (12:23, 27); and the washing of the feet, which in John takes the place of the institution of the Eucharist: "When Jesus knew that his hour had come to depart out of this world to the Father, having loved his own who were in the world, he loved them to the end." (13:1) The latter sums up the significance of all the constituents of the hour, from the washing of the feet and the High Priestly Prayer right up to the Passion. The Great Prayer likewise solemnly stresses the moment in time: "Father, the hour has come; glorify thy Son" (17:1). And since his followers (who are so much the object of this prayer) are so overwhelmed by fear and sadness that their sharing in his hour seems to be from a distance, he compares it to the "time" of a woman about to give birth. The simile is more ecclesiological than christological, yet it echoes the christological hour: "When a woman is in travail she has sorrow, because her hour has come; but when she is delivered of the child, she no longer remembers the anguish, for joy that a child is born into the world" (16:21f.). So it will be with the disciples. Jesus' hour leaves him "deeply moved", "troubled" in spirit (13:21; cf. 11:33; 12:27), but this change in him is less a psychological detail than the signal that a new phase of his existence has begun. It is the earthquake that is beginning to separate him from this world, lifting him up on the Cross as he returns to the Father. In this phase, he is both still in the world (17:13) and yet no longer in it (17:11); he asks for the restoration of the glory he had before the foundation of the world (17:1, 5), and yet he is already once more in possession of it (17:22, 24); he foresees that the disciples will fall away (13:38; 16:32) and yet looks beyond their fall to their final confirmation in faith (17:6–8, 25). Thus the last prayer of Jesus is not really a prayer *before* and *with regard to* the Passion: it is a prayer that

---

[11] Cf. the relevant passage in Schnackenburg's commentary on the Gospel of John.

expresses the total content of the "hour"; both disaster [*Unter-gang*] *and* the new dawn [*Aufgang*], that is, it is the transition, the passing-over [*Übergang*].[12] In this transition, his insight into his mission's universality attains its greatest breadth. All the same, he has to leave his friends and commends them to the Father's care during his time of suffering (17:11, 15). The time of his transition is also that of his "self-sacrifice" (17:19) "for" (*hyper*) those who are his, so that they may be "consecrated (that is, 'sacrificed') in the truth". Here again the effective consummation of Jesus' work is clearly located in the "hour".

To sum up: there is perfect unity between the (active) life of Jesus and his "hour", but it would be wrong, for the sake of preserving continuity ("solidarity with sinners", and so forth), to gloss over the deep incision this hour represents. His life leads up to the hour. (When Mark 3:6 says that his enemies had already decided to "destroy him" as soon as be began his ministry, we cannot assume that he was unaware of this.) However, his life remains the result of his own initiative, whereas, in the hour, it is his "being given up" that dominates. He is given up by men, by Christians, Jews and Gentiles, and finally by the Father too.[13] This is a seemingly passive letting-things-happen, but once Jesus, in Gethsemane, has wrestled and won through to it, it clearly becomes a "super-action" in which he is at one with a demand that goes beyond all limits, a demand that could only be made of *him*.

What takes place in the "hour" remains a mystery and can never be reduced to a "system"—even in the interpretations attempted by the primitive Church. So there is nothing strange about the fact that the Passion narratives, and subsequently the theological interpretations of the Cross, employ different theologoumena, circling concentrically around a transcendent core. Equally, on the basis of the primal phenomenon, the tension between his "life" and the "hour", it stands to reason that later soteriology can begin either with the "life" that moves toward the "hour" or with the "hour" that always presupposes the theolog-

---

[12] A. George, " 'L'Heure' de Jean XVII" in *Rev. Bibl.* 61 (1954), 392–97.

[13] Cf. the chapter entitled "Momentum of the Cross" in *The Glory of the Lord* VII (1989), 202–35, particularly 223f.

ical significance of the life. What Jesus says of his "being sent" and "having come" holds together the two phases of his existence so tightly that the mission of the "hour" is seen to be an essential part of his entire life's path; it is its ultimate purpose. Every discerning soteriology—particularly in the Fathers—has taken account of this unity of time. It would be naïve to separate the Fathers' soteriology into "incarnational" and "staurocentric" enterprises.[14] A certain "staurocentrism" may seem to assert itself in Anselm and his successors, but Thomas Aquinas endeavors to restore the balance with his ambitious project of a theology of the mysteries of Christ's life. Today it may be that an "incarnational" tendency is trying to obliterate the borderline between the life and the Passion; this calls for renewed attention to be devoted to the Passion's inherent modalities.

We have not dwelt specifically on the Resurrection. It is the goal that corresponds to Jesus' whole existence and is in entire harmony with it. The Fathers rightly see it as the consequence of the Incarnation of the New Adam and, following Paul, as the radiant side of the Cross, correctly understood. John recognizes that the two belong together; he unites them under the single concept of Christ's "lifting-up", his "glorification". The world of the Resurrection, of the new creation, where God's kingdom has come, is the destination of Jesus' life *and* of his suffering and dying. His community will concern itself exclusively with following him toward this future.

It is God who acts decisively in Jesus' "hour", to which his life leads up. For the faith of the primitive Church, the interpretation of the "hour" was essential for an understanding of the life that led up to it. Accordingly, we must start with the primitive Church's interpretation. To do justice to it, we must put ourselves in the situation of the covenant as already described: God acts out of free grace, and so he takes the free, creaturely partner seriously. The latter is empowered and summoned to respond. But the first covenant is in twilight. It has been broken in a hundred different ways, and God's punishment of the faithless people has gone as far as the rejection of them. Yet God cannot

---

[14] This artificial division has been finally overcome by J.-P. Jossua in his "Le Salut. Incarnation ou mystère pascal" in *Cogit. Fidei* 28 (Paris: Cerf, 1968).

be unfaithful to himself and his promises (2 Tim 2:13). Men felt
that the covenant conditions were too hard, and initially they
pushed the responsibility onto the mediator (Ex 20:18–21; Dt
5:27). Then the mediators sent by God were rejected, scorned
and killed with increasing regularity—right up to the figure of
the "Suffering Servant": the people's guilt was laid on him by
God himself (Is 53:10), but evidently this mediation was rejected
by the people (Is 50:6). From both sides, the *pro nobis* is the central theme of the purification of the covenant and the creation of
a New Covenant. Here the apparently irreconcilable postulates
come together: on the one hand, there is a judgment, and there
must be atonement; on the other, there is the triumph of grace,
in and through judgment, so that the covenant may be definitely
reestablished in a totally new way.

Even before Paul (1 Cor 15:3; Rom 4:25), this *pro nobis* yields
the central interpretation of the "hour".[15] It unlocks not only all
Christology but the entire trinitarian doctrine of God that flows
from it, as well as the doctrine of the Church. At the heart of the
Nicene Creed stands the *crucifixus etiam pro nobis*; it already contains the words *propter nostram salutem descendit de caelis*. However,
insofar as it sums up the covenant, this central concept implies
the activity of God in calling for the redemptive obedience of
Jesus; but it also involves those on whose behalf these things are
done. It is really a case of bringing the covenant to fulfillment,
men cannot be passive while action is taken on their behalf; they
themselves must be actively involved, yet in a way that does
not blur the distinction between Christ's preeminence and his
followers and collaborators. (It will be a major problem for
Christian thought and articulation to make this indisputable
preeminence clear, while doing justice to man's cooperation
and discipleship.) The "pro nobis" contains the innermost core
of the interplay between God and man, the center of all theo-
drama.[16]

---

[15] No theology of the Cross can make sense if it is based purely on the "divine
dei" (that is, "such was the divine counsel"); this position yields no meaningful
insight, particularly in the context of the covenant. Cf. M. Hengel, "Der stellvertretende Sühnetod Jesu" in *Int. kath. Zft. Communio* 9 (1980), 1–29, 135–47.

[16] *Theo-Drama* III, 244f.

Toward this center all the main themes of election in the Old Covenant converge. They point to the mystery: they do not exhaust it. There are, for instance, the themes of the election (of the people) to divine sonship, of the Mediator, of the (High) Priest, of vicarious sacrifice, of the prophet and his destiny, of the Suffering Servant; there are the Jewish themes of the atoning quality of the just man's suffering and death, of the devil's domination of the world, of the resurrection of the dead. . . . All these ideas create a vocabulary that circles around the unique reality and helps to express it. Old and New Covenants belong together; this means that later atonement theology will not be able to jettison parts of this vocabulary without suffering harm and impoverishment. (And the old vocabulary can hardly be replaced by a new one.) We need to remember, furthermore, that the old concepts point toward a fulfilled reality that, as such, has transcended the temporal and conditional nature of these motifs (for example, the Old Testament priesthood and sacrificial cult) and attained a sphere of permanent validity and intelligibility.

b. The Main Features of
Atonement in the New Testament

Here we must take the New Testament as a whole. However original may be the perspectives opened up by its respective parts, these parts are closely interrelated. Only in a very limited sense can we produce relatively self-contained theories of the atonement; they are clearly open to one another. This is particularly true of the pre-Easter Jesus' own understanding of his death, as portrayed by the post-Easter Church. As we have shown elsewhere,[17] his self-understanding is an essential part of the meaning of the whole event. What is intrinsically impossible is that, if God has imparted universal scope and efficacy to an event, Jesus should be unaware of its essential meaning.

1. The reconciliation with the world achieved by God presupposes that God's "only Son" has "*given himself up* for us all", so

---

[17] *Theo-Drama* III, 163ff.

that, as a result, he "gives us all things" (Rom 8:32). John says the same (Jn 3:16). First and foremost, Jesus is the one whom God has "given up", "delivered up" (Mt 17:22 parr.; 20:18, 19 parr., and so forth). He *allows* himself to be handed over. But, at the heart of this obedient letting-things-happen, there is an active consent, deliberate action: "I lay down my life" (Jn 10:17) "of my own accord" (18). Thus the idea arises that he is both the (sacrificial) "Lamb" who is "given up" (Jn 1:29) and the (sacrificial) Priest who surrenders himself (Heb 2:14ff.); he is both at the same time (Heb 9:14). In virtue of this identity, he supersedes the whole sphere of previous ritual sacrifice, but not, however, at a merely "notional" or "intellectual" level: the Cross is essentially a matter of the "shedding of blood" (the "life substance" of Jn 10:17ff.). This "shedding of blood" is understood as the atoning (Rom 3:25), justifying (Rom 5:9) and purifying factor (1 Jn 1:7; Rev 7:14) at all levels of the New Testament. The words of institution show that Jesus' eucharistic self-surrender is prior to any action on men's part to send him to his death and that God's final and definitive covenant with men is sealed in the self-surrender of Jesus (Mt 26:28 parr.; 1 Cor 11:25).

2. He gives himself "for us" to the extent of *exchanging places with us*. Given up for us, he becomes "sin" (2 Cor 5:21) and a "curse" (Gal 3:13) so that we may "become—that is, share in—God's [covenant] righteousness" and receive "the blessing of Abraham" and the "promised Spirit". He who is rich becomes poor for our sake so that we may become rich through his poverty (2 Cor 8:9). In his body, our sin and hostility are condemned (Rom 8:3; cf. Eph 2:14). The "Lamb of God who takes away the sins of the world" (Jn 1:29; cf. 1 Jn 3:5) may refer back to the Suffering Servant who bears sins (Is 53:4) or to the Passover lamb (or the scapegoat, cf. Lev 16:7ff.); at all events, he must genuinely take them upon himself if he is to be able to carry them away (*airein*). And it must be really the Lamb of "God", *God's* Lamb, who occupies the place of sin, otherwise he could not so occupy it. On the basis of this exchange of place, we are already "reconciled to God" (Rom 5:18) in advance of our own consent, "while we were yet sinners". This means that

we are ontologically "transferred" (Col 1:13) and expropriated
(1 Cor 6:19; 2 Cor 5:15; Rom 14:7), insofar as, in the Paschal
event, we have died with Christ and are risen with him (Rom
6:3ff.; Col 3:3; Eph 2:5). The "indicative" of this event is always
expressing itself as an "imperative": we are to let what is true
in itself be true in us and for us, and this is not only a result
[*Ergebnis*] but also an event [*Ereignis*] (cf. Col 3:7–11), in whose
active fruitfulness we can actually receive a share (Col 1:24;
Phil 2:17).

3. First of all, the fruit of the reconciliation event can be seen
more negatively, as man being *liberated* from something: from
slavery to sin (Rom 7; Jn 8:34), from the devil (Jn 8:44; 1 Jn
3:8), from the "world powers" (Gal 4:3; Col 2:20), from the
power of darkness (Col 1:13), from the law (Rom 7:1) and from
the "law of sin and death" (Rom 8:2) and, finally, from the
"wrath to come" (1 Th 1:10). This liberation recalls the "ran-
soming" (= redemption) of Israel from the "house of slavery"
in Egypt (1 Cor 1:30) and is described as the paying of a high
"price" (the blood of Christ: 1 Cor 6:20; 7:23; 1 Pet 1:18ff.), or
"ransom" (Mk 10:45 par.); in cultic terms it is a "propitiation"
(Rom 3:25) producing an "eternal redemption" (Heb 9:12). In
continuity with the Old Testament, again, expiation is seen in
terms of "blood", without which "there is no forgiveness" (Heb
9:22); but what is meant here is death (Heb 9:15), possibly violent death, or, more accurately, the surrendering of life (Jn 10),
which leads back to the former meaning.

4. However, this loosing of bonds (Lk 13:16; Mt 12:29) is very
much more than the mere restoration of a lost freedom. It takes
place through the Holy Spirit and imparts to us God's Holy
Spirit, who calls "Abba, Father!" in us, assuring us that we share
a fellow-sonship with Christ vis-à-vis God the Father (Gal 4:6f.;
Rom 8:10ff.). The positive side, therefore, is that we are *drawn
into the divine, trinitarian life*. From the highest perspective, the
"redemption through his blood, the forgiveness of sins" is only
one element within the all-embracing divine purpose. God's purpose is to enable us, by grace, to share in Christ's sonship (Eph
1:5ff.) by becoming "members of his body" (1 Cor 12; Eph 4,

and so forth). The New Testament knows nothing of any other kind of freedom than this, which is imparted by the Holy Spirit and lived by the power of the same Spirit (Gal 5:13, 18ff.; cf. Jn 8:31f.).

5. Whereas, in connection with man's desperate plight, there are many references to "God's anger" (Mt 3:7 par.; Rom 1:18; Eph 2:3; Rev passim), the entire reconciliation process is attributed to God's merciful *love*. On the basis of the love of the Father (Rom 8:39) and of Christ (Rom 8:35), the Son was given up "for us all" (Rom 8:32) by the Father. It is God's immense love for the world that has caused him to give up his only Son (Jn 3:16) and thereby to reconcile the world to himself (2 Cor 5:19; Col 1:20). He has empowered his Son to give his life "for his sheep" (Jn 10:15), to hand on to those who are his the kingdom that has been delivered to him (Lk 22:30). While this work of redemption must have something to do with God's covenant "righteousness" (since it is concerned with restoring and fulfilling the covenant, which is a two-sided reality), it remains true that everything flows from the primary source: God's gracious love.

Surveying these five aspects, it is clear that they belong together. It is also clear that they cannot be reduced to an allegedly higher integration, to a "system". They demonstrate their significance for an ecclesial soteriology by showing their coherence and by applying this to the proclamation of the mystery and to the defense of the Christian faith. This can only happen, however, if all aspects are given adequate room.

These are the dangers to be avoided. (1) No aspect must be allowed to dominate and so diminish the significance of the others. (2) The full content of the central assertion (which is the goal of all five aspects) may not be replaced by some alleged equivalent that is more "intelligible" to the spirit of a different epoch but in fact lacks the center of gravity of the biblical assertion. (3) The tension that exists between two aspects must not be slackened, let alone dissolved, in the interests of an illusory synthesis: rather, it must be *endured*.

The history of soteriology gives us examples of all three dangers. With regard to the first danger, there was a theology of the "exchange" (see aspect 2 above), which failed to do justice to the first aspect; a theology of liberation (aspect 3 above), which failed to pay sufficient attention to aspects 1, 2 and 4; and a theology of reconciliation (aspect 5), which did not take aspects 1 and 2 seriously enough.

As to the second danger, certain theologians have thought it sufficient to replace the notions of the "exchange of places" (3) or "self-immolation" (1) with that of the "solidarity" of God (or Jesus) with sinners.

We see the third danger in a theology that tries to interpret the "self-surrender" (1) as a mere symbol for God's love (5), so failing to give full weight to the reality of the "exchange of places" (2).

An examination of the major attempts to construct a doctrine of redemption will reveal a number of these one-sided approaches. In each case, they infallibly result in a loss of theodramatic tension in the whole. We shall limit ourselves to three periods, antiquity, the Middle Ages and modern times, each of which shows a relative internal consistency. The latter period splits into two opposite tendencies.

2. Models in the History of Theology

a. The Fathers

Varied as the theologies of the Fathers are, they are related in their fundamental approach. The basic institution, common to them all, is the "exchange". He who was God becomes man, so that man can be taken up to God's place: "*Verbum Dei . . . factus est quod nos sumus, uti nos perficeret esse quod est ipse*" (Irenaeus).[1] This dominant theme—see above, aspect 2—automatically involves aspect 4: redemption is not simply liberation but initiation into the divine, triune life;[2] but it also does justice to aspect 3:

---

[1] *Adv. Haer.* V prol. (SC 153/2, 14).
[2] This is very clear in Athanasius: *Or. II c. Arian.* 68 (PG 26, 292C–293A).

redemption from the powers hostile to God must be "paid for". (In this context, the idea found in some of the Fathers, of the devil having power—rightly or wrongly—over man, should be seen rather as symbolizing the element of "justice" that governs the relationship between God and the creation, as set forth later by Anselm. The devil epitomizes the enslaving powers; the "price" can also be paid to "death".)[3] The fifth aspect (the Father's love, that is, the love of the triune God) and the first (the Son's self-sacrifice) are always implied in the dominant second aspect.

Its dominant position is explained by the urgent need—because of the christological heresies—to assert the covenant Mediator's full divinity and unabbreviated humanity. As has been adequately shown by now,[4] this aspect is not due to some irruption of Greek thought into the biblical milieu: it results from the effort made to secure the full soteriological meaning of the New Testament's *pro nobis*. This necessity of securing the reality of the Incarnation—and "incarnation" here means less the unique act of *becoming* man than the abiding condition of *being* man (and having become man)—must not give the impression that, as far as the Fathers were concerned, the Passion and Resurrection had a lesser significance. Nor should we term their christological endeavors their "theology" and their contemplation of the Cross their "spirituality".[5] The real question we should address to the Fathers' theology is this: given that they selected the "exchange" as their central theme (or had it thrust upon them from outside), did they follow it through as radically as the New Testament requires? And, accordingly, did they fully include all the other themes and so unfold the whole dramatic potentiality of this central element of the theo-drama?

---

[3] Cf. Irenaeus, *Epideixis* 23 and 38.

[4] A. Grillmeier, "Hellenisierung-Judaisierung . . ." in *Mit Ihm und in Ihm, Christolog. Forschungen u. Perspektiven* (Herder, 1975), 423–88.

[5] As Wilhelm Breuning seems to do rather too one-sidedly in his *Gemeinschaft mit Gott in Jesu Tod und Auferstehung: Christi erlösendes Leben und Sterben* (Aschaffenburg: Pattloch, 1971): "Easter is not so absolutely at the center of the Fathers' theology as it was in the New Testament" (30).

"Admirabile Commercium"

Initially, as we have said, the model of the "exchange", expressed at the time of the Council of Ephesus by the term *commercium*[6] —replacing unfortunate, earlier terms such as *mixis* and *krāsis*[7] —seems "formal" or "neutral", allowing of different concrete expressions. All the same, the essential thrust of the interpretations remains constant. Below we briefly indicate the various stages.

α. Initially, we have purely christological baptismal "exchange" formulas: "He, being God, becomes man; men that we are, we become divine." The goal here is the *pro nobis*. Significantly, these formulas are current even before the explicit definition of Christ's divinity at Nicea and are primarily concerned with the (divine) Logos:

Irenaeus: "The Logos became man so that man should lay hold of the Logos in himself; thus, receiving sonship, he should become a son of God" (*Adv. Haer.* 3, 19, 1). Even the *Letter to Diognetus* (SC 74, IX, 5) speaks of the "sweet exchange" (*antallagē*) between the guilt of the many and the righteousness of the one.

Cyprian: "Christ wanted to be what man is so that man could be what Christ is" (*Idol.* 11).

Athanasius: "The Logos became man so that we might become divinized" (*De Inc.* 54). "He made men gods (*etheopoiēse*) by himself becoming man" (*Or. c. Arian.* I, 38; cf. *Ep. ad. Adelph.* 4).

Hilary: "(In becoming man), he who is God does not lose his divinity but makes it possible for man to become God" (*Trin.* IX, 3).

Gregory Nazianzen: "So he clothed himself with thy coarse materiality, . . . that I might become God just as much as he became man" (*Or.* 40, 45).

---

[6] M. Herz, "Sacrum commercium" in *Münchener theol. Studien* II, 15 (Munich: Zink, 1958).

[7] For example, Tertullian: "*homo Deo mixtus*" (*Apol.* 21, 14); Cyprian: "*hic in virginem delabitur, . . . Deus cum homine miscetur*" (*Idol.* 11); Gregory Nazianzen: beyond the first mixture of body and immortal soul there is a "new *mixis* and paradoxical *krasis*" between flesh and (divine) Spirit (*Or.* 38, 13).

Augustine: "In order to make gods of those who were men, he who was God became man" (*Sermo* 192, 1).

Leo I: "The Redeemer became the son of a man so that we could become sons of God" (*Sermo* 26, 2). "He became a man of our race so that we might become sharers of the divine nature" (*Sermo* 29, 5).

Cyril of Alexandria: "God became man so that we should become gods and sons" (*Thes. ass.* 25).

Ever since Nicea, these exchange formulas have been reiterated according to the constant maxim that only what has been adopted (by God in Christ) can be redeemed. For example, Proclus of Constantinople: "If he had not adopted me, he would not have saved me" (*Or.* 1: PG 65, 699D).

β. As we have said, "Incarnation" means not only the act by which the Son enters into humanity but the acceptance of an entire human life, prone to suffering. Right from the outset, therefore, it heads toward Passion and death.

Tertullian: "*forma moriendi causa nascendi est*" (*Carn.* 6, 6).

Irenaeus: "How could he take on man's end if he did not first take on man's beginning?" (*Epid.* 38).

Hilary: "Adopting us is of no advantage to God, but his will to endure humiliation signifies our advancement" (*Trin.* 9, 3).

Augustine: "His Passion belongs to his Incarnation" (*Sermo* 22, 1, 1). "Strength became weak so that weakness might become strong" (*Sermo* 190, 4).

Gregory Nazianzen: "He took the worse part so that he might give you the better part. . . . He let himself be scorned so that you should be glorified" (*Or.* 1, 5).

Gregory of Nyssa: "Anyone who ponders the mystery will be more inclined to say that it was not his death that resulted from his birth, but that he accepted to be born so that he might be able to die" (*Or. cat.* 32).

Leo I: "The Son of God became the Son of Man in order to die . . . and rise again" (*Christmas Sermon* 10).

γ. In the act of Incarnation, the Redeemer expresses his solidarity with all mankind, whose nature he shares; yet, according to the Fathers, it is the *Passion/Resurrection* (together with the sending of the Spirit) that achieves concrete, objective (and subjective) redemption.

Irenaeus: "Having become man, he summed up the long succession of human generations in himself; thus he was the epitome of salvation and as such [*in compendio*] offered it to us" (*Adv. Haer.* 3, 18, 1).

Athanasius: "He carries us all so that we all may carry the One God" (*De Inc. et c. Arian.* 8).

Leo I: "Thus he incorporated himself in us, and us in him, so that God's descent into humanity should constitute man's ascent into the divine" (*Sermo* 27, 2).

However, there are nuances in the assertion that the enfleshment of the Logos is the presupposition for God's gracious acceptance and redemption of man:

Cyril of Alexandria: "I have become one body with them [believers], and accordingly I am able to accept them [that is, bestow grace upon them] because they are physically united and bound to me in a relationship of the flesh" (*Thes. ass.* 15; PG 75, 292A; cf. *In Joh.* 1:14; PG 73, 161). This is also the point of the distinction between being joined to the Son *physikōs* and *methektikōs*, "according to grace" (*Rec. fid. ad Theod.* 13).

Gregory of Nyssa: the Incarnation is God's union with mankind, which results in the latter being joined *dynamei* (in germ) to the Godhead (*Or. cat.* 32, 5; 16, 9).[8]

Athanasius sees the assumption of human nature as "mediating" the required redemption (*De Inc.* 44); it could not take place on a mere "signal" from God—a fact that Anselm will later emphasize. Many Fathers see Paul's assertion that Jesus was "made to be sin" and "a curse" for us (2 Cor 5:21; Gal 3:13) as referring to this assumption of sinful human nature: thus Gregory of Nyssa (*Vita Moysis* 2, 33) and Gregory Nazianzen, who says that in this way Jesus became *autoamartia* and *autokatara* (the epitome of sin and a curse—*Or* 37; PG 36, 284).

Later we shall have to assess how far such expressions, when applied to the Cross (above all by Origen and Chrysostom), anticipate the theology of the Reformers. For the moment we sim-

---

[8] Cf. R. Hübner, *Die Einheit des Leibes Christi bei Gregor von Nyssa* (Leiden: Brill, 1974), 109–11.

ply observe that Origen's theory, according to which the body as such is connected with some premundane sin (*Hom. 22 in Lc*; Rauer 9, 173f.), plays no part in the theology of the Fathers quoted above.

At all events, therefore, the "exchange" has a history, whether it is seen as stretching from the Incarnation to the death and Resurrection of Christ or from man's fundamental *relation* to Christ (in the sense of 2 Corinthians 5:14f.) to his being effectively *incorporated* into him.

δ. Given the above implications, the *commercium* formula can unfold. It was probably coined in the East at the time of the Council of Ephesus (Proclus of Constantinople: *phrikton syallagma: Or.* 1; PG 65, 688D−689A) and from there entered into the Roman liturgy (*admirabile commercium*) under Leo I.[9] But the metaphor is common in Augustine too. Christ is the "heavenly merchant" who buys our pains from us in exchange for his grace. Or Christ "ransoms us" (from the "powers") and goes on to "offer in sacrifice" what he has thus bought, cf. the ancient Gelasian preface: "*Beati lege commercii divinis humana mutantur, quia nostrorum omnium mors cruce Christi redempta [!] est.*"[10] Note the introduction of scriptural themes here. While it is true that Christ, in his whole humanity, is also our pattern and teacher, it is not the theme of *paideia* but of the "exchange" that is in the foreground with the Fathers.[11] The events of salvation constitute a "*commercium caritatis*" (Augustine, *C. Faust.* 5, 9), "*commercium salutare*" (Leo, *Sermo* 54, 4). Augustine: "From what is ours he takes death, so that from what is his he may give us life" (*Sermo* 232, 5). The gift of Christ is utterly beyond value; this is self-evident, given his divinity. But the price paid is so high that he thereby ransoms the entire earth (as we find in the anti-Donatist *En. in Ps.* 147, 16). "*Assumpsit pro te quod offeret [!] pro te. . . . O magna mutatio* ['exchange']: *vive de ipsius, quia de tuo mortuus est*" (*Sermo* Morin, 664).

---

[9] Further details in Herz (note 6 above), 24ff., 7off.

[10] *Ibid.*, 155.

[11] Contrary to Greshake: "Der Wandel der Erlösungsvorstellungen in der Theologiegeschichte" in L. Scheffczyk (ed.) *Erlösung und Emanzipation*, QD 61 (Herder, 1973), 69−101.

The Fathers do not consciously impose any limits on the idea of the "exchange". In harmony with their christological ideas, however, they are bound unconsciously to assume a limit. When he takes on "the likeness of our sinful nature" (Rom 8:3), he who is perfectly sinless can only adopt the *consequences* of sin that attach to this nature. These *pathē* (*affectus*) are weaknesses, yet they are not culpable; and—as is often asserted—he adopts them only insofar as he makes us present "in himself".

The seminal text is from the pen of Gregory Nazianzen. Origen's idea was that Christ is not fully subject to the Father if "I, the last sinner" (and yet a member of Christ) am not yet fully subject to him (*Lev. hom.* 7, 1–2).[12] Gregory takes up this idea and says that Christ is not subject to the Father to the extent that he represents us ("*en heautōi . . . typoi to hēmeteron*"). "He has appropriated [*oikeioumenos*] our madness and our sins. He plays our role [*dramatourgeitai*] in our name [*hyper hēmōn*]." For, as the Logos, he was neither obedient nor disobedient but only subordinate. Now that he has taken on "the form of the slave", however, "he fashions within himself what is foreign to him by carrying me and all that belongs to me; thus he consumes whatever is evil in me just as fire consumes wax, or as the sun disperses the mist that covers the earth. For my part, as a result of this mixing [*synkrāsin*], I become a partaker of his goods" (*Or.* 30, PG 36, 108C–109C). Here Christ becomes the central figure of the world stage. He plays his dramatic role, portraying not only himself but us too in him, on the basis of an appropriation (*oikeiōsis*) whereby he images and imprints (*typoun*) our fallen nature within himself; what is defective is thus consumed, so that it can be genuinely incorporated.

The crucial question here is this. How internal is this role-playing in the suffering Christ, and how far does he identify himself with the role? The relationship between Christ the Head and his members (which we are), to which Gregory Nazianzen also refers, must surely point us in the direction of a true identification.

---

[12] Baehr. VI, 370–80. Ambrose imitated this idea in his *De Trin. ad Gratian.* Cf. Gerhoh von Reichersberg, *L. cont. duo haer.* chap. 4.

Augustine wrestles with the problem in the wake of Hilary and Ambrose, whose treatment of the subject was less clear. Jesus adopts human emotions, for example, mortal fear in Gethsemane, these "stirrings of human weakness, not because of a weakness in his constitution, but from a willing compassion" (*En. in Ps.* 87, 3). Since he is sinless, he does not need to fear death; but, as Head, he adopts the language of his members ("*non enim timebat mori qui venerat mori, . . . sed loquebantur membra in capite*": *In Ps.* 40, 6; cf. *In Ps.* 90, 19). Jesus experiences fear on the basis of a free-will appropriation, but the latter is implicit in his acceptance of concrete, fallen human nature ("*moriturus ergo ex eo quod nostrum habebat, non in se, sed in nobis pavebat*": *In Ps.* 30, en. II, s. 1, 3). For this "appropriation", Augustine uses words like *repraesentare, transfigurare, personam agere* (that is, to act a role).[13] He wants to maintain both the realism of Christ's emotions and the fact that they are deliberately willed by him (*In Joh. tr.* 49, 18). In himself, Jesus did not need to be tempted; but we and our temptations are in his flesh (*In Ps.* 60, 3). He is not fallen and so does not need to fear death; but he freely undergoes the fear of death, which is not his but ours (*In Ps.* 93, 19). Similarly, he experiences dereliction on the Cross, not in himself, but in us. The Son could not be abandoned by the Father,[14] but since we are *really* in him, his mortal cry is *real*.

It is possible to ask whether what is meant here by Christ's "will" to represent his sinful members in himself actually covers what Gregory meant by *synkrāsis*, that is, including men's guilt, as expressed strongly by Ambrose: "*Peccata nostra non usu, sed qualitate suscepit*" (*Explan. Ps.* 38, 5). Augustine makes a careful distinction here: "*Invenit [Christus] nos iacentes in culpa et poena, suscepit solam poenam, et culpam solvit et poenam*" (*S. Guel.* 31, 3, Morin 558; cf. *Sermo* 171, 3, 3).[15] In fact, the "mystical realism"

---

[13] Tarc. J. van Bavel, "Recherches sur la christologie de s. Augustin" in *Paradosis* X (Fribourg, 1957), 127–45. On earlier, similar interpretations, cf. G. Jouassard, "L'Abandon du Christ en croix dans la tradition grecque du IVᵉ et Vᵉ siècle" in *RSR* (1925), 609–33.

[14] Which prevented Augustine "d'admettre l'abandon comme sentiment réel, c'est qu'il n'y a pas d'abandon véritable de Dieu". Van Bavel, 143.

[15] Further texts in van Bavel (note 13 above) and L. Sabourin, *Rédemption sacri-ficielle* (Desclée de Brouwer, 1961), 55ff.

of the unity of Head and members will subsequently play a considerable part (in Thomas).

It becomes clear from his reiterated interpretation of 2 Corinthians 5:21 that Augustine wanted to avoid any inner contact between the purity of the Head and the sins of the members. The fact that, "for our sake" God "made him to be sin who knew no sin" could only mean that God made him "a sacrifice for sin": "*sacrificandus ad diluenda peccata*" (*Enchir.* 41; *Sermo* 152, 11; 134, 4-5; *Expos. Gal.* 11). Apparently Ambrosiaster was the first to put forward this explanation;[16] after Augustine, it was handed on without a break, persisting until the Middle Ages.[17]

The Greeks had to come to grips with Gregory's strong language in Address 30, already quoted: "*Holon en heautōi eme pherōn meta tou emou*": "He bore me in my entirety within himself, together with all that is mine" (PG 36, 109C). But Maximus is careful to distinguish between the consequences of sin (which can be termed *tēn di'eme hamartian*), that is, the "corruption of nature" that Jesus took upon himself, and sin itself (*tēn emēn hamartian*), which he could not assume. It is only in the sense of bearing the effects of sin that Jesus submits to judgment together with us (*synkatakrinas hēmīn heauton: Quaest. ad Thal.* 42; PG 90, 408A; *Ambig.* 42; PG 91, 1348BC). Nonetheless, his adoption of our mortal fear is real; it is not merely simulated, not *monon ephantase* (*Op.* 16; PG 91, 196D). When Jesus makes his prayer on the Mount of Olives, he first of all manifests real horror on the part of his human will, before this same will bows and consents to the divine will; Maximus sees this as a proof of his own two-wills doctrine.[18] Certain Monothelites, following

---

[16] "For the first time, it seems, Ambrosiaster explicitly introduces the notion 'sin-offering' for 'sin' in the exegesis of 2 Corinthians 5:21": S. Lyonnet and L. Sabourin, "Sin, Redemption and Sacrifice. A Biblical and Patristic Study" in *Anal. Bibl.* 48 (Rome, 1970), 205. Pelagius, in his commentary on Paul's Epistles, follows Ambrosiaster. Cf. also K. H. Schelkle, *Paulus, Lehrer der Väter* (Düsseldorf: Patmos, 1956), 207ff.

[17] Lyonnet-Sabourin (see previous note), 215ff. The same applies to the assumption of sinners' fear during the Passion: "Passioni appropinquans Dominus infirmantium in se voces sumpsit eorum timorem ut abstraheret suscepit": Gregory the Great, *Mor.* 12, 12 (PL 75, 994).

[18] Cf. François-Marie Léthel, O.C.D., *Théologie de l'Agonie du Christ. La Liberté humaine du Fils de Dieu et son importance sotériologique mises en lumière par Maxime*

Pyrrhus, based themselves on Gregory's *oikeiōsis* and assumed that Jesus had only "ascribed" a human will to himself. Maximus asks his opponents whether this consent on Jesus' part is substantial (*ousiōdēs*) or merely a matter of an external attitude (*schetikē*), as, for instance, when friends attribute what they do or suffer to each other, without really experiencing it? Pyrrhus, of course, is obliged to affirm the former (*Disp. c. Pyrrho*, PG 91, 304AB). As we have seen, however, Jesus' physical, created will only assumes the *consequences* of sin, even if, according to Maximus (quoted here word for word by Gregory), "he bore me in my entirety within himself, together with all that is mine, so that he could impart redemption to all of me, taking the whole curse of sin away from me" (*Op.* 9; PG 91, 128D). Nor is Maximus slow to describe Jesus' taking of sin's consequences upon himself as "self-sacrifice" (*Ad Thal.* 36; PG 90, 380B), and as the annihilation of the powers hostile to God (*Ad Thal.* 21, PG 90, 316A).

For John Damascene, Christ's substantial, creaturely will was something to be taken for granted; he can use *schetikōs* in a new sense, linking up with what Maximus said in his "Disputation": "Jesus takes upon himself the non-sinful *pathē* and, moreover, *kat' oikeiōsin schetikēn*, the debts thus incurred." The latter is done in this way: it is as if a person "represents someone else [*prosōpon hypodytai*] out of compassion or love and in his stead speaks for him in words that do not in any way apply to the speaker himself. In accordance with this *oikeiōsis*, he [Christ] has taken on our curse and our forsakenness, not as if he had actually been or become these things himself, but by taking on the role [*prosōpon*] and making himself like us. This is what is meant when Scripture says, 'He became a curse for us'" (PG 94, 1003).

Everywhere this formula, "me in my entirety and all that is mine", is similarly restricted to the consequences of sin and the punishment due to sin, whereas sin itself is *not* taken on by him. In this way the *admirabile commercium* comes up against an uncon-

---

le *Confesseur* (Paris: Beauchesne, 1979). Léthel here builds on the work of M. Doucet, *La Dispute de Maxime le Confesseur avec Pyrrhus* (Montreal, 1972, typescript). Maritain has also drawn attention to the importance of Jesus' human freedom in the Passion in his *De la grâce et de l'humanité du Christ* (Paris-Bruges, 1967).

scious limit—unconscious because it is taken for granted. The Redeemer acting on the world stage does not completely fill out his role of representing the sinner before God. On the other hand, the fact that this limitation is unconscious means that, with their *commercium* formula, the Fathers are desirous of holding fast to the whole, unabbreviated realism of the gospel. The *pro nobis* formula is constant from the earliest to the latest times, and is subject to no restriction. So we find it in 1 Clement,[19] the Didachē,[20] Pseudo-Barnabas[21] and right up to Ignatius of Antioch,[22] Polycarp[23] and the Shepherd of Hermas,[24] where there is further development of Isaiah 53.[25] From Origen[26] and Cyprian,[27] it comes down to Athanasius[28] and Cyril of Alexandria.[29] As well as the *pro nobis*, Ambrose goes on to emphasize the Pauline *pro me* in a particularly intense and personal way;[30] but this is also familiar to the Antioch Fathers[31] and, of course, Augustine.[32] The liturgy continually recalls and is aware of it. There is continuous use of nouns with the prefix *anti-* (cf. the *antilytron*, "ransom", of 1 Timothy 2:6, following Mark 10:45, Matthew 20:28); from Eusebius onward, we have *antipsychon*,[33] similarly in the sense of "ransom"—actually "scapegoat".[34] Athanasius speaks of this too (*Inc.* 8; cf. *antididous*: *C. Arian.* 2, 66), whereas in Gregory of Nyssa the biblical *antallagma* (Mk 8:37 par.) returns, applied to Christ (*C. Eunom.* 11; PG 45, 860).

[19] 7, 4. [20] 9, 5. [21] 11.
[22] Rom 6:1; Sm 1, 2; 71; Eph 16:2.
[23] 1, 2.
[24] Vis III, 5, 3; sim IX, 12, 4.
[25] 1 Clem 16; Ps.-Barn. 7, 3.
[26] *Comm. Joh.* VI, 53–58.
[27] *Or.* 34.
[28] *De Incarn.* 7, 20, 31, 37, and so forth.
[29] *De recta fide ad Reginas* (PG 76, 1293; *Or. altera, ibid.*, 1344).
[30] *Expos. Ps.* 118, 8, 7; *ibid.*, 12, 37; *Expos. Luc.* 2, 41; *De bono mortis* 6, 25.
[31] Theodore, *hom. cat.* (Tonneau) V, 1–6.
[32] *De Trin.* IV, 13, 17, and so forth.
[33] References in L. Sabourin, *Rédemption sacrificielle* (Desclée de Brouwer, 1961), 22f. Sabourin also discusses the origin of the word, which is already found in Ignatius (Eph 21:1; Sm 10:2; *Ad Polyc.* 2, 3) and can be traced back to 4 Maccabees.
[34] "Eusèbe . . . adopte l'interprétation 'substitutive'." Sabourin, 25.

b. The Medieval Model

Anselm

Anselm is the first to develop a systematic soteriology, endeavoring to bring together motifs inherited from Scripture and the Fathers, and to integrate them. He makes his task more difficult by trying to operate *remoto Christo* when demonstrating to unbelievers (and believers who are none too sure) that the Incarnation of the Son of God was "necessary". There are things that seem entirely natural once we presuppose God's historical covenant with Israel (and the Noah covenant with mankind); that is, the two-sided relationship between God and his people and the juridical elements that are implicit even in a covenant that has come about through grace. These become more abstract and less perspicuous once salvation history is excluded from consideration on methodological grounds and the relation (*ordo*) of God to his creation is held to be the sole foundation. It must immediately be said, however, that current polemical attacks on Anselm's alleged "legalism" are foolish, whether they come from Protestant or Catholic theologians. Such an approach fails to do justice to the juridical categories that are intrinsic to God's personal freedom and to that of the creature. Anselm becomes substantially more accessible if we approach him after having been schooled in the Old Covenant, where, in free divine grace, a two-sided, reciprocal standard of just conduct is established. This standard is maintained unconditionally on God's side because of his covenant faithfulness, even when man proves unfaithful.

As a result of his methodological restriction, Anselm also makes it hard for himself when it comes to synthesizing the five central biblical themes. At the heart of his reflections, he places the concept of *satisfactio*, taken over from the Latin Fathers, Tertullian,[1] Hilary[2] and Ambrose.[3] His use of this concept causes him to favor the third biblical aspect, that is, man's

[1] On *satisfactio* and *meritum* in Tertullian, cf. Braun, *Deus Christianorum*, 2d ed. (Paris, 1976), 475ff.

[2] *Tr. in Ps.* 53, 12.

[3] *In Ps.* 38, nos. 46 and 53. On this whole issue: J. Rivière, "Sur les premières applications du terme 'satisfactio' à l'oeuvre du Christ" in *BLE* 25 (1924), 285–97, 353–69.

liberation by "ransom" or "satisfaction", and the "exchange" aspect is pressed into service in this context: he who is both God and man must actually take man's place if the latter, given his insolvency through sin, is to find relief. This by no means causes Anselm to forget the fifth aspect (God's love) or the first, which flows from it (the delivering-up of the Son); he traces everything back to the Father's mercy and the Son's free self-surrender: "*Quid misericordius intelligi valet, quam cum peccatori . . . unde se redimat non habenti Deus Pater dicit: Accipe Unigenitum meum et da pro te; et ipse Filius: Tolle me et redime te?*"[4] As for the fourth scriptural aspect, that is, man's initiation, achieved by the redemption, into the life of the Trinity, it remains implicit, it is not treated explicitly. Similarly, there is no express treatment of Christ's Resurrection or of the Holy Spirit.

Anselm openly admits his self-imposed methodological limits. He is precisely aware of the atonement's mystery-quality and indeed seeks to commend this quality to faith by pointing out certain rational aspects that it manifests.[5] He rightly presupposes that God's "external" honor—and in concrete terms this means his position in the covenant made with man—can be restored neither by mere forgiveness of sin on God's part (I, 12)[6] nor by

---

[4] *Cur Deus homo*, I, II, chap. 20.

[5] "Plus . . . persuadebis altiores in hac re rationes latere, si aliquam te videre monstraveris": *CDH* II, 16.

[6] Cf. Athanasius, *Or. c. Arian.* II, 64 (PG 26, 291). Characteristically, Athanasius links this impossibility with the theme of *theiōsis*, which Anselm does not do. At this point, Anselm's critics (Harnack, Ritschl) confuse God with a mere private citizen or a feudal lord. In fact, God, as Creator, has invested his honor and authority in his creation. Accordingly, his requirement of satisfaction serves to maintain that honor and authority, just as Athanasius says in the passage quoted. Cf. R. Hermann, "Anselms Lehre vom Werke Christi in ihrer bleibenden Bedeutung" in *Zft. syst. Theol.* I (1923), 376–96; Hans-Ulrich Wiese, "Die Lehre Anselms von Canterbury über den Tod Jesu in der Schrift 'Cur Deus homo'" in *Wiss. u. Weisheit* 41 (1978), 149–79; 42 (1979), 34–55. Wiese undertakes a thorough discussion of the entire literature, aiming to discover a balanced vantage point, though it may be that he is looking for a rather too "personal" mode of thought behind Anselm's "juristic" categories. To the present author, it seems futile to set these two poles against each other. Cf. also Wilhelm Breuning, *Gemeinschaft mit Gott in Jesu Tod und Auferweckung* (Aschaffenburg, 1972). Breuning asks the question, "Juristic or personal categories?" (59) and rightly discovers the latter in the former.

mere remorse on the part of the sinner (I, 21). (As for God's "interior" honor, it remains unassailable.) It follows that an initiative is required on the part of the merciful God to encourage man to play his part. For Anselm himself, there is no opposition between the juridical and personal aspects of the God-man relationship. In view of the foregoing, all polemics against Anselm in this area should be dropped.

Since Anselm was the first to try to bring Scripture's soteriological motifs into a coherent rational "system", the dramatic dimension of the world's redemption in Christ came out in his theology as never before, in terms not only of content but also of form. He describes an action that takes place between God and the world; through the unity of "freedom" (on God's side) and "necessity", this action has the vibrancy of a closed dramatic action with an inner logic that comes, not from the necessity of fate that overwhelms freedom (*necessitas antecedens*), but from a necessity arising from the free character of the parties concerned (*necessitas sequens*, II, 17). This formally fulfills the demand for a well-built dramatic action,[7] such as we have already shown in connection with Calderon's drama of destiny, a drama that is continually being burst open from within so that justice may be done to the reality of freedom.[8] Anselm was not afraid of taking great pains to show that, in God, freedom cannot be other than identical with "rightness" (*rectitudo*), which contains not only absolute truth and goodness but also justice and mercy: they have a common source. This is reflected in the order (*ordo*) that sustains the world created by God: it follows that God owes it to himself (his "honor") to put an end to the disorder introduced into the world by man's created freedom, and this he does by intervening with both his righteousness and his mercy. As in the Bible, this is done with a view to the relationship between God and sinful man, who stands in need of redemption; in Anselm, the question of the fallen angels who are beyond redemption remains in shadow, as in Scripture, and is raised only insofar as man has to fill the gap thus created in the angel ranks (I, 16–18)

[7] *Theo-Drama* I, 250f.; 353f.

[8] *Theo-Drama* I, 361–69. In considering the identity of God's "freedom" and "necessity" in Anselm, it is essential to refer to the *Proslogion* and *Monologion* as well as to *Cur Deus homo*. Cf. Wiese, 157.

—a theme taken up by Augustine. This theme remains a "sub-plot" that neither disturbs the self-contained course of the main action nor adds anything substantial to it. There is a necessary transition in theology from an aesthetic to a dramatic view of the world; rarely has it been as clear as this: Anselm's *"honor"* is the *"glory"* of God in a contemporary form, and Augustine's *"pul-chritudo universi"*, which Anselm takes over (I, 15), is the same thing as the *"ordo"* that must be established one way or another, whether by *poena* or *satisfactio* (I, 15). Man cannot provide the latter, for he owes everything to God—even his death, since he is a sinner. On the other hand, man's guilt calls for recompense through a work of supererogation.[9] It follows, therefore, that the Son of God must become incarnate; this is solely the work of the merciful God, yet it is performed by the man Jesus. Like all Anselm's individual themes, this is a traditional one. But the way the motifs fit together and lead one to another is new; it brings out the dramatic dimension in the "beauty" of the divine world plan—a dimension that was latent hitherto. In fact, the inter-play of this interlocking necessity (*necessitas*) and God's perfect, unabridged freedom—and this applies to the triune God as well as to the Father and the Son separately—brings out the aesthetic dimension that is preserved and nurtured by the dramatic.[10]

With regard to the freedom of the divine action, its "necessity" resides solely in the nature of God and the inner relation-ship between him and the work he has undertaken with the world and with man. Everything, including the death of Jesus, follows from it (*necessitas sequens*) in accord with the free de-cision to enable man to enjoy the beatific vision of God. Of course this decision is a trinitarian one, originating in the Son just as much as in the Father and the Spirit.[11] Thus "[the Fa-ther] did not compel Christ to die: Christ himself suffered death voluntarily [*sponte*]" (I, 9). This recurrent *sponte* is the leitmotif of the dramatic action. Again and again it is attributed to the

---

[9] "Non ergo satisfacis, si non reddis aliquid maius quam sit id pro quo pec-catum facere non debueras" I, 21.

[10] On Anselm's aesthetic view (particularly with regard to the interplay of ne-cessity and freedom), cf. *The Glory of the Lord* II, 211–59.

[11] "Ipse [Filius] cum Patre Sanctoque Spiritu disposuerat se non aliter quam per mortem celsitudinem omnipotentiae suae mundo ostensurum" I, 9.

Son, even after his Incarnation, even in his strict obedience to the Father (the kind of obedience man owes to God, even unto death); the result is that the "command" that God addresses to the Son seems increasingly to have the form of a "granting", a "ratification" of the Son's will.[12]

If the Son becomes man—not through a kenosis on God's part, since this is impossible given the immutability of the divine essence[13]—he owes God (the Father) a life of perfect righteousness. Indeed, he owes him more: he owes it to him to suffer for this righteousness to which he holds fast so tenaciously. In negative terms, this means that, for Anselm, neither Jesus' life nor even his sufferings represent a work of supererogation, but only his death. For, since he was not a sinner, dying was not a debt he was required to pay. (This view will need critical examination.) Positively, it means that Jesus' death was not an isolated event but the final consequence of a righteousness he had maintained throughout his life (*perseveranter servando iustitiam*, II, 11; *veritatem et iustitiam vivendo et loquendo indeclinabiliter tenebat*, I, 9). This aspect, which sees Jesus' death as the ultimate consequence of his initiative on behalf of righteousness, could provide a link with a theology of liberation. At all events, it shows that it is not only the Son's divine nature that exercises free volition (*sponte*), whereas his human will "merely obeys". On the contrary, the humanity of Jesus, with its free will (as is clear from Maximus onward), participates in his free-will, atoning death: its goal is man's final liberation (*liberatio*). On the other hand, this liberation cannot be automatic: it cannot override man's naturally constituted freedom, even if he *is* a sinner. Anselm makes an important distinction between an objective restoration of the world's

---

[12] "Vult quod *non prohibet*. Quoniam ergo Patri Filii voluntas placuit, *nec prohibuit* eum velle aut implere quod volebat, recte voluisse ut Filius mortem . . . sustineret —quamvis poenam eius non amaret—affirmatur. . . . Immo maxime decet talem Patrem tali Filio *consentire* . . ." I, 10. It is clear from this and similar passages how foolish it is to accuse Anselm of having invented a cruel Father-God, who, in order to restore his own honor, demanded that this Son should be slaughtered. Anselm himself rejects such a repulsive picture of God: "It would be very strange if God were to delight in the blood of an innocent man—or actually needed it— and would (or could) only pardon the guilty after killing the innocent" I, 10.

[13] "Divinam enim naturam . . . [n]ullatenus posse a sua celsitudine humiliari" I, 8.

order through Christ's death and the subjective appropriation of redeeming grace by the sinner who repents and is converted (II, 16; II, 19). In principle, this conversion can occur after or before Jesus' death on the Cross, but it takes place because of the merits of the latter, as Anselm illustrates.[14] In Jesus, a man has made such satisfaction that, on the basis of his achievement, all others can be given a share in it. This is only possible because Jesus is also God, which means that whatever he does has a surpassing worth and fruitfulness. Since, being God, he cannot himself profit from the reward, he makes it available to sinful man, on whose behalf the entire work was undertaken: "*solvit pro peccatoribus quod pro se non debebat*" (II, 18). The *pro nobis* (I, 6), *propter salvandos* (II, 19) is a constant theme, and the triune God's initiative in the work of redemption is just as evident as that of the man Jesus.

Anselm's interpretation of the mystery of redemption fascinated all who came after him, but it has its flaws. The idea of the "exchange" is no longer at the center but a variant of the ransom motif. (*Satisfactio*, undertaken as a free-will act of penance, is ultimately a "ransom", *redemptio*, I, 1; I, 3; I, 6; II, 16; II, 21, paid for by a "price", *pretium*, II, 20). Consequently, what for the Fathers was an unconscious limitation is now a conscious and indispensable element: the Innocent One who suffers death must not come into contact with the sins of the others if his work is to be effective. Christ's death is placed on one side of the scales and the sins of the world on the other; his death overbalances the world's sin because of the free-will nature and divine value of the former.[15] Here Jesus is less than ever the "Bearer of sin". Hence Anselm's strange view—in the face of the Gospel accounts of

[14] II, 16: "Since not all who need reconciling can come together on a [single] day, the King grants that, in virtue of the greatness of that work [performed by him who is alone innocent], all who—whether before or after that day—confess their desire to attain forgiveness through that work and join the pact there concluded, shall be loosed from all past sin. . . ."

[15] "The death of Christ is seen exclusively as a vast credit over against the debit signified by sin", says Felix Hammer in his harsh criticism of Anselm in *Genugtuung und Heil. Absicht, Sinn und Grenzen der Erlösungslehre Anselms von Canterbury* (Vienna, 1967), 145. Cf. similarly Hans Kessler, *Die theologische Bedeutung des Todes Jesu* (Düsseldorf, 1970).

the Passion—that Christ's sufferings are not expiatory but only exemplary (*exemplum*, II, 11).[16] In restricting himself solely to the factor of death, Anselm is at one with the theology of Karl Rahner, who frequently attacks him on other issues.[17] Such a view can only be understood insofar as the concept of "merit" is not yet clarified in Anselm. Contrary to many Fathers, he does not see that Jesus' entire life, work and suffering are meritorious. Nor does he think in terms of a representative, atoning suffering for the sins of men. His Christology is Chalcedonian and thoroughly orthodox (I, 8), but what remains obscure is the relationship between the Godhead's sovereign decision, a decision that involves suffering, and mankind's obedient acceptance of that decision. What is lacking is the link with the Son's trinitarian *missio*, his "sending" by the Father on the basis of his *processio*. Thus Anselm cannot explain why Jesus' obedience is addressed emphatically to the Father rather than to the whole Trinity.[18] What is also missing is the organic connection between Christ and all other human beings, which is established by the Incarnation and on which the Fathers lay such stress. The fact that Christ is the New Adam, possessing the *gratia capitis*, is more assumed than declared. Consequently, according to Anselm, Christ's redemptive grace is made available to his brothers only because he cannot use it himself (since all glory is his already). True, the *pro nobis* is an integral part of the aims of the Incarnation and of Christ's atoning death, but, by contrast with the Fathers, Anselm does not see it grounded organically in the act of Incarnation.

---

[16] Here Anselm is probably drawing on the Augustinian distinction between *sacramentum* and *exemplum: De Trin.* I, IV, chap. 3, no. 6.

[17] H.-U. Wiese, *loc. cit.*, (1979), 53–54: After setting forth the theology of death of Karl Rahner (who sees death as "personal self-fulfillment" and "man's final, unshakable Yes to God"), Wiese observes: "For Rahner, Jesus' death achieves redemption *as death*, whereas, for von Balthasar, it does so *as an acceptance of suffering* (for which we have no analogy). Anselm's view is that of Rahner. . . . Death is a greater self-surrender than suffering. . . . Anselm and Rahner—unlike von Balthasar—approach the death of Jesus in a predominantly abstract way, not on the basis of a biblical reflection on the suffering and death of Jesus."

[18] Hence the somewhat risky formulation: "Quoniam idem [Filius] ipse est Deus, . . . ad honorem suum se ipsum sibi sicut Patri et Spiritui Sancto obtulit, id est humanitatem suam divinitati suae": II, 18.

Anselm's fundamental idea is that Christ's work outweighs all the sin of the world, incomparably so (*praevalet* II, 14; *incomparabiliter superat* II, 18; *recompensat* II, 18).[1] In this way, it constitutes the perfect "satisfaction" for sin. This view is also central to Aquinas' ambitious christological synthesis. While he keeps Anselm as his point of reference, he opens up the latter's self-imposed methodological limits and, as far as possible, brings in all the themes of Scripture and the Fathers. All the time he is aware that all the concepts applied to the *mysterium* are more pointers and images than exhaustive definitions, which is why he refers in the same breath to *meritum, satisfactio, sacrificium, redemptio* (*S. Th.* III, 48, 1–4; 6 ad 3). Like Anselm, he lays the emphasis on God's love, which "inspires" (*inspiravit*)[2] the Incarnate One with the loving will to carry out the eternal decree, and on the love of Christ, who, fulfilling the commandment of love to the very end, dies for his friends (*C. G.* III, 158 end; IV, 55 resp. 13, 20). He also stresses the divine dignity of his person (*ibid.*, resp. 23, 24). But, at the same time, he is at pains, right from the outset, to resist the idea of a ransom-price to be paid to the "powers"[3] or of punitive action designed to appease the divine anger.[4]

Anselm had emphasized the first, third and fifth scriptural themes. Thomas has a longer stride than Anselm. He gives greater emphasis to the fourth theme, namely, the grace of sonship[5] that is given to sinners as a result of the work of reconciliation (Pas-

[1] The idea of Christ's work "outweighing" sin is already present in the Fathers, cf. Cyril of Alexandria's commentary on 2 Corinthians 5:21: *antaxios* (PG 74, 945; another ref. in Sabourin, 35, note 1).

[2] In the body of 47, 3, it is the Father who inspires the incarnate Son with this will; in ad 2, it is the whole triune God who does so, that is, including the Son himself as God. There is no contradiction between these two expressions. The Trinity inspires Jesus to suffer: 48, 5.

[3] *S. Th.* III, 48, 4 ad 2 and 3.

[4] Anger, properly speaking, is never attributed to God: *S. Th.* I, 19, 11; II, II, 162, 3, etc. Nonetheless, it is possible to speak of God "hating" sin (and sinners), and so of being "reconciled" (*placatus est* III, 49, 4) in the context of a work of atonement that proceeds from his love (*ibid.*, obj. 2, resp. 2). We shall return to this.

[5] "Spiritus adoptionis filiorum": 49, 3 ad 3.

sion and Resurrection seen as *superabundans satisfactio*), opening heaven (49, 5) and giving access to eternal blessedness in God and participation in his nature (22, 1). Yet his attachment to Anselm prevents him from taking account of the patristic theme of the "exchange of places". Scholars have rightly pointed out that Thomas gives a felicitous theological treatment of the whole life of Jesus, and particularly of his glorification, integrating it into the events of reconciliation.[6] Thus, like the Fathers, he deals thoroughly with the question of the *passiones* adopted by Jesus[7] and justifies Jesus' prayer on the grounds that he is the Priest of mankind (*fons totius sacerdotii*, 22, 4); indeed, he could even pray for himself, since he possessed *similitudinem peccati in carne* (*ibid.*, ad 1). All the same, in Thomas, as in Anselm, we find the same lack of any inner contact between Jesus and the reality of sin as such.

This missing connection in Anselm between Christ and the mankind "for whom" he suffers[8] is established on a grand scale by the patristic idea of the organic link between Christ, who is the Head, and the Church (and potentially all mankind) as his Body. Christ's personal grace is simultaneously *gratia capitis*, overflowing onto the members of his Body (49, 1: *Ecclesia quasi una persona cum suo capite*; III, 8, 1–3: *virtutem habet influendi gratiam in omnia membra: ibid.*, 1, *ut . . . ab ipso (gratia) redundaret ad membra*: 48, 1). Like no other,[9] Christ is the effective Mediator between God and human beings. But this assertion, which suffices for the operation of satisfaction, is all there is: when Thomas comes to speak of Christ's sufferings—which, in contrast to Anselm, he does regard as having a value as *satisfactio*

---

[6] Cf. L. Bouyer, *Das Wort ist der Sohn. Die Entfaltung der Christologie* (Einsiedeln: Johannes Verlag, 1976), 434ff.; W. Breuning, 116ff. "Christus a principio suae conceptionis meruit nobis salutem aeternam" (48, 1 ad 2).

[7] III, 14, 4 (the acceptance of all the bodily frailties that affect all men because of original sin); 15, 4 (the acceptance, in addition, of the *pathē* of the soul; these are different in Christ from what they are in us, since in him these motions of the senses never overwhelm the *ratio*. Thus Jerome calls them only *pro-passiones*). But we can be sure that Jesus experienced genuine pain, grief, fear (15, 7) and anger (in the sense of ardor, 15, 9).

[8] For Thomas, the *pro nobis* formula is just as much a basic assumption as it was in the antecedent tradition: 47, 3; 48, 4, etc.

[9] III, 26, 1 + ad 1; 48, 5.

(49, 1–5)—his portrayal is strangely flat, almost moralizing in tone, in spite of all the superlatives he employs. He goes through the Passion narratives (46, 5) and gives reasons why Christ has endured "all human sufferings" (if not *secundum speciem*, then *secundum genus*); he suggests why his pains were greater than any that can be experienced in this life (explicitly excluding hell: 46, 6, cf. obj. 3); but all the time he is careful to insist that, during the Passion, Christ could not lose the blessed vision of God: "God was never a cause of grief to his soul": 46, 7. As for the reasons for the Passion, the first is to demonstrate God's love for man; the second is to give "an example of obedience, humility, courage, justice and the other virtues"; next, it is to merit justification; then, to remind man to keep away from sin. The patristic and Anselmian reason comes last: it was appropriate that man, conquered by the devil, should now triumph as man over the devil[10] (46, 3). Finally, it is strange that Thomas, who had given a thorough account of the sufferings of Christ's soul, should later prefer to describe the Passion as a bodily event[11] in a way that almost recalls Athanasius. There is no emphasis whatsoever on Christ's abandonment by God as the center of the Passion.[12]

Nonetheless, Thomas gives us this astonishing turn of phrase: Jesus suffered so much "because in suffering he made satisfaction for all mankind's sins, *unde ea quasi sibi adscribit*" (46, 6), "*pro omnibus peccatis simul doluit*" (*ibid.*, ad 4): in each case he quotes the Old Testament. However, we should understand this "attribution" of sin in the same sense as the Fathers' *oikeiōsis*.

Thomas warns us against understanding the Anselmian *necessitas* (of Incarnation and Passion) too strictly: God was free to devise other ways of reconciling the world to himself. Only if we keep in mind his *free* decision to save the world can we speak of a (consequent) "necessity" (46, 2) in view of the goal: the liberation of man from the "powers", Christ's exaltation on the basis of his humiliation and the fulfilling of the prophecies

[10] This theme is already present in Irenaeus, and then in Cyril and Maximus.

[11] "Passio Christi, licet sit corporalis, habet tamen spiritualem virtutem ex divinitate unita" 48, 6 ad 2; cf. 49, 1: "passio Christi, licet sit corporalis. . . ."

[12] It is mentioned once, in order to show that the Father did not hinder the Son from suffering: 47, 3.

(46, 1). But Thomas agrees with Anselm that atonement as a result of satisfaction through suffering shows a "more superabundant mercy" on God's part "than if he had forgiven sins without satisfaction" (*ibid.*, ad 3). If we ask whether it would have been sufficient for the Incarnate One to pay a lesser price, the immediate answer is Yes, because of the *infinita dignitas personae Christi*. However, Thomas keeps returning to God's free and eternal purpose, which fixed this price, and no other, for the world's reconciliation (*Quodl.* II, q 1, a 2). Satisfaction is achieved through the suffering of the humanity of the Second Divine Person; this humanity is the "organ" (*instrumentum*) through which the God-man accomplishes it; according to Paul (1 Cor 1:25), it is precisely the weakness of the suffering man that channels and demonstrates the greater strength of God (III, 48, 6). This "weakness" is that of the entire human being Jesus, suffering in mortal anguish; his obedience and readiness to embrace death have a mysterious and reconciling influence on God (*ut per ipsum placetur Deus. . . . Propter hoc bonum in natura humana inventum Deus placatus est super omni offensa generis humani. . . . Per passionem Christi est sublata odii causa:* 49, 4). There is a circle of mystery here, analogous to the circle of which Thomas speaks in connection with intercessory prayer. On the one hand, God has always included the free human being's intercession in his eternal, immutable plans of salvation; and, on the other hand, he allows himself to be "swayed" by such prayer. With regard to Christ's Passion, it is more than a sign of God's constant and antecedent desire to be reconciled with the world; it is more than a sacramental sign that God *is* reconciled to the world and is applying the fruits of this reconciliation to the world: it is in very truth the event *whereby* God's anger is turned away from the sinner, even if it remains the case that, from before all time, God has already specified Christ's Passion and satisfaction as the means whereby this is to be brought about. Thomas brings the two poles of the paradox (that is, that God is untouchable and yet can be touched by some earthly event) toward each other: God's eternal love appoints that the work of love, accomplished in the dimension of time, shall achieve reconciliation, for "*mors Christi virtutem satisfaciendi habuit ex caritate ipsius qua voluntarie mortem sustinuit*" (*C. G.* IV, 55, resp. 22–23). As in Anselm, the whole emphasis lies on the freedom of the divine love. This manifests itself, at the highest level, in the freedom of Christ's love-death on behalf of sinners.

c. Contemporary Models

There are two ways of approaching the contemporary models. Concepts such as "sacrifice", "ransom" and "satisfaction", that is, aids to understanding employed by biblical and ancient thought that are now no longer intelligible, can be replaced by other concepts that are clearer to modern man. Alternatively, the attempt can be made to bridge the gulf that yawns wider and wider (up to Anselm and his successors) between the person and work of Jesus and the rest of mankind, contrary to the Fathers' original intuition of the *commercium*, the union of God and man through the "exchange of places". If both attempts are taken together, it should be possible to come up with a promising new approach that would present the original theologico-historical plan in a radical (retrospective) form. This would promote the most satisfactory reflection possible on the biblical themes we have enumerated.

Looking at the history of modern times, we are inclined to doubt whether these two new paths, each of which has led to appreciable individual results, can be said to converge automatically on a synthesis (and, in any case, such a synthesis, of its very nature, cannot and must not be a "system"). In fact, the two approaches seem to be essentially opposed. The first model, which aims to provide a new set of aids to understanding centering on the idea of Jesus' *solidarity* with mankind, takes its bearings primarily from his humanity and his active ministry. The second model, which wants to follow up the *commercium* theme in a radical way and insist on full *substitution*, looks primarily at the Cross as interpreted by Paul: here the full Godhead of the person of Jesus is the decisive factor.

Like the ancient and medieval worlds, the modern world is quite aware, when it comes to contemplating the mystery of Christ, that it is circling around the center of the drama in which God and man are involved. Even in the purely human drama, the two themes concern central, dramatic situations. On the one hand, we have the kind of solidarity that goes the whole way—that is, to death—as at the end of Dostoyevsky's *Idiot* or in *King Lear*; and, on the other hand, there is the representative suffering that is found (both in its religious and in its social aspect) in Euripides, which Faulkner and Camus (*Requiem for a Nun*) have convincingly portrayed in our own time. Here too death is the horizon.[1] What if these two lines, which initially seem to diverge, should ultimately converge? We shall have to reflect upon this at the end of our soteriology.

SOLIDARITY

This word is a late arrival, but what it signifies is found at an early stage. However, it requires some comment. It is very persuasive, in that what was previously formulated in primarily ontological terms is now put in terms of personal consciousness: in Jesus, God himself wishes to share fully in the human destiny; he desires to be there "for" man. This biblical "for" is what is expressed by another new coining, that is, "pro-existence"; it has a similar immediacy, and (after some reflection) its meaning is accessible to everyone. Karl Barth has done this in the simplest way, describing the average man as "man *with* others", and Jesus as "the man *for* others".[2] However, this immediately raises the question of the content of this "pro", or "for". Should it be understood as a primarily social investment of himself or as something more—and, if so, what? This shows that the concept of "solidarity" we are to examine is by no means unambiguous. It can be used in a more or a less exclusive or inclusive way.

First of all, it should be said that many Catholic authors use the concept of "solidarity" as a vivid expression for Jesus' communion with our (sinful) nature. Two examples will illustrate this. F. Prat takes the "fundamental principle of solidarity" to be the cornerstone of soteriology,[3] "recognized more and more

---

[1] On Euripides, cf. *The Glory of the Lord* IV, 131–54; on the dramatic theme, cf. *Theo-Drama* I, 392ff.: "Death on behalf of someone else", including the reworking of the Alcestis theme, Claudel's *Annonce*, *Repos* and *L'Otage*, Marcel's *Monde cassée* and G. Kaiser's *Die Bürger von Calais*, as well as Le Fort/Bernanos, *Carmel dialogues*.

[2] *Church Dogmatics* III/2, 203–324.

[3] *La Théologie de s. Paul*, 15th ed. (1939) II, 240ff.

by modern theologians". "Christ took the sins of men upon himself in order to save them; he has entered into communion with their sinful nature, and, in order to save the Jews, and subsequently the Gentiles, he takes their curse upon himself, or rather, he causes himself to share in the curse that is upon them." "There is no exchange of persons, but there is a solidarity of action. Sin is not transferred from men to Christ but extends from men to include Christ." We can leave to one side the question of whether such assertions are adequate; but, at all events, Prat has Catholic teaching in mind here (in contradistinction to the Lutheran theology).

J. Alfaro also sees the concept of "solidarity" as the central element of patristic theology, which Thomas attempted to express by the *gratia capitis*: "The ultimate reason for the redemption lies in God's love for sinful man and in Christ's solidarity with mankind, that is, in his grace as Head and in his identification with mankind through his love."[4] It is significant that Alfaro rejects the view of Rivière (and de Montcheuil) that what is redemptive about the Cross consists exclusively in Jesus' love and obedience, not in his sufferings, and that the latter are "only a consequence of his humanity and of his life's historical circumstances". According to Alfaro, this opinion, which comes from Anselm and is also to be found in K. Rahner, "forgets the incarnate Son of God's solidarity with *sinful* humanity and the narrow boundary that exists between sin and death."[5]

Such a use of the concept is beyond criticism. Unfortunately, it easily slides unnoticed into misuse at the hands of a liberal Christology that puts the emphasis on Jesus' solidarity—expressed in his life and teaching—with the poor, sinners and the marginalized and sees the Cross as nothing more than the ultimate consequence of this "social" solidarity. This shift of emphasis occurs as early as Socinius (*De Jesu Christo Servatore*), with his main thesis that Jesus became the Redeemer, not by his death on the

[4] *Myst. Sal.* III/1, 682–85. Further examples: E. Hocedez, "Notre solidarité en Jésus Christ et en Adam", *Greg.* (1930), 373–413; L. Malevez, "L'Eglise dans le Christ", *RSR* 25 (1935), 257–91, 418–40; Y. Congar, "Sur l'inclusion de l'humanité dans le Christ", *RSPhTh* 25 (1936), 489–95. P. Galtier, *Les Deux Adams* (Paris, 1947).

[5] *Ibid.*, 686.

Cross, but by his moral example and his teaching. As is well known, the Socinians, expelled from Poland, had a considerable influence in Holland and England and on the Enlightenment. In different ways, the Jesus of Herder, Kant, Schleiermacher and Ritschl can be described in terms of "solidarity"; the concept is found in many of the more recent Christologies that see the core of the Christ-event in Jesus' paradigmatic fellowship with sinners.

We find this, for instance, in the work by H. Kessler to which we have already referred.[6] For Kessler, the Passion of Jesus is the direct "consequence of his ministry", the direct consequence of his solidarity with the "outcast"[7] (direct: without any kind of theological caesura). "What the earthly Jesus lived out, brought to mankind and endured right up to his death, Paul predicates (exclusively) of his death",[8] namely, that, in Jesus, God turns toward sinners and the lost. This idea must replace the theories of sacrifice and expiation that are no longer tenable today.[9] Thus the idea of "solidarity" is at the heart of H. Küng's *On Being a Christian*:[10] Jesus was the "partisan for the handicapped"; he "existed for *all* men",[11] including professional swindlers. We are presented with grace, not achievement; the "God with a human face",[12] not the lofty, righteous God of Torah and Temple. In this role, Jesus can be portrayed essentially as God's "Advocate" ["*Sachwalter*"]; as such, he need not have understood his death, in advance, as a "vicarious atonement for the many".[13]

Küng has maintained a certain reserve toward liberation theology: Jesus was not a revolutionary. But radical liberation theology—in all its nuances—will tend in the same direction, putting Jesus' solidarity with the poor at the center. The Cross, set up

---

[6] *Theo-Drama* III, 107ff: *Die theologische Bedeutung des Todes Jesu* (Düsseldorf: Patmos, 1970).

[7] H. Kessler, 229ff.

[8] *Ibid.*, 328.

[9] *Ibid.*, 309. Kessler thinks he can demonstrate that Paul is no longer interested in these obsolescent formulas (324).

[10] English translation (New York: Doubleday, 1984).

[11] *Ibid.*, 266.

[12] *Ibid.*, 300, 308.

[13] *Ibid.*, 325.

between the two criminals, means simply that Jesus is in deadly earnest in carrying out his life's manifesto.[14] This is not the place to go into this theology in detail. We only need to draw attention to the feedback effect it has on Christology, as in the case of C. Duquoc, for instance.[15] Duquoc rejects a univocal interpretation of the events of the Cross, saying that only a pluralistic interpretation can be adequate; yet his final sentence is this: "Jesus renounces his own liberation. The liberation of others is more important to him. It is for this reason that he is both liberated [by the Resurrection] and Liberator."[16] Duquoc, too, regards concepts like satisfaction, redemption and sacrifice as unintelligible. They "introduce a hiatus between the way we understand faith and the way we understand the world".[17] What remains intelligible is the thought that God has liberated the world *not without* man's cooperation.[18] However, Jesus has already conquered death in his earthly deeds and attitudes.[19] Our understanding of the Cross must start with the stance Jesus adopted in history: "Jesus is the Liberator in his Passion, since it results from his word and attitude." But our understanding must also start from the fact that, confronted with the suggestion of using power for the purposes of liberation, he rejects it as a temptation; in this way, he makes man a genuine "coworker with God" in bringing about the kingdom. (But "to die because of men's sins does not mean dying for the forgiveness of sins.")[20] Finally, our understanding of the Cross must proceed from the Resurrection, which confirms Jesus' "hope" of God's forgiveness.[21] Thus the meaning of the Cross is hope in, and collaboration toward, the growth of the kingdom; the obsolete concepts are remodeled to fit in with this program.[22]

---

[14] On the necessity of a caesura between the life and the Passion: Thomas, *S. Th.*, III, 48, 1 ad 2, ad 3. By contrast, Bultmann sees no caesura between the two (at least in the Gospel of John): "Death . . . has no extraordinary significance for salvation; it is a fulfillment of the *ergon* that begins with the Incarnation and the final proof of that obedience under which Jesus' whole life stands", *Theologie des Neuen Testamentes*, 399.

[15] *Christologie II* (Paris: Cerf, 1972).   [16] *Ibid.*, 225–26.

[17] *Ibid.*, 191, 220.   [18] *Ibid.*, 192.

[19] *Ibid.*, 203.   [20] *Ibid.*, 203

[21] *Ibid.*, 205.   [22] *Ibid.*, 216.

As we might expect, this theology looks for covering fire from the angle of exegesis, which, according to Bultmann, assures us "that we cannot know how Jesus understood his end, his death".[23] We have already mentioned A. Vögtle's repeated attempts to show that, during his mission to Israel, Jesus could not have thought in terms of an expiatory death, let alone one that would have been effectual for all mankind.[24] From the very outset, however, Jesus made the unique claim to be the "Mediator of salvation"; this need not have undergone any qualitative change in the face of disaster. It is enough for this long-established claim "to remain open to the future, even in the face of death. It only needs to remain open for the revelation (cited by the apostolic preaching) of the saving mediatorship of that Jesus who, going to his death, assures his disciples of the coming of the eschatological kingdom."[25]

If we reduce Jesus' "claim to be the Mediator of salvation" to the notion of "solidarity", treated as a central concept, we encounter E. Schillebeeckx' view of Jesus' understanding of his death. "Jesus felt his death to be (in some way or other) part of the salvation offered by God, as a historical consequence of his caring and loving service of and solidarity with people."[26] We can get no farther than this minimal formula since "no certain logion is to be found in which Jesus himself might be thought to ascribe a salvific import to his death." "He understands . . . his death as a final and extreme service to the cause of God as the cause of men. . . . The 'for you' [*hyper* formula], in the sense of Jesus' whole pro-existence, had been the historical intention of his whole ministry."[27]

Our last witness to this "solidarity" Christology is J. Moingt, who, like the aforementioned, interprets the Passion from the standpoint of Jesus' active life, endeavoring to stick to the prohi-

---

[23] *Das Verhältnis der urchristlichen Christusbotschaft zum historischen Jesus*, 3d ed. (Heidelberg, 1962), 11.

[24] *Theo-Drama* III, 101, 108, 140.

[25] "Der verkündende und der verkündigte Jesus 'Christus' " in *Wer ist Jesus Christus* (Herder, 1977), 43, 69f.

[26] *Jesus. An Experiment in Christology* (London: Collins, 1979), 310.

[27] *Ibid.*, 311.

bitions issued by the exegetes. Like Duquoc and Schillebeeckx,[28] he initially excludes the biblical terminology of sacrifice as being unintelligible to modern man.[29] What Israel hopes for, within its particular horizon, is that God, the Creator and Lord of the covenant, will bring about (in connection with the Messiah) a lifting and abolition of all its sin, understood as alienation from God and rebellion against him. On the basis of his personal claim, his direct contact with God and his eschatological time dimension, the historical Jesus is a comprehensive symbol of the hoped-for new creation,[30] particularly since he includes in his act of faith those elements of unfaith that had persisted hitherto— distance from traditional religion, temptation, being forsaken by God.[31] If we ask what is the significance for salvation of Christ's death "for us", we can distinguish three stages: (1) Because of the universality of his mission (including his death), Jesus' task is to manifest God's will to save all men (the "representative" *pro nobis*). In his perfect, eschatological faith, he goes beyond the zone of alienation from God and *"grâce à sa solidarité avec nous, nous devenons tous solidaires de sa foi qui peut vaincre désormais en chacun de nous l'incrédulité humaine."*[32] (2) The immediate effect of this is that the future is open to us, who are justified before the God who has "delivered up" Jesus for us (*pro nobis* here means "for our advantage"). (3) Finally, there is a genuine representation or exchange of place (substitution):[33] although the entire salvation initiative rests with God, there is in Jesus' consciousness an awareness that all mankind is included in him. But this does not mean that he has to offer himself to God as a "sacrifice" for all—the maximalist thesis—nor that he saw his death simply as his last ministry to mankind—the minimalist thesis: *"Ce qui est requis, . . . c'est qu'il fasse de sa mort l'expression absolue de sa foi en Dieu. . . . Il n'est pas nécessaire qu'il se sente comptable devant Dieu de la multitude des hommes, il est nécessaire et il suffit qu'il ait*

---

[28] *Menschliche Erfahrung und Glaube an Jesus Christus* (Herder, 1979), 33, 35f.

[29] "La Révélation du salut dans la mort du Christ. Esquisse d'une théologie systématique de la rédemption" in *Mort pour nos péchés* (Brussels: Fac. St. Louis, 1976), 117–72. Since the transition to faith in the Church's message presupposes a conversion, Moingt presents only a phenomenology of Jesus' death on the Cross.

[30] *Ibid.*, 126–41.   [31] *Ibid.*, 144.
[32] *Ibid.*, 155.   [33] *Ibid.*, 150ff.

conscience d'avoir reçu de Dieu une mission qui engage la totalité de l'histoire."[34]

In this last sentence, the boundary between a "solidarity Christology" and a "substitution Christology" becomes very narrow, but Moingt feels it is important not to overstep it.[35] This reticence is justified, on the one hand, by the allegedly insufficient scriptural support and, on the other hand, by a concept of autonomy taken over from the Enlightenment, according to which the kind of inner representation attributed by Paul to the Crucified Savior seems impossible. All the same, in their own way, these Christologies are trying to do justice to the theology of the Fathers; yet the *commercium* no longer operates at the ontological plane but only at the social and psychological level.

Excursus: The Soteriology of Karl Rahner

Karl Rahner sees the theological sciences falling apart in hopeless pluralism. At a "first stage of reflection", therefore, prior to these disciplines, he seeks to put theology's fundamental structure into a tightly ordered system—together with the philosophy that is inseparable from it.[1] As a

---

[34] *Ibid.*, 153.

[35] It is important to bear his starting point in mind, that is, the *epochē* with regard to faith in the divinity of Jesus: the author only presents a phenomenology of the Cross. Jesus' "representation" remains symbolic (Jesus is the universally "normative" human being), and to that extent it expresses the solidarity of all mankind. In the same book as Moingt, X. Léon-Dufour writes on "La Mort rédemptrice du Christ selon le NT" (11–44). He admits that the Pauline *pro nobis* means "in the place of", and not only "for the sake of" (18). But he goes on to say that "representation", particularly where it involves death, is "hard to imagine in a world where the person is fully responsible for his acts". So he suggests that we should speak of "solidarity" rather than substitution (22), even in the case of the Suffering Servant of Isaiah 53. In that case, however, the *mortuus pro nobis* simply means that Jesus lived his life for us, even in death. "*Relativiser ici, ce n'est pas dévaloriser*" (26). The "late" sacrifice theories in the NT are to be traced back to earlier views. In the end, he attributes Jesus' pro-existence to the "mystery of the human person", which as such "is characterized by self-surrender to others". Each man's solidarity with others renders him "kenotic" (43). Much of this recalls the theorems of K. Rahner.

[1] *Foundations of Christian Faith* (New York: Crossroad, 1984) (referred to as F). Volume and page numbers refer to Rahner's *Schriften zur Theologie* (Einsiedeln, Zurich and Cologne: Benziger, 1960). References are to the German edition.

result, many elements of the organism of Christian faith that have been handed down to us must either drop out or be entirely reinterpreted. Here we can illustrate this only with regard to soteriology; we shall uncover the fundamentals of this system by examining particular positions within it. Right at the start, Rahner warns us against "mere biblicism".[2] This, as we shall show, is ultimately because, for him, the verbal revelation is only one "species", one sector, within an overall history of revelation. It is only "the most successful instance of the necessary self-interpretation of transcendental revelation",[3] "only the explicit account of what, by grace, we already are and what we already experience —at least implicitly—in the infinitude of our transcendence".[4]

1. In Scripture, in the Fathers and in Anselm, the *pro nobis*, preeminently in the Cross of Christ, is interpreted as a representative expiation. Rahner rejects this interpretation. This theory "requires man's place to be taken by Jesus *in a way that is ultimately beyond our powers to conceive*; it contradicts a proper understanding of man's self-redemption. Moreover, such a view interprets the Pauline *hyper hēmōn* in a strained and unconvincing way. How, in view of the first disciples' experience of Jesus' death and Resurrection, could the Apostle of the Gentiles know and speak about this '*hyper*'?"[5] Rahner fails to take account of the fact that this formula has been demonstrated to be pre-Pauline; indeed, he speaks of a "late" theology that includes "explicit Logos theology, the doctrine of preexistence, the Johannine 'I' sayings, the explicit application of titles of exaltation, explicit soteriologies, and so on."[6] Against all this, he urges a "return to the original revelation" (the simple Easter experience of the disciples),[7] when the death of Jesus was not yet regarded as having a "redemptive significance. . . , [blotting out] our sinfulness before God".[8]

If we ask how Rahner arrives at this downgrading of practically the entire high theology of the New Testament—a theology from which members of the Church down through the centuries have drawn their

---

There is an English edition, *Theological Investigations* (New York: Herder, 1961–1979). (Volume numbers differ after Volume III.) On this topic, cf. A. Grün, *Erlösung durch das Kreuz. K. Rahners Beitrag zu einem heutigen Erlösungsverständnis* (Münsterschwarzach, 1975).

[2] F 14.   [3] F 155.   [4] IV, 549.

[5] XII, 26f. It is well known that the Socinians rejected the "exchange of debts" —for reasons similar to Rahner's: merit, guilt and punishment are all nontransferable. Cf. W. Pannenberg, *Grundzüge der Christologie* (1964), 171–72, English edition: *Jesus, God and Man* (Philadelphia: Westminster Press, 1968).

[6] F 264–65.   [7] F 265–66.   [8] F 282.

spirituality, whether they were ordinary folk or the great saints—we find two elements. The first, of lesser importance, is an exegetical consideration; the second (and for Rahner it is crucial) is speculative.

With regard to the first consideration: "It is not established historically beyond all dispute whether the pre-Resurrection Jesus himself already interpreted his death as an expiatory sacrifice (and did this in the context of the servant of God suffering in expiation in Deutero-Isaiah and of the just man suffering innocently and in expiation in late Jewish theology)." [9] The short answer to this view (for which A. Vögtle is often cited) is that it would have been tactless of Jesus to—as it were—threaten the Jewish people, which resisted conversion, with his forthcoming death, a death by which he would be able to overcome all the resistance of sin. It must also be borne in mind that, if we say that Jesus had no knowledge of the true meaning of his suffering and dying (in accordance with the pre-Pauline *pro nobis*), we are also obliged to delete those words in which he authoritatively explains the meaning of his institution of the Eucharist. However, the second aspect is much more important.

Rahner tirelessly repeats—contrary to what he asserts to be Anselm's view—that God, who is unchangeable, cannot be caused to "change his mind" by an event in the world like the Cross of Christ; he cannot be changed from an insulted, wrathful God to a reconciled God. [10] Now both Scripture and Anselm were well aware of this when they spoke of the whole work of salvation proceeding from the loving Father, a Father who does not need to reconcile himself with the world but undertakes to reconcile the world to himself. All the same, it would be wrong to take the almost countless scriptural references to God's anger with the sinner, and those that speak of judgment (particularly in the New Testament), and submerge or dissolve them in "God's free, salvific will", which is also "the a priori cause . . . of the Incarnation and the Cross of Christ". [11] This is what actually happens, as we shall see very clearly

---

[9] F 283. In IX, 200, Rahner correctly postulates that the way the pre-Easter Jesus understood himself, when confronted with the Resurrection, must produce a Pauline Christology. It seems utopian to think that exegesis can seriously demonstrate "a certain historical development of this self-consciousness [of Jesus] . . . for example, with regard to the integration of his death": IX, 206f. Elsewhere Rahner says that, provisionally, the Resurrection suffices to provide us with all the theological insights of the New Testament (and of the later Church) concerning Jesus Christ: X, 223f.

[10] F 211 (a "change of mind on God's part" would be mythology), 255, 288 (against Anselm); I, 212f.; VIII, 224f.; X, 360; XII, 261.

[11] F 317.

later on: for Rahner—and we follow him here—the order of creation exists for the sake of the supernatural, free self-disclosure of God, but this does not mean that the creature as such has any claim on grace. If (*per impossibile*) grace were not offered to him, man *would be* under "judgment" at the hands of a God who was somehow "dumb"; but since God has determined to give himself, man stands within "salvation".[12]

Starting from the principle of God's immutability ("we cannot change his mind"), Rahner concludes that, on the one hand, God is he-who-is-always-reconciled: he is the One who, by his offer of grace, forgives sin and justifies man.[13] Consequently, the Incarnation and death of Jesus Christ can only be described as a final cause[14] or as a "quasi-sacramental" cause[15]—something that only becomes clear in the context of Rahner's whole Christology. According to the latter, Jesus is the only human being fully to accept God's self-giving; he does this in his death, commending himself totally to the darkness of God's hidden mystery. It was in view of this event (to which the Resurrection is God's answer) that God risked bringing the world, and salvation history, into being.

This does not mean that the perfect Yes to God on the part of the man Jesus is the condition without which neither world nor salvation would be possible. Rather, it is primarily that God desires to "be there" for everyone; this is substantiated in the categories of history by the "exemplary" death of Jesus.[16] In this system, the *pro nobis* is traced from Christ back to God himself: God is "for us"[17] in that he "offers to everyone as a sinner *salvation* and nothing less";[18] "hence God is reconciled as one reconciled by himself".[19] So it is not Christ who, in virtue of his uniqueness, embraces and contains mankind in order to reconcile it to God through his suffering—for we have already heard that such "representative" action is inconceivable; rather, the universal "effect" of his death is attributed to the intertwining of all human destinies. It is

---

[12] F 210 (If God "refuses himself", we stand under judgment); F 216-18 (If man is left to his own transcendence, God's mystery is only "the infinitely far horizon, that which judges, rejects and keeps him at a distance", whereas, if God reveals himself, he is also a "holy mystery of protective nearness").

[13] F 116ff.

[14] F 195, 227, 316.

[15] F 211, 283; cf. I, 204 and XII, 266ff.

[16] F 211.

[17] F 119 ("God is present for us . . . in the mode of closeness"), 122 ("God becomes immediate to the subject").

[18] F 250.   [19] F 283.

sufficient "that the destiny of one person has significance for others". [20] In Jesus, however, because of his total self-surrender to God, we have the *unio hypostatica*, in which "a human reality belongs absolutely to God". Accordingly, we can say that Jesus is "the offer for us"; nor is this "moral": Jesus embodies both God's absolute will to save man and man's acceptance of it. [21] However, he continually stresses that "the humanity of God, in which the God-Man as individual exists for every individual person, neither is nor can be graced in itself with a closeness to God and an encounter with God that is essentially different from *the* encounter and self-communication of God that in fact is intended for *every* person in grace and has its highest actualization in man in the beatific vision. [22] Here again it becomes clear that Jesus could not represent men in any other way but that in which one man is able to "be there" for another. By contrast, Rahner has no difficulty in using the concept of Jesus' *solidarity* with us. [23]

In view of this doctrine of God's absolute immutability, we are bound to ask Rahner why he clings with the same tenacity to the theologoumenon that God, who is not subject to development *in himself*, "is changeable *in another*" and that the "primal phenomenon of self-emptying is the *kenosis* and *genesis*" of God. [24] In this perspective

---

[20] *Ibid.*; cf. 201: the "unique event" is "an intrinsic moment within the whole process by which grace is bestowed upon all spiritual creatures . . . [emanating] in time and space from one point." On the basis of this universal solidarity of all men, Rahner explains original sin (F 106–15: each person is codetermined by the results of others' freedom, and this necessarily goes right back to the origin). "If we understand this not merely in a biological sense but also historically, the individual, notwithstanding his personality and freedom, is a member of the single, concrete humanity. Accordingly, the historical decision taken by every man is already a codeterminant of the situation of all men." "Exkurs über Erbsünde" in Weger, *Theologie der Erbsünde*, QD 44 (1970), 201. See also XII, 257.

[21] F 200.

[22] F 218–19.

[23] XIII, 200: "His death [must] take place for us, he must die sharing our destiny and in solidarity with us." XIII, 180: "unconditional solidarity of love for all men". Cf. also XII, 264, 270.

[24] I, 202; IV, 147–48. It is interesting, therefore, that Rahner, in discussing the *hyper* of Christ, can also speak of a "reciprocity whereby each conditions the other" (for example, the relationship between grace and the sign in sacraments): "The sign is actually produced by grace as its *Realsymbol*; thus grace attains its fulfillment" XII, 268. Cf. also *Sacramentum Mundi* II (1968), 951: "It is only a half-truth to say that the incarnate Logos died 'merely' in his human nature, with the implication that this death *does not affect* God; in fact, it leaves out the specifically Christian truth." (Further passages from Rahner are quoted in J. Moltmann,

(and here Rahner resembles Bulgakov), creation is only a first realization, "secondary in rank", of that self-emptying that will attain fullness through the Incarnation, with the adoption of the weakness it implies. Does not God's self-emptying mean that he *can* be affected? We recall the doctrine of intercessory prayer as set forth by Thomas, concerned to preserve the freedom of the *causa secunda*: the immutable God is affected by the freedom of his creature insofar as, from eternity, he has included the latter's prayers in his providence as a contributory cause. Could we not assume something analogous in the case of "representation" by Jesus (should it prove possible)?

2. Representation is rejected as "inconceivable" because, for Rahner, the concept of personal freedom means self-activation of the subject in its totality; it occupies a central position in his thought, as in Kant.[25] What act, we may ask, on the part of creaturely freedom could "cause" God to give himself, definitively and without reservation, to the world? Answer: Only an act in which a human being would surrender himself equally absolutely to God—the infinite mystery over which man has no control.[26] In concrete terms, this means the act of Jesus Christ's death. This death is the indissoluble union of two things: his self-surrender and his acceptance by God; it is the place where Jesus' entire act of freedom finally coincides with God's free self-giving.[27] And here we must remember that the concrete death that Jesus dies (not only his "natural" death) is "the connatural manifestation" of human nature's "sinful alienation from God". Thus it is a vivid "sign of absolute obedience to God".[28] In concentrating everything—the Incarnation of the Word of God—on the death, as we have already observed, Rahner is following the Anselm he so harshly criticizes. For Anselm, everything else, even Christ's suffering on the Cross, was something "owed to God". Rahner too directs our attention away from the suffering: everything important comes about "through his death itself, and not, in the watered-down and superficial way it is often put, through his 'mortal suffering'." The latter is "ultimately fortuitous and could be replaced by some other

---

The Crucified God, 201f.) If God can be "affected", then he can be influenced—always providing he so wills.

[25] F 35f. Of course Rahner brings out the creaturely nature of freedom much more clearly than Kant; cf. VI, 215–37.

[26] XII, 260. The ability to make free decisions is an inalienable accompaniment of free subjectivity: F 90, cf. 94. Freedom is "the self-actualization of the single subject": F 95. The subject's "formal freedom" means that "no one can take his place": F 111.

[27] VIII, 216.   [28] I, 216.

circumstance that would 'bring out' Christ's obedience."[29] Logically, then, on this basis, the only path of "discipleship of the Crucified" is for the Christian to "die with Christ"; for only in death are all our creaturely categories withdrawn, only in death does the world dissolve, only in death does the free subject irrevocably hand himself over (if he so wills) to God.[30] Moreover, it is a matter of indifference "whether and to what extent and in what sense the pre-Resurrection Jesus explicitly ascribed a soteriological function to his death." It is enough that "he accepted it at least as the inevitable consequence of fidelity to his mission and as imposed on him by God."[31] Thus, in his death, he "really becomes the creative pattern of our death".[32] It is clear that, in this view, all pious devotions centering on Christ's sufferings[33] miss the main point. On the other hand, it remains unclear in what sense— if Christ is to be more than an example—Rahner wishes to speak of "sharing" in the death of Christ. It is also unclear, assuming Jesus had a restricted understanding of his own death, how seriously we should take the eucharistic words of institution, with their clear use of the

---

[29] *Ibid.* "Why are we redeemed solely by Christ's death?" I, 215.

[30] XIII, 192; 195–97. Of course this self-surrender must be practiced and prepared for by every free act in life.

[31] F 249, 248.

[32] XIII, 199. "To that extent, his death is identical with ours": *ibid.* Cf. the various reflections on death in VII, 137–56, 275–80. Here all Jesus' "sufferings" are seen in advance in the context of his death (137); this is essentially because we ourselves only exist in a movement toward death; we are always saying farewell, always heading for the "zero point of our lives" (143). Death is "only the end of a lifelong dying" (149), and since it is the dying of a sinner, it can seem utterly meaningless. In a relatively early passage (1955), Rahner actually says of Jesus: "It is a terrible thing to fall into the hands of the living God, having wanted— in a love that is incomprehensible—to be one with the world's sin" (140). But this "being one" is that of solidarity, not of being in our place. And, behind that sinfulness, which is the ground of death, there is that "most profound of abysses: spiritual freedom", which desires the "ultimate validity" of its acts (275) and thus (as the philosophers have always said) makes life into a rehearsal for death (142). In this way, Jesus becomes simply the man who accepts his death, forsaken by God, and who is "crucified and resurrected in the baffling darkness of God": X, 263. Cf. also *Zur Theologie des Todes*, QD 2 (1958) and X, 181–99: "Zu einer Theologie des Todes". Thomas speaks in similar terms (*Comp. Theol.*, 226): "Passus est autem pro nobis ea quae ut nos pateremur ex peccato primi parentis meruimus, quorum praecipuum est mors, ad quam omnes aliae passiones ordinantur sicut ad ultimum."

[33] Such as K. Rahner himself had earlier produced: cf. *Heilige Stunde und Passionsandacht* (1949; 4th ed., Herder, 1965).

term *hyper*. Should they be regarded as authentic and binding upon faith?

At this point, we cannot avoid this question: Why is Jesus' self-surrender to death on the Cross regarded as absolutely unique?[34] Is it not enough that the pre-Easter Jesus claimed to be the One to whom God had entrusted himself in a way that was unique, far above his dealings with the prophets?[35] Or what of the word from the Cross that speaks of handing the Spirit over into the Father's hands?[36] Or what of the Resurrection as the Father's witness? Does this not show us, indirectly, the quality of his surrender to God?

Furthermore, we would have to ask why the death of Mary (and her life, which was a preparation for it) did not lead to the same hypo-static union. Was she not free, according to Catholic teaching, from all inherited and personal guilt? And, as such, since she was perfect, was her death not of the same quality as that of Jesus? It is noteworthy that Mary is not mentioned once in the entire *Foundations of Christian Faith*. Exegetical problems (that is, concerning the "brothers and sisters" of Jesus and the historicity of the infancy narratives) cause Rahner to re-treat noticeably from the understanding of Mary's place in the work of salvation that has prevailed hitherto (and that has found expression in the Marian dogmas).[37]

Occasionally Rahner does speak of a participation in the death of Jesus, a death he sees subject to the darkness of infralapsarian human death, weighed down by guilt. Here we must ask what justifies the veto against Jesus genuinely "representing" sinners. Rahner says that human freedom must necessarily be objectified in alien material, material that for the most part is characterized by guilt (at least collective guilt), in such a way that "this material, which is determined in part by others' guilt, . . . does not remain external to the free act"; "by saying Yes to God", the individual "*endures* and overcomes" the entail of sin.[38] If this is so, there seems to be no reason why the freedom that "has

---

[34] VII, 144.   [35] F 245–46, 252.

[36] "If there is one word that is inherently worthy of belief, it is this": VII, 140. But this very word, which Luke uses similarly at the death of Stephen, is suspected of having been toned down by Luke (as compared with Mark and Matthew).

[37] XIII, 361–377. Here again, he operates with the term "amalgam" (367), that is, an amalgam of the original faith-understanding and time-bound concepts. Today this amalgam would have to be dissolved in the wake of a progressive "enlightenment". Cf. XIII, 11–47. See also our *New Elucidations* (San Francisco: Ignatius Press, 1979), 46–60.

[38] VI, 234–35. Rahner actually says that this "endurance" involves a "participation in the Cross of Christ".

become alienated from itself" through alien matter[39] should not be set free by someone authorized by God who, on our behalf (that is, as our representative), should *endure* the alienating alienation (whether it arises through inheritance—original sin—or personal guilt); in liberating man from alienation, far from relieving him of responsibility for his own self-actualization, he would actually be making it possible. This leaves the question open whether the liberating grace that is imparted to the sinner on the basis of the "final cause" of God's saving will (*intuitu meritorum Christi*) is given more in the Anselmian sense or more in the sense of genuine "representation" (that is, on behalf of, and in the place of, the sinner).

3. Properly speaking, we would need to analyze all this with a view to establishing the fundamental model employed by Rahner in his Christology. However, this would go beyond the limits we have adopted in the present work. A few indications must suffice. His constant attacks on a one-sided, crypto-Monophysite view of the God-man, which portrays him as a God in human disguise and hence a figure of mythology, lead us to suspect that what Rahner is proposing, by contrast, is an extreme Antiochene emphasis. At the limit, this emphasis leads to the idea that, in the total surrender of the man Jesus to God and God's total ("uniquely sublime") self-giving to him, an "encounter" takes place that brings about a (kind of) identity: "If, therefore, the reality of Jesus, in whom as offer and as acceptance God's absolute self-communication to the whole human race 'is present' for us, is really to be . . . unsurpassable and definitive . . ., then we have to say: it is not only established by God, but it is God himself."[40] However, on the one hand, we must take into account the paradox that, as the creature becomes more independent, it also becomes increasingly self-dependent,[41] which throws light on Jesus' autonomy vis-à-vis God. On the other hand, we must say that this (hypostatic) unity is only the highest instance—and why, incidentally, is it so far above other instances?—of the unity that comes about in the coincidence of the human transcendence toward the divine horizon and God's self-disclosure (which, in the concrete world order, is always a matter of antecedent grace). "The transcendental term of transcendence and its object, its 'in-itself', coincide in a way that subsumes both—term and object—and their difference into a more original and ultimate unity that can no longer be distin-

---

[39] *Ibid.*, 234.   [40] F 202.
[41] F 78–9, 226; I, 182, cf. I, 190: Jesus' presence-to-himself is his total expropriation to the Logos; IV, 151; VIII, 215; IX, 211.

guished conceptually." [42] In view of this statement, is not Rahner's axiom that anthropology is a defective Christology [43] simply too weak? Surely we already have a formal identity? And does this not make it clear, once again, why the *pro nobis* can be said merely of God, and only *katachrēstikōs* of Christ?

This also enables us to see that God, because he is the Subject who is blissful and perfect in himself, can *for that very reason* communicate himself to another; this ability of his is one, whole, in the identity of the *transeunt* and immanent Trinity, because in the former "God really gives himself and really appears as he is in himself." [44] As his own self-utterance, God is the Logos; as the self-gift, given in a final and definitive way, continually "coming" to the innermost core of the creature, he is the holy Pneuma. It is only on the basis of God's "transeunt" movement, therefore, that light is shed on the Trinity; God appears in the Trinity in "three modes of presence". [45] It is not clear whether this *transeunt* movement absorbs the whole immanent movement into itself ("We may not duplicate these three modes of God's presence for us by postulating a different presupposition for them in God"), [46] or whether, on the contrary, "The immanent self-expression of God in its eternal fullness" is "the condition that makes possible God's self-expression outward and outside himself". [47] As for the second mode of subsistence, if we say that it is "simply identical with the God who expresses himself in time", [48] it means that the *transeunt* self-utterance dominates the immanent self-utterance, similar to what we find in ante-Nicene teaching on the Trinity. From this viewpoint, the positing of a subject outside God becomes, quite logically, simply a first step in God's self-utterance to this subject. [49] Rahner says that this subject *could* exist without a supernatural goal; [50] God *could* have "kept silent" and not communicated with him; [51] but such considerations are completely abstract and only

---

[42] F 119; cf. IV, 154: the unity of God's "self-utterance" and his "being heard". IX, 138f.: "The last, eschatological self-transcendence [is] that in which the world freely opens itself to God's self-communication and, in virtue of the latter, accepts it." The "unity of these two acceptances" is the climax of world history.

[43] F 122.   [44] F 136.   [45] F 137.

[46] *Ibid.*; cf. IV, 149.

[47] F 223.   [48] F 304.

[49] F 197: "We are entirely justified in understanding creation and Incarnation —not as two disparate and juxtaposed acts of God 'outward' that have their origins in two separate initiatives of God—but, rather, in the world as it actually is, as two moments and two phases of the *one* process of God's self-giving and self-expression, although it is an intrinsically differentiated process."

[50] F 173.   [51] IV, 149; F 173.

serve to underline God's freedom in communicating himself (and this self-communication begins with the creation).[52] It is possible to insist, like Rahner, on the difference between the finite spirit's naturally given horizon of transcendence and one that has been elevated by a "supernatural *existentiale*" and deepened and opened toward the living God —and then go on to relativize the difference between these two perspectives.[53] With regard to God's gracious freedom, his self-giving— which in Jesus Christ, within history, is "irrevocable", "irreversible" —was always such, right from the foundation of the world. In fact, the promises to Noah and to Abraham, and the Sinai covenant, were all "irrevocable".

In sum, we can say that Rahner's entire system is concerned with God's absolute *pro nobis* for the world as a whole and mankind in particular. He affirms that, in terms of finality, this has come about exclusively on the basis of Jesus Christ's existence-unto-death. However, this approach fails to shed much light on the issue since, in fact, what we call the "Hypostatic Union" is so deeply involved with the concrete human nature that it appears to be only the "most successful instance" of the latter.[54] Like all systems that fail to take the *sacrum commercium* seriously, Rahner's soteriology lacks the decisive dramatic element. Thus God's "wrath" is always, antecedently, overtaken by his will to save

[52] "The possibility that there be men is grounded in the greater, more comprehensive and more radical possibility of God to express himself in the Logos which becomes a creature": F 223.

[53] F 298: When it comes to speaking of the *desiderium naturale in visionem*, "it makes no difference . . . to what extent and in what sense this ontological orientation [*desiderium*] toward immediacy to God belongs to man's 'nature' in the abstract or to his historical nature as elevated in grace by the supernatural *existential*[e]." The second view, which Rahner mostly puts forward, presupposes Neo-Thomism. This assumes a purely natural "preunderstanding" [*Vorgriff*] on the part of the human spirit, by which it embraces the "*esse ut sic*". However, this does not arrive at the living God; accordingly, what is needed is the complement of the "*existentiale*" [*Existential*]. The first view, which H. de Lubac has always upheld, is rooted in the Augustinian doctrine of the *imago Dei*; man has a direct yearning for the living Original of which he is the image.

[54] "The Incarnation of God is the unique and *highest* instance of the actualization of the essence of human reality": F 218; cf. I, 184. The extreme formulation that the humanity of Jesus "is so expropriated that it becomes the humanity of God himself" (*ibid*.; cf. F 202; IV, 142) comes in for exacting criticism in the context of the limits of the *communicatio idiomatum*: F 290. Moreover, the death of Jesus can be interpreted, not primarily as an infralapsarian death, but as an expression of the fundamental philosophical law that the greater God's nearness, the greater he is veiled from us: I, 187.

men, a will that is always ahead of all human resistance to God (in the direction of *apokatastasis*).[55]

SUBSTITUTION

The Radicalism of Luther

For the most part, the Christology of "solidarity" slips into a more psychological or philosophical vein. By contrast, the second possibility in modern times, the Christology of "substitution", strikes like a thunderbolt. It is as if Luther's thought, right from its very beginnings, was bent upon filling precisely the gap that patristic theology had left open in the *admirabile commercium*. His Christology follows the doctrine of the *pro nobis* to its ultimate, exclusive conclusion, and here it is understood as an exchange (*mirabilis mutatio*,[1] *opus conversum*,[2] *transmutatio*,[3] *suavissimum commercium*),[4] but no longer an exchange of divine and creaturely nature. The aspect of divinization is relegated completely. Now the exchange is between the sinner and Christ, the bringer of grace. No one could take 2 Corinthians 5:21 more literally: "For our sake he made him [Christ] to be sin who knew no sin, so that in him we might become the righteousness of

---

[55] Cf. F 102: "Yes and No to God are not parallel"; this is because of the self-contradiction involved in the No: man attempts to deny his own being, an attempt doomed to failure. Rahner holds fast to the (abstract) possibility of "eternal loss" (F 443), but in such a way that the world "stands before an offer of God that transcends an ambivalent situation of freedom on God's part": F 299. "What is the meaning of our life, a life that, by our own efforts, we fundamentally do not understand, . . . if, first and last, it is the life of God?": I, 212. Hence he adopts a radically "Scotist" point of view: "Salvation history, that is, the history of forgiveness and reconciliation imparted to guilty mankind, is embraced and integrated by God's relationship with the world: prior to all sin, God envisages his own incarnational history in the world; sin in the world is only permitted as the condition whereby God's all-embracing and undergirding relationship to the world can be radicalized.": X, 233.

[1] References are to the Weimar edition throughout. Here: 31, II, 435, 11. Practically all the following quotations are taken from Theobald Beer, *Der fröhliche Wechsel und Streit. Grundzüge der Theologie Martin Luthers* (Leipzig: Benno, 1974); here I give only a rudimentary outline of his very detailed interpretation.

[2] 57 Hebr 166, 13.   [3] 5, 311.

[4] 5, 253, 11.

God." In Luther's *On the Freedom of a Christian Man* (1520), the exchange is presented in bridal imagery:

> Faith . . . unites the soul with Christ like a bride with her bridegroom. From this marriage it follows, as St. Paul says, that Christ and the soul become one body. Thus they have all things in common, all benefits, fortunes and ill-fortunes. What Christ has belongs to the faithful soul, and what the soul has becomes Christ's. Thus if Christ possesses all goods, all blessedness, they are the soul's also. And if the soul is laden with all manner of vice and sin, they become Christ's. Now the joyous exchange and contest begin. Christ is both God and man; he has never sinned, and his holiness is invincible, eternal and all-powerful; in giving the faithful soul its wedding-ring [that is, faith], he makes its sin his own, as if he himself had committed it. Thus sin is swallowed up and drowned in him. For his righteousness is too strong for sin; the soul is purged of all its sins and, on account of this betrothal gift [that is, faith], it becomes free and lissom, endowed with the eternal righteousness of Christ, its Bridegroom. Is this not a joyous bargain, in which the rich, noble, holy Bridegroom, Christ, takes the poor, despised, wretched little harlot to wife, removing all evil from her and adorning her with all that is good? Sins can no longer damn the soul, therefore, for they now lie on Christ and have been swallowed up in him.[5]

Sins "lie" on Christ: this is something that must be taken seriously. In bearing the sin of the entire world, he, "the sole just and holy man", becomes simultaneously "the sole, the greatest sinner on earth".[6] "Christ is more damned and forsaken than all the saints; he did not merely suffer somewhat, as certain people imagine. In all reality and truth, he submitted to God the Father's eternal damnation for us."[7] "Christ felt all the evil that is in us following the act of sin, namely, death and the fear of hell."[8] "He felt the anger of God, more than any other man. Indeed, he felt hell's punishment."[9] Luther speaks of the evil that "follows" the act of sin. Consequently, he distinguishes between two states of sin in us: "While sin is being committed, it is not experienced as sin; it is not experienced as what, at

[5] 25, 26ff.   [6] 49, 121, 10.
[7] 56, 392, 7ff.   [8] 8, 87, 34ff.
[9] 40, III, 716, 6.

its worst, it is: the forgetting and scorning of God." Once law is roused, however, once "the spiritual law is revealed", there awakes in the sinner too a "consciousness [*conscientia*] of what sin is". Full awareness is found in the damned: this is "the descent to hell". When 2 Corinthians 5:21 speaks of Christ being "made to be sin", it refers, not to the first sin, that is, sin as committed, but to the second sin, that is, that "which is taken over on our behalf".[10]

Thus Christ himself is the archetype of the *simul justus et peccator*.[11] This, for Luther, is the logical consequence of the Chalcedonian formula, for the adopted human nature is essentially sinful and subject to God's judgment. Christ is also, however, the precise counterimage of the soul redeemed by him, so that Karl Rahner's maxim applies to Luther as well: every theological proposition is also anthropological, and vice versa. The only difference is that here everything—the whole of theology and anthropology—is basically reduced to soteriology, and the latter is basically reduced to the central *commercium*. The pattern for everything else is set by the dramatic event of the "conjugal" exchange between God (in the kenotic Jesus Christ) and man (whose lostness is taken over by Christ so that man can receive the latter's righteousness). Here, as has been shown,[12] a decisive role is played by the ancient patristic image of man's liberation from evil powers, that is, the image of Leviathan: it swallows mankind, which is the bait proffered by Christ's Godhead, and, having no right to this prey, is overwhelmed by it.[13] In terms of Christology, this picture represents Christ's sin-bearing,

[10] 5, 604, 1–11.

[11] 49, 121, 10; 3, 226, 36f.; 5, 602, 32–603, 5.

[12] Beer, 213 21.

[13] This graphic theory was developed, beginning with Origen, by the Fathers, particularly Gregory of Nyssa, Augustine, and Gregory the Great. In the latter case, it was probably used to combat Marcion's view that, unknown to the Demiurge, the true God had sent the Redeemer into the nether world, thereby tricking the Demiurge and depriving him of power. Cf. the beginnings of such a view in Ignatius, Ephesians 19 (and see H. Schlier, *Religionsgeschichtliche Untersuchungen zu den Ignatiusbriefen* [1929], 5–32). In the *Hortus Deliciarum* of Herrad von Landsberg, the "luring" of the devil is vividly portrayed. Cf. J. Zellinger, "Der geköderte Leviathan im Hortus Deliciarum der Herrad von Landsberg" in *Hist. Jahrbuch* 45 (1925), 161–77.

crucified humanity as purely passive in the dramatic process: it is the bait that is "swallowed"; victory lies with the deity that, hidden from the devil, holds the "fishing line". "Through divine immortality, he has absorbed everything [that is, hell] into himself."[14] Again Luther is quite consistent when, having treated the *commercium* as absolute and as the sole normative theologoumenon, he sees the "communication of qualities" in Christ's being plunged into damnation: "The *communicatio idiomatum* means that Christ, in his humiliation, devours the devil, hell and everything." In this way the *communicatio idiomatum*[15] is "estranged" from the two-natures doctrine and made into a purely here-and-now drama.

Luther not only portrays the clash of opposites (light and darkness) in Christ in abstract paradoxes; he also endeavors to come to grips with it using a christological psychology. The paradoxes are more concentrated and more extreme forms of assertions found in the Fathers. "The poor and the rich, the strong and the weak, the confused and the composed, the sad and the merry, the forsaken and the powerfully protected, the rejected and the chosen, and, ultimately, fearful man and God—all these meet in one and the same Person."[16] But these extremes are in concrete conflict: the struggle is between "spirit" and "flesh" (as depicted by Paul), but also, at a deeper level, the struggle is "in a certain sense with God himself".[17] If Jesus undergoes the "experience" of sin on our behalf, he also endures "genuine fear of death and hell".[18] On the Cross, he is acquainted with the temptation to blaspheme God, but he "stifles and swallows it".[19] In this struggle, grace is, as it were, "embroiled in sin" (*impeccatificatum*), and sin is imbued with grace (*gratificatum*);[20] sin becomes a "sin engraced" (*peccatum gratiae*),[21] a sin under dominion (*peccatum regnatum*).[22] The struggle is again formulated as a paradox, and Christ is both "dead and living, damned and blessed, in pain and in joy; thus he absorbs into himself all that is evil and radiates from

---

[14] 57 Hebr 128, 13–19.   [15] 43, 579, 40ff.

[16] *Unbekannte Fragmente aus Luthers zweiter Psalmenvorlesung 1518*, ed. E. Vogelsang (Berlin, 1840), 45. The paradoxes apply to both Christ and Christians.

[17] 5, 202, 22ff.   [18] 8, 87, 34ff.

[19] 5, 612, 26ff.   [20] 8, 126, 30.

[21] 8, 102, 6.   [22] *Ibid.*, 5–8; 44, 473, 12ff.

himself all that is good."[23] He is the execution of judgment,[24] which is thus directed away from us. (For Luther, the image of Christ as Judge is an especially terrifying one, to be replaced by the image of Christ the Reconciler and Savior.)

If we turn from this Christology to the corresponding anthropology (and each forms a pattern for the other), we see that, in the Lutheran theology of the *commercium*, Christ's "becoming sin" is matched by man's becoming righteous through faith alone (*sola fide*). The latter expresses the absolute priority of Christ's work for man over any synchronous action on man's part. It is at this point that the obscurities and illogicalities of the Lutheran doctrine of the "exchange" begin. For, in the first place, the *sola fides* as such is not synchronous with Christ's act; in fact, the only thing synchronous with it is the objective change of status of sinful humanity, prior to the faith or unbelief of the individual, as expressed in 2 Corinthians 5:14f. ("if one has died for all, then all have died") and Romans 14:7f. On the other hand, Luther, as a result of a "fortunate non sequitur", cannot restrain himself from urging the believer actively to "seize" and "lay hold of" faith and the benefits it contains—which, doubtless, looks very much like something achieved by man.[25]

In any case, Luther reckons throughout with a "double righteousness" (and correspondingly with a "double sin"). The first is that righteousness that is acquired from Christ through pure exchange on the basis of pure faith. The second, rigorously distinguished from the first, is that righteousness that is to be acquired on the basis of the call to holiness, inherent in grace and the fulfillment of the law; here Luther is unabashed in using the language of "merit" and "reward".[26] Luther bases his "double" case on a passage in Augustine on which he lays great stress; here Augustine distinguishes between Christ as *sacramentum* and as *exemplum* (a pattern for life).[27] Even in his marginal notes to

---

[23] 3, 426, 34–36.   [24] 3, 463, 26.

[25] Apprehendere Deum . . . placatum in Christo: 39, I, 439, 18–440, 1. Arripere Evangelium: 40, I, 592, 19. In his despair, man can become "shameless" and "seize the Savior's hand in spite of the law": 22, 397, 1. 15.

[26] Cf. the "Sermo von der doppelten Gerechtigkeit" (1519) and the wealth of texts quoted by T. Beer, 10, 17–46; on merit and reward: 82–97.

[27] *De Trin.* IV, 3 (PL 42, 891).

Augustine (1509), the parallel concept of a "double" sin crops up: on the one hand, there is the sin that, in the exchange of death, murders Christ; and, on the other, there is the sin that man, crucified to the world in his discipleship of Christ, has to overcome.[28] In this exchange, however, both man and Christ share the same *simul.* Man cannot replace the here-and-now "exchange" process by some state of sinlessness that he has supposedly attained. That is, he cannot conceive such sinlessness apart from the sin that clings to him: "Sin both remains and does not remain; it is both taken away and not taken away";[29] at the same time, there is a *peccatum gratiae* and a *peccatum extra gratiam.*[30]

Thus, if we look only at the "first righteousness" and "first sin", we can speak of Christ (and of man) only in dialectical terms, as we have already seen in the case of the "estranged" *communicatio idiomatum.* And since this first horizon is decisive for Luther, the union of opposites affects his entire theology. We can speak of God only *sub contrario*: grace appears only in wrath; "God cannot be God without first becoming a devil; we cannot get into heaven without first going to hell."[31] Compared with this purely actualized dialectic of the *commercium*, the "second righteousness" and "second sin" (that is, that sin that remains to be dealt with) which Luther takes most seriously can only present an aspect which can no longer be seriously held to. Certainly, in the wake of *gratia* (the grace of justification), there is the *donum* (the gift of the Holy Spirit), which sanctifies and makes meritorious action possible; however, taken in isolation , and reified, this aspect would lead directly back to that holiness of works of the law that attracts such detestation, unless it were continually grounded on the union of opposites of the original exchange. The law, in itself, would expose us to, and terrify us with, the naked demands of God's majesty, before which no one can stand;[32] we must seek refuge in Christ, who enables us to meet God's grace *sub contrario.*

---

[28] 9, 18, 18–32.   [29] 56, 270, 10–13.

[30] 8, 102, 5–8.

[31] Cf. the entire passage from the interpretation of Psalm 117: 31, I, 249, 16–250, 37.

[32] 40, II, 330, 1–2; 5–6; 39, I, 391, 3–4.

The high drama of Luther's reduction in fact suppresses that *other* drama, which presupposes the existence of persons, with their proper being and constitution. We can no longer tell whether man, who is both a sinner and righteous, is one or two; we can no longer tell whether he is a subject enjoying continuity. Formally Luther holds fast to Christ's two natures, but he makes no connection between Christ's Incarnation and his "becoming sin" (which does not begin, in Luther's view, until he accepts his mission at his baptism).[33] Thus the entire traditional view of Christ as the Head of mankind falls to the ground. It is only faith that lays hold of justification; love is only involved in the works of "second righteousness". Consequently, there is no place for the primary love of the redeemed for the person of the Redeemer. Artificially, but very deliberately, the unity of grace—which justifies *and* sanctifies—is torn asunder. Finally, in reducing theology to the *pro nobis* between Christ and sinners, Luther obscures the entire horizon of God's self-disclosure in Christ, everything the Fathers understood by *oikonomia* and the "divinization" of man through the grace of participation.

Luther's radicalism found no direct disciples among the other reformers. Melanchthon's interpretation of the *commercium*, that is, grace as *imputatio*, by no means expresses Luther's original intuition. However, another side of his theology of the "exchange" does continue to exert an influence, although it was not his discovery but was known before his time. This is his teaching on Christ's penal suffering on our behalf (or his experience of hell). To this we shall now turn.

Vicarious Punishment

The interpretation of Christ's suffering as a *punishment* accepted "for us", that is, in our place and merited by us, is one that appears early in some of the Church Fathers. In many cases, it can be questioned whether they mean anything more, by this interpretation, than what is already expressed in the word "representation". Origen sees the Lord weighed down by the sins of

[33] 20, 219, I. 5–8; 49, 120, 9. 14.

all[1] and taking the punishment (*kolasis*) for it. Victorinus Afer, on one occasion, refers to the "sins punished in him [Christ]";[2] "In his catholic body—for his body has reference to all men— he catholicized [universalized] all he suffered, so that all flesh should be crucified in him."[3] Gregory of Elvira also speaks of punishment.[4] We have already mentioned Augustine's dictum that Jesus found us *in culpa et poena*, taking the *poena* alone upon himself and freeing us from both.[5] Chrysostom speaks in the most serious vein of Christ being punished on our behalf; he refers to God's anger, which is vented on Christ,[6] insofar as the latter is punished in place of the guilty.[7] Thomas occasionally still speaks of *poena*, and even of *maledictio*, but without wanting to imply any more than is expressed by the phrase "vicarious suffering".[8]

Rupert of Deutz sounds much more consciously aware when, in the context of the *commercium*,[9] he speaks several times of Christ being genuinely accursed,[10] while Abelard softens the

---

[1] *Comm. in Joh.* 11, 50 (Pr. 4, 413, referring to Isaiah 53). Cf. Osmo Tiililä, "Das Strafleiden Christ. Beitrag zur Diskussion über die Typeneinteilung der Versöhnungsmotive" in *Finnische Akad.* 47, 1 (Helsinki, 1941). Texts also in L. Sabourin, *loc. cit.*

[2] *In Gal.* 2, 21 (PL 8, 1166).

[3] *In Gal.* 6, 16 (*ibid.*, 1196).

[4] *Tract. Origenis*, ed. Batiffol, tr. 2.

[5] *Sermones*, Morin I, 558.

[6] *In 2 Cor.* 11 (PG 61, 480); *In 1 Tim.* 2, 2, h 7 (PG 62, 537); *In Gal.* 2, comm. 8 (PG 61, 646).

[7] *In Gal.* 3, 13 (PG 61, 655).

[8] *Super Gal.* c 3, 1, 1 and *Comp. Theol.*, 226: "Vere maledictus a Deo quia Deus ordinavit quod hanc poenam sustineret [he means death], ut nos liberaret." Christ did not assume those deficiencies of nature that would have made him less able to make satisfaction for us, such as the lack of grace, ignorance, and so forth. Death, for Thomas, is the epitome of *poena*.

[9] Commutatio gratiosa (maledictio-benedictio): *De Vict. Verbi Dei* 12, 25 (PL 169, 1483).

[10] "Quia vere solus est hic a Deo maledictus", not like Cain, who was accursed through his sins and through his brother's blood, but by God himself loading all our sins and curses upon him: *In Dt.* 1, 6 (PL 167, 923–24). The same distinction is made between *maledictus a Deo* and *a suo peccato*: 1, 6; only the first applies to Christ: *In Jonam* 1, 2 (PL 168, 414) and *In Joh.* 13 (PL 169, 793): "Deo . . . transponente maledictiones humani generis in illo."

imputation of a *maledictio* by using the word *quodammodo*.[11] Rupert was the first to apply to Christ the image of the scapegoat,[12] an image that was to have such a long history.[13] It reappears in Denys the Carthusian, who depicts Christ as the scapegoat walking toward the Cross;[14] he also sees God's penal justice venting itself upon Christ.[15] Hence, strangely enough, it becomes customary for both Reformers and decided anti-Reformers to speak of Christ suffering our "punishment".

Calvin[16] does not take the narrow path followed by Luther but simply accentuates the traditional themes we have already discussed; he speaks of "transferring to Christ the curse that was due to us" (*per translationem imputativam*)[17] and refers to God's wrath, several times employing the image of the scapegoat,[18] which "condemns Jesus to the terrible agonies that were intended for the damned".[19]

In his Apologia to the *Confessio Augustana* (1537), Melanchthon endeavors to shed light on the wrath of God—which needs to be appeased—using the analogy of pagan sacrifice.[20] Like Luther, he speaks of Christ "diverting" (*derivare*)[21] the eternal Father's wrath onto himself: "Thus he became like us, and we like him; he joined human nature to himself in an eternal covenant so that it should share in his triumph."[22] Similarly Beza speaks of

---

[11] *S. de Cruce* 12 (PL 178, 480).

[12] L. Sabourin, "Le Bouc émissaire, figure du Christ?" in *Sc. Eccl.* 11 (1959), 45–79. The author rejects the use of this image.

[13] *In Lev.* 2, 30 (PL 167, 819). Suggestions of this can be already found in Rabanus Maurus, *De Univ.* 7, 8 (PL 11, 203).

[14] *In Lev.*, c 1; *Opp.* 2, 144.

[15] *In Rom.* 3, 25 (13, 31).

[16] Cf. P. van Buren, *Christ in Our Place. The Substitutionary Character of Calvin's Doctrine of Reconciliation* (Edinburgh, 1957).

[17] *Institutes* II, 16, 6.

[18] *In Isaiam. BCR* 37, 262; *In Joh.*, ibid., 47, 413f.; *In 2 Cor.*, ibid., 50, 74.

[19] *Institutes* II, 16, 10; *BCR* 31, 586f.

[20] *Apol.* 12, 23; cf. *In Rom.* Corp. Ref. 15, 656.

[21] On Luther, cf. the passage quoted by Sabourin, *loc. cit.*, 85: "peccata nostra in se derivavit" (*Enarr. Uberior in cap. 53 Isaiae* [Wittenberg, 1574], vol. 4, 216ff.).

[22] *Apol.* 3, 58; *De defin. just.*, Corp. Ref. 11, 999.

the *imputatio* of sins, of God's whole anger being poured out on the Son, who is made a scapegoat for the sins of all.[23] Grotius thinks in more juridical terms: for him, Jesus' Passion is simply an example provided by God for sinners.[24]

At this point, we quote Quenstedt's nuanced passage on Jesus' hell-sufferings, since it forms a transition to later reflection: "*Sensit mortem aeternam, sed non in aeternum. Aeterna ergo mors fuit, si spectes essentiam et intensionem poenarum; sin respicias infinitam personae patientis sublimitatem, non tantum aequipollens, sed et omnes omnium damnatorum aeternas mortes infinities supergrediens fuit.*"[25]

Right down to our own time, there has been no break in the line of Protestant exegetes and dogmaticians speaking in terms of Jesus' penal suffering.[26] As chief witnesses here, we can mention K. Barth, W. Pannenberg and J. Moltmann.

Barth sees the two sides of the *commercium*: "It is one thing for God to elect and predestinate himself to fellowship with man, and quite another for God to predestinate man to fellowship with himself. Both are God's self-giving to man. But, if the latter means unequivocally that a gift is made to man", the former signifies "God's hazarding of his Godhead and power and status. . . . God wills to lose in order that man may gain." "God has ascribed to man the former, election, salvation and life; and to himself he has ascribed the latter, reprobation, perdition and death."[27] Historically, then, this results in the "exchange that took place on Golgotha . . . when the Son of God bore what

---

[23] *Jesu Chr. D. N. Nov. Test.* (1558), 241.

[24] *Defensio fidei cath.*; de satisf. Christi, c. 4.

[25] *Theologia didacto-polemica* III, 346.

[26] Many quotations in L. Sabourin, *Rédemption sacrificielle*. J. B. Lightfoot is impressive in his *Galatians* (1939), 138, as are Holtzmann, Pfleiderer, Windisch, *2 Korinther*, 198: "In the first place, 'made to be sin' means 'condemned to become incarnate. . . .' Secondly, sin is not only imputed to him: somehow he has taken it upon himself in its whole reality, like the scapegoat 'for sin' [*Sündenbock*] (Lev 16), in the primal, awesome sense of this word. . . . Then, in death, he 'became acquainted' at least with the curse of sin, the alienation from God that comes through sin, the divine anger at sin and the divine punishment for it, in all its hideous depths." Cf. Pannenberg, *Das Glaubensbekenntnis* (Siebenstern, 1972), on the phrase "descended into hell", 98–103.

[27] CD II/2, 162–63.

the son of man ought to have borne. . . . Man is not rejected. In God's eternal purpose, it is God himself who is rejected in his Son. The self-giving of God consists, the giving and sending of his Son is fulfilled, in the fact that he is rejected in order that we might not be rejected."[28] Thus Jesus is the one whom God judges in our stead.[29] "He gives himself (like a *rara avis*) to the fellowship of those who are guilty of all these things, and not only that, but he makes their evil case his own." "He as One can represent all and make himself responsible for the sins of all. . . . He can conduct the case of God against us in such a way that he takes from us our own evil case, taking our place and compromising and burdening himself with it."[30] "It was to fulfill this judgment on sin that the Son of God as man took our place as sinners . . . by treading the way of sinners to its bitter end in death, in destruction, in the limitless anguish of separation from God, by delivering us sinful men and sin in his own person to the *nonbeing* that is properly theirs, the nonbeing, the nothingness to which man has fallen victim as a sinner and toward which he relentlessly hastens. We can say indeed that he fulfills this judgment by suffering the *punishment* we have all brought on ourselves."[31]

Pannenberg associates himself with this tradition. Some have questioned whether he is right to do so, since his deduction —that Jesus suffered universally for Jews and pagans alike— seems too external: the Jews, following the logic of their law, condemn Jesus as a blasphemer; the pagans, in accord with their view of the divine authority of the earthly kingdom, remove him as someone who questioned this. God, in raising Jesus from the dead, shows Jesus to be right and all the others to be wrong. Just as he is rejected by mankind (because he runs counter to the latter's ideals), his vicarious death includes all men. (Pannenberg takes up P. Marheineke's concept of "inclusive representation".) Pannenberg jumps from the sociological assertion that Jesus was

---

[28] *Ibid.*, 167.   [29] CD IV/1, 222.

[30] *Ibid.*, 236.

[31] *Ibid.*, 253. The theme of the exchange of places is given extensive treatment by Barth (in connection with 2 Corinthians 5:19f.) in CD IV/1, 73ff.

"totally forsaken" by men and equates this with the theological assertion of "eternal damnation".[32] Finally, following Luther, he holds fast to the penal quality of Jesus' suffering.[33]

In J. Moltmann's *The Crucified God*,[34] the *pro nobis* is given considerably more theological foundation.[35] The whole calamitous history of mankind is brought into the trinitarian history of God himself, with its climax in the Cross and the dereliction of the "crucified God", so that it is primarily God— and only secondarily mankind—who "loads the world's sin" on Jesus. The Son's bearing of guilt is vicarious;[36] he has endured "rejection"[37] and hence "hell" for us;[38] thus, within the life of God, God is genuinely against God.[39] But for Moltmann, this kind of alienation within God is nothing other than the suffering of absolute love: the Father, in his own way, is just as much affected by the Cross as the Son is: "The Son suffers dying, the Father suffers the death of the Son."[40] An impassible God could not be the God of this world.[41] What was borne on the Cross? "If God has taken upon himself death on the Cross, he has also taken upon himself all of life and real life, as it stands under death, law and guilt."[42]—Nonetheless, there is little mention of sin as such; as the final chapter on liberation theology shows,

[32] *Grundzüge der Christologie*, loc. cit., 271, 270.

[33] *Ibid.*, 286.

[34] London: SCM, 1974.

[35] Cf. *ibid.*, 172ff., 176 on the differences between Moltmann and Pannenberg.

[36] Since Jesus "first died for the victims and then also for the executioners" (178), so that, in spite of possible misunderstandings, "these ideas of expiation are important in that they show", among other things, "that, as the Christ of God, Jesus took the place of helpless man as his representative" (183). "He made him sin for us": this must be taken seriously (242).

[37] *Ibid.*, 276.   [38] *Ibid.*, 263, 276.

[39] *Ibid.*, 190. "The Cross of the Son divides God from God to the utmost degree of enmity and distinction" (152). This is the center of all Christian theology (153).

[40] *Ibid.*, 243.

[41] *Ibid.*, 200–278. Protestant polemics is directed, not against the natural knowledge of God, but against a picture of God understood as *apatheia* along the lines of the ancient world, which is then elevated into a norm for Christianity. Moltmann is right to protest against this, pointing to God's "pathos" in the Old Covenant (as interpreted by A. Heschel and even by the Rabbis).

[42] *Ibid.*, 277.

the author is more concerned with the hopeless, tragic, vicious circles of human history, poverty, violence, alienation, the exploitation of nature, meaninglessness.[43] It is things such as these that Christian action in the world must help to remedy, starting from the Resurrection of Jesus and the universal hope of salvation; a "new political theology" is called for. No less than Teilhard, Moltmann does see that Christ faces mankind with a momentous choice; but in view of the Resurrection, he puts all the emphasis on God's will to save the whole world and, within this will, on the power of Christian hope and the action that stems from it.[44]

The Catholic tradition, starting with Rupert and Denys, extends without a break from Erasmus,[45] Cajetan,[46] Salmeron,[47] to the twentieth century. Estius provides three interpretations of 2 Corinthians 5:21: Christ being "made to be sin" for us can mean that he became a "victim of sin" (Augustine); that he "assumed sinful flesh" (Thomas); or finally, "that God treated him as the epitome of sin and corruption, as a scapegoat."[48] Many writers followed this line: here we mention only Cornelius a Lapide, who speaks of punishment, retribution and the scapegoat in connection with Jesus' sufferings.[49] The great French orators do the same, as do many of the more modern exegetes like

---

[43] *Ibid.*, 318–19.

[44] Cf. the differences between this and the "model of exoneration" (whereby the Church relieves the state of religious responsibilities) and the "model of correspondence" (K. Barth: political action as a reflection—in the form of "small hopes"—of the "great hope" of transcendent salvation): *ibid.*, 308ff. By contrast, "the beyond is *in* the here-and-now": the latter is to be seen as a "sacrament" of God's real presence.

[45] Voluit pati supplicium perinde quasi peccasset omnia. *Annot. in NT*, in 2 Corinthians 5:21; cf. *Paraphrasis*, Opera (Basel, 1540), 667–68. On Galatians 3:13: execrationem quae nos tenebat obnoxios, in se transtulit.

[46] Transtulit [Deus] autem peccata nostra in Christum (*Ep. Pauli*, in 2 Corinthians 5:21).

[47] Ipse sumpsit omnium peccatorum personam et nostrorum delictorum reatum in se transtulit. . . . Posuit Dominus in eo iniquitatem omnium nostrorum. *Disp. in Ep. D. Pauli* III, Opera 15 (Cologne, 1604), 311. On the image of the scapegoat, cf. vol. 16, 200).

[48] *Comm. in omnes S. Pauli Ep.* (1679), 467.

[49] *Comm. in S. Script.* (1868), vol. 18, 455.

Allo, Lagrange, Huby, Cornely,[50] Prat, d'Alès.[51] We shall have to consider how far it is legitimate to use the widespread notion of "penal substitution"; initially, however, we should be reluctant to oversimplify and speak of "external, juridical ideas", even if this juridical aspect is softened by the concept of solidarity.[52]

The idea that Jesus, in being forsaken by God, experienced the *poena damni*, at least analogously, is also found in Catholic thinkers such as Blondel,[53] Daniélou[54] and Martelet.[55]

However we view the idea of "punishment" when applied to the Cross, we must agree with J. Galot when he says that the idea of solidarity is insufficient, without that of representative ("vicarious") suffering, to express the force of the biblical affirmation. "There is solidarity, it is true, but it extends as far as substitution: Christ's solidarity with us goes as far as taking our place and allowing the whole weight of human guilt to fall upon him."[56] How are we to imagine this substitution? (For there is no analogy to it in the natural realm, and the theory and practice of "sacrifice" and "expiation" as found among ancient peoples, which offers an approximation to it, is apparently alien to the modern mind.) Help comes from an unexpected quarter here in the thesis of René Girard. Girard's background is in literature, ethnology and psychoanalysis; he shows that the theme of the

---

[50] In his commentary on 2 Corinthians 5:20 and Galatians 3:13, he speaks of Jesus as "vir maledictissimus, in quo praeter maledictionem nihil invenitur".

[51] Article "Rédemption" in DAF IV, 558: "Le Christ courbé sous le poids de la colère et de la malédiction." Further examples in Sabourin.

[52] L. Sabourin, 78–79. The author even quotes a passage from Hesychius that presupposes a much more internal relationship: "Portat enim iniquitates nostras quia ignis proprium est foenum consumere, et divinitatis peccatum perimere, unde et ignis consumens Deus dicitur." *Comm. in Lev. 16* (PG 93, 998).

[53] "Il a sympathisé avec tout et tous, jusqu'avec l'abandon du damné" (quoted by X. Tilliette in *Quatre Fleuves* 4, 53). "Vous avez pris en vous et connu par votre amour tout ce dont les hommes ont souffert et surtout tout ce dont ils ont eu tort de ne pas souffrir, jusqu'au dam. . . . Je vous adore, Homme de la Douleur divine", *Carnets Intimes* (1883–1894), Nov. 6, 1894 (Paris: Cerf, 1961), 540.

[54] "Seul Jésus franchit cet abîme, descend dans l'abîme de la misère, s'enfonce au plus profond des enfers." *Les Saints paiens* (1955), 126.

[55] Martelet is right to distinguish Jesus' experience of the abyss from that of the damned: *L'Au-delà retrouvé; Christologie des fins dernières* (Paris: Desclée, 1975), 96.

[56] *La Rédemption, mystère d'alliance* (Paris-Bruges: Desclée de Brouwer, 1965), 268.

"scapegoat" has become relevant in a new way. He uses it to throw light on the mechanisms operating in all human culture and religion.

The "Scapegoat" Mechanism

In their own way, René Girard's endeavors, in his two volumes, *La Violence et le sacré*[1] and *Des choses cachées depuis la fondation du monde*,[2] can be compared to the systems of Teilhard de Chardin and Karl Rahner. He too distills the basis of a total anthropology from an all-embracing Christology. However, his is purely staurological, that is, it is marked by sharp antitheses: Christ is the fulfillment of "all the things that have been hidden since the foundation of the world", but only insofar as he takes their meaning (a meaning that is necessarily self-concealing), uncovers it, completes it and radically reverses it. This becomes clear in the opposition between the two "logos"-principles of Heraclitus and John: the former is the logos of harmony through violence; the latter is the logos that renounces violence, which the world "cannot understand", "cannot know" and "did not accept" (Jn 1:5, 10, 11), and which thus becomes the universal scapegoat. "So Jesus is the only man to reach the goal that God intended for the whole of mankind",[3] since he is the only one to "live out agapē right to the end".[4] If his existence is to be of significance for all, "representation" must be central.[5] But in what sense?

We can distinguish in this system between starting point and goal. The goal was the unveiling of truth in Christ—although the first volume does not contain the word "God", let alone "Christ"; *La Violence et le sacré* was written with Christ in mind.[6] The stimulus was doubtless Freud's *Totem and Taboo*. This book seems somehow strange and isolated within Freud's *oeuvre* (Freud

---

[1] Paris: Grasset, 1972. References here are given solely by page number.

[2] *Recherches avec J.-M. Oughourlian et Guy Lefort* (Paris: Grasset, 1978). References here are given as II plus page number.

[3] II, 236.   [4] II, 239.

[5] Initially Girard rejects the concepts "expiation" and "substitution" (II, 203f.) but goes on to accept "redemption" in the full sense: II, 205.

[6] II, 198f.

does not connect the murder of the primal Father with the Oedipus complex),[7] yet, with the instinct of genius, it touches on the drama that is fundamental to everything[8] but unable to unveil it completely.[9] Girard's main campaign is to supersede and demolish psychoanalysis; his aim to overcome the structuralism of Lévi-Strauss,[10] the Hegelian-Marxist dialectic,[11] Heidegger[12] and rationalist ethnology (Frazer)[13] is only secondary.

Girard's is surely the most dramatic project to be undertaken today in the field of soteriology and in theology generally. In his view, world history and all the values realized in it are based on a primal tragedy that has now been disclosed; it comes to a climax —and this is also its turning point—in the tragedy of the rejection of Christ. "All religious ritual is rooted in the scapegoat, and all human institutions, sacred or profane, come from ritual. This is true of political power, judicial authority, the art of medicine, the theatre, philosophy, even anthropology."[14] Note particularly his considerable use of great drama, especially Greek drama: he quotes practically all the plays of the three great tragedians;[15] but he also cites Shakespeare,[16] Corneille and scenes from Cervantes and Dostoyevsky.[17] Theatre, Greek theatre, is essentially

---

[7] 166, 203, 235ff., 281; he rejects the Oedipus complex.

[8] 134, 169. "Totem et tabou, qui passe plus près sans doute de la thèse développée ici": 297. Girard acknowledges the connection between sex and power but sees the former subordinated to the latter: 301; II, 30.

[9] Cf. primarily the quotation from Freud on tragedy, and his critique: 277ff.

[10] 305ff. The main criticism is that the inexplicable "sacral" is spirited away, II, 14, 75, 114ff.

[11] 426 (critique of the master-servant dialectic); II, 66, 71.

[12] He gets as far as "salvation" but cannot explain what it presupposes: II, 72.

[13] 49f. and passim.

[14] 425.

[15] First of all, Oedipus (75, 103ff.) and Dionysus (the Bacchae, 63, 95, 170ff., 226); but also Ajax (23f.), Medea (24), Iphigeneia (26, 63), Oresteia (35), Ion (61), the raving Heracles (64f., 69, 71), the Seven against Thebes (70f., 94f.), Alcestis (73, 98), Andromache (119, 214), The Trachinian Women (65, 203), The Phoenician Women (73), The Suppliant Women (93).

[16] 100, 378, 418ff., II, 45.

[17] 66 (Corneille). Girard had already discussed the great writers (Dante, Cervantes, Hölderlin, et al.) in his first book, Mensonge romantique et vérité romanesque (Paris, 1961), and Dostoyevsky in his second, Critique dans un souterrain (Lausanne, 1967). Both are in the tradition of psychoanalysis.

rooted in myth and ritual;[18] it is fundamentally religious,[19] although it signals a crisis in the myth. If great drama only thrives in particular, privileged, diachronic periods, when the sense of myth and ritual, though fading, continues to reecho through man's world, Girard sees all other cultural institutions thriving on the humus of the primal tragedy that underlies everything: that of the scapegoat. If its "mechanism" is to operate, it must essentially be hidden, unrecognized—as he repeats tirelessly[20] —but it must not "be conceived in terms of repression and the unconscious".[21] The great poets—Sophocles, Euripides, Shakespeare—come very close to discovering what it is, but at the last moment they draw back within the veils of myth.[22] The aspect of concealment is an integral part of the primal drama itself, of its essential ambivalence. Thus Girard always presents the primal event, to which the whole baffling multiplicity of rites and myths refers,[23] as mere "hypothesis": it remains something indirectly ascertained, something around which we circle; yet, because of the phenomenon of convergence, we can claim scientific "certainty" for it.[24]

Initially, the dramatic element seems to be the primal tragedy that grounds all culture, that is, the scapegoat, profoundly ambivalent, which is epitomized in the case of Christ. But, at a deeper level, we see that the real drama lies in the effect this epitome has: it revolutionizes and unmasks everything that precedes and follows it. Nietzsche's antithesis—Dionysus versus the Crucified—is correct, but only in its reverse form: the Crucified versus Dionysus.

Here we can do no more than give a rough outline of Girard's complex arguments. Man's fundamental desire (*désir*), as such, is unlimited and has no object (in contrast to the Freudian *li-*

[18] 108; on Japanese theatre, II, 156.

[19] 438f.

[20] 21, 97 (in tragedy), 122 (naked truth is not to be borne), 124, 149 ("a fundamental dimension of religion is man's failure to penetrate the veil"), 168, 192, 222, 385, 396. We must reckon with the most stubborn resistance (442) when it comes to unveiling the mechanism (430).

[21] 431.   [22] 118, 184, 194f.

[23] 379–428.   [24] 128f., 149, 229; II, 43, 137.

bido); it is hedged about by its imitative character: "Rivalry is not the result of a chance convergence of two desires toward the same object; the subject desires the object because its rival desires it. . . . The other has to show the subject what it should desire; confronted with the example of an apparently superior being that desires something, the subject must conclude that the object of this desire is something even more fulfilling. . . . Desire is essentially imitative."[25] Hence the "power" element in the desirability of the object: "Power endows objects with their value";[26] it is "simultaneously the universal instrument, object and subject of all desires".[27] There is no such thing as desire without power.

Thus we have the primal phenomenon of the struggle between "two brothers", Cain and Abel, Romulus and Remus, Eteocles and Polyneices, and so forth. Here the struggle becomes absolutized and detached from its object.[28] In the stychomythy of Greek tragedy, which is a blow-by-blow battle in words, we can discern power's *indifference*, which arises in this way.[29] All tragedy is built upon the reciprocal opposition of symmetrical forces; the pervading atmosphere and milieu is one of power or "anger".[30] This is the origin of the phenomenon of the *Doppelgänger*, or "double", filling the threatened man with utter dread.[31] The reciprocal intensification in the battle of desire is profoundly ambivalent: on the one hand, it eliminates all differences and prepares the way for a reciprocity that could prove fruitful, yet on the condition that the tension of anger and power be discharged.[32] The model of "brothers in enmity" is only the prototype of something that is always going on in the group, the clan, in society; the accumulated tension can only be dispersed by being discharged, quasi-fortuitously,[33] onto a victim common

---

[25] 204–5. This is in fact a *mimésis d'approbation*; Plato had an inkling of this in his attack on mimesis, but he did not bring it out clearly: II, 16.

[26] 202.   [27] 203.   [28] II, 34–35.

[29] 70.   [30] 75, 95, 103.

[31] 220–26. On the phenomenon of twins in primitive cultures: 88ff. On the effect of similarities: 90; cf. II, 43. On the "monstrous": 98, 113, 226f., 348–49; II, 44. On the mask that mediates the monstrous: 232f.

[32] On good and bad reciprocity: II, 228, 241.

[33] On chance (*hasard*) or the drawn "lot" as a specifically human element: 433ff.,

to both sides, a "scapegoat". The "unanimity" created by the "lynching" (which dissolves the tension) is fundamental; both sides' spontaneous acknowledgment and designation of the victim reestablishes peace through "catharsis"; the negative reciprocity of power becomes a positive reciprocity.[34]

The victim now takes on all the accumulated ambivalence. On the one hand, it is accursed, the personification of amassed evil; on the other, it is "consecrated" and "holy",[35] its death guaranteeing peace and making civilization possible, at least for a time. Its unique position in the community means that it extends upward into the transcendent realm; it allows man to discover the sacral (*sacri-ficium*: something made both accursed and holy) and hence the realm of the religious. Both aspects, that which brings destruction and that which brings blessing, are identical: Oedipus Rex is found to be responsible for plague and for all ill-fortune in Thebes; he is blinded; yet it is from his grave (in *Oedipus at Colonos*) that blessing proceeds. The one chosen to be cut off is often enough the one who, prior to being sacrificed, was venerated as divine.[36] There is an alternation of humiliation and exaltation,[37] as we see in the example of the African king who is chosen as a sacrifice[38] or the Greek "*pharmakos*" who is kept in reserve to be sacrificed when necessity arises.[39] The victim is "*sacer*",[40] it embodies that essentially ambivalent sacral quality, that mysterious substance that pervades and governs all things (in the form of power),[41] but which must be kept within bounds and at a distance and which must be pacified.[42] The victim exhibits a twofold transcendence, toward the demonic and the divine; bearing the curse, it is also the bringer of salva-

---

II, 111; 435; on trial by ordeal: 439. What decides the issue is "almost nothing": 117.

[34] On the question of unanimity: 116f., 120, 144f., 159. It is not difficult to interpret the celebrated "catharsis" in Aristotle in medical terms, as a "purgation" (W. Schadewaldt); cf. *Theo-Drama* I, 315 note 20.

[35] 19.   [36] 417.   [37] 380.

[38] 140f., II, 59f.   [39] 29f., 137f.   [40] 356.

[41] 52, at least in a society prior to the introduction of an objective legal order: 335.

[42] 54, 369. Thus the victims chosen were often outsiders or those on the margin: 374f.

tion.[43] This, according to Girard, is sufficient to account for the emergence of the religious and the sacral; the phenomenon of sacrifice explains divinity, not divinity the phenomenon of sacrifice.[44] The picture of divinity that thus arises is an ambivalent one, like all primitive images of gods, but also like the chimeras of every Olympus: they demand revenge and victims, they accept sacrifice[45] and desire to be "honored" in this way;[46] in return, they grant peace and prosperity. The ambivalent god *kat'exochen* is Dionysus; his celebration is that of power, destroying all institutions.[47] He calls for the rending (*sparagmos*) of the victim with the votaries' bare hands (thus King Pentheus in the *Bacchae*), yet at the same time he is the most tender of all gods.[48] He is "the god of felicitous murder".[49] Heraclitus equates him, the god of inebriation, with Hades.[50]

Girard identifies "essential power" (*violence essentielle*)[51] with (anthropological) being[52] and, no less, with "the holy" (in R. Otto's sense),[53] that is, that which is the object of worship.[54] According to Girard, the primal murder of the scapegoat is behind all the myths that half-conceal and half-reveal it. More importantly, it is also behind all ritual. For ritual is basically man's way of regulating a "sacrificial crisis" that recurs periodically: this happens when, in a group, after a period of relative peace, a new period of imitative violence needs to be discharged. Here ritual has a ready-made solution: a victim is unanimously chosen to be sacrificed to the god's wrathful violence. In the first instance, this victim is human, but secondarily[55] it can be an animal, often one assimilated to the human being as far as possible. All rituals, including ritual proscriptions (incest) and regulations, even can-

---

[43] 125–28.

[44] On the definition of "the religious": 42 ("the religious coincides with the obscurity that ultimately encircles all man's resources against his own violent propensity. . . . This obscurity coincides with the effective transcendence of sacred, legitimate power over against culpable, illegal, immanent power"), 85, 130f., 147, 426 ("Human society begins, not with the 'slave's' fear of his 'master', but with the religious").

[45] 368.   [46] 369, II, 64.   [47] 170ff.

[48] 348.   [49] 190.

[50] 354. Dionysus, of course, can be torn apart and put together again: 196.

[51] 446, 450.   [52] 211, 279.   [53] 357.

[54] 358.   [55] 149f.

nibalism,[56] point back to the cathartic repetition of the primal drama of the scapegoat.[57]

Girard's argument for this hypothesis, which is presented as the "only solution" for the problem of sacrality and the possibility of culture,[58] is crowned by a fascinating chapter on hominization. Here he shows that the threshold to the human is passed when imitation of the leading animal becomes (by contrast with the animal kingdom) a *mimesis d'appropriation*. The realm of the instinct is left behind; now the question is how to find a mechanism that will regulate the struggle of all against everyone.[59] Civilization is only possible on this basis;[60] thus Chinese wisdom expressly sees the peace of the realm grounded in ritual.[61] The "evil" symmetry of the crisis gives way to the relaxed differentiation found in "good" society.[62] Here Girard takes up the Idealist (post-Kantian) thesis that the Fall—the transgression of the paradise proscription—coincides with man's acquisition of consciousness. In the transition from animal to human being, the first trace of real murder indicates that man is now on the stage.

Given these presuppositions, it can plausibly be argued that all institutions are based on the phenomenon of religion (defined in this way as "ambivalent"). Equally, it is plausible that all social insurances against the repetition of "sacrificial crises" —primarily the public exercise of law, but also scientific medicine, and so forth—go hand in hand with the secularization of religious realities. All the same, Girard insists that the legal system (which he sees as a technologizing of power) remains basically just as ambivalent as its primitive stage[63] and that the mechanism continues to operate through all facets of society. Indeed, as we shall see, secularization actually intensifies its operation.

---

[56] 379.
[57] 379–428.
[58] 122, 192.
[59] 203, 429, II, 93–108.
[60] II, 27, 36, 40.
[61] 22, 77.
[62] Cf. the interpretation of the speech of Odysseus in Shakespeare's *Troilus and Cressida*: the obliteration of the distinction ("degree") leads to parricide. 79ff.
[63] 32–41.

There is of necessity an abrupt transition from the foundation of civilization, which calls for the mechanism to be hidden, to its unveiling in the Old and New Testaments.[64] This unveiling takes place along the lines of Freud and his uncovering of repressed matter. Though not exclusively, "knowledge" is essentially involved, namely, knowledge of "what has been hidden since the foundation of the world" (Ps 78:2 = Mt 13:35). The only link between civilization and Christianity is the scapegoat mechanism, albeit in Jesus it is brought to peerless fulfillment and given a totally new significance and value (by being unveiled).

The Old Testament remains *in via*, yet after only a few large strides it reaches to Jesus. As early as the story of Cain and Abel we have (for the first time) no mention of the sacralization of the victim; here and later, Scripture sides with the innocent party. All the same, Cain, on the basis of his murder, becomes the founder of towns (and hence of culture).[65] In Lamech (Gen 4:24), an escalation of violence is evident. In the prophets, Girard observes (though here he is too one-sided) "a clearer and clearer challenge to the great pillars of ancient religion, namely, cultic sacrifice" and the Law, understood as an awesome list of prohibitions.[66] The climax is the "Suffering Servant", the scapegoat rejected by all and for all; he, however, is not a "ritual victim" but "a spontaneous historical event".[67] This figure, however, the Old Testament's last word, remains overshadowed by an ambivalent picture of God: if the "Servant" himself no longer has "any connection with power", it is God who "makes" him a scapegoat: "Yahweh has caused all our sins to fall upon him", or even (if we accept this reading as the correct one):[68] "It was the will of the Lord to bruise him" (Is 53:6, 10). Yet, on the other hand, all guilt is laid upon men: "*We* esteemed him stricken, smitten by God, and afflicted" (Is 53:4). For Girard, as far as the removal of the scapegoat mechanism from the sphere of magic is con-

---

[64] On the following, cf. part 2 of vol. 2, II, 163–304.

[65] II, 170–72.   [66] II, 177.

[67] II, 179.

[68] It can equally well be translated: "But Yahweh was pleased in his Stricken One." Cf. C. Westermann, "Das Buch Jesaja, Kp. 40–66" in *Das Alte Testament deutsch* 19 (1966), 215.

cerned, the God of the Old Covenant stops half-way: the God of violence has not yet arrived at the powerless God of Jesus and the New Covenant. If it is objected that the New Testament also has its apocalypses, which are marked by violence, Girard says that it is not God who applies violence to sinners: rather, all violent action here is described as simply the consequence of sin itself.[69] There is a paradigmatic opposition between the beginning of Genesis, where God drives man from paradise, and the beginning of John, where the incarnate Logos is the One whom the world does not accept and drives out.[70]

Only Jesus fully unveils the nature of the "sacral", when he names Satan as the "murderer from the beginning", who is also "the father of lies", that is, in that he conceals the true nature of the scapegoat mechanism (Jn 8:43f., 59). His "woes" addressed to the Pharisees plainly call them "whitewashed graves",[71] those who are guilty of "the blood of all the prophets, shed from the foundation of the world" (Lk 11:50), and yet erect monuments to those they have murdered: "by means of religious and legal institutions", they obliterate the traces of murder and sacralize the tradition.[72] This psychoanalysis (or rather, "cosmo-analysis") is matched by the complete purification of the image of God from all traits of violence. Violence is forbidden to man because the heavenly Father does not employ it; his kingdom will be a kingdom of love, not of ritual institutions and interdicts.[73]

The world has one last chance to respond to this radical unveiling on the part of Jesus, and again it does so in "unanimity" (Christians, Jews and pagans)[74] by issuing the death sentence—thereby involving everyone in an injustice that cries to heaven. Something analogous takes place in the killing of Stephen: first he makes his accusation, unveiling and analyzing Israel's history: "As your fathers did, so do you. Which of the prophets did not

---

[69] II, 210. In view of the conclusion of the parable of the vineyard, where the lord of the vineyard has the wicked laborers killed, this thesis is harder to defend. Girard prefers the Matthean text, where it is the listeners, not Jesus, who give this verdict.

[70] II, 298f.   [71] II, 186.   [72] II, 188.

[73] II, 220. Accordingly, in Paul, the "principalities and powers" are made responsible for the violence manifested in history: II, 214ff.

[74] II, 190.

your fathers persecute?" (Acts 7:51ff.). Then they all rush upon him "as one man" and stone him "outside the city", just as Jesus was crucified outside the Holy City.[75]

In this perspective, the "religious dimension in mankind", all sacrifice and ritualism, is unmasked as satanic, something diametrically opposed to the message of Jesus. So Girard calls for a "nonsacrificial conception" of the death of Jesus and rejects all attempts to reintroduce concepts of sacrifice. This applies even to the New Testament (Hebrews)[76] as well as to the sacrificial practices of the later Church and to the theology of sacrifice such as Anselm's. (Girard's presentation of Anselm's theories is as distorted as that of K. Rahner and many others.)[77] Girard says that the Church's concrete history was only possible because of an (at least) partial return to covert "mechanism". First Judas was branded as a scapegoat,[78] then Jews in general[79] and many others in the course of history (the Inquisition, witches, and so forth). Why was there this regression from the message of Jesus, this quasi-Old Testament attitude right in the middle of the New? Girard says it is because pagan peoples lack the pedagogical background of the Old Covenant and thus have to go through their own pre-Christian period. They have yet to make their final "choice" in favor of Christian defenselessness.[80]

Cannot the Cross of Jesus also be read as a "sacrifice", that is, in the sense of a self-surrender? Girard has no hesitation in saying Yes.[81] But only on condition that we maintain the abyss between this latter self-surrender and the old ritual sacrifice, which is intended to placate a god who requires violence. "This complete self-sacrifice must be understood in a nonsacrificial sense. Or, if the word 'sacrifice' must be retained, it should not be applied

[75] II, 193–96.

[76] II, 206. Girard dismisses Paul's clearly sacrificial terminology in a mere aside: "Tout ce qui, chez lui déjà, pourrait à la rigueur annoncer la lecture sacrificielle": 216. We have noted the same tendency in H. Kessler, cf. Theo-Drama III, 107f., n. 29.

[77] As if, in Hebrews and in Anselm, God is someone "who finds it necessary to avenge his honor" and "demands an even more precious and beloved victim, namely, his own Son": II, 206.

[78] "Whose betrayal has the same episodic character as Peter's denial": II, 206.

[79] II, 196ff.   [80] II, 276.   [81] II, 259.

to any other sacrifice apart from the Cross—which is clearly impossible."[82]

And what of world history in the wake of Christ? The unveiling of the mechanism operates as history's "secret motor".[83] The sacral and the religious fade more and more, in proportion to the unmasking of power and man's awareness of it.[84] But this does not mean that man has got "beyond" power: on the contrary, his knowledge of power leads to holocausts on an unimaginable scale.[85] The disappearance of the myths of reconciliation and of veneration for the victim[86] leads to the growth of naked power. The latter can actually stifle the new awareness and create new pseudo-sacral institutions (the quasi-myths of Nazism and Communism)[87] designed to obliterate both the traces and the awareness of murder.[88] However, even if ideologies enjoin silence, the facts speak for themselves,[89] and they do so in the language of the Apocalypse.[90] If the solution provided in Jesus is rejected, man's progressive and irreversible understanding of civilization's foundations is bound inevitably to destroy that same civilization.[91]

Girard's synthesis is a closed system, since it wants to be "purely scientific", jettisoning all "moribund metaphysics".[92] All philosophy is secularized religion, and religion owes its existence to the covert scapegoat mechanism.[93] There is therefore no such thing as a "natural" concept of God.[94] This brings us back to the "theology" of the young Karl Barth (and it is also Barth's later theology insofar as he regards the *analogia entis* as *the* invention of the Antichrist"); for Girard, religion is the invention of Satan. Here the transition from the sacral to Christ takes place without man's understanding being involved at all; thus Christ exhibits no intelligibility either. The only possibility would be

---

[82] II, 475.   [83] II, 233.   [84] 121.

[85] II, 150.   [86] II, 41, 45f.   [87] 124, 445.

[88] II, 73.   [89] II, 158.

[90] II, 160. Since everything is fundamentally open, the modern attack on prohibitions and taboos is ridiculous: II, 48.

[91] II, 153.

[92] "Métaphysique funéraire": II, 159. "C'est ici pour la première fois que cette métaphysique est complètement *réduite* à des rapports purement humains": II, 50.

[93] II, 24.   [94] II, 65.

for Christ's unveiling of the primal mechanism to uncover some substratum of "natural religion", however distorted; but Girard dismisses this out of hand and so introduces an ineradicable contradiction into his system. For, by acknowledging Christ's divinity (and even his birth of the Virgin),[95] he is positing a theological dimension that explodes his allegedly pure scientism. Only on the basis of this dimension can we understand that there is in man "an obscure but radical protest against power and the lie, these two elements that are inseparable from every human order".[96] We constantly meet the words "power" and "violence", never the word "justice".[97] Can it be proved scientifically that the justice for which men long is nothing but power in disguise? His initial concept is *"désir"*, a desire that, compared to animal instinct, has absolutely no bounds. Formerly, in Augustine, this unbounded aspect was the *desiderium* (*naturale in Deum*), pointing to God. In Girard, as in Barth, it must be totally corrupt, for at the very start of human history it unleashes a war in which everyone is struggling against all, in a way that is reminiscent of Hobbes. The dramatic tension between the world and God is so overstretched that the link breaks, rendering impossible a drama that involves the two sides. This is clear from the fact that the self-concealing "mechanism" eliminates all freedom on man's part. Girard maintains a complete hiatus between naturalism and theology; they are not even linked by an ethics. In his view, the "omnipresence of violence" means that distinction between "good" and "evil" is illusory.[98] Accordingly, he does not speak of "sin" but of "hostility", and so forth; the concept of sin is secondary.[99] So too it is not clear how Christ, the ultimate scapegoat, can bear the world's sin, unless we suppose that men themselves load this sin onto him.

This raises a question that is crucial in the present context: What takes place on the Cross, according to this theory, if the transferral of the world's guilt to Jesus is only a psychological unloading (as it was in all ritual sacrifice), and if—on the other hand—the power-less Father-God demands nothing in the na-

---

[95] II, 238ff., 243ff.   [96] 246.
[97] Only once does the phrase "violence et persécution injuste" slip out: II, 149.
[98] 280.   [99] 142.

ture of an "atoning sacrifice"? To put it more concretely: the Church regards the eucharistic celebration as a representation of the "sacrifice of the Cross", in which Christ has effectively offered himself for mankind; how then can she present and offer Christ's self-surrender to the divine Father if the latter, who is no longer an Old Testament God, has "no pleasure" in it, since he did not *want* the Cross, and even less *commanded* his Son to accept it?

Girard's system, with its clear, inherent contradiction, has brought us face to face with this very concrete question, and to that extent it has rendered us a service.

In his book *Brauchen wir einen Sündenbock?*,[100] the theologian Raymund Schwager has tried to provide answers to some of the questions left open by Girard.[101] He agrees to a large degree with Girard's theses, including the psychoanalytical tendency to interpret redemption as "uncovering", "unveiling", "laying bare" and "seeing through"[102] the hidden mechanisms. He even refutes arguments proposed against Girard.[103] Yet, at a point of prime significance, he attempts an important correction: the fundamental transcendence of the "sacral" cannot (ultimately) be explained solely on the basis of mere power. Schwager goes quite far in his concessions (even to the borders of Barthianism),[104] but he finds it necessary to designate Girard's rejection of all metaphysics as a methodological *epochē*.[105] Positively, and here he goes beyond Girard, he says that, at root, God himself is the real scapegoat

---

[100] *Gewalt und Erlösung in den biblischen Schriften* (Munich: Kösel, 1978).

[101] The book appeared before Girard's second volume but is based throughout on conversations with him. As a result, most of the themes found in Girard's second volume (including the details) are already to be found in Schwager.

[102] 162, 180, 185, 192, 228, 230. "The Sermon on the Mount should be seen in the context of the biblical psycho-social analysis of the lie and of power": 180. Like Girard, Schwager interprets the "key of knowledge", which the Pharisees have thrown away and which is rediscovered in Jesus, as the "mechanism": 146.

[103] 36–53.

[104] Cf. the polemics against the Catholic teaching of society being built up out of "positive family relationships" that arise "directly out of human nature" (162).

[105] "Whether there is such a thing as transcendence or not cannot be answered at this level of reflection. Methodologically, therefore, . . . Girard excludes it": 51.

on behalf of sinful humanity.[106] Thus he distances himself from the thesis that the scapegoat is essentially "fortuitous".[107]

In his first volume, Girard seems to put forward the view that the unanimous transferral of human guilt to the ultimate scapegoat, Jesus, should be evaluated just like all the other, earlier acts of transference, that is, as a socio-psychological transaction. Schwager rejects this. In his second volume, however, Girard portrayed this unique and definitive transferral of guilt in concrete terms. For Schwager, the crucial thing is that, on the Cross, "not only the punishment of sin but sins themselves were transferred to the Holy One",[108] "physically and morally, not merely juridically".[109] At this point, Schwager is close to the thought of Luther and his followers and criticizes Anselm. Unfortunately, while he makes criticism that seems justified to the present writer, he mixes it up with the usual polemics against the alleged distortion, at Anselm's hands, of the image of the divine Father:[110] "The idea of a God who requires satisfaction is . . . of pagan origin." The Christian "God forgives without requiring anything in return, without requiring satisfaction."[111]

So why the Cross? Schwager is right to ask the question. The only answer—and it must presuppose that mankind's sin really is transferred to Jesus—is this: in order to get rid of their sin, men must "transfer their hostility to God concretely to him [Jesus] through the crucifixion".[112] Thus Jesus takes sin and holds on to it, lest it should fall in vengeance on the heads of those who have committed it.[113] This is the conclusion of the largely convincing analyses of Old Testament texts in which God moves progressively from being a God of violence and wrath (ca. 1,000 instances) to being a God who does not himself wield power but only allows the power wielded by men to have its effect on them. But, after discussing each aspect, Schwager rightly points out that the Old Testament does not reach any clear view, for example, of war, or of the way in which God undertakes to

[106] 202–4, in connection, particularly, with Romans 1. It seems perverse to me to refer to the Book of Job in this connection; the "distortion" of the picture of God in the case of the suffering Job is in a quite different context.
[107] 196ff.   [108] 210.   [109] 139.
[110] 210.   [111] 211.   [112] 214, cf. 215, note.
[113] 139.

reconcile and gather his people. Are Israel's enemies to be anni-hilated or converted, for instance?[114] And even where the vio-lence done to the Suffering Servant is concerned, it remains an open question whether "God laid on him the iniquity of us all" (Is 53:6) or whether the passage should be translated: "Yet the Lord permitted us all to lay our sins on him." Girard had also noted this ambivalence.

Why the Cross, if God forgives in any case? The answer given hitherto is unsatisfactory. It concerns only men's attitude to the Crucified, as if God's attitude to him did not exist. If we juxta-pose the two possible interpretations of Isaiah 53:6, we cannot fail to discern a relationship between God and his Servant: either he *wills* to burden him with sins, or he *allows* it. The difference, perhaps, is not great. Schwager uses a formula that points to both sides: "God is at work in this event, *enabling* the Smitten One freely to offer himself and by so doing to take upon him-self the trespasses of the others."[115] The resuscitation of Jesus, symbolically anticipated in the exaltation of the Suffering Ser-vant, shows clearly enough that God is involved in this event of ultimate significance. Thus God's forgiveness and the Cross (that is, the bearing of sin) cannot be left in mutual isolation: they are related. In this case, therefore, it will not be enough to follow Girard and Schwager in demythologizing the Old Testa-ment picture of God so that he changes from a violent, wrathful God and becomes a powerless God who does not engage in ret-ribution. What we have, in fact, is a new form of the problem latent in both Old and New Covenants: What is the relationship between God's love and his justice, particularly in the case of the Cross? God's justice, which Girard never acknowledges as something primal, is evidently quite different from power. If we recognize this, Anselm's presentation of the problem acquires a new significance. So far the whole question of what Paul calls "judgment", John calls "*krisis*" and the Book of Revelation calls "the wrath of God" has not been thoroughly explored.[116]

---

[114] 127.   [115] 140, 141.

[116] Schwager (202) says that "God did not hold man's resentment against him. He allowed himself, in the person of his Son, to be the target of everyone's hos-tility; he allowed himself to be made the scapegoat." This is far too weak. It is by no means evident that the Book of Revelation can be set aside as being "of its

Girard's perspective and Schwager's discovery that it is sins (not only the punishment due to sin) that are transferred, on the Cross, to the scapegoat have brought us to the final elements of the drama of reconciliation, yet without offering a satisfying conclusion. Before attempting to look for it ourselves, we must mention two further authors who have approached the mystery of vicarious suffering with great circumspection.

Final Approaches

In his doctrine of redemption,[1] *Sergei Bulgakov* tries to grasp the kenosis of the Cross as the last of God's self-utterances. It begins within the Trinity, with God the Father's self-dispossession in favor of the Son, and proceeds via the kenosis involved in creation.[2] Christ will bear the world's sin: this is the rationale underlying all creation.[3] It remains a mystery how Christ bears sin, but it takes place because, ontologically, the New Adam[4] bears within him the totality of human nature—in this, Bulgakov is following the Greek Fathers—and because Christ's humanity, as a result of the Hypostatic Union with the whole of humanity (through kenosis), is empowered "in a supra-empirical manner"[5] to appropriate all the sins of the world: "*acceptation comme les Siens propres*",[6] "*il les admet à l'intérieur de lui-même*",[7] "*le péché semble lui devenir propre*",[8] "*Le Christ n'est nullement 'un autre' pour tout homme, car le Nouvel Adam comprend chaque individu humain . . .* naturellement *dans son essence, et* compassionnellement *dans Son amour. Et le péché . . . n'est déjà plus pour Lui le péché d'autrui, mais le Sien propre.*"[9]

However, this is because of his obedience to the Father. Thus, "in a kind of *oboedientia passiva*",[10] a "sacrificial obedience",[11] he

---

time" (222f.), nor is it obvious that the angels who pour out the bowls of wrath over the earth are essentially symbols of human communities (223).

[1] *Le Verbe incarné: Agnus Dei* (Paris: Aubier, 1943).
[2] *Ibid.*, 138ff., 259ff.   [3] *Ibid.*, 280.
[4] *Ibid.*, 298.   [5] *Ibid.*, 282.
[6] *Ibid.*, 290.   [7] *Ibid.*, 290.
[8] *Ibid.*, 292.   [9] *Ibid.*, 298.
[10] *Ibid.*, 289.   [11] *Ibid.*, 300.

allows himself to be placed under God's anger against sin.[12] Thus he "drinks the chalice" and is "forsaken by God".[13] Through this experience of sin he "destroys" the "reality" of sin that men have created.[14] His suffering is hypostatic and, as such, its intensity is supra-temporal (*surtemporal . . . étendu au passé et à l'avenir*)[15] and, in that sense, "eternal" (*l'éternel est qualité, et non quantité*).[16] Although this suffering is the endurance of something utterly alien,[17] something that is simply "accepted" and hence "*quelque chose d'incomparable et même de contraire aux souffrances des pécheurs*" (the damned), in its own way it is "*l'équivalent de ce qui eût été propre à l'humanité, c.à.d. les tourments de l'enfer*".[18] By this concept of "intensive equivalence", Bulgakov expresses the identity and difference between Christ's suffering and that due to sinners. He strongly emphasizes that the Cross is an event involving the whole Trinity;[19] we shall have to devote some attention to this in our concluding remarks.

A. *Feuillet*, in his *L'Agonie de Gethsémani, enquêtes exégétiques et théologiques*,[20] calls for "*un dialogue profond entre exégètes et théologiens*", particularly with regard to the Passion of Jesus.[21] Exegesis, he asserts, can only be objective if it is conducted on the basis of faith,[22] not in an ivory tower.[23] As far as the meaning of the Passion is concerned, Lagrange's interpretations are "*souvent pauvres du point de vue doctrinal*".[24] Prat tries in vain to reduce everything to "solidarity";[25] and it is not enough to say, with A. Plummer, "*que Jésus a tellement sympathisé avec ceux qui souffrent que leurs souffrances devenaient comme les siennes propres*".[26]

Feuillet undertakes a minute analysis of the Mount of Olives narratives (especially that of Mark) in order to show the theological depths they contain. The Fathers were too timid to draw out all the implications; modern exegetes, on the other hand,

[12] *Ibid.*, 286, 292, 297.
[13] *Ibid.*, 287, 291.
[14] *Ibid.*, 286–87.
[15] *Ibid.*, 283.
[16] *Ibid.*, 297.
[17] *Ibid.*, 295.
[18] *Ibid.*, 296.
[19] *Ibid.*, 289, 299, 305f.
[20] Paris: Gabalda, 1977.
[21] *Ibid.*, 225.
[22] *Ibid.*, 231.
[23] *Ibid.*, 237.
[24] *Ibid.*, 229.
[25] *Ibid.*, 196.
[26] *Ibid.*, 245.

who see nothing but Jesus' fear of death,[27] or even merely legendary features[28] or a literary montage, fail to do justice to the whole import of the texts. It is essential to see how Jesus is "set upon" by suffering,[29] finds himself suddenly "alienated"[30] and is literally "thrown to the ground".[31] The "hour" is the hour of the final judgment,[32] the "Day of the Lord";[33] the cup he must drink is doubtless the eschatological "chalice of the wrath of Yahweh",[34] not unconnected with the eucharistic chalice.[35] It is offered to Jesus, yet he must accept it voluntarily.[36] Once Jesus has struggled through and reached his consenting Yes—in "great agitation",[37] in complete isolation and forsakenness[38]— "it is all over" ("apechei").[39]

The songs of the Suffering Servant[40] show that the only solution is for him vicariously to take on himself the world's sin. "Jésus accepte de se faire qu'un avec le monde coupable et d'apparaître aux yeux de Dieu chargé des péchés du monde. . . . Il se trouve comme atteint par la lèpre du péché (cf. Is 53:3), comme véritablement plongé dans la fange des iniquités des hommes de tous les temps."[41] His vision of the Father is veiled from him.[42] We must speak of "penal substitution" here, while being clear that the Victim is innocent and freely takes the others' punishment on himself.[43] Feuillet quotes a great number of theologians in his favor, not without making a critical assessment of them: Moltmann, Cullmann, Taylor, Cranfield, Albertz, and many others. This brings him to the question of suffering in God and the Trinity's participation in the Son's Passion.[44] In the triune God, who has created man in his own image, "quelque chose . . . correspond à la souffrance. . . ."[45] In the ek-stasis of suffering on the Cross, we see God's total self-giving

[27] Ibid., 25f.

[28] Ibid., 54.

[29] Ibid., 80, 188.

[30] Ibid., 82.

[31] Ibid., 83.

[32] Ibid., 84–86.

[33] Ibid., 227f.

[34] Ibid., 87–92.

[35] Ibid., 202.

[36] Ibid., 99, 212f., 254.

[37] Ibid., 168.

[38] Ibid., 197.

[39] Ibid., 116.

[40] Ibid., 29–40.

[41] Ibid., 205f.

[42] Ibid., 199.

[43] Ibid., 195.

[44] Ibid., 258, cf. the quotation from Maritain, 259.

[45] Ibid., 258.

in his triune life and in his love for his creatures.[46] The disciples on the Mount of Olives are summoned (and fail) to do their part; this shows that man is enjoined to participate in his redemption: "*Rédimés et co-rédempteurs, tous le sont, les pécheurs et les saints.*"[47] The book concludes with an analysis of Pascal's *Mystère de Jésus*, showing it to have a timeless relevance.

---

[46] *Ibid.*, 260.
[47] *Ibid.*, 248.

C. DRAMATIC SOTERIOLOGY

As the preceding historical outline showed, the quintessence of Scripture is found in five motifs. We must take account of all five motifs if our reflection is to be truly ecclesial. (1) The Son gives himself, through God the Father, for the world's salvation. (2) The Sinless One "changes places" with sinners. While, in principle, the Church Fathers understand this in a radical sense, it is only in the modern variations of the theories of representation that the consequences are fully drawn out. (3) Man is thus set free (ransomed, redeemed, released). (4) More than this, however, he is initiated into the divine life of the Trinity. (5) Consequently, the whole process is shown to be the result of an initiative on the part of divine love.

We have seen that it did not prove easy to do equal justice to all these aspects. The Fathers stressed that it was through the "exchange of places" (2) that man was initiated into "divinization" (4); in this context, it was quite possible to see man's liberation from the "powers" (3) as a work of God's love (5). But did this view also encompass the Son's self-giving (1) in all its ultimate and necessary consequences? Anselm, for instance, endeavored to put more weight on this aspect (1); but, in doing so, did he not undervalue the second aspect (2), causing Christ's merit, which is actually "superabundant", simply to *balance* the reality of the sin that requires to be "cancelled"? And as for those who, like Luther, were absolutely serious about the Son's self-surrender to sin's reality (1), was their insistence on this "punishment of the Innocent One" consistent with God's love (5)? Then there were those who, like Girard and Schwager (and Pannenberg too), proposed that it was not God but men who cast their sins onto the Lamb of God; this, however, seemed to give men the initiative in the redemptive process, while God, whose part it is always to love and forgive (K. Rahner), simply looked on, failing to measure up to the divine action of self-giving (1). A final criticism is this: the Cross was not an event that came straight down from heaven but rather the culmination of God's covenant history with mankind (epitomized by Israel): it was a genuine "*mystère d'alliance*" (Galot). Accordingly, the "partner" cannot be simply

317

the object of God's action: rather, in a mysterious way that in no way undermines God's initiative—and this does not come out in Galot—he must participate in uttering God's word. In other words, there must be an interplay, in the liberation of man (3), between the *gratia sola*, on the one hand, and man's creaturely freedom, on the other—a freedom that has *not* been eradicated by sin.

Are the systems hitherto attempted sufficiently dramatic? Or have they always failed to include or to give enough weight to one element or another that is essential to the complete dramatic plot? For no element may be excluded here: God's entire world drama is concentrated on and hinges on this scene. This is the theo-drama into which the world *and* God have their ultimate input; here absolute freedom enters into created freedom, interacts with created freedom and acts *as* created freedom. God cannot function here as a mere Spectator, allegedly immutable and not susceptible to influence; he is not an eternal, Platonic "sun of goodness", looking down on a world that is seen as a "*gigantomachia*", a "vast, perpetual scene of slaughter".[1] Nor, on the other hand, can man, guilty as he is in God's sight, lie passive and anaesthetized on the operating table while the cancer of his sin is cut out. How can all this be fitted together?

This is the climax and the turning point of the theo-drama, and as such it already contains and anticipates the final act, the "eschatology".[2] Here, more than ever, it is clear that the boundaries between the theological "loci" and "treatises" must come down. All these elements are involved simultaneously: each has its role, each belongs on stage. We need to appreciate a number of complementary aspects if the central action, that is, the relationship between the guilty and the Lamb who bears their sin, is to be interpreted: these arise, on the one hand, from internal relationships within the Godhead, that is, the doctrine of the Trinity, which forms the backdrop of the entire action, and, on the other hand, from extension within the world of time, that is, the covenant theology of the Old and New Testaments. It

---

[1] Plato, *Soph.*, 246 a, c; cf. *The Glory of the Lord* IV, 185.

[2] We have dealt with this aspect in detail in *Theo-Drama* III, 109ff.; 135ff.; 165ff., and also in *Zuerst Gottes Reich* (Benziger, 1966).

is not simply that the full doctrine of the Trinity can be un-
folded only on the basis of a theology of the Cross (and here
and in what follows, the "Cross" is always used in the Pauline-
Johannine sense—which is also that of the Synoptics—that is,
including the Resurrection) and is inseparable from it: rather, we
must see the doctrine of the Trinity as the ever-present, inner
presupposition of the doctrine of the Cross. In the same way,
and symmetrically to it, the doctrine of the covenant or of the
Church (including sacramental doctrine) must not be regarded
as a mere result of the Cross-event but as a constituent element
of it.

In what follows, we shall reflect on the way in which all the
constituent elements are concentrated and combined. To this
end, we shall try to see all the biblical data together, along with
all the valid and fruitful motifs that arise during the history of
theology. Our aim is not to erect a system, for the Cross explodes
all systems. Moreover, we are operating at the "essential" level,
excluding the question of how, given the death of the absolute
Word, it is still possible to utter meaningful words. We have
already addressed this issue[3] and will have to return to it in our
Theo-Logic.

1. The Cross and the Trinity

a. The Immanent and the Economic Trinity

Scripture clearly says that the events of the Cross can only be
interpreted against the background of the Trinity and through
faith; this is the thrust of its first and fifth motifs, namely, that
God (the Father) gave up his Son out of love for the world and
that all the Son's suffering, up to and including his being forsaken by God, is to be attributed to this same love. All soteriology must therefore start from this point. Of course, we must
not leave consideration of the Hypostatic Union aside, for how
could the man Jesus have borne away the world's sin, except
as God? But Jesus understands his "hour" as something given

---

[3] In *The Glory of the Lord* VII.

him by the Father; it is only on the basis of this "hour" that the Spirit will be set loose in and for the world.

It is only from the Cross and in the context of the Son's forsakenness that the latter's distance from the Father is fully revealed; when the unity between them is exposed, the uniting Spirit, their "We", actually appears in the form of mere distance. The surrendered Son, in bearing sin, that is, what is simply alien to God, appears to have lost the Father; so it seems as if this revelation of the "economic" Trinity brings out, for the first time, the whole seriousness of the "immanent" Trinity. This is why Hegel incorporates the world process into the internal "history of God":[4] the true life of the Spirit is not that which preserves itself from death and dissolution but that which looks negativity in the eye. Many theologians, in attempting to establish the relationship between immanent and economic Trinity, seem to lay such weight on the latter that the immanent Trinity, even if it is still distinguished from the other, becomes merely a kind of precondition for God's true, earnest self-revelation and self-giving.

In *K. Rahner*, this may be because he sees God primarily in terms of mystery; accordingly, he is concerned to preserve God's inner, triune nature as the mystery of mysteries. In his axiom, "The economic Trinity *is* the immanent Trinity, and vice versa",[5] the accent clearly lies on the divine Trinity that is genuinely revealed (uttered) and given to the world in the economy of grace: the Son is the self-utterance of the Father, the Spirit is the Father's self-giving together with the Son. Why not leave it at this (as, at times, P. Schoonenberg has done)? Surely this self-communication on God's part adequately shows him to be love, free and perfect? Why is the Son always held to be not only the *logos prophorikós* but also the *logos endiáthetos* of the Father? Because in the Gospel, says Rahner, Jesus experiences and proclaims himself to be *the* Son, not only vis-à-vis the Father but also in regard to men. That is, he thus distinguishes himself from the latter.[6] Is this sufficient to distinguish

---

[4] *Phänomenologie des Geistes* (1832), 26.

[5] *Theological Investigations* (London and Baltimore: Helicon, 1961–1979), *Myst. Sal.* 2 (1967), 327f.

[6] *Myst. Sal.* 2, 359.

Jesus from a mere "advocate of God on earth", particularly if the "late" descendence-Christology of the New Testament is regarded as an over-interpretation? We cannot deal with this question here. On the other hand, Rahner maintains that God utters himself *substantially* in the (incarnate) Logos and communicates himself equally *substantially* in the Holy Spirit. This shows, in contrast to H. Küng, that "the immanent (and necessary) Trinity is the necessary condition for God to be able freely to communicate himself."[7] And, with regard to this "necessary condition", Rahner can only say: "In one and the same God there exist real distinctions between him who is necessarily without origin, mediating himself to himself (the Father), him who is truly uttered to himself (the Son), and him who, for himself, is conceived and accepted in love (the Spirit). It is *because of this* that God can freely communicate himself 'ad extra'."[8] These concrete modes of being of the one God are not like self-consciousness (in the modern "personalist" sense), for God has only one self-consciousness. They cannot address each other as "Thou".[9] Hence it is only as man, not as the Son of God, that Jesus calls the Father "Thou". The process whereby "self-communication" takes place in God retains a strangely formal aspect,[10] which is hardly credible as the infinite prototype of God's "economic" self-squandering. In Rahner, it is only in the realm of the economic Trinity that the concept of "self-communication" has a convincing ring about it.

In *Moltmann*, we come across another form of identification, nearer to Hegel. For him, the Cross is not the privileged (and ultimately the solely valid) locus of the Trinity's self-revelation. Rather, it is the locus of the Trinity's authentic actualization. "The briefest expression of the Trinity is the divine act of the Cross, in which the Father causes the Son to sacrifice himself through the Spirit."[11] Moltmann bases himself on Rahner's formula but goes beyond the latter's position: "The 'bifurcation' in God must contain within it the whole turmoil of history."[12]

[7] *Ibid.*, 384, note 21. [8] *Ibid.*, 384.
[9] *Ibid.*, 366, note 29.
[10] It is related to Augustine's *imago Trinitatis* within the soul (the ground of the soul, reason, will/love).
[11] *The Crucified God* (London: SCM, 1974), 241.
[12] *Ibid.*, 246.

Thus "the Trinity is not a closed circle in heaven but an open eschatological process for men on earth, with the Cross as its origin."[13] So Moltmann is sucked into the undertow of White-head's "process theology",[14] which "overcomes the dichotomy between immanent and economic Trinity, as well as that between God's nature and his inner tri-unity".[15] It overcomes this latter dichotomy, according to Moltmann, since the attempt to approach God on the basis of a "one-nature" knowledge of God actually blocks the path to the genuine, Christian knowledge of God; God is known in the true dimensions of his love, not by analogy, but in the contradiction of the Cross, that is, *sub contrario*.[16] The Son's forsakenness on the Cross becomes a directly trinitarian event: the Father himself is forsaken,[17] death is located in God,[18] Jesus' death on the Cross is "God's death and God's suffering".[19] The most profound communion between Father and Son is "expressed at the very point where they are most profoundly separated, when Jesus dies on the Cross, forsaken by God and accursed."[20] "In the Christ-event", therefore, in the genuinely Hegelian manner, salvation is to be defined as a "negation [expiation] of the negation [sin]".[21]

Interpretations of this kind, like all talk of God's suffering, become inevitable wherever the internal divine process, "procession", is lumped together with the process of salvation history. Thus God is entangled in the world process and becomes a tragic, mythological God. A way must be found to see the immanent Trinity as the ground of the world process (including the crucifixion) in such a way that it is neither a formal process of self-communication in God, as in Rahner, nor entangled

---

[13] *Ibid.*, 249.   [14] *Ibid.*, 256.

[15] *Ibid.*, 245.

[16] *Ibid.*, 69; 32: "God is only [!] revealed as 'God' in his opposite: godlessness and abandonment by God." By contrast, "Man seeks to know God in the works and ordinances of the cosmos . . . in order to become divine himself . . . in pursuit of his own interests" (69). However, Moltmann does not stop at the level of these contradictions; for him, "the basis and starting point of analogy is this dialectic" (28); "Christian theology is not the 'end of metaphysics'"; rather, "it is free to take up metaphysics as a task of theology" (218).

[17] *Ibid.*, 192.   [18] *Ibid.*, 215f.

[19] *Ibid.*, 190, cf. 192.   [20] *Ibid.*, 243f.

[21] *Ibid.*, 261, cf. 230.

in the world process, as in Moltmann.[22] The immanent Trinity must be understood to be that eternal, absolute self-surrender whereby God is seen to be, in himself, absolute love; this in turn explains his free self-giving to the world as love, without suggesting that God "needed" the world process and the Cross in order to become himself (to "mediate himself").

It is possible to say, with Bulgakov, that the Father's self-utterance in the generation of the Son is an initial "kenosis" within the Godhead that underpins all subsequent kenosis. For the Father strips himself, without remainder, of his Godhead and hands it over to the Son; he "imparts" to the Son all that is his. "All that is thine is mine" (Jn 17:10). The Father must not be thought to exist "prior" to this self-surrender (in an Arian sense): he *is* this movement of self-giving that holds nothing back. This divine act that brings forth the Son, that is, the second way of participating in (and of *being*) the identical Godhead, involves the positing of an absolute, infinite "distance" that can contain and embrace all the other distances that are possible within the world of finitude, including the distance of sin. Inherent in the Father's

---

[22] The innumerable critical appraisals of Moltmann's work often raise this objection (yet perhaps not often enough!). Cf. *Diskussion über Jürgen Moltmanns Buch "Der gekreuzigte Gott"* (Munich: Kaiser, 1979: Ricoeur [25], Lochmann [33], Denbowski [36], Bauckham [52], Klappert, including an important comparison with K. Barth [70ff.], Miskotte [93], W. Kasper [146f.], Markus Barth [161]). Moltmann's reply, which retracts nothing of his identification of the "economic" with the "immanent" Trinity, is unsatisfying. How can we know about a radical distinction between the world and God if the creature (whether in communication with God or "forsaken" by God) does not have a fundamental awareness that it is *not* God? Moltmann may reject the "two-natures" theology in connection with the concrete phenomenon of Jesus, but it remains the inner presupposition of his trinitarian theology of the Cross. Kasper has pointed out that this primary distinction is indispensable (147) and that it frustrates any attempt to equate God-in-himself (understood as inner-divine "process") with God's intervention in the world process. Moltmann's speculations concerning God's freedom are inconsistent—he suggests that the idea that God enjoys freedom of choice is a Nominalist impossibility (170). Questions such as, "Can God content himself with being self-sufficient?"; "Could God be really satisfied to enjoy his own, untouched glory?" (170), show that, for him, considered apart from the world process, God is only an "abstract, self-contained Being" (155) and that he can only be "love" by "doing the good", in the free "overflowing of goodness" (172–73). Hence the really naïve question, "What right have we to say that the revealed Trinity must have, as its presupposition, an independent, 'essential' Trinity?" (179).

love is an absolute renunciation: he will not be God for himself
alone. He lets go of his divinity and, in this sense, manifests a
(divine) God-lessness (of love, of course). The latter must not be
confused with the godlessness that is found within the world,
although it undergirds it, renders it possible and goes beyond
it. The Son's answer to the gift of Godhead (of equal substance
with the Father) can only be eternal thanksgiving (*eucharistia*)
to the Father, the Source—a thanksgiving as selfless and unreserved as the Father's original self-surrender. Proceeding from
both, as their subsistent "We", there breathes the "Spirit" who
is common to both: as the essence of love, he maintains the infinite difference between them, seals it and, since he is the one
Spirit of them both, bridges it.

We cannot entertain any form of "process theology" that identifies the world process (including God's involvement in it, even
to the extent of the Cross) with the eternal and timeless "procession" of the Hypostases in God. Accordingly, there is only
one way to approach the trinitarian life in God: on the basis of
what is manifest in God's kenosis in the theology of the covenant
—and thence in the theology of the Cross—we must feel our
way back into the mystery of the absolute, employing a negative
theology that excludes from God all intramundane experience
and suffering, while at the same time presupposing that the possibility of such experience and suffering—up to and including its
christological and trinitarian implications—is grounded in God.
To think in such a way is to walk on a knife edge: it avoids all
the fashionable talk of "the pain of God" and yet is bound to
say that something happens in God that not only justifies the
possibility and actual occurrence of all suffering in the world
but also justifies God's sharing in the latter, in which he goes
to the length of vicariously taking on man's God-lessness. The
very thing that negative ("philosophical") theology prohibits
seems to be demanded by the *oikonomia* in Christ: faith, which
is beyond both yet feels its way forward from both, has an intuition of the mystery of all mysteries, which we must posit as the
unfathomable precondition and source of the world's salvation
history.

The action whereby the Father utters and bestows his whole
Godhead, an action he both "does" and "is", generates the Son.

This Son is infinitely Other, but he is also the infinitely Other *of the Father.* Thus he both grounds and surpasses all we mean by separation, pain and alienation in the world and all we can envisage in terms of loving self-giving, interpersonal relationship and blessedness. He is not the direct identity of the two but their presupposition, sovereignly surpassing them. Hence, too, he is not the mere foundation of a potential "history of God", a God who would achieve unity through the pain involved in "bifurcation" (within himself and/or in the world): he is the concrete, complete presupposition ("prepositing") of this bifurcation. God the Father can give his divinity away in such a manner that it is not merely "lent" to the Son: the Son's possession of it is "equally substantial". This implies such an incomprehensible and unique "separation" of God from himself that it *includes* and grounds every other separation—be it never so dark and bitter. This is the case even though this same communication is an action of absolute love, whose blessedness consists in bestowing, not only some thing, but itself. However, though we may have a stereoscopic view of these two aspects, we have no right to regard the Trinity one-sidedly as the "play" of an absolute "blessedness" that abstracts from concrete pain and lacks the "seriousness" of separation and death. Such a view would lead necessarily to a Hegelian process theology. "Love is as strong as hell" (". . . as death" AV, RSV): no, it is stronger, for hell is only possible given the absolute and real separation of Father and Son.

If, with believing hearts, we are to come to a deeper grasp of the primal divine drama—which is not a matter of temporal process—we must remember this: the Father, in uttering and surrendering himself without reserve, does not lose himself. He does not extinguish himself by self-giving, just as he does not keep back anything of himself either. For, in this self-surrender, he *is* the whole divine essence. Here we see both God's infinite power and his powerlessness; he cannot be God in any other way but in this "kenosis" within the Godhead itself. (Yet what omnipotence is revealed here! He brings forth a God who is of equal substance and therefore uncreated, even if, in this self-surrender, he must go to the very extreme of self-lessness.) It follows that the Son, for his part, cannot *be* and *possess* the absolute nature of

God except in the mode of receptivity: he receives this unity of omnipotence and powerlessness from the Father. This receptivity simultaneously includes the Son's self-givenness (which is the absolute presupposition for all the different ways in which he is delivered up to the world) and his filial thanksgiving (Eucharist) for the gift of consubstantial divinity. The world can only be created within the Son's "generation"; the world belongs to him and has him as its goal; only in the Son can the world be "recapitulated". Accordingly, in whatever way the Son is sent into the world (*processio* here is seen to be *missio*, up to and including the Cross), it is an integral part of his "co-original" thanksgiving for the world. He is delivered up to the world, yet the world is already his, even if it does not accept him. His thanksgiving is the eternal Yes to the gift of consubstantial divinity (that is, a divinity that is equally absolute). It is a Yes to the primal kenosis of the Father in the unity of omnipotence and powerlessness: omnipotence, since he can give all; powerlessness, since nothing is as truly powerful as the gift. Here, spanning the gulf of the Divine Persons' total distinctness, we have a correspondence between the Father's self-giving, expressed in generation, and the Son's thanksgiving and readiness (a readiness that goes to the limit of forgiveness). It is a profound mystery of faith. Thus the absolute is manifest as "We" in the identity of the gift-as-given and the gift-as-received in thanksgiving, which can only be such by attesting, maintaining and fueling the infinite distinction between Father and Son. Thus, within the distinction, the gift is not only the presupposition of an unsurpassable love: it is also the realized union of this love.

It is pointless to call this primal drama, which is above all time, "static", "abstract", "self-enclosed". Those who do so imagine that the divine drama only acquires its dynamism and its many hues by going through a created, temporal world and only acquires its seriousness and depth by going through sin, the Cross and hell. This view betrays a hubris, an exaggerated self-importance, on the part of creaturely freedom; it has succumbed to the illusion that man's ability to say No to God actually limits the divine omnipotence. It imagines that, by saying No to God, it is *man* who has drawn God into a momentous drama and made him consider how he (God) may extract himself from a trap he himself has set. On the contrary, it is the drama of the "emptying" of the Father's heart, in the generation of the Son, that contains and surpasses all possible drama between God and a world. For any world only has its place within that distinction between Father and Son that is maintained and bridged by the Holy Spirit. The drama of the Trinity lasts forever: the Father was never without the Son, nor were Father and Son ever without the Spirit. Everything temporal takes place within the embrace of the eternal action and as its consequence (hence *opera trinitatis ad extra communia*). So it is unnecessary—in fact, it is nonsense—to imagine a point of time within infinity when the triune God decides to create a world.[23]

We are not saying that the eternal separation in God is, in itself, "tragic" or that the Spirit's bridging of the distinction is the sublation of tragedy, that is, "comedy". Nor are we saying, in a Hegelian sense, that the trinitarian drama needs to pass through the contradictions of the world in order to go beyond the "play", to go beyond the "abstract", and become serious and concrete. Rather, we approach the mystery from two sides, that is, from that of negative theology, which excludes as "mythology" any notion that God *has to* be involved in the world process; and from the point of view of the world drama, the possibilities of which must be grounded in God. In pursuing these paths, we are led by the hand through the trinitarian passages of Scripture, particularly John, whose writings are most transparent to the Trinity. It is irrelevant to suggest that the Father's generation of the Son involves no risk and is therefore "undramatic": a world that is full of risks can only be created within the Son's *processio* (prolonged as *missio*); this shows that every "risk" on God's part is undergirded by, and enabled by, the power-less power of the divine self-giving. We cannot say that the Father is involved in "risk" by allowing his Son to go to the Cross, as if only then could he be sure of the earnestness of the Son's indebtedness and gratitude. However, if we ask whether there is

---

[23] This renders questionable Moltmann's assertion: "By assuming that God makes a decision with regard to himself (that is, to create a world), one is projecting time into God's eternity, for every 'decision' is characterized by the before-and-after structure of time." "Antwort auf die Kritik an 'Der gekreuzigte Gott' " in *Diskussion* (see previous note) 171–72.

suffering in God, the answer is this: there is something in God that can develop into suffering. This suffering occurs when the recklessness with which the Father gives away himself (and *all* that is his) encounters a freedom that, instead of responding in kind to this magnanimity, changes it into a calculating, cautious self-preservation. This contrasts with the essentially divine recklessness of the Son, who allows himself to be squandered, and of the Spirit who accompanies him.

b. The Creation, the Covenant, and the Cross-Eucharist

In creation, God fashions a genuine creaturely freedom and sets it over against his own, thus in some sense binding himself. It is possible to call this creation, together with the covenant associated with it—in Noah, and more patently in Abraham and Moses—a new "kenosis" on God's part, since he is thereby restricted, implicitly by creaturely freedom and explicitly by the covenant with its stated terms. He is "bound" in two ways. First, he has endowed man with a freedom that, in responding to the divine freedom, depends on nothing but itself. Like the ultimate ground that cannot have some further rationale beyond it and is hence ground-less—that is, the Father's self-surrender to the Son and their relationship in the Spirit (which grounds everything)—human freedom participates in the divine autonomy, both when it says Yes and when it says No. This is analogous to the way in which the Son receives the autonomy of the divine nature in the mode of receptivity (not, like the creature, in being created): the Father "has granted the Son also to have life in himself" (Jn 5:26).

The creature can refuse to acknowledge that it owes its freedom to the Creator. This is because freedom has no other origin but itself; it is not "caused" by anything but itself; in refusing, it deliberately ignores the fact that it did not acquire this self-origin by its own efforts. Absurdly, it tries to arrogate divine nature to itself without sharing in the Person who is always endowing, receiving, pouring forth and giving thanks for that nature—and who embodies its self-giving. Man's refusal reveals that abyss in the creature whereby it contradicts its own character as analogy and image, a character that arises necessarily from its position within the trinitarian relations. As a result of the creation, the most positive God-lessness on God's part has produced a real, negative godlessness; the latter is impossible to God because he is always in a covenant relationship with his creation, and particularly because of his formal covenant with Noah and Israel. It is "unbearable" for the rebellious, sinful, self-sufficient creature to look divine love in the face; this means that God too finds it "unbearable"—precisely because he has to "bear" it and it causes him to suffer. Man's refusal was possible because of the trinitarian "recklessness" of divine love, which, in its self-giving, observed no limits and had no regard for itself. In this, it showed both its power and its powerlessness and fundamental vulnerability (the two are inseparable). So we must say both things at once: within God's own self—for where else is the creature to be found?—and in the defenselessness of absolute love, God endures the refusal of this love; and, on the other hand, in the omnipotence of the same love, he cannot and will not suffer it.

We must remember that the creature's No, its wanting to be autonomous without acknowledging its origin, must be located within the Son's all-embracing Yes to the Father, in the Spirit; it is the refusal to participate in the autonomy with which the Son is endowed. This negation, however, is restriction: it is the refusal to follow truth to the very end. It is the lie, which only exists by courtesy of the truth and has already been overtaken by it. For the Son, following truth to the end means making a fitting response to the Father's total gift of himself[24] by freely

[24] Some object that the "generation" of the Son, as his identification with the "Word" of God shows, is intellectual by nature, whereas the volitional (love) only appears at the procession of the Holy Spirit. This view is partly based on arguments from anthropology (Augustine, Thomas) or from the Old Testament (the "word" that Yahweh addresses to Israel is primarily an instruction). But the latter argument forgets that Yahweh's word to Israel presupposes his election of Israel in an unfathomable love, and the former fails to realize that the entire psychological process of self-consciousness is initiated by the prior address of a "thou": it cannot, therefore, be applied to God, who has no antecedent conditions. In the Wisdom literature, there is a definite link between man's love for the divine word (as Wisdom) and the word that God himself communicates to man out of love; love is not limited to the gift of *ruach* (spirit). In the New Covenant, God (primarily as Father) *is* utter love, particularly in the sending (the surrender)

and thankfully allowing himself to be poured forth by the Father, a response that is made in absolute spontaneity and in absolute "obedience" to the Father (and "obedience" here means the readiness to respond and correspond to the Father). Both take place in a generous, eucharistic availability [*Gelöstheit*] that matches the limitless proportions of the divine nature. The creature's No is merely a twisted knot within the Son's pouring-forth; it is left behind by the current of love.

We can indeed say, as Greek "emanation" theology does, that the Father expresses his own fullness in the Son, so that the Son imitates God (his "world of ideas") in every possible way. At the same time, we must maintain that the Son, in responding to and accepting his Father's self-giving, is ready to pour *himself* forth in any way the Father may determine. Given the plan to bring about creatures endowed with freedom, the ultimate form of this pouring-forth will be that of the Eucharist, which, as we know it, is intimately connected with the Passion, *pro nobis*. This "readiness" (active, eager obedience) can and must also be understood as a spontaneous "offer", so that there can be no question of the Son being "forced" to do something by a will that is exclusively the Father's. Creation, if it is to be free, can only be envisaged and decided upon by the entire triune God; it follows that this decision must be regarded as standing from all eternity.

This being so, we are justified in thinking backward from the Eucharist—the Son's ultimate self-giving—to the covenant that it makes possible, and from there again to the creation that gains its meaning from the covenant. Covenant and creation are not only rendered possible by the Son's "eucharistic" response to the Father: they are "surpassed" by it, since both of them can only become reality within the embrace of the Son's response. This does not rob the creature of its inherent freedom, its freedom to act within the covenant with God; its own ground-lessness is not expropriated and stifled by the "omnipotence" of divine goodness (as in Islam, for instance). Within the Trinity, God's all-powerful love is also powerlessness, not only giving the Son

---

of the Son. The Son's sending refers back to his coming forth from the Father (cf. the context of John 1:13, according to the reading "*hos . . . egennēthē*").

an equal, divine freedom but also giving the creature itself—
the image of God—a genuine power of freedom and taking it
utterly seriously. What it *does* mean is that, because of the Son's
all-embracing *eucharistia*, God cannot be entangled in some kind
of tragic role; he is not torn in two, which would signify a per-
sistent, unconquerable hell in God.

We spoke of a first "kenosis" of the Father, expropriating
himself by "generating" the consubstantial Son. Almost automatically, this first kenosis expands to a kenosis involving the
whole Trinity. For the Son could not be consubstantial with the
Father except by self-expropriation; and their "We", that is, the
Spirit, must also be God if he is to be the "personal" seal of
that self-expropriation that is identical in Father and Son. For
the Spirit does not want anything "for himself" but, as his revelation in the world shows, wants simply to be the pure manifestation and communication of the love between Father and
Son (Jn 14:26; 16:13–15). This primal kenosis makes possible
all other kenotic movements of God into the world; they are
simply its consequences. The first "self-limitation" of the triune
God arises through endowing his creatures with freedom. The
second, deeper, "limitation" of the same triune God occurs as
a result of the covenant, which, on God's side, is indissoluble,
whatever may become of Israel. The third kenosis, which is not
only christological but involves the whole Trinity, arises through
the Incarnation of the Son alone: henceforth he manifests his
eucharistic attitude (which was always his) in the *pro nobis* of the
Cross and Resurrection for the sake of the world.

Man's freedom is left intact, even when perverted into sin.
This has been a patristic theologoumenon since the time of Irenaeus: God does not overwhelm man; he leads him to his goals
peithei, suadelā.[25] This indicates no inability on God's part; it is
not that he is uncertain whether he can convince rebellious man.
It arises from the power-lessness that, as we have seen, is identical with his omnipotence: he is above the necessity to dominate,
let alone use violence. This identity of powerlessness and omnipotence sheds much light on what we have already said about

[25] The motif appears in a different form in Augustine and his "*voluptate trahi*"
(*In Joh.* tr. 26).

God's "holiness" and on John's use of the term "glorification", where the powerlessness of the Cross and the omnipotence of the Resurrection are seen together.

The fact that human freedom and its perversion are always exercised within the Son's *eucharistia*—since, reading backward from the Cross to the covenant and from there to the creation, the latter is the precondition for every possible and real world —shows the confrontation between ground-less divine love and ground-less human sin: "It is to fulfill the word. . . . 'They hated me without a cause'". But "If I had not come and spoken to them, they would not have sin" (Jn 15:24, 22). Here, the "light" that has come into the world shines in the darkness from the beginning of creation (Jn 1:4–5) and "lightens every man" (v. 9).

All this is preparatory to a doctrine of salvation that—by providing what we might call a trinitarian substructure—endeavors to avoid all the one-sidedness found in the historico-theological systems. Now that the patristic "exchange of places" no longer stands unsupported and unprepared, it is not in need of the Lutheran complement (which is in fact just as unsupported). The second motif, the *commercium*, is now firmly based on the first, that is, *the Son's self-surrender*, insofar as the latter is the "economic" representation of *the Father's trinitarian, loving self-surrender* (the fifth motif). In this context, the third scriptural topic, that is, *redemption, understood as liberation and ransom*, becomes accessible. It will be discussed in connection with the motif of the "exchange". Finally, the context also accommodates the fourth motif, namely, *initiation into the life of the Trinity*, which arises directly from the foregoing.

2. Sin and the Crucified

a. On the Nature of "Representation"

The foregoing complements and completes the many observations on the Trinity to be found in both parts of the second volume [that is, volumes two and three of the English edition— TRANS.].[1] How can someone "represent" sinners? We saw this

---

[1] Cf. *Theo-Drama* II, 203, 244, 256, 266ff., 284, 295f., 330; III, 168ff., 172, 183–91, 199f., 224–28.

"representation" of sinners primarily in the traditional motifs of "head" and "body", according to the Pauline *en Christōi*, and in Christ's mediatorship in creation,[2] but as yet the preliminary model of the *admirabile commercium* lacked an adequate theological foundation. However, our discussion of the latter in the present volume has shown us how to see the "exchange of places" as ultimately grounded in the immanent Trinity: the Trinity does not hover "unmoved" above the events of the Cross (the view that Christ is somehow "above" his abandonment by God and continues to enjoy the beatific vision), nor does it get entangled in sin as in a process theology à la Moltmann or Hegel, becoming part of a mythology or cosmic tragedy.

In endeavoring to strike a path between these extremes, we do not imagine that we have "seen through" the mystery of God's redemptive *kenosis*. It consists in the identification of the divine Logos with the man Jesus (*Theo-Drama* III, 228), an event that is itself in continuity with the antecedent *kenōsis* of the Word of God in his covenant with Israel. (The latter continues the covenant with mankind as a whole, which is itself based on the prior creation of creatures endowed with freedom.) This *kenosis*, in all its ever-intensifying and ever more concentrated stages, remains God's very own secret; he thereby reveals and communicates his own nature to the world. We are only establishing negative limits, so to speak, by eliminating the two above-mentioned extremes: if Jesus can be forsaken by the Father, the conditions for this "forsaking" must lie within the Trinity, in the absolute distance/distinction between the Hypostasis who surrenders the Godhead and the Hypostasis who receives it. And while the distance/distinction between these two is eternally confirmed and maintained ("kept open") by the Hypostasis who proceeds from them, it is transcended in the Godhead that is the absolute gift they have in common.

Since the world cannot have any other *locus* but within the distinction between the Hypostases (there is nothing outside God: *Theo-Drama* II, 260ff.), the problems associated with it—its sinful alienation from God—can only be solved at this *locus*. The creature's No resounds at the "place" of distinction within the

---

[2] *Theo-Drama* III, 230ff.

Godhead. The Son, the "light" and "life" of the world, who enters into this "darkness" of negation by becoming man, does not need to change his own "place" when, shining in the darkness, he undertakes to "represent" the world. He can do this on the basis of his *topos*, that is, of his absolute distinction, within the Trinity, from the Father who bestows Godhead.

If, once the Incarnation has taken place, we ask who burdens the Son, the "Lamb of God", the "Lamb as though it had been slain", with the unimaginable load of all the world's No to divine love, the answer—a preliminary answer, but nonetheless real— must be: men themselves in their darkness. Girard's "scapegoat mechanism" can prove helpful here to some degree: neither Christians, Jews nor pagans are prepared to admit to being responsible. Further light may be shed here by Pannenberg: precisely because they have followed the divine Law to the very end (with regard to the letter), the Jews are bound to reject this Messiah as a blasphemer (confirming what Paul says in Galatians 2:19),[3] and the Romans are bound to crucify him as an agitator against the divinely appointed state order.[4] But it is equally clear that nothing would be achieved by men unloading their sin if the one onto whom they load it were incapable of receiving it in its totality, as *what it is*: it presupposes that he is both willing and able to bear sin. His willingness springs from the mission given him by the Father, which is rooted in his coming-forth from the Father; more profoundly, it is grounded in the distinction we have established, within the mission, between the "life", which is preparatory, and the "hour", which is the goal of his expectation.

The "hour" is the hour of the penetrating "power of darkness" (Lk 22:53). Like no other hour, it is an integral part of the Son's mission; whatever it may contain, he affirms it from the very outset. *He* accepts it: it is not imposed on him from the outside. However, it is entirely different in quality from what preceded it: it calls for an *inner* appropriation of what is ungodly and hostile to God, an identification with that darkness of alienation from God into which the sinner falls as a result

---

[3] Cf. the context established by H. Schlier, *Der Galaterbrief*, 96–101.
[4] *Grundzüge der Christologie*, 215ff.

of his No. Consequently, in accepting the "hour", the Son—
essentially bound to the Father in loving obedience—can only
be totally overwhelmed by it. All he can do, in the trembling
weakness of mortal fear, is to pray for it to pass him by and then,
"strengthened" (even in weakness) by the angel, to affirm it as
his Father's will, not his own. Indeed, it cannot be the Son's will
to appear before the Father bearing the No of the whole world;
his will is only to carry out the Father's will—his mission—
into ultimate darkness. This will is the *sponte* of which Anselm
continually speaks; according to Anselm, the Son exhibits it in
heaven (in the trinitarian decision concerning the Incarnation),
in becoming man and in suffering. But because, in the economy of salvation, the trinitarian decision can only be carried out
by the Father making the divine will known to the incarnate
Son through the Holy Spirit (in the "trinitarian inversion", cf.
Theo-Drama III, 183ff.), the impression is given that the Father[5]
—*cooperante Spiritu Sancto*—loads the Son with the sins of the
world (to the annoyance of all Anselm's opponents). However,
as Thomas rightly says, it is not a question of God overpowering
either the suffering Son or the vanquished worldly powers but
of that powerlessness that is indivisible from the divine omnipotence. *As such*, because it is God's truth and righteousness, this
powerlessness is more powerful than all worldly power.[6]

Here the God-man drama reaches its acme: perverse finite freedom casts all its guilt onto God, making him the sole accused, the
scapegoat,[7] while God allows himself to be thoroughly affected
by this, not only in the humanity of Christ but also in Christ's
trinitarian mission. The omnipotent powerlessness of God's love
shines forth in the mystery of darkness and alienation between
God and the sin-bearing Son; this is where Christ "represents"

[5] Desideravit quidem anima hominis illius salutem nostram, quam in morte
sua consistens sciebat, et propter illam quam desiderabat, hanc tolerabat. . . . Sed
quia etiam Christus ipse alibi profitetur non se venisse voluntatem suam facere
sed voluntatem Patris, . . . quando eam (mortem) videlicet pro angustia sua re-
formidabat et transire potius quam venire volebat, quasi nolens sustinuit iniunc-
tam sibi a Patre oboedientiam. Abelard, *In Rom*. lib. 2 (PL 178, 876).

[6] Christus venerat dissolvere opera diaboli non potestative agendo, sed magis
ab eo et eius membris patiendo, ut sic diabolum vinceret iustitia, non potestate.
S. Th. III, 41, 1 ad 2.

[7] Schwager, 202.

us, takes our place: what is "experienced" is the opposite of what the facts indicate.[8]

It is a mistake to speak of Christ's work on our behalf as something removed from the darkness of sin, something that overthrows sin through pure merit. This is the idea of the "undeserved", perfect death of Jesus as put forward by Anselm and K. Rahner. Nor, on the other hand, can it be interpreted as an identification of the Crucified with the actual No of sin itself; Luther says that this No at least begins to surface in Jesus, but he "swallows it down". Jesus does experience the darkness of the sinful state,[9] not in the same way as the (God-hating) sinner experiences it (unless the sinner is spared such experience), but nonetheless in a deeper and darker experience. This is because it takes place in the profound depths of the relations between the divine Hypostases—which are inaccessible to any creature.

Thus it is just as possible to maintain that Jesus' being forsaken by God was the opposite of hell[10] as to say that it *was* hell (Luther, Calvin) or even the ultimate heightening of hell (Quenstedt). If, contemplating the Cross, we read the terrible warnings that Yahweh addresses to his people if it breaks the covenant (Lev 26; Dt 28:15−68)—and the covenant is broken more radically than ever before in the rejection of the Messiah—we get some idea of what it means for Jesus to be under the "curse" of the Law and to be "made to be sin". At all events, his experience of being abandoned on the Cross is timeless. Here too it is anal-

---

[8] "The depths of the saying [Christ's cry of dereliction on the Cross] are too deep to be plumbed, but the least inadequate interpretations are those that find in it a sense of desolation in which Jesus felt the horror of sin so deeply that for a time the closeness of his communion with the Father was obscured. Glover writes: 'I have sometimes thought there never was an utterance that reveals more amazingly the distance between feeling and fact.' " V. Taylor, *St. Mark*, 2d ed. (1966), 594.

[9] Here we should look back to the Temptations of Jesus: they are an anticipation of the Passion, an inner experiencing, with sinners, of what the attraction of sin is: cf. *Theo-Drama* III, 168f. On the dramatic dimension of the history of temptation: Duquoc, *Christologie* I (Cerf, 1972), 52−71; Lohmeyer, *Vater Unser*, 3d ed. (Göttingen, 1952), 134−46; Michl in *Handbuch der Dogmengeschichte* II, 26, 16 (refs. note 21).

[10] C'est exactement dans le sens opposé à l'enfer que va l'oeuvre opérée par Jésus. L'enfer est haine, . . . l'oeuvre du Christ est une oeuvre d'amour et d'union. La mort qu'elle demande est tout le contraire de ce qu'est la mort éternelle. E. Mersch, 345.

ogous to hell. This is why its actuality persists through all ages of the world. Jesus' agony lasts until the end of the world (Pascal); in fact, it goes right back to the world's beginning. His mortal wounds are eternally open (Bérulle). This timelessness is confirmed, in some precision, by those Christian mystics who were privileged to experience something of the dark night of the Cross.[11]

Whether or not the concept of "punishment" is to be applied to Christ's sufferings on the Cross is largely a matter of language. If we say that an innocent man as such cannot be "punished", even if he is atoning for the guilty,[12] we shall avoid the term. It is possible to distinguish, like Hilary,[13] between the *sensus poenae*, which Christ experienced, and the *vis poenae*, for *pietatis est susceptio peccatorum ista, non criminis* (Ambrose).[14] It is essential to maintain, however, that the Crucified does not bear the burden as something external: he in no way distances himself from those who by rights should have to bear it. (Indeed, he is *in*

---

[11] "When the soul is seized by purifying contemplation, it feels in the most vivid manner death's shadow, its groanings and the pains of hell. For it feels God-less, punished and rejected by God, the object of his displeasure and anger. The soul feels all this and more: it seems to the soul that this condition will last for ever." St. John of the Cross, *The Dark Night* II, 6, 2 to II, 9. St. John does not give a directly christological interpretation of his experiences; however, they are underpinned by the principle that the more vigorously the fire of God's love burns in the soul, the more the soul is plunged into darkness because of its imperfections. Each attack of darkness seems eternal.

[12] "Le principe de la substitution pénale, inacceptable en thèse générale et en droit strict (car il est de l'essence du châtiment de tomber sur le coupable) prend une toute autre valeur à l'égard de la Rédemption:

"d'abord à raison de la solidarité de nature qui fait du Christ le représentant né de l'humanité entière,

"puis à raison de la générosité qui le fait s'offrir spontanément seul pour tous, aux coups de la justice divine,

"enfin à raison du bon plaisir divin qui agrée la substitution." A. d'Alès, *Le Dogme catholique de la Rédemption*, 2d ed. (1913), 180. Similarly F. Prat, *Théologie de Saint Paul* (1925) II, 256; Galtier, *De Incarnatione et Redemptione* (1926): "Ille proinde qui, sine ullo sui debito, poenam assumit ex mera pro reo charitate, dici sane potest aliquo modo puniri pro alio, nam patitur materialiter poenam alii debitam, sed tamen illa poena non habet pro illo rationem poenae", 398.

[13] *Comm in Ps.* 54, 13 (PL 9, 554C). Cf. *Ps.* 69 (68) 9; *De Trin.* 10, 47.

[14] *In Ps.* 37, 6, quoted in H. G. W. Turner, *The Patristic Doctrine of Redemption* (London: Mowbray, 1952), 104, 107.

them eucharistically!) Subjectively, therefore, he can experience it as "punishment", although objectively speaking, in his case, it cannot be such. The sufferings of Christ on man's behalf are far above all possible sufferings entailed by sin. Human speech is inadequate to express this: our best course is to follow the biblical language of A. Feuillet[15] and the carefully balanced words of S. Bulgakov,[16] who establishes an analogy between what the sinner would have to expect from God's wrath and the Son's forsakenness by God—which, in a truly divine manner, utterly surpasses the sinner's expectation. If we realize the ground-lessness of man's free No in the face of the purely gracious (and hence ground-less) Yes of God's love, it is clear that the expiation, the expurgation of this ground-less sin must involve a transfiguration through suffering that is surpassingly "ground-less" [etwa Über-Grundloses] in a way we cannot imagine.

Here again we are confronted with the fundamental theodramatic law of world history: the greater the revelation of divine (ground-less) love, the more it elicits a groundless (Jn 15:25) hatred from man. No end to this escalation can be envisaged, so the Cross must be deferred to an endless end (since Jesus has atoned for all sin). The Cross is raised up at the end of evil, at the end of hell.[17] The Cross, like the Son of God himself, is unique, peerless.

b. The Cup of Wrath

The cup mentioned on the Mount of Olives is God's cup of wrath, often referred to in the Old Covenant,[1] filled with the wine of his anger.[2] It enters into the one who drinks it[3] (by contrast with the other images of God's wrath, that is, fire or

---

[15] See above, 314f.

[16] See above, 313f.

[17] Gregory of Nyssa realized this (PG 46, 1132), cf. the commentary by Jerôme Gaith, La Conception de la liberté chez Grégoire de Nysse (Paris: Vrin, 1953), 143f., 147.

[1] Is 51:17, 22; Jer 13:13; 25:15–17, 27ff.; 48:26; 49:12; 51:7; Ezek 23:32–34; Hab 2:15–16; Obad 16; Zech 12:2; Ps 79:9; Lam 4:21.

[2] Jer 25:16; Rev 14:8.

[3] Job 21:20; Is 51:17: "to the dregs".

inundation,[4] and makes him "reel". God alone himself treads this wine of wrath in the wine press.[5]

God is angry with the sinner on account of his sin. This is a constant theme of Scripture, from the first book to the last. Enlightenment philosophy campaigned against God being portrayed as having "emotions", but with only limited justification.[6] Lactantius, in his courageous writing "On the Wrath of God", countered the adoption by many Church Fathers of the notion of God's *apatheia*; modern Protestant theology (since Schleiermacher) and Catholic theology too would do well to reread Lactantius. He says that a God who was not involved with the world could not enjoy happiness in himself.[7] And a God who only loved and did not hate evil ("a plausible and appealing suggestion") would contradict himself: "If God is not angry with the godless and unrighteous, he cannot love the God-fearing and righteous."[8] In such a case, we would not owe him reverence, which is the foundation of religion. And religion in turn is the foundation of all wisdom, morality, justice and social order.[9] Furthermore, it is impossible for God to announce to the world a law of reward for the good and punishment for evil, and then let this law operate so to speak without his own active participation.[10] Having established the world order, he cannot renounce his freedom nor retire from his obligation to punish and forgive. Moreover, since God is gracious, he must be able to show anger too, "for grace cannot exist without wrath"; "it is in very wrath that grace is demonstrated."[11] But God's anger is not an irrational emotion (which in man's case would have to be held in check): "he is not ruled by anger but directs it according to his good pleasure."[12]

---

[4] Texts in Stählin, art. *orgē*, in *ThW* V, 399, 438.

[5] Is 53:1–6; Rev 19:15. The image of the wine press is common to the whole of the Old Testament as an expression of the crushing of the guilty in God's wrathful judgment: Gen 49:9–12; Jer 25:30; Is 63:1–6; Joel 4:13.

[6] Cf. M. Pohlenz, "Vom Zorne Gottes" in *FRL* 12 (1909).

[7] *De ira Dei* 4.   [8] *Ibid.*, 5.

[9] *Ibid.*, 7, 8, 12.

[10] This objection is finally raised in no. 19. God's will is one with the law he has established: no. 16.

[11] *Ibid.*, 16.   [12] *Ibid.*, 21.

In the Old Testament, God's "anger" is very close to his "jealous" watch (*zēlos*) over his covenant, his "jealousy" regarding his chosen Israel. He has committed himself to Israel, and yet it continually betrays him.[13] Thus Yahweh's anger is primarily directed against Israel: even at the making of the covenant (Ex 19), he threatens anyone who would presume to come too close to the divine majesty. Through all Israel's history, this "anger" is constantly being provoked by the people's falling-away and by the failure of its representatives. The pre-Exilic prophets announce God's anger upon those who, on account of their election, indulge in a false sense of security and feel that they are safe from God's wrathful judgment.[14] This judgment may be delayed, it may be averted by conversion, but it can also become fixed and irrevocable, so that all intercession is futile, even forbidden. True, "God's anger is the urging of the Holy Spirit, asserting his absolute claim of sovereignty",[15] but it does so within his gracious and ultimately loving covenant. So in no way does it exclude his mercy; in fact, it should be regarded as a function of mercy, as we find in certain daring expressions of the divine mercy: "In overflowing wrath for a moment I hid my face from you, but with everlasting love I will have compassion on you" (Is 54:8); "For his anger is but for a moment, and his favor is for a lifetime" (Ps 30:5). God's divinity actually requires that grace should triumph in him over wrath (Hos 11:8ff.; Jer 31:20).[16] Ultimately, however, God's anger cannot be contained within any system: Sirach wisely lets the two stand juxtaposed: "With him are both mercy and wrath" (5:6). Within the horizon of the Old Testament, it is unthinkable that the "Day of the Lord", which brings everything to light, could be a revelation solely of mercy and not also of wrath.

Contrary to the unconsidered utterances of modern theologians, we must maintain that "anger is an essential and ineradicable feature . . . even in the New Testament picture of God.

---

[13] There is a discussion of these texts in the article "*zēlos*" in *ThW* (Stumpff).

[14] Fichtner in the article "*orgē*" in *ThW*, 398. Of course, God's anger is also directed against the nations (cf. the oracles concerning the nations in Amos, Isaiah, Jeremiah, Ezekiel, Obadiah, Nahum, Habakkuk and Joel).

[15] *Ibid.*, 408–9.

[16] Cf. also 2 Macc 5:17, 20; 7:33; Wis 11:9; 16:5; 18:20–25.

As the entire New Testament knows, it is a terrible thing to fall into the hands of the living God (Heb 10:31); God has the power to save and to destroy (James 4:12); he is feared because, beyond bodily death, he has the power to consign body and soul to hell (Lk 12:5; Mt 10:28)—and all this presupposes an awareness of God's anger."[17] The love in God's heart is laid bare in all its radicality, showing its absolute opposition to anything that would injure it. And it is precisely the trinitarian form of this revelation of love in Jesus Christ that allows us to discern the necessary unity of love and anger. Jesus' anger, which breaks through in so many places, flares up wherever there is resistance to his mission and the tasks arising from it, for such resistance offends the Father's love manifest within him, the triune Holy Spirit. His anger is not a purely human anger; it is an anger that is part of his ministry, and so it is a revelation of the divine attitude. He, the world's Lord, is angry with the rebellious enemies of God: he angrily dismisses Satan (Mt 4:10; cf. in Peter also, Mt 16:23); threatens demons (Mk 9:25), is "deeply moved" in the face of the power of death (Jn 11:33, 38); he is appalled at the demonic in man (Jn 8:44), particularly the hypocrisy of the Pharisees (Mt 15:7 passim), this "brood of vipers" (Mt 12:34), these murderers of those sent by his Father (Mt 23:31). We read that Jesus, "in warm indignation" (Mk 1:41–42 NEB) at a leper's condition, "sternly charged him" not to make him known, anticipating the leper's subsequent disobedience. This latter turn of phrase (cf. Mk 3:12; 8:30) may also underline the gravity of the event (cf. Mt 9:30). A similar interpretation should be given to Jesus' constant rebuking of the disciples (even after the Resurrection) at their lack of faith. Matthew 17:17: "How long am I to bear with you?"; Mark 7:18: "Then are you also without understanding?" "And he upbraided them for their unbelief and hardness of heart, because they had not believed those who saw him after he had risen" (Mk 16:14). He is filled with "anger" and "grief" (Mk 3:5) at the Pharisees' hard-heartedness, which increases with every new sign he gives of God's love, until they eventually determine that he must die. In the parable, the "master of the house" becomes angry (Lk 14:21) because his invi-

---

[17] Stählin in the article "orgē", ThW, 424.

tation is refused with cheap excuses. Ultimate wrath overtakes
the murderous vineyard workers ("He will put those wretches
to a miserable death", Mt 21:41), a symbol of the divine anger
at Israel's rejection of the Son. It also overtakes the hireling who
has so crassly offended against Jesus' new commandment: "In
anger his lord delivered him to the torturers, till he should pay
all his debt. So also my heavenly Father will do to every one
of you, if . . ." (Mt 18:34f.). In both these cases, we are already
confronted with the reciprocal escalation of love and sin: ever-
greater mercy arouses ever-greater anger. The same polarization
is indicated by the terrible "woes" against the towns that had refused the invitation to penance (Mt 11:20ff.); a parable speaks of
the cursing of an unfruitful tree, a symbol of Israel (Mk 11:14),
while in the very next verses the desecrated Temple is violently
cleansed ("he overturned the tables . . ." Mk 11:15ff.), Jesus
actually making a whip of cords for the purpose (Jn 2:15). In
Jesus, too, anger is mixed with compassion, just as the prophets
find both aspects merging into each other in the covenant God's
attitude to Israel. It is true that Yahweh's anger is directed primarily at the evil shepherds of his people, just as Jesus' anger is
primarily against the leaders of the nation, whereas his compassion and his ministry apply to the "sheep who have no shepherds" (Mk 6:34), the "lost sheep of the house of Israel" (Mt
15:24). But it is also true that, right from the start, entire towns
(including Nazareth) refuse to accept Jesus' message, and in the
end the whole nation "as one man" will cry "Crucify him!"

There is no doubt about it: the coming of Jesus has aroused
the world's slumbering No. It is no accident that the demons are
the first to recognize him: they must appear in the eschatological
confrontation "before the time" (that is, of the Last Judgment:
Mt 8:29). Their resistance, but even more the growing resistance
of the Chosen People, this "sinful and adulterous generation"
(Mk 8:38), provokes the eschatological wrath of the Son of Man.
On the day of his glory, he will be ashamed of those who now
are ashamed of him and his words (*ibid.*).

In the Synoptics, we discern something like a dramatic plot
in which the progressive revelation of Jesus' love provokes the
resistance of those addressed, and this in turn heightens wrath.

Mention of ultimate perdition comes mostly toward the end.[18] In John, however, the confrontation of light and darkness has become somehow fixed, immobile; the light is love and, when it meets darkness, is both *krisis* and "anger" at the same time. To that extent, the atmosphere informing Jesus' disputations with the Jews can be compared to that in Greek tragedy, where anger enfolds and governs all the characters and all the action.[19] The difference is that, in tragedy, anger is the ultimate horizon (even if, through catharsis, the victim becomes "holy"), whereas, in John, the severity of the clash manifests the severity of offended divine love. *Krisis* contains a tacit element of anger; it comes to light, unveiled, in the Johannine Apocalypse with all the paraphernalia of Old Testament "wrath" symbolism: the fires of anger, the cups of God's anger that cause men to stagger, the bowls of wrath poured out on the earth, the wine presses spurting blood; what is depicted here is not only the wrath of God but, explicitly, the "wrath of the Lamb" (Rev 6:16; cf. 14:10).

The Lamb can only ride out to battle as the "Lion of Judah" (Rev 5:5) and tread "the wine press of the fury of the wrath of God the Almighty" because he stands on God's throne as the "slain" and "slaughtered" Lamb. He has diverted onto himself all the anger of God at the world's faithlessness. He himself has drained the cup and experienced the full extent of what, in an inchoate and anticipatory way, the Old Testament prophets underwent. This immeasurably expands the hiatus in Jesus' being between his *life*, in which he manifests both the love and the anger of God, and the *hour*, in which God's wrath is poured out on the representatives. In his work *The Prophets*, A. Heschel has convincingly set forth God's passionate initiative (his "pathos") on behalf of his creation, his saving plan, his chosen ones.[20] This "pathos" is not an "attribute of being", some

---

[18] Mt 21:19; 23:13–46; 22:12f.; 23:13–39; 24:51; 25:12, 29, 41.

[19] Cf. the descriptions in R. Girard, *La Violence et le sacré* (Paris: Grasset, 1972), 102–25. Also Kleinknecht in *ThW* V, 383: in Attic tragedy, anger is "important and an element of the tragic"; it is "not blind anger but a demonic excess of will inherent in the nature of the tragic person, going hand in hand with *ananke*, that is, necessity and fate."

[20] Abraham J. Heschel, *The Prophets* (New York/Evanston: Harper and Row, 1955. A short preliminary sketch had already appeared in Cracow [1936], enti-

"immutable quality" of God,[21] but an aspect of his personal engagement for creation and covenant. It is his "constant care and concern",[22] distinguishing him from other national and covenant gods. He is "moved and affected" by events in the world; he is "involved, even stirred by the conduct of man".[23] Thus he experiences delight or grief, shows agreement or indignation, knows reciprocal love or its opposite, namely, that "suspended love"[24] that is anger. This "pathos" on God's part is the opposite of a supposedly a-pathetic divinity. It is not an irrational emotion but, on the contrary, identical with God's ethos,[25] which can never be detached from his free involvement that is controlled by love and righteousness. "Before the Torah, there was the covenant, which was entered out of God's love for the Patriarchs."[26] ("Law" arises where God's "ethos" *is* so detached.) Thus God's pathos is *not* anthropomorphic.[27] The prophet is a man who is sym-pathetically open, by divine design, to God's divine pathos toward his world.[28] What such a man experiences, thinks and utters comes from God to the world; it does not ascend from the world to God.[29] So, like Jeremiah, he can be filled with the tension in God between wanting to love and having to punish;[30] he is filled with a sense of the offense offered to God,[31] of the fate prepared for him in the world.[32] He can be

---

tled *Die Prophetie*.) Moltmann has tried to fit Heschel into his system (that is, the identity of immanent and economic Trinity), but Heschel explicitly rejects any attempt to interpret the prophetic utterances in terms of Western metaphysics, cf. esp. chapters 13–18, and particularly p. 483. God's *pathos* has nothing whatever to do with any mythological suffering, dying and rising God (Tammuz, Osiris, and so forth). Rather, it is his "moral abhorrence" of the failure of his people (or of individuals) to respond to his covenant.

[21] *Ibid.*, 231.   [22] 279.   [23] 224.

[24] 295.   [25] 219.

[26] 230. "Pathos denotes, not an idea of goodness, but a living care; not an immovable example, but an outgoing challenge, a dynamic relation between God and man; not mere feeling or passive affection, . . . but a passionate summons", 224. On righteousness as the measure of this *pathos*, cf. 288. Where God's free love (the foundation) is offended, his indignation is just: Jer 1:16; Ps 7:11f.

[27] 271, cf. 234: unlike that of other gods.

[28] 301–23.   [29] 271.   [30] 44, 108.

[31] Hosea's experience of marriage, Jeremiah's loincloth: 52, 117f.

[32] 112.

filled to "inebriation"[33] with God's brooding grief at the hardness of heart of the man to whom he wishes to speak[34] and with God's anger, which (as in Jeremiah) can epitomize a whole age of the world.[35] And since the prophet is a mediator, representing God to his people, but also the guilty people to God, he is, as it were, rent asunder and burned by this anger (Jer 20:9). "I am full of the wrath of the Lord; I am weary of holding it in"(Jer 6:11). The prophet feels himself "deceived", even "violated" by God (Jer 20:7).[36] So he comes to hate his calling,[37] since it means that he, with his message, is hated and persecuted by the people, whereas God fills him with the "bitterness" of his words of wrath.

Previously we described the path from prophecy, via the Suffering Servant, to Christ, as an ever-deeper descent down the "ladder of obedience", ultimately arriving at the perfect Incarnation of the divine Word.[38] Now this view is complemented and confirmed by the ever-deeper descent of God's wrath upon the mediatorial man. This descent of God's anger goes so far that the mediator may no longer announce the world of wrath (like Jeremiah and like Jesus during his public ministry). Now he may not even pray for those who are rejected and undergoing punishment. Thus Jeremiah is explicitly forbidden to intercede, and Jesus too does not pray for the world: John 17:9; cf. 1 John 5:16. Now all the Suffering Servant can do is endure the anger, like accepting poison (Jer 8:14; 9:14, 23, 15).[39] It would be better if he had not been born than to end in such ruin at God's hands and at the hands of men (Jer 20:14–18).

Can we seriously say that God unloaded his wrath upon the Man who wrestled with his destiny on the Mount of Olives and was subsequently crucified? Indeed we must. Even in life, Jesus had been the revealer of the whole pathos of God—of his love and his indignation at man's scorning of this love—and now he has to bear the ultimate consequence of his more-than-prophetic

---

[33] 218.   [34] 119, 125, 188.

[35] 106: "Jeremiah lived in an age of wrath."

[36] 113–19.   [37] 123.

[38] *The Glory of the Lord* VI, 215ff.

[39] On the connection between anger and poison, cf. H. Gressmann, *Der Ursprung der israelitisch-jüdischen Eschatologie* (Göttingen, 1905), 130f.

mediation. "What was suffered there on Israel's account and ours was suffered for Israel and for us. [Namely,] The wrath of God that we had merited. . . . The reason why the No spoken on Good Friday is so terrible, but why there is already concealed in it the Eastertide Yes of God's righteousness, is that he who on the Cross took upon himself and suffered the wrath of God was none other than God's own Son, and therefore the eternal God himself in the unity with human nature that he freely accepted in his transcendent mercy."[40] He endured the conflict between God and man "from both sides: not only as the God who had been offended by man but also as the man whom God threatens with death, the man who is subject to death in the face of God's judgment, . . . who has entered into the likeness [homoiōma] of the 'flesh of sin' and is actually 'made to be sin' for us." The everlasting flame that burns in this judgment is the very light that enables us to see the true and terrifying nature of the judgment threatened and executed in the Old Testament.[41] All that happened to Israel then and since in terms of divine judgment is "only a faint reflection compared with the infinitely more terrible happenings that took place on Good Friday". Israel (and all who have to suffer in world history) is only "the representative of Someone very different . . ., who bears the wrath and judgment of God." "The real judgment of God is alone the crucifixion of Christ. . . . In it, the real essence of all the Old Testament threats and executions of judgment, that is, the revelation of the wrath of God against all ungodliness and unrighteousness of man (Rom 1:18)—without which revelation is not divine revelation—was embodied in a unique event."[42]

This unity between the outpouring of wrath upon the "Lamb of God" on the Cross, and the Father's love for the world that it manifests, throws light on the otherwise baffling riddle presented by two passages in Romans.

First of all, the revelation of God's covenant-righteousness is presented—inconceivably—as parallel and simultaneous to a revelation of his anger. Thus, in the gospel, "God's righteousness is revealed [apokalyptetai] through faith for faith; as it is written, 'He who through faith

[40] K. Barth, *Church Dogmatics* II/1, 396.
[41] *Ibid*.   [42] *Ibid*.

is righteous shall live.' For the wrath of God is revealed [*apokalypte-tai*] from heaven against all godlessness and wickedness of men" (Rom 1:17–18). Godlessness: that is, not only do the pagans "suppress" (v. 18) the knowledge of God they have actually acquired from the cosmos (v. 19), but the Jews have failed to observe the law of God revealed to them (2:1–3, 8). Thus all are guilty before God, and every mouth must fall silent in his presence (3:9–19). However, while this truth always existed in God, it was kept hidden because of his patience (2:4) and "forbearance" (3:25), to be revealed eschatologically in the "righteousness of God" in Christ, the "expiation" (3:25). Only this expiation, the Cross, shows the real nature of God's wrath regarding the entire world, Jews and Gentiles. *Apokalyptetai* seems to be used here in opposite senses, yet the two meanings converge on the same cognitive reality, which can only be grasped by man "through faith for faith". This is expounded in Romans 5:9: since Jesus died for us while we were yet sinners, "much more shall we be saved by him from the wrath of God". But the very fact that we were saved by his blood shows what a "store of wrath" (2:5) had accrued to mankind's account.[43]

Romans 9:22–23, with its highly compressed thought, can be explicated in the same way. Paul was speaking of the absolute priority of God's right to create his subjects for lofty or lowly purposes, just as the potter has control over the form and purpose of the vessels he makes. Then, looking ahead, on the one hand, to the election of the "true" Israel and the people's rejection of Christ and, on the other, to the ultimate shape of his "true" Israel into which, from Christ onward, all believers are incorporated, he says, "What if God, desiring to show his wrath and to make known his power, has endured with much patience the vessels of wrath made for destruction, in order to make known the riches of his glory for the vessels of mercy, which he has prepared beforehand for glory. . .?" (And the next sentence continues: "even us whom he has called, not from the Jews only but also from the Gentiles. . . .") Israel's hardness of heart vis-à-vis its Messiah is part of God's overall design of salvation, which is to bring forth the "Israel of God" (Gal 6:16); the anger that breaks out against Israel is an eschatological anger (since the vessels are "destined for perdition"—cf. the collapse of Jerusalem and Jesus' judgment on and turning away from the people in Luke 13:35), which is nonetheless encompassed by God's "endurance" and "great forbearance". Thus he grants hard-hearted Israel a time for repentance (cf. Rom 2:4), a time that is still running "today" (Rom

---

[43] On this whole passage: G. Bornkamm, "Die Offenbarung des Zornes Gottes" in *ZNW* 34 (1935), 239–362, reprinted in *Das Ende des Gesetzes* (Munich: Kaiser, 1952), 9–33.

11:31, *kai autoi nyn eleēthōsin*). Indeed, he will eventually reinstate "all Israel" in its original vocation, not by Israel's own efforts: "The Deliverer will come from Zion, he will banish ungodliness from Jacob; and this will be my covenant with them when I take away their sins" (11:26f.). This is the only possible Deliverer: by removing godlessness and taking God's wrath upon himself, he will actually transcend God's plans for history, which had created "vessels of wrath, appointed for destruction". It was for his sake that God's wrath was kept within the bracket of his "patience" and "great forbearance";[44] it belonged—and this creates a partial tension with the text we have just discussed (Rom 1-2)—to God's preeschatological "restraint" (*anochē*: Rom 3:25, cf. 2:4).

Passages such as this indicate a vanishing point where the lines of God's anger and his love meet. This is only possible if the object of God's righteous anger is seen in the context of the eternal, trinitarian love relationship between Father and Son. The Son does not deviate an inch from the Father's will; he carries it out to the very end. But neither does he deviate from his solidarity with all his sinful brothers, ". . . so that by the grace of God he might taste death for every one. . . . That is why he is not ashamed to call them brethren" (Heb 2:9, 11). In love and obedience, he will not surrender this solidarity; in consequence, he drinks deeply of the darkness of man's God-forsakenness, "because he knows union with God".[45] God's anger strikes him instead of the countless sinners, shattering him as by lightning and distributing him among them; thus God the Father, in the Holy Spirit, creates the Son's Eucharist. Only the Eucharist really completes the Incarnation. It takes place at a point where the estranged world, having been drawn in all seriousness into the relationships within the Godhead, seems to create a contradiction in God. "Here we are faced with the deepest mystery of the Trinity in its salvation-historical reality. Here, furthermore, the trinitarian relationships in God attain their greatest clarity: God is confronted with God; God is opposed by God. So the Father allows the Son to endure dereliction among sinners; the Son, suffering at the Father's hand, cries out to him. But all

---

[44] Cf. Schlier's remarks in his *Der Römerbrief*, 300-303, and E. Peterson, *Die Kirche aus Juden und Heiden* (Salzburg, 1933).

[45] P. Althaus, *Die christliche Wahrheit*, 3d ed. (Bertelsmann, Gütersloh), 471.

the while he is wholly God, not only moved by the Father's love but also borne and enveloped by it."[46] In this wrathful alienation —from the "economic" point of view, that is, in their common work of love for the world—Father and Son are closer together than ever. On the one hand, in cultic terms, the Son is the High Priest offering himself for the world. On the other hand, it is also true that "God himself is the Offerer, sacrificing himself for man."[47] In the Eucharist of his surrendered Son, God concludes his new and eternal covenant with mankind, committing himself to it utterly and with no reservation.

The Son bears sinners within himself, together with the hopeless impenetrability of their sin, which prevents the divine light of love from registering in them. In himself, therefore, he experiences, not their sin, but the hopelessness of their resistance to God and the graceless No of divine grace to this resistance. The Son who has depended [sich verlassen] entirely on the Father, even to becoming identified with his brothers in their lostness, must now be forsaken [verlassen] by the Father. He who consented to be given [ver-geben] everything from the Father's hand must now feel that it was all "for nothing" [vergebens]. There is no balancing or cancelling-out, no "squaring" of light and darkness; there can be no weighing-up of the "for nothing" of sin's hatred and the "for nothing" of the grace that gives and forgives. At the end of night, a night that is experienced as endless, light breaks forth in primal creativity; at the end of absolute futility [Vergeblichkeit] comes forgiveness [Vergebung]. But the night that was endured as endless was the absolute light: as John of the Cross says, it becomes invisible when it encounters no resistance in the air. Forgiveness does not come as a return for some achievement: it comes because any such achievement was impossible.

It is a miracle of transfiguration that the world's darkness can be taken into the inner light of the Trinity; so the estrangement of the sinful No is overtaken and encompassed by the free-will, obedient estrangement of the divine Yes. God's anger at the rejection of divine love encounters a divine love (the Son's) that exposes itself to this anger, disarms it and literally deprives it of

---

[46] Ibid., 471–72.
[47] H. Thielicke, Der Evangelische Glaube II (Tübingen: Mohr, 1973), 487.

its object. However, these summary, abstract formulations contain hidden and unsolved problems.

One problem—the more somber one—is found at the limit: a sinner might so identify himself with his No to God that trinitarian love would be unable to loosen the resultant snarl, with the result that the fiery torrent of eternal love that flows around and through him would remain a torrent of eternal wrath. Hence the words, "it is a terrible thing to fall into the hands of the living God" (Heb 10:31). These words apply, not to just any sinners, but to those who resist the triune work of atonement with full consciousness and realization. "For it is impossible to restore again to repentance those who have once been enlightened, who have tasted the heavenly gift, and have become partakers of the Holy Spirit, and have tasted the goodness of the word of God and the powers of the age to come, if they then commit apostasy" (Heb 6:4ff.); a person such as this has "spurned the Son of God, and profaned the blood of the covenant by which he was sanctified, and outraged the Spirit of grace" (10:29). Scripture prohibits us from saying that this deliberate No is impossible. "Whoever speaks against the Holy Spirit will not be forgiven, either in this age or in the age to come" (Mt 12:31f.). Once again we are confronted with the mystery of the reciprocal heightening of Yes and No. "If you were blind, you would have no guilt; but now that you say, 'We see', your guilt remains" (Jn 9:41). For this to take place, a creature must be able to identify itself with its refusal.

The other remaining problem is of lighter hue: How does Christ's work on man's behalf ("representation") affect the sinner? Paul Althaus produced the formula that, in natural life, this representation is primarily "exclusive": the representative (for example, the soldier at the battlefront) saves others the trouble or the suffering involved, although, even in this kind of representation, "there is an inclusive element . . . in the ethical preconditions and results. When someone else does something for us, it not only relieves us of a burden but also imposes a burden on us." In personal life, by comparison, representation is inclusive right from the outset. "A person is called to experience the mystery of the divine fellowship in a deeper way, on behalf of many. . . . The waking person takes upon his soul the sickness and guilt of the one who slumbers. The free man, to whom 'all is permitted', all is pure, exercises renunciation on behalf of those who are less free and in danger." Here and in similar cases, "the meaning and goal of representation . . . is to draw those who are being represented into the inner attitude of the one representing them"; it is "inclusive".[48] And when someone suffers for the sake of another's moral life or relationship with God, "the representative consciously founds and animates the fellowship [that thus results]". It is possible for the person being represented to turn his back on the representative and go his own oblivious way. "This is representation at its height. Here it is *exclusive*. The representative remains entirely alone, which makes his suffering so hard. But this apparently exclusive quality only goes to show that the representation is encountering resistance. Essentially, intentionally, it is inclusive."[49] For Althaus, a Protestant theologian, it is the power of this inclusion that draws the sinner (in his self-exclusion) into a fellowship of life with Jesus. Insofar as Jesus does what we cannot do, his action is primarily exclusive; but insofar as, on the Cross, he vouches for us in God's presence—and vouches for us effectively—his action becomes inclusive.[50] We need to ask ourselves whether this transition is presented with adequate clarity and insight in Catholic dogmatics. Is it simply a matter of a transition from the *indicative* of justification to the *imperative* of laying hold of it in faith, whereby we allow ourselves to be inwardly healed by it[51] and join with Christ and his followers in the practice of repentance? But where can the "unbelieving" sinner find the faith to lay hold of this justification?

c. The Church's Mediation

In the climactic scene of the drama of redemption there is still one actor missing. We have considered the action of Father and Son in the Spirit who is common to both of them and the action that takes place between Christ and the sinners who cast their

[48] P. Althaus, "Das Kreuz Christi" in *Theologische Aufsätze* (Gütersloh: Bertelsmann, 1929), 36ff. The idea and terminology come from H. Thielicke, 495-96.
[49] *Ibid.*, 42.
[50] P. Althaus, "Die Christliche Wahrheit", 274.
[51] Cf. Thielicke, 496.

sins upon him. But it is not yet clear how, on the basis of this deed (which is itself the epitome of their sinfulness), they could be made sharers in the grace of God and attain the freedom of the children of God.

One character is missing. This emerges from a twofold presupposition of the Passion scene. The making of the covenant with Abraham and the people was something far too positive and final to be represented solely (now) by the perverted unbelief of the Jews and the false hypostatizing of the law vis-à-vis the sheer grace of the covenant God. What has happened to the faith of Abraham, which was vindicated by the sacrifice of Isaac? Where is the prophetic faith of all those who followed Abraham and lived in hope of redemption (Heb 11)?

This faith has already been fulfilled and over-fulfilled in the consent of the lowly handmaiden to the Incarnation of the "Son of the Most High", the merciful Word of God "to Abraham and his seed" (Lk 1:32, 55). Her consent was so pure, so far above the failings of even the great figures of the Old Testament, so unlimited and definitive, that it included all that was to befall the Son who was the object of her consent. That is why we rightly conclude that Mary was free from every shadow of mankind's guilt.

In the perspective of this once-for-all Yes, we begin to see the unity of both themes and their relevance to the Passion scene. Mary's consent represents the pure faith of Abraham and the people; it is the fruit of Israel's positive history, proving that God has not made his covenant for nothing: now the covenant becomes concrete reality beneath the Cross, with the same actuality as it had in Nazareth thirty-three years before. The sword that was to pierce Mary "so that the thoughts of many hearts should be revealed" (Lk 2:35) has not ceased piercing her; it has kept the whole insistence of her consent awake for this day, on which its terrible depths are to be plumbed. Mary's consent, her spiritual and physical readiness, is responsible for the earthly existence of Jesus, who perfects the Old Covenant and brings the promise of the New and Eternal Covenant; it prefigures the coming Church of Jesus; and it has a decisive role to play on the Cross. It is to mediate between Yahweh's faithless covenant-partners, who have adopted Gentile ways ("we have no king but Caesar", Jn 19:15), and the future covenant-partners, who will come to faith through the grace of the "Lamb as though it had been slain". It is not easy to situate this role in the whole drama.

First of all, we must exclude the theory that, reflecting on the New Covenant concluded on the Cross, sees Jesus (whose Person is divine) as the "divine factor" and Mary as the representative of consenting mankind. In such a scheme, the two would be related as fashioning act and fashioned potency. In the realm of objective redemption, Mary would do by anticipation what every individual has to do in subjectively appropriating the redemption.[1] It has been objected, rightly, that the Christology presupposed here undervalues the humanity of Christ: Christ is fully empowered to ratify the covenant in the name of and on behalf of mankind.[2] It may be true, however, that this retort does not take sufficient account of the fact that Mary's consent, a perfect representation of Old Covenant faith, was a precondition of the possibility of the Incarnation; to that extent, it cannot be simply swallowed up in the human Yes of Jesus.

We must also remember the old patristic teaching on the *connubium* of the divine and human natures, at the Incarnation, in Mary's womb (most clearly developed in Augustine and Gregory the Great):[3] while it spoke of the Mother only as the "place", as it were, where this marriage is made, it continually and increasingly emphasized the Virgin's active role in this union. This was most lucidly expressed by Aquinas' celebrated observation: "It was appropriate that the Blessed Virgin should be told that she would conceive the Messiah . . . , for thus it was made plain that there was to be a spiritual marriage between the Son of God and human nature. So, at the Annunciation, the Virgin's consent was awaited, for it represented human nature in its entirety."[4] And even more clearly, showing the objective bond between the Virgin's personal Yes and the covenant made with the entire nature: "The Blessed Virgin's consent, which was elicited by

---

[1] Heinrich M. Köster, *Die Magd des Herrn* (Limburg: Lahnverlag, 1947).

[2] Thus K. Rahner against Köster: "Probleme heutiger Mariologie" in *Aus der Theologie der Zeit*, ed. G. Söhngen (Regensburg, 1948), 85–113.

[3] Augustine, *In Ep. 1 Joh.*, tr. 1 n. 2; Gregory, *Hom 38 in Ezech.*

[4] *S. Th.* III, 30, 1 c.

the Annunciation, was the act of a single person, yet overflowing [*redundans*] for the salvation of the multitude, indeed, of all
human nature."[5] Mary cannot be the impersonal "place" where
the covenant between the natures is concluded: God does not
overpower his creature, least of all the woman who represents
his covenant, but respects her dignity as a person. She epitomizes
that human nature that will receive God's Word and Son, and to
that extent she shares responsibility for him. In part, therefore,
we have rehabilitated the thesis criticized above; yet its distinction of the divine and the human roles in terms of "act" and
"potency" remains inadequate. Of course, Mary *has* a "potentiality", but it is not passive or material: it represents the highest
act that a creature can perform in love of God. It is the firm,
responsible readiness to accept the will of God with all its consequences.

On the other hand, we must exclude totally any suggestion
that God is "obliged" or that Mary exercises any "morally determining influence" on the redemptive acts of Jesus. It was not her
"yearning" for redemption that moved the Son of God to become man, nor did it give the new Adam "the courage to accept
death on the Cross".[6] Nor can we speak of the Mother having
any "rights over her Son",[7] rights that she renounced (thereby
acquiring "merit") so that the redemptive sacrifice could take
place. All these theories misconstrue the character of this original, constant Yes: it is an act of perfect self-surrender to God
in faith. Nothing is extorted from God, nor is any claim made
vis-à-vis him. God, in infinite and merciful freedom, has looked
down upon the lowliness of his Handmaiden.

What is of essential importance is that Mary, in giving her firm
and abiding Yes to the Incarnation and all its consequences, of
which the greatest is the Cross, has done so "in the name of

[5] 3, d 3, q 2, sol 2.

[6] On these ideas, cf. C. Dillenschneider, *Marie au service de notre Rédemption*
(Haguenau, 1947); also his *Pour une Corédemption mariale bien comprise* (Rome, ed.
"Marianum", 1949), and *Le Principe premier d'une théologie mariale organique* (Alsa-
tia, 1955); H. Seiler, *Corredemptrix* (Rome, 1939); P. Sträter (in: Seiler-Sträter),
"De modalitate Corredemptionis B.M.V.", *Gregorianum* 28 (1947).

[7] T. Gallus, "Ad B. M. Virginis in redemptione cooperationem", *Div. Thom.*
(Piac.) 31 (1948).

the entire human race". She has consented on behalf of the very sinners who reject the Incarnation. "He came to his own home, and his own people received him not" (Jn 1:11). If there had been no exceptions to this statement, he would not have come at all. So the text continues: "but to all who received him. . . ." (1:12). One stands out among all these: Mary. And it is to her that the next passage points (for originally it must have referred to the Mother/Son relationship): "who believed in his name, . . . who were born, not of blood nor of the will of the flesh nor of the will of man, but of God".[8] This form of "receiving", that is, the Virgin Birth, is qualitatively different from all the subsequent forms that, in part, it makes possible. All subsequent "receiving" will always involve former sinners. The Mother's advance Yes vouches for sinners, whether they will receive or not. She is in solidarity with them, unconditionally, precisely *because* she is "immaculately conceived" and hence, in love, infinitely at their disposal, infinitely available. When she gratefully says Yes to the coming Savior, she does not do so for herself alone but for all who stand in need of the "salvation of Israel".

However, this essential solidarity, in accord with Jesus' solidarity with all sinners—to the extent of taking upon him their sinful condition—means that the Mother is given the "last place", *behind* the last sinner, to whom she does not refuse her solidarity. Since the Woman's "hour" does not coincide with the Man's, her Son's (Jn 2:4), this relegation of the Mother, which results from her consent, can begin long before the Cross. We see it in those instances that mark the entire public life of Jesus, where he keeps her at a distance. This begins when the twelve year old distances himself from the Mother who comes looking for him; she is relegated to the old aeon of "flesh and blood". Thus he refuses to allow her physical motherhood to be extolled (Lk 11:27f.). These are all anticipations of the "last place" that she will occupy beneath the Cross. She occupies this last place as an objective consequence of her Yes; for she was wedded to human nature *in its entirety*, that is, not primarily because of her subjective, personal strength of faith. The Handmaiden *does* pos-

---

[8] I. de la Potterie, *La Mère de Jésus et la conception virginale du Fils de Dieu. Etude de théologie johannique* (Rome, ed. "Marianum", 1978).

sess this strength of faith, but it comes from the Lord, who has sovereign control over her. Indeed, she does represent the people of the covenant: but the covenant was entered into solely with a view to her Son; he alone will fulfill it.

The Son hangs between earth and heaven, utterly forsaken by men and God. The darkness of the world's guilt that he bears within him veils and obscures all sight of a meaning to his suffering. He has no sense of it achieving anything. For sin, in the face of God's freely given love, is meaningless and groundless. Objectively, though the Son cannot know this, at the end of his suffering there stands man redeemed, man immaculate, incarnationally present within history. Though for the present it is beyond his perception, this redeemed man is anticipated, by the Father's design, in Mary. Hidden behind the multitude of sinners, embracing them all, she is objectively closest to him: she makes his suffering possible and guarantees its goal. Now, however, he can only see her as the farthest from him; this is how he *must* see her. He is forsaken *absolutely*, and the only way of fellowship with him is to take leave of him and plunge into forsakenness. He must withdraw from his Mother just as the Father has withdrawn from him: "Woman, behold your son." We could put it this way: the Son's *missio* is his *processio* extended in "economic" mode; but, whereas in his *processio* he moves toward the Father in receptivity and gratitude, in his *missio* (thanks to the "trinitarian inversion"),[9] he moves away from him and toward the world, into the latter's ultimate darkness. In fact, since all is obedience, he *is* moving toward the Father through this utter estrangement, but for the present he must not be allowed to know this. And as for the truth about the lowly Handmaiden, who occupies the last place, behind sin, in the most complete expropriation and poverty, though she is the sign of his own pure origin and the symbol of his radiant future (in which he will attain his full stature, given him by the Father), it must be hidden from him. On the contrary, he sends her forth as she is, as his Mother and as the anticipation of his triumph, into a relationship that is new and initially alien. Alien, because he has always made a clear distinction between her fundamental,

[9] *Theo-Drama* III, 183–202.

antecedent purity and the lostness of sinners; the fact that Mary is always there in her purity (and always has been) means that, from his point of view, his own "achievement" seems superfluous. It is not due to him that she is what she is, for she was thus before him. In this way, the Father who determined to give him this Mother in the first place[10] has kept the Son from seeing his own redemptive achievement. Because of the darkness of sin, the Son cannot see that Mary owes her being to him as well as to the Father and that only in this way can she be the chosen vessel of the Holy Spirit. Darkness conceals the goal that is concretely embodied in Mary; in fact, the Son himself bids farewell to it. Only thus, in the pure *gratis* of grace, in the pure superfluity [*Überflüssigkeit*] of love, can the Son be eucharistically poured out, beyond measure [*über-verflüssigt*]; only thus can he become all the world's sin. And, from his vantage point, all is in vain since, carrying the darkness of sin, he can no longer see any light, any meaning.

And yet Mary is there, the Immaculate One, and hence the entire divine project of the Incarnation is there too. God can no longer be banished to his heaven and regarded as inaccessible, perhaps in the form of the "immanent Trinity". Sinners always try to do this; we tend to put Yahweh and Allah in the other world and to keep this world to ourselves. It is all the more terrifying for the Son, therefore, in the darkness of his anguish, to see that this whole work, which has begun to be realized in Mary, is pointless (because of his gratuitous suffering) and doomed to failure. The Son is not simply alone with sinners in that absolute exchange envisaged by Luther: he is accompanied by a witness to God's activity (which always operates *sola gratia*), and this robs the Man of Sorrows of all hope of completing his mission. It also robs the theologians (Moltmann) of any possibility of expounding the Trinity on the basis of the Cross alone.

---

[10] We must not forget that redemption is not a work of the Son in isolation but of the entire Trinity, naturally with a view to the fruitfulness of the Incarnation and of the Cross. The Mother's preredemption is due to the sheer unmerited grace of the Trinity. While this preredemption (like all redemption) is essentially due to the Son's life and suffering, the Mother's anticipated redemption (which is a precondition for the Son's Incarnation) can appear to the Son equally as a prior gift from the Father, in the Spirit.

Not even on the basis of a dialectic of the Cross that is formally multiplied to infinity, of a "speculative Good Friday".

However, we must also contemplate the same scene from Mary's point of view. In Nazareth, she was the poor handmaiden, characterized by a threefold poverty. She had been given away to Joseph, which meant that she could not respond to God's choosing of her by any autonomous gesture of self-dedication: in any case, God took what was his, beyond all creaturely pacts. Furthermore, she had been given away to the overshadowing Spirit, in accordance with what had been announced to her; thus her consent was not a kind of anxiously awaited free decision (a view that is common since Ambrose, Autpert and Bernard), but more like a natural self-giving arising from a long-accepted availability. And, finally, she is poor because she is fruitless, unfecundate, surpassing the barrenness of Sarah, Hannah and Elizabeth in the Old Testament (these figures provide the only way of approaching what happened to Mary). And, into this thrice-poor womb, God, through his Spirit, placed the seed of his Word, so that Mary would fulfill all the paradoxical promises that assert that "the barren woman has borne seven" (1 Sam 2:5; cf. Is 54:1; Ps 113:9).

The same Word of God whom she conceived in silence has himself now fallen silent: he is the "lamb that is led to the slaughter, who opens not his mouth" (Is 53:7; Mt 26:63; Acts 8:32f.); he is distributed—beyond all measure—to sinners, squandered on them in their darkness, for it is for them that he suffers. Mary, however, has remained what she was from the beginning: she is the poverty of the dispossessed womb. The Son has kept her at a distance, and now he does so even more: in her "open" poverty, she embraces and envelops the "closed" and negative poverty of all sinners. She is in solidarity with them all in their poverty, but, behind them and in them, she is the only one able to receive the seed of God, eucharistically multiplied—thousands-fold—into her womb. Thus repeated and perfected, her conception is translated into suffering; this makes Mary the "bride of the (slain) Lamb" and the "womb of the Church"—a nuptial relationship that begins in the utter forsakenness and darkness they both experience. In her first conception, she was the "vessel (not the bride) of the Spirit" for the sake of her virginal motherhood vis-à-vis the Son; in her second conception, she becomes the equally virginal Bride of the Son of God himself, who gives himself away eucharistically.

All this takes place in a silence in which even God the Father withdraws into invisibility. In a similar way, in creation, the Creator withdrew in silence from the creatures he had endowed with fruitfulness, in order to speak to them through their own speech, through their own faculties, and thus to move them to acknowledge their indebtedness to him. This withdrawal on the part of the Father reaches its acme—brutally, one might say—in the dereliction of the Cross, in which Mary has her share. In this dereliction, the Father gives no word of answer to the Son; and his Word, that is, the Son himself, sinks into the silence of death. This silence of death is the indefinable moment in which the "new man" is conceived and born of the Church's womb, a womb that has become so poor that, spiritually, it shares the Son's death.

With only a slight reinterpretation of the Book of Wisdom's vision of the nocturnal visitation of the Word, we arrive at a vision of ultimate salvation: "When deep silence lay over all, and night had run the half of her swift course, down from the heavens, from the royal throne, leapt your all-powerful Word; into the heart of a doomed land the stern warrior [no: the Lamb-as-though-it-had-been-slain] leapt. Carrying your irrevocable command [which was to send him to ruin] like a sharp sword, he stood [he hung], and filled the universe with [his] death" (Wis 18:14ff. JB adapted). By means of the Eucharist, he distributes his death, spilling it as life into the womb of his Church. In the transition from the Old to the New Covenant, "night" has become intensified; at the crucifixion, it covers the whole universe (Mt 27:45); the sword has become sharper, death more radical: now, once for all, is the judgment of this world (Jn 12:31). And, in the midst of it, and precisely because of it, the marriage of the Lamb and his Bride and Spouse is celebrated: this union rends the "curtain" that separated God from the earth, tearing it in two "from top to bottom; and the earth shook, and the rocks were split; the tombs also were opened . . ." (Mt 27:51).

We can only avoid the misunderstandings associated with words such as "coredemption" if we hold on to the paradox to the very end. First of all, this paradox means that Mary's virginity, which goes beyond the sterility of those Old Testament women who were made fruitful by the power of God, is of such poverty that it takes the "last place", behind the sterility and barrenness of all sin. (The Son explicitly indicates this "last place" by sending her away and handing her over to another.) She takes her place behind the rupture of the Old Covenant (which now becomes manifest), behind the godlessness of all paganism. For the Cross, in the judicial proceedings against Jesus, lays everything bare, to its very foundations. All is shown to be of no use to God: God's Word and Son is utterly isolated in the face of this barrenness, which invades and permeates him, making his suffering seem equally hopeless and fruitless. Behind all this unusable material, indeed, hidden in it, there is the *womb* to which he owes his existence, rightly described thus: "The Lord created me at the beginning of his work, the first of his acts of old" (Prov 8:22). If it is true that "the Lamb without spot or blemish", with his "precious blood", has been "destined before the foundation of the world" (1 Pet 1:19f.), and if all the world's darkness is only permitted because of the antecedent *idea*, *offer* and *mission* of the Lamb, which undergird it and make it possible, it follows that this providence must include the *womb* that facilitates all that belongs to the world and the Incarnation of the Lamb himself. Now, however, hidden behind, hidden in the futile, negative darkness of sin, this *womb* is banished to universal futility by the Dying Man. This final farewell—in judgment—is now the only possible form of relationship.

Thus the mystery of Mary's source-function is unveiled (together with all the other unveilings associated with judgment). Furthermore, just as in the first creation God is silent, only addressing the creature by enabling him to speak, to act and to recognize his own indebtedness, so in the second creation the Virgin is empowered to new motherhood by the Word who falls silent in death: she is to bring forth redeemed creation's answer to this silenced Word. And just as Mary's Yes was expropriated right from the outset, having been uttered "in the name of the whole human race", so now she brings forth this response in the name, too, of all those who refuse to respond. All of them, as individuals, are undergirded and sustained not only by the Word of God who dies in darkness "for them" and on their behalf but also by the response of the Church; she acts as a source, representing them and answering for them, in her darkness, at the Cross. Deep down, man's attempt to banish God from finitude in order to avoid receiving (and conceiving) from him, his endeavor to bring forth fruit on his own, is undergirded and sustained by the "wisdom of the poor", that wisdom which was "the first of God's acts" and which, in creation, has always said Yes to being made fruitful by God and his Word. At the Cross, Mary's Yes consents to her being totally stripped of power (Mary can do nothing to help her Son); and what is more, she is sent away into utter uselessness: Mary cannot even remind her Son of the mystery of his coming forth from her, for she is handed over to another son. This is the graveyard of all those theories that try to establish a direct connection between the suffering of the Mother and that of the Son, however much the former is subordinated to the latter. God, from the lonely heights of his almighty power, can take the "nothingness" of unfruitful virginity (to which, in the Old Covenant, the odor of shame was attached) and make of it the fruitful motherhood of the Virgin, with a fruitfulness that extends to the whole world. He does this through his divine-human Son who, by means of his Eucharist, embodies the miracle of divine omnipotence and universal fruitfulness and makes it a reality in the Father's entire creation. Here, finally falling silent, the Word is empowered to make his whole body into God's seed; thus the Word finally and definitively becomes flesh in the Virgin Mother, Mary-Ecclesia. And the latter's physico-spiritual answer is more fruitful than all the attempts on the part of the sinful world to fructify itself— attempts that are doomed to sterility.

3. Resurrection, Spirit and Life in God

a. The Risen and Crucified One

The change that takes place at Easter is as abrupt as it is organic. The extreme distance between Father and Son, which is endured as a result of the Son's taking on of sin, changes into the most profound intimacy; but it always *was* such because the distance was a work of trinitarian, loving obedience, and in this obedience Father and Son were always one in a reciprocal relationship in the Spirit. All the same, Good Friday is not just the same as Easter: the economic Trinity objectively acts out the drama of the world's alienation. So we should not say that the Cross is nothing other than the ("quasi sacramental") manifestation of God's reconciliation with the world, a reconciliation that is constant, homogeneous and always part of the given: rather we should say that God, desiring to reconcile the world to himself (and hence himself to the world), acts dramatically in the Son's Cross and Resurrection. This dramatic aspect does not entangle the immanent Trinity in the world's fate, as occurs in mythology, but it *does* lift the latter's fate to the level of the economic Trinity, which always presupposes the immanent. This is because the Son's eternal, holy distance from the Father, in the Spirit, forms the basis on which the unholy distance of the world's sin can be transposed into it, can be transcended and overcome by it. The dramatic interplay between God and the world is enacted in the temporal acts of the concrete Christ-event and its consequences: it cannot be reduced to philosophical or timelessly abstract principles.

Within the Son's absolute, loving obedience (which persists in the realm of the immanent Trinity), according to which he walks into an utter forsakenness that surpasses the sinner's isolation, we find the most radical change from eternal death to eternal life, from the absolute night of the Spirit to the Spirit's absolute light, from total alienation and remoteness to an unimaginable closeness. That is why John sees both extremes as one and the same "glory" and "exaltation"; they interpenetrate, yet without cancelling out that highest dramatic quality described by Paul, in overflowing words, as "the immeasurable greatness of [God's] *power* in us who believe, according to the *working* of the *strength* of his great *might* which he accomplished in Christ when he raised from the dead and made him sit in the heavenly places" (Eph 1:19–20). On the one hand, in the realm of the immanent Trinity, the glory the Son has regained through his passing through darkness is the same glory he possessed with the Father "before the foundation of the world" (Jn 17:5). On the other hand, it is also true that his humanity only comes to share in this glory through the dramatic act of the economic Trinity, by being finally opened to all (in the Eucharist) and drained (ultimately, in the opening of his heart).

It is essential, therefore, that his wounds feature in his Resurrection and transfiguration. Not only to prove to the disciples the identity of this tortured body that has become bafflingly spiritualized, able to walk through closed doors, but, more importantly, because it is through his opened body (a hand can be reached inside his body through the wound: Jn 20:27) and the infinite distribution of his flesh and shedding of his blood that men can henceforth share in the substantial infinitude of his Divine Person. And here again it must be emphasized: the fact that his (now eucharistic) body has passed to a state of eternal life beyond all death (Rom 6:9) does not remove him from the drama of his passage through the world of sin. His wounds are not mere reminders of some past experience. Since this drama is experienced by the economic Trinity, which is one with the immanent Trinity, it is constantly actual; all the more since the drama of the Passion, to which the Eucharist belongs, embraces all past and future points of world time. Thus, wherever sin and death reign in the world, the revolution effected by Christ becomes operative, "the death he died he died to sin [that is, to sin's disadvantage], once for all" (Rom 6:10). And not only is this definitive event being continually rendered concrete from below, as it were, by continued sin: it is continually being implanted from above into all times, in the sacrament instituted by Christ. We shall speak of this shortly.

First, however, we must remember that he who "died to sin once for all" (because he was made the epitome of sin, 2 Cor 5:21) now "lives to God" (Rom 6:10), that is, for God and his saving designs. He lives both for God and also through him, for it is God who changed death into life. This means that Christ's "living for God" simultaneously implies that God lives for him, superabundantly, since he "made him sit . . . far above all rule and authority and power and dominion, and above every name that is named, not only in this age but also in that which is to come; and he has put all things under his feet" (Eph 1:21f.; cf. Col 1:16). For, after Christ has passed through ultimate darkness, he is given "the keys of death and hell" (Rev 1:18); because of his obedience unto death on the Cross, he is given authority over heaven, earth and the nether world (Phil 2:9ff.). He now "stands at the right hand of God" (Acts 7:55) and has the divine freedom to judge the whole world as seems right to him. We must stress this sovereign freedom on the part of the risen man Jesus Christ, since it is the revelation of that hidden freedom that is expressed in his total obedience to the Father, a freedom that is not only divine but also human. Anselm underlined this with his recurrent theme of the "*sponte*"; Maximus the Confessor was the first to give it full and explicit treatment in accord with Chalcedonian theology.[1]

We see the freedom of the Risen One most clearly in the end of what we have described as the "trinitarian inversion", which is nothing other than Jesus' submission to the Holy Spirit who communicated the Father's will to him. Of course, he possessed the Spirit in fullness (Jn 3:34), but the Spirit had been visibly sent down upon him, so he allowed himself to be "driven" by him, even toward something that he, as man, could only anticipate with horror, that is, the "baptism" with which he had to be baptized. This economic form of the Trinity comes to an end with the Resurrection. As early as Easter, we see Jesus as the one who, even as man, has control of the Spirit and sovereignly breathes him into the disciples (Jn 20:22). His sovereignty is such that he can entrust the Spirit (who is his) to his Church, so that, whether forgiving or retaining sins, she can share in his Resurrection freedom and communicate the power of the Spirit.

In "economic" terms, the Spirit was in and above Jesus. Jesus obeyed the Spirit, but not according to a law above him: he obeyed the Spirit who united him with the Father. Now, in freedom, he sends the Spirit forth, who is *his* Spirit, the Spirit of both freedom and obedience to the Spirit. The Exalted One can grant his friends a share in his Spirit, for now he possesses the Spirit in himself—and "where the Lord is, there is the Spirit"— and he can give them a share in the Spirit's freedom, the Spirit's direct access to God: "Where the Spirit of the Lord is, there is

[1] François-Marie Léthel, "Théologie de l'Agonie du Christ" in *Théologie historique* 52 (Paris: Beauchesne, 1979).

freedom" (2 Cor 3:17). Such direct access liberates man from the mediation of the law (Gal 3:12f.; Acts 7:38); the Father's bosom, which, in infinite generation, brought forth the Son, is henceforth the only law for those who have been endowed with the Spirit, the milieu of love's absolute freedom. From this wide perspective of the "Spirit of God", "the spiritual man judges all things, but is himself to be judged by no one" (1 Cor 2:15).

At this point, we discern the profound connection between the Spirit of Christ, being born of God, and *baptism*, which is indicated in the mysterious words of the interview with Nicodemus. Jesus says that the only ones to reach the kingdom of God are those who are born again of water and the Spirit; yet, while we can hear the rushing of the Spirit, blowing where he will, we cannot know whence he comes and whither he goes. "So it is with every one who is born of the Spirit" (Jn 3:2–8). How is this possible? In answer, we must refer to the distance between the Crucified and the Father, which "infiltrates" that distance created by sin, guided by the "driving" of the Spirit. This is the Spirit whom the Risen One gives to those who are his, the Spirit of sonship and of new birth from God (Jn 1:13). He himself was not born from the desire of the flesh but of God (Jn 1:12–13), and so he possesses the "power" to make others "children of God". This takes place through the communication of the Spirit of Christ, for he is the "spirit of sonship, who causes us to cry, 'Abba! Father!' . . . the Spirit himself bearing witness with our spirit that we are children of God . . . predestined to be conformed to the image of his Son" (Rom 8:15f., 29). In his freedom, the man who is reborn of the primal bosom of the Father becomes a riddle to worldly men; no one can find out where he comes from and where he goes.

Ultimately, however, this freedom comes from the Son's all-embracing obedience on the Cross. He himself describes this as the baptism with which he must be baptized and which fills him with dismay (Lk 12:50). Baptism, as Jesus knows it from John and to which he submitted himself, is a total plunging beneath the waves of sin (cf. the Old Testament images of God's inundating waters: Ps 42:8; 69:2, and the parallels in Mark 10:38f., which speaks of drinking God's cup of wrath as well as of baptism). Baptism expresses solidarity with all sinners; it recapitu-

lates their plunging into sin and thus makes it possible for them
to emerge saved and purified. There is an ambivalence in baptism: on the one hand, it signifies the "perishing of the ancient
world in the Flood" (2 Pet 3:6) and, on the other, the "ark, in
which a few . . . were saved by water" (1 Pet 3:20). Not only
does the ark prefigure baptism: baptism "saves through the Resurrection of Jesus Christ" (1 Pet 3:21). The Son, totally buried
in the baptism of sin, rises again to the Father's bosom (which,
in trinitarian terms, he never left), taking with him those he has
saved from the tide of sin, who are "destined to be sons" (Eph
1:5). This is why, in baptism, Christians are essentially "baptized into Christ's death", "buried with him" under the waters
that submerged him. Baptism is a "copy of his death", uniting
us with him; thus, in baptism, Christ's death is understood not
only as something "historical" but as a "present" and effectual
reality.[2] Passing through death in this way, we come to a "new
life", a "new creation" (2 Cor 5:17; Gal 6:15) that is the result
of Christ's Resurrection and the pledge of our own resurrection.
Again, it is "new life of the Spirit" (Rom 7:6) and hence freedom
"from our old self", from "sin" (Rom 6:6); we are no longer
"under law but under grace" (Rom 6:14).

This entire context of Spirit, freedom and baptism—realities
that converge on the redeemed human being's sharing in the
Risen Christ's sonship—throws light on the latter's freedom to
give others a share in his drama. He draws them into his destiny
by communicating his Spirit to them; by doing this, as we shall
see in more detail, he gives *himself* eucharistically. Since he is
the Son, he can only give himself if he also enables them to participate in his proceeding from the Father. However, the grace
of sonship is always identical with the bestowal of the Spirit of
Christ. The Spirit is not given prior to the Paschal Triduum
(Jn 7:39), when Jesus "breathes out" the Spirit along with his
"accomplished" mission and gives him back to the Father (Lk
23:46; cf. Mk 15:37; Mt 27:50; Jn 19:30). Subsequently, as the
Risen Christ, he wields the Spirit and breathes him into the
Church (Jn 20:22); this Spirit is one and the same Spirit of both
Passion and Resurrection, initiating the band of followers into

---

[2] Schlier, *Römerbrief* (Herder, 1977), 196.

an entirely new, dramatic way of life. This new form of existence is most clearly profiled in Paul's destiny and teaching. It is no longer a one-way movement from the epoch of the Passion to that of the Resurrection (although, in the total context, this sequence does form the backdrop, cf. Phil 3:11). Rather, our dying-with-Christ is something that happens retroactively, so to speak, in virtue of and sustained by the grace of the Resurrection. So all suffering points toward a resurrection with Christ (cf. 2 Cor 5:8ff.). We shall have to examine in more detail this dramatic context, which owes itself to the indivisible Spirit of Christ.

Initially, therefore, we have two conceptual complexes to discuss. First, following the sequence of topics in the second volume of *Theo-Drama*, there is the soteriological liberation of finite freedom in its negative and positive aspects, that is, liberation from the "powers", on the one hand, and "divinization", on the other. Second, according to the sequence in the third volume of *Theo-Drama*, we have the soteriologically constituted form of the Christian's personal existence-in-discipleship in its inner dynamic of dying and rising again.

b. Freedom Liberated

The theme announced by this heading is an extensive one; we can give only a brief account of it here. Yet such a treatment has advantages: it is only too easy for highly detailed investigations of the constituent topics to lead us into a theological half-light where suppositions and arbitrary constructs can be taken for solid structures.

Under this heading—and it is essential to grasp this—two of the five biblical themes can only be discussed in undivided unity, namely, the third and the fourth. The third is man's liberation through the Cross, that is, everything we mean by "ransom", "redemption", "liberation" from the powers of sin, of the world, of death, of the demonic; and the fourth is the liberated man's initiation into the trinitarian life of God, described by the Greek Fathers, in their reflection on the theology of Paul and John, as *theosis*. Man's freedom, hitherto enslaved, is liberated "from" something and liberated "for" something. We have already established this unity of themes in the second volume of *Theo-Drama*, pages 207–316;[3] we can develop and deepen it here.

First: liberation from the "powers". It is well known how important a role this theme plays not only in the Gospel (cf. for example, Mt 12:28ff.; Lk 13:16, and so forth) and in Paul but also in the theory often found (since Origen) in the Fathers, according to which sinners are "ransomed" from Satan, who rightly or wrongly claims power over them. It has been suggested, no doubt correctly, that here Origen has christianized an ancient Marcionite belief, that is, that the Redeemer "bought" from the Demiurge the souls that were to be saved.[4] We should be slow to dismiss this theme as historically obsolete[5] and should remember how G. Aulén considered it to be a constituent element of the "classical" doctrine of atonement.[6] In fact, whether or not the theme can be demythologized remains an open question, and one that is surely insoluble. If we go back beyond Origen and his many followers (first and foremost Gregory of Nyssa and Augustine) and come to Marcion himself, we find that the questions he asked presuppose even earlier and more radical questions: To what extent, even before the human paradise, was creation disordered and in the grip of fallen powers? And what of the struggle for existence that characterizes creation? What of death?—for the cosmos is unthinkable apart from death. Should they not be regarded as the result of some primal revolt, a revolt that the Bible announces first of all in muted terms (the serpent in paradise) but finally proclaims with full volume: "the ancient serpent, who is called the Devil and Satan, the deceiver of the whole world" (Rev 12:9)? Here, once again, we come up against the question of the personal being of some extra-human evil; and in the light of our earlier discussion of it (and within the limits

---

[3] In that context, we already discussed the Christian doctrine of the Holy Spirit, who "brings about two things at the same time: he liberates finite freedom so that it may embrace its own, ultimate freedom; and he does so by initiating it into a participation in infinite freedom" (230–31).

[4] A. von Harnack, *Markion*, 158–72; also his *Dogmengeschichte* I, 682, note 3; B. Studer, "Soteriologie" in *HDG* III, 2a, 71.

[5] As J. Rivière is wont to do in his numerous works.

[6] Cf. *Theo-Drama* II, 159–63.

we there established), we must recognize that the reality will not go away just because we refuse to entertain the idea.[7] It is right to criticize (as Anselm himself did) the extravagant depiction of the "price" paid to the devil but not the kernel of the notion itself, which is that the devil's power is broken by the Cross: "Now is the ruler of this world cast out" (Jn 12:31); for Christ "disarmed the principalities and powers and made a public example of them [as prisoners], triumphing over them . . ." (Col 2:15). However we envisage the concentrated power of evil—whether as a depersonalized spiritual power or as the world's sin, heightened to the level of quasi-personality—its undeniable dominance over human freedom is fundamentally broken as a result of the Passion. That "whole world" that "is in the power of the evil one" (1 Jn 5:19) is "passing away" (1 Jn 2:17); "darkness is passing away" (1 Jn 2:8).

What is here called evil, the demonic, the devil, is the power that is hostile to God. And God did not intend death, as we experience it (Wis 2:23–24), so that the Fathers will use the words "sin", "the devil", "hell" and "death" interchangeably.[8] Of course, to say that this hostile power is broken is and remains an eschatological affirmation. This is shown by Paul when he says that Christ must reign "until he has put all his enemies under his feet. The last enemy to be destroyed is death" (1 Cor 15:26). Or the Book of Revelation, which says that the devil, having been cast out of heaven when Christ is "caught up to God," is "in great wrath, because he knows that his time is short" (Rev 12:12). In principle, the devil's works have been abolished (1 Jn 3:8), even if, confronted with Christ, he intensifies his enslavement of mankind more than ever (Jn 8:34; 13:2, 27). We shall return to this confrontation in the context of the theology of history. For man's eschatological liberation from wretched servitude exposes him, by that very fact, to danger, as the Johannine Jesus insists: "See, you are well! Sin no more, that nothing worse befall you" (Jn 5:14). More explicitly, the evil spirit, having been driven out, finds no resting place in the wilderness and returns to its former habitation, which is "empty,

---

[7] *Theo-Drama* III, 495ff.

[8] J. Rivière, "Mort et démon chez les Pères" in *RSR* 10 (1930), 579–621.

swept and put in order. Then he goes and brings with him seven other spirits more evil than himself, and they enter and dwell there; and the last state of that man becomes worse than the first" (Mt 12:43–45). This eschatological intensification *within* the victory of Christ, which is already won, *within* Christ's proclaimed plan to "release the captives" (Lk 4:18), is the central problem of the theology of history.

Looking back to volume two of *Theo-Drama*, we understand not only how man's finite freedom can be fettered by "powers" and subsequently released from them but also, at a deeper level, what is involved in such liberation—which the Bible speaks of as grace, divine sonship, being born of God. Finite freedom revealed itself in an indissolubly twofold aspect: it is the gift of "beginning from oneself" (*autexousion*),[9] yet it always contains the second dimension, namely, the obligation to leave room (in the vast expanse of being) for an unimaginable number of others, equally free. Associated with the latter is the obligation to acknowledge one's indebtedness[10] to the source of unconditional freedom, for finite freedom must return to this source in order to reach its goal (that is, its own total liberation, which can only be found in unconditional, infinite freedom). The interpenetration of these two aspects gave a precise indication of the finite structure of genuine freedom (a freedom genuinely given responsibility for itself): if it is to avoid self-contradiction, it cannot affirm itself as a loving source unless it acknowledges that it owes its being to a profound abyss of freedom (God's love), which has given it this being-in-responsibility, *and* simultaneously affirms and makes room for the freedom of others (love of neighbor).[11] Of course, finite freedom can attempt to live out this contradiction: it can lay such stress on the pole of the *autexousion* (*liberum arbitrium*) that the other pole, that is, the affirmation of the source and the breadth of freedom, is reduced to the former. In such a case, the *autexousion* is reinterpreted as *autarkia*, "total self-subsistence". This freezes the movement of finite freedom, which can only remain vital in the current flowing from the

---

[9] *Theo-Drama* II, 215, 220.
[10] *Ibid.*, 227–29; 284–85.
[11] *Ibid.*, 208f., 239f.

infinite source to the infinite goal (the two are identical). This "freezing" amounts to what Paul calls the "suppression" of a self-evident truth, the refusal to give "honor" or "thanks" to the God who is "known" (Rom 1:18, 21); by so doing, men enslave themselves once more, and this time they cannot get free by their own efforts. For finite freedom, essentially, cannot control absolute freedom: it is the latter that is free, in grace, to speak to every being that, sent forth into the realm of finite freedom, tries to suffice unto itself.

So, on the basis of the brief account in the second volume of *Theo-Drama*, pages 312–16, we must go over the relationship between freedom and grace in more detail. Initially it might seem that the structure of finite freedom we have indicated is so much a part of its "created" essence that there is neither reason nor space for any distinction between its nature and the realm of the "supernatural", that is, what is "of grace" in the true sense. After all, the bi-polar structure we have demonstrated—man's realization that he is "for himself" and yet owes his being to Another and also that he must allow room for other (finitely free) beings—belongs so much to the "nature" of this freedom that it must be defined by the very unity of rest and self-motion (*stasis* and *kinēsis*, as we found in Gregory of Nyssa).[12]

Gregory clearly understood his theory of the Spirit and of freedom as a Christian development of Plotinus' doctrine of Spirit. For Plotinus, the Spirit is the interminable upward movement of the *nous* to the *hen*, performed in finite steps: its return-to-itself is its longing for the All-One.[13] The formulations are similar, but there is a crucial difference. Plotinus' "One" is infinitely free only in itself and for itself; this means that the Spirit, the One's "Other", can only approach this freedom asymptotically; the philosopher is "compelled to equate the fulfilled with the unfulfilled, the joy of finding with the torment of seeking". The Spirit yearns for the One and circles around it, only encountering the *ousia*, that is, "determinate, intelligible being that has already found logical form".[14] Gregory of Nyssa is quite

---

[12] *Ibid.*, 236f.
[13] Texts: *ibid.*, 234f.; cf. *The Glory of the Lord* IV, 293.
[14] *The Glory of the Lord* IV, 297.

different: here absolute freedom freely and sovereignly communicates itself to finite freedom; in the Incarnation of Christ, it
descends to a level below itself, making itself available to finite
freedom as the latter's source and final goal. We can see the same
in Augustine.[15] The concept of yearning (*desiderium*) is central
for him; thus, while pointing to the innermost dynamism of finite freedom, he also makes it clear that such movement cannot in any way force the divine self-disclosure. Yearning is "the
soul's thirst . . . for God",[16] and it is by thirsting that the soul
becomes able to seize him: "The whole life of a proper Christian
is holy yearning. You yearn for what you do not yet see, but
the yearning itself makes you ready for being filled by it when
it eventually presents itself to your sight."[17] Yearning is not a
demand: it is a plea: "Your yearning is your prayer; if it is constant, so is your prayer. You will fall dumb if you stop loving. If
love remains awake, you will always be crying out; and as long
as you thus cry out, your yearning remains."[18] And in order to
show that genuine yearning is always directed toward a divinely
planned and divinely willed encounter with God's free grace in
the world, Augustine stresses that the saints of all ages, even
before Christ, yearned for the advent of the Son in the flesh.[19]

Right from the outset, God had decided to reveal and so give
himself to the creature he had endowed with finite freedom.
(He could not manifest himself except by giving himself.) This
means that we do not need to wonder whether or how finite
freedom would be possible in the absence of such a decision on
God's part. In fact, the New Testament testifies that God's will
to give himself has been the real motive of his creation from
all eternity. Thus the creature's yearning for a God who freely
reveals himself is not a demand: it can only be seen as a response
to God's decision.

How can God freely communicate himself to the creature he

---

[15] In *Theo-Drama* II, 231ff., we set forth Augustine's position as it appears primarily in *De Spiritu et Littera*. Here we are illuminating it from a complementary
angle.

[16] *En. in Ps. 62*, n. 4 (PL 36, 750–51).

[17] *In 1 Ep. Joh.*, tr. 4, c. 2, 6 (PL 35, 2008–9).

[18] *En. in Ps. 37*, n. 14 (PL 36, 404).

[19] *En. in Ps. 118*, s. 20 n. 1 (PL 37, 1557).

has endowed with freedom? The only way to envisage such self-communication is this: it must mysteriously heighten and fulfill the law of "natural" philosophy that says that God is completely immanent in his complete transcendence. For, even in the pure order of creation, the free creature cannot be conceived to be "outside" God (by God "withdrawing" or "making room" for the creature: *zimzum*); it must be understood to be *in* him, in his own infinite realms of freedom, sustained, accompanied and totally permeated by God; and so the creature's *being-over-against-God* grows in proportion to its *being-in-God*. Accordingly, at the level of God's personal self-giving to his free creature, there can be no place for a one-sided finite personalism that sees God as the mere "Thou", my self's "Other", however much weight personal categories may acquire at this level. Augustine's dictum *"interior intimo meo et superior summo meo"* retains its undiminished force, in both its assertions. And this, despite the difficulty involved in expressing, in the philosophical categories of causality, this new indwelling of God in the creature to whom he gives himself. (Even at the level of creation, "efficient causality" was not able to express God's essential immanence in the creature or the creature's immanence in him.) Yet it is precisely this intimacy with God on the part of the creature, preeminently of the creature endowed with grace—an intimacy for which there is no analogy and which persists despite the infinite distance between the *ens a se* and the *ens ab alio*—that forms the basis for the incomparable dramatic interplay of both.

Since this relationship has no analogy, it is very hard to distinguish the different forms of act and attitude that manifest God's grace. Basically, they only acquire meaning in the context of the creature's finitude, and even more in the context of its sinful resistance to the advances by which God seeks to woo it. Only in this way can we distinguish "internal" graces from "external" graces (that is, coming from the environment); only thus can we distinguish "indwelling" ("habitual") graces from those that inform acts ("actual"). God embraces his creature equally from within and from without, in duration and in act. It is not God, although he is eternal life and eternal freedom, who changes vis-à-vis the finite: it is the finite that alters its stance vis-à-vis him, coming closer to him or moving farther away. This, of course, raises once more the question that has been discussed all down the centuries: Why should we distinguish the areas of "nature" and (supernatural) "grace", if, from the creature's point of view, its existence [*Dasein*] and existence-in-this-form [*Sosein*] come to it as a gift from "outside" just as much as the benefits it receives from God? Bernanos concludes his *Diary of a Country Priest* with a quotation from St. Thérèse: "Everything is grace": Does this truth not transcend all theological hair-splitting? The decisive struggle between this monism or dualism of grace takes place between Pelagius and Augustine, but it is quite wrong to say that there was no dualism before Augustine.[20] On the contrary, the history of theology shows that the two areas were clearly distinguished right from the beginning. Nature is what God freely creates, *ens ab alio*; however much grace it receives, it remains eternally *nondivine*, the receptive subject of God's free bestowal of grace, which enables it to participate in the divine goods. The spiritual creature's ability to make free decisions is an integral part of its nature just as much as its reason; without this ability, it could neither understand nor spiritually receive God's self-giving. As early as Tertullian, we have the distinction between "to create" (*facere*) and "to form, establish" (*condere*): "*Quantum enim ad substantiam fecit* [*Deus*]*, quantum ad gratiam condidit.*"[21] And, with regard to the relationship between divine grace and our freedom: "*Haec erit vis divinae gratiae, potentior utique natura, habens in nobis subiacentem sibi liberi arbitrii potestatem.*"[22] Cyril of Jerusalem stresses that we are children of God, not by nature, but by adoption, that is, by grace.[23] The "divinization" so extolled by the Greek Fathers[24] is always the result of a grace that is rig-

---

[20] Gisbert Greshake, *Gnade der konkreten Freiheit. Eine Untersuchung zur Gnadenlehre des Pelagius* (Mainz: Grünewald, 1972): Greshake, indebted to Harnack, says that "Augustine was the first to distinguish nature from grace" (251). The following presentation of the argument between Pelagius and Augustine is based on Greshake's learned and informative study, although we are obliged to distance ourselves from his central thesis.

[21] *Adv. Marc.* l. 5, c. 17 (PL 2, 514C).

[22] *De anima* n. 21 (PL 2, 685).

[23] 3rd Catechesis (PG 33, 444).

[24] J. Gross, *La Divinisation du chrétien d'après les Pères Grecs* (Paris, 1938); P. Brezzi, "La Teopoiesi nel pensiero cristiano dei primi secoli" in *Rend. Acc. Linc.* 8, 2 (1947), 222–28; A. Theodoru, "Die Lehre von der Vergöttlichung des Mensch-

orously distinguished from nature, a grace that elevates us to a "super-natural dignity" (*hyper physin axiōma*).[25] The distinction insisted upon by Augustine is thoroughly traditional; even if, in creating the angels, God simultaneously establishes their nature and bestows grace upon them, the two elements must be clearly distinguished.[26]

The conflict between Pelagius and Augustine may well be full of misunderstandings, and the various more recent attempts to rehabilitate Pelagius are not without justification. In certain passages, Augustine, in later life, abbreviated his earlier positions for polemical reasons,[27] and he may have interpreted Pelagius in the sense of his more radical pupils such as Coelestius (from whom Pelagius distanced himself) and Julian of Eclanum. In Pelagius' favor, Greshake established that, while being profoundly dependent on the (pantheistic) Stoic concept of nature, he saw human nature, even in its God-given freedom, enjoying the most intimate connection—a kind of osmosis—with the divine Ground. True, the Stoics put heavy stress on the first pole, finite freedom, and pushed the notion of *autexousion* as far as the idea of *autarkia*, but they did not ignore the second pole: finite freedom is imbued with an inclination toward the ethically good (Chrysippus), and "impressions enter men from outside; there they join themselves to the seeds of the Logos that were originally implanted in man's 'memoria'." The law first established by Zeno does not impugn the autonomy of the ethically free human being; it "only articulates the inner, rational law of nature that is inherent in man. A considerable part is played, in addition to the

en bei den griechischen Kirchenvätern" in *Kerygma und Dogma* 7 (1961), 283–310; H. Rahner, "Die Gottesgeburt" in *Symbole der Kirche* (Salzburg, 1964); O. Faller, "Griechische Vergottung und christliche Vergöttlichung" in *Gregoriana* 6 (1925), 419–39; J. M. Garrigues/A. Riou, "Théophanie selon Jean Scot Erigène et divinisation selon s. Maxime le Confesseur" in *Annuaire de l'Ecole Prat. des Hautes Etudes*, 5th sec., 77 (1969–1970), 312–13.

[25] Cyril of Alexandria, *In Joh. 1, 9* (PG 73, 153).

[26] Simul in eis et condens naturam et largiens gratiam: *De Civ. Dei* 12, 9 (PL 41, 357).

[27] Cf. H. Jonas, *Augustin und das paulinische Freiheitsproblem. Eine philosophische Studie zum pelagianischen Streit*, 2d ed. (Göttingen, 1965), 62.

law, by the example of the man in whose works and life the Logos is especially concentrated and manifested; such a man is like a divine ambassador, able to educate and assist others."[28] On the one hand, with Pelagius, we can give the term "primal grace"[29] to the original gift of freedom to man, whereby God hands man over to himself. On the other hand, we can remind ourselves that it is precisely in his autonomy that man is an "image of God" and that he is surrounded by God's *pronoia*, his *cura*, his accompanying providence and care. Taken together, these two aspects give us practically all the basic elements of Pelagius' view of freedom. Not quite all, for, as a Christian and an extensive commentator on the Pauline Letters, Pelagius will make a clear distinction, in the manner of the Latin Fathers (beginning with Tertullian),[30] between the personal freedom of the creature and the personal freedom of God. Pantheistic Stoicism was unable to do this. Thus his basic position is a "unique combination of a Greek concept of salvation history and a Latin anthropology", in which the latter is "determined by the pathos of the individual's freedom and responsibility".[31]

This pathos is of an undoubtedly religious hue; it yields something that is crucial for Pelagius: his whole understanding of grace (in creation and redemption) centers on the primary gift of freedom to the creature in the original act of creation. Even when, after the Fall, nature is "blocked" in its relationship of freedom vis-à-vis God and so needs the help of the law and, finally, of Christ, Pelagius underlines the fact that God's activity as Creator and his redemptive *cura* constitute "one operation". This shows that "Pelagius' whole theology is grounded in the theology of creation."[32] The specifically Christian grace is always given solely in order to reestablish and strengthen man's original freedom—which is, of course, a religious freedom. In

---

[28] Greshake, 170–71.   [29] *Ibid.*, 287.

[30] Tertullian says that man enjoys a "bonum emancipatum sibi a Deo", that is, a good that God has given to be his own—or even a good that is independent of God, although the latter translation must be highly questionable on account of the "sibi". Julian, who takes an extreme Pelagian position, can speak of the man who possesses a "libertas arbitrii, qua a Deo emancipatus homo est" (PL 45, 1102).

[31] Greshake, 191–92.   [32] *Loc. cit.*, 130.

other words, all Pelagius' Christian spirituality is decidedly anthropocentric. God comes to fallen man's aid with the *correcto-
rium* of the law, holding up a mirror to him, as it were, in which
man can see his true essence and so strive for it anew;[33] in this
context, Pelagius is thinking less of God's covenant with Israel,
in which God reveals his essence, than of a means whereby man
can return to himself and find himself. Pelagius does acknowledge that Christ forgives sin *gratis*,[34] but, as Augustine will object, such forgiveness does not contain the inner grace to help
men to avoid new sins or the grace that prompts us to pray that
we may not fall into temptation.[35] Again, Christ remains primarily the *exemplum*, not in a purely external sense, but in the
way a significant model is able powerfully to transform our inner
orientation toward God. This model, however, is again traced
back to the very first grace by which, in creation, man is given
freedom.[36] On the one hand, there is the sinner's concrete inability to do the good (because of a certain superior power on the
part of the image of sin that confronts him in his environment
and in his own life). On the other hand, the absolved sinner is
concretely empowered to do the good because of the superior
power of attraction exercised by Christ's *exemplum*. In Pelagius,
these two sides are skillfully balanced between determinism and
indeterminism,[37] since the original gift of grace whereby man
possesses the ability to act freely (*posse*) is only "blocked", not
withdrawn.

But is this not simply how it is? Pelagius distinguishes three
things. First there is *posse*, that is, our nature, with its God-given
freedom, its "*possibilitas* always sustained by God's help"; but "it
is by God's activity alone that man can do the good." Secondly

---

[33] Texts in Greshake, 96, note 13.

[34] *Ibid.*, 101-2.

[35] *De natura et gratia*, 34, 39 (PL 44, 266).

[36] "The effective power of [Christ's] grace must be seen in connection with the
fundamental grace of creation. When man encounters the word and example of
Jesus Christ, who is the image of God in an absolute sense, he is presented with a
'mirror', as it were, that shows him what he himself is and should be." Thus the
image of God in man, which was obscured and choked by sin, is now "set free
and reanimated by a stimulus that is both mental and spiritual." Greshake, after
passages in Pelagius: 121.

[37] *Ibid.*, 86.

there is the *velle*, the power of decision-making that is inherent in man. Thirdly, there is *esse* (the effect).[38] In making these distinctions, is Pelagius not at one with Augustine (and, as we have shown,[39] with Anselm and Bernard, who followed the latter)? For Augustine distinguished between the *liberum arbitrium* —man's God-given ability to make a free choice, and the *libertas* that the will, enslaved to sin, only regains through the grace of God.[40] Augustine grants that even the sinner has the ability to make his own decisions within the space remaining to him (where he is shut out from God's love); however, so long as he refuses to admit saving grace, such decisions will be simply one form or another of self-love. Nonetheless, distinctions can be drawn here too: they emerge where, according to Pelagius' anthropocentric approach, all forms of grace can be traced back to a single form, namely, God's gift of finite freedom and his maintenance of it. Here God and man are seen in a kind of duality-in-unity that again agrees with Stoic thought and ultimately sees in sin (against which Pelagius preaches so forcefully) nothing other than a self-wounding on man's part.

For Augustine, by contrast, in accord with the biblical message, God is not only infinite freedom but also, above all, infinite love. Sin is primarily an offense against the latter; it is a turning away from it and a falling from love's sphere. The sinner cannot of his own volition return to this sphere: he needs the free initiative of divine love if he is to do so. Freedom, in its full sense, only exists in personal participation in absolute love, which presupposes that (however Augustine may have conceived the nature of the first man, Adam) this sharing in the inner fullness of God's love is distinct from the creation and gift of a natural, free power to choose. For Augustine, it is this sharing that constitutes grace in the full sense, however free and gracious creation itself may have been. Furthermore, it does not lie exclusively in the realm of the *illuminatio* of finite knowing from within—although this element is very important in Augustine and his doctrine of the internal teacher (*magister interior*). Such *illuminatio* could always

---

[38] *Ibid.*, 63.

[39] *Theo-Drama* II, 223–24.

[40] Of course, Augustine is not totally consistent in his terminology, but his teaching as such is clear throughout.

be conferred from a certain distance; it would not *have* to be the self-giving of absolute Love, which must be both noetic and ontic. Hence, for Augustine, salvation history's greatest *exemplum* of divine grace is the Cross of Christ, indissolubly connected with his Eucharist, in which Christ's essence is inwardly communicated to us, or rather, we become inwardly his members. Where Pelagius says *exemplum*, Augustine deliberately and insistently says *exemplum et sacramentum.*[41] Even if Pelagius does not mean his *exemplum* to be taken in a purely external sense, as a historical fact that exerts its influence upon us, he obstinately refuses to enter the sphere of *sacramentum* in the broader and narrower senses. For him, "being in Christ, just like man's being a son of God, is not a mystical interpenetration or identity between Christ (God) and the disciple, but a unity and community that come about through discipleship and imitation."[42] "Thus Pelagius stops at the point at which the Greek theologians' doctrine of man's askesis rises to the presence of the Pneuma, to the level of inner illumination through sacramental mystagogy, even going so far as to speak of the divinization of human nature and of the cosmos by the Incarnation of the Logos. Pelagius is satisfied with man's practical, 'ethical' approximation to Christ and with the presence of the Spirit that implies."[43] But an ethicism of this kind cannot stand without being linked to the ontic problem of the God/creature relationship, and particularly that between

---

[41] Cf. Theobald Beer, *Der fröhliche Wechsel und Streit* (Leipzig: Benno, 1974); see index under "sacramentum". The chief passage is *De Trin.* IV, 3 (PL 42, 891); cf. also *De consensu evangelistarum* I, 53–54 (PL 34, 1069f.).

[42] Greshake, 124.

[43] Greshake seems to share this Pelagian complacency, for he tries to say that the difference between Pelagius and Augustine arises from their different horizons of experience, that is, Augustine is torn asunder psychologically, and only conversion can make him whole again; he also frequently makes derogatory remarks about Augustine's concept of grace. Like Pelagius, he is concerned to "resist a mystical, nonconcrete pneumatology that would overpower subjectivity; instead, he wishes to describe Spirit as a concretely defined and definable quantity that is in part dependent on man's free action" (143). "Grace is not a mysterious, invisible, transforming power that proceeds directly from God: it is freedom . . ." (153). "Not a mystical, inward wholeness that is guaranteed by sacramental initiation, but the plain and visible walking along the path of Christ" (152). So Pelagius can "link salvation . . . to nature, whereas Augustine must have recourse beyond nature to a special, mysterious gift of grace from the hand of Christ" (205).

infinite and finite freedom. The drama involving the two kinds of freedom presupposes that the creature has been endowed with freedom and so constituted as the "image" of God;[44] it is this same presupposition that forms the basis for man's development toward "likeness" with God. However, the latter cannot be *more* than the precondition for inner participation in the essence of God, that is, in the vibrant, divine love-life of the Trinity. It is Augustine's indisputable achievement to have established this (over against Pelagius); individual one-sidednesses in the way he formulated it cannot affect this achievement.

Infinite freedom summons finite freedom to go beyond itself and share in the former. This remains a mystery, because the creature, although it is profoundly affected in its innermost essence, has no way—even at the level of speculation—of translating this offer into the terms of its own finitude. The attempt to do so characterizes all forms of Gnosticism. There is a distinction between the ineradicable nondivinity of the creaturely "image" and its vocation to participate in the divine prototype ("likeness"): Gnosticism obliterates this distinction and makes of the two a single process, comprehensible in terms of finite being and finite thought. This is all the easier because the distance between the created, nondivine "image" and the prototype seems to run parallel to the prototypical distance *within* the Trinity: accordingly, particularly since Joachim of Flora, there is a great temptation to equate the distance between God and the creature with the "distance" found within the Trinity. This temptation is addressed by the strong words of the Fourth Council of the Lateran: "*inter creatorem et creaturam non potest similitudo notari, quin inter eos maior sit dissimilitudo notanda*" (DS 806): this also applies in its highest form to the creature's "divinization" by the *lumen gloriae*. This basic formula of the *analogia entis* is also the ultimate foundation of our Christian theological dramatic theory, just as it has its concrete center in the Chalcedonian "unconfused and indivisible" with regard to the two natures in Christ.[45]

This means that we can speak concretely of *theosis* only in the

---

[44] Pelagius is quite right here: "vir ad imaginem Dei factus [est] et idcirco [!] liber est." *Expos. XIII epist. Pauli*, ed. Souter (Cambridge, 1926), 188.

[45] *Theo-Drama* II, 267–68.

context of Christology: it presupposes the no less mysterious possibility of the Incarnation of God. If we take seriously this mystery of God's descent into the form of his creature—this was the seminal intuition of the Greek Fathers—the *sarkōsis* implies the *theopoiēsis*. For now the "prototype" [*Urbild*] (the eternal Son, enjoying eternal Sonship of the Father) has indwelt the "copy" [*Abbild*] and stamped his divine form upon it once and for all.[46] We have to remember, however, that the divine penetration of the creaturely went farther than the Fathers, with their idea of the *admirabile commercium*, were inclined to admit: even the sinner's alienation from God was taken into the Godhead, into the "economic" distance between Father and Son. This consideration alone gives completeness and sharpness to the notion that *theosis* is implicit in the Incarnation of the divine Word. Even before man, the image of God, sets forth to win a share in the gracious offer of freedom and divine life, God's absolute freedom has already plumbed the *regio* (*peccaminosae*) *dissimilitudinis* and penetrated the self-enclosed servitude of finite freedom: *ascendens in altum captivam duxit captivitatem: dedit dona hominibus* (Eph 4:8). The passage continues, emphasizing the primacy of the descent: "In saying, 'He ascended,' what does it mean but that he had also descended into the lower parts of the earth? He who descended is he who also ascended far above all the heavens, that he might fill all things" (Eph 4:9–10). He also liberated finite freedom from its self-inclosed servitude, since freedom can only fulfill its inchoate *autexousion* ("of itself") within the context of the absolute, divine "of himself". And, since what

[46] Cf. for example, Athanasius, *C. Arian.* I, 38 (PG 26, 92C), *Ep. ad Adelphium* 4 ("For, in taking on the nature of a servant, the Son [who was in the divine nature] by no means forfeited the Godhead. On the contrary, he became the liberator of all flesh and of the entire creation", PG 26, 1077A). R. H. Hübner, in his *Die Einheit des Leibes Christi bei Gregor von Nyssa* (Leiden: Brill, 1974) 232ff., asked how Athanasius could see the world, on the one hand—in a Stoic sense— as animated and permeated by the Logos, while, on the other hand, he holds that mankind (and through it, the cosmos) can only be "divinized" by the Incarnation of the Logos in a particular body. The answer is an Augustinian one: the first point of reference is God's immanence, as Creator, in his creation; the second is a new, free act of God's grace, a qualitatively new and uniquely intimate form of participation in the divine life: we are given a share in his divine Spirit. But cf. also *Ep. ad Serap.* 4, 6–7; *Ep.* 4 (PG 26, 633ff.).

is inchoate (in the "image" of God) already contains an element of the absolute (for this is what freedom means), the "image" is committed to becoming "like" God if it is to realize itself. In fact, the creature's "ascent to God" has already been taken up into the entirely different, liberating "servitude" of eternal freedom by the grace (*dedit dona*) of the God who first descends to the level of the creature. Only in God's freedom can man find his "exemplary identity".[47] There is no suggestion of self-alienation here in man's orientation to divine freedom: it is actually the only way in which he can find himself. Maximus the Confessor succinctly portrays man's ascent within God's correlative descent in Christ:

> Even now man has firmness and self-identity through conduct (*hexis*) that has integrity; in the coming aeon, he will have them through the gift of divinization. Thus he loves and embraces the aforementioned *logoi*, which have preexistence in God. Indeed he thereby loves God himself, in whom all the *logoi* of the good are firmly grounded, and thus he is a "part of God":
>
> he *is*, because of the *logos* of being that is in God;
>
> he is good, because of the *logos* of his goodness that is in God;
>
> he is divine, because of the *logos* of his eternal being that is in God.
>
> He venerates these *logoi*, acts in accord with them and so translates himself entirely and solely into God. Thus he fashions and forms God, entirely and solely, within himself, so that by grace he himself is and may be called God; while God, by condescending to his level and for his sake, is and may be called Man. This is the operation of the power of mutual will: it divinizes man in God thanks to his love for God and incarnates God in man thanks to his love of men. By a wondrous exchange (*kalēn antistrophēn*), God is made man for the sake of man's divinization, and man is made divine because of God's becoming man. For the Logos of God, who is God, wills to work the mystery of his Incarnation always, and in all.[48]

---

[47] Cf. *Theo-Drama* II, 270.

[48] *Ambigua* 7 (PG 91, 1084BD). German translation after Felix Heinzer, *Sohnschaftliches Menschsein. Zur christologischen Anthropologie Maximus des Bekenners* (Fribourg: Diss., 1979, typescript), 162, who indicates parallel passages in Maximus. Cf. Augustine's brief assertion: "The elevation of human nature is of such a kind

Clearly, this portrayal of the unity of the two soteriological themes, that is, redemption as the liberation of a self-inclosed freedom (3) and initiation into the life of the Trinity (4), includes all the other biblical themes. For we have just arrived at the central theme of the "exchange of places" (2), which comes about on the initiative of God's love, which desires to reconcile the world with him (5) on the basis of the Father's sacrificial surrender of the Son, a surrender explicitly affirmed and accomplished by the Son (1). If Maximus' portrayal of the reciprocal immanence of finite and infinite freedom seems somehow undramatic, we must remember two things: first, that the *analogia entis* (the irreducible "otherness" of created nature) excludes any kind of fusion and confusion in this ever-intensifying reciprocal interpenetration: each increase in "divinization" on the part of the creature also implies an increase of its own freedom. This guarantees the abiding and ever-increasing vitality of the dramatic relationship between God and the creature. Second, as we have already indicated, finite freedom, once it has been redeemed and liberated, is now in danger of being able to utter a heightened No, even to the extent of making a total and irrevocable refusal of grace, as we must assume in the case of that angel who fell. We shall deal later with this inner, apparently inevitable process of polarization.

c. The Paradox of Christian Discipleship

The following short section forms a bridge to the next chapter by drawing from the foregoing an apparently paradoxical conclusion with regard to the structure of Christian discipleship. We have laid great stress on the caesura in the life of Jesus: on the one hand, we have his life as such (whether hidden or public), which was an ever more conscious movement toward the "hour", and, on the other hand, we have the "hour" itself, when it finally arrived, with its special, discontinuous content. If Jesus' entire life, from the moment of the Incarnation, was redemptive (in the sense put forward particularly by the Greek

---

that it could not have risen higher, just as the Godhead, for our sake, could not have descended any lower." *De praed. sanct.* 15 (PL 44, 983).

Fathers), then the "hour" that brought everything to its consummation was eminently so. Here the sinful world, alienated from God, is taken into the infinite Father/Son relationship (which is now "economic"); when the Son accomplishes his mission, as he breathes out the Spirit of his mission and gives him back to the Father, the Spirit is breathed into a mankind that has been redeemed by the Passion, namely, the Church of Christ. For the Spirit accompanies the Son's entire mission, shares in the experience of it and, as it were, enfolds this mission in himself. He is simultaneously the Spirit of the Father who surrenders his Son and that of the sacrificed and glorified Son; he is the trinitarian Spirit, yet he informs the entire "economy", and so he contains within himself, in unity, both the movement toward the Cross and the movement from Cross to Resurrection. This Spirit is the concrete grace and love of God that is "poured into our hearts" (Rom 5:5). By way of amplification, we can say that Jesus did not infuse the Spirit of his mission into his disciples in installments so that they could follow him step by step: in fact, as long as Jesus "was not yet glorified", the disciples "had not been given" the Spirit (Jn 7:39). Consequently, in spite of their "good will", the disciples could not really understand Jesus, nor could they follow him to the end, to the Cross. So Jesus says to Peter, "Where I am going you cannot follow me now; but you shall follow afterward" (Jn 13:36).

Accordingly, this "following afterward" cannot be a historical repetition of the historical sequence of Jesus' life in its movement to the Cross: the Spirit given to believers always embraces the totality—the journey to the Cross, the Passion, the Resurrection and Ascension. Paul says explicitly that the Spirit given to believers recapitulates the entire economy of salvation, since he is the Spirit of the whole historical and pneumatic Christ, crucified and risen. In many passages, the gift of the Spirit of Christ, whereby the believer is initiated into the sphere of Christ, is portrayed as a dying-with, a suffering-with, a being-crucified-with, a being-buried-with; the believer shares Christ's weakness so that he may rise with him, enjoy new life with him, reign with him, be glorified with him, ascend to heaven with him (Rom 6:4, 5, 8; 8:17; 2 Cor 4:11; 13:4; 2 Tim 2:11, 12; cf. Eph 2:5f.). But there is no suggestion that the two phases are consecutive in the earthly life of the Christian. Rather, the complete fulfillment of the second phase remains a matter of eschatological hope (cf. Phil 3:11): it is reserved for Christ's parousia. However, this applies only to the final fulfillment, not to the effects of Christ's risen and heavenly life, for the latter is expressly shown forth in the very midst of mortal existence: "We always carry in the body the death of Jesus, so that the [glorified] life of Jesus may also be manifested in our bodies" (2 Cor 4:10). "Always" refers to the fact that a certain temporal succession of phases is a natural possibility, arising out of the historical nature of our existence, but it is secondary: the most important factor is the unity and integrity of the Spirit of Christ, simultaneously bearing death and Resurrection within him. Nor does this alienate the Christian from the historical Jesus: in Jesus, the Spirit of his mission was complete at every moment, since he was ready for the Father's "hour" at all times during his earthly life—indeed, as the Transfiguration scene shows, he had the potential for resurrection life within him always, by way of anticipation—but he did not wish to preempt it. It is not the Holy Spirit who embodies the synthesis of Jesus' mission, for example, by distilling the latter's whole achievement: Jesus himself, at any one time, *is* this synthesis, for the Father willed to give him the Spirit "without measure" (Jn 3:34). In a certain respect, in his own public life, he mirrors something of the paradox of subsequent discipleship: he is revered by his disciples, feted by the crowds and watched by the leaders of the nation, *and simultaneously* he is unknown, mistaken and rejected in advance. To that extent, he anticipates something of Paul's paradoxical assertions concerning the Christian life: "When reviled, we bless; when persecuted, we endure; when slandered, we try to conciliate" (1 Cor 4:12–13); "in honor and dishonor, in ill repute and good repute. We are treated as impostors, and yet are true; as unknown, and yet well known; as dying, and behold we live . . ." (2 Cor 6:8f.).

Thus the "sphere" in which the Christian lives, which is summed up by the term *en Christōi*, embraces both the historical Jesus and equally the Risen Christ, the Christ of faith, who recapitulates in himself everything earthly.[49] In the life of the

[49] "The only way Paul is able to bridge the objective, temporal gap is by the

Christian, naturally, resurrection in the full sense belongs to the world to come, as in the case of Christ himself. So a Christian's historical path may well lead to the Cross, as did Christ's; this was predicted for Peter (Jn 21:18), and in the same way Paul was delivered up to the Jews and by them to the Gentiles (Acts 21ff.). But again, this cannot change the fact that the Christian is in principle someone who has risen and ascended into heaven (Eph 2:6; Col 3:1-4) and that Christ's Resurrection glory radiates through his whole being and activity (2 Cor 3:16-4:6), as is plain to anyone who looks, "not to the things that are seen, but to the things that are unseen" (*ibid.*, 4:18). Whether these phases of darkness and light, distress and consolation (2 Cor 1:4-7) are synchronous or diachronous for the individual Christian is a secondary matter; where the Spirit of the Lord is involved, there is nothing against these phases being simultaneous, even if particular forms of inner distress and darkness exclude a concomitant experience of consolation. The Christian is both crucified with the Lord and risen with him: both these *existentiales* stamp his existence, simultaneously and inseparably.

There is a locus at which the pneumatic unity of Cross and Resurrection is especially evident to the disciple, a locus that has become sacramental in the life of the Church. The sinner's first decisive encounter with the all-penetrating light of Christ is both things at once: a crucifying light and a liberating summons to come forth from darkness. In the sacrament of *penance*, which places the sinner in the spotlight of judgment, the pain of exposure to the two-edged sword of God's word, which "pierces to the division of soul and spirit" (Heb 4:12f.), is the precondition for the Easter absolution. Thus, in the penitential scene with the Samaritan woman, she is both humbled and liberated. Thus Paul is blinded and cast down by the light from heaven —heretofore all was error!—but at the same time he is pointed toward a new, risen existence as a "chosen vessel" (Acts 9:3ff.).

---

figure of Christ himself. On the one hand, he is always the historical Christ and, as such—in terms of salvation history—the Messiah; on the other hand, he is the pneumatic Lord who lives through all times (not 'above' time or 'timeless'), who will come again at the parousia." R. Schnackenburg, "Das Heilsgeschehen bei der Taufe nach dem Apostel Paulus" in *Münch. Theol. Stud.* I, part 1, vol. 1 (Munich: Zink, 1950), 158. Cf. the whole section 132–67.

The entire Johannine theology of light and darkness portrays this irruption of light into what was withdrawn and self-concealing, which must either surrender to the light or even more resolutely close itself to it (cf. Jn 1:5, 9; 3:19–21; 8:12 and chapter 9 by way of interpretation; 12:35–36). The penitential letters in the Book of Revelation—passing over many scenes in the Gospel—constitute a model of ecclesial penance. The Son of Man with "eyes as of flame" looks into the most hidden corners of the community, exposing it mercilessly; if it repents, he promises it things that far transcend the present world. These letters are a kind of painful and purifying precondition, necessary if the community is to share in the eschatological and heavenly visions. For their part, the apostolic Letters are practically all written within the context of discipleship on the basis of the Gospel's illumination: here the unsparing scrutiny of the light is applied not only to what the Christians were prior to their conversion (Rom 6:16ff.; Eph 2:12; 4:17–5:20, passim) but also to the individual communities' failures, in coarser or more refined ways, to live up to the gospel. Here, *parainesis* means both a grave warning and a consolation and strengthening that lifts the one to whom it is addressed. The community may experience crucifixion as it passes through the *inferno* (2 Pet, Jude) until, on the heights of the *purgatorio*, the light of Easter begins to shine. But it is always the same Spirit of Christ, who redeems by judgment and judges in order to redeem. It is God's Word—the Crucified and Risen One, eternally pierced (Rev 1:7) and yet lofty and transfigured —who thus communicates his light to others; this is an abiding, crucial aspect of the Church's sacrament: true, the sinner confesses his guilt, but he does so led (indeed, "reproved") by the Spirit, to whom he must bow if his confession is to have substance before God. Only what is "reproved is made manifest by the light, for whatsoever doth make manifest is light" (Eph 5:13f., AV).

Discipleship brings with it the gift of participation in the Cross and Resurrection of Christ, and this points to a final element. This participation is bound to extend itself, albeit in a secondary manner, to the *pro nobis* of Christ's Paschal Mystery. We have to speak of this with reticence, as does the New Testament itself. But is there not something frightening in what Jesus says to the Sons of Zebedee when, unsuspecting, they say that they can drink of the cup that he will drink: "The cup that I drink you will drink; and with the baptism with which I am baptized, you will be baptized . . ." (Mk 10:39f.)? Is it not disconcerting to hear Paul say, unabashed, that he is crucified together with Christ (Gal 2:19) and that he bears Christ's wounds (Gal 6:17)? He is quite aware, of course, of the vast gulf between Christ's crucifixion and his own ("Was Paul crucified for you?", 1 Cor 1:13) and wants to know and preach nothing but the Cross of Christ (*ibid.*, 2:2). There is a closeness *and* a distance here, as is shown by the phrase "I complete what is lacking in Christ's afflictions" (Col 1:24). The sufferings of the God-man are all-sufficient, but within those sufferings a place has been left for the disciples; thus Jesus predicts that those who are his will share his destiny (Jn 16:1-4; Mt 10:24f.). "Through grace", a fellowship of suffering and resurrection is created, and this fellowship only has meaning if the *pro nobis* is extended to the participants. The metaphor of the vine brings us as close as we can get to uttering its meaning: the man who lives *en Christōi*, from the root and stem of Christ, will bear fruit. First and foremost, of course, it is the "gospel which is bearing fruit and growing in the whole world", but immediately thereafter we hear that this is also taking place in the community at Colossae (Col 1:6); a few verses later the Colossians are urged "to bear fruit in every good work", empowered by the might of God's glory (1:10f.). The Romans are enjoined similarly to "bear fruit for God" (Rom 7:4). Paul's apostolate seems to him a "gathering of fruit" in and for Christ (Rom 1:13); the word is frequently found in the Gospels. But this bearing of fruit is not for oneself: it is for the kingdom of God; alternatively, man is "hired" by the kingdom of God to work in the harvest. It does not matter whether the laborers are few or hired at the last moment or reap where they have not sown: in all cases, they are working for the whole harvest. So, however hidden and modest their contribution is, they are working within Christ's sphere and in fellowship with him.

This brings us immediately to the final section in our consideration of New Testament soteriology: the relationship between the Redeemer and the Church.

4. The Church and the Paschal Mystery

a. The Dramatic Dimensions of the Eucharist

If the "for us" of the Cross is recognized to be inclusive,[1] mankind is part of the drama of the Cross whether it wishes to be or not. The Church of Christ, knowing this mystery and believing in it, is consciously a part of it, particularly since, on the night Jesus was betrayed, he himself endowed her with this knowledge in the form of an action that ensured her involvement: "Do this in memory of me." In her actions (*drāma*, that is, "doings", from the Greek *drāō*), the Church is always related, at least indirectly, to the Paschal drama. As a result, the celebration of the Eucharist has often been described as a dramatic action.[2] In view of the many controversies on this subject, it seems important to take time to reflect on the Church's involvement in the events of the Cross. We shall trace this involvement in five stages.

1. After all we have said about the Passion of Christ being "for us", there can be no doubt that those for whose sins Christ suffered and atoned have undergone an ontological shift. Moreover, this shift must be acknowledged to have taken place— contrary to Luther—*prior* to their embracing of the fact by an act of faith. If Jesus "died for us while we were yet . . . enemies"

---

[1] Cf. 231 above. On the phenomenon of "inclusion", cf. Phil. Jobert, O.S.B., "Fondements de la théologie du Sacré-Coeur" in *Rev. Thomiste* 4 (1976), 591–98.

[2] J. A. Jungmann, in his *Missarum Sollemnia* (Vienna: Herder, 1948), I, 4, quotes a sentence from Hugo Ball: "As far as the Catholic is concerned, there is no such thing as theatre. The spectacle that engrosses him and takes possession of him every morning is Holy Mass." Jungmann himself says that Jesus does not accomplish his sacrifice on our altars "in order to give us a spectacle but in order to draw us and his Church, everywhere on earth and in all centuries, into his *pascha*, into his movement from this world to the Father. His sacrifice, on every occasion, is meant to become the Church's sacrifice" (*ibid.* I, 239). Medieval theology, which interpreted the Mass by means of much top-heavy allegorizing, saw it not only as a spiritual battle and a judicial process but also as the performance of a drama (*tragoedia*): Honorius Augustodunensis, *Gemma animae*, c. 72–83 (PL 172, 566C–570C; cf. PL 213, 144D).

(Rom 5:8, 10), something has happened to us as a result. Paul formulates it with great clarity: "If one has died for all, then all have died" (2 Cor 5:14). It follows that, "if we live, we live to the Lord; and if we die, we die to the Lord" (Rom 14:8), even before those who thus believe and know are addressed by the imperative: "And he died for all, that those who live might live no longer for themselves but for him who for their sake died and was raised" (2 Cor 5:15). Note that the inclusion of mankind, and of the Church in particular, is here portrayed solely as the work of him who suffers and dies "for" the others; it is not, for instance, already the action of the "Mystical Body of Christ" —regarded as a single action because of the organic unity of "Head" and "members". For the Mystical Body is only formally established on the basis of that "inclusion" that flows from the "for us". It is important to maintain this against an exclusively incarnational rationale; at the same time, we should not simply attribute the latter to the Greek Fathers without making a careful distinction. We must make the same distinction in the thought of Aquinas too: he begins with the *gratia capitis* given to Christ; this grace *redundat ad membra*. Thus Thomas endeavors to get beyond Anselm's all-too-juridical theory of the transfer of merit, for he too knows that, while Jesus possessed this *gratia capitis* "from the very beginning of his conception", it only became operative through his Passion.[3]

2. The next thing for consideration is the abiding actuality of the historical Passion, not primarily because it affects every human being who enters history at any time, but rather because— as we have already shown[4]—what takes place in the "economic" Trinity is cherished and embraced by the "immanent" Trinity and, in particular, by the Holy Spirit, who, as the Spirit of Jesus' entire temporal existence and preeminently of his Passion and Resurrection, is poured out upon the Church and the world.[5] But this presence of the salvific drama is only fully brought about through the continual representation of Christ, bodily delivered up "for us". As Johannes Betz (incorporating the insights of Odo

---

[3] *S. Th.* III, 48, 1 c and ad 2.
[4] Cf. 319ff. above.
[5] Cf. 364ff. above.

Casel) has demonstrated, the Greek Fathers discerned clearly that Christ, in surrendering his sacrificed flesh and shed blood for his disciples, was communicating, not the merely material side of his bodily substance, but the saving events wrought by it. The central issue, for them, is "the real presence, in the Supper of the Lord, of the Person and saving work of Jesus".[6] On the one hand, then, there is the *person*, for, as in particular John Chrysostom emphasizes, it is the Person of Jesus who acts in the ministerial priest;[7] as we shall go on to see, this does not exclude the contribution of the Church.[8] On the other hand, there is the *saving work*; the Fathers equally affirm that this saving work is identical, in the here-and-now celebration, with what was accomplished on the Cross.[9] The liturgy constantly connects these two words: "we recall and offer",[10] repeating the words of institution and showing the relationship between the present action and what took place then. It is unwise to polarize the various theories that try to define the nature of this "making-present"; most of them stress one particular aspect, but all the aspects converge on a mystery that is not fully accessible to our reason. The fundamental

[6] *Die Eucharistie in der Zeit der griechischen Väter*, vol. I/1 (Freiburg: Herder, 1955). Cf. primarily chapter 2 on the "Real Presence of the Person of Christ in the Eucharist as Kyrios and High Priest" (65–139). Betz shows how important the "suppers of the Risen One" were and have remained "for an understanding of the Church's Eucharist"; they represent "a link between the Last Supper of the historical Jesus and the Eucharist of the Church" (82, quoting Markus Barth).

[7] "The sacred action takes place before us by human power. He who accomplished it then, at that supper, performs it now also. Our part is only to be servants. It is he who consecrates and transforms." *In Mt. hom.* 82, 5 (PG 58, 744); cf. *In 2 Tim. hom.* 2, 4 (PG 62, 612): "Anyone who thinks that this [sacrifice] is less than that [on the Cross] fails to understand that Christ is present and acting here and now."

[8] The same Chrysostom establishes the link: Christ's word transforms the gifts at every Eucharist, and he has entrusted this word to the Church. The illustration he uses is highly significant: "Just as that other command, 'Be fruitful and multiply and fill the earth' empowered our nature [!] for all time to procreate children, so this command, issued once for all, accomplishes the sacrifice on every altar in every church." *De prod. Judae* 1, 6 (PG 49:380).

[9] "The sacrifice we offer is not a different one from that offered by the High Priest then: it is the same one we continually offer [*poioumen*]. Or rather, we make the memorial of that sacrifice." Chrysostom, *In Heb. hom.* 17, 3 (PG 63, 131).

[10] Texts in J. Betz, 204–11.

presupposition is that the Person of Jesus is really present; but along with the Person comes his entire temporal history and, in particular, its climax in Cross and Resurrection.[11] Indeed, in the context of the Cross, his whole existence can be understood as a perpetual, eternal self-offering to the Father on behalf of mankind; thus the Church's eucharistic sacrifice would refer to this eternal gesture of his.[12] Thus the Church's part in Christ's sacrifice would seem, not so much to "make present" the latter, but rather to "relate the faithful to the supertemporal presence of the saving mystery".[13] But can we sensibly distinguish between these two forms of relationship? After all, it is a relationship between something temporal and something eternal. Does it make any difference whether, in this encounter, we place more emphasis on the Person of the Redeemer (the objective agent) or on the effects of grace found in the Church and in believers?[14]

---

[11] "The transfigured Christ is characterized by his death and his Resurrection. These are not mere past events of his life: they are ever alive and present." M. Schmaus, *Kath. Dogmatik* IV/1, 3–4 (1952), 56. ". . . Cette réalité que furent la passion, la mort, la résurrection et l'ascension du Christ, incarnées dans cette chair et ce sang ici présents, qui sont dans l'état où ils sont aujourd'hui au ciel, c.à.d. glorieux, mais qui ne sont glorieux que parce qu'ils *ont été* et *continuent* d'avoir été souffrants, morts et ressuscités." E. Masure, *Le Sacrifice du corps mystique* (Paris: Desclée de Brouwer, 1950), 56.

[12] Texts in M. de la Taille, *Mysterium Fidei* (Paris: Beauchesne, 1931), eluc. XXI (265ff.). So also Cajetan: "Perseverat immolatitio modo unicum sacrificium. . . . Quemadmodum continua intercessio Christi pro nobis in coelo non derogat unicae intercessioni mortis Christi, ita non, immo multo minus eidem derogat perseverantia Christi immolatitio modo ad intercedendum pro nobis, ut participes simus remissionis peccatorum in ara crucis factae, quando ista intercessio fit per mysterium sub specie panis et vini: illa autem in coelo fit per Christum in propria specie, in qua crucifixus est." *De sacrif. missae* (1531), c. 6. On the relationship between the Eucharist and the "heavenly altar", cf. *ibid.*, 271–83.

[13] Thus V. Warnach, interpreting O. Casel's theory: "It is *we* who, by carrying out the cultic symbol with faith, are 'made present' to the saving action; we are transferred into its reality." "Zum Problem der Mysteriengegenwart" in *Lit. Leben* 5 (1938), 35.

[14] As Scholasticism did. Cf. Thomas, *S. Th.* III, 83, 1: ". . . alio modo quantum ad effectum passionis Christi, quia scilicet per hoc sacramentum participes efficimur fructus dominicae passionis." Similar is G. Söhngen's view of the way Jesus' historical sacrifice is made present in the Eucharist: it is "brought into the here and now by being performed *in* and *by* us inwardly, that is, by the life-giving Spirit of the Lord." *Der Wesensaufbau des Mysteriums* (Bonn: Hanstein, 1938), 47.

While this view is right to locate the historical work of Jesus in the realm of the eternal, or, as we have said, the economic Trinity in the immanent Trinity, we must ask whether it is sufficient. Must there not be some direct relationship between the historical Last Supper, with the historical Cross, and the celebration of the Eucharist in history here and now? Is it enough to say that "We are in touch with salvation history and its past through the divine mystery and its supertemporal present reality"?[15] The words of institution point to a unique series of events, ending in the Cross: the command to repeat this action ("Do this . . .") refers to those same events. Attempts to refer the present back to the past (Kierkegaard's "simultaneity") are unconvincing;[16] Casel's idea that the historical saving act is made present *secundum modum substantiae*, in its essential core, *non tamquam in tempore*, is equally unconvincing, unless we adopt the kind of Platonism[17] that Casel is anxious to avoid.[18]

Next we learn "that it is not only in the sacramental effect that Jesus' once-for-all work is set forth and rendered present but in the Church's here-and-now sacramental *action*."[19] This must involve the interplay of two elements: the ecclesial action as such, which is clearly an offering of sacrifice, but also the symbolism of what is offered: the bread and wine are separated, constituting a "type"[20] or symbol of the dead body of Jesus, which is separated from its shed blood. There can be no doubt that these two elements, more than all the explanations given hitherto, give

---

[15] *Ibid.*, 53.

[16] As a proponent of this view, J. Betz (*loc. cit.*, 199) quotes W. T. Hahn, *Das Mitsterben und Mitauferstehen mit Christus bei Paulus* (1937), 96f., and G. Bornkamm, "Taufe und neues Leben bei Paulus" in *Th. Bl.* 18 (1939), 237.

[17] Betz at least refers to this possibility: "The symbolic presence of the past saving action . . . can be compared to the presence of the idea in the visible, individual thing in Platonism. . . . But everything depends on really understanding the image in the Platonic sense. The image is not a substitute for the archetype, . . . it *is* the archetype made radiantly visible" (202; cf. 210).

[18] Söhngen, 51; O. Casel, "Mysteriengegenwart" in *Jahrb. f. Lit. wiss.* 8 (1928), 145ff.

[19] Thus J. Betz, 200, and also the concluding view of G. Söhngen, *Das sakramentale Wesen des Messopfers* (Essen, 1946).

[20] On the different treatment of this symbolism in the Fathers (*symbolon, eikōn, homoiōma, antitypos*), cf. J. Betz, 217–42.

concrete expression to the direct historical relationship between
the Last Supper of Jesus and our celebration today. But again we
can ask whether they are sufficient. As far as the Church's act itself is concerned, to what extent does it go beyond a mere act of
offering (*oblatio*) and involve an actual sacrifice (*sacrificium*) that is
at least analogous to the sacrifice of Christ? For what is sacrificial
in this act inheres wholly in the *offerendum*, namely, Christ's sacrifice on the Cross (which the Church of God proclaims), not
in the *offerens*. It may be true that the separation of the forms of
bread and wine is a symbolic sign, referring to Christ's sacrificial
death; but it is scarcely possible to say that this sign has the power
to bring about an effective *presence* of this sacrificial death. Certainly, what is ultimately offered to God is no longer earthly food
but Christ's body and blood, but it is not obvious how such an
offering—nor its final result, that is, Communion—draws the
Church's action inwardly into the sacrifice of Christ. Nor is it
merely a learning process for the Church, whereby she learns how
to imitate her Lord's self-surrender, as Augustine says: "*Ecclesia
. . . se ipsam per Ipsum discit offerre.*" But, in the same breath, Augustine says something quite different: "*Cuius rei* [that is, of the
Cross] *sacramentum quotidianum esse voluit ecclesiae sacrificium, . . .
cum ipsius capitis corpus est.*"[21] So the question is, is the Church
already the Body of Christ in offering her sacrifice, or is it only
by her action that she becomes such? Does she already enjoy an
intimate harmony with Christ's self-sacrifice, in such a way that
her offering (*oblatio*) is part of it (*sacrificium*)?

3. In order to reach the idea that, in the eucharistic celebration,
the Church is not offering an "alien" sacrifice, that is, Christ's,
but is herself inwardly involved in it, it seems that there must
be an interplay of three elements.

a. First, there must be the recognition, on the part of believers, that Jesus' sacrifice has taken place "for us and for all". In
other words, there must be explicit faith that our situation has
been transformed through Jesus' initiative "while we were yet
sinners". This recognition is part of the creed the catechumen
had to profess; equipped with it, he was admitted to the celebra-

---

[21] *De Civ. Dei* X, 20 (PL 41, 298).

tion of the Eucharist. But there is something else latent here—
and the Gospels often speak of it in the context of discipleship
—namely, that if we are prepared to affirm and accept Jesus'
suffering for us, we must also be prepared to walk with him
along his way. This is the *Sitz im Leben* of that "learning" of
which Augustine spoke: the community's celebration of the Eucharist led to the more and more conscious insight that faith in
his sacrifice, which already includes us, "passively", by way of
anticipation, also demands our active collaboration.[22] In sinners,
however (and believers are and remain such), this *opus operantis*
remains inchoate; as such, it cannot be part of the constitutive
opus operatum. Accordingly, there is a great amount of supplica-
tion in the prayers of the Mass: we who rely on Christ's sacrifice, which he offered to God, pray that God may include us in
Christ's self-surrender.

b. Yet there is one place at which this inchoate act of the
community is already fully accomplished: in Mary's consent.
Beneath the Cross, her consent becomes the most excruciating
affirmation of her Son's sacrifice. We have already seen in some
detail how the Mother's Yes crowns that process of heightening
that affects the entirety of Old Testament faith; it gives birth to
ecclesial faith and is its pattern. Insofar as Mary's Yes is one of
the presuppositions of the Son's Incarnation, it can be, beneath
the Cross, a constituent part of his sacrifice. It is not, of course,
of equal significance: Mary is put to one side ("Behold your
son") as if she is now useless; she must take the last place, behind all the sinners. It is only in this way, at this point, that the
new Eve is the helper of the new Adam; for, insofar as he bears
the guilt of all in the presence of the Father, he is the primary
occupant of the "last place". Here, therefore, he makes room for
his Mother's part, so different and so painful, which is simply to
let his suffering happen and to accept all the pain that must happen to her too. Mary allows the Cross to take place: this is the
archetype of the Church's entire faith, which "allows things to
take place"; this is seen particularly in the event of the Eucharist,
that existentially perfect and exemplary gesture that is implanted
into the Church and handed on down the centuries. Here, and

[22] Cf. Jungmann, I, 239–43.

here alone, we discern that this "letting be" is also a sacrifice in the existential sense, that is, the most painful renunciation and forfeiting of something—which is an essential element of the concept of sacrifice even in natural religions. Only where there is the free-will transferring of something from one's own possession to the realm of the divine can we speak of sacrifice. Elsewhere we have tried to show how the Mother's perfect attitude is all of a piece with the attitude of other women in the Gospels, be they the Lord's friends Martha and Mary of Bethany, with their mission of profound spiritual suffering, or the other holy women at the foot of the Cross, in particular Mary Magdalen.[23] Nor should we forget the scene at the Presentation in the Temple: the life of Jesus begins with his Mother's "sacrificial gesture", in which she gives her firstborn back to God and is told that a sword will pierce her heart.

However, we must go farther: and what we have to say here will form the basis for the third aspect, with which we have yet to deal. We have laid stress on the caesura between Jesus' active life, in which, in accord with his mission, he acted on his own responsibility, and his suffering, the "hour of darkness", in which he allowed himself to be "led like a lamb to the slaughter", weighed down by a crushing burden (Is 53:7). As the footwashing shows, the institution of the Eucharist still belongs to the active side of his life; only on the Mount of Olives is there the abrupt transition to his being handed over to the pitiless "powers", to the designs of a Father whom he no longer understands. Naturally, Jesus' being-handed-over is the final fruit of his life of action, of his responsibility, of his free obedience to the Father's whole will. Yet something analogous to this final act did take place in the first act of his earthly life, for initially every child is entrusted, defenseless, to its mother's hands. It has to let itself be clothed, carried, fed and looked after. Similarly, those who are dying no longer have control over themselves; they must let others look after them—if indeed there *is* someone to care for them. And the Son of God, seen within the perspective of his preexistence, freely entered into this condition of dependence

---

[23] "Die Messe ein Opfer der Kirche?" in *Spiritus Creator* (Einsiedeln: Johannes Verlag, 1967), 166–217.

when he became incarnate. It is on this basis that, as he goes along his path of suffering, he can allow the Church control over him and his sacrifice. But even before this is said of the disciples and their followers, who are specially consecrated for this role, it is true of the feminine Church, to whose loving but powerless care the Crucified One is entrusted. This situation is essential to being human; the Son of God, in becoming man, cannot simply jump over it, but, in him, it is perfected by being raised to the supernatural level, and it will remain such as long as the Church exists in time. He entrusts to her administration not only the fruits of his life and suffering but himself as well. In his Passion, he allows himself to be supported by the Father's will, which is expressed concretely in the will of the sinners who "do with him whatever they wish" (cf. Mt 17:12); at the same time, he is sustained by the consent of the feminine Church, suffering with him. So he will be entrusted to the hands of the Church, particularly in his Eucharist. Finally, from this center, he will be given into the hands of anyone who becomes a "mother" to him, by doing the will of his Father and allowing him to be born in the world.[24] Christ is entrusted to the hands of Mary at birth and at his death: this is more central than his being given into the hands of the Church in her official, public aspect. The former is the precondition for the latter. Before the masculine, official side appears in the Church, the Church as the woman, the helpmate of the Man, is already there. And it is only possible for the presbyters to exercise their office in the Church of the Incarnate, Crucified and Risen One if they are sustained by the "supra-official" Woman who cherishes and nurtures this official side; for she alone utters the Yes that is necessary if the Incarnation of the Word is to take place.[25] It is from this archetypal Yes that the faith—more or less weak, more or less strong—of the other members of the Church is nourished. (We considered this faith under 1. above.) It is from this archetypal Yes that

---

[24] Cf. the wide-ranging topic of being born of God: H. Rahner, "Die Lehre der Kirchenväter von der Geburt Christi aus dem Herzen der Kirche und der Gläubigen" in *Symbole der Kirche, Die Ekklesiologie der Väter* (Salzburg: O. Müller, 1964), 13–87.

[25] On these interrelated topics, cf. my *The Office of Peter and the Structure of the Church* (San Francisco: Ignatius Press, 1986), 183–225.

believers, in the celebration of the Eucharist, draw their loving resolve—more or less consciously—to let God's will happen, painful though it may be, since his will is for the salvation of the world and the Church. Few enough, no doubt, are aware of the painful implications of the Church's sacrificial action in which they participate and that, as often as it takes place, they "proclaim the death of the Lord" (1 Cor 11:26); but there must be some implicit understanding of this insofar as they are prepared to walk in the footsteps of the Crucified. Few approach that "sacrificial" attitude of "letting be" that characterizes the original, motherly experience that lies at the Church's source.

We have spoken in term of a diastasis, a separation, between the Son's being-sacrificed and the Woman's consent; it could be objected that this gets no farther than a polar relationship that fails to bring out adequately the unity of the Eucharist, in which the "Head" and the "members" are united in sacrifice. It would be wrong, however, to play off the "Man/Woman" relationship against that of the "Head/Body": the "one flesh" is grounded on the former relationship (Eph 5:23ff.; cf. 1 Cor 6:15ff.), and the holiness of bodily existence depends on its readiness for self-surrender (1 Cor 6:18–19; 7:4f.). The diastasis we have described is a presupposition for the nuptial relationship of Christ and the Church, which is consummated on the Cross, for there the Church is represented by Mary. Insofar as the Woman plays the part allotted to her in this drama, she can be drawn in the most intimate way into the Man's fruitful activity; she can be fructified by him. Thus (and only thus) can we say that, in the Eucharist, the community is drawn into Christ's sacrifice, offering to God that perfect sacrifice of Head and members of which Augustine spoke in celebrated terms.[26] Within this perspective, the "general priesthood" of the faithful, with Mary as matrix and archetype, forms the background of the ministerial priesthood; it is the condition that makes the latter possible.

c. This can only be explained if "Do this in remembrance of me" is understood as the command whereby Jesus tells the

---

[26] *De Civ. Dei* X, 6: ". . . profecto efficitur, ut tota ipsa redempta civitas, hoc est congregatio societasque sanctorum, universale sacrificium offeratur Deo per Sacerdotem magnum, qui etiam seipsum obtulit in passione pro nobis, ut tanti capitis corpus essemus, secundum formam servi" (PL 41, 284).

Church to take action on her own initiative: this is possible because in his Passion he himself has become available; he is now at the Church's disposal. Before Jesus is delivered into the hands of sinners in accord with the Father's will, he gives himself into the hands of the Church, or more precisely into the hands of those who are to assume, in and for the Church, what had been his own personal responsibility. Sinners are not to be the only ones to send mankind's Scapegoat back, beyond their borders, to God; his Mother is there too, giving her consent, and with her stand those who, in an official capacity and in the name of the Church, offer to God "the Lamb as though it had been slain". And this is done on behalf of all those for whom the Lamb allows himself to be slain, sinners outside and inside the Church. What else could the Church offer to God? "God will never be loved more than by Christ, that is, by the humanity adopted by the eternal Word and now crucified. So we can do nothing better than offer God this boundless love with which Christ has loved him: herein lies the whole meaning of the sacrifice of the Mass."[27] But there can be no question of an offering of this nature, which now stands where Jesus had stood during his active ministry, except on the basis of an explicit command empowering the Church to take over his place and function. For, if the Church can never attain the existential perfection of Mary's Yes (which must always be the Church's precondition), the feminine Yes of consent can never take the place of the official offering in the name of Jesus himself.[28] Following Christ's command to do what he does, those who are commissioned can only repeat word for word what the Lord said: "This is *my* body, *my* blood." Similarly, it is in his place (and not in their own) that they can say, "*I* absolve you from your sins." There are no circumstances in which the (Marian) Church could speak such words on her own account. It is of the essence of the spiritual office to be thus set in the place of Christ, even if we can say that the possibility of such a relationship (that is, involving an identity of function) has the relationship between Christ and Mary as its

---

[27] J. Daniélou, *Contemplation, croissance de l'Eglise* (Paris: Fayard, 1977), 99.

[28] On the history and theology of the relationship between Mary and the priesthood, cf. R. Laurentin, *Marie, l'Eglise et le sacerdoce* I–II (Paris: Lethielleux, 1953).

presupposition. As for the priesthood of the Old Covenant, we can say that its official function is initially wholly sublated into Christ's (the Letter to the Hebrews); on the basis of his plenitude of authority, he bestows new, christological authority on his disciples. All that is true in Israel's faith is concentrated in Mary; in her, it becomes the precondition for the Incarnation; in her, it accompanies the Incarnate One right up to his Cross and glorification, so to be transformed into the faith of the Church. It is because of this faith ("Blessed is she who believed . . ." Lk 1:45), in which Peter has a share ("Blessed are you, Simon Bar-Jona! For flesh and blood has not revealed this to you . . ." Mt 16:17), that the latter can be given the keys of the kingdom, which belong to Christ alone. This function of representing Christ within the feminine modality of the Church (with her Marian faith) is reserved to the man; it takes place in the middle ground in which Man and Woman face each other on the supernatural plane: on the one hand, the Man comes forth from the body of the Woman, and, on the other—in Communion— the believing community is taken into the unifying Body of the Man Christ. This shows the mediatorial and transitory form of the official priestly function, which is nonetheless necessary if Christ is to become bodily present in transubstantiation.[29]

4. For the community of faith, the offering of Christ's self-sacrifice to God the Father in the Holy Spirit[30] is, first of all, a way of assimilating the mind of Christ, which is *eucharistia*, praise and thanksgiving to God. But this thanksgiving is not like the Old Testament "sacrifice of praise", that is, a thanksgiving for his glory and his beneficial deeds; rather, it links up explicitly with Christ's Eucharist to the Father: he thanks the Father for his divine permission to give himself on behalf of sinners, for the

[29] On the degrees of Christ's presence in the celebration of the Eucharist, cf. Everett A. Diederich, "The Unfolding Presence of Christ in the Celebration of Mass" in *Communio, Internat. Cath. Review* (Spokane, Wash., Winter 1978), 326–43.

[30] Here we can dispense with a more detailed treatment of the epiclesis and the Spirit's actualizing role, merely pointing back to what has already been said (364ff.) about the communication of the Spirit to the Church. The Church cannot be completely separated from Christ's self-communication.

privilege of thus manifesting the Father's uttermost love. True, the inner connection between the believers' prayers of praise and Jesus' sacrificial attitude and deed is not evident at a first glance; for some early Church Fathers,[31] like Justin, it was a disputed issue,[32] but again and again the connection was made.[33] Here we must remember that, as the Old Covenant drew to a close, the "sacrifice of praise" was by no means exhausted by the recitation of prayers: where the material concept of sacrifice had been spiritualized, it also included a sacrificial attitude on the part of the person praying.

Let us look backward from the famous passage in Hebrews 13:10–16. Here, in all probability, the "offering of the sacrifice of praise, . . . that is, the fruit of lips that acknowledge [God's] name" refers to the mysterious "altar of sacrifice, from which those who serve the tent [the Jews] have no right to eat". Between the mention of the altar and the summons to praise, we read first of those animals whose blood is brought into the Holy of Holies by the High Priest as an atonement for sin and which are burned outside the camp. The author goes on to speak of Jesus, who for this very reason suffered outside the city walls in order to sanctify the people through his own blood. Next the community is summoned to go forth to him outside the camp, "bearing abuse for him". The substance of the Eucharist, in its meal-aspect, is the sacrifice of Christ (replacing the animals of the Old Testament);[34] at the same time, it elicits the community's constant "sacrifice of praise". On the one hand, we here discern the original meaning of the eucharistic sacrifice of praise in the Fathers, but, on the other hand, we must remember that the Old Testament sacrifices of praise in Leviticus 7:11ff., of-

[31] P. F. Palmer, *Sources of Christian Theology I: The Eucharist as a Sacrifice* (London, 1954).

[32] F. S. Renz, *Geschichte des Messopferbegriffs* I (1961), 154; F. Wieland, *Der vorirenäische Opferbegriff* (1909).

[33] O. Casel, "Die Eucharistielehre des hl. Justinus Martyr" in *Der Katholik*, 4th series, 13 (1914), 164–76. Revised text in: O. Casel, *Das christliche Opfermysterium*, ed. V. Warnach (Styria, 1968), 102–15.

[34] Following F. J. Schierse, *Verheissung und Heilsvollendung, Zur theologischen Grundfrage des Hebräerbriefes* (Munich: Zink, 1955), 191ff., the altar's various aspects must be seen together: the Last Supper, the sacrifice of the Cross, the heavenly altar (since the Cross appears in its eternal aspect) and finally Christ himself.

fered by way of thanksgiving, included a sacrifice of food or of sacrificial animals. In Hebrews, the sacrifice of praise is ceaselessly offered to God explicitly "through him", the crucified and glorified Christ. This does two things: it avoids a "sarkic" overevaluation of the mere "eating" from the altar, and it preserves the traditional connection between the sacrifice of praise and a concrete gift-offering. For Essene spirituality, the sacrifice of praise is indeed spiritualized, in a certain sense—the bloody Temple sacrifices are replaced by the sacred meals, and prayer itself acquires a real sacrificial character—but this spiritualization goes hand in hand with an ascetic thrust of the whole life (expressed in Qumran by celibacy and poverty), which, in the understanding of the sects, transforms the whole of existence into a priestly, sacrificial work.[35]

In spite of this traditional, organic connection between the prayer of praise and the concrete sacrifice, the link between them could appear too external. In the Essene sacrifice of the lips, the sacrifice was closely united with the life of the person praying; in the Christian Eucharist, by contrast, it could seem that the sacrifice of Christ remained a mere object of the Christians' sacrifice of praise. One easily gets this impression from the eucharistic prayers of praise found in the *Didachē* (chaps. 9–10, 14), particularly since the first thanksgiving (*eucharistein*) is given to God the Father "through your servant Jesus" for all his natural and supernatural gifts, and the second speaks of the pure sacrifice prophesied by Malachi.

5. In the fourth element, just described, we have indeed discerned a relationship, in various forms, between the one who sacrifices and what is sacrificed: what is sacrificed (whether it is

---

[35] For details, cf. O. Betz, "Le Ministère cultuel dans la secte de Qumran et dans le christianisme primitif" in *La Secte de Qumrân et les origines du christianisme*, Rech. Bibl. IV (Paris: Desclée de Brouwer, 1959), 163–202. This paper is intended to correct the presentation of H. Wenschkewitz, *Die Spiritualisierung der Kultusbegriffe* (Leipzig, 1932). The sect's Rule briefly summarizes the connection between the sacrifice of praise and personal conduct: "The sacrifice of the lips according to the Rule is like a sacrifice of righteousness, and conduct that is perfect is like a well-pleasing free-will offering": 9, 4–5. This is confirmed by contemporary texts; cf. *Test. Lev.* 3, 6–8, and the Syrian Apocryphal Psalms (Noth, ZAW 1930, 5), 2, 16ff. For more details, see O. Betz, 170–72.

a thing or a simple prayer) expresses the attitude of the person sacrificing. This is clear in the Essene texts and even clearer in the Letter to the Hebrews, where the sacrifice of praise on the New Testament altar is linked with the summons to discipleship, to embrace the scandal of the Cross of Christ. To that extent, the Tridentine anathema, "*si quis dixerit, missae sacrificium tantum esse laudis et gratiarum actionis . . .*",[36] is already anticipated. No longer can there be any question of a *nuda commemoratio* here, since—at least in Hebrews—the context is that of the Christians' authentic following of Christ into his sacrifice. As yet, however, the whole movement is from below upward: from the sacrificing Church, through Christ, to God; what is missing is the descending movement from Christ's sacrifice to the Church, drawing her into what is his own.

At the same time, this was our starting point, namely, the movement whereby Christ, through suffering, takes on the world's sin and thus changes mankind's status. The first thing is that, in Jesus' death on our behalf, all have died. This is so true that it is not easy to separate this first fact from the Christian event of baptism as described in Romans 6: Christians, baptized into the death of Jesus, "united [or 'grown together'] with him in a death like his", realize in faith, but through the efficacy of the sacrament, what has already taken place objectively in the events of the Cross. They personally ratify these events and allow this death to affect them, ready to draw the conclusion that they have "died to sin once and for all". At this point, the faith of Christians, understood as consent to all that Christ has done for them, is in touch with Mary's archetypal faith, which sums up the faith of the Old and New Covenants. The more seriously Christians take this "letting be" in their lives, here and now and in the future, the more Marian is their baptismal faith. But this itself links them to the gesture whereby, from the very outset, Mary gives her Son to God the Father in the Holy Spirit—even unto the Cross. He, the Son, is to do everything the Father wills, and into this work of his he inserts Mary and all men. In this action of giving back and surrendering her Son, Mary's existential gesture coincides with the official gesture of the celebrating

[36] DS 1753.

priest: at the altar, he focuses the Church's gesture, that is, that of the concrete believers assembled, without making any distinction between his gesture and that of the people.[37] Here again we must remember the primacy of the Marian over the liturgical: in Incarnation and birth, the Word-made-man was already entrusted to the care of his Mother; only later did the Word entrust himself to the care of the Church (as ministerial office and as community).

We can put it even more concretely. The most intimate spiritual/physical communion between Mary and the Child she carries is the starting point for all her subsequent renunciations and sacrifices, right up to the Cross, even if it is true that this primary communion was the result of her Yes, which implicitly included all the sacrifices that were to follow. We have a picture of this sequence in Christ's Last Supper: there he offers himself to his disciples under the forms of bread and wine—without any antecedent sacrificial rite—in order to draw them inwardly into his coming sacrifice on the Cross. The initiative is entirely his; the command to repeat this action only comes after he has already distributed himself among them. It is preceded by the washing of the feet, a quasi-sacramental symbol signifying that he is taking his disciples' sins upon himself, a pattern for the sacrament of penance that will come into being after Easter. This latter scene is a pure initiative on Jesus' part; Peter, after his initial resistance, is only required to acquiesce. He must let this happen if he is to "have part in" the Lord. There could be no clearer demonstration of the primacy of Christ's action in gathering his Church into his own sacrifice—and this applies equally to the Church in her official aspect. It will be clearly expressed once again in his High Priestly Prayer: Jesus consecrates (sacrifices) himself so that those who are his "may be consecrated [sacrificed] in the

---

[37] "Here, as in the first prayer after the Consecration, the original text (of the Roman Canon) ascribed the offering of sacrifice to the faithful, without any restriction: *qui tibi offerunt hoc sacrificium laudis*. They are not uninvolved spectators, . . . rather, they are all together bearers of the sacred action. . . . It is characteristic that a later period . . . found this artless expression too bold and accordingly inserted the phrase *pro quibus tibi offerimus vel*. The interpolation quickly established itself from the tenth century on, though not without encountering resistance." Jungmann, II, 203–4.

truth" (Jn 17:19). The metaphor of the Vine had already said as much.

We must say, therefore, that every eucharistic sacrifice on the part of the Church always proceeds on the basis of a communion with Christ that he has already initiated and has the effect of creating a new and ever-deeper communion. This communion, given by Christ, is begun in baptism, where it is inchoate and yet real; this is why only the baptized are admitted to Communion (*Did.* 9, 5). And baptism rests on a prior deed of Christ wrought on all mankind. So the Church's eucharistic action can be read backward, from the end to the beginning. In this context, the "offering" of bread and wine at the so-called "offertory" is only an anticipation of the central action in the Canon, in which the Church primarily joins in and assimilates herself to the work of Christ; she is thus privileged to *act*, taking the place reserved for her by Christ, who *suffers* the action of others. Yet, at the same time, this action on the Church's part is wholly Marian: it consists in letting herself be drawn into Jesus' availability for the Father's will. At the feeding of the five thousand, for instance, she is ready to follow Jesus and, in order to hear his word, to renounce all comfort; this involves sacrifice, for she may have nothing more to eat that day. But there is no inner relationship between her renunciation and Jesus' subsequent miraculous feeding of the crowd; the latter occurs because "he had compassion on them, because they were like sheep without a shepherd" (Mk 6:34). Between her action and his there is the unbridgeable chasm of miracle. So the Church's entire eucharistic action—on the part of both her institutional officebearers and her faithful community—is nothing but an echo of the Lord's prior action of grace; it is the action, through the Son, of the triune God. In Pauline terms, it is faith that is privileged to act; it is not "works".

The whole purpose of the foregoing was simply to prevent an over-hasty simplification of the dramatic side of the Eucharist and to focus on the interplay (which is ultimately beyond our comprehension) between the priority of the divine action and man's subsequent "letting be", which is both active and free. We repeat: the diverse theories that are intended to illuminate this interaction, and which are often made to contradict one another, should rather be seen as different but complementary aspects of the mystery. The Christ/Church relationship is expressed both in terms of Bridegroom/Bride (n.b., as "one flesh") and of Head/ Body; no aspect should be obscured, since each throws light on the others. This in itself should warn us against rationalistic oversimplification. Incorporated into Christ's obedience, we become obedient with him; but, incorporated into his freedom, we also become truly free. As members of his Body, "which is the Church", we are equipped by the Holy Spirit with our most personal mission—and this is, as we have shown, the very core of our personal being—but this mission can be nothing other than a participation in the once-and-for-all, all-embracing mission of Christ. In this sense, grace perfects nature: if by "nature" we mean that man is free to make his own decisions and action, this freedom is perfected by the grace of a sublime participation in the absolute, divine freedom. This comes about through our being incorporated into the Eucharist that, in the Spirit, Christ makes to the Father. And it is precisely in participating in Christ's mission that our elevated freedom is placed at the service of the communion of the saints.

b. The Dramatic Dimension of
the Communion of Saints

If believers are drawn into the Body and hence into the work of Christ, it follows that they acquire a share—in the secondary way we have indicated—in his *pro nobis*. This was the whole thrust of our remarks on the essence of the theological person (as a participation in the archetypal personality of Christ):[1] ultimately the being of the theological person coincides with the person's role and influence in the community. Scripture says the same about the priesthood of believers (1 Pet 2:5, 9; Rev 1:6; 5:10; 20:6), since the priest is essentially defined by his function on behalf of people (Heb 5:1). Finally, everything we have said about our inner assimilation to the being of Jesus by faith,

---

[1] *Theo-Drama* III, 230ff., 263ff. Cf. the preliminary remarks on the "communion of saints" in *Theo-Drama* II, 409f.

which is sealed by the sacraments, including the way the power of Jesus himself is infused into the believer's mind and being, points in the same direction. True, the way Jesus is "for us" has been contrasted with the way men are (merely) "with" one another,[2] but this view is only possible at a preliminary stage in which mankind's purely natural solidarity (because it shares in a single nature) is compared with the supernatural mission of the Second Adam. This solidarity, however, is only fully actualized when Christ "recapitulates" mankind in himself, in his divine-human person, which is simultaneously pneumatic and somatic.

For all who take part in it, this involvement in Christ has dramatic consequences, even if (like the extent and range of Christ's work) these consequences remain hidden in this aeon and cannot be set forth on any earthly stage. It signals an unimaginable expansion, in the order of creation, of the individual's sphere of influence; indeed, in the image used by Paul, he is no longer an isolated individual: he is incorporated into the organism and blood-circulation of the Mystical Body. Since this theatre of action is designed, from the very outset, with a view to Christ's *pro nobis*, it includes and comprehends all the possibilities of action that arise within the inner area of freedom of all the fellow members of Christ. These possibilities far transcend the possibilities of mere "being-with": they can only be conceived in terms of the individual being a member of Christ and in the degree to which such membership becomes a reality. More precisely, it is only in the realm of the good and the salvific that this internal influence on another's inner self is possible, that is, in the *communio sanctorum*. By its very nature, no such influence is possible in the realm of evil.

There is no question, therefore, of a parallel between a *Civitas Dei* and a *Civitas diaboli*. Origen occasionally spoke as if there were such,[3] a view that arose possibly from his belief that every human being was given, at birth, a good and an evil angel.[4] This in turn may have come from the Judaeo-Christian teaching on

[2] Thus Karl Barth, *Church Dogmatics* III/2, 203, 222.

[3] *Hom. 15 in Jes. Nav.* 5 (Baehrens VII, 389–98); *Hom. 6 in Ez* 1 (Baehrens VIII, 390).

[4] *Peri Archon* III, 2, 4 (Koet. V, 251); *In Luc.* h 12 (Rau. IX, 56); *In Jes. Nav.* h 23, 3 (Baehr. VII, 4, 43), *De or.* 31, 6 (Koet. II, 399).

the "two ways".[5] In his seventh "hermeneutical rule", Ticonius spoke of a counterbody to the Body of Christ: *De diabolo et corpore eius*,[6] and we know what a strong influence his "rules" had on Augustine, although, in the latter, the "opposing kingdom" by no means bears exclusively devilish features. But Origen is also aware of the connection between sin and *schisma*, or isolation; accordingly, any notion of an *organism* of evil, analogous to the Mystical Christ, is self-contradictory. "The devil," Bernanos says, "who can do so much, will not succeed in founding his church, a church based on a communion of the merits of hell, a communion of sin. Right to the end the sinner is condemned to sin alone." That "dead community" that bursts out in laughter at the end of the sermon is an assembly of the dead and the rotting, of chaos and primeval slime, the dregs of hell.[7]

It is the good that creates unity. So the "communion of saints" can only be created on the basis of the principle of the good "in Person"; and here we cannot posit any hiatus between the action of the Holy Spirit and that of the Son who eucharistically gives himself to all (and behind whom stands and works the Primal Giver, the Father). In the foreground there is fellowship (*koinonia*) with the Trinity as such, which is the result of grace; this, as Origen concludes from 1 John 1:3–4, produces the community of believers.[8] Augustine deduces from this that the Spirit who sustains the unity of Father and Son is "somehow" the unifying principle of the *communio sancto-*

---

[5] *Didachē* 1–6, with the detailed historical commentary by J.-P. Audet, *Etudes bibliques* (Gabalda, 1958).

[6] PL 18, 15–66. We can leave it an open question to what extent the *corpus diaboli* in Ticonius is one aspect of the all-embracing *corpus bipartitum* of the Church (that is, composed of both good and bad), as his second "rule" explains. Cf. J. Ratzinger, "Beobachtungen zum Kirchenbegriff des Tyconius im 'Liber regularum' " in *Das neue Volk Gottes* (Düsseldorf: Patmos, 1969), 11–23.—Augustine will get closer to the idea of a *corpus diaboli* when he describes Babylon as a "*civitas societasque iniquorum*" (*De cat. rud.* 21, 37; *Civ. Dei* 15, I, 1; *In Ps.* 64, 2).

[7] *Monsieur Ouine* (Plon, 1946), 166, 164, 172f.

[8] Igitur si nobis cum Patre et Filio et cum Spiritu Sancto societas data est, videndum nobis est, ne sanctam istam divinamque societatem peccando abnegemus. . . . Sed et sanctorum socios nos dicit Apostolus, nec mirum, si enim cum Patre et Filio dicitur nobis esse societas, quomodo non et cum sanctis, non solum qui in terra sunt, sed et qui in caelis? *Hom. 4, 4 In Lev.* (Baehr. VI, 319).

rum.[9] Here we must not forget, however, that this Spirit is the Spirit of the self-giving Son and that the prototype of the unifying love between believers is the entire love of the Trinity.[10] Paul himself lists all three Divine Persons as giving the different gifts of the Spirit that characterize the Church's unity (1 Cor 12:4–6).

Paul observes the differentiation of the members and their function for the benefit of the unity of the "Body of Christ"; as Ephesians 4:7ff. shows even more clearly, differentiation arises from the very principle of this unity. This serves to remind us that genuine unity always creates and sustains difference; this is true of what arises from below, from organic nature and human society, but also of what comes from above, from the kingdom of eternal, triune love. Even in nature's organisms, we find that the more differentiated a being's organs of self-representation and activity are, the higher its unity is. And, as for human society, its origin is not to be sought in a seething mass of isolated individuals who eventually make an artificial pact in order to constitute a state: no, it arises from the unity of the species, which naturally and freely "forms" itself into a social organism. Here, at all points, the concept of *Gestalt*, "form", that is, that unity that is manifested as such in its structure of parts, is indispensable. At no moment in time is there either a mere unity that subsequently multiplies itself or a mere atomized plurality that, for some reason or other, "organizes" itself into a unity. Both are always equally fundamental, and in each case it is the power of unity that puts forth its own fullness in the plurality of the *Gestalt*, in the particularity of the organs. We sense that something analogous may be said of the mystery of the Trinity: God reveals the fullness of being in the trinitarian *Gestalt* of the Godhead. Although we may not say that the Godhead is prior or superior to the Father, it would be Arianism to say that the Father is he who, in order to reveal his own fullness, generates

---

[9] Ideo societas unitatis Ecclesiae Dei . . . tamquam proprium est Spiritus Sancti, Patre et Filio cooperantibus, quia societas est quodammodo Patris et Filii ipse Spiritus Sanctus. *Sermo* 71, 20 (PL 38, 463). Cf. also Peter Lombard, *In Ep. ad Ephes.* c. 4 (PL 192, 197).

[10] Bonaventure, *In 4 Sent.* l 1, d 14, a 2, q 1; *ibid.*, l 1, d 10, a 1, q 3 (Quar. 1, 249, 199).

the Son and with him sends forth the Spirit. Doubtless Christ, with his own fullness, is the origin of the Mystical Body and the communion of the saints; but, by filling his Body, he also, manifesting his fullness, fills himself.[11] This is all the more true since, in God's eternal purpose, the Son's Incarnation and redemption take place at the same time as the election of all his brethren; for it is his destiny to sum up all things in himself (Eph 1:4–10). Here too, the primacy of the unifying principle in no way obstructs the simultaneous appearance of the plurality it yields. The world attains its form [Gestalt] in him, just as he attains his full stature [Vollgestalt] in it.

We are confronted with the mystery of how, in the Mystical Body, the principle of unity seems to achieve everything in the members—"without me you can do nothing" (Jn 15:5)— while, in the same parable, the vine must be distinguished from the grapes that can be separated from it. If we are to approach this mystery, we must see the two aspects together in one: the natural, organic, and the cultural and social; the fact that the Father cultivates the vine and prunes it where necessary shows that mere organic growth and fruiting is not sufficient as an image. Just as it depends on the cooperation of the branches whether and how much they bear fruit, the element of deliberate cultivation is essential if the whole plant is to be fruitful. Both levels, taken together, are necessary to the full parable: the vine needs the grapes as its organs if it is to bear fruit; nonetheless it has produced them itself and saturated them with its own juices, thus enabling them to reach the desired condition. They owe to the vine plant both their distinct being and their activity. What is this "activity" on the part of the grapes? Primarily it is to affirm the process whereby they have been fashioned and enabled to reach their fullness. The branch's fruitfulness is indivisibly twofold: on the one hand, it is its *own* fruitfulness; but, on the other, it is a fruitfulness that has been given to it, entrusted to it.

At this point, we recall the theology of Cajetan, who was responding to the oversimplifications of the Reformers; this theology was developed by his pupil Nazarius. Seripando had suggested a "double righteousness", that is, a real but insuffi-

---

[11] The two meanings of *plēroumenou* in Ephesians 1:23 are complementary.

cient righteousness on man's part that needs to be supplemented
by the all-sufficient righteousness of Christ; this means that both
righteousnesses are external to each other. Cajetan replies that
Christ's fruitfulness "overflows" onto the members of his Body,
so that the latter are enabled to bring forth fruit for eternal life
on the basis of a power that is their own yet comes to them in
a secondary way, from Christ. Accordingly, we should not say
"that we merit eternal life because of our works, *quatenus a nobis
sunt*, but that we merit eternal life by works *quatenus a Christo in
nobis et per nos sunt*".[12] Thus Nazarius in more detail: in part, the
merits of Christ are attributed to us, since God regards Christ
and us as a single mystical Person, and, in part, they overflow
upon us, granting us, who are the living members of the vine, a
share in its power of fruitfulness (that is, Christ's merit). Thus
Christ has two modes of being: as a physical person and as the
personal bearer of all the members of his Mystical Body.[13]

These clarifications contain nothing more, essentially, than the
New Testament witness: he who drinks of Christ will himself
become a spring, welling up unto eternal life; and if anyone is
a member of Christ, he can make up in his sufferings what is
yet lacking to the sufferings of Christ; and, most of all, because
of the death of Christ, "the love of God has been poured into
our hearts by the Holy Spirit" (Rom 5:5). And this love is divine love, in which all that is particular and specific is rendered
beneficial to all, by the same Spirit who inspired the Son of the
Father to undertake his work of love for all. The crucial point,
brought out preeminently by Thomas, is that, to be genuine and
perfect, this communication of Christ's love by the Spirit must
go beyond all intermediate goals: it must communicate love's
effective dynamism. On the basis of 1 Corinthians 12, Thomas
can describe the "communion of saints" as a "sharing in all the
Church's goods". Moreover, *et inde est quod qui in caritate vivit,
particeps est omnis boni quod fit in toto mundo*.[14] In view of what
we have already said, this general observation can be refined as
follows: the more a member "lets go" and surrenders himself to

[12] Cajetan, *De fide et operibus adv. Lutheranos*, 1532.
[13] Nazarius, *Commentary on Part 3 of the Summa* Q 1, a 2, controversia 7 (ed.
Cologne, 1621), 91–99.
[14] *In Symbolum Apost.* art. 10 (Opusc. theol. II, Marietti, no. 997).

Christ, the more he is enabled to give himself on his own initiative. So Thomas (in the context of the suffrages) distinguishes between the principle of love's unity in the Body of Christ, according to which "the good of the one overflows to all", and "the intention of a particular individual, whereby his deed is applied to another"; the first takes place *per modum meriti, cuius radix est caritas,* and the other *per modum satisfactionis, prout unus pro altero satisfacere potest.* Significantly, the borders between these two cannot be sharply delineated; Thomas immediately goes on to say that, even in the latter case, where a particular intention is involved, part of it benefits everyone; and the more love the individual has, the more benefit accrues to him.[15] This means that if the implicit community aspect were to be excluded from a prayer or penance intention, in order to apply the work *only* to the specified matter or person, the Catholic sense of the *communio sanctorum* would be lacking—or, what comes to the same thing —there would be a failure in assimilating the mind of Christ in himself and in us.

How far does the power of intercession for another extend? How far can we act on behalf of someone else? Is it possible to win the grace of conversion for a person in grave sin? Thomas answers, "If by grace a man fulfills the will of God, it is appropriate, according to the laws of friendship [*secundum amicitiae proportionem*], that God should carry out the saving will of one man for another, even if there is an obstacle on the part of the person whose justification is being sought."[16] This qualification leaves everything open; all that is hidden from us is the mechanism by which the members of the Body can act on behalf of one another. God alone can know this. But it gives us a firm hope that the energies of this "acting on behalf of others" can affect the innermost regions of others' freedom. Journet says, "It is clear that the Acts of the Apostles makes a close connection between the martyrdom of Stephen and the conversion of Saul (Acts 7:58f.)", a connection pointed out by Augustine on

---

[15] *Quodlibetum* 2, q 7, a 1; put differently in *Quodl.* 8, q 5, a 2: "et sic iuvatur aliquis ex actu alterius [even if this act is proposed in a particular intention], inquantum quilibet existens in caritate gaudet de quolibet bono opere." On the question of the application of the suffrages, cf. *4 Sent* 45, q 2, a 1, ql 1, cf. Suppl. 71, 1.

[16] I–IIae, q 114, a 6.

several occasions.[17] Paul was profoundly convinced of the fruitfulness of his work and sufferings for his communities and for the Church as a whole.[18]

This highlights one of the fundamental elements of Catholic dramatic theory, even if its way of working remains hidden. There is in principle no limit to the possible influence of one member upon another within the spiritual community of goods, both in space and time.

> A particular movement of grace that saves me from some profound danger can have come from the loving act (yesterday, tomorrow, or five hundred years ago) of an entirely unknown person, whose soul stood in a mysterious relationship to mine and which thus found its reward. What we call "free will" is like those modest flowers of the field whose seeds the wind carries far away in all directions to land and germinate on God knows what mountain, in God knows what valley. The revelation of his miracles will be the spectacle of one moment in eternity.

So speaks Léon Bloy.[19] Elsewhere he says, "Every human being who performs a free act thereby projects his personality into infinity. . . . Wherever and whenever it occurs, an act of love, a movement of genuine compassion sings the praise of God from Adam to the end of time, heals the sick, consoles the despairing, quiets tempests, frees prisoners, converts the unbelieving and protects all mankind."[20]

Careful examination is necessary here, however, to discover the basis of this possibility of influence. We must not have recourse to it too soon, and the concept needs to be refined. For there is something that precedes it, something that, in some degree, it presupposes but that must not be equated with it. It is that cosmic sympathy of all the world's elements that was extolled in the ancient world by Poseidonios (to name but its most well-known proponent); it formed the basis of many ancient arts of life and healing, even down to modern times. No one, perhaps,

---

[17] Serm. 168, 6 (PL 38, 914); Serm. 49, 11 (PL 38, 325, 6).

[18] Journet, L'Eglise du Verbe incarné II (Paris: Desclée de Brouwer, 1951), 324ff. Journet gives broad treatment of the theme of the communion of saints in several places.

[19] Méditation d'un solitaire (ed. Bollery-Petit, 1909), 140f.

[20] Le Désespéré (ed. Bollery-Petit, 1964), 113.

has been more eloquent than Paul Claudel in singing the praises of this necessary, reciprocal relationship between all beings in the world, be they never so unknown to one another. This is found in Claudel's aesthetics (*Art poétique*, 1904) and right up to his *Conversations dans le Loir-et-Cher* (1934); the theme is found in practically all his other works. In his early manifesto, what fascinates the poet is the relationship between coming-to-be and knowing (*naître* and *connaître*; similarly in Greek and Latin): it is only by sharing in being born and in being defined in their distinct identity by common boundaries that beings can know about themselves and others. His "Great Odes" celebrate the fact that every thing, even the most distant star, is indispensable to my existence. The famous *Cantique de Palmyre* (one of the dialogue-partners in the *Conversations*) shows how this cosmic sympathy merges into the *communio sanctorum*:

> I have good news for you: all this pain, all this dissension, all this losing of one's way—it is not true. Just close your eyes and, in the darkness, you will find our treasure once more; you will understand that pain is impossible. For you must surrender all your rights over us to this love, a love that inseparably joins veins and arteries in us. This love is the dominant factor . . . , and it is not only we who feel the source from which we come and the pulse that throbs right through us: every second that passes imprints upon us the echo of those millions of beings with whom—on the basis of the mysterious fluid that our own person burns—we form a single body. We shall not forever escape the rose, for we already smell her perfume. I am overwhelmed by a perfume that permits me to say "We"! There is a rose that calls for a homage that is so total that it is beyond the powers of one single woman to give it; the gift of life is so great that we can only express our gratitude for it by engaging all that exists to join in our thanksgiving. None of our brethren, not even if he wanted to, is able to leave us; and in the coldest miser, in the harlot and in the dirtiest drunkard, there lives an immortal soul, occupied with holy respiration; shut out from the light of day, the soul dedicates itself to nocturnal adoration. I hear her speaking while we talk thus, and I hear her weep when I kneel down. I say Yes to the Whole! I accept them all, understand them all; not one of them is superfluous to me, nor can I do without any. There are so many stars in the sky, and their number exceeds our power to count them; yet if I am to praise

God, I need every one of them. There are so many living beings, but few of them do we see sparkle, while the others wallow in chaos, caught in the whirlpools of dark slime. There are many souls, and there is not one with which I am *not* in communion because of that sacred point in each that says *Pater noster*.[21]

Claudel has said the same thing a hundred times. As early as his *Art poétique*, he describes the individual soul's inner limitations in its knowledge of God and its a priori necessity to complement it by the insights of all other fellow creatures.[22] It is no surprise to find that there is a seamless transition from this "philosophical" intuition to the insights of Christology and ecclesiology. The latter come to the fore most clearly in his late works, dealing extensively with biblical themes. "Not one of the elect," he says, "if he is to be entirely himself, if he is completely to fulfill his duties, that is, to make of himself a child of God, can get along without all the others; nor, equally, can he withdraw from the demands they in turn make of him, in the fullness of that freedom that is called the exercise of love. This is what we call the communion of saints."[23] "If we are to be ourselves, know ourselves, realize and sacrifice ourselves, our individual soul needs the whole Church. The soul exists only in virtue of the indispensable place and function that are allotted to it. Only then does it really begin to live and function; only then can we really *read* the soul, just as the word can be read because of the sentence, and the sentence because of the whole page, and so on."[24] The requirement of love is so absolute that it "employs the concepts of debtor and creditor. We serve our neighbor, and he serves us. We live by him, in him, through him and for him. He is both our cause and our effect. He lives a particular picture of God with regard to us, and we live a particular picture of God with regard to him."[25]

What, however, is the medium of this universal mediation? The universe or the Church? Perhaps Claudel's Catholicism had

[21] *Conversations* (Gallimard, 1935), 118f.

[22] *Art poétique*, in *Oeuvre poétique* (Pléiade, 1957), 200.

[23] *P. Claudel interroge l'Apocalypse* I (Gallimard, 1950), 202.

[24] *P. Claudel interroge le Cantique des Cantiques* (Egloff, 1948), 120.

[25] *L'Evangile d'Isaïe* (Gallimard, 1951), 171.

given him a receptivity for this "cosmic sympathy", or at least sharpened it:

> In God, everything communicates with everything else; everything is reciprocal. In God's eyes, the universe is not too much to show good to me, and in my eyes the whole world is not too much to show good to God. I am moved to compassion for all creatures in their need to praise God, and in their need of me in order to do so. The universe is nothing but a vast deficiency, and this deficiency constitutes our wealth. The universe lacks God, and God has put himself into the hands of each of us, so that we can give him to the universe.[26]

On the basis of assertions such as these, it is understandable that Claudel cultivates a certain optimism with regard to the world; this causes him, like Teilhard de Chardin, to put forward utopian images of the unification of cultures and of the universal brotherhood of man, such as we find very clearly in the last act of the final version of the *Annonce*, and even more forcefully in the last of the *Conversations*, where the earth, he says, "is to be organized as one single Temple".

The danger of this kind of blurring of the boundaries between cosmic and christological universality is most immediately visible in his evaluation of the negative counterimage, where the "communion of sinners" (the *civitas diaboli*) is given analogous dignity and influence to that of the "saints". At first sight, this seems plausible: why should not the love that is rejected by the individual produce an echo throughout the universe that is the same—but negative—as that produced by the fruition of love? Bloy often speaks in these terms, and Claudel believes he can deduce a *communion des pécheurs* from the existence of the Cross that embraces them all.[27] But Bernanos has already warned us

---

[26] *Emmaüs* (Gallimard, 1949), 228.

[27] *Un Poète regarde la Croix* (Gallimard, 1935), 267. Similarly unsatisfactory is the presentation of the communion of saints given by the young *Möhler* in his *Die Einheit der Kirche*. Cf. the full exposition and criticism of the latter by J. R. Geiselmann in his *Die theologische Anthropologie Johann Adam Möhlers* (Herder, 1955), esp. 22–106. The way in which the Holy Spirit is here seen as the divine life-fluid, in which the Christians' community of spiritual goods is realized, is a product of the common Romantic idea of the cosmic, synchronic and diachronic life-context, though it must be said that Möhler (by contrast with Schleiermacher) attempts

about inferring such a parallel, and the doctrine of original sin shows that the parallel does not hold. Our solidarity "in Adam" does not exhibit the same structure as that we enjoy "in Christ". We can say that, through the sin of the race, the individual has forfeited a positive good (because of his solidarity with all his fellow men); but we cannot say that something of "Adam's" sinfulness (or of the evil that caused that forfeiture) has been forced upon him. The old theology frequently paid too little attention to this distinction between the two solidarities; thus it drew a direct parallel between the negative effect of Eve's sin and the positive effect of Mary's obedience. When considering the defect of the human race as a whole, we can only speak of "sin" or guilt by way of analogy, if at all; the person who suffers as a result of this defect has *not* received something that, under other circumstances, he could have received: he has not received something for which he personally can be held accountable. The gifts bestowed in the communion of saints are quite different and positive: they are grounded in Christ's *pro nobis*, whereby he takes into himself those he has adopted and, having taken away their guilt, endows them with goods that are not only juridically "attributed" to them but ontologically "imparted" to them. Our examination of the Church's Marian participation in the Eucharist has shown that it is possible to share in the *pro nobis* of the Cross, and indeed in the entire life of Jesus;[28] this is the foundation on which the authentic communion of saints is built.

Perhaps the best corrective to Claudel's ambiguity with regard to *communio* (that is, his blurred distinction between creation and salvation) is Péguy's view of *communio* as it appears throughout

---

to make a clearer distinction between the Holy Spirit and the "universal Spirit". Möhler has a profoundly Catholic sense of catholicity, that is, the actuality of tradition since Christ, with all its values; he is aware of the way the ecclesial, sacramental presence mediates that of the living Christ; he is convinced of the truth that Christ's fullness can only be experienced by the community of all the faithful together and that reconciliation with Christ must coincide with reconciliation with and within the community: however, all this fails to attain a theologically adequate expression because of the continued influence—increasingly overcome as time goes on—of Romantic notions of "organism".

[28] Thomas, *Expos. symboli*, no. 997.

his work.[29] Whereas Claudel's starting point is that every fellow creature is indispensable if the individual is to understand himself, Péguy begins with the fact that every individual human being is indispensable to the eternal bliss itself. All enjoy solidarity in salvation: hence no individual can be damned; thus Péguy's central figure is his (fictional) Joan of Arc, who surrenders herself to damnation and fire for the salvation of all. Initially, the poet abandons the bourgeois, individualistic Church of Christians, thinking to find the true *communio* among extreme socialists; when he fails to find it there, he goes to the lengths of total communism, where he once again encounters the Church. He too, like Claudel, regards the "osmosis" between the realm of nature and that of grace as central; for him, there can be no Christianity without the ancient world and Judaism. However, he sees this osmosis coming from a "mysterious, fleshly spiritual effluence, whereby the kingdom of grace overflows into the kingdom of genius [that is, antiquity]".[30] And when, in *Eve*, he describes the gigantic triumphal procession of the historical civilizations, this whole procession moves in homage toward the crib of Bethlehem; only in this perspective is it clear why the whole *epos* can be dedicated to Eve, the primal Mother. As the second "Joan of Arc", she is manifestly given the face of the Mater Dolorosa. Thus the first, socialist Joan, who gave herself for the sake of the whole community, including the lost, was obviously conceived by a heart that was Christian: the idea of eternal damnation was totally out of place in the context of Marxism. Péguy was bound to see that Christianity had always been his starting point: real solidarity cannot be had more cheaply than on the basis of true biblical *caritas*. Ultimately this means the Cross and the Eucharist through which it is distributed among men.

We may recall here that the expression *communio sanctorum*, which is found in the Apostles' Creed around 400 A.D. (as witness Bishop Nicetas of Remesiana) and in other texts soon afterward, was understood in the sense of the community "of the saints",

---

[29] These are only indications. For a full treatment, see the final chapter of *The Glory of the Lord* III, "Lay Styles", 440–517.

[30] *Solvuntur Objecta* (Oeuvres en Prose II, Pléiade), 752.

that is, of people living in the grace of Christ. No doubt, however, the original meaning was a sharing in the Church's sacraments, the *sancta*, first and foremost the Eucharist.[31] This view occasionally came to the fore again in the Middle Ages (Ivo of Chartres, Josselin, Abelard) and features in the great syntheses of Albert, of Bonaventure and, in particular, of Thomas. The entire development shows increasingly that the shared communion of the Church's members results not only from the fact of sharing in the Church's common goods, distributed by the Holy Spirit; what individuals themselves do, as a result of this participation in Christ's freely bestowed love, also enters into the exchange. Thus Christ's *pro nobis* perfects his members' ability to *be* and *act* on behalf of others.

It is worth dwelling for a moment on this aspect, for the hidden dramatic dimensions are truly profound. The explanation of the article given in the Roman Catechism (I, c. 10, q 20) may prove helpful. Here the unity of the faithful in the Holy Spirit is interpreted primarily as *sacramentorum communio*, but in such a way that anyone who receives a sacrament (centrally, of course, the Eucharist) receives a good that is common to all, "the fruit of which belongs to all the faithful". "For whatever is received by one person, with a pious and holy disposition, refers to all and is of benefit to all, through the love that does not seek its own." It goes on to mention the body-metaphor of 1 Corinthians 12, in which the gift and function that is personal to every member is not for its own benefit but for that of the whole Body. Such gifts include the charisms, which "are granted, not for private advantage, but for public advantage and for the upbuilding of the Church. . . . A genuine Christian possesses nothing that he cannot regard as shared with all others." Otherwise he would not have God's *caritas* within him.

Where then are the boundaries between a straightforward "being-for-one-another" and that "action" or "work" for others that theology has primarily in mind when it speaks of the reciprocal application of "merits" (*réversibilité des mérites*)? My being-in-grace (which is a being-in-love), involving being allotted and

---

[31] Texts and bibliography in Geiselmann (see note 27 above), 56ff.; cf. also A. Piolanti, *Il mistero della communione dei santi nella rivelazione e nella teologia* (Rome, 1957).

possessing a charism, personal to me, for the sake of the community, must be seen as having an influence that is ultimately universal. For, always assuming a mature consciousness, it presupposes at least the habitual act of a loving readiness for service; it is not complacent and self-absorbed but is ready to take initiatives in the social arena. Such a person is at least potentially an agent, and as such he is already fruitful.[32] However, this fruitfulness remains mediated by the Church, the sacraments, the Holy Spirit; which—to repeat what we have already observed—cannot be said of a putative "communion of evil".[33]

In the person endowed with grace, therefore, the transitions between his being and the "merit" of his actions are fluid ones. Actions are expected of him, since he is a conscious subject and all the more since he is a person in Christ; the charismatic endowment that fits him for participation in the mission of Christ is meant to be exercised consciously. In 1 Corinthians 13, where Paul describes the nature of love, sentences referring to love's *being* pass on without a break into those referring to love's attitude and action. But even in *being* there is a *doing*; christologically speaking, even Christ's being-flesh involves an act of his being-Word. When Thomas says, *qui in caritate vivit, particeps est omnis boni quod fit in toto mundo*, his *fit* need not be restricted to mere deeds: it can include good dispositions and the readiness to work for good. This applies particularly if, as from time immemorial (and this is most pronounced in Origen), the *communio sanctorum* is understood as a fellowship and exchange of goods between believers on earth and the blessed in heaven. We must imagine that the whole being of this *communio* is perpetually performing the good [*je im Akt des Guten*]; distinct individual acts on earth are only consequences flowing from it.

No doubt the performance of individual acts is the normal way in which the good radiates forth; in each case, the act calls for a free decision. One need only think of the many passages where Paul asks the communities for their explicit prayer, and of the times when Jesus urges his followers to watch and pray, and when

[32] Cf. the remarks of C. Journet, 659ff., and the beautiful passage by Bañez, *ibid.*, 664f., note 5.

[33] It is noteworthy that much intensive parapsychological research today tries to reproduce, at the natural level, the laws of the true community of saints.

the Apostle speaks of the exchange of suffering and consolation (2 Cor 1:6f.), of the way he and the community are "proud" of each other (v. 14). We have just mentioned the most important acts that are exchanged within the inner communion of the faithful: praying for others and suffering for others (besides, of course, the visible, external mutual help that is a matter of course for Christians). For Paul, the former are at least as important as the external ministrations; indeed, they are basically more necessary and more effective, since they are more closely linked to Christ's "being-for", "acting-for" and "suffering-for". The fact that Christians can thus do things for one another because such action is directly grounded in Christ's *pro nobis* means that this kind of "representation" has an efficacy that is self-evident and quite different from the Old Testament instances of representation; magnificent as they are, the latter are of doubtful efficacy (Abraham, Moses). The confidence of being linked to another person (since we are both members of the same Body of Christ) causes our efforts on one another's behalf to range much more widely than was possible in former times. Such action extends even to the place of purgation: the person undergoing the fire of Purgatory cannot intercede for others (although he will be able to do so in heaven), but there is nothing against our showing uninterrupted solidarity with him through our intercession and sufferings on his behalf. How can such purgation, which is so much the result of personal culpability, be transferred to another? This is one of the mysteries of divine justice and mercy; in all probability—as in other matters—God has many different ways and means of achieving the same goal.[34]

We owe a debt to Gertrud von Le Fort and Georges Bernanos for having reflected on death, or rather its particular "passion" quality, as one of the possibilities of suffering on behalf of others—although, of course, earlier saints knew and practiced this form of love. Bernanos, in his *Dialogues des Carmélites* (1949), subtly divides the topic. The story concerns little Blanche, who, in spite of her *angst*-ridden existence, is enabled finally to face death without fear. Mortal anguish is accepted on her behalf in

[34] On one occasion, Thomas observes: "Potest etiam fieri ut acerbitas poenae modici temporis compenset diuturnitatem poenae in aliis" (*Quodl.* 2, 7, 1 ad 4), but this is surely only one possibility among others.

four different degrees: first, there is the old prioress, Madame Croissy, who dies a strange, terrible and scandalous death; next, the sub-prioress, Marie de l'Incarnation, who initially urges the whole community to make a death-vow and is subsequently humiliated because of her arrogance: she is the only one who has to renounce this death and must live on alone on the others' behalf; then there is the new prioress, Lidoine, who takes over Marie's role, and, finally, there is little Sister Constance, who takes the place of Blanche (who is resisting) and consents on her behalf.[35]

Not only is there a great closeness to Christ's Cross here, the action has moved *inside* the Cross; nor can those involved be accused of hybris. They are very well aware that "all is grace" —the last words of the dying country priest, whose sufferings and death were on behalf of his parish.

Since the Church, as Bride and Body of Christ, shares in the "merits" of her Head's entire life and suffering, she is one with him in becoming the world's "sacrament of salvation". (And here her external activity—evangelizing and pressing for the removal of injustices in the distribution of goods or racial discrimination or the repression of classes or peoples—must not be underplayed simply because of the paramount importance, on the basis of the communion of saints, of her invisible, representative ["on-behalf"] activity.) It is like this: visible action undertaken in discipleship of Christ—*transiit benefaciendo*, Acts 10:38—does not come to an end at the point where human activity otherwise stops; in fact, Christian discipleship acquires a new intensity and efficacy in suffering and death, for this is its most decisive phase, as Bishop Ignatius of Antioch saw most clearly. Both the latter and Paul before him knew that such fruitfulness springs solely from the grapes' bond with the vine, from the overflowing of the eucharistic Cross onto the redeemed.

"Even if I am to be poured out as a libation upon the sacrificial offering of your faith, I am glad and rejoice with you all. Likewise you also should be glad and rejoice with me" (Phil

---

[35] Cf. my book *Gelebte Kirche: Bernanos*, 2d ed. (Einsiedeln: Johannes Verlag, 1954), 458-60.

2:17). In "being-for" his communities, the Apostle goes to the lengths of giving his blood, but even in death, in discipleship of Christ, he can be both priest and sacrifice.[36]

[36] E. Lohmeyer, *Der Brief an die Philipper*, 9th ed. (1953), 113.—If it is to be accepted by God, satisfaction that is imperfect presupposes the existence of a satisfaction that is perfect, that is, Christ's. In the Church, therefore, all representative being, acting and suffering is founded on Christ's representative being, acting and suffering: Thomas, *S. Th*. III, q 1, a 2 ad 2.

IV. THE BATTLE OF THE LOGOS

A. ELEMENTS OF A CHRISTOLOGICAL THEOLOGY OF HISTORY

Jesus Christ stands in world history as God's representative. In God's place, he has to campaign against recalcitrant human freedom for the sake of the coming kingdom of God. It is true that he personally emerges from this battle victorious, through his death on the Cross, his *descensus* and his Resurrection; but this does not mean that all his work is done: only when "he delivers the kingdom to God the Father after destroying every rule and every authority and power . . . and puts all his enemies under his feet" (1 Cor 15:24f.) can he hand the perfected kingdom over to the Father. Moreover, this time of the end is the time of the most bitter struggle, as we have often mentioned (*Theo-Drama* II, 417–28; III, 391–401; IV, 20, 56ff., 64ff.). Christ's utter Yes to God and to the world drives the utter No—the demonic, anti-Christian No—out of its hiding-place. "If I had not come and spoken to them, they would not have sin; but now they have no excuse for their sin. He who hates me hates my Father also. If I had not done among them the works which no one else did, they would not have sin; but now they have seen and hated both me and my Father. It is to fulfill the word that is written in their law, 'They hated me without a cause'" (Jn 15:22–25).

There may be Old Testament analogies to this situation,[1] but the alternative provoked by Jesus' word and actions is so final that it constitutes a historical event that cuts world history in two, thus making it impossible to relativize the event by the use of transcendental theology (K. Rahner). Insofar as the event, in its consequences, becomes historically tangible, it yields a nuanced dramatic theology of history. The former segment is what the New Testament calls "the time of God's long patience" (this volume, above, 205–11). And since the event's prehistory be-

---

[1] All four Evangelists give us the theme of "hardening of the heart" found in Isaiah 6:9ff., and in parallel places in other prophets. Cf. *The Glory of the Lord* VI, 248–49.

longs to Israel, cutting Israel right down the middle into a part that affirms and a part that denies, Israel will retain an eminently theological role among the actors in the drama (*Theo-Drama* III, 361ff.). To assert this is not to call into question the hidden presence of the divine Spirit in the pre-Christian and post-Christian, extrabiblical realms of humanity (*Theo-Drama* III, 410–18), but the forms of this presence cannot be theologically differentiated; only on the basis of the biblical word can there be decision [*Entscheidung*] and hence distinction [*Unterscheidbarkeit*]. The division of world history into time before and after Christ has a theological foundation, even if the historical fact of Christ's appearance on the stage points not only forward but, in the sense of a theology of the *Ecclesia ab Abel*, right back to the beginning.[2]

As for the attempt to divide the history of the Church and the world since Christ into periods, it will hardly be a fruitful undertaking. At the time when people tried to divide history into the seven ages of the world deduced from the Apocalypse, the present age was mostly regarded as the sixth of seven; theologically this may indicate that people saw themselves, in a qualitative sense, close to the events of the end. In fact, every age does well to see itself in this framework, particularly if —with Ticonius and Augustine—it has once and for all banished the expectation of a thousand-year kingdom conceived in historical terms. Even less successful were the attempts made in the last century to divide the history of the Church into Hegel's dialectical periods; these attempts generally regarded the

---

[2] I am thinking here less of F. A. Staudenmaier's *Idee in der Geschichte* (cf. Balthasar Schrott's work of the same name [Essen: Ludgerusverlag, 1976]) than of Leopold Schmid's *Der Geist des Katholizismus oder Grundlegung der katholischen Irenik* (Giessen, 1848–1850; 4 volumes), according to which the "Catholic" idea is first actualized *in itself* (as the dialectic of self-deepening [the Father], self-emptying [the Son], and self-remembering [the Spirit]—corresponding to Hegel's "pure logic"), before it enters the process of self-unfolding in world history (cf. the short presentation in K. Werner's *Geschichte der katholischen Theologie* [1866], 508–10). Here we could also mention J. N. Sepp's work (cf. Werner, 526ff.), a product of the Görres school. Ernst von Lasaulx's *Philosophie der Geschichte* (1856), initially based entirely on Romantic notions of "organism" (civilizations spring forth, blossom and die), finally arrives—led by "hope" (162)—at the three historical periods of Joachim of Flora (166f.).

present as a definitive synthesis of hitherto one-sided elements.[3] No one today would share this kind of optimism. The history of missions, if we were to apply Mark 13:10 to it, provides no evidence; in any case, this verse refers, not to the conversion of all nations, but to a sufficient awareness, on the part of the whole world, of the fact of Christ. Nor does the history of doctrine show the identifiable "progress" of the Age of the Church, as a naïve optimism has suggested: for the most part, it was erroneous teachings that made it necessary to introduce rational precision in expounding revelation; this necessity is a two-edged sword, and its advantages cannot obscure its disadvantages.[4]

The firm basis for this is provided by Christ's prophetic words, which refer both to the continued effect of his manifestation and to the fate that, sooner or later, awaits his disciples. The attempt

[3] Of course there is a kind of deepening and enrichment of faith's understanding as a result of the Church's definitions and the theological work the latter presupposes. But this explicitation has its inevitable, inherent dangers, to which Hilary gave almost too clear expression: "Because of the malicious teachings of the blasphemous heretics, we are compelled to do what is forbidden, to scale heights that are too steep, to utter things that are ineffable, to proceed boldly where we should be reticent. For, while we ought simply to observe the commandments in faith, worshipping the Father, together with him honoring the Son, made rich to overflowing by the Holy Spirit, people compel us to stretch our feeble speech to the limits of the ineffable. We are attacked from without, and so we ourselves are obliged to attack in return; as a result, what should remain hidden in the depths of the believing heart is exposed to the vicissitudes of human speech" (*De Trin.* II, 2). This shows, at least, the dialectic involved in all defining of the mystery: articulation cannot (or not without great difficulty) be separated from disintegration, nor illumination from rationalization. The new and richer synthesis so urgently demanded in the wake of analysis is infinitely harder to attain than the original, naïve juxtaposition. It is true that the living totality accompanies mankind through history (with the result that much that has been treated to analysis automatically sinks back into the unity of simple faith), but analysis remains a danger for true believers, particularly the simple; what has become too complicated is left to one side. —In some way or other this tragic dimension is implicit in the paradox of the Church's missionary command, which is to "proclaim from the rooftops" things that are ineffable, *arcana*, to pour holy things into unholy ears. When she explains things that, in themselves, are to be embraced by faith, she does so in the trembling hope that she is not profaning the "holy and manifest mystery" or casting pearls before swine.

[4] A wealth of examples can be found in P. Volz, *Die Eschatologie der jüdischen Gemeinde*, 2d ed. (Tübingen: Mohr, 1934), 147–63.

to show that he did not utter these prophecies is as foolish as the attempt to prove that he never predicted the Fall of Jerusalem. Those who would strike out his utterances on the consequences of his life and work are robbing him of his central claim and what is central to his self-awareness. So we must begin with his prophetic words if we want to say anything theologically relevant about the situation of the post-Christian world and its history.

A question may be asked at this point: Do the various periods in Jesus' life shed light on the Church's history and hence, indirectly, on world history? One fact at least could be significant here, namely, the sequence whereby an active life and work move toward the goal of the Passion. We have insisted enough on the hiatus between both "times" in the life of Jesus himself; and the destinies of Peter and Paul—according to John 21, Acts, 2 Corinthians, Galatians and 2 Timothy—are fashioned closely enough after their Lord's. Should this sequence be applied to the Church's history as a whole? People are quick to point out that Christian prophecy of the last things is clearly dependent on Jewish expectations about the future, but such considerations do not carry us very far. True, the expected arrival of the Messianic kingdom is to be preceded by the "pangs of the Messiah", and Jewish apocalyptic may have influenced Mark 13 and its Synoptic variants; such influence extends to Paul's early eschatology (1 and 2 Thessalonians). These late Jewish speculations have initially no foundation; we can ask, however, whether they are not *given* a real foundation by the fact of Christ. More precisely, must not this fact, that is, Jesus' absolute claim, demonstrate its validity through world history by unfolding its inner consequences? Thus, just as the Yes of faith to Jesus was possible from the beginning, the complete No, with all its counterdesigns, can only appear at the end. It is clear that, ever since Jesus' earthly life, the No-principle has been active; John speaks of those who reject Jesus' claim to be God's Word and Son in the flesh: they are the "Antichrist" (1 Jn 2:18, 22; 4:3; 2 Jn 7). For Paul too, the "mystery of godlessness" is already at work, though it will only emerge fully at the manifestation of him who is absolutely "lawless"—whom the returning Lord will destroy by his breath and his radiance (2 Th 2:5–8). This corresponds to the gradual intensification (described at the beginning of this volume) evident in the series of visions set forth in the Book of Revelation, terminating in the Logos going out, his garments spattered with blood, to do battle with the "trinity" of hell.

There can be no substantial objection to this view apart from what we indicated in the section on "the paradoxes of discipleship"—which forbids us to draw a direct parallel between Jesus' progress toward his "hour" and the Church's progress toward the eschatological tribulation. For, as we have shown, the Church comes from the Cross and is always heading toward it. It is in the power of the Holy Spirit, who is sent to her on the basis of Christ's Resurrection and Ascension, that she is equipped for discipleship, enabled to drink the Lord's cup (Mk 10:39). Hence, in Paul, the baffling simultaneity of transfiguration and Passion: "For while we live we are always being given up to death for Jesus' sake, so that the life of Jesus may be manifested in our mortal flesh" (2 Cor 4:11). This is a final warning against seeing post-Christian world history in terms of "periods". For, as in the life of Paul, a period of relative earthly success can lead into one of great tribulation and vice versa—which cannot be described theologically as "progress" or "regression". Thus, in different parts of the universal Church, persecution and growth can be simultaneous; indeed, it seems to be Paul's view that the glory of the Lord actually shines forth in the disciple's sharing of Christ's sufferings: "When I am weak, then am I strong" (2 Cor 12:10). "For we are weak in him [Christ], but in dealing with you we shall live with him by the power of God" (2 Cor 13:4).

What if these words refer solely to the mystery of Christ in his disciples, perhaps only in the saints, and by no means to world history, which pursues its path irrespective of Christ? Our reply must be that Jesus' words concerning himself referred to the condition of the world as a whole, not to a small group of men around him. So we cannot avoid the question: Does world history give indications that these words had a universal effect? That is, does not world history show a theological structure, a christological structure, and can it not be demonstrated even to the nonbeliever? In such a case, world history and the Church's history would be more interrelated than is commonly assumed;

not merely in the sense of an external intertwining of Church and State (since Constantine), including modern absolutism with its ideal of "throne and altar", but in a way that is more in accord with the gospel?

B. THE PROVOCATION
OFFERED BY JESUS

1. Gathering, Separating

Jesus' claim[1] is so provocative that he summons the whole world to enter the lists. It becomes clear, in him, that the *transcendental* is directly present and manifested in the *categorial*. It is impossible, therefore, to postulate an abiding mystery of transcendence *behind* the realm of the "categorial" that is accessible to reason. All non-Christian religious philosophy and mysticism does this. On the contrary, the absolute Logos is present in and through history.

"He who is not with me is against me, and he who does not gather with me scatters" (Mt 12:30; Lk 11:23). This saying occurs in the context of the struggle between the "strong man" and the "stronger" who overwhelms and despoils him. In Matthew, this "stronger" man is the "Servant of God" endowed with the Spirit, the "beloved one" who comes forth with the gentleness of the divine "still, small voice" on Horeb, "in whose name the Gentiles will hope" (Mt 12:18–21): the heightened paradox points even more clearly to the presence of the absolute. There can be no neutrality in the face of him, no avoiding his gesture of embrace, of gathering-in; if we are not "for" him, we are already against him. And there is no distance between the inner decision and the external action and its basic tendency: either we gather with him or the reverse—we scatter. Jesus is the Shepherd who gathers the leaderless, scattered sheep into the one fold (Mk 6:34; Jn 10), and he gives his life in doing so. The hireling, who does not do this because "he cares not for the sheep", flees, exposing the flock to the wolf's "snatching" and "scattering" (Jn 10:12). There is nothing automatic about these opposing basic thrusts —either toward integration and union or toward disintegration

---

[1] Cf. *The Glory of the Lord* VII, 115–29, "The Claim".

and chaos—as if a person, as a result of what he has done, were
to find himself, whether he wished to or not, going in one direction or the other; no: the particular direction taken depends
on the individual's personal and primary decision for or against
Jesus, which means that he chooses either the path toward God
or the path toward chaos.

It follows that Jesus' gathering is also a separating. Gathering
his flock to God, he brings peace (Jn 14:27); but, calling for
decision, he brings a sword. "Do not think that I have come
to bring peace on earth; I have not come to bring peace, but a
sword. For I have come to set a man against his father, and a
daughter against her mother, and a daughter-in-law against her
mother-in-law; and a man's foes will be those of his own household" (Mt 10:34–36). The sword is an image for "dividing"
and "division" (as in Lk 12:51–52), the dissolving of neutral
bonds of blood and society as a result of the individual's utterly
personal decision. This is a prerequisite if the "gathering" that
God desires is to begin. Hence the next passage in Matthew:
"He who loves father or mother more than me is not worthy
of me; and he who loves son or daughter more than me is not
worthy of me; . . . He who finds his life will lose it, and he
who loses his life for my sake will find it" (Mt 10:37–39). Luke
replaces "loves more" with the stronger "hates" (14:26); Jesus
must be preferred absolutely, not merely relatively. This choosing of Jesus also means that one's own "life" must be left behind
—which refers not only to one's physical existence but equally
to all those religious techniques that aim at the well-being of
one's own "I", "depth-ego" or "self". Later, when the work
of the Cross has been accomplished "for us", Paul will show
that, together with Christ, the Christian has been uprooted, not
only from every other bond with the world but also from his
own self, and "transferred" (Col 1:13) "to the kingdom of the
beloved Son". He has died to himself and so to all anxiety about
this self.

This word of Jesus (and it stands for many another word in the
Gospels) thus shows its provocative nature not only vis-à-vis all
those world religions that find the *theion* primarily in the social
order that is built on the clan but also, and most definitively,
vis-à-vis those that value self-discovery more highly than all so-

cial bonds, whether sought in the Jewish study of the Law[2] or in philosophy[3] or oriental meditation.

In setting out to gather all men, Jesus relativizes all religion in the world, Jewish and Gentile. He thereby separates whatever is prepared to respond to his absolute summons from what resists it. So it comes about that his peace-bringing action ("he is our peace", Eph 2:14) introduces more division in the world than any other; not through fanaticism but because of an inherent logic: the very One who has come, "not to judge, but to save" utters that "word" that judges those who reject it (Jn 3:16–21; 12:47–48). This yawning abyss is inevitable, however, if in Jesus God wishes to provoke his freed creature to the highest degree of responsibility. Man is not to despair of the world; he is not to seek to *gather himself* while jettisoning a hopelessly splintered existence; nor is he to try to *gather the world* at the cost of losing his own wholeness (Mk 8:36): he is to strive for what is impossible to man, namely, to "gather" at the same level as God and with God, since this is the offer God makes to him in Jesus. God's offer goes far beyond all mundane constructs of ethics and religion; it can only resign itself to man's No—for it seems absurd to man to transcend his own utmost possibilities by negating them. This rejection of the greatest possible opportunity, this desire to exercise freedom on the basis of one's *own* source, is the sin that comes into full consciousness through the provocation offered by Jesus.

This provocation can only end tragically for the One who desires to be God's own Word. For the *tragedy* of the Cross, elicited by the provocation itself, must have been foreseen and fore-willed from all eternity, as the only possible consequence of the premise that God creates finite freedom out of himself

[2] *Str.-Bill.* I, 587; Grundmann, *Lukas*, 303.

[3] "Do you imagine you can devote yourself to philosophy and still go on doing what you are doing? . . . You must keep vigils, overcome desires, leave your relations and friends, be despised by your servant, be laughed at by people on the street, take the lowest place in all situations, with regard to honor, rank and dignity, and in the courts. Think about these things, and then, if it seems right to you, immerse yourself in your business, if you are prepared to forfeit peace of soul, freedom, firmness of heart" (Epictetus, *Diss.* III, 15, 10–12, quoted by Grundmann, *loc. cit.*).

and gives it its own autonomy. The absolute "gathering" that leads to the Cross inevitably involves an absolute separation: the Word that summons and gathers men collapses in death, darkness and the chaos of splintered freedom; and this splintering is undergirded by the eucharistic "splintering" of God, which streams beyond all the boundaries that finite freedom can set. Thus God's "splintering" is "for us", splintered as we are and fleeing from him.

> This process, however, is the eternal design of the Trinity; it is the holy depth, the innermost sanctuary of divine life, which could not reveal itself to sinful and finite creatures unless the latter were made ready in the tragic collapse of divine life: otherwise the creature would fade away or despair or remain blind when confronted with the infinite deluge of creative love. For it is only through the love-death of the eternally offered Son that the Creator's love is communicated and expropriated, overflowing onto us. Only thus does it flow down from the majesty of that Paternal love, profoundly shattered, which eternally gave the Son in order finally to become life in the realm of personal freedom, in the realm of the divine fellowship through the Holy Spirit. In the Spirit's holy wells of love, all sighing, all suffering of the tragic creature is experienced in painful depth, in order to refine and sanctify the creature and incorporate him as a member of the Lord's holy Body. This love is not something absolutely supra-tragic: it is the creative fashioning and heightening of tragedy itself, making of it the most precious legacy of all eternities in the abyss of divine life.[4]

This fleeting glimpse of the depths shows once more how Jesus' provocation potentially contains and anticipates not only his entire destiny but also that of the world; it even embraces the powers of heaven and hell between which it hovers. Not as if the drama as a whole were predetermined by it; Jesus appeals to men to believe "that I am he" (cf. Mk 6:50), and from time to time he finds such faith inside and outside Israel. So he does not need to anticipate his own destiny: it is enough for him to know that he is sent to follow God's will—God's saving will —to the very end. And that means, of course, to follow his

---

[4] G. Siewerth, *Christentum und Tragik* (1934), 299–300, reprinted in *Grundfragen der Philosophie im Horizont der Seinsdifferenz* (Schwann, 1963).

will into the abysses opened up by his provocation, with all the monsters that lurk and slumber there. The latter already sense his approach: "What have we to do with you, Jesus of Nazareth? Have you come to destroy us? I know you: you are the Holy One of God!" (Mk 1:24). If these powers can do nothing against the uniquely Holy One, they have all the more influence over his human opponents, who immediately "take counsel how they might destroy him" (Mk 3:6): their hour of victory will be "the power of darkness" (Lk 22:53).

He did not come imagining that he could gather without introducing division. True, he addresses everyone, omitting no class of men, disputes with the scribes and "eats and drinks with tax-collectors and sinners". But he also knows where his voice is heard and where it returns to him, rebounding as from a wall: "Those who are well have no need of a physician, but those who are sick; I came not to call the righteous, but sinners" (Mk 2:17). In this sense, he learns from the way his absolute mission is received, from the play's successive acts and from the way it rushes to its final conclusion: all this shows him how he will be ultimately separated, isolated and so able—by unshakably holding fast to his mission of "gathering"—to bring in all that was scattered and divided.

2. Gathering and Sifting

A leitmotif runs through the Gospels in the form of the words of Isaiah concerning the people's "hardness of heart": "Make the heart of this people fat, and their ears heavy, and shut their eyes; lest they see with their eyes, and hear with their ears, and understand with their hearts, and turn and be healed" (Is 6:10).[1] The theme is also found in the Psalms (35:19; 69:5; 129:161): "They hate me without a cause" (Jn 15:25). There is also the whole parallelism between the theodramatic aspects of the first destruction of the Jerusalem that will not repent and its second, definitive destruction. All this shows how much Jesus' gathering of what was scattered was the conclusion of an endeavor begun long ago. It always had the same result: what *seemed* to be

---

[1] Cf. K. H. Schelkle, "Der Zweck der Gleichnisreden" in *Neues Testament und Kirche, Festschrift für Schnackenburg* (Herder, 1974), 71–75.

"gathered" was in fact a chaotic, undifferentiated amalgam: it had to be separated and distinguished. The second creation has to repeat the process of the first: it must divide and separate in order to bring order into the chaos and relate the parts to one another. *Distinguer pour unir.*

However, this is also the rule of human reason, which analyzes in order to synthesize; it is the *intellectus dividens et componens*. This gives scope for the supposition that the point in world history at which this process of reason breaks through at the universal level is not without some inner relation to the point at which Jesus' provocation of the world takes place. Among others, K. Rahner has on several occasions pointed out this coincidence: Jesus appeared at the beginning of the epoch "that saw the beginning of the history of mankind's self-appropriation through deliberate deeds, of history's conscious, active self-heightening",[2] when "in a rapid acceleration, man developed from a being both secure in nature and directly at its mercy to one who inhabits an environment he himself has created, . . . who has transformed his numinous environment into one he has rationally planned, making it a demythologized building-site for his own plans"; thus he "will become a human being in a way we cannot as yet envisage". This breakthrough may last for a few millennia, but it is plausible "to place the Christ-event within it".[3] Hegel had used similar arguments to explain Christ's appearance at this particular locus in world history. Both writers see that Christianity cannot be made responsible for secularizing and technologizing nature—a one-sided notion—but that it does have some connection with it.

This connection becomes even clearer if one observes that human reason, in its secularizing role in world history, prevents those who reject Jesus' provocation from returning to a "numinous" world view in which the divine and the worldly commingle, unseparated. Initially such a return is made difficult; ultimately it becomes impossible. This leaves the field clear for what must be called "post-Christian atheism". For when nature is deprived of divinity, the presence of the Creator within it

---

[2] *Schriften* V, 218 [*Theological Investigations* 5 (London and Baltimore)].
[3] *Grundkurs*, 172; cf. *Schriften* I, 219 and IX, 240f.

fades. To the observer who sees matter only in terms of the *utile*, God disappears into the background. This is a natural process, and to it corresponds the claim of Jesus to be "*the* way, *the* truth and *the* life" (Jn 14:6)—a claim that attracts to itself and concentrates all the religious aspirations of mankind. He goes on to say that "no one comes to the Father except by me": this is not to deny the ultimate salvation of all who do not know him and adhere to other religions; he is saying that the latter religions do not mediate salvation: he alone does. Once this has become sufficiently well known to mankind, the other religions (those that still remain) are bound to acquire a certain anti-Christian slant. They will try to appropriate all the features of the religion of Jesus that seem to commend it to mankind: they will say, for instance, that even individualistic techniques of meditation have an effect on social conditions—thus trying to isolate Christ's claim and render it abstract. But although the religions keep trying to give themselves a new stimulus (and they can actually do so, because of the yearning for God that indwells man), their symbolic and institutional substance, which is a relic of mythological times, continues to dissolve and disintegrate. Their structures, erstwhile powerful and formative, collapse in a plethora of ephemeral and private sects, continually crystallizing and dissolving. The only exceptions are those religions that are directly or indirectly dependent on the biblical revelation, first of all Judaism, and then Islam. They constitute a very strange kind of exception, however, for both of them—first of all Judaism, and then Islam—reject the full claim made by Jesus and so will be particularly susceptible to militant atheism (Judaism) or emphatically anti-Christian theism (Islam).

The crude atheism, negative and sceptical, of a civilization that has fallen back into paganism will be more than apathetic: it will act in a positively anti-Christian way, particularly where Christ's claim is put provocatively by his followers, pillorying the oppressive forms taken by the state, economics or racist fanaticism. In general, however, this kind of pagan atheism, even where it strikes an impressive pose (as in Nietzsche), will hardly manage to take energetic, concrete measures against Jesus' claim. It will go aground on delusion and self-destruction, as we see in Dostoyevsky's *The Devils* and in Nietzsche. The effective challenge comes from a secularized Israel that, frustrated in its Messianic hope, tries itself to promote salvation in and through the technological age. It is explicitly atheistic and anti-theistic vis-à-vis the ancient God, Yahweh, who has failed; and it is explicitly anti-Christian, insofar as Jesus' claim to fulfill this salvation in himself is proved to be a pitiful failure, doomed in its very concept. Marxist anti-theism organizes and channels all the pagan, diffuse, anti-Christian atheism and gives it a shape, a plan, a striking force. It may do this by interpreting the Messianic expectation as a dialectic that presses forward with iron necessity; or it may take the "watching and waiting" that is built on a concrete faith in Yahweh's promise, substituting for it an abstract "principle of hope" that is empty, cheerless and grounded on nothing but itself. There is a secular tradition that the Antichrist will be a Jew;[4] this may be more than crude anti-Semitism: it may be a genuine theological deduction, for Israel alone, among all the nations, is the abiding bearer of an absolute hope that is identical with its existence. Such a hope, consistently followed through and lived out side-by-side with the rejection of Christ, must seek to offer a countervision of world history.

It is immaterial that it is pagans (or former Christians, for example, Stalin) who build this vision, guaranteeing its implementation by the greatest possible use of all worldly force (for example, vast stockpiling of arms, police, propaganda, concentration camps); it is immaterial that all this is in flagrant contradiction to the alleged aim of a free, classless society and that this contradiction shamelessly exposes itself to the whole world: the fascination exercised by this apocalyptic beast and its propaganda prophets is such that the whole world, Christian or not, gazes as if spellbound at the deluding image. "It is shattering to behold —and characteristic of the despair of the world in which we live —that many people no longer have the strength to visualize the whole proportions, secret and veiled, of communism."[5] The latter, moreover, because of "its imperialistic expansionism and the

---

[4] Hans Preuss, *Die Vorstellung vom Antichrist im späteren Mittelalter, bei Luther und in der konfessionellen Polemik* (Leipzig: 2d ed., 1909), 41. Josef Pieper, *Über das Ende der Zeit* (Munich: Kösel, 1950), 157.

[5] G. Siewerth, "Der Triumph der Verweiflung" in "Gott in der Geschichte", *Gesammelte Werke* III (Patmos, 1971), 240.

satanic falsehoods of its propaganda", even when many have un-
covered its face, "compels the whole civilized world to take defensive measures".[6] Furthermore—and this even more clearly
unveils the apocalyptic situation—this fascination so weakens
the Christian organism that the alien wasp is able to inject its
anaesthetizing sting and lay its eggs right inside it, with the result that the body, hollowed out from inside, serves as welcome
food for the enemy. Christians are confronted with a thousand
pretexts for interpreting their own eschatological hope in purely
mundane terms; they are urged to put Third World development and liberation theology before missionary activity, instead
of performing "corporal works of mercy" in the all-embracing
spirit of the Beatitudes. Why, if we are serious about God's Incarnation in Jesus, should we not find "atheism in Christianity"?
For the latter's norm now resides in this divine impulse in man,
not in the alienating spell cast by a tyrant in heaven.

Again we find that the situations portrayed in the Book of
Revelation have a high degree of actuality. The negation that
marks the earthly life of Jesus and seals his fate has acquired the
dimensions of world history: law versus faith, political self-help
versus waiting on God. But, since the time of Jesus, the possibility of concentrated power—at an earthly, planetary level—
has increased beyond all imagining. The Hellenistic *oikoumene*
and the Roman world empire were pale anticipations of what
today can be achieved by the modern stockpiling of arms and
modern propaganda. Weapons produced on the pretext of being
for mankind's redemption would suffice to destroy the entire
world, not just once but many times over, and their material potential conceals the spiritual potential of the "plan" that opposes
the redemption effected by Christ.

Here for the first time we discern the whole theodramatic demonic context of the post-Christian situation: the secularization
that characterizes world history, which began to set in at the
same time as Christ appeared, creating a new period of history
that manifests itself in man's ever more complete domination
over nature (for man is now liberated from nature), is not some
neutral phenomenon that can be regarded as "progress" or "de-

---

[6] *Ibid.*, 242.

velopment": ultimately it is encompassed by and taken into the service of that theodramatic world decision that was provoked and triggered by Jesus. *Gaudium et spes* is under the shadow of *luctus et angor* and dominated by it. The course of history is not determined by an ever more banal rationalism that pervades thought and life but by the interaction of two mysteries: on the one hand, "the wisdom of God in a mystery" (1 Cor 2:7, AV), which calls for the surrender of faith, and that of the great Whore of Babylon, "on whose forehead is written a name of mystery" (Rev 17:5).

In Revelation, Babylon is not overthrown in the battle with the Logos, although the Lamb and his followers make war against the kings subject to Babylon (Rev 17:14): it is destroyed and burned by its own adherents, who turn against it in hatred (Rev 18). The world seems ripe for such self-destruction on the part of the *Civitas diaboli*, given that the *Civitas terrena*, with its weapons of destruction, has fallen within the ambit of the former.

We must not be afraid to utter the harsh truth. In making his provocative claim to have reconciled the world in God, Jesus never suggested that he was creating an earthly paradise. The kingdom of God will never be externally demonstrable (Lk 17:21); it grows, invisibly, perpendicular to world history, and the latter's fruits are already in God's barns. Man responds to this provocation by attempting to manufacture the kingdom of God on earth, with increasing means and methods of power; logically this power that resists the powerlessness of the Cross is bound to destroy itself, for it bears the principle of self-annihilation within it by saying No to the claim of Christ. And so we are brought to the following formulation, extravagant though it may seem: mankind's self-destruction is the only foreseeable end to the world, left to itself, and the only end it deserves, insofar as it prefers to hoard what is its own (that is, power, mammon) rather than to gather with Christ. It has already decided its own fate.

3. Mysterium Iniquitatis

Again it must be emphasized that this intensifying of the dramatic confrontation is only possible in the post-Christian age, when the diffuse religious dimension (part of the pre-Christian search for meaning) has become subordinated to the No to the claim of Jesus, who concentrates everything "religious" on himself: "No one comes to the Father except by me."

Naturally, this claim was intolerable to the quasi-religious, pagan state. Those who denied the latter's sacral nature were ipso facto atheists—as the early Christians were called. It took a long time for the state to be de-sacralized, even after it had become Christian, and the process robbed mankind of that natural protection that lay in society's being embedded in an overall cosmic order. Now it was man himself who, in order to preserve his dignity and freedom, had to produce norms for the state, taking responsibility for them and altering them as the good of all required. But where can freedom find its own norm, if it is not to wander off in empty arbitrariness, thus threatening everyone else's freedom? In the family, perhaps, where humanity and nature form an indissoluble unity: here man is generated and brought to birth by energies that are simultaneously personal and natural: this provides the matrix for an authority that is exercised and accepted in love, in the sense of that respect (grounded in the Fourth Commandment) for the deepest personal values, rooted as they are in the sustaining womb of nature and closely related to the values of religion. But can nature maintain these values once it has become technologized? Surely, if sex is subordinated to technology and man generally is emancipated from his matrix in nature, the family will be deprived of the power to sustain and cherish all that we mean by the organism of society and the state—including the authority that is indispensable to it?

In the post-Christian era, when Jesus has succeeded in gathering all religious elements to himself, there will be only two paths left. One is indicated by Paul when he says: "I bow my knees before the Father from whom every *patria* in heaven and on earth is named" (Eph 3:14f.), and here *patria* (family) strongly suggests natural and personal inheritance from the family's progenitor. In other words, the diffuse religious elements that bind men to the *theion* are deepened through Christianity, which makes man aware that he owes all that he is, both personally and in terms of nature, to the all-creating Father-God; because of the eternal

Son, we have been accepted as free sons of the Father. As a result of biblical revelation, however, the "numinous" dimension in man's relationship with the universe is finally "clarified", that is, shown to speak of Christ, and the world is "secularized" (in a correct sense) and shown to be God's "other", God's partner. Thus the world's relation to the Paternal (and trinitarian) Origin is infinitely heightened: its journey through meaning and time is illuminated by having a beginning and an end, an Alpha and an Omega. Christians must always be aware of this context whenever there is talk of a "secular world".

The other path involves the loss of natural bonds and of the handing-on of life, the loss of the heart—which is the unity in man of body and soul, *cosmos* and *idea*—and the loss of that innate proportion that enables man to shape his world responsibly and in a human and humane manner. If the inexhaustible intimacy of Jesus' relationship with his Father fulfills and transcends all "numinous" natural religion, it follows that the rejection of this relationship leads to the forfeiting of any sense of gratitude for existence: any such sense of indebtedness, even to father and mother, now seems to involve estrangement from one's own freedom. Marx, who makes this No the cornerstone of his anthropology, is only drawing the final conclusions from the Enlightenment's (anti-Christian) idea of freedom as total autonomy. This leads the way to the insatiable dialectic between a freedom that is anarchy and the withdrawal of such freedom by order of the absolutist state—ostensibly in order to arrive at a realm of absolute freedom where man is totally self-made.

Jesus says Yes to his Father's creation and goes in search of all beings lost in the world maze, in order to bring them home. (This shows the unity, in the divine-human heart of the Redeemer, of creation and redemption.) This Yes is utterly opposed, eschatologically speaking, to the No that rejects any permanent bond (*re-ligio*) with the Origin (which is the zero-point in Ernst Bloch's "Prinzip-Hoffnung"); accordingly, it resists that blind, headlong rush toward an a-topic (that is, "place-less"), u-topian Omega that has no Alpha—the luciferian usurping of absolute creative power. In opposition to a "flesh" that originates in Spirit and can become the Spirit's bearer—ultimately in the humble Incarnation of the divine Word—we see the implacable materialism that degrades matter to the mere raw material of its abstract, dis-incarnating power structures.

Again, this formal opposition only becomes lethal for mankind in that the link between natural paganism ("they are without God in the world", Eph 2:12) and a Christianity aware of the glories of grace has failed in its mediating role and thus represents the whole phenomenon of rejection in the world ("his own people did not receive him", Jn 1:11). Instead of showing Abrahamic faith and the absolute trust called for by the prophets, it preferred self-reliance and the superficial wisdom of power politics; we see this from Solomon, via Zedekiah, right down to the Zealots, of whatever stamp.

In the Old Testament, the wicked Jerusalem is regarded as the supreme Harlot, and is set lower than Sodom and Samaria (Ezek 16); finally it is destroyed and put under the control of Babylon. The other Jerusalem, more lamentable than the first, rejects its Messiah and is left forsaken (Lk 13:35) and so thoroughly destroyed that not one stone remains upon another (Lk 21:6). Here we have a twofold prophecy of the eschatological destruction of the Tower built by Titanic effort in the "great city" where Temple and altar still stand, but where the Temple forecourt has been surrendered to the trampling of the Gentiles (Rev 11:2). This is the city in which "their lord was crucified" and which is "allegorically called Sodom and Egypt" (Rev 11:8).[1] Ultimately it is called Babylon, and its "fall" is announced even before it becomes visible (Rev 14:8; 17:1; 18:2ff.), although for the present it maintains its enslaving dominance (1 Pet 5:13).

Judaism and the Gentile world both reject Jesus and—once the Gentile Christians have appropriated the early Church's knowledge and changed this holy knowledge into an elitist, arrogant Gnosticism, a process that already shows through at many points in the New Testament—the different modes of rejection of Jesus

---

[1] H. Schlier regards Revelation 10-11 as "the conclusion of Israel's history . . . , which seems to be reduced to its fundamental salvation-historical features, that is, its eschatological decisions, which become visible in the light of Christ": *Die Zeit der Kirche* (Herder, 1956), 18. At the outset, we expressed our reservations about this view of the apocalyptic visions, which endeavors to distinguish the Old and New Testaments; in the case of these chapters, however, such a distinction is not impossible.

on the part of Jews and Gentiles coalesce and become indistinguishable. It is this No that Jesus calls the unforgivable sin against the Spirit and that the Letter to the Hebrews portrays in such terrifying terms: "For it is impossible to restore again to repentance those who have once been enlightened, who have tasted the heavenly gift, and have become partakers of the Holy Spirit, and have tasted the goodness of the word of God and the powers of the age to come", for they are like barren land, fit only for burning (Heb 6:4–8; cf. 10:26). "For it would have been better for them never to have known the way of righteousness than after knowing it to turn back from the holy commandment delivered to them" (2 Pet 2:21). But it is precisely this "knowledge that puffs up" (1 Cor 8:1) that tends to "more and more ungodliness . . . like gangrene" (2 Tim 2:16f.). It is precisely the deep things of divine knowledge that are perverted by the "ignorant and unstable" (2 Pet 3:16). If purity is not persisted in, it leads to incomparably more impurity (Mt 12:43–45).

Jewish-Gentile Gnosticism is the arch-enemy of the Christian faith and of love in the Church. As a phenomenon, it epitomizes all the ever-intensifying rejections of the message of Jesus in world history. In each case, some vital aspect of this message —liberation from sin, insight into the heart of God, brotherhood among men in this heart—is taken over, manipulated and "staged" as if man himself had produced it. This can lead to the proud dualism of the gnostic "pneumatics" who separate themselves from the hopeless "psychics" and "hylics"; all subsequent dualisms (including racism) belong to this family. It can also lead to the arrogance of a monistic "Enlightenment", which, in tolerant superiority (since it knows the rules of "the progress of the human race"), addresses those who are still in bondage to faith and committed to the "kingdom of the Son" and endeavors to guide them to the "age of the spirit" that has awakened to absolute Knowledge. Joachim's successors in this field are as innumerable as the sand of the sea.[2] This attempt to bring "enlight-

---

[2] Henri de Lubac, in his two-volume work *La Postérité spirituelle de Joachim de Flore* (Lethielleux; vol. 1 [1979]: "De Joachim à Schelling"; vol. 2 [1981]: "De Saint Simon à nos jours") is the first to trace the theme right down to the present day.

enment" to a religiosity that is still imprisoned in the darkness of an alienating institution, leading it into the self-illumination of free thought, characteristically calls itself "humanism". The term profits from the fading radiance of the Christian "humanity of God" (Titus 3:4) and ultimately attributes this radiance to man himself—and directs it against God. Or else it represents this radiance as emanating from a "divine" man, as Soloviev brilliantly portrays in his story of the Antichrist.[3] The manifesto of this greatest humanist proclaims: "World peace is assured forever. Every attempt to disturb it will instantly meet with irresistible opposition; for from now on there is only a single central power on earth. . . . That power is mine."[4]

Here again we are confronted with the complete Antichrist, endowed with total power, as the No to Christ's total powerlessness. This power is concentrated more and more, until no one—great or humble, rich or poor, free or slave—"can buy or sell unless he has the mark, that is, the name of the beast" on his hand or forehead (Rev 13:16f.); increasingly, therefore, the Christian's witness becomes a witness in blood, the giving of his life. Thus the final phase of the Church's history corresponds to the end of the earthly life of Jesus, who "made the good confession [in blood] in the presence of many witnesses" (1 Tim 6:12). As we have already said, this correspondence is not grounded in Jewish apocalyptic but purely in Christology.[5] For, just as the

---

[3] In *Drei Gespräche* (1900), translated by E. Müller-Kamp (Bonn, 1947).

[4] *Ibid.*, 200.

[5] H. Schlier insists on this in his article "Thlipsis" in *ThW* III, 139ff.: the Church is essentially concerned with "the sufferings of Christ" (Col 1:24; 2 Cor 1:5), suffering "for Jesus' sake" (2 Cor 4:8–10), cf. Phil 3:10; 1 Pet 4:13, and so forth. In our discipleship of Christ, the eschatological tribulation has already begun; "when the New Testament uses the term *thlipsis*, it is not merely taking over or even developing Jewish ideas of the eschatological suffering: it is setting forth a new understanding of the eschatological facts on the basis of the concrete history of Jesus Christ" (*loc. cit.*, 146). This can be insisted on even if there is a Jewish tradition that the man persecuted (for God's sake) can rejoice. W. Nauck, in his "Freude im Leiden. Zum Problem einer urchristlichen Verfolgungstradition" in *ZNW* 48 (1955), 68–80, against Selwyn's *1 Peter* (1949), 450, finds such a tradition in texts that are not influenced by Christianity (*Syr. Bar.* 48, 48f.; 54, 16–18) and locates its *Sitz im Leben* in the Old Testament *peirasmos*, for which the believer must be grateful (cf. K. G. Kuhn in *ZThK* 49 (1952), 204–8).

power of the anti-Christian negation comes from the absolute, provocative position adopted by Christ, and just as the *mysterion* that is written on the forehead of Babylon the Great (Rev 17:5) is the perverse mirror-image of the christological *mysterion* (Eph 3:3), the Christian's ultimate (blood-) testimony can only correspond to that of his Lord: Jesus "uttered" his testimony with his whole substance, his flesh and blood, thus accomplishing the Incarnation of the Word of God and effecting the redemption.

Assuredly, the entire history of the Church is accompanied by the testimony of the martyrs, since the mystery of the Cross accompanies it from the beginning and throughout all the phases of its development. Hence Jesus addresses prophetic words to his Apostles, predicting that they will share the same fate that

---

Akira Sataka, "Das Leiden der Jünger um meinetwillen" in *ZNW* 67 (1976), 4‑19, attempts to show that Judaism is unacquainted with the notion that the just man can suffer "for the sake of" (*heneka*) anything: suffering is simply the just man's destiny. In this context, he refers to D. Rössler, *Gesetz und Geschichte* (1960), 90, 94. Sataka suggests that the historical Jesus cannot have used the formula; in any case, he rejects the idea of *shared* suffering on the part of Jesus and the disciple. The "I" that says "for my sake" is "evidently the Exalted One who addresses Christians through prophets" (13). The expression must have become current "at an early stage", however, since the disciples are unequivocally persecuted for Jesus' sake and for the same infringement of the law as he. A different view, as is to be expected, is found in Joachim Jeremias, *Neutestamentliche Theologie*, 2d ed., I (Gütersloh, 1973), 229ff. [*New Testament Theology* (SCM)]: "It is essential to the messenger's ministry that he should suffer for Christ's sake. All strata of the sources agree that Jesus continually affirmed this." Initially it is more a matter of accepting personal offenses (the slap on the cheek, the refusal of admission to a village) than of real persecution; thus "neither the persecution of Stephen nor the persecution under Agrippa I, let alone that under Nero . . . , provided the model." The logia that speak of the disciples' fate can be distinguished from those concerning the eschatological tribulation (230). Donald Riddle, "Die Verfolgungslogien in formgeschichtlicher und soziologischer Beleuchtung" in *ZNW* 33 (1934), 271‑89, shows the similarities and differences between the persecution-logia in Jewish apocalyptic and in Christianity. According to him, these logia attained wider influence because of the early persecution at the hands of Jews and then due to the way individual Christians were denounced to the state authorities and imprisoned. (On the persecution by the Jews, cf. Schnackenburg's commentary on John 15:18‑25; 16:1‑4a, with reference to Revelation 2:9; 3:9; Justin, *Dial.* 95, 4; 133, 6.) In general, it is impossible to doubt that Jesus, in sternly requiring unconditional discipleship, told his followers that suffering and even persecution would inevitably be involved: such was always the lot of the prophets.

awaits him. His words refer not only to the manner of death of the Twelve: they apply to all who will belong to his fellowship.[6] "The Church is built on the foundation of the martyrs. . . . A Church that does not suffer is not the apostolic Church. . . . Christ's mortal suffering—since it is the 'Son of Man', the Incarnate One, who suffers—permeates the whole Church, his Mystical Body."[7] The Book of Revelation shows both things at once: martyrdom as the normal badge of the Christian who is sealed with the sign of Jesus (Paul says, "baptized into the death of Jesus": Rom 6:3); and martyrdom as the preeminent destiny of the Church of the eschatological age, when Babylon the Great is "drunk with the blood of the saints and the blood of the martyrs of Jesus" (Rev 17:6). In this period, the Church will no longer be primarily a missionary Church where her blood is the "seed" of her newly planted communities (as in Acts, which gives the paradigm for all missionary epochs); now she enters the final phase, sharing in the Passion of Christ, who confronts the *mysterium iniquitatis* in an entirely new way: he disarms it from within by enduring suffering. "When I am weak, then I am strong" (2 Cor 12:10).

It is impossible to represent this final act of the Church's history in a visible form. Scripture envisages a time of tribulation in which Christians "will be hated by all nations", when "many false prophets will arise" and "men's love will grow cold" (Mt 24:9–12); and it raises the question of whether the returning Son of Man "will find faith on the earth" (Lk 18:8). But just as the eschatological conversion of Israel, of which Paul speaks, cannot be situated within history,[8] so too we do not know whether, in this final tribulation, the Church is to die with her Lord in order to rise with him to eternal life. We cannot know this, just as we cannot say whether the second coming of the Son of Man will take place as world time is ending or *after* it has ended; the first alternative may be solely apocalyptic imagery.

The Antichrist's total power will necessarily be earthly and po-

---

[6] Cf. the classic observations of E. Peterson, *Zeuge der Wahrheit* (1937), reprinted in *Theologische Traktate* (Munich: Kösel, 1951), 107–224.

[7] *Ibid.*, 167, 173, 179.

[8] As G. Fessard (*De l'actualité historique* . . .) rightly argues against many proponents of this view, such as C. Journet and also J. Pieper.

litical. So E. Peterson is right to emphasize the civil-legal nature of the eschatological witness-by-blood (and of every Christian witness-by-blood). The total embrace of political power means that there can be no remaining sanctuary, nowhere to emigrate to; this obliges the Christian to take his stand publicly. Today's "iron curtain" is an initial, clear anticipation of this: escape is impossible; the Gulag stifles all alternatives. Then there is the question of the feasibility of a counterkingdom built on pure political power (the "first beast") and the consistent lie (the "second beast"); Jesus seems to say that such a kingdom cannot survive, and he predicts its fall (Mt 12:25f.). Thus Babylon will be torn down and burned by its own adherents (Rev 17:16). But again the details are veiled from us: we do not know whether the collapse of the hostile kingdom will take place within history or not until the dawn of eternity.

The whole abyss of the *mysterium iniquitatis* yawns in the way it opposes the *mysterium Trinitatis*, which is at the heart of Jesus' claim. Jesus does not present his claim in his own name but in the name of the Father who has sent his Spirit of mission upon him. What is provocative in Jesus' message is that he manifests the glory of divine power in lowliness, defenselessness and a self-surrender that goes to the lengths of the eucharistic Cross. This unveils a totally unexpected picture of God's internal, trinitarian defenselessness: the wisdom of God that is folly yet wiser than the wisdom of men (1 Cor 1–2). Only thus can the Son really reveal the Father; only thus can the Spirit who proceeds from both be the revelation of their loving fellowship. Truth, at its origin, is unreserved self-surrender and hence the opening-up of the depths of the Father. Truth is the Son's humility, which makes room for, and expresses, the whole sublimity of the Father's love. Truth is the Spirit who both attests and seals this divine relationship and communicates it to the world. We must be quite clear that hell's attempt to produce a countertrinity must be a refutation of all structuralism that, abstracting from content, attempts to find identities or analogies of structures. The only thing that links the first beast, the Antichrist, with God is blasphemy: on its seven heads and ten horns stand "blasphemous names" (Rev 13:1); in fact, its whole body is covered with them (17:3); "it opened its mouth to utter blasphemies against God" and those who dwell in heaven (13:6), for it "was given a mouth uttering haughty and blasphemous words" (13:5). Here the opposition is so total that there is no similarity whatsoever. Thus there is the pseudo-miracle of the healing of the beast's mortal wound, in contrast to the "Lamb as though it had been slain", whose wound remains always open, manifesting the truth of the defenseless nature of the divine, trinitarian love. This "healing"—which demonstrates, as it were, that there was no wound in the first place—blasphemes the mystery of Jesus' death and Resurrection: these two are inseparable, as his Eucharist attests. (John speaks of his "exaltation", and Luke of his being "received up": Lk 9:51.) As a result, the blasphemous structure of the trinity of hell contradicts the divine Trinity in every last detail. The beast is not the image of the Dragon but a grotesque mixture of different animal species. The dragon does not bring it forth out of itself: it arises out of the sea, a product of creation (that is, it is merely human, in contrast to the God-man), and the Dragon bestows upon it its *dynamis*, great *exousia* and its throne; there is nothing here of divine self-emptying and so nothing of the Trinity's self-disclosure and truth. The Dragon, absolute evil, remains hidden behind its hideous offspring and utterance, the beast, but in such a way that the latter continues to put forth its monstrous seductive power "over every tribe and people and tongue and nation" who "worship" it (Rev 13:7f.). This is full-blown in the second beast, which stands against the Holy Spirit and is complete anti-truth, which it can only be if it simultaneously resembles the Lamb and the Dragon (13:11), for the lie must adopt the appearance of truth. So it performs miracles, but precisely those that Jesus had refused to do (13:12; Lk 9:55); it seduces people to worship idols (contrary to the Old Testament ban on images, since Jesus was to be the sole Image of the Father), until the idol itself comes alive and has the same deadly effect as the Antichrist. (So the Roman statues of the emperors killed those who refused to venerate them, as the idols of anti-Christian tyrannies of all times continue and will continue to do.) The lying "spirit" that arises from the earth to fascinate the world is not at all the spirit of reciprocal surrender between the Dragon and the Antichrist; rather, like the latter, it is a mere extension of "the great dragon, the ancient serpent, who is called the Devil and Satan" (Rev 12:9). To that extent, the countertrinity is not a true trinity but a "Sabellian" one: the same evil under three forms. However, evil, the rejection of love, is compelled to assume a perverse outward shape of love, manifested in the Arch-Whore of Babylon, "mother of harlots and of earth's abominations" (17:5), with whom "the kings of the earth have committed fornication, and the merchants of the earth have grown rich with the wealth of her wantonness" (18:3). Here love is perverted into pleasure and the accumulation of wealth, just as Paul sees licentiousness and greed together (Eph 4:19; 5:3; Col 3:5). Indeed, the accumulation of wealth—the complete opposite to God's attitude—is by far the predominant element in the great dirge on the Fall of Babylon; it is primarily the "merchants of the earth" who lament Babylon's desolation and burning, for all the products of their worldwide trade were designed to increase and glorify its harlotry (18:9–24).

In the Book of Revelation, there is only one way to combat the trinity of hell, which is the final shape of evil: believers must bear witness in their lives and in their blood, thus fully incarnating their faith as they pit it against utter, satanic dis-incarnation. The victors who are seen in heaven (7:9ff.; 14:1ff.; 15:2) "are they who have come out of the great tribulation; they have washed their robes and made them white in the blood of the Lamb" (7:14); alternatively, they are given white robes after they have been "slain for the word of God"; they cried to God for justice but had to endure "until the number of their fellow servants and their brethren should be complete, who were to be killed as they themselves had been" (6:9–11). This eschatological opposition between the apparent omnipotence of evil and the apparent mortal powerlessness of believers cannot be dismissed as a mere vision. It is genuine prophecy.

C. THE CHURCH'S FORM:
BEAUTIFUL AND MARRED

1. Polarities and Dissensions

So far, in this section on "the battle of the Logos", we have considered the Church as a homogeneous whole, simply as the "called, chosen and faithful" ones (Rev 17:14) together with whom "the Lord of lords, the King of kings" goes to war. But it is not only in the Book of Revelation that we learn that even the saints can be vanquished (11:7; 13:7); all the New Testament writings testify to internal tensions and dissensions in the Church; they are lamented, and the communities are urged to overcome them.

The Church is a community of sinners who have been sanctified through baptism; the sinfulness that continues to adhere to them or reawakens within them leads naturally to conflict. "Where sins are, there are divisions, false teachings, disputes."[1] If this is generally true, it is particularly the case in an organism as full of tensions as the Church necessarily is, since she straddles the realms of time and eternity, of the "already" and the "not yet", of visibility and invisibility, of obedience and freedom, of the order instituted by Christ and the authority and inspiration of the Holy Spirit in each of the Church's members, of tradition and constant newness, of rootedness in the Old Covenant and of that which transcends it. Ultimately the tension is between the fulfillment of the last iota of the Law and the overcoming of the Law by the new "law of freedom" or of love; once *this* law is kept, it replaces all others. We could go on to describe this network of tensions whereby the Church's organism expands. On the one hand, it is comprehensible like any other human community, with a clear profile outlined by rules of membership; on the other hand, it exceeds our comprehension, since the boundaries of the visible Church do not correspond to those of

---

[1] Origen, *In Ez. hom.* 9, 1 (Baehr., 405). "If a man falls into sin, he becomes multiple: he is separated from God, falls apart, declines from unity. But if many follow God's command, they constitute a single Man, as the Apostle says in 1 Corinthians 10:17 and Ephesians 4:5." Origen, *Comm. in Osee* (PG 13, 828C).

the living Mystical Body of Christ, for the latter can have true members outside the *Catholica* and many dead members within her. Right from the beginning, this organism of interrelated tensions could only be held together by the source that gave it shape in the first place: a living faith in Jesus Christ, justification and sanctification by his death and Resurrection, his sacraments and discipleship of him in active love. Not even sin was necessary: human limitation was sufficient to create the differing emphases among the elements in tension. One thinks of Stephen's associates with their polemics against Law and Temple; of the disputes over the coexistence of Jewish and Gentile Christians in the new "third race"; and, most obvious of all, of those tensions and polemics provoked by the preaching of Paul—though here Paul vehemently asserts that there was also a satanic element at work here, in the likeness of an "angel of light".

There is more. Even within the communities founded by Paul and stamped with his spirit, there are dissensions practically everywhere. The Letters to the Corinthians are full of accusations of strife in the community: there are *schismata* (1 Cor 1:10), there is *hairesis* (1 Cor 11:19), "for you bear it if a man makes slaves of you, or preys upon you, or takes advantage of you, or puts on airs, or strikes you in the face . . ." (2 Cor 11:20). In Philippi, two women have acquired opposing coteries; the Galatians should beware, lest in "biting and devouring one another" they are totally "consumed by one another" (Gal 5:15). And, as soon as Paul has turned his back, alien teachings insinuate themselves, Jewish teachings from Jerusalem, early gnostic teachings in Colossae and no doubt in Corinth too. Hardly is the Church founded when she is deeply rent by strife. No wonder then that Paul, having given the Corinthians and Romans a description of the Body of Christ in terms of the unity and order of her manifold members, goes on in the Letter to the Ephesians to lay the main emphasis on his doctrine of the Church, linking it even more closely than before to the doctrine on the Christ: the Church is a fullness that comes from his fullness of love, and, as such, even where there is genuine knowledge of her, she transcends all human understanding. Only he who lives in and from the fullness of Christ can lead an authentically ecclesial life, "with all lowliness and meekness, with patience, forbearing one another in love", aware that all are one body and one spirit, called to the same hope by the one Lord and destined for the same faith through the one baptism, as children of the same God and Father (cf. Eph 4:2–6). If the Johannine writings dwell so much on love, it is partly because there was serious dissension in the background (cf. 3 Jn). The latest New Testament writings openly heap curses against the wrongdoers, libertines and false teachers who are to be found in the Church, unashamed "blots and blemishes" in her love-feasts (Jude 12; cf. 2 Pet 2:13–22). In his farewell discourses, Paul predicted "that after my departure fierce wolves will come in among you, not sparing the flock; and from among your own selves will arise men speaking perverse things, to draw away the disciples after them" (Acts 20:29f.).

This brief look at the Church's beginnings was necessary if we are to understand that her history—past, present and future—is almost inevitably tragic. "For there must be factions among you in order that those who are genuine among you may be recognized" (1 Cor 11:19). Do these words perhaps go back to something said by the Lord himself?[2] Of course this does not refer to some—allegedly theologically justifiable—future development that was to come about according to a divine plan, for example, as if the multiplicity inherent in the fullness of Christ needed to unfold through world history;[3] no: schism and heresy is always due to the sin and guilt of Christians. For its chief effect is always to obscure the person and mission of Christ himself, since, as the origins of both the community and the gospel message show, he can only put forth his influence in history in tandem with the faith of his disciples. "Is Christ divided?" (1 Cor 1:13). The impression given, at least to those outside, must be that Christians themselves do not know the true nature of their own origin, the foundation on which they stand. It must seem that this Christ is a being with no clear locus in the world;

---

[2] Justin, *Dial.* 35, 3, gives us the (apocryphal) Dominical saying: "There will be divisions [*schismata*] and party wrangling [*hairesis*]." There are a number of allusions to this, cf. Schneemelcher, *Ntl. Apokryphen* I (1959), 54. The saying only makes explicit what is implicit in the Synoptic apocalypses.

[3] Karl Barth has energetically bolted the door to this view. Cf. my *Theology of Karl Barth* (San Francisco: Ignatius Press, 1992), 4.

accordingly, with regard to the vital issues of mankind, he can be put on one side and left to the interest of private sects.

The history of the Church shows increasing disintegration of ecclesial unity; there is no corresponding tendency toward a return to unity. However much—today more than ever—people strive for such a return through the ecumenical movement, the difficulties encountered are of positively supernatural proportions: there no longer exists a complete, common set of reference points for the envisaged unity. An abstract Christ, without the concrete shape of a Church that is inseparable from him, cannot provide this reference point. In concrete terms, Christ only exists together with the community of saints united in the *Immaculata*, together with the communion of the ministerial office visibly united in Peter and his successors and together with the living, ongoing tradition united in the great councils and declarations of the Church. Where these elements of integration are rejected in principle, it is impossible to return to unity, however much good will is displayed by the partners. Furthermore, these efforts dissipate on internal matters much of the Church's energy that would otherwise be available for the preaching of the gospel in the world. The energy is not entirely lost, of course, for wherever strife between Christians is overcome, it can be seen as a step toward the lost unity. But all too often the unity achieved is superficial; people imagine they have penetrated to the center when they are still on the periphery, and this is because they either have not recognized, or will not acknowledge, the real dividing issues.

The more Christianity splinters, the more unrecognizable becomes that Church that has persisted, through the splintering process, as the original, straight tree-trunk from which the branches emerge. The phenomenology of religion sees this tree trunk as one splinter group among others, which, in order to distinguish itself from the other Christian denominations, has to give itself a complicated title: Roman Catholic. But it is not only in phenomenology that the position becomes clouded: even theology is confused, because the branches contain much living sap from the original root-complex and trunk; thus they bear flowers and fruits that are undeniably part of the Christian totality. So we have a paradoxical situation: the *Catholica* finds that things that are fundamentally hers, but which she has somehow forgotten or inadequately realized, are exhibited—to her shame —by other Christian communities.

The saints are the Church's powers of regeneration; they can reanimate whole areas that seemed dead. But, as the splintering proceeds, these wide areas get narrower and narrower. Their power does not extend beyond the boundaries of the Church community, or rarely in an identifiable manner. Or a great Catholic ardor is reinterpreted as a humanistic phenomenon and given appropriate prizes. The creation of the unity commanded by the Lord—a categorical imperative for Christianity—is addressed to sinners, and as such it seems a utopian demand.

2. The Domestication of Faith

There is an even more dangerous tendency in the Church: faith is overtaken or hollowed out by knowledge. This has often been described as the distinctively tragic destiny of Christian history.[1] Even the Old Covenant had ended in wisdom literature (and its continuation in apocalyptic), in which man was very close to claiming an overall grasp of the history of revelation, that is, a gnosis; the temptation to such Gnosticism must have been even greater at the conclusion of the revelation in Christ, with the giving of the Holy Spirit, who "searches the deep things of God". However, Gnosticism's first, powerful attack in the second century was too fantastic, and the Church—particularly in the work of Irenaeus—was able to foil it. The Gnosticism that emerged from the Middle Ages and has come down to modern times is much more serious; its effects are more profound. We have already mentioned Joachim of Flora's doctrine of the "three phases", which initially seems so harmless; this quickly adopted more radical forms, aiming to overcome the institutional Church of Christ in the name

[1] Thus G. Siewerth in *Das Schicksal der Metaphysik von Thomas zu Heidegger* (Einsiedeln: Johannes Verlag, 1959); more extensively in J.-M. Le Guillou, *Das Mysterium des Vaters, Apostolischer Glaube und moderne Gnosis* (Johannes Verlag, 1974).

of the Holy Spirit, who was destined to rule the Third Age of the world. Henri de Lubac has shown how uninterruptedly and how multifariously Joachim's vision underpinned the Enlightenment, then Idealism, finally emerging in Marxism.[2] Not that Joachim can be made solely responsible for the development of modern rationalism and historicism.[3] Particularly in the universities, Averroism, quite independently of the "spirituals", had accorded pride of place to *ratio* over *fides*, thus profoundly upsetting the entire clerical world of learning; in doing so, it had also pushed the latter toward the contrary movement, an irrational mysticism that was no less dangerous to faith in the incarnate Word, or toward a voluntaristic Nominalism that was partly to blame for the break that took place in the Reformation. Then the Reformation and the religious disputes that followed it brought about the final victory of rationalism: now man and his reason were exalted as the measuring rod of a sustainable religion—even of one calling itself Christian—with the result that mystery and dogma, along with the authority that took responsibility for them, were evacuated from the Christian faith. This rational faith, which is the product of the religious wars, then mingles with another movement that comes straight from a Scholasticism that is undergoing progressive collapse. Whereas High Scholasticism had made the mistake of thinking that it had to give an appropriate answer to every inquisitive question, however untheological,[4] now, in the theology of its imitators, such

---

[2] *La Postérité spirituelle de Joachim de Flore*, vol. 1 (Lethielleux, 1979).

[3] K. Löwith's celebrated analysis *Weltgeschichte und Heilsgeschehen, die theologischen Voraussetzungen der Geschichtsphilosophie*, 2d ed. (Urban-Bücher, 1953), goes back in time from Bossuet to Joachim, whom he regards as the seminal influence. Farther back, the only interesting figures for Löwith are Augustine and Orosius. Cf. his Appendix 1: "Verwandlungen der Lehre Joachims".

[4] "One of the gravest weaknesses of Scholasticism, even in its full flowering in Thomas Aquinas or Duns Scotus, was the way it felt it necessary to answer all the questions put to it, and that on the basis of the word of God. . . . Even Thomas showed this weakness by uncritically accepting a mode of questioning that was due in part to the under-rationality of a particular cultural epoch; he should rather have said openly that such a way of proceeding is illegitimate and that the questions a man puts . . . are always more or less incorrectly put, because of his fallen state. Before God can grant an answer, he must put the question straight. And that is

questions are multiplied beyond all bounds; the answers become more and more hair-splitting as the legitimate rational method of a Thomas is increasingly distorted into an unbearable rationalism by the overweening deductions of a "theology of conclusions".[5] G. Siewerth, in his presentation of this process, spoke of it "advancing into the divine ground", because the ratio, abandoning all restraint, thinks itself empowered and authorized to plumb the ultimate mysteries of God. In the end, this leads to Hegel's God, who is without all mystery: behold the door to atheism.

The Enlightenment, which asserted itself first within Anglican and Protestant theology and then more radically in French philosophy, finally penetrated Catholic theology too. There were reactions to it, first from religious Romanticism and then, more energetically, from the revival of Thomism; but they could not prevent Enlightenment principles from forcefully asserting their dominant role in theology. The vanguard of this movement was the purely rational "historico-critical method" of exegesis applied to the inspired texts. Today, therefore, Christian thought is profoundly disturbed and divided. On the one hand, there is an understanding of faith that, in the traditional view, regards the articles of faith as the irreducible object of all Christian theologizing; on the other hand, there is the opposite view, which subjects these very articles—both their content and the act of faith that they elicit—to rationalistic scrutiny and substitutes for most of them a new and essentially reduced content that relies on anthropological plausibility. Church authority, which holds fast to ancient tradition and seeks to bind others to it, finds itself subjected to historico-critical examination and required to present its credentials. Now, firm results on the part of the historico-critical method are few and far between, while there is a superabundance of the question marks it puts over things that were once held to be unshakable; for the most part, accordingly, the "enlightened" Christian's faith can only hover uncertainly in the air. At best, in the absence of firm foundations, all it can do is

---

the first thing that God's word enables us to do." Louis Bouyer, *Das Handwerk des Theologen* (Einsiedeln: Johannes Verlag, 1980), 170–71.
[5] *Ibid.*

cling to the Church's external forms. This is an unstable and unsatisfactory result, since, for the "enlightened" Christian, the *lex orandi* can no longer be the *lex credendi*: he can in no way take literally the words that are prayed in the Canon of the Mass in the parish Eucharist.

The rationalism that has penetrated theology is a new form of Gnosticism. More categorically than ever before, it claims right of domicile in theology. It can also manifest itself as a form of the Church's *aggiornamento*, as a precondition for the evangelization of the modern world. It alone, allegedly, can create a common basis for dialogue with nonbelievers; only thus can we hope that they will give Christianity a hearing. In this way, politically speaking, the Western world is being prepared for what the "peace priests" did in the East. The kind of Christology established by historico-critical methods is generally, at root, an "ascending" Christology, that is, starting from the man Jesus of Nazareth, and the assertions of the "descending" Christology (according to which the preexistent Word of God becomes flesh) are held to be a later superstructure. So the question arises, can it ever be worthwhile or justifiable to stake one's life—since this is how faith proves itself in terms of flesh and blood—on the remaining historical core of truth?

Theologians such as these are torn between the "new theology" they have designed (on the basis of rationalistic exegesis) and their commitment to the Catholic Church; their situation is tragic, but one cannot describe it as dramatic. The situation of the Church herself, however, her heart invaded by a disintegrating rationalism, is certainly eminently dramatic. The situation is somewhat similar to Irenaeus' campaign against Gnosticism, but it is more acute insofar as the gnostic sects that claim to have the correct interpretation are no longer outside the Church: they are inside her, claiming to have the proper scientific tools and to be in authentic communication with all religions and world views. What an advantage over conservative orthodoxy, enclosed in its particularist dogmas and relying on obsolete traditions!

A "battle of the Logos" within the *Catholica* herself is today unavoidable. It cannot be avoided by the "orthodox" making a tactical retreat into their defensive positions: they must openly confront the fire from the "historico-critical" methods. This is quite possible, since, in the context of the total phenomenon of the Christian faith and the inner structure of faith's written documents, it can be shown that these methods have only a limited scope.[6] For, on the one hand, there is the certainty of the witnesses who are ready to commit themselves to a Lord who has himself shown that he comes from God (his claim is not a function of the witnesses' enthusiasm); this is quite evident to the faith of the "little" and "simple" people that is extolled in the Beatitudes. And, on the other hand, there are the literary means by which the narrators endeavor to share their conviction —which was transformed, in the wake of Easter, into a genuine faith in Christ—with us who come later. These literary means, which are in the service of the portrayal and in the service of faith, must be tested and weighed; they must be given their true position *as means*. They must not be treated in such a way as to undermine or trivialize the faith they aim to mediate, which is the faith of the first community and of the Church in all ages, the faith of the simple. This issue needs to be fought out today. Nonetheless there are instances in our time of the Old Testament miracle whereby Yahweh creates such confusion in the camp of his enemies that they annihilate one another. Many methods that call themselves "critical" in fact cancel each other out. Great rams, applied to walls or gates, prove to be hollow and are splintered. And behind the front lines of the "scientific" arguments, with their endless skirmishing, we can discern the two fundamental attitudes of faith and unbelief, in whose service the arguments are used. These fundamental attitudes are irreducible: one sees the form [*Gestalt*], the other is blind to it.

Today's struggle is more fierce than ever, but it began a long time ago. It began in Jesus' disputes with the Jews, and in part with his own disciples, and in Paul's arguments against his communities that had been infected with Gnosticism. Paul uses weapons of attack and of defense ("weapons of righteousness for the right hand and for the left", that is, for attack and pro-

---

[6] This is not the place for such proof. It is carefully developed in Heinrich Schlier's essays, "Über Sinn und Aufgabe einer Theologie des Neuen Testaments", "Biblische und dogmatische Theologie", "Was heisst Auslegung der Heiligen Schrift?" in *Besinnung auf das Neue Testament* (Herder, 1964), 7–62, and in the introductory essays in *Das Ende der Zeit* (Herder, 1971).

tection: 2 Corinthians 6:7; "the shield of faith, the helmet of salvation, the sword of the Spirit", Ephesians 6:10f.); and his chief weapon is his own existence as a believer. Finally, we see this struggle of faith in the whole course of the Church's history. Often, as in the confused Arian controversy, it takes the form of close hand-to-hand fighting, until a Council puts an end to a decades-long battle by presenting the ancient faith in a new formulation. The word of God, which is above heaven and earth (Lk 21:33), has also outlived all historico-critical theories; the latters' ostensible advances only go to make the unshakable character of God's word all the more evident. In a word, the more *relative* many forms of expression are shown to be, the more clearly we discern the "primal word" that they approximate and the appropriate "primal answer" that this word elicits.[7]

However, these victories are not achieved without fierce fighting within the Church, and the battle may be harder today, with the advance of Enlightenment ideas, and even harder tomorrow. The anthropocentric, unbelieving Enlightenment is continually acquiring more effective means of influencing public opinion and making the protagonists of unabbreviated faith adopt a defensive and minority stance. The phrase "little flock" and the image of the sheep sent out among wolves become more and more graphically relevant. But at the same time we find that the paradoxical power of the isolated individual (such a one was Kierkegaard) is vindicated time and again, confounding all quantitative calculation, in the tradition of the small round stone from the sling of David.

The swords of gnostic Enlightenment each have a cutting edge, but the sword that comes from the mouth of the Warrior-Logos is two-edged (Rev 1:16; 2:12; Heb 4:12). It parries the open attack from the front and the covert attack from behind. It rules by dividing and exposing, until "all are open and laid bare". The Warrior-Logos gives something of the power of his sword to those who fight alongside him, putting on the "armor of God" in order "to stand against the wiles of the devil". Again we can see beyond faith's struggle against Gnosticism and dis-

---

[7] Cf. H. Schlier, "Über Sinn und Aufgabe einer Theologie des Neuen Testaments", *loc. cit.*, 15.

cern the underlying struggle between Christ and the Antichrist, the hideous offspring of hell. Spiritual literature down through the Church's history is full of instructions on how to conduct oneself in the *pugna spiritualis*, how to acquire the *discretio spirituum* to distinguish God's Spirit from the hostile spirit. The duel is superhuman; therefore the believer must be in possession of divine weapons. This is no mere battle of words and ideas between human beings: here mankind is drawn into the theodramatic war that has broken out between God, in his Logos, and hell's anti-logos. That is why the combatants need "the sword of the Spirit, which is the word of God" if they are to "stand" (*stēnai*, Eph 6:11–17), that is, not to "advance" but to "stand fast, eye to eye" (*antistēnai*, *ibid.*, 13). The situation Paul here describes at the end of the Letter to the Ephesians is clearly eschatological; he is speaking of the "evil time".[8] Accordingly, the last and most effective weapon is "prayer at all times in the Spirit", not only for oneself but "for all the saints" (6:18). Here Paul is urging the community to prepare for a battle that is not limited to internal Church matters; but he himself campaigned just as resolutely against internal enemies as against external ones, particularly when he discovered that some alien element had penetrated into the Church's interior.

He compares such alien elements to the serpent in paradise, insinuating itself from outside to lead the inhabitants astray. The virginal Eve hearkened to its suggestions then, and now the virginal *Ecclesia* begins to listen to them and is in danger of being diverted from her full surrender to Christ. At this point, the Apostle is seized by "God's zeal" for his covenant, which has become a nuptial bond between Christ and the Church (2 Cor 11:1–3). How greedily the *Ecclesia* listens to these suggestions, which entice her away from the chaste love of the covenant and toward some kind of gnosis, whether it be the "know-how" of the old Law or the arcane knowledge of the pagan mysteries! This Gnosticism always opposes faithful love ("knowledge puffs up, but love builds up", 1 Cor 8:1), for Christ is no longer the One to whom the Bridal Church owes everything; he is no longer the *pro nobis*; beside him there are other, more proven,

---

[8] Cf. the relevant passages in H. Schlier's commentary on Ephesians.

more profound ways to salvation—this is the point of view of the Enlightenment. All of a sudden, man's knowledge of God (Hegel's "absolute knowledge") becomes more important than man's *being known* by God (in the concrete biblical sense of conjugal love); for the latter is impossible in the absence of love, since only "if one loves God is one known by him" (1 Cor 8:3). Anyone who fails to see in Christ the Bridegroom, God's incarnate address to man, cannot love God concretely in him. So the virginal Church necessarily tends toward the mentality of Babylon and becomes the "poor little harlot", as Luther described her.[9]

The Enlightenment in all its forms is fatal to the Church, because, starting with the "wise and clever", it gradually infiltrates the people through catechesis, preaching and mass media; it unsettles the faith of the "simple" and obscures the "sound eye" that enables the whole body to be "full of light" (Mt 6:22f.). Again the "millstone" image is appropriate: how many millstones would be needed where this kind of infection penetrates even to the simplest hearth! The gaps are closed one by one, and often it seems a miracle that there are places where Christians can still live with minds and hearts intact.

3. Fruitfulness from the Desert

The foregoing points to a final dramatic tension in the very essence of Christ's Church. The gospel concludes with a definitive handing-over of authority: the Apostles are sent out to the entire world. The whole notion of "Church", in radical contrast to the Synagogue, is centrifugal; not only is the Church open to the world, which in principle already belongs to Christ: she is also jointly responsible for it. It is not enough to preach the message of salvation to the world from outside: this message must permeate it like leaven, becoming disseminated throughout it. What we are speaking of is—in the modern expression —"inculturation". The cultural materials that exist in the world

---

[9] Cf. Origen's extensive application of the Old Testament "harlot" passages to the Church: *Hom. 6–10 in Ez.* (Baehr. VIII, 378–423).

must be taken up and adapted, albeit critically. Again, this must not be done by the forced imposition of Christianity onto a reluctant substratum; conquests of this sort continue to take their revenge centuries later. Rather, there must be a loving appreciation of the existing values; it must calmly be shown that they are genuinely fulfilled only in the message of Christ.

However, this is difficult, from both sides. It is difficult on the part of the culture that is to be transformed: particularly in its most highly developed form, its *Gestalt* exhibits an earthly perfection, like a work of art; in its own order, it seems incapable of improvement. The Christian reality, however, lives entirely in relationships of continual transcendence and in principle (not accidentally) breaks open the complacent, earthly forms, putting them in touch with a Catholic universality: thus they must open up to the world around them but also to the world above them. It is even more difficult on the part of the Church; the gospel message is embedded in the structures of the "missionized" culture, a fact that threatens to bring the movement of the missionary Church to a full stop. Inculturation threatens to adapt Christianity to the existing culture; the salt of the gospel is in danger of losing its savor. Amalgams are formed between Christianity and secular culture; at times this produces marvelous cathedrals of art, of philosophy and of piety, yet it is not clear whether these are a pure expression of the gospel.

The Church can only effectively pursue her task, therefore, if she herself alternates between two impossible poles: preaching to the world purely from without and transforming it purely from within. As Church, she must *penetrate* without becoming "establishment" and *advance* without leaving unfinished business behind. Paul represents a kind of ideal: he founds communities, moves on, then returns to his foundations, but without finally settling down there. The profile he presents should be that of every community and of each individual: the Church must put down roots where she is, yet without coming under the spell of the place. Here again we find that this paradox, which is baffling at an earthly level, reflects the discipleship of Christ, who comes into the world and leaves it (Jn 16:28) and yet stays with it until the end (Mt 28:20); for it is in his *exodos* (Lk 9:31)—which is his Eucharist—that he is killed and so remains with us.

So the Church's paradoxical task, simultaneously to penetrate the world and to avoid being held fast by it, is ultimately made possible in the christological context: she is continually being persecuted, she and her message are always being questioned or tested for consistency (sometimes unto death), which triggers a new evangelizing initiative either in the particular place or elsewhere. In such initiatives, the Church has continually to reflect anew on her fundamental values and compare them with the results of her endeavors in the field of inculturation: How far does what has been achieved constitute a harvest that can be brought into the "everlasting barns", that is, how far is it an order of creation and history that is genuinely permeated and transformed by Christianity? Or does it perhaps show that the Church has succumbed to secularism—albeit the subtlest, apparently most religious secularism—and so has betrayed the mystery of Christ?

It is surely part of the saints' task to provoke such new initiatives and examinations of conscience. The message of the saints, publicly proclaimed, is always unsettling, and so, initially, it is mostly rejected or only listened to by a small group. As a rule, its major effect is posthumous. Augustine referred to the saints as the "dung of the Church", in connection with the psalm verse that speaks of the bodies of the saints remaining on the ground.[1] Paul takes up the Lord's words concerning the "last place", where he, like the other "pillars of the Church", has been put, less by the world than by the Church herself. The Corinthians, whose "inculturation" has led to Gnosticism, are "wise", "strong" and "held in honor", whereas the holy Apostles are "fools", "weak" and "held in disrepute" (1 Cor 4:10). "Already you are filled! Already you have become rich! Without us you have become kings!": an established Church, like Kierkegaard's Danish Church. This kind of diagnosis applies at all periods of the Church's history: we always find a flying column of saints who, from without and especially from within, inspire and enliven the vast, inert multitude of "good sinners", as Péguy calls them—as well as the less good. In the Church of Christ, there is always a majority that is dragged along by the minority, or whose faith, hope and love are vacillating. Augustine comments

---

[1] *En. in Ps.* 140, 21, 37 (PL 37, 1829–30).

on the psalm verse, "We received your mercy, Lord, in the midst of your people" (47:10): Why not, "among your people"; why "in the midst of your people"? "Are those who receive different from those in whose midst they receive?" For many who receive the sacraments and have the appearance of piety are reckoned as belonging to the People of God. So Augustine says, "in the midst of your people, which refuses to accept your mercy, we received your mercy. For he came to his own, and it was his own people who did not accept him."[2] Augustine believes that the Church will remain mixed until the end of time; even if he does not adopt the teaching of the Donatist, Ticonius, who said that the Church is *bipartita*, partly Jerusalem, partly Babylon, he recognizes that there are members of the Church outside her and enemies of the Church within her.

It will never be possible to assess the relationship between genuine members and "passengers", nor can we deduce socio-logical laws for the Church's progressive, inner disintegration on the basis of aging or foreign influence; the Holy Spirit, who animates the Church, can inspire her to initiatives that are com-pletely new and cannot be foreseen. According to the laws of sociology, she should have suffered her demise long ago: "as dying, and behold, we live" (2 Cor 6:9). The Church will not succumb to desolation and ossification, though the process may seem inevitable; not even the sects' progressive hollowing-out of the *Catholica* by expropriating and exporting her goods can do this, nor, we may add, can Christianity's constant outpouring of light into the world, where it is renamed and regarded as hu-manism. Why? Because the wellsprings of the Spirit can at any time burst forth from her innermost heart. Nor is it the "insti-tution" that, appearing to be a mere fleshless skeleton, hinders the Pneuma from blowing and working[3]—although this does not give Christians the right to rely on pure institution. Again, Paul's example shows that office and existence are intended to be inseparable: whenever he is required to prove the legitimacy of his office, he always cites the credibility, the witness-quality of

[2] *En. in Ps.* 47, 8–9 (PL 37, 538–39).
[3] Cf. our volume entitled *Pneuma und Institution*, Skizzen zur Theologie IV (Einsiedeln: Johannes Verlag, 1974), and Medard Kehl, "Kirche als Institution" in *Frankf. theol. Studien* 22 (J. Knecht, 1976), 239–311.

his existence. Similarly, the archetypal call of Peter at the end of the Gospel of John is followed by the promise of martyrdom that is inseparable from it. Right from her exemplary beginnings, the Church is always being led into the fire by the Spirit. This may result in the burning of many branches that were already dry and withered (cf. Jn 15:6)—whether we can call them "martyrs" is another question—but living branches, too, are consumed in the fire, to be born again out of the flames.

From the point of view of the theology of history, the Church's outlines are hazy, in the twilight of the future. The ever-intensifying anti-Christian manifestations, as the end approaches, can achieve two things at once: the expected large-scale falling-away from the faith but also the deeper purification, through more severe testing, of the remaining "little flock". The "desert" to which the apocalyptic Woman is transferred for the remaining earth-time is also two things, as in the Old Testament: it is a place of impoverishment, distress and temptation but also a place of rejuvenation, of concentrated attention on God. So it is with Christ's time in the wilderness: he experiences want and is ministered to (invisibly) by angels; he is tempted and, in his earthly weakness, triumphs by the power of God. The desert isolates the Woman so that the Dragon's venom cannot reach her. And, in this isolation, in a way that is beyond our comprehension, she becomes fruitful; the text speaks of the Dragon in wrath making war on "the rest of her offspring" (Rev 12:13-17). In the world that has crucified the Logos, there is no room for his Church; she can only exist in the no-man's-land of the desert, where a "place" (*topos*) is prepared for her. Her children, however, have to go out to battle against the "prince of this world" and win back territory from him; their task is to implant the Spirit and truth of Christ in the world. From the world's point of view, the Woman remains u-topian and without form [*Gestalt*]; the "place" God has provided for her cannot be found on earth, just as her true face cannot be seen. But again and again something of her invisible form is discernible in her genuine children, who, in fighting with the Dragon, "keep the commandments of God and bear testimony to Jesus". However, the Church's outward form may disintegrate through the course of her history—and even the "saints" can be vanquished—the Woman is "nourished" in the desert, during the world's span of time, with a desert manna that comes from above. This not only keeps her alive, contrary to expectation, but actually renders her fruitful. It may happen that her children, bearing "testimony to Jesus", are decimated and practically annihilated; but the form [*Gestalt*], invisible to the world, remains intact, a permanent sign that Christ has conquered the world and imprinted the seal of his dominion upon it.

Once more, definitively, we find that the Christ-event is the basis of the paradoxical destiny of the Church and her children; it provides the dramatic context and resolution of this destiny.

D. SLAIN AND VICTORIOUS

1. The Two Adams

"He came to his own home, and his own people received him not. But to all who received him . . . , he gave power to become children of God" (Jn 1:11–12). Here we see the head-on clash of acceptance and nonacceptance. We cannot speak of a partial acceptance and a partial rejection: in the parable of the vineyard servants, the heir who comes to his own property is unanimously murdered. According to John, this "unanimous" action is characteristic of the "world". "The world" as a whole, not individuals within it, "knew him not". Yet in the same sentence we read, "and the world was made through him" (1:10). It is therefore the same "world" in each case. The beginning of the Prologue had already emphasized that the world, all of it without exception, was made by the Logos ("and without him was not anything made that was made": 1:3). Paul had already stressed the same point several times (1 Cor 8:6: "Jesus Christ, through whom are all things"; Col 1:16: "in him all things were created, in heaven and in earth"), even expanding the phrase "through him" by the words "and for him". Since "the world" transcends itself at both ends, that is, at its origin and its goal, it is all the more strange that, firmly embedded in this constitutive meaning (Logos) as it is, it fails to recognize the latter—and hence fails to know itself either. As the Letter to the Romans puts it, the world must and should recognize him and yet does not, thus becoming "inexcusable" (Rom 1:18–21). Failure to appreciate the world's objective transcendence at its origin and goal must betoken a profound subjective inability, as is envisaged by the teaching on the two Adams (1 Cor 15:45ff.): the first is "psychic", from the earth, he is "flesh and blood", "corruptible" and, as such, cannot "inherit the kingdom of God" (50), nor can he "put on immortality" by his own efforts.

We must not simply smooth out this paradox by citing the "supernatural *existentiale*", that is, that the "psychic" is always tending toward self-transcendence in the "pneumatic"—a process is guaranteed by its very structure. The starkness of the

paradox becomes quite tangible in the Old Testament and even
in the very midst of salvation history in the narrower sense:
the psychic man, aware that he will assuredly die—since every bond with God is broken (Ps 88:6-13), the dead are forgotten and have themselves forgotten God (Ps 6:5; Job 14:25;
Eccles 9:5-6)—nonetheless cries out to God with a hope that
flatly contradicts the certainty of his end. While in a number
of cases the individual may be merely pleading for a few years
more of "psychic" life, what is meant here is ultimately something else, something more significant: the writer senses that
the limitations of a "flesh and blood" that cannot inherit the
kingdom must be exploded—yet at the same time he is perfectly sure that these limitations must remain. Initially, imprisoned in death as he is, man's hope can only project itself "forward", into the temporal succession of generations: salvation,
the Messianic kingdom, comes when all the generations have
fallen in death. But surely this hope too comes up against a wall
that is just as unscalable as that presented by the corruptible life
of the individual? Is historical man's jump from his dreams to
their implementation in a utopian "yonder" (Bloch) any less
paradoxical than the plea of the sick or persecuted man in the
Old Testament? This would imply that mankind's situation in
the world is just as "hopeless" vis-à-vis its earthly future as the
individual is in the face of his death. "Only a fool can hope
for ultimate fulfillment in this world"[1]—and, as for penulti-
mate hopes, we are not concerned with them here. In other
words, even the Old Testament Messianic hope in the future
is self-contradictory unless it opens out to a victory over death
(both the death of the individual and the death of the world as a
whole), to a "resurrection from the dead". Such an opening-out
and opening-up, however, are no longer within the power of
the first, psychic Adam: he has stubbornly determined to find
his meaning within himself and develop it from his own potential and possibilities. (This potential is implanted in him, and,
since its development is necessary to him and gives his existence meaning—it is both a task and an achievement—he en-

---

[1] P. Tillich, "Das Recht auf Hoffnung" in *Ernst Bloch zu Ehren* (Frankfurt,
1965), 273.

trusts himself to its dynamic thrust, as if his goals could recapitulate and underpin their origin.) Accordingly, the world has
failed to recognize the Logos who created it and now enters on
its stage.

Nonetheless, the Logos rejected by the world has in fact fashioned it; the "psychic" Adam is created with a view to the Second, heavenly Adam, which means that when the Logos comes
into the world he is coming "to his own" It is his own insofar
as it comes from him and is going to him; but it is alien to him
insofar as it does not have the "pneumatic" as its first principle:
first comes the "psychic", and only then the "pneumatic". "The
first man was from the earth, a man of dust", and so "the second
man from heaven" has no place beside him (1 Cor 15:47). It
follows that the One who comes "to his own", and who from
the beginning possesses the world he has created—and hence
is its "Victor"—is also, from the very outset, "vanquished" by
it. Only on the basis of his Resurrection does he show that he
has "overcome the world" (Jn 16:33); only thus does it emerge
that he, the transcendent Omega, is also the transcendent Alpha,
the world's *raison d'être*; only thus does it become finally clear
that the world is not its own but owes itself ultimately to him.
Moreover it owes itself to him *just as it is*, that is, enclosed in its
finitude, with no way out: this is so that *he* can show himself to
be the way out, "the Way".

So the circle of relationships between the two Adams is both
tragic—the Cross is unavoidable—and anti-tragic (we cannot
use the word "comic" here), since he who is infallibly vanquished is also infallibly Victor. From the world's point of view,
the first Adam was there first and defends his domain against
"thieves" (it is remarkable how freely Jesus uses the word in
his parables, Matthew 6:19, 24:43 par., and is himself compared
to a thief: 1 Thessalonians 5:2, 4; 2 Peter 3:10; Revelation 3:3;
16:15), but all the same the first Adam is indebted to the Second,
who is not only his *goal* but also his *source* of meaning.

Whatever actual meaning there is in the created world (and
whatever potential meaning there is hidden in man's constitution) comes from that Wisdom that plans the world and is infused into it (Wis 7:22ff.), which is simultaneously that silent
word of God that is implanted in things (Ps 19:4) and the word

of Wisdom that speaks here and now in Jesus.[2] According to the Prologue of John's Gospel, however, the creating Word does not become flesh "out of the blue", as it were, but mediated by the Mosaic law and finally by the prophetic words of the Baptist, both of which spoke of and for the Word (Jn 5:33, 46). The Incarnation has its prehistory in creation through the Logos and proceeds to his Cross and Resurrection. The great proponent of this history is the anti-gnostic Irenaeus: he describes it as the Logos becoming accustomed to live with men and rest upon them,[3] in turn accustoming men to be bearers of God's Spirit.[4] We do not need to say that the entry of the Logos into his work began in Abraham:[5] it can be traced much farther back. We can see its signs scattered throughout human history, as the *logos spermatikos*. The final, concentrated and ever-intensifying preparation, however, takes place in Israel.

Becoming flesh, the Word experiences two things: he appropriates what is his, what came forth from him and is to be taken beyond itself, to "immortality"; and he also appropriates what is alien to him, what is finite, mortal and, moreover, self-enclosed and turned away from God. In this latter sense, the *sōma-sēma* is a prison. "O faithless and perverse generation, how long am I to be with you and bear with you?" (Lk 9:41). The world, too, will find him alien and intolerable and so will kill him. Within the realm of the first Adam (which yet belongs to him, the Second), victory is impossible; he cannot transform this realm as such into his own realm: "My kingdom is not of this world" (Jn 18:36). This remains true despite all the possibilities of sowing the seeds of the nonworldly in this world and seeing them sprout and blossom. It remains true despite our efforts to make

---

[2] Cf. Lk 7:35; 11:49; on the equation of Jesus with Wisdom, cf. Wilkens, art. "Sophia" in *ThW* 7, 514–26; A. Feuillet, "Le Christ Sagesse de Dieu dans les Epîtres pauliniennes", *Etudes bibliques*, (1966).

[3] *Adv. Haer.* III, 17, 1.

[4] *Ibid.* IV, 14, 2.

[5] However, it is unmistakably clear that the Logos becomes concrete in Israel's law: thus we find it putting an end to the "naïve entanglement in guilt" on the part of the Gentiles: "If it had not been for the law, I should not have known sin. I should not have known what it is to covet if the law had not said, 'You shall not covet'" (Rom 7:7). This is the direct antecedent of Jesus' words: "If I had not spoken to them, they would not have sin" (Jn 15:22).

what is worldly serviceable for the kingdom of the Logos, as it were, to transpose it from the sphere of the old Adam into that of the New. These things are possible because even the strictly worldly has the Logos as its origin and goal. But such transposition can only take place through a "dying with" the Logos and a "rising with" him. As an example, we can use the cardinal virtues that were taken over from Greek life and thought and translated into Christian terms. The model for this transposition is the Logos-made-flesh in his entire destiny—earthly life, death, supra-earthly Resurrection: that is, not only the isolated pattern he represents, lived out for us on earth, but also his rejection by the "spirit of the world" and his transfigured transformation in the Holy Spirit. Unless the Model passes through death and Resurrection, even his closest disciples will fail to understand what he is really saying. This is a crucial point to be borne in mind for our next section.

A further point arises in connection with the dialectic between the realms of the first and the Second Adam. The potential with which the Logos has endowed the world he has created is meant to be recognized and activated by man as his own, in a divinely willed and increasing autonomy. Insofar as this process also implies that the natural elements, once regarded as "divine", are now distinguished from the Creator-God's free use of them, we can speak of a growing secularization of the process of civilization. What was mistakenly regarded as divine now falls back upon the world and thus within the domain of human freedom. From a religious point of view, however, this growing autonomy is not unambivalent. For it can be understood and practiced as man's increasing insight into, and increasingly energetic execution of, what God himself intended by the world process; thus man's growing, free, creative self-definition is in growing harmony (in the *analogia libertatis*) with the free, divine will. Only if man, aware of his autonomy, detaches himself from the realm of all-embracing divine freedom and sets himself up against it does this secularization (or de-sacralization) become a Titanism that is forgetful of God. If we think of the Incarnation of the Logos as the perfecting of human selfhood (that is, not as the overpowering and commandeering of human nature and human free will by a numinous divine will), we are bound to acknowledge the unity of both in Jesus Christ, providing Christians with a model: on the one hand, he displays perfect, free responsibility for his own deeds and attitudes; and, on the other hand, he is completely oriented to the absolute, divine freedom, which, for Jesus, is represented by his Father's will, mediated by the Holy Spirit. The Spirit does not force the Father's will on him; he sets it before him, and then, as the Son's own Spirit, he operates within his human freedom so that the Son may be resolutely open to the absolute will of God.

The first Adam is not perfectible in himself; he must die to himself if he is to be lifted to the level of the Second and incorporated in him. That this is possible is something he owes to the Second Adam, his goal and his source. This explains Jesus' unique freedom vis-à-vis the world; he works in the world, not in order to perfect it, but to imprint upon it the signs (*sēmeia*) of that kingdom that transcends it. He does this with his human, sovereign freedom, which he also demands of his disciples ("Be not anxious . . ."); but this is a sign neither of flight from the world nor of superiority to matter nor of condescension— for he is in solidarity with all men. Rather, it betokens a docile sensitivity to the Father's will, whose coming kingdom is to be foreshadowed. It is in this same freedom, ultimately, that he is able to accept the fact that he is *persona non grata*, to accept being banished to the Cross and to accept this utter rejection of him, this self-enclosed rigidity on the part of the world, which is so closely connected with his having to die. He accepts all this freely and obediently in order to refashion the ending of the old Adam into his genuine beginning in the New. This is the mystery of the pro nobis, the mystery of the Eucharist, in which his death on the Cross, which is laid upon him, is transformed from the outset into the "remedy of immortality".

2. Theodramatic Dimensions of Liberation

The man who is reborn in Christ is given a share in the analogy of Christ's freedom: freed for a responsibility, before God and the world, that is genuinely within his grasp, he possesses the Holy Spirit, who enables him to be a docile follower of absolute, divine freedom. In this exercise of this analogy, we see the perfecting of something that was present in germ in creaturely freedom: for, if Adam was created really free, he was not fettered in the way that is characteristic of man's fallen state. That is, he was not imprisoned with a freedom that can only circle round and round within the confines of the world, relating only to itself, its advantage and its achievements.[1] His gift of freedom came from the creative Logos and thus imparted a real possibility of transcending the internal world and heading for God. Now, however, since the Logos himself took on fallen Adam's "likeness of sinful flesh" (Rom 8:3), and thus "condemned sin in the flesh", the Christian is liberated to enjoy a freedom that far outstrips Adam's. He is freed from the chains of a freedom that circles around itself and endowed by the Son of God with the freedom of the sons of God (Jn 8:36; Gal 5:1). A paradox remains: though a "new creation", he has to watch and wait within the restrictions of the "old creation" until "hope" has dissolved in the vision of the "reality": "If Christ is in you, although your bodies are dead because of sin, your spirits are alive because of righteousness" (Rom 8:10). This paradox, which is irreducible, will govern everything that follows. "The body is dead because of sin": we live within a world that is fallen and that is therefore not merely biologically but theologically moribund, with its unbreakable finitude and with all the hard and equally unbreakable structures that sin—which starts up again with each new-born life—lays upon it. It is *in* this world that we live as those who have died in Christ; we are not *of* this world, but Christ bids us join him in it, to be heralds of the new reality, to live it and, indeed, imprint the new life upon the world.

So we are faced with a grave question: Given this essentially self-enclosed world, how far is it possible to sow in it the seeds of an openness that comes from God and goes to him? Can immortal seeds be sown in earth that is "dead", that is, subject to death in all its dimensions? If man knows and seeks a freedom that refers only to himself (whether individually or socially), is it possible to implant in him an entirely different, God-given free-

---

[1] Cf. on this issue, H. Schlier, "Zur Freiheit gerufen. Das paulinische Freiheitsverständnis" in *Das Ende der Zeit* (Herder, 1971), 216–33.

dom with God as its goal? It cannot be impossible; otherwise
Christ, rejected by the world but bodily risen from the dead,
would not have merely warned his followers against men (Mt
10:17) and predicted that they would be hated by the world (Jn
15:19): he would not have sent them out, either, to the whole
world to preach his message (Mt 10; 28:19), like sheep among
wolves (Mt 10:16). But in actual fact he did, since to him, the
New Adam, was given all power not only in heaven but also
on earth, on the old, recalcitrant earth (Mt 28:18). Things are
possible by the grace of Christ that are impossible by the world's
grace and favor. We have set forth the aspect of impossibility
in the chapters on the world's growing refusal and the abiding
necessity of blood-martyrdom. Should we not add something
on the aspect of possibility? Nor should such possibility be restricted to the private realm of example and interpersonal influence (for there have always been instances of radiant holiness,
there have always been striking conversions): surely it should
also address the public realm that is ruled by the laws of society,
of economics and of politics? Can there be such a thing as a
strictly internal, worldly fullness of meaning? Can there be an
influential "politics of the sheep", for example, via a "politics of
powerlessness"?

   Gaudium et spes, luctus et angor struggled with this paradox and
tried to put things as positively as it could (albeit by setting to
one side the apocalyptic law of the ever-growing No that opposes the ever-growing Yes). Appealing to man's common humanity, the Pastoral Constitution spoke much of what can be
"genuinely human" (1), "fully human" (11, 1), "supremely human" (11, 3), and "reasonable and human" (63, 3), if it takes the
standard for what is human from the God-man: "In reality, it is
only in the mystery of the Word-made-flesh that the mystery of
man truly becomes clear", for the first Adam was a "type" of the
Second, who, by revealing the mystery of God's love, declares
to man his nature and his calling (22, 1). This, at last, solves the
question of the meaning and truth of human existence (41, 1), a
question that the Constitution continually raises in new forms
and that every purely world-immanent answer fails to address
(4, 1; 10, 1; 33, 2; 36, 3, and so forth). Man can only exist if he
is able to attribute a meaning to his actions within the world,

even if this meaning does not ultimately satisfy him. Thus the question of meaning provides the real basis for dialogue between the Church and the world (40, 1).

Man is characterized as "the meeting point of many conflicting forces": he is aware of his "shortcomings" (and his limited achievements), and at the same time he is driven about by "unlimited longings". At a deeper level, he feels that he is a "sinner", obstructed in his freedom, finding himself doing things he wishes he did not do. Furthermore, all the "discords in social life" come from his own being. Ideologies, regrettably, as well as the oppressive weight of suffering distract men from seeing "the *dramatic nature* of this state of affairs", so that they either hope for "a genuine and total emancipation of mankind through human effort alone . . . and an earthly paradise where all the desires of their hearts will be fulfilled" or else, "having lost faith in life, extol the kind of foolhardiness that would empty life of all significance in itself and invest it with a meaning of their own devising" (10).[2] The issue is not one of finite goods. It concerns the Yes or No to the absolute good, with which freedom is always concerned (even where it fails to seek this good in God). Accordingly, human existence is described as a battlefield: "Man therefore is divided in himself. As a result, the whole life of men, both individual and social, shows itself to be a struggle, and a *dramatic one*, between good and evil, between light and darkness." The tragedy is that man "finds that he is unable of himself to overcome the assaults of evil" and so feels "bound by chains" (13, 1), despite the universal aspiration for freedom and justice that is stronger now than ever before (9).

Our age is primarily characterized by the successes of technology (5, 1–3; 6; 20, 1; 23, 1; 35, 1; 57, 3), which is founded on the "advance of science" (44, 2) and provides the conditions for "economic progress" (64f.). Does this also create favorable conditions for a "cultural progress" that "humanizes social life both in the family and in the whole civic community through the improvement of customs and institutions" (53)? At this point the Constitution begins to show those weaknesses that have been

[2] *Vatican Council II: The Conciliar and Post-Conciliar Documents*, ed. A. Flannery, O.P. (Dublin, 1975).

acknowledged in part (but only in part). It rightly notes the tendency to uniformity that characterizes the technologizing of the earth (54) and the problems associated with it, that is, the loss of tradition; the splintering of knowledge into individual disciplines; specialization and the loss of an overall education; the increased tension between mass culture and the genuine education of the few; the tension between a "humanism that is purely earthbound and even hostile to religion" and genuine transcendence (56; 61, 1). At the same time—and this is the unacknowledged problem area—an ideal convergence is assumed between this "one-world culture" (*universalis cultura*, 61, 3) and the catholicity of the Church's mission (58, 2). This assumption is highly abstract. For instance, it is said that the results of psychology and sociology in particular should be applied by Christians, but there is no mention of the fact that these anthropological sciences are not neutral but are stamped by the Christian or anti-Christian principles that inform them; the Council does not point out that their results, whether spurious or genuine, need to be examined with regard to the axioms upon which they rest, and may even need to be dismantled and rebuilt.

Of course it is right to encourage "dialogue" (25, 1) between those who build a purely worldly culture and the Christian proclamation of the kingdom of God in order to promote the search for meaning. It is essential for Christians to pay attention to the valid results of human research and achievement (44), to put their efforts into shared projects for the benefit of mankind (31, 3; 43, 2; *libenter cooperari*) and not to engage in "religious" evasions (43). But, on the other hand, there is too little awareness of the demonisms at work in the total technologizing of nature, society and the individual; there is too little appreciation of the problems encountered by Christians in cooperating with such "Titanist" projects. On the one hand, the arms race is branded and condemned (81), but what of the havoc wrought by the mass media? There is an insistence on the absolute obligation to diminish the gap between rich and poor, the yawning gulf between rich and poor nations is roundly criticized, (66; cf. 8), and there is great emphasis on the inalienable human rights of all (26); but, if ever all men reach a comfortable level of existence, will they be moved to regard their manufactured cultural goods "as flowing from God's hand", to be used and enjoyed "in a spirit of poverty and freedom" (37)?[3]

The Constitution is aware that the *individual*, with his inner contradiction, will have to keep up the "dour combat with the powers of evil, stretching . . . until the last day" (37). However, with its assumption of the aforementioned convergence between the world culture and the Church's catholic ideal, there is no reference to a corresponding combat at the *social* level, at the level of culture and politics, where the battle is bound to be even more severe, since, per se, the world-immanent social structures do not transcend this world. There is continual reference to Jesus Christ as the crown of Christian humanism, who has provided the fundamental principle of mankind's socialization in his commandment of love, and even more in his death "for all" (32, 3; 22, 3, 5); but, when it comes to the creation of solidarity among the family of nations, he seems to be a mere *deus ex machina* (26, 4; 30, 2; 32, 5). Through the influence of Christians, the earthly world is to become *materia regni coelestis* (38), and the energies of nature are to be rendered serviceable, so that, in "that future day", "mankind itself will become an offering accepted by God" (*ibid.*). True, the document asserts that "we must be careful to distinguish earthly progress clearly from the increase of the kingdom of Christ"; nonetheless, it speaks of the growth of the "body of a new human family", "foreshadowing in some way the age that is to come" (*aliqualem novi saeculi adumbrationem*) and extols worldly progress as "of vital concern to the kingdom of God, insofar as it can contribute to the better ordering of human society" (39). These simplistic affirmations surely gloss over the whole range of problems raised by the eschatological passages of Scripture.[4] Does not Paul give the ultimate verdict on the world's destiny, and all man's achievements in it, when he says that all man's work must go through the fire

---

[3] There is another contradiction: on the one hand, it is emphasized that Christ took the part of the poor and that he himself must be found in them (81, 1); poverty in the spirit of the Beatitudes is extolled (72, 1). On the other hand, it is said that poverty restricts freedom (31, 2) and should thus be combated (cf. *Decree on Ecumenism*, 12).

[4] On K. Rahner's objections to a preliminary draft of the final text, cf. J. Ratzinger's commentary in the Herder edition, part 3 (1968), 395, col. 1.

of judgment, which will test how much of it was built on the foundation of Jesus Christ and how much was not (1 Cor 3:11–15)? All that mankind will have amassed will hardly merit being called an "offering" acceptable to God; at most, as Teilhard de Chardin agreed with Maurice Blondel, it will go to make a pyre, ready to receive the transforming fire of God.[5]

From this vantage point, we can take a look at so-called *liberation theology* and appreciate its urgency and its complex nature. Its greatest danger lies in its tendency to link together the relationships of the first and the Second Adam, earthly action and the kingdom that comes down from God, within a single system or overview; in so doing, it succumbs in a new way to theological rationalism. Nor does its appeal to "the primacy of praxis" do anything to change the situation. But, since this appeal to Christians, this summoning of their crucial, world-transforming cooperation, is at the heart of Christianity, it reveals the dramatic situation of the Christian in this world as perhaps nothing else does. We shall show this in four steps.

1. Ever since Genesis, man has been called to shape the earth after his own likeness, which is the likeness of God. The gospel does not remove this imperative but gives it a direction and a concrete reference: the words, the deeds, the work wrought by the Logos are to be proclaimed to all nations sharing in the building of the world. Paul does not regard himself as dispensed from work (nor does Jesus, the craftsman); he has "with toil and labor worked night and day" and "did not eat anyone's bread without paying" (2 Th 3:8). His example is normative: "If any one will not work, let him not eat" (3:10). What, however, if the organization of human toil uses the latter in order to increase a power that is exercised, not by the workers, but by those who reap its fruits? Work, as such, aims at gaining power over nature, and the will-to-power increases with each success; thus it is hardly possible to say where working for sheer survival turns into work-

---

[5] "J'accorde d'abord, sans difficulté, que l'Effort universel du Monde peut être compris comme *la préparation d'un holocauste*. . . . Tout notre travail, finalement, aboutit à former l'hostie sur qui doit descendre le Feu divin": Teilhard, December 21, 1919, in Henri de Lubac, *Blondel et Teilhard de Chardin, Correspondance commentée* (Paris: Beauchesne, 1965), 43.

ing for the sake of pure domination. It does not matter whether such domination aims at boundless affluence or the boundless stockpiling of arms (in order to achieve even greater power): in either case, the threshold has been crossed to a purpose that is immoral because it is inhuman. The inhuman aspect is immediately seen in the exploitation of the workers, who are regarded and treated as mere means to power. Clearly, the Christian must throw himself into the cogs of this pitiless machinery and, as the Pastoral Constitution tirelessly insists, urge the human proportions (which he has discerned in Jesus Christ) against the twofold disproportions of excessive power (in affluence and imperialism) and powerlessness (in poverty). Whether he has any chance of at least restraining the demonic forces inherent in the twofold disproportions, or whether the power-spiral will keep turning relentlessly and crush him, is another question. He must try, having equipped himself with adequate knowledge and skill, to appeal to the human dimension that is alive in all men who are not entirely corrupt and spiritually dead. Any success will always be precarious in earthly terms, however: power, in the hands of essentially covetous men, remains ambivalent. The best that can be achieved is a temporary balance, not between intolerable misery and senseless luxury or a Titanic will-to-power, but between a bearable poverty and a comfortable existence that is concerned about the world in its wholeness. This Christian attempt to help every human being to live in a way that accords with universal human rights and the dignity of the person will become more and more questionable the nearer it gets to its goal. This is because the cultural goods that are now available to be foisted on the poor (and for which they themselves are striving) originate in that very realm of technology that is characterized by an insatiability and a mass culture (or nonculture!) that are destructive of the person. These destructive features are passed on by the rich countries to the poor all the more easily since the latter have hardly experienced an age of any kind of "personal" culture.

This means that Christian liberation in the name of the freedom of Christ *also* has to rely on the (inadequate) means of the old aeon and must resign itself to failure, however much earthly effort it puts into the task. Claudel's oft-repeated axiom applies here once more: Christians are required, not to achieve victory, but to resist and to stand fast. In earthly terms, their Master is a Victor who was vanquished.

2. What kind of victory was Christ's? Ultimately, surely, in the Passion he *no longer* resisted the superior power of evil but allowed it to rage in him, the defenseless One, and so burn itself out. Is the nonresistance put forward by Christ in the Sermon on the Mount meant to apply only to the private and interpersonal sphere and not also to the social and political arena? "Christ provided the spirit and the motivation, Gandhi the method"— Martin Luther King once said. Today's tactics of nonviolence,[6] employed in many different ways and for many different purposes, and before which unjust violence must finally capitulate, can constitute a stirring appeal to the human dimension in the heart of every man; ultimately the Christian element will rarely be lacking (even in the case of Gandhi) in such appeals. Two questions arise, however. Can a state realistically do without organs of power if it is to uphold public order against criminals of all kinds? How can such organs of power (police, army) be prevented from misuse at the hands of those who wield power? The other question is a deeper one: Can the Cross of Christ be changed into a "tactical" instrument in issues that are purely this-worldly? Can the *agapē* that suffers and endures all things (1 Cor 13:7) provide a technique for the attainment of political goals? Is this not the attempt to take "divine virtue"—that is, something that is and remains God's own possession—and manipulate it on the human stage? Put like this, it is clear that we have already crossed a boundary, however hard it is to define. The Christian can try to exercise influence in the spirit of the Sermon on the Mount, and also to reach the masses, and probably he will not be too anxious if occasionally, in this spirit, he finds himself across the frontier into political tactics. At the frontier, however, he will have to reflect on the realities of earthly power relationships. As far as he himself is concerned, he can choose the path of martyrdom for Christ's righteousness, but it is

---

[6] A wealth of portrayals in *Politik ohne Gewalt? Beispiele von Gandhi bis Câmara*, ed. Hans Jürgen Schulte, Suhrkamp Taschenbuch 330 (1976).

questionable whether he can legitimately impose this choice on a large multitude for the sake of political goals, or even human goals. This "politics of the Cross" may become a mere partial ingredient in overall political calculations as to the practicality of earthly justice. It is significant that, the more Gandhi proceeded along his path, the more isolated his role became.

3. Must violence after all be opposed by violence? The strategy of the Cross was a strategy in death, at the border-crossing into the kingdom beyond. As a strategy, it cannot be applied in its totality—or as the only one—in the midst of earthly power struggles. On the other hand, we have no example from the life of Jesus in which he fought for his cause with earthly means of power. (Not even the cleansing of the Temple.) And it is quite irrelevant to attempt to revive the Old Testament theology of Yahweh's "holy" wars; at most they can be regarded as *typoi*, anticipations (1 Cor 10:6); Christians cannot claim them as their own à la Islam. Quite simply, however, there is the order of the old aeon with its severe laws (including the state, which wields the sword in the name of a higher justice: Rom 13), and Christians still live within this old order, which, self-enclosed and inchoate as it is, cannot and must not be "theologized". The Christian politician and sociologist must have a realism that comes from a sober assessment of earthly power relationships. They are not simply justified by theology ("He who takes the sword will perish by the sword", Mt 26:52), but, in need, man may have recourse to them in self-defense. Even in the parables of Jesus, we find cool-headed calculation as to what can be achieved by earthly power and what cannot (Lk 14:31). There is the remarkable parable (Lk 16:1–9) in which the steward of "unrighteous mammon" is praised, not because of his fraudulent actions, but because of his purely human shrewdness. The "mammon of unrighteousness" is a Hebraism that refers to all riches, even those legitimately acquired, insofar as some injustice always clings to them (Sir 27:2).[7] But it is possible to be "faithful", we read, in using this "mammon of unrighteousness": accordingly, it is this kind of "faithfulness" that can be

[7] J. Ernst, *Lukas* (Pustet, 1977), 465.

entrusted with "the true riches" (Lk 16:11). Jesus' contact with tax collectors shows that he was well aware of this frontier area. Mammon, "the deceitfulness of riches" (Mk 4:19 AV), is a form of those purely worldly goods that cannot enter the kingdom of God; the use of force is another such form that, as the *ultima ratio* —in the individual and the social sphere—belongs to existence in the prison of finitude. Moreover, the boundaries of the use of force are not easily identifiable: they can begin long before blood is openly shed; and is it not a fact that many of the tactics of nonviolence are (paradoxically) a manifestation of power, a way of using unusual means to compel someone who is outwardly stronger to do what he does not want to do?

4. We have a strict Christian duty to fight for social justice on behalf of the poor and oppressed. It is a spiritual and corporal "work of mercy", a work according to which the Christian, and indeed everyone, will be judged. But since neither the goals nor the means are clear-cut—prompting us to ask at what point the assistance offered, the degree of well-being aimed at, starts becoming dangerous for the recipient—such fighting can only be one element within a more all-embracing struggle, namely, the battle of the Logos. What Luke refers to as "true riches" (16:11) is more than political and economic freedom, for this, within the tangled context of world politics (and, even more, of world economics) can only be an entirely relative freedom. "Real freedom" is granted by God through the gift of his Holy Spirit, and even someone poor and oppressed can share in it and consciously live it, no less than the prisoner of the concentration camp and the Gulag. A man such as Maximilian Kolbe manifested this freedom in the highest degree. Only if we grasp the difference between Christian freedom and ordinary, civil freedom can we understand Paul's apparent indifference to the institution of slavery; he shows how "freedom in Christ transcends all human freedom and lack of freedom". This freedom in Christ does not depend on "whether or not men allow me to be free. . . . In Jesus Christ there is neither slave nor freeman" (Gal 3:28; Col 3:11).[8] The testimony (*martyrion*) given by Christians in the face

[8] H. Schlier (see note 1 above), 228.

of superior worldly power is an *ultima ratio* quite different from, and higher than, the one we have just discussed, even if there can be a fluid transition between nonviolence (and even the use of violence itself, understood as society's necessary self-defense) and this testimony in one's own flesh and blood. The active deed by which, in Christian freedom, a person concludes his earthly existence forms the transition from the closed sphere of the first Adam to the open sphere of the Second. And, since the Book of Revelation portrays only the extreme opposites in the battle of the Logos, it depicts all testimony to Jesus in the world in this frontier situation.

Here, however, we must remember that, in the history of the Church, the period of the martyrs was followed by that of the monks. Their lives were a testimony of total dedication and, as such, equivalent to martyrdom. The Pastoral Constitution does not miss the opportunity of mentioning this vocation besides that of directly promoting earthly liberation (38). Monastic theology, beginning with Origen, most strongly emphasized that this life has the nature of a battle and also drew out the social contribution it makes to the whole battle of the Logos: so long as Moses on the mountain lifts his hands to God, the children of Israel on the plain are able to triumph in their battle (Ex 17:8ff.).[9] On the other hand, this uppermost zone of liberation theology demonstrates that all the intermediate zones, in spite of their urgency, must be seen to be relative, at least where they have political and economic liberation in the foreground. Other liberation movements merit theological credentials only if they are carried on within the horizon of that ultimate liberation won by Christ and for him.

3. A Duel between Two Deaths

1. "The last enemy to be destroyed is death" (1 Cor 15:26). It is the last because death itself is the universal, radical annihilator. But how can an annihilator be annihilated unless by itself? A profound abyss is opened up by this idea, and only there,

---

[9] W. Völker, *Das Vollkommenheitsideal des Origenes* (Tübingen: Mohr, 1931), 175ff.

in its deep darkness, can the final dramatic (and theodramatic) dénouement take place. In following the "battle of the Logos", our gaze has shifted from Jesus, who gathers by separating and whose gathering provokes an increasing separation. Initially, it turned toward the dramatic shape of his work, the Church. Then it addressed that strange twilight zone between the two aeons, in that never-ending campaign to bring the freedom of the kingdom of God into the kingdom of this world—a campaign that seemed to lead nowhere. Is this all the Christian can point to in the end—Jesus' work in decay, his program incapable of full implementation? Does his message not have a crippling effect at the crucial moment when ultimate courage is required of the warrior? Are Camus' *Les Justes* not right to push Christianity aside as something ineffectual, while they resolve to do the absolute deed and "die impersonally for justice in the world"?[1] In conclusion, therefore, we must turn away from the Church's protagonists and their doings and look once more at the "Forerunner" (*prodromos*, Heb 6:20), who, in single combat, will decide the outcome of the entire battle.

In the *Prolegomena* (*Theo-Drama* I, 369–408), we examined the astonishing many-sidedness of death in some detail. Many aspects—all equally valid—circled around its mystery, and, although they often interpenetrated and intersected, they could not be made to coincide. The same thing showed itself, even more tantalizingly, in our examination of death within the horizon of the drama of human action (this volume, 117–35): we found it impossible to get beyond the contradiction between the certainty of death and the vague hope of survival. This was no less true of the Old Testament, where the line of death is more pitilessly drawn than in those cultures that veil death's radicalism with postulates and dreams of immortality and where the believer who hopes in the covenant God is faced with the certainty of losing everything in death.

It has been said that we do not know how Jesus understood his own death. And if we accept Paul's statement that Jesus, by dying, conquered death and drew its sting, it follows that we also cannot be sure of knowing that. For, in that case, he must

---

[1] Analysis in *Theo-Drama* I, 382–83.

have succeeded in reconciling all death's contradictory masks and faces into a single countenance, even getting beyond the Old Testament contradiction. This in turn must have resulted in an invisibility and intangibility that affected him, the Actor, just as much as us, the spectators, at least in the scene of the decisive confrontation. In order to approach the meaning of this concluding scene, we shall view the various dramatic aspects of death (as set forth in the *Prolegomena*) together with the soteriology we have presented in this volume. Gradually we shall see emerging the fundamental concept that proved to be the center of Christology as developed in the third volume of *Theo-Drama*, a concept that sustains and explains everything.

We distinguished seven aspects of death, illustrating them with examples from drama: death as destiny; death as the interpreter of life; death immanent in all human existence; death as the decisive act of life; death as atonement; death as the expression of love; death on behalf of another. These interrelated aspects can be reduced to three main ones: (1) Death as destiny. Death is what is always threatening us from outside, both uncertain and absolutely certain; men act this out in "dances of death" (Ionesco), and at the same time they anxiously try to conceal it from them. (2) Death, immanent in every moment of life, becomes per se the *interpreter* of life, of the significance or nonsignificance, the meaning or meaninglessness of the whole of a lived life and all its parts. Here it remains uncertain whether death, the annihilator (and hence the only real element), plunges everything into its nonmeaning, or whether, in the face of death's annihilating activity, finite situations stand out in a kind of tragic finitude [final validity: *End-Gültigkeit*]. (3) Death is a final *deed*, with many facets, but it is always a self-suspension, a deed that is so all-embracing that it can only be performed by the investment of one's whole existence. It is related to, or identical with, absolute love, which ultimately calls for the suspension of the isolated self; it can consist in atonement (required by others or undertaken by oneself) for some transgression that cannot otherwise be expunged; finally, it can be representative, where one person dies on behalf of someone else or even takes over the latter's terrible manner of death.

The three aspects are both exclusive and inclusive. If death is a fate that threatens from outside, it cannot be a deed; and, if it threatens life and questions it, it cannot be its interpreter. But, insofar as man knows that he will assuredly die, and has his death always before him consciously or unconsciously, he is bound to evaluate all he experiences and does against the background of this ever-present threat; it will enable him to attach greater or lesser value to things and the possibilities they suggest. It is true that death is mostly something undergone, and so it cannot explicitly be a *deed*. Nonetheless, there is always something of the deed in it: death, as a fact, draws out the consequences of the way a man has seen and appreciated it as something that is both *within* him, as an *existentiale*, immanent in his life, and *ahead of* him, as an ineluctable destiny. Thus we see that, while the innumerable facets of death present in empirical reality are mutually irreducible, there is a kind of osmosis between them in virtue of the omnipresence of the one death.

Whether death can be seen as the interpreter of a life that has come to its end or as the deed par excellence of the living person in the act of self-surrender, it remains the fate of all men. This is even true of the suicide who freely chooses it as the lesser of two evils. In committing suicide, a man embraces death, not because it destroys him, but *in spite of* the fact that it destroys him. In Dostoyevsky's *The Devils*, Kirilov's suicide, the deed that is supposed to prove that man is equal to God, equates the absolute of his chosen fate with the absoluteness of the divine being —a meaningless equation that illustrates Dostoyevsky's *apologia* for God. Where someone sacrifices himself for another (*Alcestis*, Faulkner's *Requiem for a Nun*), for the city (*Die Bürger von Calais*), for the country (*Iphigeneia*), fate strikes him now, but sooner or later it will strike those who have been thus spared. Whether death is passively endured or actively embraced, whether it is feared or longed for, it remains man's destiny, the axe that one day, without fail, will descend on all finite human life—life that was once not even there at all.

There is something of the "execution" about death as such. It reveals an inner connection with the guilt associated with existence, a conscious guilt mostly felt by the individual but one that also includes all those for whom the connection is not evident (for example, children). Somehow or other, death always seems to be *merited*; people are fond of attributing an atoning value to it: the punishment of death, or even a death taken upon oneself, seems to balance out the guilt a man has acquired. "A freely chosen death alone can break the chains of destiny."[2] Such a view is only possible, however, in the context either of purely societal considerations (the state can do no more than kill the criminal for the common good) or of a religious world view that posits a connection between guilt and destiny (as in Greek tragedy and its successors). Does this connection still hold, however, if the One before whom man is primarily guilty is neither society nor sovereign destiny but the living God before whose judgment seat he must appear? Whether death, as fate, is suffered by a man or deliberately performed by him (by way of atonement?), he cannot manipulate its meaning. He can accept it as a merited punishment, but he cannot know whether or not it cancels out his guilt.

We repeat: as long as death is fate, the sword of Damocles hanging over every moment of life, sure to fall one day, its status as an interpreter of life and as a deliberate act remains questionable.

It is a questionable interpreter: in the face of a heaven that is veiled, it may impart a certain impressive pathos to the uniqueness of a rounded human character (as in Greek drama), but how rarely this happens, and how often destiny's thread is cut off before the fabric is complete—or else the whole fabric remains confused. And in both cases, where a figure doomed to ruin is forced into immortality or where such an attempt fails, the question arises: Are we justified, on the basis of the fragments of meaning discovered in our finitude, in concluding that there is an eternal fulfillment of meaning on the yonder side of destiny? Passionate religious and philosophical efforts have been made again and again to demonstrate this. But in most cases, surely, this involved a shift of meaning from the earthly and unique toward the longed-for eternity or recurrence (reincarnation). This is even so in the case of Plato, despite his attachment to the world: the kaleidoscope of life, even political life with its important consequences, is ultimately a puppet play. Compared

[2] Schiller, *Die Braut von Messina* IV, 9.

with this shift of emphasis, the momentous deeds we find in
Homer (against the background of the shadowy Hades), and,
even more, in Israel's momentous dealings with its God (against
the background of oblivion in Sheol), are of quite a different
caliber and weight. God, who puts so much importance on the
life (Ps 72:14) and death (Ps 116:15) of his faithful, could demand an utterly absolute relationship with man within his finite existence, without any prospect of a future life. For these
faithful souls, privileged to bask in Yahweh's favor, the latter
was so overwhelmingly significant that any question of an af-
terlife was simply superfluous. Complaints about the inevitable
fate of death, heralded in various ways even in life, simply did
not occur. Does this not put a question mark, again, over all the
intimations and postulates (up to and including the reflections
of G. Marcel) that seek to "eternalize" whatever has been begun
in this life?

Next we come to death as a deliberate act. Here man actively
lays hold of the fate [*Verhängnis*] that hangs over him; death,
accordingly, can be interpreted as the taking-down [*Ab-Hängen*]
of what was hanging above him [*das Verhängte*], as the reconciliation of the ultimate conflict in Being (Hölderlin gives it its
highest expression in his *Empedokles*). Or he can break the power
of his own fate by suffering it in advance, in life (this is most
beautifully set forth in Kleist's *Prinz von Homburg*). Or, included
in the equation in advance, he can take upon himself the expiation for some monstrous deed for the sake of universal justice
(as in Camus' *Les Justes*). The question is always whether this
anticipation of death, this advance undergoing of it, can really
rob it of its fate-character. Empedocles may throw himself into
Etna, but does not the redemption of the world remain pure
phantasmagoria?

2. Death, therefore, must be stripped of its fate-character, or the
latter must be so changed that its sting is drawn. (For its sting
always remained, even when it was transformed into the interpreter of life, or life's ultimate deed.) A qualitatively different and
more profound kind of fate must be found in order to overcome
the deadliness of death from within.

Thus, without noticing it, we have come close to the theology of Anselm. He too was looking for a death that was unmerited, undergone by someone entirely guiltless and that, as such, was not subject to fate. In addition, this death was to be accepted freely (*sponte*) by the most precious person imaginable, thus outweighing all the fate-bound deaths incurred through guilt. Anselm's approach was correct, but he did not take it far enough; he compared only the external value of the two kinds of death, not their inner quality. We must remember this: if Jesus' atoning death is to be really representative ("for us"), he must share the experience we have of fate; he must comprehend and embrace it. Death as fate must be overcome from within, by something more deadly than itself. Death as fate, in all its dimensions and aspects, must be surpassed by a greater degree of deadliness; thus death, profoundly and mortally wounded, can be "swallowed" up in the more all-embracing reality. Insofar as death is overcome in this struggle, we can speak of a duel between life and death (*mors et vita duello conflixere mirando*), but equally, and at a deeper level, it is a duel between death and itself, a duel between two forms of death. The more intensive, more radical form vanquishes the other and then takes it over. This differs from and complements the Anselmian version.

Jesus must therefore submit to the fate of death. He does not reach out for death in advance by his own action; he awaits it, not knowing when his "hour" will strike. At this point, he differs essentially from that most uncanny imitation of him we find in Camus' *Les Justes*, where the "just" seize death for the sake of world justice: "We pay more than we owe. That means dying twice." With great perceptiveness, however, one of them realizes that this deed, so close to Jesus' own death, is actually, as a *deed*, the opposite of it: "We have taken the world's misfortune on ourselves. That's what he did. What courage! But it often seems to me to be a kind of pride, which has to be punished. . . . We pay for this pride with our lives."[3]

Jesus' death, whereby he took upon himself the misfortune, the guilt of the world, was not the result of Titanist pride; it was no Atlas-like feat. We see this in the way he left the "hour" to

---

[3] *Theo-Drama* I, 383.

the Father. In any case, he does not load the world's guilt upon himself (as *Les Justes* do) but allows the "hour", in due course, to load it upon him. His approach is not heroic: he does not match himself against this guilt and resolve to shoulder it; he experiences it as something unbearable that can only be borne *in obedience* to the Father's will.

This is the crucial word. Anselm had already identified obedience as the higher unity of free will (*sponte*) and docility (above, pp. 255–61). If this obedience is to be different from that of any dying man who accepts his inevitable fate, it must be the fundamental mode of Jesus' entire life. Above all, it must govern his Incarnation (his *becoming* man), in which he is "thrown toward death", and so distinguish him from all other human beings who are thus "thrown". He must become man in free obedience if *his* death is to overcome death. At this precise point, moreover, his death becomes the legitimate interpreter of his whole existence. Not as if (as in Anselm) this life spent in obedience to his mission were insignificant by comparison with the unmerited death that alone counts. No: every moment counts, every expression of active life, hidden and public, since it all goes to make up that unique, peerless Person who, inseparable from death and Resurrection, is the revelation of God's glory in the world. Even in Paul, who reads the figure of Christ from its center in the Cross-Easter, the life of obedience is always presupposed (Phil 2:7); John reads it from the very beginning as the "manifestation of glory" (2:11), "accomplished" in the exaltation of the Cross (19:30). The Synoptics mark the steps of Jesus' life as he moves toward the Cross, emphasizing how much his death was the key to his life. This is not only true for the disciples, for whom the true figure of Jesus cannot be separated from this death that interprets everything; it is true for Jesus himself. On the one hand, the coming "hour" and "baptism" were always present to his mind; on the other hand, he could only utter and perform his astonishing words and deeds if they were backed up, "covered" in advance, by his dying, his "glorious testimony" (1 Tim 6:13). Never was a death so much the interpreter of a life as here, where obedience to his mission was his life's inner form; it emerged unveiled in death, bringing to light every lived moment of life.

To that extent, this unique death was also uniquely immanent in his life. Not, we repeat, as if it had been changed into some independent act over and above the rule of obedience. But his death was omnipresent in his active life; it was its inner form. Indeed, at the last frontier—in ultimate obedience—it became possible for him to *do* something with this death of his, by eucharistically sharing out his flesh and blood. However, it was only possible for him to use his own death in this way after God and men had already decided upon it. Thus it has nothing in common with suicide—a suspicion voiced by the Jews (Jn 8:22).

3. Having said all this, however, we have not mentioned the central fact, which is that Jesus by his obedient death takes over the guilty death that is our fate. This, and this alone, can undermine death from within and draw its sting. We have already indicated the essential points in the chapters on "Cross and Trinity" (above, 319–32) and "Representation" (above, 332–38). The forsakenness that prevails between the Father and his crucified Son is deeper and more deadly than any forsakenness, temporal or eternal, actual or possible, that separates a creature from God. Every sin committed in the world is borne and atoned for on the Cross, including that sin that by its very nature "brings forth" the "second death" (Rev 21:8; James 1:15); it follows that the Cross must be erected at the end of hell, without being equated with the latter. For the Cross is the pure obedience that remains intact even when God withdraws himself. In every death, we can see an entire world collapsing in ruin, for it signals the demise not only of a man's own world and context but of the entire horizon of being that gave him meaning and being in the first place.[4] The divine, to be sure, is an implicit part of that horizon for every man, and, if he is a believer, this means the living God—yet only as the goal of his faith. For the Son of God, by contrast, this horizon is the Father by and from whom he lives in the Holy Spirit at every moment and from whom, in eternal love, he receives his mission. We have already shown

[4] Georg Scherer, *Das Problem des Todes in der Philosophie* (Darmstadt: Wiss. Buchgesellschaft, 1979); also his "Leben, Tod und Todestranszendenz" in *Internat. Kath. Zeitschrift Communio* 9 (1980), 193–208.

(*Theo-Drama* III, 191–202) in what sense this receptivity can be understood as his "beholding" of the Father and how variable such beholding may be. On the Cross, the constant relationship between them has assumed the modality of "forsakenness" by the Father and hence of irremediable "lostness" on the part of the Son; as a result, the Son experiences the loss of a horizon of meaning and being such as no ordinary creature can either possess or lose.

The Son dies through being estranged from the Father, "made to be sin" (2 Cor 5:21). This can only be a once-for-all act, an act that embraces and undergirds everything, in which sin is once and for all drowned in the abyss of absolute obedience. As Paul puts it, "The death he died he died to sin, once for all;" so "death no longer has dominion over him" (Rom 6:9f.). And here we must not forget that, in thus "dying to sin", the Son underwent death *in and through* each individual sin that makes up the total-ity of the world's evil, insofar as the holy God cursed (and so banished) in him everything hostile to the Divinity. Of course we can say that the Son dies "because of sin", but at a deeper level he dies "because of God", because God has definitively rejected what cannot be reconciled with the divine nature.[5]

The Son "humbled ("diminished") himself and became obe-dient unto death", not an ordinary death, but "death on a cross" (Phil 2:8), which undergirds the former and drags it down into its own abyss. In this sense, "death will be swallowed up for ever" (Is 25:8 Symm) or, as Paul says, following Aquila: "Death is swallowed up in victory" (1 Cor 15:54). The "sting of death", that is, its chastising spur, its inescapable fate-aspect, is "sin": and sin too is swallowed up "for ever" and "in victory". And if "the

---

[5] In this paragraph, and not for the first time, von Balthasar, like Paul in similar circumstances, is having to coin new words and expressions to express aspects of the mystery of the Son's atoning work. First, he refers to the Son's *Weg-Sterben*, "dying away" from the Father, like a flower cut off from the plant. Next he makes the verb "to die", *sterben*, transitive and speaks of sin being "died", *hinuntergestor-ben*: this is not possible in English, hence our rather tame "drowned". More im-portant is his coining of the verb *durchsterben*, again in a transitive sense: if *durchlei-den* means to "deal with something by enduring the suffering associated with it", *durchsterben* suggests "dealing with something by enduring the death it entails". This may explain our paraphrase in the text. *Wegfluchen* is another coining: "to banish or annihilate by cursing"—TRANS.

power of sin is the law" (1 Cor 15:56), it is stripped of power by the power of absolute obedience. For the power of the Son's absolute obedience is love, which underpins and transcends all law.

Once faith has grasped this, it becomes clear why Jesus describes himself as "the resurrection and the life", drawing the sting from every death. And—which comes to the same thing —we can understand how, since One "has died for all", then "all have died", so that "those who live might live no longer for themselves but for him who for their sake died and was raised" (2 Cor 5:14f.).

4. In conclusion we can once again go through the seven facets of death in the human drama and show that all of them are marvelously enfolded in the unique, peerless death of Jesus.

Destiny was an aspect of his death in several regards. In the first place, he was predestined from birth, indeed, from *before* birth, so that some Fathers could say that the Son was born *in order to* die.[6] But even at the purely earthly level, the claim Jesus makes by his words and actions provokes and "entices" his death. From the very beginning of his public ministry (Mk 3:6), people are discussing how they may destroy him, and a first attempt is made (Lk 4:29). The net is drawn tighter and tighter around him, for example, in John's account of the disputes: "You seek to kill me" (Jn 8:40), until the catastrophic final act begins with treason from his own ranks. And this final act is not the idealistic victory of the hero who must perish (as in most tragedy; for instance, in *Maria Stuart*): here, fateful sin breaks out in the hero himself; he trembles in mortal anguish and, forsaken by God and men, dies after uttering a great cry. His inward destiny [*Verhängnis*], which had always hung over him [*verhängte*], dominates his outward destiny, which simply ministered to it.

Jesus' death was the *interpreter* of his life. The whole nature of the gospel shows this. Never was a life interpreted so much from the vantage point of its end, in the all-illuminating light of the subject's death—a death that yet contains the Resurrection.

---

[6] Cf. above, 247f.

His unique death, of universal significance, imparts a universal significance to every detail of his life. He himself knows that every episode will echo endlessly through history: "Truly, I say to you, wherever this gospel is preached in the whole world, what she has done will be told in memory of her" (Mt 26:13). He can hear in his own words an exhortation that transcends every death: "Heaven and earth will pass away, but my words will not pass away" (Mt 24:35). Not in the sense of timeless, sublime words of wisdom, for these are the words of One who is profoundly aware of the finitude of his allotted time span: "I cast out demons and perform cures today and tomorrow, and the third day I finish my course" (Lk 13:32). What is this "finishing" of the "course"? It is shown by the next sentence: "Nevertheless I must go on my way today and tomorrow and the day following; for it cannot be that a prophet should perish away from Jerusalem" (Lk 13:33). "The light is with you for a little longer. Walk while you have the light, lest the darkness overtake you" (Jn 12:35). Jesus' light is "*the* light of the world" within a milieu that is limited by death and so calls for urgent action. It is a completely historical and dramatic milieu, neither epic nor lyrical. Nothing can be repeated; the unique, *ephapax*, is infinitely concentrated, and this *concentration* includes and embraces all *extension*. Moreover, it seems to be getting more concentrated as time goes on: from the hidden thirty years to the public three years, and then the crucial three days that recapitulate all that has gone before.

The third aspect, the *immanence* of death in life, borders on the foregoing. Jesus' entire life is saturated with his death.[7] But it is not only that death, the *causa finalis* of his existence at every moment of his life, gives it ultimate meaning; it is also that his existence itself rests on a kenotic act of obedience that moved him to let go of the "form of God" and embrace the "form of a slave". The final goal of this kenosis was the particular death of Jesus, designed to outstrip and "conquer" death itself. Death, therefore, is uniquely immanent in this act of self-emptying and what flows from it, in his creaturely existence before the Father.

---

[7] Cf. Tennessee Williams: "life saturated with death", quoted in *Theo-Drama* I, 377.

In spite of the hiatus between the Passion and Jesus' antecedent life, something of the dignity and centrality of the death-situation enters into all the situations of his life from the very outset. Many words of Jesus (particularly in John) give a direct sense of this omnipresence of death. Death is very much an integral part of Jesus' reflections on his mission (for example, the eucharistic discourse in John 6 or the reference to the water that comes forth from him, John 4 and 7). If death is the central locus of tragedy (A. Gehlen), the existence of Jesus unites two things: it is the *approach* to a climax and the *presence* of this climax at all intermediate points.

This unique death of Jesus is final, unsurpassable. Thus it is also immanent (in an entirely different way) in his risen life, in spite of Paul's categorical assertion that "we know that Christ being raised from the dead will never die again; death no longer has dominion over him" (Rom 6:9). Rather, it is Christ who now holds the keys to the prison of death and Sheol: "Behold, I have the keys of Death and Hades" (Rev 1:18). But he lives as the "Lamb as though it had been slain"; we are not told that his scars will last only until the Last Judgment or that the Last Judgment will put an end to his eucharistic self-giving—a practice that presupposes his death. It would be more correct to say that his earthly life and death are transcended and transfigured to become the eternal life of the *Kyrios*. In this way (and only thus), he becomes the creaturely prototype and sacrament of the omnipresence and total self-giving of the triune God. At the same time, he becomes the *vinculum substantiale*[8] of all creation, which he recapitulates in himself.

Our outline of soteriology has shown sufficiently that the death of Jesus is a superabundant *atonement*. We must again emphasize that Anselm's two postulates (that is, death must be unmerited and undergone by a person of the highest dignity; and it must contain an element of infinite pain, which alone can purge and destroy the monstrous quality of the world's guilt) do not attain the fullness of this atoning value. Indeed it can be asked whether a man's death—laid on him from without or freely accepted by him—has an intrinsic atoning value or only acquires it on the

---

[8] In the sense of Maurice Blondel and his interpretation of Leibniz.

basis of an agreed convention. (In which case it would seem to be
a relatively mild punishment, compared with the endless torture
undergone by the living.) We cannot imagine in what way the
death of Jesus contained the element of torture that is immanent
in the world's guilt. It is pointless to speculate about the finitude
or infinitude of the pain he endured. One thing is certain: this
atoning torment must have consisted in unfathomable depths of
forsakenness by the Father; we have shown how the resultant
tensions within the Trinity include and embrace all distance between the sinner and God. It is impossible to depict this from the
outside. There are experiences that point in this direction, but
they are reserved for specially chosen souls who are drawn more
deeply into the mystery of redemption, including, no doubt, all
the "humiliated and abused" people of the world, the oppressed,
imprisoned and tortured.

We must never forget that the task of atonement displays a
unique combination: it is both accepted in free will *and* laid on
him from without. It cannot be a deliberately planned action
(again in contrast to Camus' *Les Justes*), because in that case the
person would have control over his own death—and God alone
can govern such matters. But what was accepted by the Son in
naked obedience on the Mount of Olives—a burden that seemed
beyond bearing—ultimately goes back to a decision made by the
entire Trinity for the sake of man's salvation. The Son, who is
now so obedient, was (and is) just as actively involved in this decision as Father and Spirit. Indeed, in a certain sense, he was *most*
involved, since the triune decision contained a personal "initiative" by which he offered himself for the task. In that respect,
that utterly alien reality he bears, in his work of atonement, is his
very own; it is something envisaged by him and for him from
the start.

It is obvious that, in his atoning work, Jesus dies *out of love.*
He dies essentially "for" us. "Greater love has no man than
this, that a man lay down his life for his friends", says Jesus to
his disciples (Jn 15:13); and these "friends" are what Paul calls
the "enemies" of Jesus since they are sinners: "One will hardly
die for a righteous man . . . , but God shows his love for us in
that while we were yet sinners Christ died for us" (Rom 5:7f.).
We were sinners, that is, "in rebellion against God" (*asebeis*),

hopelessly "incapable" (*asthenēs*) of extricating ourselves from the situation (Rom 5:6). So we are not friends but sinners and "enemies" (cf. Rom 8:7).

Again we find that this death, which is both freely embraced by him *and* laid on him from outside, presupposes a twofold love: the love of the Father, who lays this burden on him, and the love of the Son who bears it. In the context of this death, there is so much insistence on the Father's love for us that there seems to be no place for the kind of misunderstanding (for example, of the Anselmian teaching) according to which the Father is thought to be concerned solely for his honor and surrenders his Son on that account. It all goes back once more to the loving decision made by the Trinity, in which the Holy Spirit of love is just as involved as the Father and Son, guaranteeing and fulfilling the unanimity of their love in the deadly abandonment of the Cross.

We have already said that, in his obedient death, Jesus dies of the sin that murders him but that he also dies because God forsakes him. Nothing prevents us from understanding the Son's death in obedience to the Father as a death *for love of* the Father, for the implementation of his will to the uttermost. In the end, therefore, it is the human expression of a shared love-death in a supereminently trinitarian sense: the One who forsakes is just as much affected (in his eternal life) as the One who is forsaken, and just as much as the forsaking and forsaken love that is One in the Holy Spirit.

At this point, we must not omit a reference to the community of love and forsakenness that unites Jesus and his Mother, the prototype and embodiment of the Church of the redeemed. It shows two things: that a one-sided love-death remains unintelligible and ineffectual unless it encounters some (simultaneous) response; and that it can only be realized through a shared forsakenness. In part, the remote human parallels we cited earlier (Pyramus and Thisbe, Pelleas and Melisande, the Irish sagas, the death of Romeo and Juliet, Antony and Cleopatra, Tristan and Isolde, Rodrigue and Prouèze)[9] made this twofold aspect clear: each partner dies alone, yet death is shared. So too Jesus and Mary are separated from each other in their deaths, in his

---

[9] *Theo-Drama* I, 388–92.

physical death and her spiritual death; the mocking crowd comes between them. But, in this way, the mystery of ultimate fruitfulness between Man and Woman comes to fulfillment: at the very point where the Eucharist wells up and springs forth, the ecclesial womb that will receive that Eucharist takes shape.

Finally, we come to *representative* death, an aspect that is deeply rooted in human civilization and of which, therefore, man has some preliminary understanding.[10] Examples from the ancient world are largely political in theme, apart from *Alcestis*. *Die Bürger von Calais*, indubitably influenced by Christianity, also sets forth a political action. The other great models (Wilder's *Alcestis*, Claudel's *L'Annonce*, *Le Repos* and *L'Otage*, Greene's *The Potting Shed*, the Faulkner/Camus *Requiem for a Nun*, and the Le Fort/Bernanos *Dialogues des Carmélites*) are echoes of the unique representative death that took place on the Cross. They are meditations on the death of Jesus, his perfect, selfless self-giving for the sinful "other", who is thereby healed (as in Faulkner/Camus and in Claudel's *L'Annonce*). But they also reflect on the way he is utterly overstretched and exhausted by a guilt that is not his— the terrible, alien death of the old prioress in Bernanos, Sygne's breakdown under overwhelming pressure in Claudel. By such steps as these, the dramatists feel their way from man's preliminary understanding of representation toward a sharing in the Christian understanding of the Cross. The path is an inward path: what is taken over is not "having-to-die", as in the ancient *Alcestis*: now it is the inner fear of death that is transferred from one person to another. On the Cross, man's fear of God has become God's anxiety for man, which allows little Blanche de la Force, who has been liberated from this fear, boldly to sing the Te Deum as she finally mounts the scaffold. Thus the sting is drawn from death, inevitable though it be: "If Christ is in you, although your bodies are dead because of sin, your spirits are alive because of righteousness" (that is, the righteousness that has been attained) (Rom 8:10). So the martyrs can go to their deaths courageous and rejoicing because of the representation performed on the Cross, but they owe this courage to the anguish of him who wrestled on the Mount of Olives, utterly bereft

[10] *Theo-Drama* I, 392–400.

of courage. How many of our fellow men have been admitted into the mystery of this terrible anguish and God-forsakenness remains God's own secret.

We conclude this volume on the theodramatic action with the Cross; it outstrips the "last enemy, death", and death's defeat automatically makes way for eternal light to burst into the outer darkness, since

> What is sown is perishable, what is raised is imperishable.
> It is sown in dishonor, it is raised in glory.
> It is sown in weakness, it is raised in power.
> It is sown a physical body, it is raised a spiritual body.
>
> (1 Cor 15:42ff.)

INDEX OF PERSONS